LINUX

IN A NUTSHELL

Sixth Edition

*Ellen Siever, Stephen Figgins, Robert Love,
and Arnold Robbins*

O'REILLY®

Beijing • Cambridge • Farnham • Köln • Sebastopol • Taipei • Tokyo

Linux in a Nutshell, Sixth Edition

by Ellen Siever, Stephen Figgins, Robert Love, and Arnold Robbins

Copyright © 2009 Ellen Siever, Stephen Figgins, and Robert Love. All rights reserved.
Printed in the United States of America.

Published by O'Reilly Media, Inc., 1005 Gravenstein Highway North, Sebastopol, CA 95472.

O'Reilly books may be purchased for educational, business, or sales promotional use. Online editions are also available for most titles (*http://my.safaribooksonline.com*). For more information, contact our corporate/institutional sales department: (800) 998-9938 or *corporate@oreilly.com*.

Editors: Simon St.Laurent and Andy Oram

Production Editor: Rachel Monaghan

Indexer: Angela Howard

Production Services: Octal Publishing, Inc.

Cover Designer: Karen Montgomery

Interior Designer: David Futato

Illustrator: Robert Romano

Printing History:

January 1997:	First Edition.
February 1999:	Second Edition.
August 2000:	Third Edition.
June 2003:	Fourth Edition.
July 2005:	Fifth Edition.
September 2009:	Sixth Edition.

ISBN: 978-0-596-15448-6

[M]

Table of Contents

Preface

This is a book about Linux, a freely available clone of the Unix operating system whose uses range from embedded systems and personal data assistants (PDAs) to corporate servers, web servers, and massive clusters that perform some of the world's most difficult computations.

Whether you are using Linux for personal software projects, for a small office or home office (the so-called SOHO environment), to provide services to a small group of colleagues, or to administer a site responsible for millions of email and web connections each day, you need quick access to information on a wide range of tools. This book covers all aspects of administering and making effective use of Linux systems. Among its topics are booting, package management, and revision control. But foremost in *Linux in a Nutshell* are the immeasurable utilities and commands that make Linux one of the most powerful and flexible systems available.

In addition to the tools and features written specifically for it, Linux has inherited many from the Free Software Foundation's GNU project, the Berkeley Software Distribution (BSD), the X Window System, and contributions from major corporations as well as the companies that created the major Linux distributions. More recent projects extend Linux in exciting ways, some through changes to the kernel and some through libraries and applications that radically change the user's experience.

This book is a quick reference for the basic commands and features of the Linux operating system. As with other books in O'Reilly's "In a Nutshell" series, this book is geared toward users who know what they want to do and have some idea how to do it, but can't always remember the correct command or option. The sixth edition has been examined from start to end and checked against the most common Linux distributions (Debian, Ubuntu, Fedora, and SUSE) so that it reflects the most useful and popular commands.

Organization of This Book

This book is a reference to the most important commands and utilities available on Linux systems.

Chapter 1, *Introduction*, explains Linux's strengths and the key aspects of working with Linux, and lays out the scope of this book.

Chapter 2, *System and Network Administration Overview*, introduces TCP/IP networking and the Linux commands used for system administration and network management.

Chapter 3, *Linux Commands*, is the core of the book, a reference listing of hundreds of the most important shell commands available on Linux.

Chapter 4, *Boot Methods*, covers the commands used to control booting on Linux, particularly LILO and GRUB.

Chapter 5, *Package Management*, explains the **apt** series of commands that manage updating and installation on Debian, and the RPM system and **yum** used by Red Hat/Fedora, Novell/SUSE, and several other distributions of Linux.

Chapter 6, *The Bash Shell*, documents Bash, the default command-line interpreter on Linux.

Chapter 7, *Pattern Matching*, introduces regular expressions and explains how different tools interpret these powerful tools for searching and text processing.

Chapter 8, *The Emacs Editor*, provides reference information on Emacs, a text editor and full-featured development environment.

Chapter 9, *The vi, ex, and vim Editors*, describes the classic **vi** editor that is the most popular text-manipulation tool on Linux.

Chapter 10, *The sed Editor*, describes this "stream editor" that is useful for processing files in standardized ways.

Chapter 11, *The gawk Programming Language*, documents another valuable tool for processing text files, the GNU version of **awk** that is the default on Linux systems.

Chapter 12, *Source Code Management: An Overview*, provides the background for understanding Subversion and Git, which are valuable tools for tracking changes to files and projects, and are discussed in the following two chapters.

Chapter 13, *The Subversion Version Control System*, provides a description of a popular source code management and version-control tool.

Chapter 14, *The Git Version Control System*, describes a distributed version control system with many advanced features including the ability to access project history even when not connected to a central server.

Chapter 15, *Virtualization Command-Line Tools*, describes virtualization on Linux, which allows multiple virtual servers to run on a single physical server. Tools covered include Xen, KVM, the libvirt API, and the VMware command-line interface.

Other Resources

This book doesn't tell you how to install and get up to speed on a Linux system. For that, you'll probably want O'Reilly's *Running Linux*, by Matthias Kalle Dahlheimer and Matt Welsh, an in-depth guide suitable for all major distributions. For networking information, check out *Linux Network Administrator's Guide* by Tony Bautts et al. (O'Reilly). If you're new to Linux/Unix concepts, O'Reilly's *Learning the Unix Operating System*, by Jerry Peek et al., provides introductory information. In addition to these and other Linux titles, O'Reilly's wide range of Unix, X, web-related, and scripting and programming language titles may also be of interest.

Online Documentation

The Internet is full of information about Linux. One of the best resources is the Linux Documentation Project at *http://www.tldp.org* (or one of the dozens of mirror sites around the world), which has numerous short guides called HOWTOs, along with some full manuals. For online information about the GNU utilities covered in this book, consult *http://www.gnu.org* (also widely mirrored). The Free Software Foundation, which is in charge of the GNU project, publishes its documentation in a number of hardcopy and online books about various tools.

Each distribution maintains its own website, and contains documentation for the software it provides as well as guides to maintaining your system under that distribution.

Websites

As befits a hot phenomenon, Linux is the central subject of several websites and a frequent topic of discussion on others. Some sites offer original content; others just have links to articles posted elsewhere and threaded discussions (which can be a useful service). Among the sites frequented by Linux users are:

http://lwn.net
:   Linux Weekly News, a site with weekly in-depth articles and frequent news updates

http://www.linuxgazette.net
:   Linux Gazette, a site published monthly with articles and tips in many languages

http://www.linuxquestions.org
:   A very popular source for technical guidance, including a growing wiki (site maintained by user contributions) at *http://wiki.linuxquestions.org*

http://linuxsecurity.com
:   Linux Security, a collection of security-related news

http://linuxinsider.com
:   Linux Insider, a news feed

http://linuxtoday.com
:   Linux Today, another news feed

http://slashdot.org
:   Slashdot, a famous discussion list

Linux Journal and Linux Magazine

Linux Journal and *Linux Magazine* are monthly magazines for the Linux community, written and published by a number of Linux activists. These magazines are two of the oldest among many monthly print and online magazines devoted to Linux. With both print editions and websites, they offer articles ranging from questions and answers for novices to kernel programming internals. *Linux Journal*, at *http://www.linuxjournal.com*, is the older magazine. *Linux Magazine* is at *http://www.linux-mag.com*.

Usenet Newsgroups

Most people can receive Usenet news at work or through their ISPs. While this communications technology has lost ground in the past several years to web-based threaded discussions, it is still a valuable source of help and community connections on many topics. The following Linux-related newsgroups are popular:

comp.os.linux.announce
> A moderated newsgroup containing announcements of new software, distributions, bug reports, and goings-on in the Linux community. All Linux users should read this group. Submissions may be mailed to *cola@stump.algebra.com*.

comp.os.linux.development.apps
> Guidance for using features of Linux for application development, and for understanding the effects of the operating system on user-space programs.

comp.os.linux.development.system
> Discussions about developing the Linux kernel and the system itself.

comp.os.linux.networking
> Discussions relating to networking with Linux.

comp.os.linux.x
> Help on getting the X graphical window system to work. This list used to see some of the highest traffic of any Linux group back when distributions had more trouble setting up graphics automatically. This is no longer the case, thanks to the increasing sophistication of autodetection and configuration software.

There are also several newsgroups devoted to Linux in languages other than English, as well as newsgroups and online forums for the different distributions.

Online Linux Support

There are many ways of obtaining help online, where volunteers from around the world offer expertise and services to assist users with questions and problems.

The freenode IRC service is an Internet relay chat network devoted to so-called "peer-directed" projects, particularly those involving free software. Some of its channels are designed to provide online Linux support services.

Internet relay chat is a network service that allows you to talk interactively on the Internet to other users. IRC networks support multiple channels where different groups of people type their thoughts. Whatever you type in a channel is seen by all other users of that channel.

There are a number of active channels on the freenode IRC network, where you will find users 24 hours a day, 7 days a week who are willing and able to help you solve any Linux problems you may have, or just chat. You can use this service by installing an IRC client (some distributions install them by default), connecting to server name *irc.freenode.org:6667*, and joining a channel focusing on Linux, such as:

#linpeople
> General help and discussion

#debian
> Help for Debian distribution

#gentoo
> Help for Gentoo distribution

#redhat
> Help for Red Hat distribution

#suse
> Help for SUSE distribution

And so on. Please be sure to read up on the rules of chat etiquette before chatting. In particular, the participants in these groups tend to expect people to read documentation and do some experimentation before asking for help with a problem. Some IRC clients include Xchat, Konqueror, and KVirc. Note that these are all graphical programs and as such are not described in this book.

Linux User Groups

Many Linux User Groups around the world offer direct support to users. Typically, Linux User Groups engage in such activities as installation days, talks and seminars, demonstration nights, and purely social events. Linux User Groups are a great way of meeting other Linux users in your area. There are a number of published lists of Linux User Groups. Linux Online (*http://www.linux.org*) has a list of Linux user groups organized by country at *http://www.linux.org/groups*.

Using Code Examples

This book is here to help you get your job done. In general, you may use the code in this book in your programs and documentation. You do not need to contact O'Reilly for permission unless you're reproducing a significant portion of the code. For example, writing a program that uses several chunks of code from this book does not require permission. Selling or distributing a CD-ROM of examples from O'Reilly books does require permission. Answering a question by citing this book and quoting example code does not require permission. Incorporating a significant amount of example code from this book into your product's documentation does require permission.

We appreciate, but do not require, attribution. An attribution usually includes the title, author, publisher, and ISBN. For example: "*Linux in a Nutshell*, Sixth Edition, by Ellen Siever, Stephen Figgins, Robert Love, and Arnold Robbins. Copyright 2009 Ellen Siever, Stephen Figgins, and Robert Love, 978-0-596-15448-6."

If you feel your use of code examples falls outside fair use or the permission given above, feel free to contact the publisher at *permissions@oreilly.com*.

Conventions

This desktop quick reference follows certain typographic conventions:

Bold
> Used for commands, programs, and options. All terms shown in bold are typed literally.

Italic
> Used to show arguments and variables that should be replaced with user-supplied values. Italic is also used to introduce new terms, indicate filenames and directories, and to highlight comments in examples.

`Constant width`
> Used to show the contents of files or the output from commands.

`Constant width bold`
> Used in examples to show commands or other text that should be typed literally by the user.

`Constant width italic`
> Used in examples to show text that should be replaced with user-supplied values.

$
> Used in some examples as the **bash** shell prompt ($).

[ ]
> Surround optional elements in a description of syntax. (The brackets themselves should never be typed.) Note that many commands show the argument [*files*]. If a filename is omitted, standard input (e.g., the keyboard) is assumed. End with an end-of-file character.

EOF
> Indicates the end-of-file character (normally Ctrl-D).

|
> Used in syntax descriptions to separate items for which only one alternative may be chosen at a time.

This icon indicates a note, which is an important aside to its nearby text.

 This icon indicates a warning.

A final word about syntax. In many cases, the space between an option and its argument can be omitted. In other cases, the spacing (or lack of spacing) must be followed strictly. For example, **-w***n* (no intervening space) might be interpreted differently from **-w** *n*. It's important to notice the spacing used in option syntax.

How to Contact Us

We have tested and verified all of the information in this book to the best of our ability, but you may find that features have changed (or even that we have made mistakes!). Please let us know about any errors you find, as well as your suggestions for future editions, by writing:

O'Reilly Media, Inc.
1005 Gravenstein Highway North
Sebastopol, CA 95472
800-998-9938 (in the United States or Canada)
707-829-0515 (international or local)
707-829-0104 (fax)

There is a web page for this book, which lists errata, examples, or any additional information. You can access this page at:

http://www.oreilly.com/catalog/9780596154486

To comment or ask technical questions about this book, send email to:

bookquestions@oreilly.com

For more information about books, conferences, Resource Centers, and the O'Reilly Network, see the O'Reilly website at:

http://www.oreilly.com

Safari® Books Online

 Safari Books Online is an on-demand digital library that lets you easily search over 7,500 technology and creative reference books and videos to find the answers you need quickly.

With a subscription, you can read any page and watch any video from our library online. Read books on your cell phone and mobile devices.

Access new titles before they are available for print, and get exclusive access to manuscripts in development and post feedback for the authors. Copy and paste code samples, organize your favorites, download chapters, bookmark key sections, create notes, print out pages, and benefit from tons of other time-saving features.

O'Reilly Media has uploaded this book to the Safari Books Online service. To have full digital access to this book and others on similar topics from O'Reilly and other publishers, sign up for free at *http://my.safaribooksonline.com*.

Acknowledgments

This sixth edition of *Linux in a Nutshell* is the result of the cooperative efforts of many people. Many thanks to Avery Pennarun for writing the Git chapter. Thanks also to Simon St.Laurent and Andy Oram for their editorial skills. For technical review, thanks go to Greg Goddard, Leam Hall, Forrest Humphrey, Josh More, and Dave Pawson.

1

Introduction

It is hard to chart the rise of Linux without risking the appearance of exaggeration and hyperbole. During the past few years alone, Linux has grown from a student/hacker playground to an upstart challenger in the server market to a well-respected system taking its rightful place in educational and corporate networks. Many serious analysts claim that its trajectory has just begun, and that it will eventually become the world's most widespread operating system.

Linux was first developed by Linus Torvalds at the University of Helsinki in Finland. From his current location in Silicon Valley, Linus continues to centrally coordinate improvements. The Linux kernel continues to develop under the dedicated cultivation of a host of other programmers and hackers all over the world, joined by members of programming teams at major computer companies, all connected through the Internet.

By "kernel," we mean the core of the operating system itself, not the applications (such as the compiler, shells, and so forth) that run on it. Today, the term "Linux" is often used to mean a software environment with a Linux kernel, along with a large set of applications and other software components. In this larger meaning, many people prefer the term GNU/Linux, which acknowledges the central role played by tools from the Free Software Foundation's GNU project as complements to the development of the Linux kernel.

Linux systems cannot be technically referred to as a "version of Unix," as they have not undergone the required tests and licensing.[*] However, Linux offers all the common programming interfaces of standard Unix systems, and, as you can see from this book, all the common Unix utilities have been reimplemented on Linux. It is a powerful, robust, fully usable system.

---

[*] Before an operating system can be called "Unix," it must be branded by The Open Group.

The historical impact of Linux goes beyond its role as a challenge to all versions of Unix as well as Microsoft Windows, particularly on servers. Linux's success has also inspired countless other free software or open source (defined at *http://opensource.org*) projects, including Samba, GNOME, and a mind-boggling collection of innovative projects that you can browse at numerous sites like SourceForge (*http://sourceforge.net*) and Freshmeat (*http://freshmeat.net*). As both a platform for other developers and a development model, Linux gave a tremendous boost to the GNU project and has also become a popular platform for Java development. In short, Linux is a focal point in the most exciting and productive free-software movement ever seen.

If you haven't obtained Linux yet, or have it but don't know exactly how to get started using it, see "Other Resources" on page xvii.

The Excitement of Linux

Linux is, first of all, free software: anyone can download the source from the Internet or buy it on a low-cost CD-ROM. But Linux is becoming well known because it's more than just free software—it's unusually good software. You can get more from your hardware with Linux and be assured of fewer crashes; even its security is better than many commercial alternatives.

Linux first appeared in organizations as ad hoc installations by hackers running modest web servers or development systems at universities and research institutions, but it now extends deeply into corporations around the world. People deploying Linux for mission-critical systems tend to talk about its ample practical advantages, such as the ability to deliver a lot of bang for the buck and the ease of deploying other powerful tools on Linux, such as Apache, Samba, and Java environments. They also cite Linux's ability to grow and sprout new features of interest to large numbers of users. But these advantages can be traced back to the concept of software freedom, which is the root of the broad wave of innovation driving Linux.

As free software, Linux revives the grand creativity and the community of sharing that Unix was long known for. The unprecedented flexibility and openness of Unix—which newcomers usually found confusing and frustrating, but eventually found they couldn't live without—continually inspired extensions, new tools, and experiments in computer science that sometimes ended up in mainstream commercial computer systems.

Many programmers fondly remember the days when AT&T provided universities with Unix source code at no charge and the University of Berkeley started distributing its version in any manner that allowed people to get it. For these older hackers, Linux brings back the spirit of working together—all the more so because the Internet is now so widespread. And for the many who are too young to remember the first round of open systems or whose prior experience has been constricted by trying to explore and adapt proprietary operating systems, now is the time to discover the wonders of freely distributable source code and infinitely adaptable interfaces.

The economic power behind Linux's popularity is its support for an enormous range of hardware. People who are accustomed to Microsoft Windows are often amazed at how much faster their hardware appears to work with Linux—it makes efficient use of its resources.

For the first several years after its appearance, users were attracted to Linux for a variety of financial and political reasons, but soon they discovered an unexpected benefit: Linux works better than many commercial systems. With the Samba file and print server, for instance, Linux provides stable Windows-based networking to a large number of end-user PCs. With the Apache web server, it provides more of the useful features web administrators want than competing products do. Embedded versions of the Linux kernel are growing in use because, although they are larger than the most stripped-down operating systems, they deliver a range of powerful features within a remarkably small footprint.

Opinions still differ on how suitable Linux is as a general-purpose desktop system. But the tremendous advances in usability and stability of the desktop software and its applications are undisputed. Soon (if not today), one will find Linux in many offices and other end-user environments. Meanwhile, the strides made by Linux in everyday computing tasks are reflected in the many new commands found in this edition.

Distribution and Support

Because of the vast number and variety of tools beyond the kernel required for a functional computing environment, building a Linux installation from scratch is quite complex. Over the years, therefore, commercial and noncommercial packages called *distributions* have emerged. The first distribution consisted of approximately 50 diskettes, at least one of which would usually turn out to be bad and have to be replaced. Since then, CD and DVD drives, as well as high-speed Internet connections, have become widespread and sharing Linux has become much easier.

After getting Linux, the average user is concerned next with support. While online newsgroups and forums offer quick responses and meet the needs of many intrepid users, you can also buy support from the vendors of the major distributions and a number of independent experts. Linux is supported at least as well as commercial software. When you buy a distribution from a vendor, you typically are entitled to a period of free support as well.

Intel's x86 family and other compatible chips are still by far the most common hardware running Linux, but Linux is also now commercially available on a number of other hardware systems, notably the PowerPC, the Intel Itanium processor, and Sun Microsystems' SPARC.

Commands on Linux

Linux commands are not the same as standard Unix ones. Most of the commands are provided by the GNU project run by the Free Software Foundation (FSF). GNU means "GNU's Not Unix"—the first word of the phrase is expanded with infinite recursion.

Benefiting from years of experience with standard Unix utilities and advances in computer science, programmers on the GNU project have managed to create versions of standard tools that have more features, run faster and more efficiently, and lack the bugs and inconsistencies that persist in the original standard versions.

While GNU provided the programming utilities and standard commands such as **grep**, many of the system and network administration tools on Linux came from the Berkeley Software Distribution (BSD). In addition, some people wrote tools that specifically allow Linux to deal with special issues such as filesystems. This book documents the standard Unix commands that are commonly available on most Linux distributions.

The third type of software most commonly run on Linux is the X Window System, ported by the XFree86 and X.org projects to standard Intel chips. This book does not discuss the X Window System; see the O'Reilly book *Running Linux*, by Matthias Kalle Dalheimer and Matt Welsh, for an introduction to X.

What This Book Offers

Originally based on the classic O'Reilly quick reference, *Unix in a Nutshell*, this book has been expanded to include much information that is specific to Linux. These enhancements include chapters on:

- Package managers (which make it easy to install, update, and remove related software files)
- Boot methods
- The Subversion and Git version control systems
- Virtualization

The book also contains dozens of Linux-specific commands, along with tried-and-true Unix commands that have been supporting users for decades (though they continue to sprout new options).

This book does not cover the graphical tools contained in most distributions of Linux. Many of these, to be sure, are quite useful and can form the basis of everyday work. Examples of these tools include OpenOffice (Sun Microsystems' free, open source version of the StarOffice suite), Evolution (a mail, calendar, and office productivity tool from Novell), Firefox and Thunderbird (a browser and mail program from Mozilla), and the GIMP (a graphic image-manipulation program and provider of a powerful library used by the GNOME project). But they are not Linux-specific, and their graphical models do not fit well into the format of this book.

While you probably log in to one of the graphical desktop environments such as GNOME or KDE and do much of your work with the graphical applications, the core of Linux use is the text manipulation and administration done from the command line, within scripts, or using text editors such as **vi** and Emacs. Linux remains largely a command-driven system, and this book continues to focus on this level of usage; for many tasks, the command line is the most efficient and flexible tool. In your day-to-day work, you'll likely find yourself moving back and forth between graphical programs and the commands listed in this book.

Every distribution of Linux is slightly different. There are variations in directory structure, choice of standard utilities, and software versions, but you'll find that the commands we document are the ones you use most of the time, and that they work the same on all distributions. Note, though, that some commands are only available with certain devices or configurations, or have alternatives that may be preferred in your environment. Basic commands, programming utilities, system administration, and network administration are all covered. However, some areas were so big that we had to leave them out. The many applications that depend on the X Window System didn't make the cut. Nor did the many useful programming languages—such as Java, Perl, and Python—with which users can vastly expand the capabilities of their systems. XML isn't covered here, either. These subjects would stretch the book out of its binding.

Linux in a Nutshell doesn't teach you Linux—it is, after all, a quick reference—but novices as well as highly experienced users will find it of great value. When you have some idea of what command you want but aren't sure just how it works or what combinations of options give you the exact output required, this book is the place to turn. It can also be an eye-opener, making you aware of options that you never knew about before.

Once you've installed Linux, the first thing you need to do is get to know the common utilities run from the shell prompt. If you know absolutely nothing about Unix, we recommend you read a basic guide (introductory chapters in the O'Reilly books *Learning Red Hat Enterprise Linux and Fedora*, by Bill McCarty, and *Running Linux*, mentioned previously, can get you started). This chapter and Chapter 2 offer a context for understanding different kinds of commands (including commands for programming, system administration, and network administration). Chapter 3 is the central focus of the book, containing about one half its bulk.

The shorter chapters immediately following Chapter 3 help you get your system set up. Since most users do not want to completely abandon other operating systems (whether a Microsoft Windows system or some Unix flavor), many users opt for a dual-boot system, with Linux residing on the same computer as other operating systems. Users can then boot to the system they need for a particular job. Chapter 4 describes the commonly used booting options on Intel systems, including LILO (Linux Loader) and GRUB (the GRand Unified Bootloader). Chapter 5 covers the Red Hat package manager (**rpm**)—which is supported by many distributions, including Red Hat Enterprise Linux, Fedora, SUSE, and Mandriva—and the Debian package-management system, which is used by such distributions as Ubuntu, Knoppix, and Gnoppix. It also describes some of the frontend package-management tools that simplify package management and automatically resolve dependencies. These tools include **yum** for **rpm**-based systems and **aptitude** and **synaptic** for Debian-based systems. Package managers are useful for installing and updating software; they make sure you have all the files you need in the proper versions.

All commands are interpreted by the *shell*. The shell is simply a program that accepts commands from the user and executes them. Different shells sometimes use slightly different syntax to mean the same thing. Under Linux, the standard shell is **bash**. Others, such as the **ksh** Korn shell, the **tcsh** enhanced C shell, and zsh, are available. Chapter 6 provides thorough coverage of **bash**; you may decide to read this chapter after you've used Linux for a while, because it mostly covers powerful, advanced features that you'll want when you're a steady user. Chapter 7 covers pattern matching, which is used by the Linux text-editing utilities for searching based on a pattern rather than an explicit string.

To get any real work done, you'll have to learn some big, comprehensive utilities, notably an editor and some scripting tools. Two major editors are used on Linux: **vi** and Emacs. Emacs is covered in Chapter 8, and **vi** is discussed in Chapter 9. Chapter 9 also describes **vim**, an extended version of **vi**, commonly found on Linux systems. Chapters 10 and 11 cover two classic Unix tools for manipulating text files on a line-by-line basis: **sed** and **gawk** (the GNU version of the traditional **awk**). O'Reilly offers separate books about these topics that you may find valuable, as they are not known for being intuitive upon first use. (Emacs does have an excellent built-in tutorial, though; to invoke it, press **Ctrl-h** followed by **t** for "tutorial.")

The Subversion and Git version control systems manage files so you can retrieve old versions and maintain different versions simultaneously. Originally used by programmers, who have complicated requirements for building and maintaining applications, these tools have turned out to be valuable for anyone who maintains files of any type, particularly when coordinating a team of people. Version control systems have become a distribution channel for thousands of free software projects. Chapter 12 offers a brief overview of version control, including basic terms and concepts. Chapter 13 presents Subversion commands, and Chapter 14 presents Git commands.

Chapter 15 covers virtualization and examines several virtualization systems such as Xen and VMWare and their command-line tools.

Our goal in producing this book is to provide convenience, and that means keeping the book (relatively) small. It certainly doesn't have everything the manual pages have, but you'll find that it has what you need 95 percent of the time. See the **man** command in Chapter 3 for information on reading the manpages. They can also be read with the **info** command, the GNU hypertext documentation reader, also documented in Chapter 3.

Sources and Licenses

Some distributions contain the source code for Linux; it is also easily available for download at *http://www.kernel.org* and elsewhere. Source code is similarly available for all the utilities on Linux (unless your vendor offers a commercial application or library as a special enhancement). You may never bother looking at the source code, but it's key to Linux's strength. Under the Linux license, the source code has to be provided or made available by the vendor, and it permits those who are competent at such things to fix bugs, provide advice about the system's functioning, and submit improvements that benefit everyone. The license is the GNU project's well-known General Public License, also known as the GPL or "copyleft," invented and popularized by the Free Software Foundation (FSF).

The FSF, founded by Richard Stallman, is a phenomenon that many people might believe to be impossible if it did not exist. (The same goes for Linux, in fact—20 years ago, who would have imagined a robust operating system developed by collaborators over the Internet and made freely redistributable?) One of the most popular editors on Unix, GNU Emacs, comes from the FSF. So do **gcc** and **g++** (C and C++ compilers), which for a while set the standard in the industry for optimization and the creation of fast code. One of the most ambitious projects within GNU is the GNOME desktop, which encompasses several useful general-purpose libraries and applications that use these libraries to provide consistent behavior and interoperability.

Dedicated to the sharing of software, the FSF provides all its code and documentation on the Internet and allows anyone with a whim for enhancements to alter the source code. One of its projects is the Debian distribution of Linux.

To prevent hoarding, the FSF requires that the source code for all enhancements be distributed under the same GPL that it uses. This encourages individuals or companies to make improvements and share them with others. The only thing someone cannot do is add enhancements, withhold the source code, and then sell the product as proprietary software. Doing so would be taking advantage of the FSF and users of the GPL. You can find the text of the GPL in any software covered by that license, or online at *http://www.gnu.org/copyleft/gpl.html*.

As we said earlier, many Linux tools come from BSD instead of GNU. BSD is also free software. The license is significantly different, but that probably doesn't concern you as a user. The effect of the difference is that companies are permitted to incorporate the software into their proprietary products, a practice that is severely limited by the GNU license.

Beginner's Guide

If you're just beginning to work on a Linux system, the abundance of commands might prove daunting. To help orient you, the following lists present a sampling of commands on various topics.

Communication

Command	Action
dig	Query DNS server.
ftp	File Transfer Protocol.
login	Sign on.
rsync	Transfer files, particularly across a network.
scp	Securely copy files to remote system.
sftp	Secure file transfer program.
ssh	Run shell or single command on remote system (secure).

Comparisons

Command	Action
cmp	Compare two files, byte by byte.
comm	Compare items in two sorted files.
diff	Compare two files, line by line.
diff3	Compare three files.
sdiff	Compare and interactively merge two files.

File Management

Command	Action
cat	Concatenate files or display them.
chattr	Change attributes on an ext2 file.
chgrp	Change group of files.
chmod	Change access modes on files.
chown	Change ownership of files.
chsh	Change login shell.
cp	Copy files.
csplit	Split a file into pieces with a specific size or at specific locations.
dd	Copy files in raw disk form.
file	Determine a file's type.
head	Show the first few lines of a file.
hexdump	Display files in hexadecimal format.
less	Display files by screenful, forward and backward.
ln	Create filename aliases.
ls	List files and directories.
md5sum	Compute MD5 checksum.
merge	Merge changes from different files.
mkdir	Create a directory.
more	Display files by screenful, forward only.
mv	Move or rename files or directories.
newgrp	Change current group.
od	Display files in octal format.
pwd	Print working directory.
rm	Remove files.
rmdir	Remove directories.
sha1sum	Compute SHA1 checksum
shred	Securely delete files.
split	Split files evenly.
tac	Print lines of a file in reverse order.

Command	Action
tail	Show the last few lines of a file.
tailf	Follow the growth of a logfile.
touch	Update file timestamps and create the file if it doesn't exist.
wc	Count lines, words, and characters.

Media

Command	Action
cdparanoia	Rip a CD while providing extra features.
cdrdao	Copy a CD.
eject	Eject a removable disk or tape.
genisoimage	Generate a binary image from a directory tree.
icedax	Rip a CD or DVD to create a computer-friendly WAV format.
readom	Read or write a data CD or DVD.
volname	Provide the volume name of a CD-ROM.
wodim	Record to a CD or DVD.

Printing

Command	Action
lpq	Show status of print jobs.
lpr	Send to the printer.
lprm	Remove print job.
lpstat	Get printer status.
pr	Format and paginate for printing.

Programming

Command	Action
ar	Create and update library files.
as	Generate object file.
bison	Generate parsing tables.
cpp	Preprocess C code.
flex	Lexical analyzer.
g++	GNU C++ compiler.
gcc	GNU C compiler.
ld	Link editor.
ldd	Print shared library dependencies.
m4	Macro processor.

Command	Action
make	Create programs.
ranlib	Regenerate archive symbol table.
rpcgen	Translate RPC to C code.
yacc	Generate parsing tables.

Program Maintenance

Command	Action
ctags	Generate symbol list for use with the **vi** editor.
etags	Generate symbol list for use with the Emacs editor.
gdb	GNU debugger.
git	Scalable, distributed revision control system.
gprof	Display object file's profile data.
make	Maintain, update, and regenerate related programs and files.
nm	Display object file's symbol table.
objcopy	Copy and translate object files.
objdump	Display information about object files.
patch	Apply patches to source code.
pmap	Print the memory map of a process.
size	Print the size of an object file in bytes.
strace	Trace system calls and signals.
strip	Strip symbols from an object file.
svn	Subversion revision control system.

Searching

Command	Action
apropos	Search manpages for topic.
egrep	Extended version of **grep**.
fgrep	Search files for literal words.
find	Search the system for files by name and take a range of possible actions.
grep	Search files for text patterns.
locate	Search a preexisting database to show where files are on the system.
look	Search file for string at the beginning of lines.
strings	Search binary files for text patterns.
updatedb	Update the **locate** database.
whereis	Find command.
which	Print pathname of a command.

Shell Programming

Command	Action
basename	Remove leading directory components from a path.
echo	Repeat command-line arguments on the output.
envsubst	Substitute the value of environment variables into strings.
expr	Perform arithmetic and comparisons.
mktemp	Generate temporary filename and create the file.
printf	Format and print command-line arguments.
sleep	Pause during processing.
test	Test a condition.

Storage

Command	Action
bunzip2	Expand compressed *.bz2* files.
bzip2	Compress files to free up space.
cpio	Create and unpack file archives.
gunzip	Expand compressed (*.gz* and *.Z*) files.
gzip	Compress files to free up space.
tar	Copy files to or restore files from an archive medium.
zcat	Display contents of compressed files.
zforce	Force **gzip** files to have *.gz* extension.

System Status

Command	Action
at	Execute commands later.
atq	Show jobs queued by **at**.
atrm	Remove job queued by **at**.
crontab	Automate commands.
date	Display or set date.
df	Show free disk space.
du	Show disk usage.
env	Show environment variables.
finger	Display information about users.
free	Show free and used memory.
hostname	Display the system's hostname.
kill	Terminate a running command.
printenv	Show environment variables.

Command	Action
ps	Show processes.
quota	Display disk usage and limits.
stat	Display file or filesystem status.
stty	Set or display terminal settings.
top	Display tasks currently running.
tty	Display filename of the terminal connected to standard input.
uname	Display system information.
uptime	Show how long the system has been running.
vmstat	Show virtual memory statistics.
who	Show who is logged in.

Text Processing

Command	Action
col	Process control characters.
cut	Select columns for display.
emacs	Work environment with powerful text-editing capabilities.
ex	Line editor underlying **vi**.
expand	Convert tabs to spaces.
fmt	Produce roughly uniform line lengths.
fold	Break lines.
gawk	Process lines or records one by one.
groff	Format **troff** input.
gs	Display PostScript or PDF file.
ispell	Interactively check spelling.
join	Merge different columns into a database.
paste	Merge columns or switch order.
rev	Print lines in reverse.
sed	Noninteractive text editor.
sort	Sort or merge files.
tr	Translate (redefine) characters.
unexpand	Convert spaces to tabs.
uniq	Find repeated or unique lines in a file.
vi	Visual text editor.
vim	Enhanced version of **vi**.

Miscellaneous

Command	Action
bc	Arbitrary precision calculator.
cal	Display calendar.
clear	Clear the screen.
info	Get command information from the GNU hypertext reader.
man	Get information on a command.
nice	Reduce a job's priority.
nohup	Launch a command that will continue to run after logging out.
openvt	Run a program on the next available virtual terminal.
passwd	Set your login password.
script	Produce a transcript of your login session.
su	Become a different user, often the superuser.
sudo	Execute an authorized command as root or another user.
tee	Simultaneously store output in file and send to screen.
time	Time the execution of a command.
wall	Send a message to all terminals.
whoami	Print the current user id.
xargs	Process many arguments in manageable portions.

2

System and Network Administration Overview

Common Commands

Following are lists of commonly used system administration commands.

Clocks

Command	Action
hwclock	Manage hardware clock.
rdate	Get time from network time server.

Daemons

Command	Action
apmd	Advanced Power Management daemon.
atd	Queue commands for later execution.
bootpd	Internet Boot Protocol daemon.
cupsd	Printer daemon.
ftpd	File Transfer Protocol daemon.
imapd	IMAP mailbox server daemon.
klogd	Manage **syslogd**.
mountd	NFS mount request server.
named	Internet domain nameserver.
nfsd	NFS daemon.
pppd	Maintain Point-to-Point Protocol (PPP) network connections.

Command	Action
rdistd	Remote file distribution server.
rexecd	Remote execution server.
rlogind	**rlogin** server.
routed	Routing daemon.
rpc.rusersd	Remote users server.
rpc.statd	NFS status daemon.
rshd	Remote shell server.
rsyslogd	Alternate system logging daemon.
rwhod	Remote who server.
sshd	Secure shell daemon.
syslogd	System logging daemon.
xinetd	Extended Internet services daemon. Starts other services as needed.
ypbind	NIS binder process.
yppasswdd	NIS password modification server.
ypserv	NIS server process.

Hardware

Command	Action
agetty	Start user session at terminal.
arp	Manage the ARP cache.
fdisk	Maintain disk partitions.
hdparm	Get and set hard drive parameters.
kbdrate	Manage the keyboard's repeat rate.
ramsize	Print information about RAM disk.
setkeycodes	Change keyboard scancode-to-keycode mappings.
slattach	Attach serial lines as network interfaces.

Host Information

Command	Action
arch	Print machine architecture.
dig	Query Internet domain nameservers.
domainname	Print NIS domain name.
free	Print memory usage.
host	Print host and zone information.
hostname	Print or set hostname.
uname	Print host information.

Installation

Command	Action
cpio	Copy files to and from archives.
install	Copy files into locations providing user access and set permissions.
rdist	Distribute files to remote systems.
tar	Copy files to or restore files from an archive medium.

Mail

Command	Action
formail	Convert input to mail format.
mailq	Print a summary of the mail queue.
makemap	Update **sendmail**'s database maps.
newaliases	Rebuild **sendmail**'s alias database.
rmail	Handle **uucp** mail.
sendmail	Send and receive mail.

Managing Filesystems

To Unix systems, a *filesystem* is a device (such as a partition) that is formatted to store files. Filesystems can be found on hard drives, floppies, CD-ROMs, USB drives, or other storage media that permit random access.

The exact format and means by which the files are stored are not important; the system provides a common interface for all *filesystem types* that it recognizes. By default, almost all modern distributions of Linux use a journaling filesystem. When the kernel interacts with a journalling filesystem, writes to disk are first written to a log or journal before they are written to disk. This slows down writes to the filesystem, but reduces the risk of data corruption in the event of a power outage. It also speeds up reboots after a system unexpectedly loses power.

Most current Linux distributions default to the Third Extended (ext3) Filesystem. The ext3 filesystem was developed primarily for Linux and supports 256-character filenames and 4-terabyte maximum filesystem size. This ext3 filesystem is essentially a Second Extended (ext2) filesystem with an added journal. Since it is in all other ways identical to the ext2 system, it is both forward- and backward-compatible with ext2—all ext2 utilities work with ext3 filesystems.

Although not covered in this edition of *Linux in a Nutshell*, Linux supports other open source journaling filesystems including: IBM's Journaled Filesystem (JFS), SGI's Extensible Filesystem (XFS), and the Naming System Venture's Reiser Filesystem (ReiserFS). In some situations these can be faster than ext3. Some Linux distributions use these alternative filesystems by default. Other common filesystems include the FAT and VFAT filesystems, which allow files on partitions and floppies of Microsoft Windows systems to be accessed under Linux, and the ISO 9660 filesystem used by CD-ROMs.

Command	Action
debugfs	Debug ext2 filesystem.
dosfsck	Check and repair a DOS or VFAT filesystem.
dump	Back up data from a filesystem.
dumpe2fs	Print information about superblock and blocks group.
e2fsck	Check and repair an ext2 filesystem.
e2image	Store disaster-recovery data for an ext2 filesystem.
e2label	Label an ext2 filesystem.
edquota	Edit filesystem quotas with **vim**.
fdformat	Format floppy disk.
fsck	Another name for **e2fsck**.
fsck.ext2	Check and repair an ext2 filesystem.
mke2fs	Make a new ext2 filesystem.
mkfs	Make a new filesystem.
mkfs.ext2	Another name for **mke2fs**.
mkfs.ext3	Yet another name for **mke2fs**.
mklost+found	Make *lost+found* directory.
mkraid	Set up a RAID device.
mkswap	Designate swapspace.
mount	Mount a filesystem.
quotacheck	Audit stored quota information.
quotaon	Enforce quotas.
quotaoff	Do not enforce quotas.
quotastats	Display kernel quota statistics.
rdev	Describe or change values for root filesystem.
repquota	Display quota summary.
resize2fs	Enlarge or shrink an ext2 filesystem.
restore	Restore data from a **dump** to a filesystem.
rootflags	List or set flags to use in mounting root filesystem.
setquota	Edit filesystem quotas.
showmount	List exported directories on a remote host.
swapoff	Cease using device for swapping.
swapon	Begin using device for swapping.
sync	Write filesystem buffers to disk.
tune2fs	Manage an ext2 filesystem.
umount	Unmount a filesystem.
warnquota	Mail disk usage warnings to users.

Managing the Kernel

Command	Action
depmod	Create module dependency listing.
lsmod	List kernel modules.

Command	Action
modinfo	Print kernel module information.
modprobe	Load and remove a module and its dependent modules.
sysctl	Examine or modify kernel parameters at runtime.

Networking

Command	Action
ifconfig	Manage network interfaces.
iptables	Administer firewall facilities (2.4 kernel).
named	Translate between domain names and IP addresses.
nameif	Assign names to network devices.
netstat	Print network status.
nfsstat	Print statistics for NFS and RPC.
nsupdate	Submit dynamic DNS update requests.
portmap	Map daemons to ports (renamed **rpcbind**).
rarp	Manage RARP table.
rndc	Send commands to a BIND nameserver.
route	Manage routing tables.
routed	Dynamically keep routing tables up to date.
rpcbind	Map daemons to ports (replaces **portmap**).
rpcinfo	Report RPC information.
traceroute	Trace network route to remote host.

Printing

Command	Action
accept	Tell printer daemon to accept jobs.
lpadmin	Configure printer and class queues.
lpinfo	Show available printers and drivers.
lpmove	Move a print job to a different queue.
reject	Tell printer daemon to reject jobs.
tunelp	Tune the printer parameters.

Security and System Integrity

Command	Action
badblocks	Search for bad blocks.
chroot	Change root directory.

Starting and Stopping the System

The job of booting and rebooting a machine falls to a special program called *init*. Init is responsible for finishing the boot process once the kernel is done loading, launching the services necessary to run the computer. Init is also responsible for stopping services when needed and for shutting down or rebooting the computer when instructed.

For decades, the software handling these duties was called *SysVinit*, or System V init. Modern Linux distributions have begun switching to a replacement called *Upstart* (a less common replacement, *init-ng*, we will not discuss). The traditional model, facilitated by *SysVinit*, divides potential system states into multiple *runlevels*, each with a distinct purpose. Runlevel 3, for example, indicates a standard booted system; runlevel 6 indicates a reboot. When entering a runlevel *N*, SysVinit runs all of the commands in the directory */etc/rcN.d*. In this manner, the scripts in */etc/rc3.d* handle a system's booting while those in */etc/rc6.d* handle a reboot. Various commands (see accompanying table) allow a system administrator to force the system into a given runlevel. The file */etc/inittab* specifies what runlevel is entered on boot, as well as configuration for the system's tty's.

Upstart replaces this functionality with a more general mechanism for the stopping, starting, and monitoring of services. Upstart operates asynchronously and is a much more powerful system than SysVinit. Thankfully, however, it is backward compatible with SysVinit and most distributions use it in a way in which much of the preceding paragraph remains accurate. Indeed, most modern Linux distributions have moved to Upstart but still manage runlevels via SysVinit-style scripts in */etc/rcN.d*.

The biggest change with Upstart is with configuration. Instead of an *inittab*, Upstart maintains a directory of configuration scripts, */etc/event.d*. Files within this directory describe how Upstart should handle tty's and SysVinit-style runlevels: */etc/event.d/ttyN* configures ttyN while */etc/event.d/rcN* configures runlevel N.

Command	Action
chkconfig	Manage which services run in a runlevel.
ctrlaltdel	Shut down and then soft reboot system.
halt	Stop or shut down system.
initctl	Manage the Upstart init daemon.
reboot	Shut down and then hard reboot system.
runlevel	Print system runlevel.
shutdown	Shut down system.
telinit	Change the current runlevel.
uptime	Display uptimes of local machines.

System Activity and Process Management

A number of additional commands in Chapter 3 are particularly useful in controlling processes, including **kill**, **killall**, **pidof**, **ps**, and **who**.

Command	Action
fuser	Identify processes using file or filesystem.
renice	Change the priority of running processes.
top	Show most CPU-intensive processes.
vmstat	Print virtual-memory statistics and process statistics.

Users

Command	Action
chpasswd	Change multiple passwords.
groupadd	Add a new group.
groupdel	Delete a group.
groupmod	Modify groups.
grpck	Check the integrity of group system files.
grpconv	Convert group file to shadow group file.
lastlog	Generate report of last user login times.
newusers	Add new users in a batch.
pwck	Check the integrity of password system files.
pwconv	Convert password file to shadow passwords.
rusers	Print who-style information on remote machines.
rwall	Print a message to remote users.
useradd	Add a new user.
userdel	Delete a user and that user's home directory.
usermod	Modify a user's information.
w	List logged-in users.
wall	Write to all users.
whoami	Show how you are currently logged in.

Miscellaneous

Command	Action
anacron	Schedule commands for periodic execution.
atrun	Schedule commands for later execution.
cron	Schedule commands for specific times.
dmesg	Print bootup messages after the system is up.
ldconfig	Update library links and do caching.
logger	Send messages to the system logger.
logrotate	Compress and rotate system logs.
run-parts	Run all scripts in a directory.

Overview of Networking

Networks connect computers so that the different systems can share information. For users and system administrators, Unix systems have traditionally provided a set of simple but valuable network services that let you check whether systems are running, refer to files residing on remote systems, communicate via electronic mail, and so on.

For most commands to work over a network, one system must be continuously running a server process in the background, silently waiting to handle the user's request. This kind of process is called a *daemon*. Common examples, on which you rely for the most basic functions of your Linux system, are **named** (which translates between numeric IP addresses and more human-readable alphanumeric names), **cupsd** (which sends documents to a printer, possibly over a network).

Most Unix networking commands are based on *Internet protocols*, standardized ways of communicating across a network on hierarchical layers. The protocols range from addressing and packet routing at a relatively low layer to finding users and executing user commands at a higher layer.

The basic user commands that most systems support over Internet protocols are generally called TCP/IP commands, named after the two most common protocols. You can use all of these commands to communicate with other Unix systems in addition to Linux systems. Many can also be used to communicate with non-Unix systems, almost all systems support TCP/IP.

This section also covers NFS and NIS—which allow for transparent file and information sharing across networks—and **sendmail**.

TCP/IP Administration

Command	Action
arp	Manipulate address resolution protocol tables.
dig	Query domain nameservers.
ftpd	Server for file transfers.
host	Print host and zone information.
ip	Network configuration tool with Cisco IOS-like syntax. Replaces **ifconfig**, **route**, and **arp** on some systems.
ifconfig	Configure network interface parameters.
named	Translate between domain names and IP addresses.
netstat	Print network status.
ping	Check that a remote host is online and responding.
pppd	Create PPP serial connection.
quagga	Routing daemon.
rdate	Notify time server that date has changed.
route	Manage routing tables.

Command	Action
routed	Dynamically keep routing tables up to date.
slattach	Attach serial lines as network interfaces.
sshd	Server for secure shell connections.
tcpdump	Write network packet information to screen or file.
telnetd	Server for Telnet sessions from remote hosts.
tftpd	Server for restricted set of file transfers.
zebra	Routing daemon.

NFS and NIS Administration

Command	Action
domainname	Set or display name of current NIS domain.
makedbm	Rebuild NIS databases.
rpcbind	DARPA port to RPC program number mapper.
portmap	The old name for **rpcbind**.
rpcinfo	Report RPC information.
ypbind	Connect to NIS server.
ypcat	Print values in NIS database.
ypinit	Build new NIS databases.
ypmatch	Print value of one or more NIS keys.
yppasswd	Change user password in NIS database.
yppasswdd	Update NIS database in response to **yppasswd**.
yppoll	Determine version of NIS map at NIS server.
yppush	Propagate NIS map.
ypserv	NIS server daemon.
ypset	Point **ypbind** at a specific server.
yptest	Check NIS configuration.
ypwhich	Display name of NIS server or map master.
ypxfr	Transfer NIS database from server to local host.

Overview of TCP/IP

TCP/IP is a suite of communications protocols that define how different types of computers talk to one another. It's named for its foundational protocols, the Transmission Control Protocol and the Internet Protocol. The Internet Protocol provides logical addressing as data moves between hosts: it splits data into packets, which are then forwarded to machines via the network. The Transmission Control Protocol ensures that the packets in a message are reassembled in the correct order at their final destination and that any missing datagrams are re-sent until they are correctly received. Other protocols provided as part of TCP/IP include:

Address Resolution Protocol (ARP)
Translates between Internet and local hardware addresses (Ethernet, etc.).

Internet Control Message Protocol (ICMP)
  Error-message and control protocol.

Point-to-Point Protocol (PPP)
  Enables TCP/IP (and other protocols) to be carried across both synchronous and asynchronous point-to-point serial links.

Reverse Address Resolution Protocol (RARP)
  Translates between local hardware and Internet addresses (opposite of ARP).

Simple Mail Transport Protocol (SMTP)
  Used by **sendmail** to send mail via TCP/IP.

Simple Network Management Protocol (SNMP)
  Performs distributed network management functions via TCP/IP.

User Datagram Protocol (UDP)
  Transfers data without first making a persistent connection between two systems the way TCP does. Sometimes called unreliable transport.

TCP/IP is covered in depth in the three-volume set *Internetworking with TCP/IP* (Prentice Hall). The commands in this chapter and the next are described in more detail in *TCP/IP Network Administration* and *Linux Network Administrator's Guide*, both published by O'Reilly.

In the architecture of TCP/IP protocols, data is passed down the stack (toward the Network Access Layer) when it is sent to the network, and up the stack when it is received from the network (see Figure 2-1).

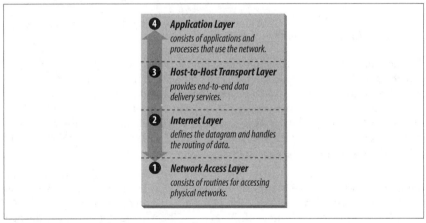

Figure 2-1. Layers in the TCP/IP protocol architecture

IP Addresses

The IP (Internet protocol) address is a binary number that differentiates your machine from all others on the network. Each machine on the Internet must have a unique IP address. The most common form of IP address used currently (IPv4) uses a 32-bit binary address. An IPv4 address contains two parts: a network part and a host part. The number of address bits used to identify the network and host differ according to the class of the address. There are three main address classes: A, B, and C (see Figure 2-2). The leftmost bits indicate what class each address is.

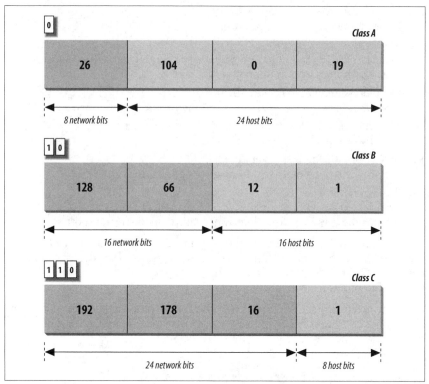

Figure 2-2. IP address structure

A standard called Classless Inter-Domain Routing (CIDR, or supernetting) extends the class system's idea of using initial bits to identify where packets should be routed. Under CIDR, a new domain can be created with any number of fixed leftmost bits (not just a multiple of eight). A CIDR address looks like a regular IPv4 address followed by a slash and a number indicating the number of network bits. For example: 192.168.32.1/24 or 128.66.128.1/17. Virtually all Internet gateway hosts now use CIDR.

IPv6, a newer standard, changes the method of addressing and increases the number of fields. An IPv6 address is 128 bits. Part of an IPv6 address is based on the Media Access Control (MAC) address of the network interface. The MAC address is unique for each network interface. When written, it is usually divided into eight 16-bit hexadecimal blocks separated by colons. For example:

```
FE80:0000:0000:0000:0202:B3FF:FE1E:8329
```

To shorten this, leading zeros may be skipped, and any one set of consecutive zeros can be replaced with double colons. For example, the above address can be reduced to:

```
FE80::202:B3FF:FE1E:8329
```

When IPv4 and IPv6 networks are mixed, the IPv4 address can be packed into the lower four bytes, yielding an address like 0:0:0:0:0:0:192.168.1.2, or ::192.168.1.2, or even ::C0A8:102.

Because improvements in IPv4, including CIDR, have relieved much of the pressure to migrate to IPv6, organizations have been slow to adopt IPv6. Some use it experimentally, but communication between organizations using IPv6 internally is still usually encapsulated inside IPv4 datagrams, and it will be a while before IPv6 becomes common.

If you wish to connect to the Internet, contact an Internet Service Provider (ISP). For most users, an ISP dynamically assigns an IP address to their systems. If you wish to always have the same address, have them assign you a static network address or range of addresses. If you are not connecting to an outside network, you can choose your own network address as long as it conforms to the IP address syntax. You should use the special reserved addresses provided in RFC 1597, which lists IP network numbers for private networks that don't have to be registered with the IANA (Internet Assigned Numbers Authority). An IP address is different from an Ethernet address, which is assigned by the manufacturer of the physical Ethernet card.

Gateways and Routing

Gateways are hosts responsible for exchanging routing information and forwarding data from one network to another. Each portion of a network that is under a separate local administration is called an *autonomous system* (AS). Autonomous systems connect to each other via exterior gateways. An AS also may contain its own system of networks, linked via interior gateways.

Gateway protocols

Gateway protocols include:

EGP (Exterior Gateway Protocol)

BGP (Border Gateway Protocol)
> Protocols for exterior gateways to exchange information

RIP (Routing Information Protocol)
> Interior gateway protocol; most popular for LANs

Hello Protocol

OSPF (Open Shortest Path First)
> Interior gateway protocols

Routing daemons

While most networks will use a dedicated router as a gateway, routing daemons like quagga and GNU Zebra, can be run on a host to make it function as a gateway. Thes replace the older gated daemon. Only one of them can run on a host at any given time. They allow a host to function as both an exterior and interior gateway and simplify routing configuration by combining the protocols RIP, Hello, BGP, EGP, and OSPF into a single package. We do not cover quagga or GNU Zebra in this book.

routed, a network routing daemon that uses RIP, allows a host to function only as an interior gateway, and manages the Internet routing tables. For more details on **routed**, see Chapter 3.

Routing tables

Routing tables provide information needed to route packets to their destinations. This information includes destination network, gateway to use, route status, and number of packets transmitted. Routing tables can be displayed with the **netstat** command.

Name Service

Each host on a network has a name that points to information about that host. Hostnames can be assigned to any device that has an IP address. A name service translates the hostnames (which are easy for people to remember) to IP addresses (the numbers the computer deals with).

DNS and BIND

The Domain Name System (DNS) is a distributed database of information about hosts on a network. Its structure is similar to that of the Unix filesystem—an inverted tree, with the root at the top. The branches of the tree are called *domains* (or *subdomains*) and correspond to IP addresses. The most popular implementation of DNS is the BIND (Berkeley Internet Name Domain) software.

DNS works as a client/server application. The *resolver* is the client, the software that asks questions about host information. The *nameserver* is the process that answers the questions. The server side of BIND is the **named** daemon. You can interactively query nameservers for host information with the **dig** and **host** commands. See Chapter 3 for more details on **named**, **dig**, and **host**.

The nameserver of a domain is responsible for keeping (and providing on request) the names of the machines in its domain. Other nameservers on the network forward requests for these machines to this nameserver.

Domain names

The full domain name is the sequence of names from the current domain back to the root, with a period separating the names. For instance, *oreilly.com* indicates the domain *oreilly* (for O'Reilly Media, Inc.), which is under the domain *com* (for commercial). One machine under this domain is *www.oreilly.com*. Top-level domains include:

aero
Air-transport industry

biz
Commercial organizations

com
Commercial organizations

coop
Cooperatives

edu
> United States educational organizations

gov
> United States government organizations

info
> Informative sites

int
> International organizations

mil
> United States military departments

museum
> Museums

name
> Names of individuals

net
> Commercial Internet organizations, usually Internet service providers

org
> Miscellaneous organizations

pro
> Professionals, including accountants, lawyers, and physicians

Countries also have their own two-letter top-level domains based on two-letter country codes. For example, the web server for the British Broadcasting System (BBC) in the United Kingdom has the following domain name: *www.bbc.co.uk*. Some domains (e.g., *edu*, *gov*, and *mil*) are sponsored by organizations that restrict their use; others (e.g., *com*, *info*, *net*, and *org*) are unrestricted. One special domain, *arpa*, is used for technical infrastructure purposes. The Internet Corporation for Assigned Names and Numbers (ICANN) oversees top-level domains and provides contact information for sponsored domains.

Configuring TCP/IP

Certain commands are normally run in the system's startup files to enable a system to connect to a network. These commands can also be run interactively.

Network interfaces

The network interface represents the way that the networking software uses the hardware: the driver, the IP address, and so forth. To configure a network interface, use the **ip** command. This command replaces the older **ifconfig** command. It has a Cisco IOS-like command syntax that will be familiar to many network administrators. With **ip**, you can assign an address to a network interface, setting the netmask, broadcast address, and IP address at boot time. You can also set network interface parameters, including the use of ARP, the use of driver-dependent debugging code, the use of one-packet mode, and the address of the correspondent on the other end of a point-to-point link. For more information on **ip**, see Chapter 3.

Serial-line communication

There are two protocols for serial-line communication: Serial Line IP (SLIP) and Point-to-Point Protocol (PPP). These protocols let computers transfer information using the serial port instead of a network card, and a serial cable instead of an Ethernet cable. SLIP is rarely used anymore, having been replaced by PPP.

PPP was intended to remedy some of SLIP's failings; it can hold packets from non-Internet protocols, it implements client authorization and error detection/correction, and it dynamically configures each network protocol that passes through it. Under Linux, PPP exists as a driver in the kernel and as the daemon **pppd**. For more information on **pppd**, see Chapter 3.

Troubleshooting TCP/IP

The following commands can be used to troubleshoot TCP/IP. For more details on these commands, see Chapter 3:

dig
> Query the DNS name service.

ifconfig
> Provide information about the basic configuration of the network interface.

ifup *and* **ifdown**
> On many systems used to start or stop a network interface.

iwconfig, iwlist, *and* **wlancfg**
> Tools commonly used to configure a wireless network interface.

nc
> Read and write data across a network connection.

netstat
> Display network status.

ping
> Indicate whether a remote host can be reached.

route
> Allows you to read and set default gateway information, as well as static routes.

tcpdump
> Dump network packet information to the screen or to file.

traceroute
> Trace route taken by packets to reach network host.

Overview of Firewalls and Masquerading

A firewall is a secure computer that sits between an internal network and an external network (i.e., the Internet). It is configured with a set of rules that it uses to determine what traffic is allowed to pass and what traffic is barred. While a firewall is generally intended to protect the network from malicious or even accidentally harmful traffic from the outside, it can also be configured to monitor traffic leaving the network. As the sole entry point into the system, the firewall makes it easier to construct defenses and monitor activity.

The firewall can also be set up to present a single IP address to the outside world, even though multiple IP addresses may be used internally. This is known as *masquerading*. Masquerading can act as additional protection, hiding the very existence of a network. It also saves the trouble and expense of obtaining multiple IP addresses.

IP firewalling and masquerading are implemented with *netfilter*, also known as **iptables**. Tthe facilities provided by *netfilter* are designed to be extensible; if there is some function missing from the implementation, you can add it.

The packet filtering facilities provide built-in rule sets. Each network packet is checked against each rule in the rule set until the packet either matches a rule or is not matched by any rule. These sets of rules are called *chains*. These chains are organized into tables that separate filtering functions from masquerading and packet mangling functions. If a match is found, the counters on that rule are incremented and any target for that rule is applied. A target might accept, reject, or masquerade a packet, or even pass it along to another chain for processing. Details on the chains provided in **iptables** can be found in Chapter 3.

In addition to these chains, you can create your own user-defined chains. You might want a special chain for your PPP interfaces or for packets from a particular site. To call a user-defined chain, you just make it the target for a match.

It is possible to make it through a chain without matching any rules that have a target. If no rule matches the packet in a user-defined chain, control returns to the chain from which it was called, and the next rule in that chain is checked. If no rule matches the packet in a built-in chain, a default policy for that chain is used. The default policy can be any of the special targets that determine what is done with a packet. The valid targets are detailed in Chapter 3.

You use the **iptables** command to define the rules. Once you have the rules defined you can use **iptables-save** to create a file with all the rule definitions, and **iptables-restore** to restore those definitions when you reboot.

For more information on the kinds of decisions you need to make and the considerations that go into defining the rules, see a general book on firewalls such as *Building Internet Firewalls* (O'Reilly) by Elizabeth D. Zwicky et al. For more details on **iptables**, consult the *Linux Network Administrator's Guide* (O'Reilly) by Tony Bautts et al., *Linux iptables Pocket Reference* (O'Reilly) by Gregor N. Purdy, or one of the relevant HOWTOs, such as the "Packet Filtering HOWTO." These HOWTOs and a number of tutorials are available on the Netfilter website at *http:// www.netfilter.org/*.

Overview of NFS

The Network File System (NFS) is a distributed filesystem that allows users to mount remote filesystems as if they were local. NFS uses a client/server model in which a server exports directories to be shared and clients mount the directories to access the files in them. NFS eliminates the need to keep copies of files on several machines by letting the clients all share a single copy of a file on the server. NFS is an RPC-based application-level protocol. For more information on the architecture of network protocols, see "Overview of TCP/IP" on page 22.

Administering NFS

To set up NFS clients and servers, you must start the NFS daemons on the servers, export filesystems from the NFS servers, and mount the filesystems on the clients. The */etc/exports* file is the NFS server configuration file; it controls which files and directories are exported and which kinds of access are allowed. Names and addresses for clients that should be allowed or denied access to NFS are kept in the */etc/hosts.allow* and */etc/hosts.deny* files.

Daemons

NFS server daemons, called *nfsd daemons*, run on the server and accept RPC calls from clients. NFS servers also run the **mountd** daemon to handle mount requests. On the client, caching and buffering are handled by **biod**, the block I/O daemon. The **rpcbind** daemon maps RPC program numbers to the appropriate TCP/IP port numbers. If the **rpcbind** daemon is not running properly, NFS will not work either. On older systems **rpcbind** is named **portmap**.

Exporting Filesystems

To set up an NFS server, first check that all the hosts that will mount your filesystem can reach your host. Next, edit the */etc/exports* file on the server. Each entry in this file indicates the name of a directory to be exported, domain names of machines that will have access to that particular mount point, and any options specific to that machine. A typical entry looks like:

    /projects hostname1(rw) hostname2(ro)

If you are running **mountd**, the files will be exported as allowed by the permissions in */etc/exports*. See the **exports** manpage for all available export options.

Mounting Filesystems

To enable an NFS client, mount a remote filesystem after NFS is started, either by using the **mount** command or by specifying default remote filesystems in */etc/fstab*. For example:

    #mount servername:/projects /mnt/nfs/projects

A **mount** request calls the server's **mountd** daemon, which checks the access permissions of the client and returns a pointer to a filesystem. Once a directory is mounted, it remains attached to the local filesystem until it is unmounted with the **umount** command or until the local system is rebooted.

Usually, only a privileged user can mount filesystems with NFS. However, you can enable users to mount and unmount selected filesystems using the **mount** and **unmount** commands if the **user** option is set in */etc/fstab*. This can reduce traffic by having filesystems mounted only when needed. To enable user mounting, create an entry in */etc/fstab* for each filesystem to be mounted. You can verify filesystems that have been mounted by using the **mount** or **showmount** commands. Or, you can read the contents of the */etc/mtab* file.

Overview of NIS

The Network Information System (NIS) refers to the service formerly known as Sun Yellow Pages (YP). It is used to make configuration information consistent on all machines in a network. It does this by designating a single host as the master of all the system administration files and databases and distributing this information to all other hosts on the network. The information is compiled into databases called maps. NIS is built on the RPC protocol.

Another version of NIS, NIS+, adds encryption and strong authentication to NIS. NIS+ is a proprietary standard created by Sun Microsystems. This chapter discusses standard NIS, which is supported by most Linux systems. There are currently two NIS servers freely available for Linux, **yps** and **ypserv**. We describe **ypserv** in this book.

Servers

In NIS, there are two types of servers: master servers and slave servers. Master servers are responsible for maintaining the maps and distributing them to the slave servers. The files are then available locally to requesting processes.

Domains

An NIS domain is a group of hosts that use the same set of maps. The maps are contained in a subdirectory of */var/yp* having the same name as the domain. The machines in a domain share password, host, and group file information. NIS domain names are set with the **domainname** command.

NIS Maps

NIS stores information in database files called *maps*. Each map consists of a pair of **dbm** database files, one containing a directory of keys (a bitmap of indices) and the other containing data values. The non-ASCII structure of **dbm** files necessitates using NIS tools such as **yppush** to move maps between machines.

The file */var/yp/YP_MAP_X_LATE* contains a complete listing of active NIS maps, as well as NIS aliases for NIS maps. All maps must be listed in this file in order for NIS to serve them.

Map Manipulation Utilities

The following utilities are used to administer NIS maps:

makedbm
> Make **dbm** files. Modify only **ypserv**'s map and any nondefault maps.

ypinit
> Build and install NIS databases. Manipulate maps when NIS is being initialized. Should not be used when NIS is already running.

yppush
> Transfer updated maps from the master server.

Administering NIS

NIS is enabled by setting up NIS servers and NIS clients. The descriptions given here describe NIS setup using **ypserv**, which does not support a master/slave server configuration. All NIS commands depend on the RPC **rpcbind** program, so make sure it is installed and running before setting up NIS.

Setting Up an NIS Server

Setting up an NIS server involves the following steps:

1. Set a domain name for NIS using **domainname**.
2. Edit the *ypMakefile*, which identifies which databases to build and what sources to use in building them.
3. Copy the *ypMakefile* to */var/yp/Makefile*.
4. Run **make** from the */var/yp* directory, which builds the databases and initializes the server.
5. Start **ypserv**, the NIS server daemon.

Setting Up an NIS Client

Setting up an NIS client involves only the following steps:

1. Set the domain name for NIS using **domainname**, which should be the same name used by the NIS server.
2. Run **ypbind**.

NIS User Accounts

NIS networks have two kinds of user accounts: distributed and local. Distributed accounts must be administered from the master machine; they provide information that is uniform on each machine in an NIS domain. Changes made to distributed accounts are distributed via NIS maps. Local accounts are administered from the local computer; they provide account information unique to a specific machine. They are not affected by NIS maps, and changes made to local accounts do not affect NIS. When NIS is installed, preexisting accounts default to local accounts.

RPC and XDR

RPC (remote procedure call) is the session protocol used by both NFS and NIS. It allows a host to make a procedure call that appears to be local but is really executed remotely on another machine on the network. RPC is implemented as a library of procedures, plus a network standard for ordering bytes and data structures called XDR (eXternal Data Representation).

3

Linux Commands

This chapter presents the Linux user, programmer, and system administration commands. These are entered into a shell at the console or on a virtual terminal on a graphical desktop.

Each entry is labeled with the command name on the outer edge of the page. The syntax line is followed by a brief description and a list of available options. Many commands come with examples at the end of the entry. If you need only a quick reminder or suggestion about a command, you can skip directly to the examples.

Typographic conventions for describing command syntax are listed in the preface. For help in locating commands, see the index at the back of this book.

We've tried to be as thorough as possible in listing options. The basic command information and most options should be correct; however, there are many Linux distributions and many versions of commands. New options are added, and occasionally old options are dropped. You may, therefore, find some differences between the options you find described here and the ones on your system. When there seems to be a discrepancy, check the manpage. For most commands, you can also use the option --**help** to get a brief usage message. (Even when it isn't a valid option, it will usually result in an "invalid option" error along with the usage message.)

Traditionally, commands take single-letter options preceded by a single hyphen, such as -**d**. A more recent convention allows long options preceded by two hyphens, such as --**debug**. Often, a feature can be invoked through either the old style or the new style of options.

Alphabetical Summary of Commands

accept

accept [*option*] *queue*

System administration command. Instruct printing system to accept jobs for the specified print queue or queues. Depending on queue settings, the system may prompt for a password.

Option
-E   Force encrypted connection.

-h *host* [*port*]
　　Connect to specified server.

-U *username*
　　Use alternate username when connecting to server.

access

access [*mode*] [*filename*]

Check whether a file is available for the action specified with the mode argument: **r** for read, **w** for write, **x** for execute. Used mostly in scripting, **access** works better than **test** because it uses a direct system call rather than looking at the file permissions, which can be misleading when a filesystem is mounted read-only.

Options
--help
　　Display help message, then quit.

--version
　　Display version, then quit.

aclocal

aclocal [*options*]

GNU **autoconf** tool. Place **m4** macro definitions needed by **autoconf** into a single file. The **aclocal** command first scans for macro definitions in **m4** files in its default directory (*/usr/share/aclocal* on some systems) and in the file *acinclude.m4*. It next scans for macros used in the *configure.in* file. It generates an *aclocal.m4* file that contains definitions of all **m4** macros required by **autoconf**.

Options
--acdir=*dir*
　　Look for macro files in directory *dir* instead of the default directory.

--help
　　Print help message, then exit.

-I *dir*
　　Additionally, search directory *dir* for **m4** macro definitions.

--output=*file*
　　Save output to *file* instead of *aclocal.m4*.

--print-ac-dir

Print the name of the directory to be searched for **m4** files, then exit.

--verbose

Print names of files being processed.

--version

Print version number, then exit.

---

aconnect

aconnect [*options*] [*sender*] [*receiver*]

aconnect [*options*]

Like its GUI relative **alsa-patch-bay**, **aconnect** connects ports in MIDI hardware and software to route events, similar to running patch cables between different mixers and synthesizers in an all-hardware audio system. **aconnect** is part of the ALSA (Advanced Linux Sound Architecture) system.

Options

-d, --disconnect

Undo the connection described.

-e, --exclusive

The connection being created must be exclusive: the sender and receiver ports may not connect to any other port.

-i, --input

List all input (sender) ports. This flag is used without any other arguments or flags.

-o, --output

List all output (receiver) ports. This flag is used without any other arguments or flags.

-r, --real *queue-name*

All events processed through this connection get new time-stamps from the named real-time queue. The receiving port must have access to, and use, the real-time queue.

-t, --tick *queue-name*

All events processed through this connection get new time-stamps from the specified tick queue.

-x, --remove-all

Cancel all connections. This flag is used without any other arguments or flags.

---

acpi

acpi [*options*]

Displays information about the ACPI (Advanced Configuration and Power Interface) system, based on the */proc/acpi* file. Most kernels after 2.4 support ACPI hardware, and in both hardware and software, ACPI is gradually replacing the older APM (Advanced Power Management) system. Some operating systems, including SUSE, ship a combined ACPI/APM power interface called **powersaved**. Most, however, require either ACPI or APM software.

Note that some ACPI systems have special events that are not available on others. For example, some laptops have events related to their docking stations and keyboard lights that are not used on nondocking or unlighted laptops. On all systems, the */proc/acpi* directory must be present for **acpi** commands to work.

Options

--a, --ac-adapter
Show whether the AC adapter is connected.

-A, --without-ac-adapter
Do not show information about the AC adapter.

b, --battery
Display battery information.

-B, --without-battery
Do not display battery information.

-c, --celcius
Use degrees Celsius as the temperature unit. This is the default unit.

-d, --directory *path*
Use the specified path to ACPI information. The default is */proc/ acpi*.

-f, --fahrenheit
Use degrees Fahrenheit as the temperature unit.

-h, --help
Display help information.

-k, --kelvin
Use degrees Kelvin as the temperature unit.

-s, --show-empty
Display information even on devices that are not available or not installed, such as empty slots for extra batteries.

-S, --hide-empty
Do not display information on devices that are not operational or not installed.

-t, --thermal
Display temperature information.

-T, --without-thermal
Do not display temperature information.

-v, --version
Display version information.

-V, --everything
Show all information on every device.

acpid

acpid [options]

Daemon that informs user-space programs about ACPI (Advanced Configuration and Power Interface) events, such as battery warnings, power-supply changes, and laptop lid closings. As ACPI hardware replaces older APM (Advanced Power Management) hardware, **acpid** replaces **apmd**. Like other daemons, this application is controlled primarily through a configuration file that determines which events merit action, and what those actions are.

Options

-c *directory*, **--confdir**=*directory*
> Set the directory used for configuration files. The default directory is */etc/acpi/events*. All files in this directory, except those beginning with a period (.), are parsed as configuration files. Typically, a single file is used for each ACPI event to be acted upon.
>
> In the configuration files, blank lines and those beginning with # are ignored. Other lines are expected to consist of a regular expression and a command to be executed when an ACPI event matches the expression.

-d, **--debug**
> Debug mode: run the daemon in the foreground and send all log output to stderr and stdout, rather than a logfile.

-e *filename*, **--eventfile**=*filename*
> Set the file used to find events. Normally this is */proc/acpi/ event*.

-g *group*, **--socketgroup**=*group*
> Set the group ownership of the socket to which **acpid** publishes events. This allows you to restrict which users on the system can access ACPI event information.

-l *filename*, **--logfile**=*filename*
> Set the logfile location. Normally, it is */var/log/acpid*.

-m *mode*, **--socketmode**=*mode*
> Set the permission mode of the socket. Normally, it is 666, with the sticky bit off.

-s *filename*, **--socketfile**=*filename*
> Set the file used to define the socket. Normally, this is */var/ run/acpid*.socket.

-S, **--nosocket**
> Tells **acpid** not to open a socket at all. Overrides all other socket options.

-v, **--version**
> Print version information and quit.

-h, **--help**
> Print help message and quit.

---

addr2line

addr2line [*options*] [*addresses*]

Translate hexadecimal program addresses into filenames and line numbers for the executable given with the **-e** option, or *a.out* if **-e** is not specified. If *addresses* are given on the command line, display the filename and line number for each address. Otherwise, read the addresses from standard input and display the results on standard output (useful for use in a pipe). **addr2line** prints two question marks (??) if it cannot determine a filename, and 0 if it cannot determine the line number. **addr2line** is used for debugging.

Options

-b *bfdname*, **--target**=*bfdname*
> Set the binary file format using its binary file descriptor name, *bfdname*. Use the **-h** option for a list of supported formats for your system.

-C, **--demangle**[=*style*]
> Decode (demangle) low-level symbol names into usernames. See the **-h** help output for a list of styles supported by your compiler.

-e *file*, **--exe**=*file*
> Specify the filename of the executable to use. The default filename is *a.out*.

-f, **--functions**
> Display function names in addition to filenames and line numbers.

-h, **--help**
> Display help information and exit.

-s, **--basenames**
> Strip directories off filenames and show only the basenames.

agetty

agetty [*options*] *port baudrate* [*term*]

System administration command. **agetty** opens a tty port, prompts for login, and invokes the **login** command with the user's name as an argument. While reading the name, **agetty** attempts to adapt the system to the speed and type of device being used. **agetty** is usually invoked by **init** using parameters specified in the */etc/inittab* file, or in newer distributions of linux by an **upstart** event using parameters given in */etc/event.d/tty*[1–6] files. On some systems this command may also be invoked as **getty** or replaced by an alternative command like **mingetty**. (See discussion of **upstart** in Chapter 2.)

You must specify a *port*, which **agetty** will search for in the */dev* directory. You may use -, in which case **agetty** reads from standard input. You must also specify *baudrate*, which may be a comma-separated list of rates through which **agetty** will step. Optionally, you may specify the *term*, which is used to override the TERM environment variable.

Options

-8   Disable parity detection and assume tty is 8-bit clean.

-f *file*
> Specify the use of *file* instead of */etc/issue* upon connection to terminal. It is overridden by **-i**.

-h   Specify hardware, not software, flow control.

-H *hostname*
> Write login *hostname* into the *utmp* file. By default, no login host is specified.

-I *string*
> Specify *string* to be sent to the tty or modem.

-i   Suppress printing of */etc/issue* before printing the login prompt.

-l *program*
> Specify the use of *program* instead of */bin/login*.

-L   Do not require carrier detect; operate locally only. Use this when connecting terminals.

-m   Attempt to guess the appropriate baud rate.

-n   Don't prompt for a login name.

-t *timeout*
> Specify that **agetty** should exit if the **open** on the line succeeds and there is no response to the login prompt in *timeout* seconds.

-U   Enable uppercase-only terminal detection. This will turn on some upper- to lowercase conversions if the login name is given in all capitals.

-w   Wait for carriage return or linefeed before sending login prompt. Use when sending an initialization string.

alsactl

alsactl [*options*] [*command*] [*card*]

Control advanced configuration settings for sound cards using the ALSA (Advanced Linux Sound Architecture) system. Driver settings are written to and loaded from configuration files. The card can be specified as a card number, id, or device. If no card is specified, the configuration for all cards is saved or loaded. The default configuration file is */etc/asound.state*.

Commands

init
> Attempt to initialize all sound cards to a default state.

restore
> Load the driver information from the configuration file.

store
> Save the current driver information to the configuration file.

Options

-d, --debug
> Debug mode: increased information output to the console.

-E *var=value,* **--env** *var=value*
> Set an environment variable. Useful for **init** or to override ALSA_CONFIG_PATH.

-f *file,* **--file**=*file*
> Specify the use of *file* instead of */etc/asound.state* as a configuration file.

-F, --force

Force the restoration of settings; used with **restore**. This is the default.

-g, --ignore

With **store** and **restore**, do not display errors and do not set error exit codes.

-h, --help

Display help message and quit.

-i *file*, **--initfile=***file*

Specify the configuration file for **init**. The default is */usr/share/alsa/init/00main*.

-p, --pedantic

Ignore mismatched control settings; used with **restore**.

-r *file*, **--runstate=***file*

Save **restore** and **init** errors to the specified file, appending new errors to the end of the file (unless **-R** is specified).

-R, --remove

Remove the runstate file first, before running the **restore** or **init**.

-v, --version

Display version information and quit.

---

alsamixer

alsamixer [*options*]

An ALSA mixer with an ncurses interface, for use with ALSA soundcard drivers. **alsamixer** supports multiple sound cards with multiple drivers. Use ESC or Alt-Q to exit.

Options

-c cardnum

Specify the number or id of the soundcard to use, if there are multiple cards. Card numbers start from 0 (the default).

-D *deviceid*

Specify the id of the mixer device to control.

-g   Toggle use of color or monochrome in the **alsamixer** window.

-h, --help

Display brief usage message and exit.

-s   Minimize the mixer window.

-V *mode*

Select the starting view mode. The possible modes are **playback**, **capture**, or **all**.

---

amidi

amidi [*options*]

Read and write raw MIDI files (*.syx* format, without timing information) to ALSA ports. For standard MIDI (*.mid*) files, use **aplaymidi** and **arecordmidi**.

Options

-a, --active-sensing
> Record and send active-sensing (FEh) bytes in MIDI commands. By default, these bytes are ignored.

-d, --dump
> Output received data directly to the screen as hexadecimal bytes.

-h, --help
> Display help information and quit.

-l, --list-devices
> List all hardware MIDI ports.

-L, --list-rawmidis
> List all RawMIDI definitions. Useful for debugging configuration files.

-p, --port=_name_
> Use the specified port. This overrides the port set in the configuration file. If neither this flag nor the configuration file sets a port, the default is port 0 on device 0, which may or may not exist.

-r, --receive=_filename_
> Write data from the port specified with the **-p** or **--port** flag to the file named here, which is a raw file, and should end in _.syx_. Unless you use the **-a** option, the data does not include Active Sensing (FEh) bytes.

-s, --send=_filename_
> Send the file to the port specified with the **-p** or **--port** flag. Use raw (_.syx_) MIDI files only.

-S, --send-hex="_hex-numbers..._**"**
> Send a string of hexadecimal numbers to the port specified with the **-p** or **--port** flag.

-t, --timeout=_n_
> Stop listening after _n_ seconds of receiving no data.

-V, --version
> Display version information and quit.

---

amixer

amixer [_options_] [_command_]

Command-line ALSA mixer. For an ncurses interface, use **alsamixer**. **amixer** displays or changes the current mixer settings for the current sound card and sound device. To display all mixer settings, use with no flags or commands.

Commands

contents
> List card controls and their contents.

controls

> Display a complete list of card controls. These controls can be set with the **cset** command, in contrast to simple mixer controls, which use **set** or **sset**.

cget [*control*]

> Display the contents of the specified card control.

cset [*control*] [*parameter*]

> Set the card control to the value specified in the parameter. Card controls may be identified by **iface**, **name**, **index**, **device**, **subdevice**, or **numid**. The parameter is normally a number or percentage value. For example, the command **amixer -c 1 cset numid=16 50%** sets the 16th element of the first sound card to 50%.

get, sget [*control*]

> Display the current values for the specified simple mixer control.

help

> Display help message and quit.

info

> Display information about the current card or the card specified with the -c flag.

scontents

> Display a complete list of simple mixer controls and their contents.

scontrols

> Display a list of simple mixer controls. Simple mixer controls can be set with the **set** or **sset** commands, in contrast to card controls, which use the **cset** command.

set, sset [*control*] [*parameter*]

> Set one of the controls listed by **scontrols**. You can specify the volume with a percentage from 0% to 100%, or a specific hardware value. Append + or − to the number to increase or decrease the volume by that amount. To set recording and muting values, use the parameters **cap** (meaning capture, or record), **nocap**, **mute**, **unmute**, or **toggle**. To specify individual channels, use the parameters **front**, **rear**, **center**, or **woofer**. For example, the command **amixer -c 1 sset Line,0 100% unmute** sets Line 0 on the first sound card to 100% and unmutes it.

Options

-c *n*

> The number of the card to adjust.

-D *devicename*

> Specify the name of the device. By default, the name is *default*.

-h   Display help information and quit.

-q   Quiet mode: do not show the results of changes made.

-s, --stdin
> Read command lines from standard input and execute sequentially.

---

anacron

anacron [*options*] [*job*]

System administration command. Normally started in a system startup file. Execute commands periodically. By default, **anacron** reads a list of jobs from a configuration file, */etc/anacrontab*. The file consists of shell variables to use when running commands, followed by a list of tasks to run. Each task specifies how often in days it should be run, a delay in minutes to wait before running the task, a unique job identifier used to store a timestamp, and the shell command to execute. Timestamps for the last run of each task are stored in the */var/spool/anacron* file. For each task, **anacron** compares the stored timestamp against the current time. If the command has not been executed within the specified frequency, the command is run. Upon completion, **anacron** records the new date in the timestamp file. Limit **anacron** to a specified task by providing the task's unique *job* identifier on the command line.

The **anacron** command is often used to support the **cron** daemon on systems that do not run continuously.

Options

-d   Run in foreground rather than as a background process. Send messages to standard error.

-f   Run tasks ignoring timestamps.

-h   Print help message, then exit.

-n   Run tasks now, ignoring delay specifications.

-q   Suppress messages to standard error when using the **-d** option.

-s   Execute tasks serially. Do not start new task until previous task is completed.

-S *directory*
> Store timestamps in *directory* instead of */var/spool/anacron*.

-t *file*
> Read tasks from *file* instead of from */etc/anacrontab*.

-T   Test validity of configuration file. Can be used with **-t**.

-u   Update timestamps for tasks, but don't run them.

-V   Print version number, then exit.

---

aplay

aplay [*options*] [*file*]

Play sound files using the ALSA sound system. The related **arecord** records sound files.

Options

-c, --channels=*n*
> Use *n* channels: 1 for mono, 2 for stereo.

-d, --duration=n
> Set an interrupt for n seconds after playback begins.

-D, --device=_devicename_
> Select a PCM device by name.

-f, --format=_format_
> Specify the sample format. The sample formats available will depend on hardware. For CD and DAT output, use the **cd** and **dat** shortcuts, which set the sample rate, format, and channel numbers all at once.

-h, --help
> Print help message, then exit.

-l, --list-devices
> List available sound cards and digital audio devices.

-L, --list-pcms
> List all PCM (pulse-coded modulation, or digital audio) devices that have been defined. PCMs may be defined in the _.asoundrc_ file.

-q, --quiet
> Run quietly. Do not display messages.

-r, --rate=n
> Set the sample rate in Hertz. The default is 8000 Hertz.

-s, --sleep-min=n
> Set the minimum number of ticks to sleep. The default is not to sleep.

-t, --file-type=_type_
> Name the file type used. Files may be **voc**, **wav**, **raw**, or **au**.

--version
> Print version and quit.

---

aplaymidi

aplaymidi [_options_] [_file_]

Play MIDI files using the ALSA sound system; output is to ALSA sequencer ports.

Options

-d, --delay=n
> Delay n seconds at the end of a file to allow for reverberation of the final notes.

-h, --help
> Print help message, then exit.

-V, --version
> Print version and quit.

-l, --list
> List output ports available.

-p, --port=_client:port_
> Specify the port to which the MIDI file will be sent. If no port is specified, the file will be sent to port 0.

---

apmd

apmd [*options*]

System administration command. **apmd** handles events reported by the Advanced Power Management BIOS driver. The driver reports on battery level and requests to enter sleep or suspend mode. **apmd** will log any reports it gets via **syslogd** and take steps to make sure that basic sleep and suspend requests are handled gracefully. You can fine-tune the behavior of **apmd** by editing the **apmd_proxy** script, which **apmd** runs when it receives an event. Note that the APM hardware standard has been replaced by the ACPI (Advanced Configuration and Power Interface) standard, and **apmd** by **acpid**.

Options

-c *n*, --check *n*
> Set the number of seconds to wait for an event before rechecking the power level. Default is to wait indefinitely. Setting this causes the battery levels to be checked more frequently.

-p *n*, --percentage *n*
> Log information whenever the power changes by *n* percent. The default is 5. Values greater than 100 will disable logging of power changes.

-P *command*, --proxy *command*
> Specify the **apmd_proxy** command to run when APM driver events are reported. This is generally a shell script. The *command* will be invoked with parameters indicating what kind of event was received. The parameters are listed in the next section.

-T [*n*], --proxy-timeout [*n*]
> Set time-out for proxy to *n* seconds. Without this option apmd will wait indefinitely for the proxy to finish. Default value of *n* is 30 seconds.

-v, --verbose
> Verbose mode; all events are logged.

-V, --version
> Print version and exit.

-w *n*, --warn *n*
> Log a warning at ALERT level when the battery charge drops below *n* percent. The default is 10. Negative values disable low-battery-level warnings.

-W, --wall
> Use **wall** to alert all users of a low battery status.

-q, --quiet
> Disable low-battery-level warnings.

-?, --help
> Print help summary and exit.

Linux Commands

Parameters

The **apmd** proxy script is invoked with the following parameters:

start
> Invoked when the daemon starts.

stop
> Invoked when the daemon stops.

standby [system | user]
> Invoked when the daemon receives a standby request. The second parameter indicates whether the request was made by the system or by the user. Standby mode powers off the monitor and disks, but the system continues to run and use power.

suspend [system | user]
> Invoked when the daemon receives a suspend request. The second parameter indicates whether the request was made by the system or by the user. Suspend, also known as "hibernate," effectively powers the system down but has a quicker recovery than a normal boot process.

resume [suspend | standby | critical]
> Invoked when the system resumes normal operation. The second parameter indicates the mode the system was in before resuming. **critical** suspends indicate an emergency shutdown. After a **critical** suspend, the system may be unstable, and you can use the **resume** command to help you recover from the suspension.

change power
> Invoked when system power is changed from AC to battery or from battery to AC.

change battery
> Invoked when the APM BIOS driver reports that the battery is low.

change capability
> Invoked when the APM BIOS driver reports that some hardware that affects its capability has been added or removed.

---

apropos

apropos *string* ...

Search the short manual page descriptions in the **whatis** database for occurrences of each *string* and display the result on standard output. Similar to **whatis**, except that it searches for strings instead of words. Equivalent to **man -k**.

---

apt

apt

The Advanced Package Tool, the Debian package management system. A freely available packaging system for software distribution and installation. For detailed information on **apt** and its commands, see Chapter 5.

---

ar

ar *key* [*args*] [*posname*] [*count*] *archive* [*files*]

Maintain a group of *files* that are combined into a file *archive*. Used most commonly to create and update static library files, as used by the link editor (**ld**). Compiler frontends often call **ar** automatically. Only one key letter may be used, but each can be combined with additional *args* (with no separations between). *posname* is the name of a file in *archive*. When moving or replacing *files*, you can specify that they be placed before or after *posname*. **ar** has largely been superseded by **tar** and **bzip2**.

Keys

d   Delete *files* from *archive*.

m   Move *files* to end of *archive*.

p   Print *files* in *archive*.

q   Append *files* to *archive*.

r   Replace *files* in *archive*.

t   List the contents of *archive* or list the named *files*.

x   Extract contents from *archive* or only the named *files*.

Arguments

a   Use with **r** or **m** key to place *files* in the archive after *posname*.

b   Same as **a**, but before *posname*.

c   Create *archive* silently.

f   Truncate long filenames.

i   Same as **b**.

l   For backward compatibility; meaningless in Linux.

N   Use *count* parameter. Where multiple entries with the same name are found, use the *count* instance.

o   Preserve original timestamps.

P   Use full pathname. Useful for non-POSIX-compliant archives.

s   Force regeneration of *archive* symbol table (useful after running **strip**).

S   Do not regenerate symbol table.

u   Use with **r** to replace only *files* that have changed since being put in *archive*.

v   Verbose; print a description of actions taken.

V   Print version number.

Example

Replace **mylib.a** with object files from the current directory:

```
ar r mylib.a `ls *.o`
```

arch   arch

Print machine architecture type to standard output. Equivalent to
uname -m.

arecord   arecord [*options*] [*filename*]

Records sound using ALSA. Accepts the same arguments and options
as **aplay**.

arecordmidi   arecord [*options*] [*filename*]

Records midi files using ALSA. You must specify the port using the
-p flag.

Options

-b, --bmp=*n*
   Set the tempo value to *n* beats per minute. The default is 120.

-f, --fps=*n*
   Set timing (SMPTE resolution) to *n* frames per second. The
   value is normally 24, 25, 29.97 (NTSC dropframe), or 30.

-h, --help
   Display help message.

-i, --timesig=*numerator:denominator*
   Set the time signature for the file and the metronome, specified as the numerator and the denominator separated by a
   colon. The denominator must be a power of 2. Defaults to 4:4.

-l, --list
   List available ports.

-m, --metronome=*client:port*
   Play a metronome signal on the specified sequencer port.

-p, --port=*host:port*
   Set the sequencer host and port used. The default host is the
   local host, and the default port is port 0.

-s, --split-channels
   For each channel of input, create a separate track in the MIDI
   output file.

-t, --ticks=*n*
   Set the frequency with which timestamps, or ticks, are used in
   the file. For MIDI files using musical tempo, timestamps are
   set in ticks per beat (default 384), while those with SMPTE
   timing use ticks per frame (default 40).

-v, --version
   Display version number.

arp

arp [*options*]

TCP/IP command. Clear, add to, or dump the kernel's Address Resolution Protocol (ARP) cache (*/proc/net/arp*). ARP is used to translate protocol addresses to hardware interface addresses. Modifying your ARP cache can change which interfaces handle specific requests. ARP cache entries may be marked with the following flags: **C** (complete), **M** (permanent), and **P** (publish). While **arp** can create a proxy for a single system, subnet proxies are now handled by the **arp** kernel module, *arp*(7). See the "Linux Advanced Routing & Traffic Control HOWTO" for details.

Options

host option arguments may be given as either a hostname or an IP address. With the **-D** option, they may also be given as a hardware interface address (e.g., eth0, eth1).

-a [*hosts*], --all [*hosts*]
Display entries in alternate (BSD) style for *hosts* or, if none are specified, all entries.

-d *host* [pub], --delete *host* [pub]
Remove the specified *host*'s entry. To delete a proxy entry, add the **pub** argument and specify the interface associated with the proxy using **-i**.

-D, --use-device
Use the hardware address associated with the specified interface. This may be used with **-s** when creating a proxy entry.

-e   Display entries in default (Linux) style.

-f *file*, --file *file*
Read entries from *file* and add them.

-H *type*, --hw-type *type*, -t *type*
Search for *type* entries when examining the ARP cache. *type* is usually **ether** (Ethernet), which is the default, but may be **ax25** (AX.25 packet radio), **arcnet** (ARCnet), **pronet** (PROnet), or **netrom** (NET/ROM).

-i *interface*, --device *interface*
Select an interface. If you are dumping the ARP cache, this option will cause the command to display only the entries using that interface. When setting entries, this will cause the interface to be associated with that entry. If you do not use this option when setting an entry, the kernel will guess.

-n, --numeric
Display host IP addresses instead of their domain names.

-s *host hardware-address* [**netmask** *mask*] [**pub**], --set *host hardware-address* [**netmask** *mask*] [**pub**]
Add a permanent entry for *host* at *hardware-address*. A *hardware-address* for type **ether** hardware is 6 hexadecimal bytes, colon-separated. The **pub** argument can be used to set the publish flag, creating a proxy entry.

-v, --verbose
> Verbose mode.

Examples

Display entry for host **eris**:

```
arp -a eris
```

Set a permanent cache entry for host **illuminati**, whose hardware address you know:

```
arp -s illuminati 00:05:23:73:e6:cf
```

Set an ARP proxy for host **fnord** using the eth0 interface's hardware address:

```
arp -Ds fnord eth0 pub
```

Remove the **fnord** ARP proxy:

```
arp -i eth0 -d fnord pub
```

---

as

as [*options*] *files*

Generate an object file from each specified assembly-language source *file*. Object files have the same root name as source files but replace the *.s* suffix with *.o*. There may be some additional system-specific options.

Options

-- [| *files*]
> Read input files from standard input, or from *files* if the pipe is used.

-a[**cdhlmns**][=*file*]
> With only the **-a** option, list source code, assembler listing, and symbol table. The other options specify additional things to list or omit:
>
> **-ac** Omit false conditionals.
>
> **-ad** Omit debugging directives.
>
> **-ah** Include the high-level source code, if available.
>
> **-al** Include an assembly listing.
>
> **-am** Include macro expansions.
>
> **-an** Suppress forms processing.
>
> **-as** Include a symbol listing.
>
> =*file*
> > Set the listing filename to *file*.

--defsym *symbol=value*
> Define the *symbol* to have the value *value*, which must be an integer.

-f   Skip whitespace and comment preprocessing.

--fatal-warnings
> Treat warnings as errors.

--gstabs
> Generate debugging information in stabs format.

--gdwarf2
> Generate DWARF2 debugging information.

-o *objfile*
> Place output in object file *objfile* (default is *file*.o).

--statistics
> Print information on how much time and space assembler uses.

-v Display the version number of the assembler.

-I *path*
> Include *path* when searching for **.include** directives.

-J Don't warn about signed overflow.

-R Combine both data and text in text section.

-W Don't show warnings.

-Z Generate object file even if there are errors.

---

at

at [*options*] *time* [*date*]

Execute commands at a specified *time* and optional *date*. The commands are read from standard input or from a file. (See also **batch**.) End input with EOF. *time* can be formed either as a numeric hour (with optional minutes and modifiers) or as a keyword. It can contain an optional *date*, formed as a month and date, a day of the week, or a special keyword (**today** or **tomorrow**). An increment can also be specified.

The **at** command can always be issued by a privileged user. Other users must be listed in the file */etc/at.allow* if it exists; otherwise, they must not be listed in */etc/at.deny*. If neither file exists, only a privileged user can issue the command.

Options

-c *job* [*job...*]
> Display the specified jobs on the standard output. This option does not take a time specification.

-d *job* [*job...*]
> Delete the specified jobs. Same as **atrm**.

-f *file*
> Read job from *file*, not from standard input.

-l Report all jobs that are scheduled for the invoking user. Same as **atq**.

-m Mail user when job has completed, regardless of whether output was created.

-q *letter*
> Place job in queue denoted by *letter*, where *letter* is any single letter from a-z or A-Z. Default queue is **a**. (The batch queue defaults to **b**.) Higher-lettered queues run at a lower priority.

-V Display the version number.

Time

hh:[*mm*] [*modifiers*]

> Hours can have one digit or two (a 24-hour clock is assumed by default); optional minutes can be given as one or two digits; the colon can be omitted if the format is *h*, *hh*, or *hhmm* (e.g., valid times are 5, 5:30, 0530, 19:45). If modifier **am** or **pm** is added, *time* is based on a 12-hour clock.

midnight | **noon** | **teatime** | **now**

> Use any one of these keywords in place of a numeric time. **teatime** translates to 4:00 p.m.; **now** must be followed by an *increment* (described in a moment).

Date

month num[, *year*]

> *month* is one of the 12 months, spelled out or abbreviated to its first three letters; *num* is the calendar date of the month; *year* is the four-digit year. If the given *month* occurs before the current month, **at** schedules that month next year.

day

> One of the seven days of the week, spelled out or abbreviated to its first three letters.

today | **tomorrow**

> Indicate the current day or the next day. If *date* is omitted, **at** schedules **today** when the specified *time* occurs later than the current time; otherwise, **at** schedules **tomorrow**.

Increment

Supply a numeric increment if you want to specify an execution time or day *relative* to the current time. The number should precede any of the keywords **minute**, **hour**, **day**, **week**, **month**, or **year** (or their plural forms). The keyword **next** can be used as a synonym of **+ 1**.

Examples

In typical usage, you run **at** and input commands that you want executed at a particular time, followed by EOF.

```
$ at 1:00 am tomorrow
at> ./total_up > output
at> mail joe < output
at> <EOT>        Entered by pressing Ctrl-D
job 1 at 2003-03-19 01:00
```

The two commands could also be placed in a file and submitted as follows:

```
$ at 1:00 am tomorrow < scriptfile
```

More examples of syntax follow. Note that the first two commands here are equivalent:

```
$ at 1945 December 9
$ at 7:45pm Dec 9
$ at 3 am Saturday
$ at now + 5 hours
$ at noon next day
```

atd

atd *options*

System administration command. Normally started in a system startup file. Execute jobs queued by the **at** command.

Options
-b *n*

Wait at least *n* seconds after beginning one job before beginning the next job. Default is 60.

-d   Print error messages to standard error instead of using **syslog**.

-l *average*

When system load average is higher than *average*, wait to begin a new job. Default is 0.8.

-n   Don't fork. Run in foreground.

-s   Process queue once, then exit.

atq

atq [*options*]

List the user's pending jobs, unless the user is a privileged user; in that case, list everybody's jobs. Same as **at -l**, and related to **batch** and **atrm**.

Options
-q *queue*

Query only the specified queue and ignore all other queues.

-V   Print the version number.

atrm

atrm [*option*] *job* [*job...*]

Delete jobs that have been queued for future execution. Same as **at -d**.

Option
-V   Print the version number and then exit.

autoconf

autoconf [*options*] [*template_file*]

Generate a configuration script from **m4** macros defined in *template_file*, if given, or in a *configure.ac* or *configure.in* file in the current working directory. The generated script is almost invariably called *configure*.

Options
-d, --debug

Don't remove temporary files.

-f, --force

Replace files generated previously by **autoconf**.

-h, --help

Print help message, then exit.

-i, --initialization

> When tracing calls with the **-t** option, report calls made during initialization.

-o *file*, **--output**=*file*

> Save output to *file*.

-t *macro*, **--trace**=*macro*

> Report the list of calls to *macro*.

-v, --verbose

> Verbosely print information about the progress of **autoconf**.

-B *dir*, **--prepend-include**=*dir*

> Prepend directory *dir* to the search path.

-I *dir*, **--include**=*dir*

> Append directory *dir* to the search path.

-V, --version

> Print version number, then exit.

-W *category*, **--warnings**=*category*

> Print any warnings related to *category*. Accepted categories are:

> **cross**
>> Cross compilation.

> **obsolete**
>> Obsolete constructs.

> **syntax**
>> Questionable syntax.

> **all**
>> All warnings.

> **no-***category*
>> Turn off warnings for *category*.

> **none**
>> Turn off all warnings.

> **error**
>> Treat warnings as errors.

---

autoheader   autoheader [*options*] [*template_file*]

GNU **autoheader** tool. Generate a template file of C **#define** statements from **m4** macros defined in *template_file*, if given, or in a *configure.ac* or *configure.in* file in the current working directory. The generated template file is almost invariably called *config.h.in*.

Options

-d, --debug

> Don't remove temporary files.

-f, --force

> Replace files generated previously by **autoheader**.

-h, --help

> Print help message, then exit.

-o *file*, **--output=***file*
> Save output to *file*.

-v, --verbose
> Verbosely print information about the progress of **autoheader**.

-B *dir*, **--prepend-include=***dir*
> Prepend directory *dir* to the search path.

-I *dir*, **--include=***dir*
> Append directory *dir* to the search path.

-V, --version
> Print version number, then exit.

-W *category*, **--warnings=***category*
> Print any warnings related to *category*. Accepted categories are:

obsolete
> Obsolete constructs.

all
> All warnings.

no-*category*
> Turn off warnings for *category*.

none
> Turn off all warnings.

error
> Treat warnings as errors.

---

automake

automake [*options*] [*template_file*]

GNU **automake** tool. Create GNU standards-compliant *Makefile.in* files from *Makefile.am* template files and can be used to ensure that projects contain all the files and install options required to be standards-compliant. Note that versions 1.4 and 1.6 differ enough that many distributions include an *automake14* package for backward compatibility.

Options

-a, --add-missing
> Add any missing files that **automake** requires to the directory by creating symbolic links to **automake**'s default versions.

-c, --copy
> Used with the **-a** option. Copy missing files instead of creating symbolic links.

--cygnus
> Specifies project has a Cygnus-style source tree.

-f, --force-missing
> Used with the **-a** option. Replace required files even if a local copy already exists.

--foreign
> Treat project as a non-GNU project. Check only for elements required for proper operation.

--gnu

Treat project as a GNU project with the GNU project structure.

--gnits

A stricter version of **--gnu**, performing more checks to comply with GNU project structure rules.

--help

Print help message, then exit.

-i, --ignore-deps

Disable automatic dependency tracking.

--libdir=*dir*

Used with the **-a** option. Search in directory *dir* for default files.

--no-force

Update only *Makefile.in* files that have updated dependents.

-v, --verbose

List files being read or created by **automake**.

--version

Print version number, then exit.

-Werror

Treat warnings as errors.

---

autoreconf   autoreconf [*options*]

GNU **autoreconf** tool. Update configure scripts by running **autoconf**, **autoheader**, **aclocal**, **automake**, and **libtoolize** in specified directories and subdirectories. This command is seldom invoked manually. It is usually called automatically from other **autoconf** tools.

Options

-d, --debug

Don't remove temporary files.

-f, --force

Remake all configure scripts, even when newer than their template files.

-h, --help

Print help message, then exit.

-i, --install

Add any default files missing from package by copying versions included with **autoconf** and **automake**.

-s, --symlink

Used with the **-i** option. Create symbolic links to default files instead of copying them.

-v, --verbose

Verbosely print information about the progress of **autoreconf**.

-I *dir*, --**include**=*dir*
>   Search in directory *dir* for input files.

-V, --**version**
>   Print version number, then exit.

-W *category*, --**warnings**=*category*
>   Print any warnings related to *category*. Accepted categories are:

cross
>   Cross compilation.

obsolete
>   Obsolete constructs.

syntax
>   Questionable syntax.

all
>   All warnings.

no-*category*
>   Turn off warnings for *category*.

none
>   Turn off all warnings.

error
>   Treat warnings as errors.

---

autoscan

autoscan [*options*] [*directory*]

GNU **autoscan** tool. Create or maintain a preliminary *configure.ac* file named *configure.scan* based on source files in specified *directory*, or current directory if none given. If a *configure.ac* file already exists, **autoconf** will check it for completeness and print suggestions for correcting any problems it finds.

Options

-d, --**debug**
>   Don't remove temporary files.

-h, --**help**
>   Print help message, then exit.

-v, --**verbose**
>   Verbosely print information about the progress of **autoscan**.

-I *dir*, --**include**=*dir*
>   Search in directory *dir* for input files. Use multiple times to add multiple directories.

-B *dir*, --**prepend-include**=*dir*
>   Search *dir* for input files before searching in other directories. Use multiple times to add multiple directories.

-V, --**version**
>   Print version number, then exit.

autoupdate

autoupdate [*options*] [*file*]

GNU **autoupdate** tool. Update the configure template file *file*, or *configure.ac* if no file is specified. This command is seldom invoked manually. It is usually called automatically from other **autoconf** tools.

Options

-d, --debug

Don't remove temporary files.

-f, --force

Remake all configure scripts, even when newer than their template files.

-h, --help

Print help message, then exit.

-v, --verbose

Verbosely print information about the progress of **autoupdate**.

-I *dir*, **--include**=*dir*

Search in directory *dir* for input files.

-V, --version

Print version number, then exit.

---

badblocks

badblocks [*options*] *deviceblock-count*

System administration command. Search *device* for bad blocks. You must specify the number of blocks on the device (*block-count*). **e2fsck** and **mke2fs** will invoke **badblocks** automatically when given the -c option.

Options

-b *blocksize*

Expect *blocksize*-byte blocks.

-c *blocksize*

Test *blocksize*-byte blocks at a time. Default is 16.

-e *number*

Abort test after finding specified *number* of blocks.

-f   Force a read/write or nondestructive write test on a mounted device. Use only when */etc/mtab* incorrectly reports a device as mounted.

-i *file*

Skip test of known bad blocks listed in *file*.

-n   Perform a nondestructive test by writing to each block and then reading back from it while preserving data.

-o *file*

Direct output to *file*.

-p *number*

Repeat search of device until no new bad blocks have been found in *number* passes. Default is 0.

-s   Show block numbers as they are checked.

-t *pattern*
      Test blocks by reading and writing the specified *pattern*. You may specify *pattern* as a positive integer or as the word **random**. If you specify multiple patterns, **badblocks** tests all blocks with one pattern, and then tests all blocks again with the next pattern. Read-only mode accepts only one pattern. It does not accept **random**.

-v   Verbose mode.

-w   Test by writing to each block and then reading back from it. This option will destroy data. Don't use it on devices that contain filesystems.

---

base64   base64 [*option*] [*file*]

Use base64 encoding to encode or decode the specified file and print the results to standard output. With no file or with a dash (-), read the data from standard input.

Options

-d, --decode
      Decode the data.

--help
      Print help message and exit.

-i, --ignore-garbage
      When decoding, ignore nonalphabetic characters except newline.

--version
      Print version information and exit.

-w *cols*, **--wrap**=*cols*
      When encoding, wrap lines after *cols* characters. The default is 76, while 0 disables line wrap.

---

basename   basename *name* [*suffix*]

basename *option*

Remove leading directory components from a path. If *suffix* is given, remove that also. The result is printed to standard output. This is useful mostly in a script when you need to work with a filename but can't predict its full path in every instance.

Options

--help
      Print help message and then exit.

--version
      Print the version number and then exit.

Examples

```
$ basename /usr/lib/libm.a
libm.a

$ basename /usr/lib/libm.a .a
libm
```

---

bash

bash [*options*] [*file* [*arguments*]]

sh [*options*] [*file* [*arguments*]]

Standard Linux shell, a command interpreter into which all other commands are entered. For more information, see Chapter 6.

---

batch

batch

Execute commands entered on standard input. Commands are run when the system load permits (when the load average falls below 0.8). Very similar to **at**, but takes no parameters on the command line. See **at** for details.

---

bc

bc [*options*] [*files*]

bc is a language (and compiler) whose syntax resembles that of C, but with unlimited-precision arithmetic. **bc** consists of identifiers, keywords, and symbols, which are briefly described in the following entries. Examples are given at the end.

Interactively perform arbitrary-precision arithmetic or convert numbers from one base to another. Input can be taken from *files* or read from the standard input. To exit, type **quit** or EOF.

Options

-h, --help
> Print help message and exit.

-i, --interactive
> Interactive mode.

-l, --mathlib
> Make functions from the math library available.

-s, --standard
> Ignore all extensions, and process exactly as in POSIX.

-w, --warn
> When extensions to POSIX **bc** are used, print a warning.

-q, --quiet
> Do not display welcome message.

-v, --version
> Print version number.

Identifiers

An identifier is a series of one or more characters. It must begin with a lowercase letter but may also contain digits and under-scores. No uppercase letters are allowed. Identifiers are used as

---

names for variables, arrays, and functions. Variables normally store arbitrary-precision numbers. Within the same program you may name a variable, an array, and a function using the same letter. The following identifiers would not conflict:

x   Variable *x*.

x[i]
> Element *i* of array *x*. *i* can range from 0 to 2047 and can also be an expression.

x(y,z)
> Call function *x* with parameters *y* and *z*.

Input-output keywords

ibase, **obase**, **scale**, and **last** store a value. Typing them on a line by themselves displays their current value. You can also change their values through assignment. The letters A–F are treated as digits whose values are 10–15.

ibase = *n*
> Numbers that are input (e.g., typed) are read as base *n* (default is 10).

obase = *n*
> Numbers that are displayed are in base *n* (default is 10). Note: once **ibase** has been changed from 10, use A to restore **ibase** or **obase** to decimal.

scale = *n*
> Display computations using *n* decimal places (default is 0, meaning that results are truncated to integers). **scale** is normally used only for base-10 computations.

last
> Value of last printed number.

Statement keywords

A semicolon or a newline separates one statement from another. Curly braces are needed when grouping multiple statements:

if (*rel-expr*) {*statements*} [**else** {*statements*}]
> Do one or more *statements* if relational expression *rel-expr* is true. Otherwise, do nothing, or if **else** (an extension) is specified, do alternative *statements*. For example:

```
if (x= =y) {i = i + 1} else {i = i - 1}
```

while (*rel-expr*) {*statements*}
> Repeat one or more *statements* while *rel-expr* is true. For example:

```
while (i>0) {p = p*n; q = a/b; i = i-1}
```

for (*expr1*; *rel-expr*; *expr2*) {*statements*}
> Similar to **while**. For example, to print the first 10 multiples of 5, you could type:

```
for (i=1; i<=10; i++) i*5
```

GNU **bc** does not require three arguments to **for**. A missing argument 1 or 3 means that those expressions will never be evaluated. A missing argument 2 evaluates to the value 1.

break

Terminate a **while** or **for** statement.

print *list*

GNU extension. It provides an alternate means of output. *list* consists of a series of comma-separated strings and expressions; **print** displays these entities in the order of the list. It does not print a newline when it terminates. Expressions are evaluated, printed, and assigned to the special variable **last**. Strings (which may contain special characters—i.e., characters beginning with \) are simply printed. Special characters can be:

a   Alert or bell

b   Backspace

f   Form feed

n   Newline

r   Carriage return

q   Double quote

t   Tab

\   Backslash

continue

GNU extension. When within a **for** statement, jump to the next iteration.

halt

GNU extension. Cause the **bc** processor to quit when executed.

quit

GNU extension. Cause the **bc** processor to quit whether line is executed or not.

limits

GNU extension. Print the limits enforced by the local version of **bc**.

Function keywords

define *f(args)* {

Begin the definition of function *f* having the arguments *args*. The arguments are separated by commas. Statements follow on successive lines. End with }.

auto *x, y*

Set up *x* and *y* as variables local to a function definition, initialized to 0 and meaningless outside the function. Must appear first.

return(*expr*)

Pass the value of expression *expr* back to the program. Return 0 if (*expr*) is left off. Used in function definitions.

sqrt(*expr*)

> Compute the square root of expression *expr*.

length(*expr*)

> Compute how many significant digits are in *expr*.

scale(*expr*)

> Same as **length**, but count only digits to the right of the decimal point.

read( )

> GNU extension. Read a number from standard input. Return value is the number read, converted via the value of **ibase**.

Math library functions

These are available when **bc** is invoked with -l. Library functions set **scale** to 20:

s(*angle*)

> Compute the sine of *angle*, a constant or expression in radians.

c(*angle*)

> Compute the cosine of *angle*, a constant or expression in radians.

a(*n*)

> Compute the arctangent of *n*, returning an angle in radians.

e(*expr*)

> Compute **e** to the power of *expr*.

l(*expr*)

> Compute the natural log of *expr*.

j(*n, x*)

> Compute the Bessel function of integer order *n*.

Operators

These consist of operators and other symbols. Operators can be arithmetic, unary, assignment, or relational:

arithmetic

> + - * / % ^

unary

> - ++ --

assignment

> =+ =- =* =/ =% =^ =

relational

> < <= > >= == !=

Other symbols

/* */

> Enclose comments.

( ) Control the evaluation of expressions (change precedence). Can also be used around assignment statements to force the result to print.

{ }   Use to group statements.

[ ]   Indicate array index.

"text"

Use as a statement to print *text*.

Examples

Note in these examples that when you type some quantity (a number or expression), it is evaluated and printed, but assignment statements produce no display.

ibase = 8	*Octal input*
20	*Evaluate this octal number*
16	*Terminal displays decimal value*
obase = 2	*Display output in base 2 instead of base 10*
20	*Octal input*
10000	*Terminal now displays binary value*
ibase = A	*Restore base-10 input*
scale = 3	*Truncate results to 3 decimal places*
8/7	*Evaluate a division*
1.001001000	*Oops! Forgot to reset output base to 10*
obase = 10	*Input is decimal now, so A isn't needed*
8/7	
1.142	*Terminal displays result (truncated)*

The following lines show the use of functions:

define p(r,n){	*Function p uses two arguments*
auto v	*v is a local variable*
v = r^n	*r raised to the n power*
return(v)}	*Value returned*
scale = 5	
x = p(2.5,2)	$x = 2.5 ^ 2$
x	*Print value of x*
6.25	
length(x)	*Number of digits*
3	
scale(x)	*Number of places right of decimal point*
2	

---

bison

bison [*options*] *file*

Given a *file* containing context-free grammar, convert into tables for subsequent parsing while sending output to *file.c*. To a large extent, this utility is compatible with **yacc**, and is in fact named for it. All input files should use the suffix *.y*; output files will use the original prefix. All long options (those preceded by --) may instead be preceded by +.

Options

-b *prefix*, **--file-prefix**=*prefix*

Use *prefix* for all output files.

-d, **--defines**

Generate *file.h*, producing **#define** statements that relate **bison**'s token codes to the token names declared by the user.

-r, --raw

Use **bison** token numbers, not **yacc**-compatible translations, in *file.h*.

-k, --token-table

Include token names and values of YYNTOKENS, YYNNTS, YYNRULES, and YYNSTATES in *file.c*.

-l, --no-lines

Exclude **#line** constructs from code produced in *file.c*. (Use after debugging is complete.)

-n, --no-parser

Suppress parser code in output, allowing only declarations. Assemble all translations into a switch statement body and print it to *file.act*.

-o *file*, **--output-file**=*file*

Output to *file*.

-p *prefix*, **--name-prefix**=*prefix*

Substitute *prefix* for **yy** in all external symbols.

-t, --debug

Compile runtime debugging code.

-v, --verbose

Verbose mode. Print diagnostics and notes about parsing tables to *file.output*.

-V, --version

Display version number.

-y, --yacc, --fixed-output-files

Duplicate **yacc**'s conventions for naming output files.

---

bzcmp

```
bzcmp [options] file1 file2
```

Apply **cmp** to the data from files in the **bzip2** format without requiring on-disk decompression. See **bzip2** and **cmp** for usage.

---

bzdiff

```
bzdiff [options] file1 file2
```

Apply **diff** to data from files in the **bzip2** format without requiring on-disk decompression. See **bzip2** and **diff** for usage.

---

bzgrep

```
bzgrep [options] pattern [file...]
```

Apply **grep** to data from files in the **bzip2** format without requiring on-disk decompression. See **bzip2** and **grep** for usage.

---

bzip2

```
bzip2 [options] filenames
bunzip2 [options] filenames
bzcat [option] filenames
bzip2recover filename
```

File compression and decompression utility similar to **gzip**, but uses a different algorithm and encoding method to get better compression. **bzip2** replaces each file in *filenames* with a compressed version of the file and with a *.bz2* extension appended. **bunzip2** decompresses each file compressed by **bzip2** (ignoring other files, except to print a warning). **bzcat** decompresses all specified files to standard output, and **bzip2recover** is used to try to recover data from damaged files.

Additional related commands include **bzcmp**, which compares the contents of bzipped files; **bzdiff**, which creates diff (difference) files from a pair of **bzip** files; **bzgrep**, to search them; and the **bzless** and **bzmore** commands, which apply the **more** and **less** commands to **bzip** output, as **bzcat** does with the **cat** command. See **cat**, **cmp**, **diff**, and **grep** for information on how to use those commands.

Options

--   End of options; treat all subsequent arguments as filenames.

-dig
> Set block size to *dig* × 100 KB when compressing, where *dig* is a single digit from 1 to 9. For **gzip** compatibility, you can use **--fast** as an alias for **-1** and **--best** for **-9**, but they have little effect on the compression speed.

-c, --stdout
> Compress or decompress to standard output.

-d, --decompress
> Force decompression even if invoked by **bzip2** or **bzcat**.

-f, --force
> Force overwrite of output files. Default is not to overwrite. Also forces breaking of hard links to files.

-k, --keep
> Keep input files; don't delete them.

-L, --license, -V, --version
> Print license and version information, and exit.

-q, --quiet
> Print only critical messages.

-s, --small
> Use less memory, at the expense of speed.

-t, --test
> Check the integrity of the files, but don't actually compress them.

-v, --verbose
> Verbose mode. Show the compression ratio for each file processed. Add more **-v**s to increase the verbosity.

-z, --compress
> Force compression, even if invoked as **bunzip2** or **bzcat**.

Examples

To produce two files: *fileone.txt.bz2* and *filetwo.ppt.bz2*, while deleting the two original files:

```
bzip2 fileone.tzt filetwo.ppt
```

To produce a single compressed file, *output.bz2*, which can be decompressed to reconstitute the original *fileone.txt* and *filetwo.txt*:

```
bzip2 -c fileone.txt filetwo.txt > output.bz2
```

The tar command, combined with the **-j** or **--bzip2** option, creates the output file *nutshell.tar.bz2*:

```
tar -cjf nutshell.tar.bz2 /home/username/nutshell
```

---

bzless   bzless [*options*] *file*

Applies **less** to datafiles in the **bzip2** format without requiring on-disk decompression. See **bzip2** and **less** for usage.

---

bzmore   bzmore [*options*] *file*

Applies **more** to datafiles in the **bzip2** format without requiring on-disk decompression. See **bzip2** and **more** for usage.

---

c++   c++ [*options*] *files*

See **g++**.

---

c++filt   c++filt [*options*] [*symbol*]

Decode the specified C++ or Java function name *symbol*, or read and decode symbols from standard input if no symbol is given. This command reverses the name mangling used by C++ and Java compilers to support function overloading, multiple functions that share the same name.

Options

-_, --strip-underscores
> Remove initial underscores from symbol names.

--help
> Print usage information, then exit.

-j, --java
> Print names using Java syntax.

-n, --no-strip-underscores
> Preserve initial underscores on symbol names.

-s *format*, **--format=***format*
> Expect symbols to have been coded in the specified format. Format may be one of the following:

> **arm**
>> C++ Annotated Reference Manual.

> **edg**
>> EDG (Intel) compiler.

> **gnu**
>> Gnu compiler (the default).

> **gnu-new-abi**
>> Gnu compiler with the new application binary interface (for **gcc** 3.x.)

hp
> HP compiler.

lucid
> Lucid compiler.

--version
> Print version number, then exit.

---

cal

cal [*options*] [[[*day*] *month*] *year*]

Print a 12-month calendar (beginning with January) for the given *year*, or a one-month calendar of the given *month* and *year*. With a day specified as well, print the calendar for that month and year, with the day highlighted. *month* ranges from 1 to 12. *year* ranges from 1 to 9999. With no arguments, print a calendar for the current month.

Options

-3 Display the previous, current and next month.

-j Display Julian dates (days numbered 1 to 365, starting from January 1).

-m Display Monday as the first day of the week (the default is Sunday).

-y Display entire year.

Examples

```
cal 12 2006
cal 2006 > year_file
```

---

cat

cat [*options*] [*files*]

Read (concatenate) one or more *files* and print them on standard output. Read standard input if no *files* are specified or if - is specified as one of the files; input ends with EOF. You can use the > operator to combine several files into a new file, or >> to append files to an existing file. When appending to an existing file, use Ctrl-D, the end-of-file symbol, to end the session.

Options

-A, --show-all
> Same as -vET.

-b, --number-nonblank
> Number all nonblank output lines, starting with 1.

-e Same as -vE.

-E, --show-ends
> Print $ at the end of each line.

-n, --number
> Number all output lines, starting with 1.

-s, --squeeze-blank
> Squeeze down multiple blank lines to one blank line.

-t   Same as **-vT**.

-T, --show-tabs
    Print TAB characters as ^I.

-u   Ignored; kept for Unix compatibility.

-v, --show-nonprinting
    Display control and nonprinting characters, with the exception of LINEFEED and TAB.

Examples

`cat ch1`	*Display a file*
`cat ch1 ch2 ch3 > all`	*Combine files*
`cat note5 >> notes`	*Append to a file*
`cat > temp1`	*Create file at terminal. To exit, enter EOF Ctrl-D).*
`cat > temp2 << STOP`	*Create file at terminal. To exit, enter STOP.*

---

cc

cc [*options*] *files*

See **gcc**.

---

cdda2wav

cdda2wav [*options*] [*files*]

Convert Compact Disc Digital Audio (CDDA) to the WAV format. This process is often called "ripping" a CD-ROM and is generally performed before using an encoder to convert the file to a compressed music format, such as OGG or MP3.

cdda2wav is now generally a symbolic link to **icedax**.

---

cdparanoia

cdparanoia [*options*] *span* [*outfile*]

cdparanoia records Compact Disc audio files as WAV, AIFF, AIFF-C, or raw format files. It uses additional data-verification and sound-improvement algorithms to make the process more reliable and is used by a number of graphical recording programs as a backend. The output is written to *outfile* if specified; otherwise it is written to one of *cdda.wav*, *cdda.aifc*, or *cdda.raw* depending on the output-format option given.

The command takes one argument, *span*, which describes how much of the CD to record. It uses numbers followed by bracketed times to designate track numbers and time within them. For example, the string **1[2:23]-2[5]** indicates a recording from the two-minute and twenty-three-second mark of the first track up to the fifth second of the second track. The time format is demarcated by colons, *hours:minutes:seconds:.sectors*, with the last item, *sectors*, preceded by a decimal point (a sector is 1/75 of a second). It's best to put this argument within quotes.

If you use the **-B** option, the span argument is not required.

Linux
Commands

Options

-a, --output-aifc

Output in AIFF-C format.

-A, --analyze-drive

Analyze and log drive caching, timing and reading. Implies **-vQL**.

-B, --batch

Split output into multiple files, one per track. Each file begins with the track number. This is the most commonly used flag for this command.

-C, --force-cdrom-big-endian

Force **cdparanoia** to treat the drive as a big-endian device.

-c, --force-cdrom-little-endian

Force **cdparanoia** to treat the drive as a little-endian device.

-d, --force-cdrom-device *devicename*

Specify a device name to use instead of the first readable CD-ROM available.

-e, --stderr-progress

Send all progress messages to standard error instead of standard output; used by wrapper scripts.

-f, --output-aiff

Output in AIFF format. The default format is WAV.

-h, --help

Display options and syntax.

-l, --log-summary *[file]*

Write results to *file* if specified, otherwise to *cdparanoia.log*.

-L, --log-debug *[file]*

Write device autosensing and debugging output to *file* if specified, otherwise to *cdparanoia.log*.

-p, --output-raw

Output headerless raw data.

-R, --output-raw-big-endian

Output raw data in big-endian byte order.

-r, --output-raw-little-endian

Output raw data in little-endian byte order.

-Q, --query

Display CD-ROM table of contents and quit.

-q, --quiet

Quiet mode.

-S, --force-read-speed *n*

Set the read speed to *n* on drives that support it. This is useful if you have a slow hard disk or not much RAM.

-s, --search-for-drive

Search for a drive, even if */dev/cdrom* exists.

-V, --version

Print version information and quit.

-v, --verbose
> Verbose mode.

-w, --output-wav
> Output in WAV format. This is the default.

-X, --abort-on-skip
> If a read fails and must be skipped, skip the entire track and delete any partially completed output file.

-z, --never-skip[=*retries*]
> If a read fails (for example, due to a scratch in the disc), keep trying. If you specify a number, **cdparanoia** will try that number of times. If you do not, **cdparanoia** will retry until it succeeds. The default number of attempts is 20.

Progress symbols

The output during operation of **cdparanoia** includes both smiley faces and more standard progress symbols. They are:

:-) Operation proceeding normally.

:-| Operation proceeding normally, but with jitter during reads.

:-/ Read drift.

8-| Repeated read problems in the same place.

:-O SCSI/ATAPI transport error (hardware problem not related to the disc itself).

:-(Scratch detected.

;-(Unable to correct a problem.

8-X Aborted read due to uncorrectable error.

:^D Finished.

> Blank space in the progress indicator means that no corrections were necessary.

-    Jitter correction was required.

+   Read errors.

!   Errors even after correction; repeated read errors.

e   Corrected transport errors.

V   An uncorrected error or a skipped read.

---

cdrdao

cdrdao *command* [*options*] *toc-file*

Write all content specified in description file *toc-file* to a CD-R disk drive in one step. This is called disk-at-once (DAO) mode, as opposed to the more commonly used track-at-once (TAO) mode. DAO mode allows you to change the length of gaps between tracks and define data to be written in these gaps (like hidden bonus tracks or track intros). The toc file can be created by hand or generated from an existing CD using **cdrdao**'s **read-toc** command. A cue file, as generated by other audio programs, can be used instead of a toc file. The file format for toc files is discussed at length in the **cdrdao** manpage.

Commands

The first argument must be a command. Note that not all options are available for all commands. Run **cdrdao** *command* **-h** to see the options that apply to a particular command.

blank

> Blank a CD-RW. The default is to do minimal blanking; use **--blank-mode** to change to full blanking.

copy

> Copy the CD. If you use a single drive, you will be prompted to insert a CD-R after reading. An image file is created unless you use the **--on-the-fly** flag and two CD drives.

discid

> Display CDDB information.

disk-info

> Display information about the CD-R currently in the drive.

drive-info

> Display information about the drive.

msinfo

> Display multisession information. Useful mostly for wrapper scripts.

read-cd

> Read from a CD and create a disk image and toc file that will allow creation of duplicates. Use **--datafile** to specify a filename.

read-cddb

> Check a CDDB server for data about the CD represented by a given toc file; then write that data to the toc file as CD-TEXT data.

read-test

> Check the validity of the audio files described in the toc file.

read-toc

> Create a toc file from an audio CD.

scanbus

> Scan the system bus for devices.

show-data

> Print out the data that will be written to the CD-R. Useful for checking byte order.

show-toc

> Print a summary of the CD to be created.

simulate

> A dry run: do everything except write the CD. Equivalent to **write --simulate**.

toc-info

> Display a summary of the toc file.

toc-size

> Display the total toc blocksize.

unlock

Unlock the recorder after a failure. Run this command if you cannot eject the CD after using **cdrdao**.

write

Write the CD.

Options

--blank-mode *mode*

Set the blanking mode to **full** or **minimal**. The default is **minimal**.

--buffers *n*

Set the number of buffers. Since each buffer holds 1 second of data, this is equivalent to setting the number of seconds of data to be buffered. The default is 32; set to a higher number if your read source is unreliable or is slower than the CD-R. The minumum is 10.

--cddb-servers *server,server*

Enter hosts for servers. Servers may include ports, paths, and proxies; you can list multiple servers separated by spaces or commas.

--cddb-timeout *s*

Set the timeout for CDDB server connections to *s* seconds.

--cddb-directory *localpath*

CDDB data that is fetched will be saved in the directory *localpath*.

--datafile *filename*

When used with the **read-toc** command, this option specifies the datafile placed in the toc file. When used with **read-cd** and **copy**, it specifies the name of the image file created.

--device *bus,id,logicalunit*

Set the SCSI address of the CD-R using the bus number, ID number, and logical-unit number.

--driver *driver-id:option-flags*

Force **cdrdao** to use the driver you choose with the driver options named, instead of the driver it autodetects.

--eject

Eject the disc when done.

--force

Override warnings and perform the action anyway.

--keep

On exit, keep any temporary WAV files created.

--keepimage

Keep the image file created during the copy process. Used only with the **copy** command.

--multi

Record as a multisession disc.

-n   Do not wait 10 seconds before writing the disc.

--on-the-fly
Do not create an image file: pipe data directly from source to CD-R.

--overburn
If you are using a disc with more storage space than **cdrdao** detects, use this option to keep writing even when **cdrdao** thinks you're out of space.

--paranoia-mode *n*
Specify the amount of error correction in the CD read, where *n* is a value from 0 to 3. **0** is none; **3** is full. Set error correction to a lower number to increase read speed. The default is 3.

--read-raw
Used only with the **read-cd** command. Write raw data to the image file.

--reload
Allow the drive to be opened before writing, without interrupting the process. Used with simulation runs.

--save
Save current options to the settings file *$HOME/.cdrdao*.

--session *n*
Used only with the **read-toc** and **read-cd** commands when working with multisession CDs. Specify the number of the session to be processed.

--source-device *bus,id,logicalunit*
Used only with the **copy** command and two drives. Set the SCSI address of the source device.

--source-driver *driver-id:option-flags*
Used only with the **copy** command. Set the source device driver and flags.

--speed *value*
Set the write speed to *value*. The default is the highest available speed; use a lower value if higher values give poor results.

--swap
Swap byte order for all samples.

-v *verbose-level*
Set the amount of information printed to the screen. **0**, **1**, and **2** are fine for most users; greater numbers are useful for debugging.

--with-cddb
Use CDDB to fetch information about the disc and save it as CD-TEXT data. Used with the **copy**, **read-toc**, and **read-cd** commands.

Examples

To find devices on the system:

```
cdrdao scanbus
```

To copy from a CD device (at 1,1,0) to a CD-R device (at 1,0,0):

```
cdrdao copy --source 1,1,0 --device 1,0,0 --buffers 64
```

cdrecord

cdrecord [*options*] *track1,track2...*

Record data or audio compact discs. This program normally requires root access. **cdrecord** is now generally a symbolic link to **wodim**.

cfdisk

cfdisk [*options*] [*device*]

System administration command. Partition a hard disk using a full-screen display. Normally, *device* will be */dev/hda*, */dev/hdb*, */dev/sda*, */dev/sdb*, */dev/hdc*, */dev/hdd*, and so on; the default is the first device on the system. See also **fdisk**.

Options

-a   Use an arrow on the left side to highlight the currently selected partition, instead of reverse video.

-c *cylinders*
      Specify the number of cylinders to use to format the specified *device*.

-g   Ignore driver-provided geometry; guess one instead.

-h *heads*
      Specify the number of heads to use to format the specified *device*.

-s *sectors*
      Specify the number of sectors per track to use to format the specified *device*.

-v   Print version number and exit.

-z   Do not read the partition table; partition from scratch.

-P *format*
      Display the partition table in *format*, which must be **r** (raw data), **s** (sector order), or **t** (table format). See the manpage for the meaning of the fields in the raw format, which shows what will be written by **cfdisk** for each partition. The sector format shows information about the sectors used by each partition. The table format shows the starting and ending head, sector, and cylinder for each partition.

Commands

up arrow, down arrow
      Move among partitions.

left arrow, right arrow
      Move among commands at the bottom of the screen.

Enter key
      Select currently highlighted command or value.

b   Toggle flag indicating whether selected partition is bootable.

d Delete partition (allow other partitions to use its space).

g Alter the disk's geometry. Prompt for what to change: cylinders, heads, or sectors (**c**, **h**, or **s**, respectively).

h Help.

m Attempt to ensure maximum usage of disk space in the partition.

n Create a new partition. Prompt for more information.

p Print the partition table to the screen or a file. Possible formats are the same as for the **-P** option.

q Quit without saving information.

t Prompt for a new filesystem type, and change to that type.

u Change the partition-size units. The choice of units rotates from megabytes to sectors to cylinders and back.

W Save information. Must be uppercase, to prevent accidental writing.

---

chage

chage [*options*] *user*

Change information about user password expirations. If run with no option flags, **chage** prompts for values to be entered; you may also use option flags to change or view information. Requires a shadow password file. An unprivileged user can only run **chage** with the **-l** option.

Options

-d *lastday*, **--lastday**=*lastday*
Date of last password change. This may be expressed as a date in *YYYY-MM-DD* format, or as the number of days between January 1, 1970 and the last password change.

-E *expiredate*, **--expiredate**=*expiredate*
Set the date when the account will be locked. This is not a date for password expiration, but for account expiration. It may be expressed in *YYYY-MM-DD* format or as a number of days since January 1, 1970.

-I *inactivedays*, **--inactive**=*inactivedays*
If a password expires and the user does not log in for this number of days, the account will be locked and the user must contact a system administrator before logging in. Set to **0** to disable the feature.

-l, **--list**
This flag is used without any others and causes **chage** to display the current password expiration attributes for the user.

-m *mindays*, **--mindays**=*mindays*
Specify the minimum number of days between password changes. Default is zero, meaning that the user may change the password at any time.

-M *maxdays*, **--maxdays**=*maxdays*
> Maximum number of days between password changes.

-W *warndays*, **--warndays**=*warndays*
> The number of days before password expiration that a user will be warned to change passwords.

chattr

chattr [*options*] *mode files*

Modify file attributes. Specific to Linux Second and Third Extended Filesystems (ext2 and ext3). Like symbolic **chmod**, **chattr** specifies attributes with +, -, and = but it operates on extended file attributes (see the upcoming section "Attributes"). *mode* is in the form *opcode attribute*. See also **lsattr**.

Options

-R   Modify directories and their contents recursively.

-f   Suppress most error messages.

-V   Verbose; print modes of attributes after changing them.

-v *version*
> Set the file's version.

Opcodes

+   Add attribute.

-   Remove attribute.

=   Assign attributes (removing unspecified attributes).

Attributes

A   Don't update access time on modify.

a   Append only for writing. Can be set or cleared only by a privileged user.

c   Compressed.

D   Write changes synchronously to disk.

d   No dump.

H   The file's blocks are stored in units of the filesystem blocksize, not of sectors. The file is or was at one time larger than 2 TB.

I   A directory is indexed using hashed trees.

i   Immutable. Can be set or cleared only by a privileged user. A file marked as immutable cannot be deleted, renamed, modified, or linked to until the setting has been cleared.

j   Journalled file. This is useful only in cases where you are using an ext3 filesystem mounted with the **data="ordered"** or **data="writeback"** attributes. The **data="journal"** option for the filesystem causes this operation to be performed for all files in the system and makes this option irrelevant.

S   Synchronous updates.

s Secure deletion. The contents are zeroed on deletion, and the file cannot be undeleted or recovered in any way.

u Undeletable. This causes a file to be saved even after it has been deleted, so that a user can undelete it later.

Example

chattr +a myfile   *As superuser*

---

chfn

chfn [*options*] [*username*]

Change the information that is stored in */etc/passwd* and displayed to the **finger** query. With no *options*, **chfn** enters interactive mode and prompts for changes. To blank a field, enter the keyword **none**. Only a privileged user can change information for another user. For regular users, **chfn** prompts for the user's password before making the change.

Options

-f *name*, --**full-name** *name*
  Specify new full name.

-h *homephone*, --**home-phone** *homephone*
  Specify new home phone number.

-o *office*, --**office** *office*
  Specify new office number.

-p *officephone*, --**office-phone** *officephone*
  Specify new office phone number.

-u, --**help**
  Print help message and then exit.

-v, --**version**
  Print version information and then exit.

Example

chfn -f "Ellen Siever" ellen

---

chgrp

chgrp [*options*] *newgroup files*

Change the group of one or more *files* to *newgroup*. *newgroup* is either a group ID number or a group name located in */etc/group*. Only the owner of a file or a privileged user may change the group.

Options

-c, --**changes**
  Print information about files that are changed.

--**dereference**
  Change the group of the file pointed to by a symbolic link, not the group of the symbolic link. This is the default behavior.

-f, --**silent**, --**quiet**
  Do not print error messages about files that cannot be changed.

-h, --no-dereference
> Change the group of the symbolic link.

-H Used with **-R**. If a command-line argument is a symbolic link to a directory, traverse the directory.

--help
> Print help message and then exit.

-L Used with **-R**. Traverse every symbolic link that points to a directory.

--no-preserve-root
> Do not treat / as special. This is the default behavior.

-P Used with **-R**. Do not traverse any symbolic links. This is the default behavior.

--preserve-root
> Do not operate recursively on /.

-R, --recursive
> Traverse subdirectories recursively, applying changes.

--reference=_filename_
> Change the group to that associated with _filename_. In this case, _newgroup_ is not specified.

-v, --verbose
> Verbosely describe ownership changes.

--version
> Print version information and then exit.

---

chkconfig

chkconfig [_options_] [_service_ [_flag_]]

System administration command. Manipulate symbolic links in the _/etc/rc.d/rc[0–6].d_ directories. **chkconfig** manages which services will run in a specified runlevel. Valid flags are **on**, **off**, **reset** or **resetpriorities** to reset the service to default on/off or priorities given in its initialization script in _/etc/rc.d/init.d_. This command is available in Fedora and RedHat-style distributions, including SUSE and SUSE-based distributions. To specify defaults in a standard initialization script, add a comment line to the script beginning with **chkconfig:** followed by the runlevels in which the service should run, and the start and kill priority numbers to assign—e.g., **chkconfig: 2345 85 15**. To override defaults specified in init files, you can create a file with the same service name in _/etc/chkconfig.d_. Place a **chkconfig** line in this override file. This allows you to safely customize package maintained services.

Options

--add _service_
> Create a start or kill symbolic link in every runlevel for the specified service according to default behavior specified in the service's initialization script.

--del _service_
> Remove entries for specified service from all runlevels.

--level *numbers*

Specify by number the runlevels to change. Provide *numbers* as a numeric string: e.g., **016** for levels 0, 1, and 6. Use this to override specified defaults.

--list [*service*]

Print whether the specified service is on or off in each level. If no service is specified, print runlevel information for all services managed by **chkconfig**.

--override *service*

If service is configured according to defaults in */etc/rc.d/init.d* and an override file exists in */etc/chkconfig.d*, reconfigure service to match the override settings.

---

chmod

chmod [*options*] *mode files*

chmod [*options*] --reference=*filename files*

Change the access *mode* (permissions) of one or more *files*. Only the owner of a file or a privileged user may change the mode. *mode* can be numeric or an expression in the form of *who opcode permission*. *who* is optional (if omitted, the default is **a**); choose only one *opcode*. Separate multiple modes by commas.

Options

-c, --changes

Print information about files that are changed.

-f, --silent, --quiet

Do not notify user of files that **chmod** cannot change.

--help

Print help message and then exit.

--no-preserve-root

Do not treat / as special. This is the default behavior.

--preserve-root

Do not operate recursively on /.

-R, --recursive

Traverse subdirectories recursively, applying changes.

--reference=*filename*

Change permissions to match those associated with *filename*.

-v, --verbose

Print information about each file, whether changed or not.

--version

Print version information and then exit.

Who

u   User.

g   Group.

o   Other.

a   All (default).

Opcode

+   Add permission.

-    Remove permission.

=   Assign permission (and remove permission of the unspecified fields).

Permissions

r   Read.

w   Write.

x   Execute.

X   Execute if file is a directory or already has execute permission for some user.

s   Set user (or group) ID.

t   Sticky bit; used on directories to prevent removal of files by nonowners.

u   User's present permission.

g   Group's present permission.

o   Other's present permission.

Alternatively, specify permissions by a three-digit octal number. The first digit designates owner permission; the second, group permission; and the third, other's permission. Permissions are calculated by adding the following octal values:

4   Read.

2   Write.

1   Execute.

Note that a fourth digit may precede this sequence. This digit assigns the following modes:

4   Set user ID on execution to grant permissions to process based on the file's owner, not on permissions of the user who created the process.

2   Set group ID on execution to grant permissions to process based on the file's group, not on permissions of the user who created the process.

1   Set sticky bit.

Examples

Add execute-by-user permission to *file*:

```
chmod u+x file
```

Either of the following assigns read/write/execute permission by owner (7), read/execute permission by group (5), and execute-only permission by others (1) to *file*:

```
chmod 751 file
chmod u=rwx,g=rx,o=x file
```

Any one of the following assigns read-only permission to *file* for everyone:

```
chmod =r file
chmod 444 file
chmod a-wx,a+r file
```

The following makes the executable setuid, assigns read/write/execute permission by owner, and assigns read/execute permission by group and others:

```
chmod 4755 file
```

chown

chown [*options*] *newowner files*

chown [*options*] --reference=*filename files*

Change the ownership of one or more *files* to *newowner*. *newowner* is either a user ID number or a login name located in */etc/passwd*. **chown** also accepts users in the form *newowner:newgroup* or *newowner.newgroup*. The last two forms change the group ownership as well. If no owner is specified, the owner is unchanged. With a period or colon but no group, the group is changed to that of the new owner. Only the current owner of a file or a privileged user may change the owner.

Options

-c, --changes

Print information about files that are changed.

--dereference

Follow symbolic links.

-f, --silent, --quiet

Do not print error messages about files that cannot be changed.

--from=*currown:currgroup*

Only change owner and/or group if the current owner and group match those specified in **--from**. If *currown* or *currgroup* is omitted, a match is not required for that attribute.

-h, --no-dereference

Change the ownership of each symbolic link (on systems that allow it), rather than the referenced file.

-v, --verbose

Print information about all files that **chown** attempts to change, whether or not they are actually changed.

-R, --recursive

Traverse subdirectories recursively, applying changes.

-H With **-R**, traverse symbolic link to a directory.

-L With **-R**, traverse every symbolic link that leads to a directory.

-P With **-R**, do not traverse any symbolic links. This is the default.

--reference=*filename*
> Change owner to the owner of *filename* instead of specifying a new owner explicitly.

--help
> Print help message and then exit.

--version
> Print version information and then exit.

---

chpasswd

chpasswd [*options*]

System administration command. Change user passwords in a batch. **chpasswd** accepts input in the form of one *username:password* pair per line. Unless the **-e** option is specified, *password* is encrypted before being stored. This command doesn't use PAM. It updates the */etc/passwd* and */etc/shadow* files.

Option

-e, --encrypted
> Passwords given are already encrypted.

-m, --md5
> Use MD5 Encryption

---

chroot

chroot *newroot* [*command*]

System administration command. Change root directory for *command* or, if none is specified, for a new copy of the user's shell. This command or shell is executed relative to the new root. The meaning of any initial / in pathnames is changed to *newroot* for a command and any of its children. In addition, the initial working directory is *newroot*. This command is restricted to privileged users.

---

chrt

chrt [*options*] [*prio*] [*pid* | *command* ...]

Set or retrieve the real-time scheduling properties of a given process, or run a new process with the given real-time scheduling properties.

Options

-b, --batch
> Use the batch scheduling policy.

-f, --fifo
> Use the FIFO (first-in, first-out) scheduling policy.

-h, --help
> Display usage information and then exit.

-m, --max
> Show the minimum and maximum valid scheduling priorities.

-o, --other
> Use the normal (called "other") scheduling policy.

-p, --pid
> Operate on the given, existing PID and do not execute a new command.

-r, --rr
> Use the round-robin scheduling policy.

-v, --version
> Display version information and then exit.

---

chsh

chsh [*options*] [*username*]

Change your login shell, either interactively or on the command line. Warn if *shell* does not exist in the file */etc/shells*. Specify the full path to the shell. **chsh** prompts for your password. Only a privileged user can change another user's shell.

Options
-l, --list-shells
> Print valid shells, as listed in */etc/shells*, and then exit.

-s *shell*, **--shell** *shell*
> Specify new login shell.

-u, --help
> Print help message and then exit.

-v, --version
> Print version information and then exit.

Example
chsh -s /bin/tcsh

---

chvt

chvt *N*

Switch to virtual terminal *N* (that is, switch to */dev/ttyN*). If you have not created */dev/ttyN*, it is created when you run this command. There are keyboard shortcuts for this functionality as well. From a graphical desktop, you can press Ctrl-Alt-F1 through F12 to switch to different virtual terminals. In text mode, you can skip the Ctrl key and just use Alt-F1 through F12. To switch back to graphical mode, use Alt-F7.

---

cksum

cksum [*files*]

Compute a cyclic redundancy check (CRC) checksum for all *files*; this is used to ensure that a file was not corrupted during transfer. Read from standard input if the character - is given or no files are given. Display the resulting checksum, the number of bytes in the file, and (unless reading from standard input) the filename. Also see **md5sum** and **sha1sum**.

---

clear

clear

Clear the terminal display. Equivalent to pressing Ctrl-L.

---

cmp

cmp [*options*] *file1* *file2* [*skip1* [*skip2*]]

Compare *file1* with *file2*. Use standard input if *file1* is - or missing. This command is normally used for comparing binary files, although files can be of any type. (See also **diff**.) *skip1* and *skip2* are optional offsets in the files at which the comparison is to start.

Options

-i *num*, --ignore-initial=*num*
> Ignore the first *num* bytes of input. *num* can be given as *num1:num2* to skip a different number of bytes in *file1* and *file2*.

-l, --verbose
> Print offsets and codes of all differing bytes.

-s, --quiet, --silent
> Work silently; print nothing, return an exit code:

> 0 Files are identical.

> 1 Files are different.

> 2 Files are inaccessible.

Example

Print a message if two files are the same (exit code is 0):

```
cmp -s old new && echo 'no changes'
```

col

col [*options*]

A postprocessing filter that handles reverse linefeeds and escape characters, allowing output from **tbl** or **nroff** to appear in reasonable form on a terminal.

Options

-b Ignore backspace characters; helpful when printing manpages.

-f Process half-line vertical motions, but not reverse line motion. (Normally, half-line input motion is displayed on the next full line.)

-l *n*
> Buffer at least *n* lines in memory. The default buffer size is 128 lines.

-p Do not filter out unrecognized control sequences, but pass them through.

-x Normally, **col** saves printing time by converting sequences of spaces to tabs. Use **-x** to suppress this conversion.

Examples

Run *myfile* through **tbl** and **nroff**, then capture output on screen by filtering through **col** and **more**:

```
tbl myfile | nroff | col | more
```

Save manpage output for the **ls** command in *out.print*, stripping out backspaces (which would otherwise appear as ^H):

```
man ls | col -b > out.print
```

---

colcrt

colcrt [*options*] [*files*]

A postprocessing filter that handles reverse linefeeds and escape characters, allowing output from **tbl** or **nroff** to appear in reasonable form on a terminal. Put half-line characters (e.g., subscripts or superscripts) and underlining (changed to dashes) on a new line between output lines.

Options

- Do not underline.

-2 Double space by printing all half-lines to make subscripts and superscripts visible.

---

colrm

colrm [*start* [*stop*]]

Remove specified columns from a file, where a column is a single character in a line. Read from standard input and write to standard output. Columns are numbered starting with 1. Begin deleting columns at (including) the *start* column, and stop at (including) the *stop* column; if *stop* is not given, delete all columns to the end. Entering a tab increments the column count to the next multiple of either the *start* or *stop* column; entering a backspace decrements it by 1.

Example

```
colrm 3 5 < test1 > test2
```

---

column

column [*options*] [*files*]

Format input from one or more *files* into columns, filling rows first. Read from standard input if no files are specified.

Options

-c *num*
:   Format output into *num* columns.

-s *char*
:   Delimit table columns with *char*. Meaningful only with **-t**.

-t Format input into a table. Delimit with whitespace, unless an alternate delimiter has been provided with **-s**.

-x Fill columns before filling rows.

---

comm

comm [*options*] *file1 file2*

Compare lines common to the sorted files *file1* and *file2*. Output is in three columns, from left to right: lines unique to *file1*, lines unique to *file2*, and lines common to both files. **comm** is similar to **diff** in that both commands compare two files. But **comm** can also

---

be used like **uniq**; **comm** selects duplicate or unique lines between *two* sorted files, whereas **uniq** selects duplicate or unique lines within the *same* sorted file.

Options

-num
> Suppress printing of column *num*. Multiple columns may be specified and should not be space-separated.

--**help**
> Print help message and exit.

--**version**
> Print version information and exit.

Example

Compare two lists of top-10 movies, and display items that appear in both lists:

```
comm -12 siskel_top10 ebert_top10
```

cp

cp [*options*] *file1 file2*

cp [*options*] *files directory*

Copy *file1* to *file2*, or copy one or more *files* to the same names under *directory*. If the destination is an existing file, the file is over-written; if the destination is an existing directory, the file is copied into the directory (the directory is *not* overwritten).

Options

-**a**, --**archive**
> Preserve attributes of original files where possible. The same as -**dpr**.

-**b**, --**backup**[*=control*]
> Back up files to be overwritten. As -**b**, takes no argument. For --**backup**, control specifies the type of backup and can also be set with the environment variable VERSION-CONTROL. The default is **existing**. Valid arguments are:
>
> **t, numbered**
>> Always make numbered backups.
>
> **nil, existing**
>> Make numbered backups of files that already have them; otherwise, make simple backups.
>
> **never, simple**
>> Always make simple backups.
>
> **none, off**
>> Never make backups, even if --**backup** is specified.

-**c** The same as --**preserve=context**.

--**copy-contents**
> Copy contents of special files when recursive.

-**d** The same as --**no-dereference** --**preserve=links**.

-f, --force

Remove an existing file in the destination if it can't be opened. See also **--remove-destination**.

-H Follow command-line symbolic links in the source.

-i, --interactive

Prompt before overwriting destination files. On most systems, this flag is turned off by default except for the root user, who is normally prompted before overwriting files.

-l, --link

Make hard links, not copies, of nondirectories.

-L, --dereference

Always follow symbolic links.

--no-preserve[*=attribs*]

Do not preserve the specified attributes. See **--preserve** for the list of possible attributes.

-p The same as **--preserve=mode,ownership,timestamps**.

--preserve[*=attribs*]

Preserve the specified attributes. By default, preserve **ownership**, **permissions**, and **timestamps**. Other possible attributes include **context, links, all**.

-P, --no-dereference

Never follow symbolic links.

--parents

Preserve intermediate directories in source. The last argument must be the name of an existing directory. For example, the command:

```
cp --parents jphekman/book/ch1 newdir
```

copies the file *jphekman/book/ch1* to the file *newdir/jphekman/ book/ch1*, creating intermediate directories as necessary.

-r, -R, --recursive

Copy directories recursively.

--remove-destination

Remove existing destination files without attempting to open them. See also **--force**.

-s, --symbolic-link

Make symbolic links instead of copying. Source filenames must be absolute.

-S *backup-suffix*, **--suffix**=*backup-suffix*

Set suffix to be appended to backup files. This may also be set with the SIMPLE_BACKUP_SUFFIX environment variable. The default is ~. You need to explicitly include a period if you want one before the suffix (for example, specify *.bak*, not *bak*).

--sparse=[always|auto|never]

Handle files that have "holes" (are defined as a certain size but have less data). **always** creates a sparse file, **auto** creates one if the input file is sparse (the default), and **never** creates a nonsparse file without holes.

--strip-trailing-slashes
> Remove trailing slashes from each source file argument.

-u, --update
> Do not copy a file to an existing destination with the same or newer modification time.

-v, --verbose
> Before copying, print the name of each file.

-x, --one-file-system
> Stay on the current filesystem.

Example

Copy the contents of the *guest* directory recursively into the */archives /guest/* directory, and display a message for each file copied:

```
cd /archives && cp -av /home/guest guest
```

---

cpio

cpio *mode* [*options*]

Copy file archives from or to tape or disk, or to another location on the local machine. Each of the three modes **-i**, **-o**, or **-p** accepts different options.

Mode

-i, --extract [*options*] [*patterns*]
> Copy in (extract) from an archive files whose names match selected *patterns*. Each pattern can include Bourne shell file-name metacharacters. (Patterns should be quoted or escaped so that they are interpreted by **cpio**, not by the shell.) If *pattern* is omitted, all files are copied in. Existing files are not overwritten by older versions from the archive unless **-u** is specified.

-o, --create [*options*]
> Copy out to an archive a list of files whose names are given on the standard input.

-p, --pass-through [*options*] *directory*
> Copy (pass) files to another directory on the same system. Destination pathnames are interpreted relative to the named *directory*.

Comparison of valid options

Single-character options available to the **-i**, **-o**, and **-p** modes are shown here (the - is omitted for clarity):

```
i:  bcdf mnrtsuv B SVCEHMR IF
o: 0a c        vABL VC HM O F
p: 0a d lm     uv  L V    R
```

Options

-0, --null
> Expect list of filenames to be terminated with null, not newline. This allows files with a newline in their names to be included.

-a, --reset-access-time
>   Reset access times of input files after reading them.

-A, --append
>   Append files to an existing archive, which must be a disk file.
>   Specify this archive with -O or -F.

-b, --swap
>   Swap bytes and half-words to convert between big-endian and
>   little-endian 32-bit integers.

-B   Block input or output using 5120 bytes per record (default is
>   512 bytes per record).

--block-size=*size*
>   Set input or output size to *size* × 512 bytes.

-c   Read or write header information as ASCII characters, which
>   is useful when source and destination machines are different
>   types.

-C *n*, --io-size=*n*
>   Like -B, but block size can be any positive integer *n*.

-d, --make-directories
>   Create directories as needed.

-E *file*, --pattern-file=*file*
>   Extract from the archives filenames that match patterns in *file*.

-f, --nonmatching
>   Reverse the sense of copying; copy all files *except* those that
>   match *patterns*.

-F *file*, --file=*file*
>   Use *file* as the archive, not stdin or stdout. *file* can reside on
>   another machine, if given in the form [*user@*]*hostname:file*
>   (where *user@* is optional).

--force-local
>   Assume that *file* (provided by -F, -I, or -O) is a local file, even
>   if it contains a colon (:) indicating a remote file.

-H *type*, --format=*type*
>   Use *type* format. Default for copy-out is **bin**; default for copy-
>   in is autodetection of the format. Valid formats (all caps also
>   accepted) are:

bin
>   Binary.

odc
>   Old (POSIX.1) portable format.

newc
>   New (SVR4) portable format.

crc
>   New (SVR4) portable format with checksum added.

tar
>   Tar.

ustar
POSIX.1 tar (also recognizes GNU tar archives).

hpodc
HP-UX portable format.

-I *file*
Read *file* as an input archive. May be on a remote machine (see **-F**).

-k   Ignored. For compatibility with other versions of **cpio**.

-l, --link
Link files instead of copying.

-L, --dereference
Follow symbolic links.

-m, --preserve-modification-time
Retain previous file modification time.

-M *msg*, **--message**=*msg*
Print *msg* when switching media, as a prompt before switching to new media. Use variable **%d** in the message as a numeric ID for the next medium. **-M** is valid only with **-I** or **-O**.

-n, --numeric-uid-gid
When verbosely listing contents, show user ID and group ID numerically.

--no-absolute-filenames
Create all copied-in files relative to the current directory.

--no-preserve-owner
Make all copied files owned by yourself, instead of the owner of the original. Can be used only if you are a privileged user. Valid in copy-in and pass-through modes.

-O *file*
Archive the output to *file*, which may be a file on another machine (see **-F**).

--only-verify-crc
For a CRC-format archive, verify the CRC of each file; don't actually copy the files in.

--quiet
Don't print the number of blocks copied.

-r, --rename
Rename files interactively.

-R [*user*][*:group*], **--owner** [*user*][*:group*]
Reassign file ownership and group information to the user's login ID (privileged users only).

--rsh-command=*cmd*
Use the specified command to communicate with remote systems.

-s, --swap-bytes
Swap bytes of each two-byte half-word.

-S, --swap-half-words
Swap half-words of each four-byte word.

--sparse

> For copy-out and copy-pass, write files that have large blocks of zeros as sparse files.

-t, --list

> Print a table of contents of the input (create no files). When used with the **-v** option, resembles output of **ls -l**.

--to-stdout

> In copy-in mode, extract files to standard output.

-u, --unconditional

> Unconditional copy; old files can overwrite new ones.

-v, --verbose

> Print a list of filenames processed.

-V, --dot

> Print a dot for each file read or written (this shows **cpio** at work without cluttering the screen).

--version

> Print version number and then exit.

Examples

Generate a list of files whose names end in *.old* using **find**; use the list as input to **cpio**:

```
find . -name "*.old" | cpio -ocBv > /dev/rst8
```

Restore from a tape drive all files whose names contain **save** (subdirectories are created if needed):

```
cpio -icdv "*save*" < /dev/rst8
```

Move a directory tree:

```
find . -depth | cpio -padm /mydir
```

---

cpp

cpp [*options*] [*ifile* [*ofile*]]

GNU C language preprocessor. **cpp** is normally invoked as the first pass of any C compilation by the **gcc** command. The output of **cpp** is a form acceptable as input to the next pass of the C compiler. The *ifile* and *ofile* options are, respectively, the input and output for the preprocessor; they default to standard input and standard output.

Options

-$** Do not allow **$ in identifiers.

-ansi

> Use 1990 ISO C standard. This is equivalent to **-std=c89**.

-dD

> Similar to **-dM**, but exclude predefined macros and include results of preprocessing.

-dM

> Suppress normal output. Print series of **#define**s that create the macros used in the source file.

-dN

Similar to **-dD**, but don't print macro expansions.

-dI

Print **#include** directives in addition to other output.

-fpreprocessed

Treat file as already preprocessed. Skip most processing directives, remove all comments, and tokenize file.

-ftabstop=*width*

Set distance between tabstops so columns will be reported correctly in warnings and errors. Default is 8.

-fno-show-column

Omit column numbers in warnings and errors.

-gcc

Define _ _GNUC_ _, _ _GNUC_MINOR_ _, and _ _GNUC_ PATCHLEVEL_ _ macros.

--help

Print usage message and exit.

-idirafter *dir*

Search *dir* for header files when a header file is not found in any of the included directories.

-imacros *file*

Process macros in *file* before processing main files.

-include *file*

Process *file* before main file.

-iprefix *prefix*

When adding directories with **-iwithprefix**, prepend *prefix* to the directory's name.

-isystem *dir*

Search *dir* for header files after searching directories specified with **-I** but before searching standard system directories.

-iwithprefix *dir*

Append *dir* to the list of directories to be searched when a header file cannot be found in the main include path. If **-iprefix** has been set, prepend that prefix to the directory's name.

-iwithprefixbefore *dir*

Insert *dir* at the beginning of the list of directories to be searched when a header file cannot be found in the main include path. If **-iprefix** has been set, prepend that prefix to the directory's name.

-lang-c, -lang-c++, -lang-objc, -lang-objc++

Expect the source to be in C, C++, Objective C, or Objective C++, respectively.

-lint

Display all lint commands in comments as **#pragma lint** *command*.

-nostdinc

Search only specified, not standard, directories for header files.

-nostdinc++

Suppress searching of directories believed to contain C++-specific header files.

-o *file*

Write output to *file*. (Same as specifying a second filename in the command line.)

-pedantic

Warn verbosely.

-pedantic-errors

Produce a fatal error in every case in which **-pedantic** would have produced a warning.

-std=_standard_

Specify C *standard* of input file. Accepted values are:

iso9899:1990, c89

1990 ISO C standard.

iso9899:199409

1994 amendment to the 1990 ISO C standard.

iso9899:1999, c99, iso9899:199x, c9x

1999 revised ISO C standard.

gnu89

1990 C Standard with gnu extensions. The default value.

gnu99, gnu9x

1999 revised ISO C standard with gnu extensions.

-traditional

Behave like traditional C, not ANSI.

-trigraphs

Convert special three-letter sequences, meant to represent missing characters on some terminals, into the single character they represent.

-undef

Suppress definition of all nonstandard macros.

-v   Verbose mode.

-version

Print version number, then process file.

--version

Print version number, then exit.

-w   Don't print warnings.

-x *language*

Specify the language of the input file. *language* may be **c**, **c++**, **objective-c**, or **assembler-with-cpp**. By default, language is deduced from the filename extension. If the extension is unrecognized, the default is **c**.

-A *name*[*=def*]

Assert *name* with value *def* as if defined by **#assert**. To turn off standard assertions, use **-A-**.

-A *-name[=def]*
> Cancel assertion *name* with value *def*.

-C   Retain all comments except those found on **cpp** directive lines. By default, **cpp** strips C-style comments.

-D*name[=def]*
> Define *name* with value *def* as if by a **#define**. If no *=def* is given, *name* is defined with value 1. **-D** has lower precedence than **-U**.

-E   Preprocess the source files, but do not compile. Print result to standard output. This option is usually passed from **gcc**.

-H   Print pathnames of included files, one per line, on standard error.

-I*dir*
> Search in directory *dir* for **#include** files whose names do not begin with / before looking in directories on standard list. **#include** files whose names are enclosed in double quotes and do not begin with / will be searched for first in the current directory, then in directories named on **-I** options, and last in directories on the standard list.

-I-   Split includes. Search directories specified by **-I** options preceding this one for header files included with quotes (**#include "file.h"**) but not for header files included with angle brackets (**#include <file.h>**). Search directories specified by **-I** options following this one for all header files.

-M [-MG]
> Suppress normal output. Print a rule for **make** that describes the main source file's dependencies. If **-MG** is specified, assume that missing header files are actually generated files, and look for them in the source file's directory.

-MF *file*
> Print rules generated by **-M** or **-MM** to *file*.

-MD *file*
> Similar to **-M**, but output to *file*; also compile the source.

-MM
> Similar to **-M**, but describe only those files included as a result of **#include "***file***"**.

-MMD *file*
> Similar to **-MD**, but describe only the user's header files.

-MQ *target*
> Similar to **-MT**, but quote any characters that are special to **make**.

-MT *target*
> Specify the *target* to use when generating a rule for **make**. By default, the target is based on the name of the main input file.

-P   Preprocess input without producing line-control information used by next pass of the C compiler.

-U*name*
> Remove any initial definition of *name*, where *name* is a reserved symbol predefined by the preprocessor, or a name defined on a **-D** option. Names predefined by **cpp** are **unix** and **i386** (for Intel systems).

-**Wall**
> Warn both on nested comments and trigraphs.

-**Wcomment, -Wcomments**
> Warn when encountering the beginning of a nested comment.

-**Wtraditional**
> Warn when encountering constructs that are interpreted differently in ANSI than in traditional C.

-**Wtrigraphs**
> Warn when encountering trigraphs, which are three-letter sequences meant to represent missing characters on some terminals.

Special names

cpp understands various special names, some of which are:

_ _**DATE**_ _
> Current date (e.g., Jan 10 2003).

_ _**FILE**_ _
> Current filename (as a C string).

_ _**LINE**_ _
> Current source line number (as a decimal integer).

_ _**TIME**_ _
> Current time (e.g., 12:00:00).

These special names can be used anywhere, including in macros, just like any other defined names. **cpp**'s understanding of the line number and filename may be changed using a **#line** directive.

Directives

All **cpp** directive lines start with **#** in column 1. Any number of blanks and tabs is allowed between the **#** and the directive. The directives are:

#assert *name (string)*
> Define a question called *name*, with an answer of *string*. Assertions can be tested with **#if** directives. The predefined assertions for **#system**, **#cpu**, and **#machine** can be used for architecture-dependent changes.

#unassert *name*
> Remove assertion for question *name*.

#define *name token-string*
> Define a macro called *name*, with a value of *token-string*. Subsequent instances of *name* are replaced with *token-string*.

#define *name(arg, ... , arg) token-string*

    This allows substitution of a macro with arguments. *token-string* will be substituted for *name* in the input file. Each call to *name* in the source file includes arguments that are plugged into the corresponding *args* in *token-string*.

#undef *name*

    Remove definition of the macro *name*. No additional tokens are permitted on the directive line after *name*.

#ident *string*

    Put *string* into the comment section of an object file.

#include *"filename"*, **#include**<*filename*>

    Include contents of *filename* at this point in the program. No additional tokens are permitted on the directive line after the final " or >.

#line *integer-constant "filename"*

    Cause **cpp** to generate line-control information for the next pass of the C compiler. The compiler behaves as if *integer-constant* is the line number of the next line of source code and *filename* (if present) is the name of the input file. No additional tokens are permitted on the directive line after the optional *filename*.

#endif

    End a section of lines begun by a test directive (**#if**, **#ifdef**, or **#ifndef**). No additional tokens are permitted on the directive line.

#ifdef *name*

    Lines following this directive and up to matching **#endif** or next **#else** or **#elif** will appear in the output if *name* is currently defined. No additional tokens are permitted on the directive line after *name*.

#ifndef *name*

    Lines following this directive and up to matching **#endif** or next **#else** or **#elif** will appear in the output if *name* is not currently defined. No additional tokens are permitted on the directive line after *name*.

#if *constant-expression*

    Lines following this directive and up to matching **#endif** or next **#else** or **#elif** will appear in the output if *constant-expression* evaluates to nonzero.

#elif *constant-expression*

    An arbitrary number of **#elif** directives are allowed between an **#if**, **#ifdef**, or **#ifndef** directive and an **#else** or **#endif** directive. The lines following the **#elif** and up to the next **#else**, **#elif**, or **#endif** directive will appear in the output if the preceding test directive and all intervening **#elif** directives evaluate to zero, and the *constant-expression* evaluates to nonzero. If *constant-expression* evaluates to nonzero, all succeeding **#elif** and **#else** directives will be ignored.

#else

Lines following this directive and up to the matching **#endif** will appear in the output if the preceding test directive evaluates to zero, and all intervening **#elif** directives evaluate to zero. No additional tokens are permitted on the directive line.

#error

Report fatal errors.

#warning

Report warnings, but then continue processing.

---

crond

crond [*options*]

System administration command. Normally started in a system startup file. Execute commands at scheduled times, as specified in users' files in */var/spool/cron*. Each file shares its name with the user who owns it. The files are controlled via the command **crontab**. The **crond** command will also read commands from the */etc/crontab* file and from the */etc/cron.d/* directory. See **anacron** for scheduling events on systems that are frequently rebooted or powered off, such as notebook computers.

Options

-m *command*

User *command* to send mail instead of **sendmail**.

-n   Run the command in the foreground.

-p   Remove security restrictions on crontab file permissions.

---

crontab

crontab [*options*] [*file*]

View, install, or uninstall your current *crontab* file. A privileged user can run **crontab** for another user by supplying -**u** *user*. A *crontab* file is a list of commands, one per line, that will execute automatically at a given time. Numbers are supplied before each command to specify the execution time. The numbers appear in five fields, as follows:

Minute	0-59
Hour	0-23
Day of month	1-31
Month	1-12
	Jan, Feb, Mar, ...
Day of week	0-6, with 0 = Sunday
	Sun, Mon, Tue, ...

Use a comma between multiple values, a hyphen to indicate a range, an asterisk to indicate all possible values, and a slash (/) to indicate a repeating range. For example, assuming these *crontab* entries:

```
59 3 * * 5        find / -print | backup_program
0 0 1,15 * *      echo "Timesheets due" | mail user
```

---

the first command backs up the system files every Friday at 3:59 a.m., and the second command mails a reminder on the 1st and 15th of each month.

The superuser can always issue the **crontab** command. Other users must be listed in the file */etc/cron.allow* if it exists; otherwise, they must not be listed in */etc/cron.deny*. If neither file exists, only the superuser can issue the command.

Options

The **-e**, **-l**, and **-r** options are not valid if any *files* are specified.

-e   Edit the user's current *crontab* file (or create one).

-l   Display the user's *crontab* file on standard output.

-r   Delete the user's *crontab* file.

-u *user*
>Indicate which *user*'s *crontab* file will be acted upon.

---

csplit

csplit [*options*] *file arguments*

Separate *file* into context-based sections and place sections in files named xx00 through xx*n* (*n* < 100), breaking *file* at each pattern specified in *arguments*. The byte count for each section is written to standard output. See also **split**.

Options

-   Read from standard input.

-b *format*, **--suffix-format**=*format*
>Use sprintf format instead of %02d for the suffix.

-f *prefix*, **--prefix**=*prefix*
>Name new files *prefix*00 through *prefixn* (default is xx00 through xx*n*).

-k, **--keep-files**
>Keep newly created files even when an error occurs (which would normally remove these files). This is useful when you need to specify an arbitrarily large repeat argument, {*n*}, and you don't want an out-of-range error to cause removal of the new files.

-n *num*, **--digits**=*num*
>Use output filenames with numbers *num* digits long. The default is 2.

-s, **-q**, **--silent**, **--quiet**
>Suppress display of character counts.

-z, **--elide-empty-files**
>Do not create empty output files. However, number as if those files had been created.

Arguments

Any one or a combination of the following expressions may be specified as arguments. Arguments containing blanks or other special characters should be surrounded by single quotes.

/expr/[offset]

> Create file from the current line up to the line containing the regular expression *expr*. *offset* should be of the form +*n* or -*n*, where *n* is the number of lines below or above *expr*.

%expr%[offset]

> Same as /*expr*/, except no file is created for lines before a line containing *expr*.

num

> Create file from current line up to (but not including) line number *num*. When followed by a repeat count (number inside { }), put the next *num* lines of input into another output file.

{n}

> Repeat argument *n* times. May follow any of the preceding arguments. Files are split at instances of *expr* or in blocks of *num* lines. If * is given instead of *n*, repeat argument until input is exhausted.

Examples

Create up to 20 chapter files from the file *novel*:

```
csplit -k -f chap. novel '/CHAPTER/' '{20}'
```

Create up to 100 address files (xx00 through xx99), each four lines long, from a database named *address_list*:

```
csplit -k address_list 4 {99}
```

---

ctags

ctags [*options*] *files*

Create a list of function and macro names defined in a programming source *file*. More than one file may be specified. **ctags** understands many programming languages, including C, C++, FORTRAN, Java, Perl, Python, flex, yacc, and bison. The output list (named *tags* by default) contains lines of the form:

> name   file   context

where *name* is the function or macro name, *file* is the source file in which *name* is defined, and *context* is a search pattern that shows the line of code containing *name*. After the list of tags is created, you can invoke **vi** on any file and type:

```
:set tags=tagsfile
:tag name
```

This switches the **vi** editor to the source file associated with the *name* listed in *tagsfile* (which you specify with -t).

etags produces an equivalent file for tags to be used with Emacs.

Options

-a   Append tag output to existing list of tags.

-e   Create tag files for use with **emacs**.

-h *extensionlist*

Interpret files with filename extensions specified in *extension-list* as header files. The default list is ".h.H.hh.hpp.hxx.h++. inc.def". To indicate that files without extensions should be treated as header files, insert an additional period in the list before another period or at the end of the list, or use just a period by itself. To use this option multiple times and have the specified lists ANDed together, use a plus sign as the first character in the list. To restore the default, use the word "default".

-n   Use numeric **ex** commands to locate tags. Same as **--excmd= number**.

-o *file*, -f *file*, **--output**=*file*

Write to *file*.

--packages-only

Include tag entries for members of structure-like constructs.

-R   Recursively read files in subdirectories of the directory given on the command line.

-u   Don't sort tag entries.

-x   Produce a tabular listing of each function, and its line number, source file, and context.

-B   Search for tags backward through files.

-I *tokenlist*

Specify a list of tokens to be specially handled. If *tokenlist* is given as a file, use **ex** pattern commands to locate tags. Same as **--excmd=pattern**.

-N   Use **ex** pattern commands to locate tags. Same as **--excmd= pattern**.

-S, **--ignore-indentation**

Normally **ctags** uses indentation to parse the tag file; this option tells **ctags** to rely on indentation less.

-T, **--typedefs-and-c++**

Include tag entries for typedefs, structs, enums, unions, and C++ member functions.

-V, **--version**

Print the version number and exit.

---

cupsd

cupsd *options*

System administration command. Start the print scheduler for the Common UNIX Printing System.

Options

-c file
> Use specified configuration *file* instead of */etc/cups/cupsd.conf*.

-f   Run scheduler in foreground.

-F   Run scheduler in foreground but detach it from the controlling terminal and current directory. Sometimes used when running **cupsd** from **init**.

---

cut

cut *options* [*files*]

Cut out selected columns or fields from one or more *files*. With no *file*, or if *file* is -, read from standard input. In the following options, *list* is a sequence of integers. Use a comma between values, and a hyphen to specify a range (e.g., **1-10,15,20** or **50-**). See also **paste** and **join**.

Options

-b *list*, **--bytes** *list*
> Specify *list* of positions; only bytes in these positions will be printed.

-c *list*, **--characters** *list*
> Cut the column positions identified in *list*. Column numbers start with 1.

-d *c*, **--delimiter** *c*
> Use with **-f** to specify field delimiter as character *c* (default is tab); special characters (e.g., a space) must be quoted.

-f *list*, **--fields** *list*
> Cut the fields identified in *list*.

-n   Don't split multibyte characters. Use with **-b**.

-s, **--only-delimited**
> Use with **-f** to suppress lines without delimiters.

--output-delimiter=*string*
> Use *string* as the output delimiter. By default, the output delimiter is the same as the input delimiter.

--help
> Print help message and exit.

--version
> Print version information and exit.

Examples

Extract usernames and real names from */etc/passwd*:

```
cut -d: -f1,5 /etc/passwd
```

Find out who is logged on, but list only login names:

```
who | cut -d" " -f1
```

Cut characters in the fourth column of *file*, and paste them back as the first column in the same file:

```
cut -c4 file | paste - file
```

date

date [options] [+format] [date]

Print the current date and time. You may specify a display *format*, which can consist of literal text strings (blanks must be quoted) as well as field descriptors, whose values are described in the following entries (the listing shows some logical groupings). A privileged user can change the system's date and time.

Options

+format

Display current date in a nonstandard format. For example:

```
$ date +"%A %j %n%k %p"
Friday 051
23 PM
```

The default is **%a %b %e %T %Z %Y** (e.g., Fri Feb 20 22:59:43 EST 2009).

-d *date*, **--date** *date*

Display *date*, which should be in quotes and may be in the format *d* **days** or *m* **months** *d* **days**, to print a date in the future. Specify **ago** to print a date in the past. You may include formatting (see the following section).

-f *datefile*, **--file**=*datefile*

Like **-d**, but printed once for each line of *datefile*.

-r *file*, **--reference**=*file*

Display the time *file* was last modified.

-R, **--rfc-2822**

Display the date and time in RFC 2822 format.

--rfc-3339=*timespec*

Display the date and time in RFC 3339 format. The value of *timespec* can be one of **date**, **seconds**, or **ns** (nanoseconds) to get the desired degree of precision.

--help

Print help message and exit.

--version

Print version information and exit.

-s *date*, **--set**=*date*

Set the date.

-u, **--utc**, **--universal**

Set the date to Coordinated Universal Time, not local time.

Format

The exact result of many of these codes is locale-specific and depends upon your language setting, particularly the **LANG** environment variable. See **locale**.

%%

Literal **%**.

- (hyphen)
    Do not pad fields (default: pad fields with zeros).

_ (underscore)
    Pad fields with space (default: zeros).

^   Use uppercase if possible.

Use the opposite case if possible.

%a Abbreviated weekday.

%A Full weekday.

%b Abbreviated month name.

%B Full month name.

%c Country-specific date and time format.

%C Century; like **%Y** but show only the two-digit century (e.g., show 20, not 2009).

%d Day of month (01–31).

%D Date in **%m/%d/%y** format.

%e Day of month padded with spaces.

%h Same as **%b**.

%H Hour in 24-hour format (00–23).

%I Hour in 12-hour format (01–12).

%j Julian day of year (001–366).

%k Hour in 24-hour format, without leading zeros (0–23).

%l Hour in 12-hour format, without leading zeros (1–12).

%m Month of year (01–12).

%M Minutes (00–59).

%n Insert a new line.

%N Nanoseconds (000000000–999999999).

%p String to indicate a.m. or p.m.

%P Like **%p** but lowercase.

%r Time in **%I:%M:%S %p** (12-hour) format.

%R Time in **%H:%M** (24-hour) format.

%s Seconds since "the Epoch," which is 1970-01-01 00:00:00 UTC (a nonstandard extension).

%S Seconds (00–59).

%t Insert a tab.

%T Time in **%H:%M:%S** format.

%u Day of the week (1–7, Monday = 1).

%U Week number in year (00–53); start week on Sunday.

%V Week number in year (01–52); start week on Monday.

%w Day of week (0–6, Sunday = 0).

%W Week number in year (00–53); start week on Monday.

%x Country-specific date format.

%X Country-specific time format.

%Y Four-digit year (e.g., 2006).

%y Last two digits of year (00–99).

%z RFC 822-style numeric time zone.

%Z Time-zone name.

Strings for setting date

Strings for setting the date may be numeric or nonnumeric. Numeric strings consist of *time*, *day*, and *year* in the format *MMDDhhmm*[[*CC*]*YY*][.*ss*]. Nonnumeric strings may include month strings, time zones, a.m., and p.m.

time
> A two-digit hour and two-digit minute (*hhmm*); *hh* uses 24-hour format.

day
> A two-digit month and two-digit day of month (*MMDD*); default is current day and month.

year
> The year specified as either the full four-digit century and year or just the two-digit year; the default is the current year.

Examples

Set the date to July 1 (**0701**), 4 a.m. (**0400**), 2009 (**09**):

    date 0701040009

The command:

    date +"Hello%t Date is %D %n%t Time is %T"

produces a formatted date as follows:

    Hello   Date is 02/20/09
              Time is 17:53:39

---

dd

dd *options*

Make a copy of an input file (**if**) using the specified conditions, and send the results to the output file (or standard output if **of** is not specified). Any number of options can be supplied, although **if** and **of** are the most common and are usually specified first. Because **dd** can handle arbitrary block sizes, it is useful when converting between raw physical devices.

Options

bs=*n*
> Set input (**ibs**) and output (**obs**) block size to *n* bytes; this option overrides **ibs** and **obs** set separately.

cbs=*n*
> Set the size of the conversion buffer (logical record length) to *n* bytes. Use only if the conversion *format* is **ascii**, **ebcdic**, **ibm**, **block**, or **unblock**.

conv=_format_

Convert the input according to one or more (comma-separated) _format_s listed next. The first five _format_s are mutually exclusive.

ascii

EBCDIC to ASCII.

ebcdic

ASCII to EBCDIC.

ibm

ASCII to EBCDIC with IBM conventions.

block

Variable-length records (i.e., those terminated by a newline) to fixed-length records.

unblock

Fixed-length records to variable-length records.

excl

Fail if the output file already exists.

fdatasync

Physically write the output file before finishing.

fsync

Physically write both the output file and the metadata before finishing.

lcase

Uppercase to lowercase.

nocreate

Do not create an output file.

noerror

Continue processing after read errors.

notrunc

Don't truncate output file.

swab

Swap each pair of input bytes.

sync

Pad input blocks to **ibs** with trailing zeros.

ucase

Lowercase to uppercase.

count=_n_

Copy only _n_ input blocks.

ibs=_n_

Set input block size to _n_ bytes (default is 512).

if=_file_

Read input from _file_ (default is standard input).

obs=_n_

Set output block size to _n_ bytes (default is 512).

of=_file_

Write output to _file_ (default is standard output).

seek=*n*
> Skip *n* output-sized blocks from start of output file.

skip=*n*
> Skip *n* input-sized blocks from start of input file.

--help
> Print help message and then exit.

--version
> Print the version number and then exit.

You can multiply size values (*n*) by a factor of 1024, 512, or 2 by appending the letter **k**, **b**, or **w**, respectively. You can use the letter **x** as a multiplication operator between two numbers.

Examples

Convert an input file to all lowercase:

```
dd if=caps_file of=small_file conv=lcase
```

Retrieve variable-length data and write it as fixed-length to **out**:

```
[data_retrieval_cmd]| dd of=out conv=sync,block
```

---

deallocvt
      deallocvt *N*

Deallocate and destroy the unused virtual console */dev/ttyN*. Multiple consoles may be named with additional spaces and integers: **deallocvt 1 4** deallocates the */dev/tty1* and */dev/tty4* consoles. Consoles are considered unused if they are not in the foreground, have no open processes, and have no selected text. The command does not destroy consoles that are still active.

---

debugfs
      debugfs [[*option*] *device*]

System administration command. Provide direct access to data structure of an ext2 or ext3 filesystem in order to debug problems with the device. *device* is the special file corresponding to the device containing the filesystem (e.g., */dev/hda3*). **debugfs** may be used on a mounted filesystem device.

Option

-**b** *blocksize*
> Use the specified *blocksize* for the filesystem.

-**c**
   Catastrophic mode. Open the filesystem in read-only mode; do not read the inode and group bitmaps initially.

-**f** *file*
> Read commands from *file*. Exit when done executing commands.

-**i**
   Specify filesystem *device* is an ext2 image file created by **e2image**.

-**s** *block*
> Read the superblock from the specified *block*.

-**w**
   Open the filesystem in read-write mode.

-R *request*
> Execute the given *request* (see list below), then exit.

-V   Print version number, then exit.

Requests

bmap *file logicalblock*
> Given the *logicalblock* of inode *file*, print the corresponding physical block.

cat *file*
> Dump the contents of an inode to standard output.

cd *directory*
> Change the current working directory to *directory*.

chroot *directory*
> Change the root directory to be the specified inode.

close
> Close the currently open filesystem.

clri *file*
> Clear the contents of the inode corresponding to *file*.

dump [**-p**] *file out_file*
> Dump the contents of inode *file* to *out_file*. Change ownership and permissions of *out_file* to match *file* if **-p** is specified.

expand_dir *directory*
> Expand *directory*.

feature [[**-**]*feature*]
> Set filesystem *feature* listed on the command line, then print current feature settings. Use - to clear a *feature*.

find_free_block [[*n*] *goal*]
> Find and allocate first *n* free blocks starting from *goal* (if specified).

find_free_inode [*dir* [*mode*]]
> Find a free inode and allocate it.

freeb *block* [*n*]
> Free *n* blocks beginning from *block*. Default is 1 block.

freei *file*
> Free the inode corresponding to *file*.

help
> Print a list of commands understood by **debugfs**.

icheck *block*
> Do block-to-inode translation.

imap *file*
> Print the location of the inode data structure for *file*.

init_filesys *device blocksize*
> Create an ext2 filesystem on *device*.

kill_file *file*
> Remove *file* and deallocate its blocks.

lcd *directory*
> Change current working *directory* on native filesystem.

ln *source_file dest_file*
> Create a link.

logdump [-acs] [-b*block*] [-i*inode*] [-f*journal_file*] [*out_file*]
> Print the ext3 journal contents to screen or to the specified *out_file*. Prints the superblock journal by default. Specify other journal information by *block* or *inode*. You can also specify a *journal_file* containing journal data. Use **-a** to print the contents of descriptor blocks. Use **-b** to print records referring to a specified block. Use **-c** to print the hexadecimal and ASCII contents of blocks referenced by the logdump.

ls [-l] [-d] [-p] [*pathname*]
> Emulate the **ls** command. Use **-l** for verbose format and **-d** to list deleted entries. Use **-p** for output that can be more easily parsed by scripts.

modify_inode *file*
> Modify the contents of the inode corresponding to *file*.

mkdir *directory*
> Make *directory*.

mknod *file* [**p**|[[**c**|**b**] *major minor*]]
> Create a special device file.

ncheck *inode*
> Do inode-to-name translation.

open [-b *blocksize*] [-c] [-e] [-f] [-i] [-w] [-s *block*] *device*
> Open a filesystem. The **-f** option forces the filesystem to open disregarding any unknown or incompatible features that would otherwise prevent it from opening. The **-e** option causes the filesystem to be opened in exclusive mode. The remaining options are identical to the command-line options for **debugfs**.

pwd
> Print the current working directory.

quit
> Quit **debugfs**.

rdump *directory dest_directory*
> Recursively dump *directory* and its contents to *dest_directory* on the native filesystem.

rm *file*
> Remove *file*.

rmdir *directory*
> Remove *directory*.

setb *block* [*n*]
> Mark *n* blocks as allocated, beginning from *block*. Default is 1 block.

set_block_group *number field value*
> Set descripter *field* to *value* for the block group specified by *number*.

seti *file*

Mark in use the inode corresponding to *file*.

set_super_value [-l] *field value*

Set superblock *field* to *value*. Use -l to print a list of valid fields.

show_super_stats [-h]

List the contents of the superblock and block group descriptors. Use **-h** to list only the superblock contents.

stat *file*

Dump the contents of the inode corresponding to *file*.

testb *block* [*n*]

Print whether each of *n* blocks is in use, beginning with *block*. By default, just check the specified *block*.

testi *file*

Test whether the inode corresponding to *file* is marked as allocated.

undel <*inode*> [*pathname*]

Undelete (mark as used) the specified *inode*. You must include the angle brackets. Optionally link the recovered inode with *pathname*. If undeleting multiple inodes, linking may not be safe. Use a separate pass to link the pathname after all inodes have been undeleted. Always run **e2fsck** after undeleting inodes.

unlink *file*

Remove a link.

write *source_file file*

Create a file in the filesystem named *file*, and copy the contents of *source_file* into the destination file.

---

depmod

depmod [*options*] *modules*

System administration command. Create a dependency file for the modules given on the command line. This dependency file can be used by **modprobe** to automatically load the relevant *modules*. The normal use of **depmod** is to include the line **/sbin/depmod -a** in one of the files in */etc/rc.d* so that the correct module dependencies will be available after booting the system.

Options

-a, --all

Create dependencies for all modules listed in */etc/modules.conf*.

-A, --quick

Check timestamps and only update the dependency file if anything has changed.

-b *dir*, **--basedir** *dir*

Specify a base directory to use instead of */lib/modules*.

-C *file*, **--config** *file*
> Use the specified configuration file instead of */etc/modules.dep*. May also be set using the MODULECONF environment variable.

-e, **--errsyms**
> Print a list of all unresolved symbols.

-F *file*, **--kernelsyms** *file*
> Use the specified kernel symbol file to build dependencies. Usually this is either a copy of a system's *System.map* file or the output of */proc/ksyms*.

-h, **--help**
> Print help message, then exit.

-n, **--dry-run**, **--show**
> Write dependency file to standard output instead of writing to module directory.

-q, **--quiet**
> Don't display error messages about missing symbols.

-r, **--root**
> Allow root to load modules not owned by root.

-s, **--syslog**
> Write error messages to the syslog daemon instead of to standard error.

-v   Print a list of all processed modules.

-V, **--version**
> Print version number.

Files

/etc/modules.dep, */etc/depmod.d*
> Information about modules: which ones depend on others, and which directories correspond to particular types of modules.

/sbin/insmod, */sbin/rmmod*
> Programs that **depmod** relies on.

---

devdump   devdump *isoimage*

Interactively display the contents of the device or filesystem image *isoimage*. **devdump** displays the first 256 bytes of the first 2048-byte sector and waits for commands. The prompt shows the extent number (zone) and offset within the extent, and the contents display at the top of the screen.

Commands

+   Search forward for the next instance of the search string.

a   Search backward within the image.

b   Search forward within the image.

f   Prompt for a new search string.

g   Prompt for a new starting block and go there.

q   Exit.

df df *[options]* *[name]*

Report the amount of free disk space available on all mounted file-systems or on the given *name*. (**df** cannot report on unmounted filesystems.) Disk space is shown in 1 KB blocks (default) or 512-byte blocks if the environment variable POSIXLY_CORRECT is set. *name* can be a device name (e.g., */dev/hd**), the directory name of a mounting point (e.g., */usr*), or a directory name (in which case **df** reports on the entire filesystem in which that directory is mounted).

Options

-a, --all
Include empty filesystems (those with 0 blocks).

-B *n*, **--block-size=***n*
Show space as *n*-byte blocks.

-h, --human-readable
Print sizes in a format friendly to human readers (e.g., 1.9 MB instead of 1967156).

-H, --si
Like **-h**, but show as power of 1000 rather than 1024.

-i, --inodes
Report free, used, and percent-used inodes.

-k Print sizes in kilobytes.

-l, --local
Show local filesystems only.

-m, --megabytes
Print sizes in megabytes.

--no-sync
Show results without invoking **sync** first (i.e., without flushing the buffers). This is the default.

-P, --portability
Use POSIX output format (i.e., print information about each filesystem on exactly one line).

--sync
Invoke **sync** (flush buffers) before getting and showing sizes.

-t *type*, **--type=***type*
Show only filesystems of the specified type.

-T, --print-type
Print the type of each filesystem in addition to the sizes.

-x *type*, **--exclude-type=***type*
Show only filesystems that are not of type *type*.

--help
Print help message and then exit.

--version
Print the version and then exit.

diff diff [*options*] *file1 file2*

Compare two text files. **diff** reports lines that differ between *file1* and *file2*. Output consists of lines of context from each file, with *file1* text flagged by a < symbol and *file2* text by a > symbol. Context lines are preceded by the **ed** command (**a**, **c**, or **d**) that would be used to convert *file1* to *file2*. If one of the files is -, standard input is read. If one of the files is a directory, **diff** locates the filename in that directory corresponding to the other argument (e.g., **diff** *my_dir junk* is the same as **diff** *my_dir/junk junk*). If both arguments are directories, **diff** reports lines that differ between all pairs of files having equivalent names (e.g., *olddir/program* and *newdir/program*); in addition, **diff** lists filenames unique to one directory, as well as subdirectories common to both. See also **cmp**.

Options

-*n* For context and unified **diff**, print *n* lines of context. Same as specifying a number with -C or -U.

-**a**, --**text**
Treat all files as text files. Useful for checking to see if binary files are identical.

-**b**, --**ignore-space-change**
Ignore repeating blanks and end-of-line blanks; treat successive blanks as one.

-**B**, --**ignore-blank-lines**
Ignore blank lines in files.

-**c** Context **diff**: print three lines surrounding each changed line.

-**C** *n*, --**context**[=*n*]
Context **diff**: print *n* lines surrounding each changed line. The default context is three lines.

-**d**, --**minimal**
Ignore segments of numerous changes and output a smaller set of changes.

-**D** *symbol*, --**ifdef**=*symbol*
When handling C files, create an output file that contains all the contents of both input files, including **#ifdef** and **#ifndef** directives that reflect the directives in both files.

-**e**, --**ed**
Produce a script of commands (**a**, **c**, **d**) to recreate *file2* from *file1* using the **ed** editor.

-**F** *regexp*, --**show-function-line**[=*regexp*]
For context and unified **diff**, show the most recent line containing *regexp* before each block of changed lines.

-**H**, --**speed-large-files**
Speed output of large files by scanning for scattered small changes; long stretches with many changes may not show up.

--**help**
Print brief usage message.

--horizon-lines=_n_

In an attempt to find a more compact listing, keep _n_ lines on both sides of the changed lines when performing the comparison.

-i, --ignore-case

Ignore case in text comparison. Uppercase and lowercase are considered the same.

-I _regexp,_ **--ignore-matching-lines=**_regexp_

Ignore lines in files that match the regular expression _regexp_.

-l, --paginate

Paginate output by passing it to **pr**.

-L _label,_ **--label=**_label_

For context and unified **diff**, print _label_ in place of the filename being compared. The first such option applies to the first filename and the second option to the second filename.

--left-column

For two-column output (**-y**), show only left column of common lines.

-n, --rcs

Produce output in RCS **diff** format.

-N, --new-file

Treat nonexistent files as empty.

-p, --show-c-function

When handling files in C or C-like languages such as Java, show the function containing each block of changed lines. Assumes **-c**, but can also be used with a unified **diff**.

-P, --unidirectional-new-file

If two directories are being compared and the first lacks a file that is in the second, pretend that an empty file of that name exists in the first directory.

-q, --brief

Output only whether files differ.

-r, --recursive

Compare subdirectories recursively.

-s, --report-identical-files

Indicate when files do not differ.

-S _filename,_ **--starting-file=**_filename_

For directory comparisons, begin with the file _filename_, skipping files that come earlier in the standard list order.

--suppress-common-lines

For two-column output (**-y**), do not show common lines.

-t, --expand-tabs

Produce output with tabs expanded to spaces.

-T, --initial-tab

Insert initial tabs into output to line up tabs properly.

-**u**   Unified **diff**: print old and new versions of lines in a single block, with 3 lines surrounding each block of changed lines.

-**U** *n*, --**unified**[=*n*]
Unified **diff**: print old and new versions of lines in a single block, with *n* lines surrounding each block of changed lines. The default context is 3 lines. With the -**U** form, *n* must be given.

-**v**, --**version**
Print version number of this version of **diff**.

-**w**, --**ignore-all-space**
Ignore all whitespace in files for comparisons.

-**W** *n*, --**width**=*n*
For two-column output (-**y**), produce columns with a maximum width of *n* characters. Default is 130.

-**x** *regexp*, --**exclude**=*regexp*
Do not compare files in a directory whose basenames match *regexp*.

-**X** *filename*, --**exclude-from**=*filename*
Do not compare files in a directory whose basenames match patterns described in the file *filename*.

-**y**, --**side-by-side**
Produce two-column output.

---

diff3   diff3 [*options*] *file1 file2 file3*

Compare three files and report the differences. No more than one of the files may be given as - (indicating that it is to be read from standard input). The output is displayed with the following codes:

= = = =
All three files differ.

= = = =*1*
file1 is different.

= = = =*2*
file2 is different.

= = = =*3*
file3 is different.

diff3 is also designed to merge changes in two differing files based on a common ancestor file (i.e., when two people have made their own set of changes to the same file). **diff3** can find changes between the ancestor and one of the newer files and generate output that adds those differences to the other new file. Unmerged changes occur where both of the newer files differ from each other and at least one of them differs from the ancestor. Changes from the ancestor that are the same in both of the newer files are called *merged changes*. If all three files differ in the same place, it is called an *overlapping change*.

This scheme is used on the command line, with the ancestor being *file2*, the second filename. Comparison is made between *file2* and *file3*, with those differences then applied to *file1*.

Options

-3, --easy-only
> Create an **ed** script to incorporate into *file1* unmerged, nonoverlapping differences between *file1* and *file3*.

-a, --text
> Treat files as text.

-A, --show-all
> Create an **ed** script to incorporate all changes, showing conflicts in bracketed format.

-e, --ed
> Create an **ed** script to incorporate into *file1* all unmerged differences between *file2* and *file3*.

-E, --show-overlap
> Create an **ed** script to incorporate unmerged changes, showing conflicts in bracketed format.

--help
> Print usage information and exit.

-i   Append the **w** (save) and **q** (quit) commands to **ed** script output.

-L *label*, **--label**=*label*
> Use *label* to replace filename in output.

-m, --merge
> Create file with changes merged (not an **ed** script).

-T, --initial-tab
> To line tabs up properly in output, begin lines with a tab instead of two spaces.

-v, --version
> Print version information and then exit.

-x, --overlap-only
> Create an **ed** script to incorporate into *file1* all differences where all three files differ (overlapping changes).

-X   Same as **-x**, but show only overlapping changes in bracketed format as with **-E**.

---

dig

dig [@*server*] [*options*] [*name*] [*type*] [*class*] [*query-options*]

dig @*server* *name* *type*

dig -h

TCP/IP command. The **dig** command is used to query DNS servers; it is more flexible than the deprecated **nslookup** command. When invoked with just the **-h** option, it displays a list of options

---

for the command. If you use it without any options or arguments, it will search for the root server. The standard arguments are:

server
> The server to query. If no server is supplied, **dig** will check the nameservers listed in */etc/resolv.conf*. The address may be an IPv4 dotted address or an IPv6 colon-delimited address. It may also be a hostname, which **dig** will resolve (through the nameservers in */etc/resolv.conf*).

name
> The domain name to look up.

type
> The type of query to perform, such as **A**, **ANY**, **MX**, **SIG**, and so forth. The default is **A**, but you may use any valid BIND9 query type.

Options

You may use the following option flags with **dig**:

-b *address*
> Set the source IP address for the query.

-c *class*
> Set the class of query. The default value is **IN** (internet), but you can choose **HS** for Hesiod or **CH** for CHAOSNET.

-f *filename*
> Operate in batch mode, performing the queries in the file you specify.

-k *filename*
> Specify a TSIG keyfile; used for signed transactions. You can also use the **-y** key, although this is less secure.

-p *portnumber*
> Choose the port number for the query. The default value is the standard DNS port, 53.

-q *name*
> Specify domain *name* to query. Sometimes this is needed to distinguish the domain name from other options.

-t *type*
> Set the type of query, as with the query argument. The default value is **A**, but you may use any valid BIND9 query.

-x *addr*
> Use the **-x** flag for reverse lookups, specifying an IPv4 or IPv6 address. You do not need the name, class, or type arguments if you use the **-x** flag.

-y *keyname: keyvalue*
> Enter the actual key name and value when conducting a signed transaction. Because the key and value can be seen in the output of **ps**, this is not recommended for use on multiuser systems; use **-k** instead.

Query options

There are a large number of query options for **dig**. Each query option is preceded by +, and many have an opposite version beginning with **no**. For example, the **tcp** flag is passed as **+tcp**, and negated with **+notcp**. Because there are so many options, only a few are discussed here. For greater detail, see the **dig** manpage.

+tcp, +notcp
> Use (or do not use) the TCP protocol instead of the default UDP.

+domain=*searchdomain*
> Perform a search in the domain specified; this is equivalent to using the **+search** option and having "searchdomain" as the sole entry in the search list or domain directive of */etc/resolv.conf*.

+search, +nosearch
> Use (or do not use) the search list provided in */etc/resolv.conf*. The default is not to use the search list.

+time=*t*
> Timeout for queries, in seconds. The default is 5, and the minimum is 1.

+tries=*n*
> The number of times to retry UDP queries. The default is 3, and the minimum is 1.

Examples

Query the mail exchange record for example.com:

    dig mx example.com

Ask a specific nameserver to resolve a domain:

    dig @ns.example.com smtp.example.com

Perform a reverse look up on an IP address:

    dig -x 208.201.239.37

---

dir

    dir [options] [file]

List directory contents. **dir** is equivalent to the command **ls -C -b** (list files in columns, sorted vertically, special characters escaped), and it takes the same arguments as **ls**. This is an alternate invocation of the **ls** command and is provided for the convenience of those converting from Microsoft Windows and the DOS shell.

---

dircolors

    dircolors [options] [file]

Set the color options for the **ls** command. **dircolors** outputs shell commands which, when evaluated, update the LS_COLORS environment variable. If you specify a file, **dircolors** reads it to determine which colors to use. Otherwise, it uses a default set of colors. If the shell is not specified, **dircolors** checks the SHELL environment variable.

Options
The program takes three options in addition to the standard **--help** and **--version** flags:

-b, --sh, --bourne-shell
> Use the Bourne shell syntax when setting the LS_COLORS variable.

-c, --csh, --c-shell
> Use **csh** (C shell) syntax when setting the LS_COLORS variable.

-p, --print-database
> Display the default colors. You can copy this information into a file and change it to suit your preferences, and then run the program with the file as its argument to set the colors to your new values.

Example
Set LS_COLORS using the default color database:

```
eval `dircolors`
```

---

dirname

dirname *pathname*

Print *pathname*, excluding the last level. Useful for stripping the actual filename from a pathname. If there are no slashes (no directory levels) in *pathname*, **dirname** prints . to indicate the current directory. See also **basename**.

---

dmesg

dmesg [*options*]

System administration command. Display the system control messages from the kernel ring buffer. This buffer stores all messages since the last system boot, or the most recent ones if the buffer has been filled.

Options
-c   Clear buffer after printing messages.

-n*level*
> Set the level of system message that will display on console.

-s*buffersize*
> Specify *buffersize* of kernel ring buffer. This is useful if you have changed the kernel default.

---

doexec

doexec /path/to/command [*argv*[0]] ... [*argv*[*n*]]

Execute the specified command with the specified options and arguments. Differs from the normal **exec** command in that *argv*[0] may be completely arbitrary, and in that it passes all options to the executable being run.

domainname domainname [*name*]

NFS/NIS command. Set or display name of current NIS domain. With no argument, **domainname** displays the name of the current NIS domain. Only a privileged user can set the domain name by giving an argument; this is usually done in a startup script.

dosfsck dosfsck [*options*] *device*

fsck.msdos [*options*] *device*

System administration command. Similar to **fsck**, but specifically intended for MS-DOS filesystems. When checking an MS-DOS filesystem, **fsck** calls this command. Normally **dosfsck** stores all changes in memory, then writes them when checks are complete.

Options

-a   Automatically repair the system; do not prompt the user.

-d *file*
    Drop the named file from the file allocation table. Force checking, even if kernel has already marked the filesystem as valid. **dosfsck** will normally exit without checking if the system appears to be clean.

-f   Save unused cluster chains to files.

-l   List pathnames of files being processed.

-r   Repair the system, prompting user for advice.

-t   Mark unreadable clusters as bad.

-u *file*
    Attempt to undelete the named file.

-v   Verbose mode.

-w   Write changes to disk immediately.

-y   When queried, answer "yes."

-A   Filesystem is an Atari version of MS-DOS.

-V   Repeat test to verify all errors have been corrected.

du du [*options*] [*directories*]

Print disk usage (as the number of 1 KB blocks used by each named directory and its subdirectories; default is the current directory).

Options

-0, --null
    End output lines with null, not newline.

-a, --all
    Print disk usage for all files, not just subdirectories.

--apparent-size
    Print the apparent sizes, not disk usage.

-b, --bytes
Print sizes in bytes.

-B *bytes*, **--block-size**=*bytes*
Use the specified number of bytes for the blocksize.

-c, --total
In addition to normal output, print grand total of all arguments.

-D, --dereference-args
Follow symbolic links, but only if they are command-line arguments.

--exclude=*pattern*
Exclude files that match *pattern*.

-h, --human-readable
Print sizes in human-readable format.

-H, --si
Like **-h**, but show as power of 1000 rather than 1024. **-H** also produces a warning.

--help
Print help message and then exit.

-k, --kilobytes
Print sizes in kilobytes (this is the default).

-l, --count-links
Count the size of all files, whether or not they have already appeared (i.e., via a hard link).

-L, --dereference
Follow symbolic links.

-m   Print sizes in megabytes.

--max-depth=*num*
Report sizes for directories only down to *num* levels below the starting point (which is level 0).

-P, --no-dereference
Do not follow symbolic links (the default).

-s, --summarize
Print only the grand total for each named directory.

-S, --separate-dirs
Do not include the sizes of subdirectories when totaling the size of parent directories.

--time[=*word*]
Print the last-modification time. With *word*, show the time as one of the following, not as modification time: **atime, access, use, ctime,** or **status**.

--time-style=*style*
Show times using the specified style. Possible values are: **full-iso, long-iso, iso,** +*format* (interpreted as in **date**). Used with **--time**.

--version
Print the version and then exit.

-x, --one-file-system
> Display usage of files in current filesystem only.

-X *file*, **--exclude-from=***file*
> Exclude files that match any pattern in *file*.

---

dump   dump [options] files

System administration command. This simple backup utility accesses ext2 and ext3 file devices directly, quickly backing up files without affecting file access times. *files* may be specified as a mount point or as a list of files and directories to back up. While you can use this on a mounted system, **dump** may write corrupted information to the backup when the kernel has written only part of its cached information. Dump maintains a record of which files it has saved in */etc/dumpdates*, and will perform incremental backups after creating an initial full backup. Use the **restore** command to restore a **dump** backup.

Options

-a   Write until end-of-media. Default behavior when writing to tape drives.

-A *file*
> Create a table of contents for the archive in the specified *file*.

-b*blocksize*
> Block size in kilobytes to use in dumped records. By default, it is 10, or 32 when dumping to a tape with a density greater than 6250 bpi.

-B*blocks*
> Specify number of blocks to write per volume.

-c   Treat target as a 1700-foot-long cartridge tape drive with 8000 bpi. Override end-of-media detection.

-d *density*
> Specify tape density.

-D *file*
> Write dump information to *file* instead of */etc/dumpdates*.

-E *file*
> Exclude inodes specified in *file*.

-f *files*
> Write backup volumes to the specified files or devices. Use - to write to standard output. Separate multiple files with a comma. Use *host:file* or *user@host:file* to write to a networked host using either the **rmt** program or the program specified by the RMT environment variable.

-F *script*
> Run *script* at the end of each volume other than the last. **dump** will pass the current device and volume number to the script. The script should return 0 to continue, 1 to prompt for a new tape, or any other exit value to abort the dump. The script will run with the processes real user and group ID.

-i *inodes*
> Specify a comma-separated list of *inodes* to skip.

-I *n*
> Ignore the first *n* read errors. **dump** ignores 32 read errors by default. Specify **0** to ignore all errors. You may need to do this when dumping a mounted filesystem.

-j[*level*]
> Compress each block using the bzlib library at the specified compression *level*. By default **dump** uses level 2 compression.

-k Use Kerberos authentication when writing to a remote system.

-L *label*
> Write the specified volume *label* into the dump header.

-m Save only metadata when backing up changed but not modified files.

-M Create a multivolume backup. Treat any filename provided with **-f** as a prefix.

-n Use **wall** to notify members of group **operator** when prompting for information.

-q Abort the backup instead of prompting for information when operator input is required.

-Q *file*
> Create Quick Access information in the specified file for use by **restore**.

-s *n*
> Write only *n* feet of tape in a single volume. Prompt for a new tape upon reaching this limit.

-S Calculate and print the amount of space required to perform the backup, then exit.

-T *date*
> Only back up files changed or modified since *date*. This overrides the time given in */etc/dumpdates*.

-u Update */etc/dumpdates* after completing the backup.

-v Print verbose information about the dump.

-W Generate a report on the backup status of all filesystems based on information in */etc/dumpdates* and */etc/fstab*.

-w Generate a report of filesystems that need to be backed up. Only report on filesystems listed in */etc/fstab* and */etc/mtab* that need to be backed up.

-y Compress each block using the lzo library.

-z[*level*]
> Compress each block using the zlib library. If provided, use the specified compression *level*. The default is 2.

dumpe2fs

dumpe2fs *device*

System administration command. Print ext2/ext3 information about *device*'s superblock and blocks group.

Options

-b   List blocks marked as bad.

-f   Force display of filesystems with unknown feature flags.

-h   Display superblock information only.

-i   Specify device is an image file created by **e2image**.

-o **superblock**=*superblock*
      Specify location of the superblock.

-o **blocksize**=*blocksize*
      Specify *blocksize* to use when examining filesystem.

-x   Print block numbers in hexadecimal.

-V   Print version number and exit.

dumpiso

dumpiso [*options*] [*file*]

Listen on selected channels and dump IEEE 1394 packets received into the specified file, or to standard output if *file* is not specified. The current number of packets is written to standard error.

Options

-c *nums*, --**channels**=*nums*
      Set channels to listen to, as a single number or a range. Channel numbers can be from 0 to 63, and the option can be specified multiple times to add new channels each time. Without this option, **dumpiso** defaults to all channels.

-h, --**help**
      Print usage information and exit.

-p *port*, --**port**=*port*
      Specify the IEEE 1394 port to receive on; only required if there is more than one on your system. The default is 0.

dumpkeys

dumpkeys [*options*]

Print information about the keyboard driver's translation tables to standard output. Further information is available in the manual pages under *keymaps*(5).

Options

-1, --**separate-lines**
      Print one line for each modifier/keycode pair, and prefix **plain** to each unmodified keycode.

-c*charset*, --**charset**=*charset*
      Specify character set with which to interpret character code values. The default character set is **iso-8859-1**. Use --**help** for the list of valid character sets.

--compose-only
> Print compose key combinations only. Requires compose key support in the kernel.

-f, --full-table
> Output in canonical, not short, form: for each key, print a row with modifier combinations divided into columns.

--funcs-only
> Print function-key string definitions only; do not print key bindings or string definitions.

-h, --help
> Print help message and the version.

-i, --short-info
> Print in short-info format, including information about acceptable keycode keywords in the keytable files; the number of actions that can be bound to a key; a list of the ranges of action codes (the values to the right of a key definition); and the number of function keys that the kernel supports.

--keys-only
> Print key bindings only; do not print string definitions.

-l, --long-info
> Print the same information as in **--short-info**, plus a list of the supported action symbols and their numeric values.

-n, --numeric
> Print action code values in hexadecimal notation; do not attempt to convert them to symbolic notation.

---

dvdrecord

dvdrecord [*options*] *track1,track2...*

Record data to a DVD recorder. **dvdrecord** is generally a symbolic link to **wodim**. See **wodim** for more information.

---

e2fsck

e2fsck [*options*] *device*

fsck.ext2 [*options*] *device*

System administration command. Checks and repairs a disk, as does **fsck**, but specifically designed for ext2 (Linux Second Extended) and ext3 (Third Extended, a journaling version of ext2) filesystems. **fsck** actually uses this command when checking ext2 and ext3 filesystems. Most often used after a sudden shutdown, such as from a power outage, or when damage to the disk is suspected.

Options

-b *superblock*
> Use *superblock* instead of the default superblock.

-B *size*
> Expect to find the superblock at *size*; if it's not there, exit.

-c   Find bad blocks using the **badblocks** command. Specify this option twice to perform the scan with a nondestructive read-write test.

-C *filedescriptor*
    Write completion information to the specified *filedescriptor*. If 0, print a completion bar.

-d   Debugging mode.

-D   Optimize directories by reindexing, sorting, and compressing them where possible.

-f   Force checking, even if kernel has already marked the filesystem as valid. **e2fsck** will normally exit without checking if the system appears to be clean.

-F   Flush buffer caches before checking.

-j *file*
    Use the specified external journal *file*.

-k   Preserve all previously marked bad blocks when using the -c option.

-l *file*
    Consult *file* for a list of bad blocks, in addition to checking for others.

-L *file*
    Consult *file* for list of bad blocks instead of checking filesystem for them.

-n   Ensure that no changes are made to the filesystem. When queried, answer "no."

-p   "Preen." Repair all bad blocks noninteractively.

-s   Byte-swap the filesystem if necessary to standard (little-endian) byte-order.

-S   Byte-swap the filesystem.

-t   Display timing statistics.

-v   Verbose.

-y   When queried, answer "yes."

e2image

e2image [*option*] *device file*

System administration command. Store disaster recovery data for ext2 filesystem on *device* to image file *file*. Weekly filesystem images can be an important part of a disaster recovery plan.

Option

-r   Create a raw image file that can be checked and debugged using filesystem utilities such as **e2fsck** or **debugfs**. Raw images are created as sparse files. Either compress the image file before moving it, or use the --**sparse=always** option when copying it with **cp**.

-I   Restore filesystem metadata in image to device. Note you will lose any changes to the filesystem since your image was created.

e2label

e2label *device* [*label*]

System administration command. Display the filesystem label on an ext2 filesystem *device*. Change filesystem label to *label* if specified.

echo

echo [*options*] [*string*]

Send (echo) the input *string* to standard output. This is the **/bin/echo** command. **echo** also exists as a command built into **bash**. You may have to specify the full path to run **/bin/echo** instead of the shell built-in command. The following character sequences have special meaning:

\a   Alert (bell).

\b   Backspace.

\c   Suppress trailing newline.

\f   Form feed.

\n   Newline.

\r   Carriage return.

\t   Horizontal tab.

\v   Vertical tab.

\\   Literal backslash.

nnn
    The octal character whose ASCII code is *nnn*.

Options

-e   Enable character sequences with special meaning. (In some versions, this option is not required in order to make the sequences work.)

-E   Disable character sequences with special meaning.

-n   Suppress printing of newline after text.

--help
    Print help message and exit.

--version
    Print version information and exit.

Examples

```
/bin/echo "testing printer" | lp
/bin/echo "TITLE" > file ; cat doc1 doc2 >> file
/bin/echo "Warning: ringing bell \a"
```

edquota

edquota [*options*] [*name*]

System administration command. Edit filesystem quotas using a text editor. When edits are complete, **edquota** writes the new information to the binary quota files. Uses the editor specified in the EDITOR environment variable, or **vi** by default.

Linux
Commands

Options

-f_filesystem_
> Only apply changes to the specified _filesystem_.

-F_format_
> Specify filesystem quota _format_ to use. See **quota** for a list of accepted values.

-g   Edit group quotas.

-p_prototype_
> Apply the same settings as used for the specified user or group: _prototype_.

-r   Edit quotas on remote systems.

-t   Edit grace times for block and inode quotas.

-T   Edit grace times for individual user or group _name_.

-u   Edit user quotas. (This is the default.)

---

egrep

egrep [_options_] [_regexp_] [_files_]

Search one or more _files_ for lines that match an extended regular expression _regexp_. **egrep** doesn't support the regular expressions \(, \), \n, \<, \>, \{, or \}, but it does support the other expressions, as well as the extended set +, ?, |, and ( ). Remember to enclose these characters in quotes. Regular expressions are described in Chapter 7. Exit status is 0 if any lines match, 1 if none match, and 2 for errors.

See **grep** for the list of available options. Also see **fgrep**.

Examples

Search for occurrences of **Victor** or **Victoria** in _file_:

```
egrep 'Victor(ia)*' file
egrep '(Victor|Victoria)' file
```

Find and print strings such as **old.doc1** or **new.doc2** in _files_, and include their line numbers:

```
egrep -n '(old|new)\.doc?' files
```

---

eject

eject [_options_] [_device_]

Eject removable media such as a CD, DVD, floppy, or tape. You may name the device by its _/dev_ or _/mnt_ filename. The _/dev_ and _/mnt_ prefixes are optional for any items in the _/dev_ and _/mnt_ directories. If no device is named, it is assumed that "cdrom" should be ejected.

Options

The eject command takes the following option flags:

-a, --auto on|1|off|0
> Set the auto-eject mode to **on** or **off** (equivalent to **1** or **0**, respectively). If auto-eject mode is on, the device is ejected when closed or unmounted.

-c *slotnumber*, **--changerslot** *slotnumber*
> If using a CD-ROM changer, select a CD from one of the slots. Slot numbers start with 0, and the CD-ROM drive must not be playing music or mounted to read data.

-d, **--default**
> List the default device name rather than doing anything.

-f, **--floppy**
> Use floppy commands to eject the drive. Normally, the system tries all methods (CD-ROM, SCSI, floppy, tape) to eject.

-h, **--help**
> Display help information.

-m, **--no-unmount**
> Do not try to unmount the device.

-n, **--noop**
> Do not perform any actions; merely display the actions that would be performed.

-p, **--proc**
> Use the mounted files listed in */proc/mounts* rather than in */etc/ mtab*.

-q, **--tape**
> Use tape commands to eject the drive. Normally, the system tries all methods (CD-ROM, SCSI, floppy, tape) to eject.

-r, **--cdrom**
> Use CD-ROM commands to eject the drive. Normally, the system tries all methods (CD-ROM, SCSI, floppy, tape) to eject.

-s, **--scsi**
> Use SCSI commands to eject the drive. Normally, the system tries all methods (CD-ROM, SCSI, floppy, tape) to eject.

-t, **--trayclose**
> Close the CD-ROM drive. Not all drives respond to this option.

-T, **--traytoggle**
> Close the CD-ROM drive if it's open and eject the CD if it's closed. Not all drives respond to this option.

-v, **--verbose**
> Verbose mode: display additional information about actions.

-V, **--version**
> Display version information and exit.

-x *speed*, **--cdspeed** *speed*
> Set the speed multiplier for the CD-ROM to an integer, usually a power of 2. Not all devices support this option. Setting the speed to 0 indicates that the drive should operate at its maximum speed.

-X, **--listspeed**
> Detect and list all available speeds that can be specified with **-x**. Not all devices support this option.

Linux Commands

elvtune

elvtune [*options*] *devices*

System administration command. Set the latency in the elevator algorithm used to schedule I/O activities for the specified block *devices*. If no options are given, print the current settings for *devices*.

Options

-b *n*

Set the maximum coalescing factor allowed on writes when reads are pending to *n*.

-h   Print help message, then exit.

-r *n*

Set the maximum read latency (basically, the number of sectors to read before writes are allowed) to *n*. The default is 8192.

-v   Print version number, then exit.

-w *n*

Set the maximum write latency (sectors to write before allowing a read) to *n*. The default is 16,384.

---

emacs

emacs [*options*] [*files*]

A text editor and all-purpose work environment. For more information, see Chapter 8.

---

enable

enable -E [*destination*]

Enable printers or printer classes. Part of the CUPS system. More often invoked as **accept**.

---

env

env [*option*] [*variable=value* ...] [*command*]

Display the current environment or, if an environment *variable* is specified, set it to a new *value* and display the modified environment. If *command* is specified, execute it under the modified environment.

Options

-, -i, --ignore-environment

Ignore current environment entirely.

-u *name*, **--unset** *name*

Unset the specified variable.

--help

Print help message and then exit.

--version

Print version information and then exit.

envsubst

envsubst [*options*] [*shell-format*]

Substitutes environment variables in a shell string or script. When used with no options, copies stdin to stdout, replacing any environment variable string, such as $*VARIABLE* or ${*VARIABLE*}, with the appropriate environment variable value. So, "My editor is $EDITOR" would be converted to "My editor is */usr/bin/emacs.*" Specifying a shell format limits the substitutions to those variables referenced in the shell format.

Options
-h, --help
> Print help message and then exit.

-v, --variables
> Display the variables referenced in the shell format, and then exit.

-V, --version
> Print version information and then exit.

etags

etags [*options*] *files*

Create a list of function and macro names defined in a programming source *file*. **etags** generates tags for use by **emacs**. (**ctags** produces an equivalent tags file for use with **vi**.) More than one file may be specified. **etags** understands many programming languages, including C, C++, FORTRAN, Java, Perl, Python, **flex**, **yacc**, and **bison**. The output list (named *TAGS* by default) contains lines of the form:

> *name*   *file*   *context*

where *name* is the function or macro name, *file* is the source file in which *name* is defined, and *context* is a search pattern that shows the line of code containing *name*. After the list of tags is created, you can invoke Emacs on any file and type:

> `M-x visit-tags-table`

You will be prompted for the name of the tag table; the default is *TAGS*. To switch to the source file associated with the *name* listed in *tagsfile*, type:

> `M-x find-tag`

You will be prompted for the tag you would like Emacs to search for.

Options
-a, --append
> Append tag output to existing list of tags.

-d, --defines
> Include tag entries for C preprocessor definitions.

-i *file*, **--include=***file*
> Add a note to the tags file that *file* should be consulted in addition to the normal input file.

-l *language*, --**language**=*language*
> Consider the files that follow this option to be written in *language*. Use the -**h** option for a list of languages and their default filename extensions.

-o *file*, --**output**=*file*
> Write to *file*.

-r *regexp*, --**regex**=*regexp*
> Include a tag for each line that matches *regexp* in the files following this option.

-**C**, --**c++**
> Expect .*c* and .*h* files to contain C++, not C, code.

-**D**, --**no-defines**
> Do not include tag entries for C preprocessor definitions.

-**H**, -**h**, --**help**
> Print usage information.

-**R**, --**noregex**
> Do not include tags based on regular-expression matching for the files that follow this option.

-**S**, --**ignore-indentation**
> Normally, **etags** uses indentation to parse the tag file; this option tells it to rely on it less.

-**V**, --**version**
> Print the version number.

---

ex

ex [*options*] *file*

An interactive command-based editor. For more information, see Chapter 9.

---

expand

expand [*options*] [*files*]

Convert tabs in given files (or standard input, if the file is given as -) to the appropriate number of spaces; write results to standard output.

Options

--**help**
> Print help message and then exit.

-**i**, --**initial**
> Convert tabs only at the beginning of lines.

-*tabs*, -**t** *tabs*, --**tabs** *tabs*
> *tabs* is a comma-separated list of integers that specify tab stops. With one integer, the tab stops are set to every *integer* spaces. By default, tab stops are eight spaces apart. With -**t** and --**tabs**, the list may be separated by whitespace instead of commas.

--**version**
> Print version information and then exit.

---

expr

expr *arg1 operator arg2* [*operator arg3* ...]

Evaluate arguments as expressions and print the results to standard output. Arguments and operators must be separated by spaces. In most cases, an argument is an integer, typed literally or represented by a shell variable. There are three types of operators: arithmetic, relational, and logical, as well as keyword expressions. Exit status for **expr** is 0 (expression is nonzero and nonnull), 1 (expression is 0 or null), 2 (expression is invalid), or 3 (an error occurred).

Arithmetic operators

Use these to produce mathematical expressions whose results are printed:

+   Add *arg2* to *arg1*.

-    Subtract *arg2* from *arg1*.

*   Multiply the arguments.

/   Divide *arg1* by *arg2*.

%   Take the remainder when *arg1* is divided by *arg2*.

Addition and subtraction are evaluated last, unless they are grouped inside parentheses. The symbols *, (, and) have meaning to the shell, so they must be escaped (preceded by a backslash or enclosed in single quotes).

Relational operators

Use these to compare two arguments. Arguments can also be words, in which case comparisons are defined by the locale. If the comparison statement is true, the result is 1; if false, the result is 0. Symbols > and < must be escaped.

=, ==   Are the arguments equal?

!=   Are the arguments different?

>   Is *arg1* greater than *arg2*?

>=   Is *arg1* greater than or equal to *arg2*?

<   Is *arg1* less than *arg2*?

<=   Is *arg1* less than or equal to *arg2*?

Logical operators

Use these to compare two arguments. Depending on the values, the result can be *arg1* (or some portion of it), *arg2*, or 0. Symbols | and & must be escaped.

| Logical OR; if *arg1* has a nonzero (and nonnull) value, the result is *arg1*; otherwise, the result is *arg2*.

&   Logical AND; if both *arg1* and *arg2* have a nonzero (and nonnull) value, the result is *arg1*; otherwise, the result is 0.

:   Like **grep**; *arg2* is a pattern to search for in *arg1*. *arg2* must be a regular expression. If part of the *arg2* pattern is enclosed in \(\)

(escaped parentheses), the result is the portion of *arg1* that matches; otherwise, the result is simply the number of characters that match. By default, a pattern match always applies to the beginning of the first argument (the search string implicitly begins with a ^). Start the search string with .* to match other parts of the string.

Keywords

index *string character-list*
> Return the first position in *string* that matches the first possible character listed in *character-list*. Continue through *character-list* until a match is found, or return 0.

length *string*
> Return the length of *string*.

match *string regex*
> Same as *string* : *regex*.

+ *token*
> Treat *token* as a string, even if it would normally be a keyword or an operator.

substr *string start length*
> Return a section of *string*, beginning with *start*, with a maximum length of *length* characters. Return null when given a negative or nonnumeric *start* or *length*.

Examples

Division happens first; result is 10:

```
expr 5 + 10 / 2
```

Addition happens first; result is 7 (truncated from 7.5):

```
expr \( 5 + 10 \) / 2
```

Add 1 to variable *i*. This is how variables are incremented in shell scripts:

```
i=`expr $i + 1`
```

Print 1 (true) if variable **a** is the string "hello":

```
expr $a = hello
```

Print 1 (true) if **b** plus 5 equals 10 or more:

```
expr $b + 5 \>= 10
```

Find the 5th, 6th, and 7th letters of the word *character*:

```
expr substr character 5 3
```

In the examples that follow, variable **p** is the string "version.100". This command prints the number of characters in **p**:

```
expr $p : '.*'     Result is 11
```

Match all characters and print them:

```
expr $p : '\(.*\)'  Result is "version.100"
```

Print the number of lowercase letters at the beginning of **p**:

```
expr $p : '[a-z]*'   Result is 7
```

Match the lowercase letters at the beginning of **p**:

> **expr $p : '\([a-z]*\)'** *Result is ""version""*

Truncate **$x** if it contains five or more characters; if not, just print **$x**. (Logical OR uses the second argument when the first one is 0 or null, i.e., when the match fails.)

> **expr $x : '\(.....\)' \| $x**

In a shell script, rename files to their first five letters:

> **mv $x `expr $x : '\(.....\)' \| $x`**

(To avoid overwriting files with similar names, use **mv -i**.)

---

factor

factor [*options*] *n*

Calculate and display the prime factors of number *n*, which must be a positive integer. If *n* is not specified, numbers are read from standard input, separated by commas, spaces, or tabs.

Options

--help
> Display help information.

--version
> Display version information.

Example:

```
user@systemname:~> factor 60
60: 2, 2, 3 5
```

---

false

false

A null command that returns an unsuccessful (nonzero) exit status. Normally used in **bash** scripts. See also **true**.

---

fc-cache

fc-cache [*options*] [*dirs*]

Create font information caches for fontconfig system, enabling applications that use fontconfig to load fonts more rapidly. If no directory is specified, the current font configuration directories are used. Only fonts readable by FreeType are cached.

Options

-f, --force
> Regenerate cache files, even if they seem to be up to date.

-s, --system-only
> Scan directories of fonts for the whole system, not the fonts in the user's home directory.

-v, --verbose
> Verbose mode: display status information during operation.

-V, --version
> Display version information.

-?, --help
> Display help information.

fc-list

fc-list [*options*] [*pattern*] [*element*]

Part of the fontconfig system. Lists available fonts and font styles. The first argument limits listed fonts to those matching the pattern, and the second displays the listed font attribute or element. To set the element argument without setting a pattern, use the : character to match all fonts. For example, **fc-list : family** displays all available fonts, with their font family information.

Options

-v, --verbose
Verbose mode: display status information during operation.

-?, --help
Display help message

-V, --version
Display version information and quit.

fdisk

fdisk [*options*] [*device*]

System administration command. **fdisk** displays information about disk partitions, creates and deletes disk partitions, and changes the active partition. It is possible to assign a different operating system to each of the four possible primary partitions, though only one partition is active at any given time. You can also divide a physical partition into several logical partitions. The minimum recommended size for a Linux system partition is 40 MB. Normally, each *device* will be */dev/hda*, */dev/hdb*, */dev/sda*, */dev/sdb*, */dev/hdc*, */dev/hdd*, and so on. An interactive, menu-driven mode is also available. Note that this command can be destructive if used improperly.

Options

-b *sectorsize*
Set the size of individual disk sectors. May be 512, 1024, or 2048. Most systems now recognize sector sizes, so this is not necessary.

-l   List partition tables and exit.

-u   Report partition sizes in sectors instead of cylinders.

-s *partition*
Display the size of *partition*, unless it is a DOS partition.

-v   Print version number, then exit.

-C *cylinders*
Specify the number of *cylinders* on the disk.

-H *heads*
Specify the number of heads per cylinder.

-S *sectors*
Specify *sectors* per track for partitioning.

Commands

a   Toggle a bootable flag on current partition.

b   Edit disklabel of a BSD partition.

c   Toggle DOS compatibility flag.

d   Delete current partition.

l   List all partition types.

m   Main menu.

n   Create a new partition; prompt for more information.

o   Create an empty DOS partition table.

p   Print a list of all partitions and information about each.

q   Quit; do not save.

t   Replace the type of the current partition.

u   Modify the display/entry units, which must be cylinders or sectors.

v   Verify: check for errors, and display a summary of the number of unallocated sectors.

w   Save changes and exit.

x   Switch to expert commands.

---

fgconsole

`fgconsole`

Print the number of the current virtual console. For example, if you are using */dev/tty1*, the command would return 1.

---

fgrep

`fgrep [options] string [files]`

Search one or more *files* for lines that match the specified text *string*. Exit status is 0 if any lines match, 1 if not, and 2 for errors. **fgrep** is faster than normal **grep** searches, but less flexible: it can only find fixed text, not regular expressions.

See **grep** for the list of available options. Also see **egrep**.

Examples

Print lines in *file* that don't contain any spaces:

    fgrep -v ' ' *file*

Print lines in *file* that contain the words in the file *spell_list*:

    fgrep -f spell_list *file*

---

file

`file [options] files`

Classify the named *files* according to the type of data they contain. **file** checks the magic file (usually */usr/share/magic*) to identify some file types. If the file type cannot be determined, it is shown as "data." **file** does its best to identify the file type, but it is sometimes incorrect. See also the **strings** command to search for printable strings in nontext files.

Options

-b, --brief

Brief mode; do not prepend filenames to output lines.

-c, --checking-printout

Check the format of the magic file (the *files* argument is invalid with **-c**). Usually used with **-m**.

-f *file*, **--files-from** *file*

Read the names of files to be checked from *file*.

-h, --no-dereference

Do not follow symbolic links. The default unless the environment variable POSIXLY_CORRECT is defined.

--help

Print help message and exit.

-i, --mime

Print mime strings rather than the traditional strings.

-L, --dereference

Follow symbolic links. By default, symbolic links are not followed.

-m *file*, **--magic-file** *file*

Search for file types in *file* instead of */usr/share/magic*, where *file* can be either a single file or a colon-separated list of files.

--mime-type, --mime-encoding

Like **-i**, but print only the mime type or the mime encoding.

-n, --no-buffer

Flush standard output after checking a file.

-N, --no-pad

Do not pad filenames to align in the output.

-s, --special-files

Check files that are block or character special files in addition to checking ordinary files.

-v, --version

Print the version.

-z, --uncompress

Attempt checking of compressed files.

Many file types are understood. The output lists each filename, followed by a brief classification such as:

```
ascii text
c program text
c-shell commands
data
empty
iAPX 386 executable
directory
[nt]roff, tbl, or eqn input text
shell commands
symbolic link to path
```

Examples

List all files that are deemed to be **troff/nroff** input:

file * | grep roff

Print the file type of the *status* file:

file status
status: ASCII English text

Print the file type of the *status* file in mime format:

file status
status: text/plain charset=us-ascii

---

find

find [*pathnames*] [*conditions*]

An extremely useful command for finding particular groups of files (numerous examples follow this description). **find** descends the directory tree beginning at each *pathname* and locates files that meet the specified *conditions*. The default pathname is the current directory. The most useful conditions include **-name** and **-type** (for general use), **-exec** and **-size** (for advanced use), and **-mtime** and **-user** (for administrators).

Conditions may be grouped by enclosing them in \(\) (escaped parentheses), negated with !, given as alternatives by separating them with **-o**, or repeated (adding restrictions to the match; usually only for **-name**, **-type**, or **-perm**). Note that "modification" refers to editing of a file's contents, whereas "change" means a modification, or permission or ownership changes. In other words, **-ctime** is more inclusive than **-atime** or **-mtime**.

Conditions and actions

-amin +*n*| -*n*| *n*
> Find files last accessed more than *n* (+*n*), less than *n* (-*n*), or exactly *n* minutes ago.

-anewer *file*
> Find files that were accessed after *file* was last modified. Affected by **-H** or **-L** when after them on the command line.

-atime +*n*| -*n*| *n*
> Find files that were last accessed more than *n* (+*n*), less than *n* (-*n*), or exactly *n* days ago. Note that **find** changes the access time of directories supplied as *pathnames*.

-cmin +*n*| -*n*| *n*
> Find files last changed more than *n* (+*n*), less than *n* (-*n*), or exactly *n* minutes ago.

-cnewer *file*
> Find files that were changed after they were last modified. Affected by **-H** or **-L** when after them on the command line.

-ctime +*n*| -*n*| *n*
> Find files that were changed more than *n* (+*n*), less than *n* (-*n*), or exactly *n* days ago. A change is anything that changes the directory entry for the file, such as a **chmod**.

-daystart

Calculate times from the start of the day today, not 24 hours ago. Only affects tests that come after it on the command line.

-delete

Delete files. Automatically turns on **-depth**.

-depth

Descend the directory tree, skipping directories and working on actual files first, and then the parent directories. Useful when files reside in unwritable directories (e.g., when using **find** with **cpio**).

-empty

Continue if file is empty. Applies to regular files and directories.

-exec *command*{ } \ ;

Run the Linux *command*, from the starting directory on each file matched by **find** (provided *command* executes successfully on that file—i.e., returns a 0 exit status). When *command* runs, the argument { } substitutes the current file. Follow the entire sequence with an escaped semicolon (\;). In some shells, the braces may need to be escaped as well.

-false

Return false for each file encountered.

-fstype *type*

Match files only on *type* filesystems. Acceptable types include **minix**, **ext**, **ext2**, **xia**, **msdos**, **umsdos**, **vfat**, **proc**, **nfs**, **iso9660**, **hpfs**, **sysv**, **smb**, and **ncpfs**.

-gid *num*

Find files with numeric group ID of *num*.

-group *gname*

Find files belonging to group *gname*. *gname* can be a group name or a group ID number.

-ilname *pattern*

A case-insensitive version of **-lname**.

-iname *pattern*

A case-insensitive version of **-name**.

-inum *n*

Find files whose inode number is *n*.

-ipath *pattern*

A case-insensitive version of **-path**.

-iregex *pattern*

A case-insensitive version of **-regex**.

-links *n*

Find files having *n* links.

-lname *pattern*

Search for files that are symbolic links, pointing to files named *pattern*. *pattern* can include shell metacharacters and does not treat / or . specially. The match is case-insensitive.

-maxdepth *num*

Do not descend more than *num* levels of directories.

-mindepth *num*

Begin applying tests and actions only at levels deeper than *num* levels.

-mmin *+n| -n| n*

Find files last modified more than *n* (+*n*), less than *n* (-*n*), or exactly *n* minutes ago.

-mount, -xdev

Search only for files that reside on the same filesystem as *pathname*. **-xdev** is for compatibility with other versions of **find**.

-mtime *+n| -n| n*

Find files that were last modified more than *n* (+*n*), less than *n* (-*n*), or exactly *n* days ago. A modification is a change to a file's data.

-name *pattern*

Find files whose names match *pattern*. Filename metacharacters may be used but should be escaped or quoted.

-newer *file*

Find files that were modified more recently than *file*; similar to **-mtime**. With **-H** or **-L**, if *file* is a symbolic link, use the modification time of the file the link points to.

-nogroup

The file's group ID does not correspond to any group.

-noleaf

Normally, **find** assumes that each directory has at least two hard links that should be ignored (a hard link for its name and one for "."—i.e., two fewer "real" directories than its hard link count indicates). **-noleaf** turns off this assumption, a useful practice when **find** runs on non-Unix-style filesystems. This forces **find** to examine all entries, assuming that some might prove to be directories into which it must descend (a time-waster on Unix).

-nouser

The file's user ID does not correspond to any user.

-ok command { }\;

Same as **-exec**, but prompts user to respond with **y** or **Y** before *command* is executed.

-path *pattern*

Find files whose names match *pattern*. Expect full pathnames relative to the starting pathname (i.e., do not treat / or . specially).

-perm *nnn*

Find files whose permission flags (e.g., **rwx**) match octal number *nnn* exactly (e.g., 664 matches **-rw-rw-r--**). Use a minus sign before *nnn* to make a "wildcard" match of any unspecified octal digit (e.g., **-perm -600** matches **-rw-******, where * can be any mode).

-print

> Print the matching files and directories, using their full pathnames. Return true. This is the default behavior.

-regex *pattern*

> Like **-path**, but uses Emacs-style regular expressions instead of the shell-like globbing used in **-name** and **-path**.

-regextype *pattern*

> Use an alternative regular expression syntax for **-regex** and **-iregex**. The possible types are **Emacs** (the default), **posix-awk**, **posix-basic**, **posix-egrep**, and **posix-extended**.

-size *n*[*u*]

> Find files containing *n* blocks. If *u*, is specified, measure size in one of the following units: **b** (512-byte blocks), **c** (bytes), **k** (kilobytes), **G** (gigabytes), **M** (megabytes), or **w** (two-byte words).

-true

> Return true for each file encountered.

-type *c*

> Find files whose type is *c*. *c* can be **b** (block special file), **c** (character special file), **d** (directory), **p** (fifo or named pipe), **l** (symbolic link), **s** (socket), or **f** (plain file).

-user *user*

> Find files belonging to *user* (name or numeric ID).

Examples

List all files (and subdirectories) in your home directory:

```
find $HOME -print
```

List all files named *chapter1* in the */work* directory:

```
find /work -name chapter1
```

List all files beginning with *memo* owned by *ann*:

```
find /work -name 'memo*' -user ann -print
```

Search the filesystem (begin at root) for manpage directories:

```
find / -type d -name 'man*' -print
```

Search the current directory, look for filenames that don't begin with a capital letter, and send them to the printer:

```
find . \! -name '[A-Z]*' -exec lpr { }\;
```

Find and compress files whose names don't end with *.gz*:

```
gzip `find . \! -name '*.gz' -print`
```

Remove all empty files on the system (prompting first):

```
find / -size 0 -ok rm { } \;
```

Search the system for files that were modified within the last two days (good candidates for backing up):

```
find / -mtime -2 -print
```

Recursively **grep** for a pattern down a directory tree:

```
find /book -print | xargs grep '[Nn]utshell'
```

If the files *kt1* and *kt2* exist in the current directory, their names can be printed with the command:

```
$ find . -name 'kt[0-9]'
./kt1
./kt2
```

Since the command prints these names with an initial ./ path, you need to specify the ./ when using the **-path** option:

```
$ find . -path './kt[0-9]'
./kt1
./kt2
```

The **-regex** option uses a complete pathname, like **-path**, but treats the following argument as a regular expression rather than a glob pattern (although in this case the result is the same):

```
$ find . -regex './kt[0-9]'
./kt1
./kt2
```

flex

flex [*options*] [*file*]

flex (Fast Lexical Analyzer Generator) is a faster variant of **lex**. It generates a lexical analysis program (named *lex.yy.c*) based on the regular expressions and C statements contained in one or more input *files*. See also **bison**, **yacc**, and the O'Reilly book *lex & yacc*.

Options

-b   Generate backup information to *lex.backup*.

-d   Debug mode.

-f   Use a faster scanner. The result is larger but faster.

-h   Help summary.

-i   Scan case-insensitively.

-l   Maximum **lex** compatibility.

-o *file*
    Write output to *file* instead of *lex.yy.c*.

-p   Print performance report.

-s   Exit if the scanner encounters input that does not match any of its rules.

-t   Print to standard output. (By default, **flex** prints to *lex.yy.c*.)

-v   Print a summary of statistics.

-w   Suppress warning messages.

-B   Generate batch (noninteractive) scanner.

-F   Use the fast scanner table representation. This option is usually as fast as **-f** and often generates smaller data (although for some data sets, it generates larger data).

-I   Generate an interactive scanner (default).

-L   Suppress **#line** directives in *lex.yy.c*.

Linux
Commands

-**P** *prefix*

> Change default **yy** prefix to *prefix* for all globally visible variable and function names.

-**V**   Print version number.

-**7**   Generate a 7-bit scanner.

-**8**   Generate an 8-bit scanner (default).

-**+**   Generate a C++ scanner class.

-**C**   Compress scanner tables but do not use equivalence classes.

-**Ca**

> Align tables for memory access and computation. This creates larger tables but gives faster performance.

-**Ce**

> Construct equivalence classes. This creates smaller tables and sacrifices little performance (default).

-**Cf**

> Generate full scanner tables, not compressed.

-**CF**

> Generate faster scanner tables, like -**F**.

-**Cm**

> Construct metaequivalence classes (default).

-**Cr**

> Bypass use of the standard I/O library; use **read( )** system calls instead.

---

fmt

fmt [*options*] [*files*]

Convert text to specified width by filling lines and removing newlines. Concatenate files on the command line, or read text from standard input if - (or no file) is specified. By default, preserve blank lines, spacing, and indentation. **fmt** attempts to break lines at the end of sentences and to avoid breaking lines after a sentence's first word or before its last.

Options

-**c**, --**crown-margin**

> Crown margin mode. Do not change indentation of each paragraph's first two lines. Use the second line's indentation as the default for subsequent lines.

-**p** *prefix*, --**prefix**=*prefix*

> Format only lines beginning with *prefix*.

-**s**, --**split-only**

> Suppress line-joining.

-**t**, --**tagged-paragraph**

> Tagged paragraph mode. Same as crown mode when the indentations of the first and second lines differ. If the indentation is the same, treat the first line as its own separate paragraph.

-u, --uniform-spacing

Reduce spacing to a maximum of one space between words and two between sentences.

-w *width*, **--width**=*width*

Set output width to *width*. The default is 75.

--help

Print help message and exit.

--version

Print version information and exit.

fold

fold [*option*] [*files*]

Break the lines of the named *files* so that they are no wider than the specified width. **fold** breaks lines exactly at the specified width, even in the middle of a word. Reads from standard input when given - as a file. By default, **fold** cuts at 80 columns; tab counts as multiple columns, and a backspace as negative one.

Options

-b, --bytes

Count bytes instead of columns, making tab, backspace, and return characters count as one byte instead of altering the column count, as in the default behavior.

-c, --characters

Count characters, not columns. Similar to counting by bytes.

-s, --spaces

Break at spaces only, if possible.

-w, --width *width*, *-width*

Set the maximum line width to *width*. The flags **-w 6**, **--width 6**, and **-6** all set the maximum width to six columns.

formail

formail [*options*]

Filter standard input into mailbox format. Useful for splitting mail digests or passing the contents of a mail file to another program, such as a spam filter, for additional processing. If no sender is apparent, provide the sender *foo@bar*. By default, escape bogus **From** lines with >.

Options

+skip

Do not split first *skip* messages.

-total

Stop after splitting *total* messages.

-a *headerfield*

Append *headerfield* to header, unless it already exists. If *headerfield* is **Message-ID** or **Resent-Message-ID** with no contents, generate a unique message ID.

-A *headerfield*

    Append *headerfield* whether or not it already exists.

-b   Do not escape bogus **From** lines.

-B   Assume that input is in BABYL **rmail** format.

-c   When header fields are more than one line long, concatenate the lines.

-d   Do not assume that input must be in strict mailbox format. This option disables recognition of the **Content-Length** field so you can split digests or use nonstandard mailbox formats.

-D *maxlen idcache*

    Remember old message IDs (in *idcache*, which will grow no larger than approximately *maxlen*). When splitting, refuse to output duplicate messages. Otherwise, return true on discovering a duplicate. With **-r**, look at the sender's mail address instead of the message ID.

-e   Allow messages to begin one immediately after the other; do not require empty space between them.

-f   Do not edit non-mailbox-format lines. By default, **formail** prepends **From** to such lines.

-i *headerfield*

    Like **-A**, but rename each existing *headerfield* to **Old-*headerfield***, unless it is empty.

-I *headerfield*

    Like **-i**, but also remove existing similar fields. If there is only a field name but no content, delete the field.

-k   For use only with **-r**. Keep the body as well as the fields specified by **-r**.

-l *folder*

    Generate a log summary in **procmail** format. You can then use **mailstat** to summarize the logs.

-m *minfields*

    Require **formail** to find at least *minfields* consecutive headers before recognizing the beginning of a new message. Default is 2.

-n [*max*]

    Allow simultaneous **formail** processes to run. Specify *max* to set the number of simultaneous processes allowed.

-p *prefix*

    Set off quoted lines with *prefix* instead of >.

-q   Do not display write errors, duplicate messages, or mismatched **Content-Length** fields. This is the default; use **-q-** to turn it off and display the messages.

-r   Throw away all existing fields, retaining only **X-Loop**, and generate autoreply header instead. You can preserve particular fields with the **-i** option.

-R *oldfield newfield*

    Change all fields named *oldfield* to *newfield*.

-s [*progname*]

    Must be the last option; everything following **-s** is assumed to be its arguments. Divide input to separate mail messages, and pipe them to the program specified or concatenate them to standard output (by default).

-t   Assume sender's return address to be valid. (By default, **formail** favors machine-generated addresses.)

-u *headerfield*

    Delete all but the first occurrence of *headerfield*.

-U *headerfield*

    Delete all but the last occurrence of *headerfield*.

-x *headerfield*

    Display the contents of *headerfield*; to always display on a single line, use with **-c**.

-X *headerfield*

    Like **-x**, but also display the field name.

-Y   Format in traditional Berkeley style (i.e., ignore **Content-Length** fields).

-z   When necessary, add a space between field names and contents. Remove ("zap") empty fields.

---

free

free [*options*]

Display statistics about memory usage: total free, used, physical, swap, shared, and buffers used by the kernel.

Options

-b   Calculate memory in bytes.

-k   Default. Calculate memory in kilobytes.

-m   Calculate memory in megabytes.

-o   Do not display "buffer adjusted" line. The **-o** switch disables the display "-/+ buffers" line that shows buffer memory subtracted from the amount of memory used and added to the amount of free memory.

-s *time*

    Check memory usage every *time* seconds.

-t   Display all totals on one line at the bottom of output.

-V   Display version information.

---

fsck

fsck [*options*] [*filesystem*] ...

System administration command. Call the filesystem checker for the appropriate system type to check and repair unmounted filesystems. If a filesystem is consistent, the number of files, number of blocks used, and number of blocks free are reported. If a filesystem is inconsistent, **fsck** prompts before each correction is attempted. **fsck**'s exit code can be interpreted as the sum of all conditions that apply:

0   No errors found.

1   Errors were found and corrected.

2   Reboot suggested.

4   Errors were found but not corrected.

8   **fsck** encountered an operational error.

16   **fsck** was called incorrectly.

32   **fsck** canceled by user request.

128

A shared library error was detected.

Options

--   Pass all subsequent options to filesystem-specific checker. All options that **fsck** doesn't recognize will also be passed.

-s   Serial mode. Check one filesystem at a time.

-t *fstype*

Specify the filesystem type. Do not check filesystems of any other type. Multiple filesystem types to check can be specified in a comma-separated list.

-A   Check all filesystems listed in */etc/fstab*. The root filesystem is checked first.

-C [*fd*]

Display completion (progress) bar. Optionally specify a file-descriptor to receive the progress. (Useful for a GUI frontend.)

-M   Don't check mounted filesystems. Returns a 0 exit code for mounted system.

-N   Suppress normal execution; just display what would be done.

-P   Meaningful only with -A: check root filesystem in parallel with other systems. This option is potentially dangerous.

-R   Meaningful only with -A: check all filesystems listed in */etc/fstab* except the root filesystem.

-T   Suppress printing of title.

-V   Verbose mode.

---

ftp

```
ftp [options] [hostname]
```

Transfer files to and from remote network site *hostname*. **ftp** prompts the user for a command. The commands are listed after the options. Some of the commands are toggles, meaning they turn on a feature when it is off and vice versa. Note that some versions may have different options.

Options

-d   Enable debugging.

-g   Disable filename globbing.

-i   Turn off interactive prompting.

-n   No autologin upon initial connection.

-v   Verbose. Show all responses from remote server.

Commands

!*[command [args]]*

Invoke an interactive shell on the local machine. If arguments are given, the first is taken as a command to execute directly, with the rest of the arguments as that command's arguments.

$*macro-name [args]*

Execute the macro *macro-name* that was defined with the **macdef** command. Arguments are passed to the macro unglobbed.

account *[passwd]*

Supply a supplemental password that will be required by a remote system for access to resources once a login has been successfully completed. If no argument is given, prompt the user for an account password in a nonechoing mode.

append *local-file [remote-file]*

Append a local file to a file on the remote machine. If *remote-file* is not given, the local filename is used after being altered by any **ntrans** or **nmap** setting. File transfer uses the current settings for *type*, *format*, *mode*, and *structure*.

ascii

Set the file transfer type to network ASCII (default).

bell

Sound a bell after each file transfer command is completed.

binary, image

Set file transfer type to support binary image transfer.

bye, quit

Terminate FTP session and then exit **ftp**.

case

Toggle remote-computer filename case mapping during **mget**. The default is off. When **case** is on, files on the remote machine with all-uppercase names are copied to the local machine with all-lowercase names.

cd *remote-directory*

Change working directory on remote machine to *remote-directory*.

cdup

Change working directory on remote machine to its parent directory.

chmod *[mode] [remote-file]*

Change file permissions of *remote-file*. If options are omitted, the command prompts for them.

close, disconnect
Terminate FTP session and return to command interpreter.

cr
Toggle carriage-return stripping during ASCII-type file retrieval.

delete *remote-file*
Delete file *remote-file* on remote machine.

debug [*debug-value*]
Toggle debugging mode. If *debug-value* is specified, it is used to set the debugging level.

dir [*remote-directory*] [*local-file*]
Print a listing of the contents in the directory *remote-directory* and, optionally, place the output in *local-file*. If no directory is specified, the current working directory on the remote machine is used. If no local file is specified or - is given instead of the filename, output comes to the terminal.

form *format*
Set the file transfer form to *format*. Default format is **file**.

get *remote-file* [*local-file*], **recv** *remote-file* [*local-file*]
Retrieve *remote-file* and store it on the local machine. If *local-file* is not specified, the file is given the same name as on the remote machine, subject to alteration by the current **case**, **ntrans**, and **nmap** settings. If *local-file* is -, the output comes to the terminal.

glob
Toggle filename expansion for **mdelete**, **mget**, and **mput**. If globbing is turned off, the filename arguments are taken literally and not expanded.

hash
Toggle hash sign (#) printing for each data block transferred.

help [*command*], **?** [*command*]
Print help information for *command*. With no argument, **ftp** prints a list of commands.

idle [*seconds*]
Get/set idle timer on remote machine. *seconds* specifies the length of the idle timer; if omitted, the current idle timer is displayed.

lcd [*directory*]
Change working directory on local machine. If *directory* is not specified, the user's home directory is used.

ls [*remote-directory*] [*local-file*]
Print listing of contents of directory on remote machine, in a format chosen by the remote machine. If *remote-directory* is not specified, current working directory is used.

macdef *macro-name*
Define a macro. Subsequent lines are stored as the macro *macro-name*; a null line terminates macro input mode. When **$i** is included in the macro, loop through arguments, substituting the current argument for **$i** on each pass. Escape $ with \.

mdelete [*remote-files*]
Delete the *remote-files* on the remote machine.

mdir *remote-files local-file*
Like **dir**, except multiple remote files may be specified.

mget *remote-files*
Expand the wildcard expression *remote-files* on the remote machine and do a **get** for each filename thus produced.

mkdir *directory-name*
Make a directory on the remote machine.

mls *remote-files local-file*
Like **nlist**, except multiple remote files may be specified, and the local file must be specified.

mode [*mode-name*]
Set file transfer mode to *mode-name*. Default mode is stream.

modtime *file-name*
Show last modification time of the file on the remote machine.

mput *local-files*
Expand wildcards in *local-files* given as arguments and do a **put** for each file in the resulting list.

newer *remote-file* [*local-file*]
Get the remote file if it is newer than the local file.

nlist [*remote-directory*] [*local-file*]
Print list of files in a directory on the remote machine to *local-file* (or to the screen if *local-file* is not specified). If *remote-directory* is unspecified, the current working directory is used.

nmap [*inpattern outpattern*]
Set or unset the filename mapping mechanism. The mapping follows the pattern set by *inpattern*, a template for incoming filenames, and *outpattern*, which determines the resulting mapped filename. The sequences **$1** through **$9** are treated as variables; for example, the *inpattern* **$1.$2**, along with the input file *readme.txt*, would set **$1** to **readme** and **$2** to **txt**. An *outpattern* of **$1.data** would result in an output file of *readme.data*. **$0** corresponds to the complete filename. [*string1*, *string2*] is replaced by *string1* unless that string is null, in which case it's replaced by *string2*.

ntrans [*inchars* [*outchars*]]
Set or unset filename character translation. Characters in a filename matching a character in *inchars* are replaced with the corresponding character in *outchars*. If no arguments are specified, the filename mapping mechanism is unset. If arguments are specified:

- Characters in remote filenames are translated during **mput** and **put** commands issued without a specified remote target filename.

- Characters in local filenames are translated during **mget** and **get** commands issued without a specified local target filename.

open *host* [*port*]

Establish a connection to the specified *host* FTP server. An optional *port* number may be supplied, in which case **ftp** attempts to contact an FTP server at that port.

prompt

Toggle interactive prompting.

proxy *ftp-command*

Execute an FTP command on a secondary control connection (i.e., send commands to two separate remote hosts simultaneously to allow the transfer of files between the two servers).

put *local-file* [*remote-file*], **send** *local-file* [*remote-file*]

Store a local file on the remote machine. If *remote-file* is not specified, the local filename is used after processing according to any **ntrans** or **nmap** settings in naming the remote file. File transfer uses the current settings for *type*, *file*, *structure*, and *transfer mode*.

pwd

Print name of the current working directory on the remote machine.

quote *arg1 arg2...*

Send the arguments specified, verbatim, to the remote FTP server.

reget *remote-file* [*local-file*]

Retrieve a file (like **get**), but restart at the end of *local-file*. Useful for restarting a dropped transfer.

remotehelp [*command-name*]

Request help from the remote FTP server. If *command-name* is specified, remote help for that command is returned.

remotestatus [*filename*]

Show status of the remote machine or, if *filename* is specified, of *filename* on remote machine.

rename [*from*] [*to*]

Rename file *from* on remote machine to *to*.

reset

Clear reply queue.

restart *marker*

Restart the transfer of a file from a particular byte count.

rmdir *directory-name*

Delete a directory on the remote machine.

runique

Toggle storing of files on the local system with unique filenames. When this option is on, rename files as **.1** or **.2**, and so on, as appropriate, to preserve unique filenames, and report each such action. Default value is off.

sendport

Toggle the use of PORT commands.

site [*command*]
> Run a site-specific command on the remote machine.

size *filename*
> Return size of *filename* on remote machine.

status
> Show current status of **ftp**.

struct [*struct-name*]
> Set the file transfer structure to *struct-name*. By default, stream structure is used.

sunique
> Toggle storing of files on remote machine under unique filenames.

system
> Show type of operating system running on remote machine.

tenex
> Set file transfer type to that needed to talk to TENEX machines.

trace
> Toggle packet tracing.

type [*type-name*]
> Set file transfer type to *type-name*. If no type is specified, the current type is printed. The default type is network ASCII.

umask [*mask*]
> Set user file-creation mode mask on the remote site. If *mask* is omitted, the current value of the mask is printed.

user *username* [*password*] [*account*]
> Identify yourself to the remote FTP server. **ftp** prompts the user for the password (if not specified and the server requires it) and the account field.

verbose
> Toggle verbose mode.

---

ftpd

in.ftpd [*options*]

TCP/IP command. Internet File Transfer Protocol server. The server uses the TCP protocol and listens at the port specified in the **ftp** service specification. **ftpd** is usually started by **xinetd** and must have an entry in **xinetd**'s configuration file, */etc/xinetd.conf*. It can also be run in standalone mode using the **-p** option. There are several FTP daemons available. On many Linux distributions, the default is the Kerberos-supporting DARPA version, which we document here.

Options

-a Require authentication via **ftp** AUTH. Allow anonymous users as well, if configured to do so.

-A Require authentication via **ftp** AUTH, but allow only users who are authorized to connect without a password. Allow anonymous users as well, if configured to do so.

-C   Require local credentials for nonanonymous users. Prompt for a password unless the user forwards credentials during authentication.

-d, -v

Write debugging information to **syslogd**.

-l   Log each FTP session in **syslogd**.

-p *port*

Use *port* as the FTP control port instead of reading the appropriate port from */etc/services*. This option will launch **ftpd** in standalone mode.

-q   Use PID files to record the process IDs of running daemons. This is the default. These files are needed to determine the current number of users.

-r *file*

Read Kerberos configuration from *file* instead of */etc/krb5.conf*.

-s *file*

Read Kerberos V4 authentication information from *file* instead of */etc/srvtab*.

-t *n*

Set default inactivity timeout period to *n* seconds. (The default is 15 minutes.)

-T *n*

Allow **ftp** clients to request a different timeout period of up to *n* seconds. (The default is 2 hours.)

-u *umask*

Set the default umask to *umask*.

-U *file*

Read the list of users denied remote access from *file* instead of */etc/ftpusers*.

-w *format*

Specify the format for the remote hostname passed to **login**. Use one of the following formats:

ip

Pass the IP address.

n[,[**no**]**striplocal**]

Pass hostnames less than *n* characters in length, and IP addresses for longer hostsnames. Set *n* to **0** to use the system default. The **striplocal** portion of the option determines whether or not to strip local domains from hostnames. The default is to strip them.

---

fuser   `fuser [options] [files | filesystems]`

Identifies and outputs the process IDs of processes that are using the *files* or local *filesystems*. Each process ID is followed by a letter code: **c** if process is using *file* as the current directory; **e** if executable; **f** if an open file; **F** if open file for writing; **m** if a shared library;

---

and **r** if the root directory. Any user with permission to read */dev/ kmem* and */dev/mem* can use **fuser**, but only a privileged user can terminate another user's process. **fuser** does not work on remote (NFS) files.

If more than one group of files is specified, the options may be respecified for each additional group of files. A lone dash (-) cancels the options currently in force, and the new set of options applies to the next group of files. Like a number of other administrator commands, **fuser** is usually installed to the */sbin* directory. You may need to add that directory to your path or execute the command as */sbin/fuser*.

Options

-    Return all options to defaults.

-signal
>   Send *signal* instead of SIGKILL.

-a   Display information on all specified files, even if they are not being accessed by any processes.

-i   Request user confirmation to kill a process. Ignored if **-k** is not also specified.

-k   Send SIGKILL signal to each process.

-l   List signal names.

-m   Expect *files* to exist on a mounted filesystem; include all files accessing that filesystem.

-n *space*
>   Set the namespace checked for usage. Acceptable values are **file** for files, **udp** for local UPD ports, and **tcp** for local TCP ports.

-s   Silent.

-u   User login name, in parentheses, also follows process ID.

-v   Verbose.

-V   Display version information.

---

g++

g++ [*options*] *files*

Invoke **gcc** with the options necessary to make it recognize C++. **g++** recognizes all the file extensions **gcc** does, in addition to C++ source files (*.C*, *.cc*, or *.cxx* files) and C++ preprocessed files (*.ii* files). See also **gcc**.

---

gawk

gawk [*options*] 'script' [*var=value...*] [*files*]

gawk [*options*] -f *scriptfile* [*var=value...*] [*files*]

The GNU version of **awk**, a program that does pattern matching, record processing, and other forms of text manipulation. For more information, see Chapter 11.

gcc

gcc [*options*] *files*

GNU Compiler Collection. **gcc**, formerly known as the GNU C Compiler, compiles multiple languages (C, C++, Objective-C, Ada, FORTRAN, and Java) to machine code. Here we document its use to compile C, C++, or Objective-C code. **gcc** compiles one or more programming source files; for example, C source files (*file.c*), assembler source files (*file.s*), or preprocessed C source files (*file.i*). If the file suffix is not recognizable, assume that the file is an object file or library. **gcc** normally invokes the C preprocessor, compiles the process code to assemble language code, assembles it, and then links it with the link editor. This process can be stopped at one of these stages using the **-c**, **-S**, or **-E** option. The steps may also differ depending on the language being compiled. By default, output is placed in *a.out*. In some cases, **gcc** generates an object file having a *.o* suffix and a corresponding root name.

Preprocessor and linker options given on the **gcc** command line are passed on to these tools when they are run. These options are briefly described here, but some are more fully described under entries for **cpp**, **as**, and **ld**. The options that follow are divided into general, preprocessor, linker, and warning options. **gcc** accepts many system-specific options not covered here.

gcc is the GNU form of **cc**; on most Linux systems, the command **cc** will invoke **gcc**. The command **g++** will invoke **gcc** with the appropriate options for interpreting C++.

General options

-a   Provide profile information for basic blocks.

-aux-info *file*

Print prototyped declarations and information on their origins to *file*.

-ansi

Enforce full ANSI conformance.

-b *machine*

Compile for use on *machine* type.

-c   Create linkable object file for each source file, but do not call linker.

-dumpmachine

Print compiler's default target machine, then exit.

-dumpspecs

Print built-in specification strings, then exit.

-dumpversion

Print version number, then exit.

-f*option*

Set the specified compiler *option*. Many of these control debugging, optimization of code, and special language options. Use the **--help -v** options for a full listing.

-g   Include debugging information for use with **gdb**.

-g_level_

> Provide the given _level_ of debugging information. _level_ must be **1**, **2**, or **3**, with 1 providing the least amount of information. The default is 2.

--help

> Print most common basic options, then exit. When used with option **-v**, print options for all of **gcc**'s subprocesses. For options specific to a target, use **--target-help**.

-m_option_

> Set the specified machine specific _option_. Use the **--target-help** option for a full listing.

-o _file_

> Specify output file as _file_. Default is _a.out_.

-p   Provide profile information for use with **prof**.

-pass-exit-codes

> On error, return highest error code as the exit code, instead of 1.

-pedantic

> Warn verbosely.

-pedantic-errors

> Generate an error in every case in which **-pedantic** would have produced a warning.

-pg

> Provide profile information for use with **gprof**.

-print-file-name=_file_

> Print the full path to the library specified by filename _file_, then exit. This is the library **gcc** would use for linking.

-print-search-dirs

> Print installation directory and the default list of directories **gcc** will search to find programs and libraries, then exit.

-pipe

> Transfer information between stages of compiler by pipes instead of temporary files.

-save-temps

> Save temporary files in the current directory when compiling.

-std=_standard_

> Specify C _standard_ of input file. Accepted values are:
>
> **iso9899:1990, c89**
>> 1990 ISO C standard (C89).
>
> **iso9899:199409**
>> 1994 amendment to the 1990 ISO C standard.
>
> **iso9899:1999, c99, iso9899:199x, c9x**
>> 1999 revised ISO C standard (C99).
>
> **gnu89**
>> 1990 C Standard with GNU extensions (the default value).

gnu99, gnu9x

1999 revised ISO C standard with GNU extensions.

c++98

1998 ISO C++ standard plus amendments.

gnu++98

1998 ISO C++ standard plus amendments and GNU extensions.

-time

Print statistics on the execution of each subprocess.

-v Verbose mode. Print subprocess commands to standard error as they are executed. Include **gcc** version number and preprocessor version number. To generate the same output without executing commands, use the option -###.

-w Suppress warnings.

-x *language*

Expect input file to be written in *language*, which may be **c**, **objective-c, c-header, c++, ada, f77, ratfor, assembler, java, cpp-output, c++-cpp-output, objc-cpp-output, f77-cpp-output, assembler-with-cpp**, or **ada**. If **none** is specified as *language*, guess the language by filename extension.

-B*path*

Specify the *path* directory in which the compiler files are located.

-E

Preprocess the source files, but do not compile. Print result to standard output. This option is useful to meaningfully pass some **cpp** options that would otherwise break **gcc**, such as **-C**, **-M**, or **-P**.

-I*dir*

Include *dir* in list of directories to search for include files. If *dir* is -, search those directories specified by **-I** before the **-I-** only when **#include** "*file*" is specified, not **#include** <*file*>.

-L*dir*

Search *dir* in addition to standard directories.

-O[*level*]

Optimize. *level* should be **1**, **2**, **3**, or **0** (the default is 1). 0 turns off optimization; 3 optimizes the most.

-S Compile source files into assembler code, but do not assemble.

-V *version*

Attempt to run **gcc** version *version*.

-Wa,*options*

Pass *options* to the assembler. Multiple options are separated by commas.

-Wl,*options*

Pass *options* to the linker. Multiple options are separated by commas.

-Wp,*options*

> Pass *options* to the preprocessor. Multiple options are separated by commas.

-Xlinker *options*

> Pass *options* to the linker. A linker option with an argument requires two **-Xlinker**s, the first specifying the option and the second specifying the argument. Similar to **-Wl**.

Preprocessor options

gcc will pass the following options to the preprocessor:

-$** Do not allow **$ in identifiers.

-dD, -dI, -dM, -dN

> Suppress normal output; print preprocessor instructions instead. See **cpp** for details.

-idirafter *dir*

> Search *dir* for header files when a header file is not found in any of the included directories.

-imacros *file*

> Process macros in *file* before processing main files.

-include *file*

> Process *file* before main file.

-iprefix *prefix*

> When adding directories with **-iwithprefix**, prepend *prefix* to the directory's name.

-isystem *dir*

> Search *dir* for header files after searching directories specified with **-I** but before searching standard system directories.

-iwithprefix *dir*

> Append *dir* to the list of directories to be searched when a header file cannot be found in the main include path. If **-iprefix** has been set, prepend that prefix to the directory's name.

-iwithprefixbefore *dir*

> Insert *dir* at the beginning of the list of directories to be searched when a header file cannot be found in the main include path. If **-iprefix** has been set, prepend that prefix to the directory's name.

-nostdinc

> Search only specified, not standard, directories for header files.

-nostdinc++

> Suppress searching of directories believed to contain C++-specific header files.

-trigraphs

> Convert special three-letter sequences, meant to represent missing characters on some terminals, into the single character they represent.

-undef

> Suppress definition of all nonstandard macros.

-A *name*[=*def*]
> Assert *name* with value *def* as if defined by **#assert**. To turn off standard assertions, use -A-.

-A -*name*[=*def*]
> Cancel assertion *name* with value *def*.

-C
> Retain all comments except those found on **cpp** directive lines. By default, the preprocessor strips C-style comments.

-D*name*[=*def*]
> Define *name* with value *def* as if by **#define**. If no =*def* is given, *name* is defined with value 1. -D has lower precedence than -U.

-H
> Print pathnames of included files, one per line, on standard error.

-M, -MG, -MF, -MD, -MMD, -MQ, -MT
> Suppress normal output and print *Makefile* rules describing file dependencies. Print a rule for **make** that describes the main source file's dependencies. If -MG is specified, assume that missing header files are actually generated files, and look for them in the source file's directory. Most of these options imply -E. See **cpp** for further details.

-U*name*
> Remove definition of symbol *name*.

Linker options

gcc will pass the following options to the linker:

-l*lib*
> Link to *lib*.

-nostartfiles
> Force linker to ignore standard system startup files.

-nostdlib
> Suppress linking to standard library files.

-s
> Remove all symbol table and relocation information from the executable.

-shared
> Create a shareable object.

-shared-libgcc
> Link to a shared version of **libgcc** if available.

-static
> Suppress linking to shared libraries.

-static-libgcc
> Link to a static version of **libgcc** if available.

-u *symbol*
> Force the linker to search libraries for a definition of *symbol* and to link to the libraries found.

Warning options

-pedantic
> Warn verbosely.

-pedantic-errors

Produce a fatal error in every case in which **-pedantic** would have produced a warning.

-w Don't print warnings.

-W Warn more verbosely than normal.

-Waggregate-return

Warn if any functions that return structures or unions are defined or called.

-Wall

Enable **-W**, **-Wchar-subscripts**, **-Wcomment**, **-Wformat**, **-Wimplicit**, **-Wmain**, **-Wmissing-braces**, **-Wparentheses**, **-Wreturn-type**, **-Wsequence-point**, **-Wswitch**, **-Wtemplate-debugging**, **-Wtrigraphs**, **-Wuninitialized**, **-Wunknown-pragmas**, **-Wstrict-aliasing**, and **-Wunused**.

-Wcast-align

Warn when encountering instances in which pointers are cast to types that increase the required alignment of the target from its original definition.

-Wcast-qual

Warn when encountering instances in which pointers are cast to types that lack the type qualifier with which the pointer was originally defined.

-Wchar-subscripts

Warn when encountering arrays with subscripts of type **char**.

-Wcomment

Warn when encountering the beginning of a nested comment.

-Wconversion

Warn in particular cases of type conversions.

-Werror

Exit at the first error.

-Wformat

Warn about inappropriately formatted **printf**s and **scanf**s.

-Wimplicit

Warn when encountering implicit function or parameter declarations.

-Winline

Warn about illegal inline functions.

-Wmain

Warn about malformed main functions.

-Wmissing-braces

Enable more verbose warnings about omitted braces.

-Wmissing-declarations

Warn if a global function is defined without a previous declaration.

-Wmissing-prototypes

Warn when encountering global function definitions without previous prototype declarations.

-Wnested-externs

Warn if an **extern** declaration is encountered within a function.

-Wno-import

Don't warn about use of **#import**.

-Wparentheses

Enable more verbose warnings about omitted parentheses.

-Wpointer-arith

Warn when encountering code that attempts to determine the size of a function or void.

-Wredundant-decls

Warn if anything is declared more than once in the same scope.

-Wreturn-type

Warn about violations of sequence point rules defined in the C standard.

-Wreturn-type

Warn about functions defined without return types or with improper return types.

-Wshadow

Warn when a local variable shadows another local variable.

-Wstrict-prototypes

Insist that argument types be specified in function declarations and definitions.

-Wswitch

Warn about switches that skip the index for one of their enumerated types.

-Wtraditional

Warn when encountering code that produces different results in ANSI C and traditional C.

-Wtrigraphs

Warn when encountering trigraphs.

-Wuninitialized

Warn when encountering uninitialized automatic variables.

-Wundef

Warn when encountering a nonmacro identifier in an **#if** directive.

-Wunknown-pragmas

Warn when encountering a **#pragma** directive not understood by **gcc**.

-Wunused

Warn about unused variables, functions, labels, and parameters.

Pragma directives

#pragma interface [*header-file*]

Used in header files to force object files to provide definition information via references instead of including it locally in each file. C++-specific.

#pragma implementation [*header-file*]

Used in main input files to force generation of full output from *header-file* (or, if it is not specified, from the header file with the same basename as the file containing the pragma directive). This information will be globally visible. Normally the specified header file contains a **#pragma interface** directive.

gdb

gdb [*options*] [*program* [*core*|*pid*]]

GDB (GNU DeBugger) allows you to step through the execution of a program in order to find the point at which it breaks. It fully supports C and C++, and provides partial support for FORTRAN, Java, Chill, assembly, and Modula-2. The program to be debugged is normally specified on the command line; you can also specify a core or, if you want to investigate a running program, a process ID.

Options

-b *bps*

Set line speed of serial device used by GDB to *bps*.

-batch

Exit after executing all the commands specified in *.gdbinit* and **-x** files. Print no startup messages.

-c *file*, **-core**=*file*

Consult *file* for information provided by a core dump.

-cd=*directory*

Use *directory* as **gdb**'s working directory.

-d *directory*, **-directory**=*directory*

Include *directory* in path that is searched for source files.

-e *file*, **-exec**=*file*

Use *file* as an executable to be read in conjunction with source code. May be used in conjunction with **-s** to read the symbol table from the executable.

-f, **-fullname**

Show full filename and line number for each stack frame.

-h, **-help**

Print help message, then exit.

-n, **-nx**

Ignore *.gdbinit* file.

-q, **-quiet**

Suppress introductory and copyright messages.

-s *file*, **-symbols**=*file*

Consult *file* for symbol table. With **-e**, also uses *file* as the executable.

-tty=*device*

Set standard in and standard out to *device*.

-write

Allow **gdb** to write into executables and core files.

-x *file*, **-command**=*file*

Read **gdb** commands from *file*.

Common commands

These are just some of the more common **gdb** commands; there are too many to list them all.

bt

> Print the current location within the program and a stack trace showing how the current location was reached. (**where** does the same thing.)

break

> Set a breakpoint in the program.

cd

> Change the current working directory.

clear

> Delete the breakpoint where you just stopped.

commands

> List commands to be executed when a breakpoint is hit.

c   Continue execution from a breakpoint.

delete

> Delete a breakpoint or a watchpoint; also used in conjunction with other commands.

display

> Cause variables or expressions to be displayed when program stops.

down

> Move down one stack frame to make another function the current one.

frame

> Select a frame for the next **continue** command.

info

> Show a variety of information about the program. For instance, **info breakpoints** shows all outstanding breakpoints and watchpoints.

jump

> Start execution at another point in the source file.

kill

> Abort the process running under **gdb**'s control.

list

> List the contents of the source file corresponding to the program being executed.

next

> Execute the next source line, executing a function in its entirety.

print

> Print the value of a variable or expression.

ptype

> Show the contents of a datatype, such as a structure or C++ class.

pwd

> Show the current working directory.

quit
> Exit **gdb**.

reverse-search
> Search backward for a regular expression in the source file.

run
> Execute the program.

search
> Search for a regular expression in the source file.

set variable
> Assign a value to a variable.

signal
> Send a signal to the running process.

step
> Execute the next source line, stepping into a function if necessary.

undisplay
> Reverse the effect of the **display** command; keep expressions from being displayed.

until
> Finish the current loop.

up
> Move up one stack frame to make another function the current one.

watch
> Set a watchpoint (i.e., a data breakpoint) in the program.

whatis
> Print the type of a variable or function.

---

genisoimage   genisoimage [*options*] [-o *filename*] *pathspec*...

Generate an ISO9660/Joliet/HFS hybrid filesystem for writing a CD with a program such as **wodim**. (HFS is the native Macintosh Hierarchical File System.) **genisoimage** takes a snapshot of a directory tree and generates a binary image that corresponds to an ISO9660 or HFS filesystem when it is written to a block device. Each specified *pathspec* describes the path of a directory tree to be copied into the ISO9660 filesystem; if multiple paths are specified, the files in all the paths are merged to form the image.

Options

-abstract *file*
> Specify the abstract filename. Overrides an **ABST**=*file* entry in .*genisoimagerc*.

-allow-leading-dots, -idots
> Allow ISO9660 filenames to start with a period instead of replacing it with an underscore. Violates the ISO9660 standard.

-allow-lowercase

Allow ISO9660 filenames to be lowercase. Violates the ISO9660 standard.

-allow-multidot

Allow more than one dot in ISO9660 filenames. Violates the ISO9660 standard.

-A *id*, **-appid** *id*

Specify a text string *id* that describes the application to be written into the volume header.

-b *image*

Specify the path and filename of the boot image to be used for making a bootable CD based on the El Torito specification.

-biblio *file*

Specify bibliographic filename. Overrides a **BIBL=***file* entry in *.genisoimagerc*.

-boot-info-table

Specify that a 56-byte table with information on the CD layout is to be patched in at offset 8 of the boot file. If specified, the table is patched into the source boot file, so make a copy if the file isn't recreatable.

-boot-load-seg *addr*

Specify the load segment address of the boot image for a no-emulation El Torito CD.

-boot-load-size *size*

Specify the number of virtual 512-byte sectors to load in no-emulation mode. The default is to load the entire boot file. The number may need to be a multiple of 4 to prevent problems with some BIOSes.

-c *catalog*

Specify the path, relative to the source *pathspec*, and the filename of the boot catalog for an El Torito bootable CD. Required for making an El Torito bootable CD.

-C *last-start,next-start*

Required for creating a CDExtra or a second or higher-level session for a multisession CD. *last-start* is the first sector number in the last session on the disk, and *next-start* is the first sector number for the new session. Use the command:

```
wodim -msinfo
```

to get the values. Use **-C** with **-M** to create an image that is a continuation of the previous session; without **-M**, create an image for a second session on a CDExtra (a multisession CD with audio data in the first session and an ISO9660 filesystem image in the second).

-[no-]cache-inodes

Cache [do not cache] inode and device numbers to find hard links to files. The default on Linux is to cache. Use **-no-cache-inodes** for filesystems that do not have unique inode numbers.

-check-oldnames

> Check all filenames imported from old sessions for **genisoimage** compliance with ISO9660 file-naming rules. If not specified, check only those files with names longer than 31 characters.

-check-session *file*

> Check all old sessions for **genisoimage** compliance with ISO9660 file-naming rules. This option is the equivalent of:

>   `-M file -C 0,0 -check-oldnames`

> where *file* is the pathname or SCSI device specifier that would be specified with **-M**.

-copyright *file*

> Specify the name of the file that contains the copyright information. Overrides a **COPY**=*file* entry in *.genisoimagerc*.

-d   Omit trailing period from files that do not have one. Violates the ISO9660 standard, but works on many systems.

-D   Do not use deep directory relocation. Violates the ISO9660 standard, but works on many systems.

-dir-mode *mode*

> Specify the mode for directories used to create the image. Automatically enables the Rock Ridge extensions.

-eltorito-alt-boot

> Start with a new set of El Torito boot parameters. Allows putting more than one El Torito boot image on a CD (maximum is 63).

-exclude-list *file*

> Check filenames against the globs contained in the specified file and exclude any that match.

-f   Follow symbolic links when generating the filesystem.

-file-mode *mode*

> Specify the mode for files used to create the image. Automatically enables the Rock Ridge extensions.

-force-rr

> Do not use automatic Rock Ridge detection for the previous session.

-G *image*

> Specify the path and filename of the generic boot image for making a generic bootable CD.

-gid *gid*

> Set the group ID to *gid* for the source files. Automatically enables the Rock Ridge extensions.

-graft-points

> Allow the use of graft points for filenames, which permits paths to be grafted at locations other than the root directory. **-graft-points** checks all filenames for graft points and divides the filename at the first unescaped equals sign (=).

-gui

> Switch the behavior for a GUI. Currently, the only effect is to make the output more verbose.

-hard-disk-boot

> Specify that the boot image to be used to create an El Torito bootable CD is a hard disk image that must begin with a master boot record containing a single partition.

-hidden *glob*

> Set the hidden (existence) ISO9660 directory attribute for paths or filenames matching the shell-style pattern *glob*. To match a directory, the path must not end with a trailing /. May be specified more than once.

-hidden-list *file*

> Specify a file containing a list of *globs* that are to be hidden with **-hidden**.

-hide *glob*

> Find paths or files that match the shell-style pattern *glob* and hide them from being seen on the ISO9660 or Rock Ridge directory. The files are still included in the image file. If the pattern matches a directory, the contents of the directory are hidden. To match a directory, the path must not end with a trailing /. See also the **-hide-joliet** option and the file *README.hide*. May be specified more than once.

-hide-joliet *glob*

> Hide paths or files that match the shell-style pattern *glob* so they will not be seen in the Joliet directory. If the pattern matches a directory, the contents of the directory are hidden. To match a directory, the path must not end with a trailing /. Usually used with **-hide**. See also the *README.hide* file. May be specified more than once.

-hide-joliet-list *file*

> Specify a file containing a list of *globs* to be hidden with **-hide-joliet**.

-hide-joliet-trans-tbl

> Hide the *TRANS.TBL* files from the Joliet tree.

-hide-list *file*

> Specify a file containing a list of *globs* to be hidden with **-hide**.

-hide-rr-moved

> Rename the directory *RR_MOVED* to *.rr_moved* to hide it as much as possible from the Rock Ridge directory tree. Use the **-D** option to omit the file entirely.

-input-charset *charset*

> Specify the character set for characters used in local filenames. Specify **help** in place of a *charset* for a list of valid character sets.

-iso-level *level*

> Set the ISO9660 conformance level. Possible values are:

> 1   Filenames are restricted to 8.3 characters, and files may have only one section.

2   Files may have only one section.

3   No restrictions.

4   **genisoimage** maps level 4 to ISO-9660:1999 (ISO9660 version 2).

-J   Generate Joliet directory records in addition to regular ISO9660 filenames.

-jcharset *charset*
The equivalent of **-input-charset -J**.

-l   Allow full 31-character filenames instead of restricting them to the MS-DOS-compatible 8.3 format.

-log-file *file*
Send all messages to the specified logfile.

-m *glob*
Exclude files matching the shell-style pattern *glob*. May be specified multiple times.

-M *path*, **-dev** *device*
Specify the path to an existing ISO9660 image to be merged. *path* (or the device given with **-dev**) can also be a SCSI device specified in the same syntax as **wodim**'s **dev=** parameter. May be used only with **-C**.

-max-iso9660-filenames
Allow up to 37 characters in ISO9660 filenames. Forces **-N**. Violates the ISO9660 standard.

-N Omit version numbers from ISO9660 filenames. Violates the ISO9660 standard. Use with caution.

-new-dir-mode *mode*
Specify the four-digit **chmod**-style mode to use for new directories in the image. The default is 0555.

-nobak, **-no-bak**
Do not include backup files on the ISO9660 filesystem.

-no-boot
Mark the El Torito CD to be created as not bootable.

-no-emul-boot
Specify that the boot image for creating an El Torito bootable CD is a no-emulation image.

-no-iso-translate
Do not translate the # and ~ characters. Violates the ISO9660 standard.

-no-rr
Do not use Rock Ridge attributes from previous sessions.

-o *file*
Specify the filename of the output ISO9660 filesystem image.

-output-charset *charset*
Specify the output character set for Rock Ridge filenames. The default is the input character set.

-p *prepid*

Specify a text string of up to 128 characters describing the preparer of the CD. Overrides a **PREP=** parameter set in the file *.genisoimagerc*.

-publisher *pubid*

Specify a text string of up to 128 characters describing the publisher of the CD to be written to the volume header. Overrides a **PUBL=** parameter set in *.genisoimagerc*.

-[no -]pad

Pad [do not pad] the ISO9660 filesystem by 150 sectors (300 KB). If used with **-B**, force the first boot partition to start on a sector number that is a multiple of 16. The default is **-pad**.

-path-list *file*

Specify a file that contains a list of *pathspec* directories and filenames to add to the ISO9660 filesystem. Note that at least one *pathspec* must be given on the command line. If *file* is -, read from standard input.

-print-size

Print estimated filesystem size and exit.

-quiet

Run in quiet mode; do not display progress output.

-r   Like **-R**, but set UID and GID to zero, set all file read bits to write, and turn off all file write bits. If any execute bit is set for a file, set all execute bits; if any search bit is set for a directory, set all search bits; if any special mode bits are set, clear them.

-R   Generate SUSP (System Use Sharing Protocol) and Rock Ridge records using the Rock Ridge protocol.

-relaxed-filenames

Allow ISO9660 filenames to include seven-digit ASCII characters except lowercase characters. Violates the ISO9660 standard.

-sort *file*

Sort file locations according to the rules in the specified file, which contains pairs of filenames and weights, with one space or tab between them. A higher weight puts the file closer to the beginning of the media.

-sysid *id*

Specify the system ID of up to 32 characters. Overrides a **SYSI=** parameter set in the file *.genisoimagerc*.

-T   Generate the file *TRANS.TBL* in each directory for establishing the correct filenames on non-Rock Ridge-capable systems.

-table-name *table*

Use *table* as the translation table name instead of *TRANS.TBL*. Implies -T. For a multisession image, the table name must be the same as the previous session.

-U   Allow untranslated filenames. Violates the ISO9660 standard. Forces the following options: **-d, -l, -N, -allow-leading-dots, -relaxed-filenames, -allow-lowercase, -allow-multidot, -no-iso-translate**. Use with extreme caution.

-ucs-level *num*

Set the Unicode conformance level to the specified number, which can be between 1 and 3 (default is 3).

-use-fileversion

Use file version numbers from the filesystem. The version number is a string from 1 to 32767. The default is to set a version of 1.

-v Run in verbose mode. Specify twice to run even more verbosely.

-V *volid*

Specify the volume ID (volume name or label) of up to 32 characters to be written to the master block. Overrides a **VOLI=** parameter specified in the file *.genisoimagerc*.

-volset *id*

Specify the volume set ID of up to 128 characters. Overrides a **VOLS=** parameter specified in *.genisoimagerc*.

-volset-seqno *num*

Set the volume set sequence number to *num*. Must be specified after **-volset-size**.

-volset-size *num*

Set the volume set size (the number of CDs in a set) to *num*. Must be specified before **-volset-seqno**.

HFS options

-apple

Create an ISO9660 CD with Apple's extensions.

-auto *file*

Set *file* as the Autostart file to make the HFS CD use the QuickTime 2.0 Autostart feature. *file* must be the name of an application or document at the top level of the CD and must be less than 12 characters long.

-boot-hfs-file *file*

Install *file* as the driver file that may make the CD bootable on a Macintosh.

-cluster-size *size*

Specify the size in bytes of a cluster or allocation units of PC Exchange files. Implies **--exchange** (see *--format* on page 173).

-hfs

Create a hybrid ISO9660/HFS CD. Use with **-map**, **-magic**, and/or the various **--HFS** options (see manpage).

-hfs-bless *folder*

"Bless" the specified directory (folder), given as the full pathname as **genisoimage** sees it. This is usually the System Folder and is used in creating HFS bootable CDs. The pathname must be in quotes if it contains spaces.

-hfs-creator *creator*

Set the four-character default creator for all files.

Linux Commands

-hfs-type *type*

Set the four-character default type for all files.

-hfs-unlock

Leave the HFS volume unlocked so other applications can modify it. The default is to lock the volume.

-hfs-volid *id*

Specify the volume name for the HFS partition. This name is assigned to the CD on a Macintosh and replaces the ID set with the **-V** option.

-hide-hfs *glob*

Hide files or directories matching the shell-style pattern *glob* from the HFS volume, although they still exist in the ISO9660 and/or Joliet directory. May be specified multiple times.

-hide-hfs-list *file*

The specified file contains a list of globs to be hidden.

-input-hfs-charset *charset*

Specify the input character set used for HFS filenames when used with the **-mac-name** option. The default is cp10000 (Mac Roman).

-mac-name

Use the HFS filename as the starting point for the ISO9660, Joliet, and Rock Ridge filenames.

-magic *file*

Use the specified magic file to set a file's creator and type information based on the file's *magic number*, which is usually the first few bytes of the file. The magic file contains entries consisting of four tab-separated columns specifying the byte offset, type, test, and a message.

-map *file*

Use the specified mapping file to set a file's creator and type information based on the filename extension. Only files that are not known Apple or Unix file types need to be mapped. The mapping file consists of five-column entries specifying the extension, file translation, creator, type, and a comment. Creator and type are both four-letter strings.

-no-desktop

Do not create empty Desktop files. The default is to create such files.

-output-hfs-charset *charset*

Specify the output character set used for HFS filenames. Defaults to the input character set.

-part

Generate an HFS partition table. The default is not to generate the table.

-probe

Search the contents of files for known Apple or Unix file types.

--format
> Look for Macintosh files of the specified file format type. The valid formats are **cap** (Apple/Unix File System (AUFS) CAP files), **netatalk, double, ethershare, ushare, exchange, sgi, xinet, macbin, single, dave, sfm, osx-double,** and **osx-hfs**.

getent

getent [*options*] *database key*

Search the specified database for the specified key. The database may be any one of *passwd, group, hosts, services, protocols,* or *networks*.

Options

-s *CONFIG*, **--service**=*CONFIG*
> Specify the service configuration to be used. See *nsswitch. conf(5)* for information about name-service switching.

-?, --help
> Display a help message.

--usage
> Display a very short syntax synopsis.

-V, --version
> Print version information and quit.

getkeycodes

getkeycodes

Print the kernel's scancode-to-keycode mapping table.

gpasswd

gpasswd [*options*] *group*

Administer */etc/group* and */etc/gshadow* entries. May only be used by an administrator. When used with a group name only, prompts for new group password. Defaults such as minimum and maximum group id values are specified in */etc/login.defs*.

Options

-a   Add a new group.

-A *users*
> Add administrative members.

-d   Delete a group.

-M *users*
> Add group members.

-R   Disable access to the group. Also prevent creation of a new group with the same name.

-r   Remove the password entirely.

gpg

gpg [*options*] *command* [*options*]

The GNU Privacy Guard application allows you to encrypt and decrypt information, create public and private encryption keys, and use or verify digital signatures. GPG is based on the use of a pair of keys, one public and one private (or "secret"). Data encrypted with one key can only be decrypted with the other. To encrypt a message to you, someone would use your public key to create a message that could only be unlocked with your private key. To sign information, you would lock it with your private key, allowing anyone to verify that it came from you by unlocking it with your public key.

GPG has dozens of additional options that fine-tune its available options. For a complete list, plus a guide to careful use of encryption and a deeper explanation of how public-key encryption works, visit *www.gnupg.org*.

Key commands

--check-sigs [*keyname*]
> Lists keys and signatures like **--list-sigs**, but also verifies the signatures.

--delete-key *keyname*
> Delete the specified key from the keyring.

--delete-secret-key *keyname*
> Delete the named secret key from the secret and public keyring.

--delete-secret-and-public-key *keyname*
> Delete the secret (if any) and then the public key for the specified name.

--desig-revoke *keyname*
> Create a revocation certificate for a key pair and designate authority to issue it to someone else. This allows the user to permit someone else to revoke the key, if necessary.

--edit-key [*keyname*]
> Edit key options using a menu-driven tool. Key options are too numerous to list here, but include everything from trust settings to images attached to keys for user identification purposes.

--export [*keyname*]
> Output the specified key or, if no key is named, the entire keyring. Use the **--output** flag to send the key information to a file, and **--armor** to make the key mailable as ASCII text.

--export-secret-keys [*keyname*]
> Outputs the specified secret key or keys. Operation is the same as **--export**, except with secret keys. This is a security risk and should be used with caution.

--export-secret-subkeys [*keyname*]
> Outputs the specified secret subkeys. Operation is the same as **--export**, except with secret keys. This is a security risk and should be used with caution.

--fingerprint [*keyname*]
> List keys and their fingerprints for keys named, or all keys if no name is specified. If repeated, shows fingerprints of secondary keys.

--gen-key

> Generate a new pair of keys, prompting for several preferences and a passphrase. For most purposes, the default answers to the questions about algorithm and key length are fine.

--gen-revoke *keyname*

> Create a revocation certificate for a key pair. A revocation certificate is designed to assure all parties that the key pair is no longer valid and should be discarded.

--keyserver *keyserver*

> Specifies the name of the *keyserver* holding the key.

--list-keys [*keyname*]

> List keys with the specified name, or all keys if no name is specified.

--list-public-keys [*keyname*]

> List public keys with the specified name, or all public keys if no name is specified.

--list-secret-keys [*keyname*]

> List secret keys with the specified name, or all secret keys if no name is specified.

--list-sigs [*keyname*]

> List keys as **--list-keys** does, but also list the signatures.

--gen-revoke *keyname*

> Delete the secret key (if any) and then the public key for the specified name.

--import *file*

> Read keys from a file and add them to your keyring. This is most often used with public keys that are sent by email, but can also be used to move private keys from one system to another. Combined with the **--merge-only** option, adds only new signatures, subkeys, and user IDs, not keys.

--lsign-key *keyname*

> Sign a public key, but mark it as nonexportable.

--recv-keys *keyname*

> Download and import keys from a keyserver. The key name here should be the key ID as known to the keyserver, and you must specify the server with the **--keyserver** option.

--refresh-keys [*keyname*]

> Check the keyserver for updates to keys already in the keyring. You can specify which keys to check for updates using the key IDs known to the server, and you must specify the server with the **--keyserver** option.

--search-keys [*keyname*]

> Search the names of keys on the keyserver. Specify the keyserver with **--keyserver**.

--send-keys [*keyname*]

> Send one or more keys to a keyserver. Specify the keyserver with **--keyserver**.

--sign-key *keyname*

> Sign a public key using your private key. Often used to send the public key to a third party. This is the same as selecting "sign" from the **--edit-key** menu.

Signature commands

-b, --detach-sign

> Create a signature that is not attached to anything.

--clearsign

> Create a signature in cleartext.

-s, --sign

> Create a signature. May be combined with **--encrypt** and/or **--symmetric**.

--verify [*detached-signature*] [*signed-file*]

> Verify the signature attached to a file. If the signature and data are in the same file, only one file needs to be specified. For detached signatures, the first file should be the *.sig* or *.asc* signature file, and the second the datafile. If you wish to use stdin instead of a file for the nonattached data, you must specify a single dash (-) as the second filename.

--verify-files [*files*]

> Verify one or more files entered on the command line or to stdin. Signatures must be part of the files submitted, and files sent to stdin should be one file per line. This is designed to check many files at once.

Encryption commands

-e, --encrypt

> Encrypt data. May be used with **--sign** to create signed, encrypted data.

--encrypt-files [*files*]

> Encrypt files one after another, either at the command line or sent to stdin one per line.

-c, --symmetric

> Encrypt using a symmetric cipher. The cipher is encrypted using the CAST5 algorithm unless you specify otherwise using the **--cipher-algo** flag.

--store

> Create a PGP message packet (RFC 1991). This does not encrypt data; it just puts it into the right packet format.

Decryption commands

-d, --decrypt [*file*]

> Decrypt a file. If no file is specified, stdin is decrypted. Decrypted data is sent to stdout or to the file specified with the **--output** flag. If the encrypted data is signed, the signature is also verified.

--decrypt-files [*files*]

> Decrypt files one after another, either at the command line or sent to stdin one per line.

Other commands

--check-trustdb

>   Check the list of keys with defined trust levels to see if they have expired or been revoked.

--export-ownertrust

>   Create a backup of the trust values for keys.

-h, --help

>   Display a help message.

--import-ownertrust [*file*]

>   Import trust values from a file or stdin. Overwrites existing values.

--list-packets

>   Display packet sequence for an encrypted message. Used for debugging.

--update-trustdb

>   Update the database of trusted keys. For each key that has no defined level of trust, **--update-trustdb** prompts for an estimate of how much the key's owner can be trusted to certify other keys. This builds a web of more-trusted and less-trusted keys by which the overall security of a given key can be estimated.

--version

>   Display version information and quit.

--warranty

>   Display warranty information. There is no warranty.

---

gpgsplit

gpgsplit [*options*] [*files*]

Split an OpenPGP-format message into individual packets. If no file is specified, the message is read from stdin. The split packets are written as individual files.

Options

-h, -?, --help

>   Display a short help message.

--no-split

>   Write to stdout instead of splitting the packets into individual files.

-p *string*, **--prefix** *string*

>   Begin each filename with the specified string.

--secret-to-public

>   Convert any secret keys in the message to public keys.

--uncompress

>   Uncompress any compressed packets.

-v, --verbose

>   Verbose mode. More informative.

gpgv

gpgv [*options*] [*detached-signature*] [*signed-files*]

Check the signature of one or more OpenPGP-signed files. This is similar in operation to **gpg --verify** but uses a different keyring, *~/.gnupg/trustedkeys.gpg* by default. Also, **gpgv** assumes that the keyring is trusted, and it cannot edit or update it. By contrast, **gpg --verify** can go to a keyserver to verify signatures that are not in the local keyring, and offers various levels of trust. In both cases, you can use a detached signature file

Options

-h, -?, --help
> Display a short help message.

--ignore-time-conflict
> Use this flag to ignore incorrect dates on signatures. An incorrect date can be a sign of fraud, but is often just a result of an incorrectly set clock.

--keyring *file*
> Use the specified file as a keyring, in addition to the default *~/.gnupg/trustedkeys.gpg*.

--homedir *dir*
> Use the specified directory as the GPG home directory, instead of the default (set in the GNUPGHOME variable, or, if that is unset, *~/.gnupg*).

--logger-fd *FD*
> Send log output to the specified file descriptor. By default, log output goes to stderr. Use of file descriptors is described in the DETAILS section of the GPG documentation.

-q, --quiet
> Minimal output.

--status-fd *FD*
> Send special status messages to the specified file descriptor.

-v, --verbose
> Verbose mode. More informative.

gpm

gpm [*options*]

System administration command. Provide a mouse server and cut-and-paste utility for use on the Linux console. **gpm** acts like a daemon, responding to both mouse events and client input. If no clients are connected to the active console, **gpm** provides cut-and-paste services.

Options

-2
> Force two buttons. If there is a middle button, it is treated as the right button.

-3
> Force three buttons. With a three-button mouse, the left button makes a selection, the right button extends the selection, and the middle button pastes it. Using this option with a two-button mouse results in being unable to paste.

-a *accel*

> Set the acceleration for a single motion longer than the delta specified with the **-d** option.

-A [*limit*]

> Start up with pasting disabled for security. If specified, *limit* gives the time in seconds during which a selection can be pasted. If too much time has passed, the paste is not allowed.

-b *baud*

> Specify the baud rate.

-B *seq*

> Set a three-digit button sequence, mapping the left, middle, and right buttons to buttons 1, 2, and 3. The default is **123**. The sequence **321** is useful if you are left-handed, or **132** for a two-button mouse.

-d *delta*

> Set the delta value for use with **-a**. When a mouse motion event is longer than the specified delta, use *accel* as a multiplier. *delta* must be **2** or greater.

-D Debugging mode. When set, **gpm** does not put itself into the background, and it logs messages to standard error instead of syslog.

-g *num*

> For a glidepoint device, specify the button to be emulated by a tap. *num* must be **1**, **2**, or **3** and refers to the button number before any remapping is done by the **-B** option. Applies to **mman** and **ps2** protocol decoding.

-h Print a help message and exit.

-i *interval*

> Specify the upper time limit, in milliseconds, between mouse clicks for the clicks to be considered a double or triple click.

-k Kill a running **gpm**. For use with a bus mouse to kill **gpm** before running X. See also **-R**.

-l *charset*

> Specify the **inword( )** lookup table, which determines which characters can appear in a word. *charset* is a list of characters. The list can include only printable characters. Specify a range with -, and use \ to escape the following character or to specify an octal character.

-m *filename*

> Specify the mouse file to open. The default is */dev/mouse*.

-M Enable the use of more than one mouse. Options appearing before **-M** apply to the first mouse; those appearing after it apply to the second mouse. Forces the use of **-R**.

-o *extra-options*

> Specify a comma-separated list of additional mouse-specific options. See the **gpm** info page for a description of the mouse types and the possible options.

-p   Keep the pointer visible while text is being selected. The default is not to show the pointer.

-r *num*
> Specify the responsiveness. A higher number causes the cursor to move faster.

-R *name*
> Act as a repeater and pass any mouse data received while in graphical mode to the fifo */dev/gpmdata* in the protocol specified by *name* (default is **msc**). In addition to certain protocol types available with **-t**, you can specify **raw** to repeat the data with no protocol translation.

-s *num*
> Specify the sample rate for the mouse device.

-S [*commands*]
> Enable special-command processing (see the next section). Custom *commands* can be specified as a colon-separated list to associate commands with the left button, middle button, and right button. If a command is omitted, it defaults to sending a signal to **init**.

-t *type*
> Specify the mouse protocol type. Use **-t help** for a list of types; those marked with an asterisk (*) can be used with **-R**.

-v   Print version information and exit.

-V [*increment*]
> Make **gpm** more or less verbose by the specified *increment*. The default verbosity level is 5, and the default increment is 1. A larger value of *increment* causes more messages to be logged. The increment can be negative, but must be specified with no space (e.g., **-V-3**).

Special commands

Special commands, activated with the **-S** option, are associated with each mouse button. You can also use **-S** to customize the commands. To execute a special command, triple-click the left and right buttons (hold down one of the buttons and triple-click the other). A message appears on the console, and the speaker beeps twice. At this point, release the buttons and press the desired button within three seconds to activate the associated special command. The default special commands are:

Left button
> Reboot by signaling **init**.

Middle button
> Shut down the system with **/sbin/shutdown -h now**.

Right button
> Reboot with **/sbin/shutdown -r now**.

gprof   gprof [*options*] [*object_file*]

Display the profile data for an object file. The file's symbol table is compared with the call graph profile file *gmon.out* (previously created by compiling with **gcc -pg**). Many of **gprof**'s options take a symbol-specification argument, or symspec, to limit the option to specified files or functions. The symspec may be a filename, a function, or a line number. It can also be given as *filename:function* or *filename:linenumber* to specify a function or line number in a specific file. **gprof** expects filenames to contain a period and functions to not contain a period.

Options

-a, --no-static

Do not display statically declared functions. Since their information might still be relevant, append it to the information about the functions loaded immediately before.

-b, --brief

Do not display information about each field in the profile.

-c, --static-call-graph

Consult the object file's text area to attempt to determine the program's static call graph. Display static-only parents and children with call counts of 0.

--demangle[*=style*], **--no-demangle**

Specify whether C++ symbols should be demangled or not. They are demangled by default. If profiling a program built by a different compiler, you may need to specify the mangling style.

--function-ordering

Print suggested function order based on profiling data.

--file-ordering *file*

Print suggested link line order for .o files based on profiling data. Read function name to object file mappings from *file*. This file can be created using the **nm** command.

-i, --file-info

Print summary information on datafiles, then exit.

-k *from to*

Remove arcs between the routines *from* and *to*.

-m *n*, **--min-count**[*=n*]

Don't print count statistics for symbols executed less than *n* times.

-n[*symspec*], **--time**[*=symspec*]

Propagate time statistics in call graph analysis.

-p[*symspec*], **--flat-profile**[*=symspec*]

Print profile statistics.

-q[*symspec*], **--graph**[*=symspec*]

Print call graph analysis.

-s, --sum

Summarize profile information in the file *gmon.sum*.

Linux Commands

-v, --version
> Print version and exit.

-w *n*, --width=*n*
> Print function index formatted to width *n*.

-x, --all-lines
> When printing annotated source, annotate every line in a basic block, not just the beginning.

-y, --separate-files
> Print annotated-source output to separate files instead of standard output. The annotated source for each source file is printed to *filename-ann*.

-z, --display-unused-functions
> Include zero-usage calls.

-A[*symspec*], --annotated-source[=*symspec*]
> Print annotated source code.

-C[*symspec*], --exec-counts[=*symspec*]
> Print statistics on the number of times each function is called. When used with option -l, count basic-block execution.

-F *routine*
> Print only information about *routine*. Do not include time spent in other routines.

-I *dirs*, --directory-path=*dirs*
> Set directory path to search for source files. The *dirs* argument may be given as a colon-separated list of directories.

-J[*symspec*], --no-annotated-source[=*symspec*]
> Don't print annotated source code.

-L, --print-path
> Print the path information when printing filenames.

-N[*symspec*], --no-time[=*symspec*]
> Don't propagate time statistics in call graph analysis.

-P[*symspec*], --no-flat-profile[=*symspec*]
> Don't print profile statistics.

-Q[*symspec*], --no-graph[=*symspec*]
> Don't print call graph analysis.

-T, --traditional
> Print output in BSD style.

-Z[*symspec*], --no-exec-counts[=*symspec*]
> Don't print statistics on the number of times each function is called.

---

grep

grep [*options*] *pattern* [*files*]

Search one or more *files* for lines that match a regular expression *pattern*. Regular expressions are described in Chapter 7. Exit status is 0 if any lines match, 1 if none match, and 2 for errors. See also **egrep** and **fgrep**.

Options

-a, --text

Don't suppress output lines with binary data; treat as text.

-A *num*, **--after-context**=*num*

Print *num* lines of text that occur after the matching line.

-b, --byte-offset

Print the byte offset within the input file before each line of output.

-B *num*, **--before-context**=*num*

Print *num* lines of text that occur before the matching line.

-c, --count

Print only a count of matched lines. With **-v** or **--revert-match**, count nonmatching lines.

-C[*num*], **--context**[=*num*], *-num*

Print *num* lines of leading and trailing context. Default context is 2 lines.

-d *action*, **--directories**=*action*

Define an *action* for processing directories. Possible actions are:

read

Read directories like ordinary files (default).

skip

Skip directories.

recurse

Recursively read all files under each directory. Same as **-r**.

-D *action*, **--directories**=*action*

Define an *action* for processing an input file that is a device, FIFO, or socket. Possible actions are **read** (default) and **skip**, as in **-d**.

-e *pattern*, **--regexp**=*pattern*

Search for *pattern*. Same as specifying a pattern as an argument, but useful in protecting patterns beginning with -.

-E, -extended-regexp

Act like **egrep**, recognizing extended regular expressions such as **(UN|POS)IX** to find **UNIX** and **POSIX**.

-f *file*, **--file**=*file*

Take a list of patterns from *file*, one per line.

-F, --fixed-strings

Act like **fgrep**, recognizing only fixed strings instead of regular expressions. Useful when searching for characters that **grep** normally recognizes as metacharacters.

-G, --basic-regexp

Expect the regular expressions traditionally recognized by **grep** (the default).

-h, --no-filename

Print matched lines but not filenames (inverse of -l) when multiple files are searched.

-H, --with-filename

Display, before each line found, the name of the file containing the line. This is done by default if multiple files are submitted to a single **grep** command.

-i, --ignore-case

Ignore uppercase and lowercase distinctions.

-l, --files-with-matches

Print the names of files with matches but not individual matched lines. Scanning per file stops on the first match.

-L, --files-without-match

Print only the names of files with no matches. Scanning per file stops on the first match.

-m *num*, **--max-count=***num*

Stop looking after *num* matches are found.

--mmap

Try to use memory mapping (**mmap**) to read input in order to save time.

-n, --line-number

Print lines and their line numbers.

-q, --quiet, --silent

Suppress normal output in favor of quiet mode; scanning stops on the first match.

-r, --recursive

Recursively read all files under each directory. Same as **-d recurse**.

-s, --no-messages

Suppress error messages about nonexistent or unreadable files.

-v, --invert-match

Print all lines that don't match *pattern*.

-V, --version

Print the version number and then exit.

-w, --word-regexp

Match on whole words only. Words are divided by characters that are not letters, digits, or underscores.

-x, --line-regexp

Print lines only if *pattern* matches the entire line.

-Z, --null

When displaying filenames, follow each with a zero byte instead of a colon.

Examples

List the number of users who use **tcsh**:

```
grep -c /bin/tcsh /etc/passwd
```

List header files that have at least one **#include** directive:

grep -l '^#include' /usr/include/*

List files that don't contain *pattern*:

grep –c *pattern files* | grep :0

---

groff

groff [*options*] [*files*]

troff [*options*] [*files*]

Frontend to the **groff** document-formatting system, which normally runs **troff** along with a postprocessor appropriate for the selected output device. Options without arguments can be grouped after a single dash (-). A filename of - denotes standard input.

Options

-a   Generate an ASCII approximation of the typeset output.

-b   Print a backtrace.

-C   Enable compatibility mode.

-dcs, **-d**name=s
    Define the character *c* or string *name* to be the string *s*.

-e   Preprocess with **eqn**, the equation formatter.

-E   Don't print any error messages.

-ffam
    Use *fam* as the default font family.

-Fdir
    Search *dir* for subdirectories with DESC and font files before searching the default directory */usr/lib/groff/font*.

-h, --help
    Print a help message.

-i   Read standard input after all *files* have been processed.

-l   Send the output to a print spooler (as specified by the print command in the device description file).

-Larg
    Pass *arg* to the spooler. Each argument should be passed with a separate **-L** option.

-mname
    Read the macro file *tmac.name*.

-Mdir
    Search directory *dir* for macro files before searching the default directory */usr/lib/groff/tmac*.

-nnum
    Set the first page number to *num*.

-N   Don't allow newlines with **eqn** delimiters; equivalent to **eqn**'s **-N** option.

-olist
    Output only pages specified in *list*, a comma-separated list of page ranges.

-p   Preprocess with **pic**.

-Parg

Pass *arg* to the postprocessor. Each argument should be passed with a separate **-P** option.

-rcn, *-name=n*

Set the number register *c* or *name* to *n*. *c* is a single character, and *n* is any **troff** numeric expression.

-R   Preprocess with **refer**.

-s   Preprocess with **soelim**.

-S   Use safer mode (that is, pass the **-S** option to **pic** and use the **-msafer** macros with **troff**).

-t   Preprocess with **tbl**.

-Tdev

Prepare output for device *dev*; the default is **ps**.

-v, --version

Make **groff** and programs run by it print out their version numbers.

-V   Print the pipeline on stdout instead of executing it.

-wname

Enable warning *name*. You can specify multiple **-w** options. See the **troff** manpage for a list of warnings.

-Wname

Disable warning *name*. You can specify multiple **-W** options. See the **troff** manpage for a list of warnings.

-z   Suppress **troff** output (except error messages).

-Z   Do not postprocess **troff** output. Normally **groff** automatically runs the appropriate postprocessor.

Devices

ascii

Typewriter-like device.

dvi

TEX DVI format.

html

HTML output.

latin1

Typewriter-like devices using the ISO Latin-1 character set.

lj4

HP LaserJet4-compatible (or other PCL5-compatible) printer.

ps   PostScript.

utf8

Unicode (ISO 10646) character set with UTF-8 encoding.

X75

75-dpi X11 previewer.

X100

100-dpi X11 previewer.

Environment variables

GROFF_COMMAND_PREFIX
> If set to X, **groff** runs **Xtroff** instead of **troff**.

GROFF_FONT_PATH
> Colon-separated list of directories to search for the *devname* directory.

GROFF_TMAC_PATH
> Colon-separated list of directories to search for the macro files.

GROFF_TMPDIR
> If set, temporary files are created in this directory; otherwise, they are created in TMPDIR (if set) or */tmp* (if TMPDIR is not set).

GROFF_TYPESETTER
> Default device.

PATH
> Search path for commands that **groff** executes.

---

groupadd

groupadd [*options*] *group*

System administration command. Create a new user group.

Options

-f, --force
> This option is useful for scripts. When specified the command will exit without error if the group being added already exists. If a *gid* requested with **-g** already exists and the **-o** option has not been specified, assign a different *gid* as if **-g** had not been specified. This option is not available on all distributions.

-g *gid*, **--gid** *gid*
> Assign numerical group ID. (By default, the first available number above 500 is used.) The value must be unique, unless the **-o** option is used.

-K *key=value*, **--key** *key=value*
> Override defaults in */etc/login.defs*.

-o   Accept a nonunique *gid* with the **-g** option.

-p *string*, **--password** *string*
> Set the password for the group. *string* must already be encrypted appropriately for the system.

-r, --system
> Add a system account. Assign the first available number lower than 499.

--usage
> Display a very short list of acceptable options for the command.

groupdel
    groupdel *group*

System administration command. Remove *group* from system account files. You may still need to find and change permissions on files that belong to the removed group.

groupmod
    groupmod [*options*] *group*

System administration command. Modify group information for *group*.

Options

-g *gid*, **--gid** *gid*
    Assign numerical group ID. (By default, the first available unreserved number is used. Many distributions reserve the first 500 IDs for system groups, some the first 1000.) The value must be unique, unless the -o option is used.

-n *name*
    Change the group name to *name*.

-o   Override. Accept a nonunique *gid*.

-p *string*, **--password** *string*
    Set the initial password for the group. *string* must already be encrypted appropriately for the system.

groups
    groups [*options*] [*users*]

Show the groups that each *user* belongs to (default user is the owner of the current group). Groups are listed in */etc/passwd* and */etc/group*.

Options

--help
    Print help message.

--version
    Print version information.

grpck
    grpck [*option*] [*files*]

System administration command. Remove corrupt or duplicate entries in the */etc/group* and */etc/gshadow* files. Generate warnings for other errors found. **grpck** will prompt for a "yes" or "no" before deleting entries. If the user replies "no," the program will exit. If run in a read-only mode, the reply to all prompts is "no." Alternate group and gshadow *files* can be checked. If other errors are found, the user will be encouraged to run the **groupmod** command.

Option

-r   Read-only mode.

-s   Sort entries by GID.

Exit codes

0   Success.

1   Syntax error.

2   One or more bad group entries found.

3   Could not open group files.

4   Could not lock group files.

5   Could not write group files.

---

grpconv

```
grpconv
grpunconv
```

System administration command. Like **pwconv**, the **grpconv** command creates a shadowed group file to keep your encrypted group passwords safe from password-cracking programs. **grpconv** creates the */etc/gshadow* file based on your existing */etc/groups* file and replaces your encrypted password entries with **x**. If you add new entries to the */etc/groups* file, you can run **grpconv** again to transfer the new information to */etc/gshadow*. It will ignore entries that already have a password of **x** and convert those that do not. **grpunconv** restores the encrypted passwords to your */etc/groups* file and removes the */etc/gshadow* file.

---

gs

```
gs [options] [files]
```

GhostScript, an interpreter for Adobe Systems' PostScript and PDF (Portable Document Format) languages. Used for document processing. With - in place of *files*, standard input is used.

Options

-- filename arg1 ...
    Take the next argument as a filename, but use all remaining arguments to define **ARGUMENTS** in *userdict* (not *system-dict*) as an array of those strings before running the file.

-Dname=token, **-d**name=token
    Define a name in *systemdict* with the given definition. The token must be exactly one token (as defined by the token operator) and must not contain any whitespace.

-Dname, **-d**name
    Define a name in *systemdict* with a null value.

-gnumber1x*number2*
    Specify width and height of device; intended for systems like the X Window System.

-Idirectories
    Add a list of directories at the head of the search path for library files.

-q   Quiet startup.

-r*number*, -r*number1*x*number2*

> Specify X and Y resolutions (for the benefit of devices, such as printers, that support multiple X and Y resolutions). If only one number is given, it is used for both X and Y resolutions.

-S*name=string*, -s*name=string*

> Define a name in *systemdict* with a given *string* as value.

Special names
-dDISKFONTS

> Cause individual character outlines to be loaded from the disk the first time they are encountered.

-dNOBIND

> Disable the **bind** operator. Useful only for debugging.

-dNOCACHE

> Disable character caching. Useful only for debugging.

-dNODISPLAY

> Suppress the normal initialization of the output device. May be useful when debugging.

-dNOPAUSE

> Disable the prompt and pause at the end of each page.

-dNOPLATFONTS

> Disable the use of fonts supplied by the underlying platform (e.g., the X Window System).

-dSAFER

> Disable the **deletefile** and **renamefile** operators, and the ability to open files in any mode other than read-only.

-dWRITESYSTEMDICT

> Leave *systemdict* writable.

-sDEVICE=*device*

> Select an alternate initial output device.

-sOUTPUTFILE=*filename*

> Select an alternate output file (or pipe) for the initial output device.

---

gunzip

gunzip [*options*] [*files*]

Uncompress *files* compressed by **gzip**. See **gzip** for a list of options.

---

gzexe

gzexe [*option*] [*files*]

Compress executables. When run, these files automatically uncompress, thus trading time for space. **gzexe** creates backup files with a tilde at the end (*filename~*). These backup files can be deleted once you are sure the compression has worked properly.

Option
-d   Decompress files.

gzip

gzip [*options*] [*files*]

gunzip [*options*] [*files*]

zcat [*options*] [*files*]

Compress specified files (or data read from standard input) with Lempel-Ziv coding (LZ77). Rename compressed file to *filename.gz*; keep ownership modes and access/modification times. Ignore symbolic links. Uncompress with **gunzip**, which takes all of **gzip**'s options except those specified. **zcat** is identical to **gunzip -c** and takes the options -**fhLV**, described here. Files compressed with the **compress** command can be decompressed using these commands.

Options

-*n*, --fast, --best

Regulate the speed of compression using the specified digit *n*, where -**1** or --**fast** indicates the fastest compression method (less compression), and -**9** or --**best** indicates the slowest compression method (most compression). The default compression level is -**6**.

-c, --stdout, --to-stdout

Print output to standard output, and do not change input files.

-d, --decompress, --uncompress

Same as **gunzip**.

-f, --force

Force compression. **gzip** normally prompts for permission to continue when the file has multiple links, its *.gz* version already exists, or it is reading compressed data to or from a terminal.

-h, --help

Display a help screen and then exit.

-l, --list

Expects to be given compressed files as arguments. Files may be compressed by any of the following methods: **gzip**, **deflate**, **compress**, **lzh**, or **pack**. For each file, list uncompressed and compressed sizes (the former is always -**1** for files compressed by programs other than **gzip**), compression ratio, and uncompressed name. With -**v**, also print compression method, the 32-bit CRC of the uncompressed data, and the timestamp. With -**N**, look inside the file for the uncompressed name and timestamp.

-L, --license

Display the **gzip** license and quit.

-n, --no-name

When compressing, do not save the original filename and timestamp by default. When decompressing, do not restore the original filename if present, and do not restore the original timestamp if present. This option is the default when decompressing.

Linux Commands

-N, --name

Default. Save original name and timestamp. When decompressing, restore original name and timestamp.

-q, --quiet

Print no warnings.

-r, --recursive

When given a directory as an argument, recursively compress or decompress files within it.

-S *suffix*, **--suffix** *suffix*

Append .*suffix*. Default is **gz**. A null suffix while decompressing causes **gunzip** to attempt to decompress all specified files, regardless of suffix.

-t, --test

Test compressed file integrity.

-v, --verbose

Print name and percent size reduction for each file.

-V, --version

Display the version number and compilation options.

---

halt

halt [*options*]

System administration command: turns off the computer. Inserts a note in the file */var/log/wtmp*; if the system is in runlevel 0 or 6, stops all processes; otherwise, calls **shutdown -h**.

Options

-d   Suppress writing to */var/log/wtmp*.

-f   Call **halt** even when **shutdown -nf** would normally be called (i.e., force a call to **halt**, even when not in runlevel 0 or 6).

-h   Place hard drives in standby mode before halt or power off.

-i   Shut down network interfaces before halt.

-n   No sync before reboot or halt.

-p   Perform power-off when halting system.

---

hdparm

hdparm [*options*] [*device*]

System administration command. Read or set the hard drive parameters. This command can be used to tune hard drive performance. It is primarily used with IDE drives, but some can be used with SCSI drives as well.

Options

The **hdparm** command accepts many option flags, including some that can result in filesystem corruption if misused. Flags can be used to set or get a parameter. To get a parameter, just pass the flag without a value. To set a parameter, follow the flag with a space and the appropriate value.

-a [*n*]

> Get or set the number of sectors to read ahead in the disk. The default is 8 sectors (4 KB); a larger value is more efficient for large, sequential reads, and a smaller value is better for small, random reads. Many IDE drives include this functionality in the drive itself, so this feature is not always necessary.

-A   Enable or disable the IDE read-ahead feature. Usually on by default.

-b [*n*]

> Get or set the bus state for the drive.

-B   Set the Advanced Power Management (APM) data if the drive supports it.

-c [*n*]

> Get or set 32-bit I/O values for IDE drives. Acceptable values are **0** (32-bit support off), **1** (32-bit support on), and **3** (on, but only with a sync sequence).

-C   Check the power status of the drive. This will tell you unknown, active/idle, standby, or sleeping. Use **-S**, **-y**, **-Y**, and **-Z** to set the power status.

-d [*n*]

> Get or set the **using_dma** flag for the drive, which may be **0** (not using DMA) or **1** (using DMA).

-D   Enable or disable defect-handling features that are controlled by the hard drive itself.

-E *n*

> Set CD-ROM read speed to *n* times normal audio playback speed. Not normally necessary.

-f   Flush and sync the buffer cache on exit.

-F   Flush write cache buffer on-drive.

-g   Query and display drive size and geometry information, such as number of cylinders, heads, and sectors.

-h   Display a short help message.

-i   Display the drive identification information obtained at boot time. If the drive has changed since boot, this information may not be current.

-I   Display more detailed identification information for the drive.

--Istdin

> Read identify data from standard input.

--Istdout

> Write identify data to standard output.

-k [*n*]

> Get or set the **keep_settings_over_reset** variable. Valid settings are **0** and **1**, and a value of 1 will keep the **-dmu** options when rebooting (soft reset only).

-K [*n*]

Get or set the **keep_features_over_reset** variable. Valid settings are **0** and **1**, and a value of 1 will keep settings for the flags **-APSWXZ** over a soft reset.

-L *n*

Set the door lock flag for the drive. Used for Syquest, ZIP, and JAZ drives.

-m [*n*]

Get or set the number of sectors used for multiple sector count reading. A value of **0** disables the feature, and values of **2**, **4**, **8**, **16**, and **32** are common. Drives that try to support this feature and fail may suffer corruption and data loss.

-M [*n*]

Get or set the level for Automatic Acousting Management (AAM) features. Newer drives support this feature, which can slow down head movements to reduce hard disk noise. Values range from **128** (quiet, but slow) to **254** (fast, but loud). Some drives support only **128** and **254**, while others support multiple levels between the extremes. At the time of writing, this feature was still considered experimental and not recommended for production use.

-n [*n*]

Set to **0** or **1** to disable or enable, respectively, the "ignore write errors" flag. This can cause massive data loss if used incorrectly, and is for development purposes only.

-N [*n*]

Get or set visible number of sectors. Without a parameter this will display the current maximum sectors and the hardware limit for the disk. The invisible sectors form the Host Protected Area (HPA) commonly used to hold diagnostic software or the original copy of the operating system. Changing this value will usually result in data loss.

-p *n*

Tune the IDE interface to use PIO mode *n*, usually an integer between 0 and 5. Incorrect values can result in massive data loss. Support for the PIO mode-setting feature varies between IDE chips, so tuning it is not for the faint of heart.

-P *n*

Set the internal prefetch sector count. Not all drives support the feature.

-q

Suppress output for the flag after this one, unless it is the **-i**, **-v**, **-t**, or **-T** flag.

-Q [*n*]

Set the depth of tagged queues. **0** disables tagged queues. This is supported only on specific drives, and only for kernels 2.5.x and later.

-r [*n*]

Get or set the flag for read-only on the device. A value of **1** marks the device as read-only.

-R   This option should be used by experts only. It registers an IDE interface. See the **-U** option for further details.

-S *n*

Set the amount of time a disk is inactive before it spins down and goes into standby mode. Settings from **1** to **240** represent chunks of five seconds (for timeout values between 5 seconds and 20 minutes); values from **241** to **251** are increments of 30 minutes (for 30 minutes to 5.5 hours). A value of **252** sets the timeout to 21 minutes, **253** to the vendor default, and **255** to 20 minutes and 15 seconds.

-t   Time device reads to determine performance.

-T   Time cache reads to determine performance.

-u [*n*]

Get or set the interrupt-unmask value for the drive. A value of **1** lets the drive unmask other interrupts and can improve performance; when used with older kernels and hardware, it can cause data loss.

-U   Unregister an IDE interface. Use this feature and the **-R** feature only with hot-swappable hardware, such as very high-end servers and some laptops. It can damage or hang other systems, and should be used with caution.

-v   Display all appropriate settings for device except **-i**. This is the same as the default behavior with no flags.

-w   Reset the device. Use as a last resort only; may cause data loss.

-W   Enable or disable the write-cache feature for the drive. The default varies among drive manufacturers.

-x   Sets tristate. Use only for hot-swappable devices. See the **-R** and **-U** entries.

-X *n*

Set the IDE transfer mode. Possible values include **34** (multi-word DMA mode2 transfers) and **66** (UltraDMA mode2 transfers), or any PIO mode number plus 8. This option is suggested for experts only, and is useful only with newer EIDE/IDE/ATA2 drives. Often used in combination with **-d**.

-y   Put the IDE drive into standby (spin-down) mode, saving power.

-Y   Put the IDE drive into sleep mode.

-z   Force the kernel to reread the partition table.

-Z   Disable automatic powersaving on some drives, which can prevent them from idling or spinning down at inconvenient moments. This will increase the electrical power consumption of your system.

Linux Commands

head

head [*options*] [*files*]

Print the first few lines (default is 10) of one or more *files* to standard output. If *files* is missing or -, read from standard input. With more than one file, print a header for each file showing the filename.

Options

-c *num*[**b**|**k**|**m**], **--bytes** *num*[**b**|**k**|**m**]
> Print first *num* bytes or, if *num* is followed by **b**, **k**, or **m**, first *num* 512-byte blocks, 1-kilobyte blocks, or 1-megabyte blocks.

--help
> Display help and then exit.

-n *num*, **--lines** *num*, *-num*
> Print first *num* lines. Default is 10.

-q, **--quiet**, **--silent**
> Quiet mode; never print headers giving filenames.

-v, **--verbose**
> Print filename headers, even for only one file.

--version
> Output version information and then exit.

Examples

Display the first 20 lines of **phone_list**:

```
head -20 phone_list
```

Display the first 10 phone numbers having a 202 area code:

```
grep '(202)' phone_list | head
```

hexdump

hexdump [*options*] *file*

Display specified file or input in hexadecimal, octal, decimal, or ASCII format. Option flags are used to specify the display format.

Options

-b
> Use a one-byte octal display; show the input offset in hexadecimal, followed by 16 three-column octal data bytes, filled with zeroes and separated by spaces.

-c
> Use a one-byte character display; show the input offset in hexadecimal, followed by 16 three-column entries, filled with zeroes and separated by spaces.

-C
> Canonical mode. Display hexadecimal offset, two sets of eight columns of hexadecimal bytes, then a | followed by the ASCII representation of those same bytes.

-d
> Use a two-byte decimal display. The input offset is again in hexadecimal, but the display has only eight entries per line, of five columns each, containing two bytes of unsigned decimal format.

-e *format_string*
> Choose a format string to be used to transform the output data. Format strings consist of:

> *Iteration count*
>> The iteration count is optional. It determines the number of times to use the transformation string. The number is followed by a slash (/) to distinguish it from the byte count.

> *Byte count*
>> The number of bytes to be interpreted by the conversion string, preceded by a slash character to distinguish it from the iteration count. The byte count is optional.

> *Format characters*
>> The actual format characters are required. They are surrounded by quotation marks and are interpreted as **fprintf** (see **printf**) formatting strings, although the *, **h**, **l**, **n**, **p**, and **q** options will not work as expected. Format string usage is discussed at greater length in the **hexdump** manpage.

-f *filename*
> Choose a file that contains several format strings, separated by newlines; the # character marks a line as a comment.

-n *length*
> Limit the number of bytes of input to be interpreted.

-o
> Two-byte octal display; show a hexadecimal offset followed by eight five-column data entries of two bytes each, in octal format.

-s *offset*
> Skip to specified *offset*. The offset number is assumed to be decimal unless it starts with **0x** or **0X** (hexadecimal), or **0** (octal). Numbers may also be designated in megabytes, kilobytes, or half-kilobytes with the addition of **m**, **k**, or **b** at the end of the number.

-v
> Display all input data, even if it is the same as the previous line. Normally, a duplicate line is replaced by an asterisk (*).

-x
> Display data in a two-byte hexadecimal format. The offset is in hexadecimal, and is followed by eight space-separated entries, each of which contains four-column, two-byte chunks of data in hexadecimal format.

---

host

host [*options*] *name* [*server*]

System administration command. Print information about hosts or zones in DNS. Hosts may be IP addresses or hostnames; **host** converts IP addresses to hostnames by default and appends the local domain to hosts without a trailing dot. Default servers are determined in */etc/resolv.conf*. For more information about hosts and zones, read Chapters 1 and 2 of Paul Albitz's and Cricket Liu's *DNS and BIND* (O'Reilly).

Options

-a   Same as **-t ANY**.

-c *class*

> Search for specified resource record class (**IN, CH, CHAOS, HS, HESIOD**, or **ANY**). Default is IN.

-d   Verbose output. Same as **-v**.

-l   List mode. This also performs a zone transfer for the named zone. Same as **-t AXFR**.

-n   Perform reverse lookups for IPv6 addresses using IP6.INT domain and "nibble" labels instead of IP6.ARPA and binary labels.

-r   Do not ask contacted server to query other servers, but require only the information that it has cached.

-s   Stop querying nameservers upon receiving a SERVFAIL response.

-t *type*

> Look for *type* entries in the resource record. *type* may be any recognized query type, such as A, AXFR, CNAME, NS, SOA, SIG, or ANY. If *name* is a hostname, **host** will look for A records by default. If *name* is an IPv4 or IPv6 address, it will look for PTR records.

-v   Verbose. Include all fields from resource record, even time-to-live and class, as well as "additional information" and "authoritative nameservers" (provided by the remote nameserver).

-w   Never give up on queried server.

-C   Display SOA records from all authoritative nameservers for the specified zone.

-N *n*

> Consider names with fewer than *n* dots in them to be relative. Search for them in the domains listed in the **search** and **domain** directives of */etc/resolv.conf*. The default is usually 1.

-R *n*

> Retry query a maximum of *n* times. The default is 1.

-T   Use TCP instead of UDP to query nameserver. This is implied in queries that require TCP, such as AXFR requests.

-W *n*

> Wait a maximum of *n* seconds for reply.

---

hostid

`hostid`

Print the ID number in hexadecimal of the current host.

---

hostname

`hostname [option] [nameofhost]`

Set or display name of current host system. A privileged user can set the hostname with the *nameofhost* argument.

Options

-a, --alias
> Display the alias name of the host (if used).

-d, --domain
> Display DNS domain name.

-f, --fqdn, --long
> Display fully qualified domain name.

-F *file*, **--file** *file*
> Consult *file* for hostname.

-h, --help
> Display a help message and then exit.

-i, --ip-address
> Display the IP address(es) of the host.

-s, --short
> Trim domain information from the display output.

-v, --verbose
> Verbose mode.

-V, --version
> Display version information and then exit.

-y, --yp, --nis
> Display the NIS domain name. A privileged user can set a new NIS domain name with *nameofhost*.

---

htdigest

htdigest [-c] *filename realm username*

Create or update user authentication files used by the Apache web server. The **-c** option is used if you wish to create the file, and will overwrite any existing files rather than update them. The three arguments are the file you wish to use as the authentication file, the realm name to which the user belongs, and the username you will update in the password file. You will be prompted for a password when you run the command.

The Apache manual contains information about authentication mechanisms, including more detail about using **htdigest** and the ways in which you can control access to the resources served by Apache.

---

hunspell

hunspell [*options*] [*files*]

A spell checker modeled after **ispell**. With no files specified, **hunspell** reads from standard input. See **ispell** for details of the available options and commands. Commands are single-character and case-insensitive; use them to tell **hunspell** what to do with a misspelled word.

hwclock

hwclock [*option*]

System administration command. Read or set the hardware clock. This command maintains change information in */etc/adjtime*, which can be used to adjust the clock based on how much it drifts over time. **hwclock** replaces the **clock** command. The single-letter options are included for compatibility with the older command.

Options

You may specify only one of the following options:

-a, --adjust

Adjust the hardware clock based on information in */etc/ adjtime* and set the system clock to the new time.

--getepoch

Print the kernel's hardware clock epoch value, then exit.

-r, --show

Print the current time stored in the hardware clock.

-s, --hctosys

Set the system time in accordance with the hardware clock.

--setepoch, --epoch=*year*

Set the hardware clock's epoch to *year*.

--set --date=*date*

Set the hardware clock to the specified *date*, a string appropriate for use with the **date** command.

-v, --version

Print version and exit.

-w, --systohc

Set the hardware clock in accordance with the system time.

The following may be used with the above options:

--debug

Print information about what **hwclock** is doing.

--localtime

The hardware clock is stored in local time.

--noadjfile

Disable */etc/adjtime* facilities.

--test

Do not actually change anything. This is good for checking syntax.

-u, --utc

The hardware clock is stored in Universal Coordinated Time.

icedax

icedax [*options*] [*output.wav*]

Retrieve audio tracks in CDDA (Compact Disc Digital Audio) format and convert to WAV format. **icedax** stands for InCrEdible Digital Audio eXtractor. The manpage has full details as well as hints on the options and on usage.

Options

Some of the following options use sectors as a unit of measurement. Each sector of data on a CD represents approximately 1/75 second of play time.

-a *n*, **--divider** *n*

Set the sample rate to a value equal to 44100/*n* samples per second. The **-R** option, used by itself, lists the possible values.

-A *drivename*, **--auxdevice** *drivename*

Specify a different drive for ioctl purposes.

-b *n*, **--bits-per-sample** *n*

Set the quality of samples to *n* bits per sample per channel. Possible values are 8, 12, and 16.

-B, **--bulk**, **--alltracks**

Copy each track into its own file. This is the most commonly used flag.

-c *channel*, **--channels** *channel*

Set stereo instructions. Set *channel* to **1** for mono; **2** for stereo; or **s** for stereo, but swapped left-to-right. You can also use **-s** (**--stereo**) to record in stereo and **-m** (**--mono**) to record in mono.

-C *byteorder*, **--cdrom-endianness** *byteorder*

Set the byte order, or "endianness" of the input data. You may set the order to **little**, **big**, or **guess**. This is useful when your CD-ROM drive uses an unexpected or unusual byte order for your platform.

--cddbp-server=*servername*

Set the name of the CD lookup server used. The default server is **freedb.freedb.org**.

--cddbp-port=*portnumber*

Select the port on which to access the CD lookup server. The servers at *freedb.org* use cddbp on port 8880, and http on port 80.

-d *duration*, **--duration**

Set the number of seconds duration, or follow with **f** to set the duration in frames (sectors). Set *duration* to zero to record an entire track.

-D *devicename*, **--device** *devicename*

Specify the device. The device must work with the **-I** (**--interface**) settings.

-e, **--echo**

Copy output to an audio output device. Use **-K** (**--sound-device**) to set the device (usually **/dev/dsp**).

-E *byteorder*, **--output-endianness** *byteorder*

Set the byte order or "endianness" of the output data. As with **-C**, you may set the order to **little**, **big**, or **guess**.

-g, **--gui**

Format all text output for easy parsing by GUI frontends.

-h, --help

Print usage information and exit.

-H, --no-infofile

Do not copy any info or CDDB files, only the audio files.

-i *n*, **--index** *n*

Set the start index to *n* when recording.

-I *ifname*, **--interface** *ifname*

Specify the type of interface, **generic_scsi** or **cooked_ioctl**. It's usually safest to use **generic_scsi**.

-J, --info-only

Use this option by itself to display information about the disc, but do nothing else.

-K *device*, **--sound-device** *device*

Set the sound device to use with **-e**.

-l *n*, **--buffers-in-ring** *n*

Use a ring of *n* buffers.

-L *n*, **--cddb** *n*

icedax looks up CD information online, if possible. This option determines what happens when there are multiple entries identifying the CD. If the mode is 0, the user is prompted to select an entry. If the mode is 1, the application uses the first entry returned.

-M *n*, **--md5** *n*

Create MD5 checksums for the first *n* bytes of each track copied.

-n *n*, **--sectors-per-request** *n*

Read *n* sectors in each request.

-N, --no-write

For debugging purposes, this option suppresses writing an output file.

-o *n*, **--offset** *n*

Start recording *n* sectors before the beginning of the first track.

-O *format*, **--output-format=***format*

Choose the output file format. Normal file options are *wav*, *aiff*, *aifc*, *au*, and *sun*. You can also use *cdr* and *raw* for header-less files dumped into recording devices.

-p *n*, **--set-pitch** *n*

Adjust the pitch by *n* percent when copying data to an audio device.

-P *n*, **--set-overlap** *n*

Use *n* sectors of overlap for jitter correction. Very fast systems with absolutely perfect drives and unscratched CDs can set this to 0.

--paranoia

Read and interpret the CD using the **paranoia** library instead of the **icedax** code.

-q, --quiet
Quiet mode; the program sends no data to the screen.

-r *n*, **--rate** *n*
Set the sample rate in samples per second. To get a list of possible values, use the **-R** option by itself.

-R, --dump-rates
Output a list of possible sample rates and dividers. This option is typically used with no other option flags or arguments.

-S *n*, **--speed** *n*
Specify the speed at which your system will read the CD-ROM. Set the value to the multiple of normal playback speed given as your CD-ROM drive speed (4, 16, 32, and so forth). Setting the speed lower than the maximum can prevent errors in some cases.

-t *m*[+*n*], **--track** *m*[+*n*]
Set start track to *n*. Optionally, use + and a second track number for the end track: **1+10** copies tracks one through ten.

-v *list*, **--verbose-level** *list*
Specify CD information to display in a comma-separated list. The options are: for no information, use **disable**; for all information, use **all**. Specify **toc** for the table of contents, **summary** for a summary of recording parameters, **indices** for index offsets, **catalog** for the media catalog number (MCN), **trackid** for track IDs, **sectors** for the table of contents in start sector notation, and **titles** for title information, if available.

--version
Display version and quit.

-w, --wait
Wait for a signal before recording anything.

-x, --max
Set recording quality (and amount of hard disk usage) to maximum.

---

iconv

iconv [*options*] *files*

Convert the contents of one or more *files* from one character encoding to another and write the results to standard output. Use -l to print a list of possible encodings.

Options

-c   Omit invalid output characters.

-f *code1*, **--from-code**=*code1*
Convert input characters from the *code1* encoding.

-?, --help
Print help message and exit.

-l, --list
Print a list of valid encodings to standard output.

-o *file*, --output=*file*
> Write the converted output to *file* instead of standard output.

-s, --silent
> Operate silently; don't print warning messages.

-t *code2*, --to-code=*code2*
> Convert input characters to the *code2* encoding.

--usage
> Print a brief usage message showing only the command syntax and then exit.

-V, --version
> Print version information and exit.

--verbose
> Operate verbosely; print progress messages.

---

id

id [*options*] [*username*]

Display information about yourself or another user: user ID, group ID, effective user ID and group ID if relevant, and additional group IDs.

Options

-g, --group
> Print effective group ID only.

-G, --groups
> Print supplementary groups only.

-n, --name
> With -u, -g, or -G, print user or group name, not number.

-r, --real
> With -u, -g, or -G, print real, not effective, user ID or group ID.

-u, --user
> Print user ID only.

-Z, --context
> Print security context of the current user.

--help
> Print help message and then exit.

--version
> Print version information.

---

ifconfig

ifconfig [*interface*]

ifconfig [*interface address_family parameters addresses*]

TCP/IP command. Assign an address to a network interface and/or configure network interface parameters. **ifconfig** is typically used at boot time to define the network address of each interface on a machine. It may be used at a later time to redefine an interface's address or other parameters. Without arguments, **ifconfig** displays the current configuration for a network interface. With the single option **-a** and no other arguments, it will display all current interfaces. Used with a single *interface* argument, **ifconfig** displays that particular interface's current configuration. Note that interfaces are usually numbered starting at zero: **eth0**, **eth1**, **eth2**, and so forth. Wireless network interfaces may begin with **ath0** or **wlan0**. On some systems the **ifconfig** command is deprecated in favor of the **ip** command.

Arguments

interface
> String of the form *name unit*: for example, **en0**.

address_family
> Since an interface may receive transmissions in differing protocols, each of which may require separate naming schemes, you can specify the *address_family* to change the interpretation of the remaining parameters. You may specify **inet** (for TCP/IP, the default), **ax25** (AX.25 Packet Radio), **ddp** (Appletalk Phase 2), or **ipx** (Novell).

parameters
> The following *parameters* may be set with **ifconfig**:

> **add** *address/prefixlength*
>> Add an IPv6 address and prefix length.

> **address** *address*
>> Assign the specified IP *address* to the interface.

> **allmulti/-allmulti**
>> Enable/disable sending of incoming frames to the kernel's network layer.

> **arp/-arp**
>> Enable/disable use of the Address Resolution Protocol in mapping between network-level addresses and link-level addresses.

> **broadcast/-broadcast** [*address*]
>> (**inet** only) Set or clear the address to use to represent broadcasts to the network. Default is the address with a host part of all ones (i.e., **x.y.z.255** for a class C network).

> **debug/-debug**
>> Enable/disable driver-dependent debugging code.

> **del** *address/prefixlength*
>> Delete an IPv6 address and prefix length.

> **down**
>> Mark an interface "down" (unresponsive).

> **hw** *class address*
>> Set the interface's hardware class and address. *class* may be **ether** (Ethernet), **ax25** (AX.25 Packet Radio), or **ARCnet**.

> **io_addr** *addr*
>> I/O memory start address for device.

irq *addr*
> Set the device's interrupt line.

metric *n*
> Set routing metric of the interface to *n*. Default is 0.

mem_start *addr*
> Shared memory start address for device.

media *type*
> Set media type. Common values are **10base2**, **10baseT**, and **AUI**. If **auto** is specified, **ifconfig** will attempt to autosense the media type.

mtu *n*
> Set the interface's Maximum Transfer Unit (MTU).

multicast
> Set the multicast flag.

netmask *mask*
> (**inet** only) Specify how much of the address to reserve for subdividing networks into subnetworks. *mask* can be specified as a single hexadecimal number with a leading **0x**, with a dot notation Internet address, or with a pseudo-network name listed in the network table */etc/networks*.

pointopoint/-pointopoint [*address*]
> Enable/disable point-to-point interfacing, so that the connection between the two machines is dedicated.

promisc/-promisc
> Enable/disable promiscuous mode. Promiscuous mode allows the device to receive all packets on the network.

txqueuelen *n*
> Specify the transmit queue length.

tunnel *addr*
> Create an IPv6-in-IPv4 (SIT) device, tunneling to IPv4 address *addr*.

up
> Mark an interface "up" (ready to send and receive).

addresses
> Each address is either a hostname present in the hostname database (*/etc/hosts*), or an Internet address expressed in the Internet standard dot notation.

Examples

To list all interfaces:

```
ifconfig -a
```

To add a second IP address to wlan0:

```
ifconfig wlan0:1 192.168.2.41 netmask 255.255.255.0
```

To change the hardware address (MAC address) assigned to eth0 (useful when setting up a router for a DSL or cable modem):

```
ifconfig eth0 hw ether 01:02:03:04:05:06
```

imapd

imapd [*options*]

TCP/IP command. The Interactive Mail Access Protocol (IMAP) server daemon. **imapd** is often invoked by **xinetd** and listens on port 143 for requests from IMAP clients. IMAP allows mail programs to access remote mailboxes as if they were local. IMAP is a richer protocol than POP because it allows a client to retrieve message-level information from a server mailbox instead of the entire mailbox. IMAP can be used for online and offline reading. The popular Pine mail client contains support for IMAP. There are several versions of **imapd** available. Here we document the Cyrus IMAP server with its most common command options.

Options

-**C** *file*

Read configuration options from *file* instead of */etc/imapd.conf*.

-**s** Encrypt data using the Secure Socket Layer (SSL).

-**T** *n*

Wait *n* seconds for a new connection before closing the process. The default is 60.

-**U** *n*

Reuse process for new connections no more than *n* times.

---

inetd

inetd [*options*] [*configuration_file*]

TCP/IP command. The Internet services daemon. This is an older daemon usually replaced with **xinetd**. See **xinetd**.

---

info

info [*options*] [*topics*]

GNU hypertext reader. Display online documentation previously built from Texinfo input. Info files are arranged in a hierarchy and can contain menus for subtopics. When entered without options, the command displays the top-level info file (usually */usr/local/info/dir* or */usr/local/share/dir*). When *topics* are specified, find a subtopic by choosing the first *topic* from the menu in the top-level info file, the next *topic* from the new menu specified by the first *topic*, and so on. The initial display can also be controlled by the -**f** and -**n** options. If a specified *topic* has no info file but does have a manpage, **info** displays the manpage; if there is neither, the top-level info file is displayed.

Options

-**d** *directories*, --**directory** *directories*

Search *directories*, a colon-separated list, for info files. If this option is not specified, use the INFOPATH environment variable or the default directory (usually */usr/local/info* or */usr/share/info*).

Linux Commands

--dribble *file*

Store each keystroke in *file*, which can be used in a future session with the **--restore** option to return to this place in **info**.

-f *file*, **--file** *file*

Display specified info file.

--help

Display brief help message and exit.

--index-search *string*

Display node pointed to by index entry *string*.

-k *string*, **--apropos** *string*

Search all info topics for *string* and display the results.

-n *node*, **--node** *node*

Display specified node in the info file.

-o *file*, **--output** *file*

Copy output to *file* instead of displaying it on the screen.

-O, --show-options, --usage

Display the node with the command-line options.

--restore *file*

When starting, execute keystrokes stored in *file*.

--subnodes

Display subtopics.

--version

Display version.

--vi-keys

Use **vi**-like key bindings.

---

init

```
init
```

System administration command. The **init** daemon is the parent of all processes on Linux. Traditionally Linux has used a System V Unix style boot process (SysVinit) that calls this daemon at system startup. The SysVinit daemon starts or stops other programmings depending on run level. Newer Linux distributions use a more flexible process called Upstart, but for backward compatibility many still group processes into run levels. For a System V **init** process use the **telinit** program to change run levels. For Upstart use **initctl** to communicate with the **init** daemon. For more information, see the section "Starting and Stopping the System" on page 19.

---

initctl

```
initctl [options] command
```

System administration command. **initctl** sends commands to the Upstart **init** daemon. Use it to monitor jobs or events, call jobs directly, or send custom events to the daemon.

Options

--show-ids

Show unique process id (*pid*) as well as the job id.

--by-id

Parameter passed to command is a job id.

--no-wait

When using **start, stop,** or **emit,** exit immediately instead of waiting for the request to finish.

--quiet

Only show errors when running the given command.

Commands

These generally apply to upstart jobs. Jobs are usually defined in files located in the */etc/event.d* directory. Most commands will accept multiple job names given in a space separated list.

emit *event* [*arguments*]

Emit a custom *event* to which **init** should respond. Event *arguments* may be passed in a comma separated list. If any job status changes as a result of the event, print each change.

events

Monitor system events.

list [*pattern*]

Print a list of all known jobs. If an optional shell style matching pattern is given, only those jobs matching the pattern will be shown.

log-priority *priority*

Change **init** message logging *priority* to one of **debug, info, message, warn, error,** or **fatal.**

start *job...*

Start and print *job* status changes to screen.

status *job...*

Print status. The job name, goal (to start or stop) and the current status of the job are shown, along with any associated *pids.*

stop *job...*

Stop and print *job* status changes to screen.

jobs

Monitor job changes, printing changes to the screen.

version

Print version of running **init** daemon.

---

insmod

insmod *filename* [*module-options*]

System administration command. Load the module *filename* into the kernel. Simpler but less flexible than the **modprobe** command. Error messages from **insmod** may be vague, because the kernel performs module operations internally and therefore sends error information to the kernel log instead of standard output; see **dmesg.**

install

install [*options*] [*source*] *destination*

System administration command. Used primarily in *Makefile*s to update files. **install** copies files into user-specified directories. Similar to **cp**, but attempts to set permission modes, owner, and group. The *source* may be a file or directory, or a list of files and directories. The *destination* should be a single file or directory.

Options

-b, --backup[*=control*]

Back up any existing files. When using the long version of the command, the optional *control* parameter controls the kind of backup. When no control is specified, **install** will attempt to read the control value from the VERSION_CONTROL environment variable. Accepted values are:

none, off

Never make backups.

numbered, t

Make numbered backups.

existing, nil

Match existing backups, numbered or simple.

simple, never

Always make simple backups.

-C Do not overwrite file when the target exists and is identical to the new file. Preserve original timestamp.

-d, --directory

Create any missing directories.

-D Create leading components of destination except the last, then copy source to destination.

-g *group*, **--group** *group*

Set group ID of new file to *group* (privileged users only).

--help

Print help information and exit.

-m *mode*, **--mode** *mode*

Set permissions of new file to *mode* (octal or symbolic). By default, the mode is 0755.

-o [*owner*], **--owner**[*=owner*]

Set ownership to *owner* or, if unspecified, to root (privileged users only).

-p, --preserve-timestamps

Preserve access and modification times on source files and directories.

-P, --preserve-context

Preserve SELinux security context.

-s, --strip

Strip symbol tables.

-S *suffix*, **--suffix**=*suffix*
Use *suffix* instead of the default backup suffix, usually **~**.

-t *directory*, **--target-directory** *directory*
Copy SOURCE arguments into the specified directory.

-T, **--no-target-directory**
Treat *destination* as a normal file.

-v, **--verbose**
Print name of each directory as it is created.

--version
Print version, then exit.

---

ionice

ionice [*options*] [*program* [*arg*]]

Set the I/O scheduling class and priority for a program. The three possible scheduling classes are idle, best effort, and real time. The default is best effort. With no arguments or just **-p**, query the current class and priority for the process. Without **-p**, the program is run with the specified parameters.

Options

-c *n*
Set the scheduling class, where n is 1 for real time, 2 for best effort, and 3 for idle.

-h   Print help information and exit.

-n *n*
Define the scheduling class data for classes that accept it. For real time and best effort, *n* can be in the range 0–7.

-p *pid*
Specify the process id of a running program to be changed.

---

ip

ip [*options*] object command [*arguments*]

ip [*object* [*command*]] help

System administration command. Show and manipulate network devices and routing. This command is a part of the iproute2 utilities for controlling TCP and UDP IP networking and traffic control. It's meant to replace the **ifconfig**, **route**, and **arp** commands among others. On some distributions these utilities may be deprecated in favor of **ip**.

ip's subcommand syntax is very similar to the Cisco's IOS syntax used on many Cisco routers and switches. The **ip** command can be used to configure tunnels, load balancing and other traffic shaping. For brevity, we won't cover all of its features here. For more in-depth coverage, we recommend iproute2's Linux Foundation web pages at: *http://www.linuxfoundation.org/en/Net:Iproute2*.

Options

-s, --stats, --statistics

> Print statistics or time values. Use multiple times to increase the verbosity of output even more.

-f *protocol_family*, **--family** *protocol_family*

> Specify the protocol_family to use for the commands given. This may be **inet**, **inet6**, or **link**. The protocol_family **link** may be used to indicate no protocol is involved. The **ip** command also accepts shortcut options of **-4**, **-6**, and **-0** for families **inet**, **inet6**, and **link**.

-o, --oneline

> Format output as one line, replacing linefeeds with the '\' character. This is useful when piping output of **ip** to another command.

-r, --resolve

> Resolve IP addresses to host names. The default is to use IP addresses.

Commands

We will only cover commands for address, link, neighbor and route objects, and the syntax of the **help** command. These are the commands that replace **ifconfig**, **arp**, and **route**. (In IPv4 the neighbor table is known as the arp table.) Most objects and commands have a long name (or two) as well as one or more abbreviations. For example, the object **address** can be given as **address**, **addr**, or **a**. The commands **show** and **list** are interchangeable and can be abbreviated as **sh**, **s**, **li**, or **l**. Here we show the most commonly used form in examples and documentation:

help

> List command syntax, including applicable arguments. The syntax is given in a form similar to BNF grammar notation.

addr add *address*[*/netmask*] *arguments*

> Add a new protocol *address* to a device. The format of the address depends on the protocol (inet or inet6). A netmask may be given in CIDR notation. If no netmask is given, a mask of **/32** is assumed.

addr del *address*[*/netmask*] [*arguments*]

> Remove a protocol *address*.

addr show [*arguments*]

> Print current *addresses*.

link set *device_name* [*arguments*]

> Define or change settings on a network device.

link show [*device_name*]

> Print current settings for network devices.

neigh add *address* [*arguments*]

> Add a new entry to the neighbor table for the IPv4 or IPv6 *address*.

neigh chg *address* [*arguments*]

Change an existing entry in the neighbor table.

neigh del *address* [*arguments*]

Mark as invalid then remove an entry from the neighbor table when released from all clients.

neigh list [*address*] [*arguments*]

Add a new entry or change an existing one in the neighbor table.

neigh repl *address* [*arguments*]

Add a new entry or change an existing one in the neighbor table.

neigh flush *arguments*

Flush the specified entries from neighbors table. This command requires an argument, either an *address*, address prefix, **dev**, **nud**, or **unused** argument.

route add *address* [*arguments*]

Add a new entry to the routing table.

route chg *address* [*arguments*]

Change an existing entry in the routing table.

route del *address* [*arguments*]

Remove an entry from the routing.

route list [*arguments*]

Show current routing table entries. Use arguments to limit the entries shown.

route repl *address* [*arguments*]

Add a new entry or change an existing one in the routing table.

Common arguments

The following are common arguments for the above commands:

address *address*[*/netmask*]

Set a link layer address (i.e., MAC address) for a network device.

arp on, arp off

Set the arp flag of a network device on or off.

brd *address*

Set the broadcast address. Addresses for address objects may also be given as the symbols + or – meaning to set all the host bits of the broadcast address to 1 or 0. When used with a link object, this argument sets the link layer broadcast address instead.

dev *name*

The *name* of the network device to which the command applies (e.g., lo or eth0.) For link object commands you can omit **dev** and just pass the *name* as the first argument.

down, up

Change the state of a network device, disabling or enabling it (or limit shown devices to those with the specified state).

dynamic on, dynamic off

Set the dynamic flag of a network device on or off.

label *name*

Assign a label string of *name* to an address.

local *address*

The IPv4 or IPv6 address to use with addr object commands. For these commands you can omit **local** and just pass the *address* as the first argument.

lladdr *address*

Set a link layer address for a neighbors table entry.

mtu *n*

Set the maximum transfer unit (MTU) for a network device to *n*.

multicast on, multicast off

Set the multicast flag of a network device on or off.

nud *state*

Set the neighbor unreachability detection (nud) *state* of a neighbor entry. State values include:

noarp

Mark the entry as valid and not to be checked. It may be removed when it expires.

permanent

Like *noarp*, but a permanent entry can only be removed by an administrator.

reachable

Mark the entry as valid until its reachability timeout expires.

stale

Mark a new or changed entry as valid, but suspicious. The kernel will check stale entries at the first transmission.

promisc on, promisc off

Turn promiscuous mode on or off for a network device.

proto *protocol*

Set the routing *protocol*. The protocol identifies how a route was entered. If you are manually entering a route, the appropriate value for protocol should be **static**. If not specified the protocol defaults to **boot**.

scope *value*

Set the valid scope of an address or route entry. Valid values include **global**, **site**, **link**, and **host**. If used with the **show** command, only addresses of the given scope will be shown.

src *address*

The preferred IPv4 or IPv6 source address for a routing table entry.

to *address*

The IPv4 or IPv6 address or address prefix for a neighbor table or routing table entry. For **neigh** and route object commands you can omit the **to** and pass the address as the first argument. For route object commands you may also use the special address **default**, which is equivalent to an address of **0/0** or **/0**.

tos *key*

An 8-bit hexadecimal number or the IPv4 or IPv6 address or address prefix for a neighbor table or routing table entry. For **neigh** and route object commands you can omit the **to** and pass the address as the first argument.

txqlen *n*

Set the transmit queue length of a network device to *n*.

unused

When given with **neigh show**, show only unused entries.

via *address*

The address of the nexthop router (e.g., the Ipv4 or IPv6 address of the gateway). Used with **route** commands.

Examples

Show all configured network cards:

```
# ip link show
```

Bring down eth0:

```
# ip link set eth0 down
```

Add an IP address to device eth0 and label it "internal":

```
# ip addr add 192.186.0.32/24 brd + dev eth0 label internal
```

Show current routing table entries for device eth1:

```
# ip route list dev eth1
```

Add a router table entry for a private network on eth1 with gateway via 192.168.0.254:

```
# ip route add 10.0.0.1/8 via 192.168.0.254 dev eth1
```

Put eth0 into promiscuous mode in order to sniff traffic:

```
# ip link set eth0 promisc on
```

Add a permanent entry to the neighbors table (arp table) for eth1:

```
# ip neigh add 10.0.0.5 lladdr 52:54:00:32:5e:20 dev eth1
nud permanent
```

ipcrm

```
ipcrm [options]
```

System administration command. Remove interprocess communication (IPC) message queues, shared memory segments, or semaphore arrays. These may be specified either by numeric identifier or by key, using the following options.

Options

-m *identifier*, **-M** *key*
> Remove specified shared memory segment and its associated data structures after the last detach is performed.

-q *identifier*, **-Q** *key*
> Remove specified message queue and its associated data structures.

-s *identifier*, **-S** *key*
> Remove specified semaphore array and its associated data structures.

---

ipcs

ipcs [*options*]

System administration command. Print report on interprocess communication (IPC) message queues, shared memory segments, and semaphore arrays for which the current process has read access. Options can be used to specify the type of resources to report on and the output format of the report.

Options

Resource specification options:

-a Report on all IPC facilities: shared memory segments, message queues, and semaphore arrays. This is the default.

-m Report on shared memory segments.

-q Report on message queues.

-s Report on semaphore arrays.

Output format options:

-c Print creator and owner user IDs for IPC facilities.

-l Print resource maximum and minimum limits.

-p Print creator and last operation process identifiers.

-t Print attach, detach, and change times for shared memory segments; last operation and change times for semaphore arrays; and send, receive, and change times for message queues.

-u Print summary of current resource usage.

Other options:

-h Print help message, then exit.

-i *identifier*
> Used in combination with the **-m**, **-q**, or **-s** options. Report only on the resource specified by numeric *identifier*.

---

iptables

iptables *command* [*options*]

System administration command. Configure *netfilter* filtering rules for kernels 2.4 and later. Rules for **iptables** consist of some matching criteria and a target, a result to be applied if the packet matches the criteria. The rules are organized into chains. You can use these rules to build a firewall, masquerade your local area network, or just reject certain kinds of network connections.

There are three built-in tables for **iptables**: one for network filtering (**filter**), one for Network Address Translation (**nat**), and the last for specialized packet alterations (**mangle**). Firewall rules are organized into chains, ordered checklists of rules that the kernel works through looking for matches. The **filter** table has three built-in chains: **INPUT**, **OUTPUT**, and **FORWARD**. The **INPUT** and **OUTPUT** chains handle packets originating from or destined for the host system. The **FORWARD** chain handles packets just passing through the host system. The **nat** table also has three built-in chains: **PREROUTING**, **POSTROUTING**, and **OUTPUT**. **mangle** has only two chains: **PREROUTING** and **OUTPUT**.

netfilter checks packets entering the system. After applying any **PREROUTING** rules, it passes them to the **INPUT** chain, or to the **FORWARD** chain if the packet is just passing through. Upon leaving, the system packets are passed to the **OUTPUT** chain and then on to any **POSTROUTING** rules. Each of these chains has a default target (a policy) in case no match is found. User-defined chains can also be created and used as targets for packets but do not have default policies. If no match can be found in a user-defined chain, the packet is returned to the chain from which it was called and tested against the next rule in that chain.

iptables changes only the rules in the running kernel. When the system is powered off, all changes are lost. You can use the **iptables-save** command to make a script you can run with **iptables-restore** to restore your firewall settings. Such a script is often called at bootup. Many distributions have an **iptables** initialization script that uses the output from **iptables-save**.

Commands

iptables is almost always invoked with one of the following commands:

-A *chain rules*, --**append** *chain rules*
    Append new *rules* to *chain*.

-D *chain rules*, --**delete** *chain rules*
    Delete *rules* from *chain*. Rules can be specified by their ordinal number in the chain as well as by a general rule description.

-E *old-chain new-chain*, --**rename-chain** *old-chain new-chain*
    Rename *old-chain* to *new-chain*.

-F [*chain*], --**flush** [*chain*]
    Remove all rules from *chain*, or from all chains if *chain* is not specified.

-I *chain number rules*, --**insert** *chain number rules*
    Insert *rules* into *chain* at the ordinal position given by *number*.

-L [*chain*], --**list** [*chain*]
    List the rules in *chain*, or all chains if *chain* is not specified.

-N *chain*, --**new-chain** *chain*
    Create a new *chain*. The chain's name must be unique. This is how user-defined chains are created.

-P *chain target*, **--policy** *chain target*
> Set the default policy for a built-in *chain*; the target itself cannot be a chain.

-R *chain number rule*, **--replace** *chain number rule*
> Replace a rule in *chain*. The rule to be replaced is specified by its ordinal *number*.

-X [*chain*], **--delete-chain** [*chain*]
> Delete the specified user-defined *chain*, or all user-defined chains if *chain* is not specified.

-Z [*chain*], **--zero** [*chain*]
> Zero the packet and byte counters in *chain*. If no chain is specified, all chains will be reset. When used without specifying a chain and combined with the **-L** command, list the current counter values before they are reset.

Targets

A target may be the name of a chain or one of the following special values:

ACCEPT
> Let the packet through.

DROP
> Drop the packet.

QUEUE
> Send packets to the user space for processing.

RETURN
> Stop traversing the current chain and return to the point in the previous chain from which this one was called. If **RETURN** is the target of a rule in a built-in chain, the built-in chain's default policy is applied.

Rule specification parameters

These options are used to create rules for use with the preceding commands. Rules consist of some matching criteria and usually a target to jump to (**-j**) if the match is made. Many of the parameters for these matching rules can be expressed as a negative with an exclamation point (!) meaning "not." Those rules will match everything except the given parameter.

-c *packets bytes*, **--set-counters** *packets bytes*
> Initialize packet and byte counters to the specified values.

-d [!] *address*[*/mask*] [!] [*port*], **--destination** [!] *address*[*/mask*] [*port*]
> Match packets from the destination *address*. The address may be supplied as a hostname, a network name, or an IP address. The optional mask is the netmask to use and may be supplied either in the traditional form (e.g., /255.255.255.0) or in the modern form (e.g., /24).

[!] -f, **[!]--fragment**
> The rule applies only to the second or further fragments of a fragmented packet.

-i [!] *name*[+], **--in-interface** *name*[+]

Match packets being received from interface *name*. *name* is the network interface used by your system (e.g., **eth0** or **ppp0**). A + can be used as a wildcard, so **ppp+** would match any interface name beginning with **ppp**.

-j *target*, **--jump** *target*

Jump to a special target or a user-defined chain. If this option is not specified for a rule, matching the rule only increases the rule's counters, and the packet is tested against the next rule.

-o [!] *name*[+], **--out-interface** *name*[+]

Match packets being sent from interface *name*. See the description of **-i** for the syntax for *name*.

-p [!] *name*, **--protocol** [!] *name*

Match packets of protocol *name*. The value of *name* can be given as a name or number, as found in the file */etc/protocols*. The most common values are **tcp**, **udp**, **icmp**, or the special value **all**. The number **0** is equivalent to **all**, and this is the default value when this option is not used. If there are extended matching rules associated with the specified protocol, they will be loaded automatically. You need not use the **-m** option to load them.

-s [!] *address*[/*mask*] [!] [*port*], **--source** [!] *address*[/*mask*] [!] [*port*]

Match packets with the source *address*. See the description of **-d** for the syntax of this option.

Options

-h [icmp], **--help** [icmp]

Print help message. If **icmp** is specified, a list of valid ICMP type names will be printed. **-h** can also be used with the **-m** option to get help on an extension module.

--line-numbers

Used with the **-L** command. Add the line number to the beginning of each rule in a listing, indicating its position in the chain.

-m *module*, **--match** *module*

Explicitly load matching rule extensions associated with *module*. See the next section.

--modprobe=*command*

Use specified *command* to load any necessary kernel modules while adding or inserting rules into a chain.

-n, **--numeric**

Print all IP address and port numbers in numeric form. By default, text names are displayed when possible.

-t *name*, **--table** *name*

Apply rules to the specified table. Rules apply to the filter table by default.

-v, **--verbose**

Verbose mode.

-x, --exact

> Expand all numbers in a listing (**-L**). Display the exact value of the packet and byte counters instead of rounded figures.

Match extensions

Several modules extend the matching capabilities of netfilter rules. Using the **-p** option will cause **iptables** to load associated modules implicitly. Others need to be loaded explicitly with the **-m** or **--match** options. Here we document those modules used most frequently.

icmp

> Loaded when **-p icmp** is the only protocol specified:
>
> **--icmp-type [!]** *type*
>
> > Match the specified ICMP *type*. *type* may be a numeric ICMP type or one of the ICMP type names shown by the command **iptables -p icmp -h**.

multiport

> Loaded explicitly with the **-m** option. The **multiport** extensions match sets of source or destination ports. These rules can be used only in conjunction with **-p tcp** and **-p udp**. Up to 15 ports can be specified in a comma-separated list:
>
> **--source-port** [*ports*]
>
> > Match the given source *ports*.
>
> **--destination-port** [*ports*]
>
> > Match the given destination *ports*.
>
> **--port** [*ports*]
>
> > Match if the packet has the same source and destination port and that port is one of the given *ports*.

state

> Loaded explicitly with the **-m** option. This module matches the connection state of a packet:
>
> **--state** *states*
>
> > Match the packet if it has one of the states in the comma-separated list *states*. Valid states are **INVALID, ESTABLISHED, NEW**, and **RELATED**.

tcp

> Loaded when **-p tcp** is the only protocol specified:
>
> **--source-port [!]** [*port*][*:port*], **--sport [!]** [*port*][*:port*]
>
> > Match the specified source ports. Using the colon specifies an inclusive range of services to match. If the first port is omitted, 0 is the default. If the second port is omitted, 65535 is the default. You can also use a dash instead of a colon to specify the range.
>
> **--destination-port [!]** [*port*][*:port*], **--dport [!]** [*port*][*:port*]
>
> > Match the specified destination ports. The syntax is the same as for **--source-port**.
>
> **--mss** *n*[*:n*]
>
> > Match if TCP SYN or SYN/ACK packets have the specified MSS value or fall within the specified range. Use this to control the maximum packet size for a connection.

[!] --syn

> Match packets with the SYN bit set and the ACK and FIN bits cleared. These are packets that request TCP connections; blocking them prevents incoming connections. Shorthand for **--tcp-flags SYN,RST,ACK SYN**.

--tcp-flags [!] *mask comp*

> Match the packets with the TCP flags specified by *mask* and *comp*. *mask* is a comma-separated list of flags that should be examined. *comp* is a comma-separated list of flags that must be set for the rule to match. Valid flags are **SYN, ACK, FIN, RST, URG, PSH, ALL**, and **NONE**.

--tcp-option [!] *n*

> Match if TCP option is set.

udp

> Loaded when **-p udp** is the only protocol specified:

--source-port [!] *[port][:port]*, **--sport [!]** *[port][:port]*

> Match the specified source ports. The syntax is the same as for the **--source-port** option of the TCP extension.

--destination-port [!] *[port][:port]*, **--dport [!]** *[port][:port]*

> Match the specified destination ports. The syntax is the same as for the **--source-port** option of the TCP extension.

Target extensions

Extension targets are optional additional targets supported by separate kernel modules. They have their own associated options. We cover the most frequently used target extensions below.

DNAT

> Modify the destination address of the packet and all future packets in the current connection. **DNAT** is valid only as a part of the **POSTROUTING** chain in the **nat** table:

--to-destination *address[-address][port-port]*

> Specify the new destination address or range of addresses. The arguments for this option are the same as the **--to-source** argument for the **SNAT** extension target.

LOG

> Log the packet's information in the system log:

--log-level *level*

> Set the syslog level by name or number (as defined by *syslog.conf*).

--log-prefix *prefix*

> Begin each log entry with the string *prefix*. The prefix string may be up to 30 characters long.

--log-tcp-sequence

> Log the TCP sequence numbers. This is a security risk if your log is readable by users.

--log-tcp-options

> Log options from the TCP packet header.

--log-ip-options

> Log options from the IP packet header.

MASQUERADE

Masquerade the packet so it appears that it originated from the current system. Reverse packets from masqueraded connections are unmasqueraded automatically. This is a legal target only for chains in the **nat** table that handle incoming packets and should be used only with dynamic IP addresses (like dial-up.) For static addresses use **DNAT**:

--to-ports *port*[*-port*]

Specify the port or range of ports to use when masquerading. This option is valid only if a **tcp** or **udp** protocol has been specified with the **-p** option. If this option is not used, the masqueraded packet's port will not be changed.

REJECT

Drop the packet and, if appropriate, send an ICMP message back to the sender indicating the packet was dropped. If the packet was an ICMP error message, an unknown ICMP type, or a nonhead fragment, or if too many ICMP messages have already been sent to this address, no message is sent:

--reject-with *type*

Send specified ICMP message type. Valid values are **icmp-net-unreachable**, **icmp-host-unreachable**, **icmp-port-unreachable**, or **icmp-proto-unreachable**. If the packet was an ICMP ping packet, *type* may also be **echo-reply**.

SNAT

Modify the source address of the packet and all future packets in the current connection. **SNAT** is valid only as a part of the **POSTROUTING** chain in the **nat** table:

--to-source *address*[*-address*][*port-port*]

Specify the new source address or range of addresses. If a **tcp** or **udp** protocol has been specified with the **-p** option, source ports may also be specified. If none is specified, map the new source to the same port if possible. If not, map ports below 512 to other ports below 512, those between 512 and 1024 to other ports below 1024, and ports above 1024 to other ports above 1024.

Examples

To reject all incoming ICMP traffic on eth0:

```
iptables -A INPUT -p ICMP -i eth0 -j  REJECT
```

---

iptables-restore   iptables-restore [*options*]

System administration command. Restore firewall rules from information provided on standard input. **iptables-restore** takes commands generated by **iptables-save** and uses them to restore the firewall rules for each chain. This is often used by initialization scripts to restore firewall settings on boot.

Options

-c, --counters
> Restore packet and byte counter values.

-n, --noflush
> Don't delete previous table contents.

---

iptables-save   `iptables-save [options]`

System administration command. Print the IP firewall rules currently stored in the kernel to stdout. Output may be redirected to a file that can later be used by **iptables-restore** to restore the firewall.

Options

-c, --counters
> Save packet and byte counter values.

-t *name*, **--table** *name*
> Print data from the specified table only.

---

isodump   `isodump isoimage`

Interactively display the contents of the ISO9660 image *isoimage*. Used to verify the integrity of the directory inside the image. **isodump** displays the first portion of the root directory and waits for commands. The prompt shows the extent number (zone) and offset within the extent, and the contents display at the top of the screen.

Commands

+   Search forward for the next instance of the search string.

a   Search backward within the image.

b   Search forward within the image.

f   Prompt for a new search string.

g   Prompt for a new starting block and go there.

q   Exit.

---

isoinfo   `isoinfo [options]`

Display information about ISO9660 images. You can use **isoinfo** to list the contents of an image, extract a file, or generate a **find**-like file list. The **-i** option is required to specify the image to examine.

Options

-d   Print information from the primary volume descriptor (PVD) of the ISO9660 image, including information about Rock Ridge and Joliet extensions if they are present.

dev=*target*
> Set the SCSI target for the drive.

-f Generate output similar to the output of a **find . -print** command. Do not use with -l.

-h Print help information and exit.

-i *isoimage*
  Specify the path for the ISO9660 image to examine.

-j *charset*
  Convert any Joliet filenames to the specified character set.

-J Extract filename information from any Joliet extensions.

-l Generate output similar to the output of an **ls -lR** command. Do not use with **-f**.

-N *sector*
  To help examine single-session CD files that are to be written to a multisession CD. Specify the sector number at which the ISO9660 image is to be written when sent to the CD writer.

-p Display path table information.

-R Extract permission, filename, and ownership information from any Rock Ridge extensions.

-T *sector*
  To help examine multisession images that have already been burned to a multisession CD. Use the specified sector number as the start of the session to display.

-x *path*
  Extract the file at the specified path to standard output.

isosize

isosize [*option*] iso9660-img-file

Display the length of an ISO9660 filesystem contained in the specified file. The image file can be a normal file or a block device such as */dev/sr0*. With no options, the length is displayed in bytes. Only one of the two options can be specified.

Options

-d *num*
  Display the size in bytes divided by *num*.

-x Display the number of blocks and the block size (although the output refers to blocks as sectors).

isovfy

isovfy *isoimage*

Verify the integrity of the specified ISO9660 image and write the results to standard output.

ispell

ispell [*options*] [*files*]

Compare the words of one or more named *files* with the system dictionary. Display unrecognized words at the top of the screen, accompanied by possible correct spellings, and allow editing via a series of single-character commands that are case-insensitive.

Options

-b Back up original file in *filename.bak*.

-B Count two correctly spelled words without a space between them as a spelling error.

-C Count two correctly spelled words without a space between them as a legitimate compound word.

-d *file*
Search *file* instead of standard dictionary file.

-H File is in HTML/XML format.

-L *number*
Show *number* lines of context.

-m Suggest combinations of known roots and affixes, even if the result is not known. For example, "generous" and "ly" are known, so "generously" would be suggested as a word, even if it were not in the dictionary.

-M List interactive commands at bottom of screen.

-n Expect **nroff** or **troff** input file.

-N Suppress printing of interactive commands.

-p *file*
Search *file* instead of personal dictionary file.

-P Do not guess new words using known roots and affixes. The opposite of **-m**.

-S Sort suggested replacements by likelihood that they are correct.

-t Expect TEX or LATEX input file.

-T *type*
Expect all files to be formatted by *type*.

-V Use hat notation (^L) to display control characters, and **M-** to display characters with the high bit set.

-w *chars*
Consider *chars* to be legal, in addition to a–z and A–Z.

-W *n*
Never consider words that are *n* characters or fewer to be misspelled.

-x Do not back up original file.

Interactive commands

? Display help screen.

space
Accept the word in this instance.

number
Replace with suggested word that corresponds to *number*.

!*command*
Invoke shell and execute *command* in it. Prompt before exiting.

a	Accept word as correctly spelled, but do not add it to personal dictionary.
i	Accept word and add it (with any current capitalization) to personal dictionary.
l	Search system dictionary for words.
q	Exit without saving.
r	Replace word.
u	Accept word and add lowercase version of it to personal dictionary.
x	Skip to the next file, saving changes.
^L	Redraw screen.
^Z	Suspend **ispell**.

join

join [*options*] *file1 file2*

Join lines of two sorted files by matching on a common field. If either *file1* or *file2* is -, read from standard input. Often used to merge data stored in text-based file formats such as comma-separated-value formatted spreadsheets.

Options

-1 *fieldnum1*
> The join field in *file1* is *fieldnum1*. Default is the first field.

-2 *fieldnum2*
> The join field in *file2* is *fieldnum2*. Default is the first field.

-a *filenum*
> Print a line for each unpairable line in file *filenum*, in addition to the normal output.

--check-order, --nocheck-order
> Check or do not check that the files are correctly sorted on the join fields.

-e *string*
> Replace missing input fields with *string*.

-i, --ignore-case
> Ignore case differences when comparing fields.

-o *fieldlist*
> Order the output fields according to *fieldlist*, where each entry in the list is in the form *filenum.fieldnum*. Entries are separated by commas or blanks.

-t *char*
> Specifies the field-separator character (default is whitespace).

-v *filenum*
> Print only unpairable lines from file *filenum*.

--help
> Print help message and then exit.

--version
> Print the version number and then exit.

kbd_mode

kbd_mode [*option*]

Print or set the current keyboard mode, which may be **RAW**, **MEDIUMRAW**, **XLATE**, or **UNICODE**.

Options

-a   Set mode to **XLATE** (ASCII mode).

-k   Set mode to **MEDIUMRAW** (keycode mode).

-s   Set mode to **RAW** (scancode mode).

-u   Set mode to **UNICODE** (UTF-8 mode).

---

kbdrate

kbdrate [*options*]

System administration command. Control the rate at which the keyboard repeats characters, as well as its delay time. Using this command without options sets a repeat rate of 10.9 characters per second; the default delay is 250 milliseconds. On boot, most Linux systems set the keyboard rate to 30 characters per second.

Options

-d *delay*

Specify the delay, which must be one of the following (in milliseconds): **250**, **500**, **750**, or **1000**.

-r *rate*

Specify the repeat rate, which must be one of the following numbers (all in characters per second): **2.0**, **2.1**, **2.3**, **2.5**, **2.7**, **3.0**, **3.3**, **3.7**, **4.0**, **4.3**, **4.6**, **5.0**, **5.5**, **6.0**, **6.7**, **7.5**, **8.0**, **8.6**, **9.2**, **10.0**, **10.9**, **12.0**, **13.3**, **15.0**, **16.0**, **17.1**, **18.5**, **20.0**, **21.8**, **24.0**, **26.7**, or **30.0**.

-s   Suppress printing of messages.

-V   Print version number and exit.

---

kill

kill [*options*] [*pids*]

Send a signal to terminate one or more process IDs. You must own the process or be a privileged user. If no signal is specified, TERM is sent.

This entry describes the **/bin/kill** command. There are also built-in shell commands of the same name; the **bash** version is described in Chapter 6.

In some Linux distributions, **/bin/kill** allows you to specify a command name, such as **gcc** or **xpdf**, instead of a process ID (PID). All processes running that command with the same UID as the process issuing **/bin/kill** are sent the signal.

If **/bin/kill** is issued with a *pid* of **0**, it sends the signal to all processes of its own process group. If **/bin/kill** is issued with a *pid* of **-1**, it sends the signal to all processes except process 1 (the system's *init* process).

Linux
Commands

Options

-a   Kill all processes of the given name (if privileges allow), not just processes with the same UID. To use this option, specify the full path (e.g., **/bin/kill -a gcc**).

-l   List all signals.

-p   Print the process ID of the named process, but don't send it a signal. To use this option, specify the full path (e.g., **/bin/kill -p**).

-s *SIGNAL*, *-SIGNAL*

    The signal number (from */usr/include/sys/signal.h*) or name (from **kill -l**). With a signal number of **9** (KILL), the kill cannot be caught by the process; use this to kill a process that a plain **kill** doesn't terminate. The default signal is TERM. The letter flag itself is optional: both **kill -9 1024** and **kill -s 9 1024** terminate process 1024.

---

killall

```
killall [options] names
```

Kill processes by command name. If more than one process is running the specified command, kill all of them. Treats command names that contain a **/** as files; kill all processes that are executing that file.

Options

-e, --exact

    Require an exact match to kill very long names (i.e., longer than 15 characters). Normally, **killall** kills everything that matches within the first 15 characters. With **-e**, such entries are skipped. (Use **-v** to print a message for each skipped entry.)

-g, --process-group

    Kill the process group to which the process belongs.

-i, --interactive

    Prompt for confirmation before killing processes.

-I, --ignore-case

    Ignore case when matching process names.

-l, --list

    List known signal names.

-q, --quiet

    Quiet; do not complain of processes not killed.

-r, --regexp

    Interpret process name as an extended regular expression.

-s *signal*, --signal *signal*

    Send *signal* to named processes. *signal* may be a name or a number. The most commonly used signal is **9**, which terminates processes no matter what. The default signal is SIGTERM.

-u *user*, --user *user*

    Kill only processes owned by the specified user.

-v, --verbose

Verbose; after killing process, report success and process ID.

-V, --version

Print version information.

-w, --wait

Wait for all killed processes to die. Note that **killall** may wait forever if the signal was ignored or had no effect, or if the process stays in zombie state.

---

klogd

klogd [*options*]

System administration command. Control which kernel messages are displayed on the console, prioritize all messages, and log them through **syslogd**. On many operating systems, **syslogd** performs all the work of **klogd**, but on Linux the features are separated. Kernel messages are gleaned from the */proc* filesystem and from system calls to **syslogd**. By default, no messages appear on the console. Messages are sorted into eight levels, 0–7, and the level number is prepended to each message.

Priority levels

0   Emergency situation (**KERN_EMERG**).

1   A crucial error has occurred (**KERN_ALERT**).

2   A serious error has occurred (**KERN_CRIT**).

3   An error has occurred (**KERN_ERR**).

4   A warning message (**KERN_WARNING**).

5   The situation is normal but should be checked (**KERN_NOTICE**).

6   Information only (**KERN_INFO**).

7   Debugging message (**KERN_DEBUG**).

Options

-c *level*

Print all messages of a higher priority (lower number) than *level* to the console.

-d   Debugging mode.

-f *file*

Print all messages to *file*; suppress normal logging.

-i   Signal executing daemon to reload kernel module symbols.

-I   Signal executing daemon to reload both static kernel symbols and kernel module symbols.

-k *file*

Use *file* as source of kernel symbols.

-n   Avoid auto-backgrounding. This is needed when **klogd** is started from **init**.

-o   One-shot mode. Prioritize and log all current messages, then immediately exit.

-p   Reload kernel-module symbol information whenever an Oops string is detected.

-P *file*
> Use *file* as the source for kernel messages instead of */proc/kmsg*.

-s   Suppress reading of messages from the */proc* filesystem. Read from kernel message buffers instead.

-v   Print version, then exit.

-x   Don't translate instruction pointers (EIP). **klogd** will not read the *System.map* file.

-2   Print two lines for each symbol, one showing the symbol and the other showing its numerical value (address).

Files

/usr/include/linux/kernel.h, */usr/include/sys/syslog.h*
> Sources for definitions of each logging level.

/proc/kmsg
> A file examined by **klogd** for messages.

/var/run/klogd.pid
> **klogd**'s process ID.

---

last

last [*options*] [*username*] [*ttynumber*]

Display a list of the most recent logins, taken from the file */var/log/wtmp* by default. If you specify a tty number or username, the output displays only the logins for that user or terminal.

Options

-a   Display the hostname from which logins originated in the last column.

-d   For remote logins, display both IP address and hostname.

-f *filename*
> Get the list of logins from *filename*. The default source is */var/log/wtmp*.

-i   Like **–d**, but display the IP address in numbers-and-dots notation.

-n *number*, *-number*
> Choose how many lines of logins to display. Thus, **last -7** or **last -n 7** displays seven lines.

-R   Do not show the hostname.

-x   Display shutdown messages and runlevel messages.

---

lastb

lastb [*options*] [*username*] [*ttynumber*]

Display a list of recent bad login attempts (from the */var/log/btmp* file). Accepts the same option flags and arguments as **last**.

lastlog

lastlog [*options*]

System administration command. Print the last login times for system accounts. Login information is read from the file */var/log/lastlog*.

Options

-t*n*, **--time***n*
> Print only logins more recent than *n* days ago.

-u*name*, **--user***name*
> Print only login information for user *name*.

ld

ld [*options*] *objfiles*

Combine several *objfiles*, in the specified order, into a single executable object module (*a.out* by default). **ld** is the link editor and is often invoked automatically by compiler commands. **ld** accepts many options, the most common of which are listed here.

Options

-b *format*, **--format**=*format*
> If **ld** is configured to accept more than one kind of object file, this option can be used to specify the input format. *format* should be a GNU Binary File Descriptor (BFD), as described in the BFD library. Use **objdump -i** to list available formats.

-call_shared
> Link with dynamic libraries.

-d, **-dc**, **-dp**
> Force the assignment of space to common symbols.

-defsym *symbol=expression*
> Create the global *symbol* with the value *expression*.

-demangle[*=style*]
> Force demangling of symbol names. Optionally set the demangling style. Turn off demangling with **-nodemangle**.

-e *symbol*
> Set *symbol* as the address of the output file's entry point.

-f *name*
> Set the **DT_AUXILIARY** field of ELF shared object to *name*.

-fini *name*
> Set the **DT_FINI** field of ELF shared object to the address of function *name*. The default function is **_fini**.

-h *name*
> Set the **DT_SONAME** field of ELF shared object to *name*.

--help
> Print help message, then exit.

-i Produce a linkable output file; attempt to set its magic number to OMAGIC.

-init *name*

Set the **DT_INIT** field of ELF shared object to the address of function *name*. The default function is **_init**.

-l*arch*, **--library**=*archive*

Include the archive file *arch* in the list of files to link.

-m *linker*

Emulate *linker*. List supported emulations with the **-V** option.

-n   Make text read-only; attempt to set NMAGIC.

-o *output*

Place output in *output*, instead of in *a.out*.

-oformat *format*

Specify output format.

-q   Retain relocation sections and contents in linked executables.

-r   Produce a linkable output file; attempt to set its magic number to OMAGIC.

-rpath *dir*

Add directory *dir* to the runtime library search path. Ignore additional paths normally read from the **LD_RUN_PATH** environment variable.

-rpath-link *dirs*

Specify path to search for shared libraries required by another shared library. The *dirs* argument can be a single directory, or multiple directories separated by colons. This overrides search paths specified in shared libraries themselves.

-s   Do not include any symbol information in output.

-shared

Create a shared library.

-static

Do not link with shared libraries.

-sort-common

Do not sort global common symbols by size.

-t   Print each input file's name as it is processed.

--target-help

Print target-specific options, then exit.

-u *symbol*

Force *symbol* to be undefined.

-v, **--version**

Show version number.

--verbose

Print information about **ld**; print the names of input files while attempting to open them.

--warn-common

Warn when encountering common symbols combined with other constructs.

--warn-once

Provide only one warning per undefined symbol.

-x With **-s** or **-S**, delete all local symbols. These generally begin with **L**.

-z *keyword*

Mark the object for special behavior specified by *keyword*. **ld** recognizes the following keywords:

combreloc

Object combines and sorts multiple relocation sections for dynamic symbol lookup caching.

defs

Disallow undefined symbols.

initfirst

Initialize object first at runtime.

execstack

Marks the object as requiring an executable stack.

interpose

Interpose object's symbol table before all but the primary executable's symbol table.

loadfltr

Process object's filter immediately at runtime.

multidefs

Allow multiple definitions of a single symbol. Use the first definition.

nocombreloc

Disable combining multiple relocation sections.

nocopyreloc

Disable copy relocation.

nodefaultlib

Ignore default library search path when seeking dependencies for object.

nodelete

Do not unload object at runtime.

nodlopen

Object is not available to **dlopen**.

nodump

Object cannot be dumped by **dldump**.

now

Non-lazy runtime binding.

origin

Object may contain *$ORIGIN*.

relro

Create an ELF *PT_GNU_RELRO* segment header in the object.

-E, --export-dynamic

Add all symbols to dynamic symbol table, not just those referenced by linked objects.

-EB
> Link big-endian objects.

-EL
> Link little-endian objects.

-F *name*
> Set **DT_FILTER** field of ELF shared object to *name*.

-L*dir*, **--library-path=***dir*
> Search directory *dir* before standard search directories (this option must precede the -l option that searches that directory).

-M   Display a link map on standard output.

-Map *file*
> Print a link map to *file*.

-N   Allow reading of and writing to both data and text. Mark ouput if it supports Unix magic numbers. Do not page-align data.

-O *level*
> Optimize. *level* should be **1**, **2**, **3**, or **0**. The default is 1. 0 turns off optimization; 3 optimizes the most.

-R *file*
> Obtain symbol names and addresses from *file*, but suppress relocation of *file* and its inclusion in output.

-S   Do not include debugger symbol information in output.

-T *file*
> Execute script *file* instead of the default linker script.

-Tbss *address*
> Begin bss segment of output at *address*.

-Tdata *address*
> Begin data segment of output at *address*.

-Ttext *address*
> Begin text segment of output at *address*.

-Ur
> Synonymous with **-r** except when linking C++ programs, where it resolves constructor references.

-X   With **-s** or **-S**, delete local symbols beginning with **L**.

-V   Show version number and emulation linkers for **-m** option.

ldconfig

    ldconfig [options] directories

System administration command. Examine the libraries in the given *directories*, */etc/ld.so.conf.d*, */usr/lib*, and */lib*; update links and cache where necessary. Usually run in startup files or after the installation of new shared libraries.

Options

-C *filename*
> Use *filename* instead of */etc/ld.so.cache*.

-**f** *filename*
> Use *filename* instead of */etc/ld.so.conf*.

-**l** Library mode. Expect libraries as arguments, not directories. Manually link specified libraries.

-**n** Suppress examination of */usr/lib* and */lib* and reading of */etc/ld. so.conf*; do not cache.

-**N** Do not cache; only link.

-**p** Print all directories and candidate libraries in the cache. Used without arguments.

-**v** Verbose mode. Include version number, and announce each directory as it is scanned and links as they are created.

-**X** Do not link; only rebuild cache.

Files
/lib/ld.so
> Linker and loader.

/etc/ld.so.conf
> List of directories that contain libraries.

/etc/ld.so.cache
> List of the libraries found in those libraries mentioned in */etc/ ld.so.conf*.

---

ldd

ldd [*options*] *programs*

Display a list of the shared libraries each *program* requires.

Options
-**d**, --**data-relocs**
> Process data relocations. Report missing objects (for ELF objects only).

-**r**, --**function-relocs**
> Process relocations for both data objects and functions. Report any that are missing (for ELF objects only).

-**v**, --**verbose**
> Verbose mode. Display extra information, including symbol versions.

--**help**
> Print help message, then exit.

--**version**
> Display the linker's version, then exit.

---

less

less [*options*] [*filename*]

less is a program for paging through files or other output. It was written in reaction to the perceived primitiveness of **more** (hence its name) and allows backward as well as forward paging. Some commands may be preceded by a number.

Options

-[z]*num***, --window=***num*

> Set number of lines to scroll to *num*. Default is one screenful. A negative *num* sets the number to *num* lines less than the current number.

+[+]*command*

> Run *command* on startup. If *command* is a number, jump to that line. The option ++ applies this command to each file in the command-line list.

-?, --help

> Print help screen.

-a, --search-skip-screen

> When searching, begin after last line currently displayed. (Default is to search from second line displayed.)

-b*buff***, --buffers=***buff*

> Specify the amount of buffer space to use for each file in 1 KB units. (Default is to use 64 KB per file.)

-B, --auto-buffers

> Do not automatically allocate buffer space to hold all data read from a pipe. If **-b** is specified, allocate that amount of space, or default to 64 KB. If necessary, allow information from previous screens to be lost.

-c, --clear-screen

> Redraw screen from top, not bottom.

-f, --force

> Force opening of directories and devices; do not print warning when opening binaries.

-F, --quit-if-one-screen

> Exit without displaying anything if first file can fit on a single screen.

-g, --hilite-search

> Highlight only string found by past search command, not all matching strings.

-G, --HILITE-SEARCH

> Never highlight matching search strings.

-h*num***, --max-back-scroll=***num*

> Never scroll backward more than *num* lines at once.

-i, --ignore-case

> Make searches case-insensitive, unless the search string contains uppercase letters.

-I, --IGNORE-CASE

> Make searches case-insensitive, even when the search string contains uppercase letters.

-j*num***, --jump-target=***num*

> Position target line on line *num* of screen. Target line can be the result of a search or a jump. Count lines beginning from 1 (top line). A negative *num* is counted back from bottom of screen.

-k*file*, **--lesskey-file**=*file*
> Read *file* to define special key bindings. See **lesskey** for more information.

-K, **--quit-on-intr**
> Exit immediately on interrupt (usually ^-C).

-m, **--long-prompt**
> Display **more**-like prompt, including percent of file read.

-M, **--LONG-PROMPT**
> Prompt more verbosely than with **-m**, including percentage, line number, and total lines.

-n, **--line-numbers**
> Do not calculate line numbers. Affects **-m** and **-M** options and = and **v** commands (disables passing of line number to editor).

-N, **--LINE-NUMBERS**
> Print line number before each line.

-o*file*, **--log-file**=*file*
> When input is from a pipe, copy output to *file* as well as to screen. (Prompt for overwrite authority if *file* exists.)

-O *file*, **--LOG-FILE**=*file*
> Similar to **-o**, but do not prompt when overwriting file.

-p*pattern*, **--pattern**=*pattern*
> At startup, search for first occurrence of *pattern*.

-P[**mM**=]*prompt*
> Set the prompt displayed by **less** at the bottom of each screen to *prompt*. The **m** sets the prompt invoked by the **-m** option, the **M** sets the prompt invoked by the **-M** option, and the = sets the prompt invoked by the = command. Special characters (described in the **less** manpage), can be used to print statistics and other information in these prompts.

-q, **--quiet**, **--silent**
> Disable ringing of bell on attempts to scroll past EOF or before beginning of file. Attempt to use visual bell instead.

-Q, **--QUIET**, **--SILENT**
> Never ring terminal bell.

-r, **--raw-control-chars**
> Display "raw" control characters instead of using ^*x* notation. This sometimes leads to display problems, which might be fixed by using **-R** instead.

-R, **--RAW-CONTROL-CHARS**
> Like **r**, but only output "raw" ANSI color escape characters.

-s, **--squeeze-blank-lines**
> Print successive blank lines as one line.

-S, **--chop-long-lines**
> Cut, do not fold, long lines.

-t*tag*, **--tag**=*tag*
> Edit file containing *tag*. Consult *./tags* (constructed by **ctags**).

Linux
Commands

-T *file*, **--tag-file=***file*

With the **-t** option or **:t** command, read *file* instead of *./tags*.

-u, **--underline-special**

Treat backspaces and carriage returns as printable input characters.

-U, **--UNDERLINE-SPECIAL**

Treat backspaces, tabs and carriage returns as control characters.

-V, **--version**

Display version and exit.

-w, **--hilite-unread**

Show the line to which a movement command has skipped, phrases displayed by a search command, or the first unread line during a normal scroll by highlighting text in reverse video.

-W, **--HILITE-UNREAD**

Show phrases displayed by a search command, or the first unread line of any forward movement that is more than one line, by highlighting text in reverse video.

-x *n...*, **--tabs=***n...*

Set tab stops to every *n* characters. Default is 8. If multiple values are given for *n* in a comma-separated list, set the tab stops to those values.

-X, **--no-init**

Do not send initialization and deinitialization strings from termcap to terminal.

-y *n*, **--max-forw-scroll=***n*

Never scroll forward more than *n* lines at once.

Commands

Many commands can be preceded by a numeric argument, referred to as *number* in the command descriptions.

SPACE, ^V, f, ^F

Scroll forward the specified *number* of lines (default one windowful).

ESC-SPACE

Like **SPACE**, but scroll forward a complete screenful.

z   Similar to **SPACE**, but if *number* is specified, reset the default to that number.

RETURN, ^N, e, ^E, j, ^J

Scroll forward. Default is one line. Display all lines, even if the default is more lines than the screen size.

d, ^D, PageDown

Scroll forward. Default is one-half the screen size. The number of lines may be specified, in which case the default is reset.

b, ^B, ESC-v

Scroll backward, but if *number* is specified, scroll back that number of lines. Default is one windowful.

w   Like **b**, but if *number* is specified, reset the default to that number.

y, ^Y, ^P, k, ^K
> Scroll backward. Default is one line. Display all lines, even if the default is more lines than the screen size.

u, ^U, PageUp
> Scroll backward. Default is one-half the screen size. The number of lines may be specified, in which case the default is reset.

r, ^R, ^L
> Redraw screen.

R   Like **r**, but discard buffered input.

F   Scroll forward. On EOF, continue trying to find more output, behaving similarly to **tail -f**.

g, <, ESC-<
> Skip to a line. Default is 1.

G, >, ESC->
> Skip to a line. Default is the last line.

p, %
> Skip to a position *number* percent of the way into the file.

{   If the top line on the screen includes a {, find its matching }. If the top line contains multiple {s, use *number* to determine which one to use in finding a match.

}   If the bottom line on the screen includes a }, find its matching {. If the bottom line contains multiple }s, use *number* to determine which one to use in finding a match.

(If the top line on the screen includes a (, find its matching). If the top line contains multiple (s, use *number* to determine which one to use in finding a match.

)   If the bottom line on the screen includes a), find its matching (. If the bottom line contains multiple)s, use *number* to determine which one to use in finding a match.

[If the top line on the screen includes a [, find its matching]. If the top line contains multiple [s, use *number* to determine which one to use in finding a match.

]   If the bottom line on the screen includes a], find its matching [. If the bottom line contains multiple]s, use *number* to determine which one to use in finding a match.

ESC-^F *char1 char2*
> Behave like { but substitute *char1* and *char2* for { and } in the search.

ESC-^B *char1 char2*
> Behave like } but substitute *char1* and *char2* for { and } in the search.

m *let*
> Use the specified lowercase letter to mark the current position.

Linux Commands

' (single apostrophe) *let*

Use the specified lowercase letter and to return to the position marked by that letter. With a second apostrophe, return to the previous position where the last "large" movement began. With ^, return to the beginning of the file; with $, return to the end of the file.

^X^X

Same as '.

/pattern

Find next occurrence of *pattern*, starting at second line displayed. Some special characters can be entered before *pattern*:

!, ^N

Find lines that do not contain *pattern*.

*, ^E

If current file does not contain *pattern*, continue through the rest of the files in the command-line list.

@, ^F

Search from the first line in the first file specified on the command line, no matter what the screen currently displays.

^K

Hightlight matching text on the current screen, but do not move there.

^R

Use text comparison; do not interpret regular expressions.

?pattern

Search backward, beginning at the line before the top line. The use of special characters is the same as for */pattern*.

ESC-/*pattern*

Same as /*.

ESC-?/*pattern*

Same as ?*.

n   Repeat last *pattern* search.

N   Repeat last *pattern* search in the reverse direction.

ESC-n

Repeat previous search command, but as though it were prefaced by *.

ESC-N

Repeat previous search command, but as though it were prefaced by * and in the reverse direction.

ESC-u

Toggle search highlighting.

&pattern

Display only lines that match the pattern. With ^N or !, display lines that do not match; with ^R, do not interpret regular expressions.

:d   Remove the current file from the list of files.

:e [*filename*]

Read in *filename* and insert it into the command-line list of filenames. Without *filename*, reread the current file. Replace a percent sign (%) in the *filename* with the name of the current file; replace a hash mark (#), with the name of the previous file.

^X^V, E

Same as **:e**.

:n   Read in next file in command-line list or the file indicated by *number*, if specified.

:p   Read in previous file in command-line list or the file indicated by *number*, if specified.

:x   Read in first file in command-line list or the file indicated by *number*, if specified.

s *filename*

If input is a pipe, save to the specified file.

t   Go to the next tag. See the **-t** option.

T   Go to the previous tag. See the **-T** option.

:f, =, ^G

Print filename, position in command-line list, line number on top of window, total lines, byte number, and total bytes.

- *(single dash)*

Expects to be followed by a command-line option letter. Toggle the value of that option or, if appropriate, prompt for its new value.

--   Like **-**, but takes a long option name.

-+   Expects to be followed by a command-line option letter. Reset that option to its default.

--+   Like **-+**, but takes a long option name.

_ *(underscore)*

Expects to be followed by a command-line option letter. Display that option's current setting.

__   Like **_**, but takes a long option name.

+*command*

Execute *command* each time a new file is read in.

q, :q, :Q, ZZ

Exit.

v   Not valid for all versions. Invoke editor specified by **$VISUAL** or **$EDITOR**, or **vi** if neither is set.

! [*command*]

Not valid for all versions. Invoke **$SHELL** or **sh**. If *command* is given, run it and then exit. Replace **%** with the name of the current file, **#** with the name of the previous file, and **!!** with the last shell command.

| *mark-letter command*

Not valid for all versions. Pipe fragment of file (from first line on screen to *mark-letter*) to *command*. *mark-letter* may be ^ for the beginning of the file, **$** for the end of the file, or **.** or **newline** to pipe the current screen.

Prompts

The prompt interprets certain sequences specially. Those beginning with **%** are always evaluated. Those beginning with **?** are evaluated if certain conditions are true. Some prompts determine the position of particular lines on the screen. These sequences require that a method of determining that line be specified. See the **-P** option and the manpage for more information.

lesskey

lesskey [-o *output-file* | --output=*output-file*] [*input-file*]

Configure keybindings for the **less** command using a configuration file. The input file defaults to *~/.lesskey* and the output file to *~/.less* unless you specify otherwise.

Configuration file format

The configuration file for **lesskey** has one to three sections. These are marked by a line containing a **#** symbol and the name of the section: **#command**, **#line-edit**, and **#env**.

The **#command** *section*

The command section determines the keys used for actions within **less**. Each line should contain the key or key combination you wish to define, a space or tab, and the name of the action to perform. You may also add an extra string at the end, which will be performed at the end of the first action.

Keys you define should be entered as you plan to type them, with the following exceptions:

Backspace: **\b**
Backslash: ****
Caret: **\^**
Escape: **\e**
Newline: **\n**
Return: **\r**
Tab: **\t**
Up arrow: **\ku**
Down arrow: **\kd**
Right arrow: **\kr**
Left arrow: **\kl**
Page up: **\kU**
Page down: **\kD**
Home: **\kh**
End: **\ke**
Delete: **\kx**

The actions that can be defined are:

invalid (creates error)
noaction
forw-line
back-line
forw-line-force
forw-scroll
back-scroll
forw-screen
back-screen
forw-window
back-window
forw-screen-force
forw-forever
repaint-flush
repaint
undo-hilite
goto-line
percent
left-scroll
right-scroll
forw-bracket
back-bracket
goto-end
status
forw-search
back-search
repeat-search
repeat-search-all
reverse-search
reverse-search-all
filter
set-mark
goto-mark
examine
next-file
index-file
prev-file
next-tag
previous-tag
remove-file
toggle-option
display-option
pipe
visual
shell
firstcmd
help
version (display version)
digit (display number)
quit

Linux
Commands

The #line-edit section

The line editing section lets you choose keys for the line-editing capabilities of **less** in a similar manner to the #**command** section, although without the "extra" string after the command. The line editing actions that can be defined are:

forw-complete
back-complete
expand
literal
right
left
word-left
word-right
insert
delete
word-delete
word-backspace
home
end
up
down

The #env section

The third section, like the second, is optional, and you can use it to override environment variables that affect **less**. Each line consists of a variable, the equals sign (=), and the value to which you wish to set the variable. The most important ones are **LESS**, which allows you to select additional flags to pass to **less** when you run it, and **LESSCHARSET**, which lets you choose a character set. See the **less** manpage for a complete list of environment variables that affect the program.

lftp

lftp [*options*] [*url*]

File transfer program with more features than **ftp**. The **lftp** command allows FTP and HTTP protocol transfers, plus other protocols including FISH (SSH based), FTPS, and HTTPS. It uses a shell-like command interface and offers job control in a manner similar to **bash**. **lftp** has two important reliability features: it resumes failed or interrupted transactions, and it goes into the background automatically if it is quit in the middle of a file transfer.

Options

-d Run in debug mode.

-e *commands*
   Start, execute the specified commands, and then wait for further instructions.

-p *portnumber*
   Connect to the specified port number.

-u *user*[,*pass*]

Login to the server with the username (and, optionally, password) you specify.

-f *scriptfile*

Run the specified script file of **lftp** commands, then exit.

-c *commands*

Run the commands specified, then exit.

Commands

The **lftp** commands are similar to those for **ftp**. However, **lftp** lacks or uses different mechanisms for a number of commands, including **$**, **ascii**, **binary**, **case**, and **macdef**. It also adds the following:

alias [*name* [*value*]]

Create an alias for a command. For example, you could set **dir** to be an alias for **ls -lf**.

anon

Set the username to anonymous. This is the default username.

at

Execute a command at a given time, as with the **at** command in an actual shell.

bookmark [*arguments*]

The **lftp** bookmark command used with the following arguments will add, delete, edit, import, or list bookmarks, respectively:

- **add** *name url*
- **del** *name*
- **edit**
- **import** *type*
- **list**

cache

Work with the local memory cache. This command should be followed by the arguments:

stat

Display the status for the cache.

on|off

Turn caching on or off.

flush

Empty the cache.

size *n*

Set the maximum size for the cache. Setting it to **-1** means unlimited.

expire *nu*

Set the cache to expire after *n* units of time. You can set the unit (*u*) to seconds (**s**), minutes (**m**), hours (**h**), or days (**d**). For example, for a cache that expires after an hour, use the syntax **cache expire 1h**.

close

Close idle connections with the current server. This differs from **ftp**, which closes all connections. If you have connections to multiple servers and wish to close all idle connections, add the -a flag.

command *cmd args*

Execute the specified **lftp** command, with the specified arguments, ignoring any aliases created with the **alias** command.

mirror [*options*] [*remotedir* [*localdir*]]

Copy a directory exactly. The **mirror** command accepts the following arguments:

-c, --continue

If mirroring was interrupted, resume it.

-e, --delete

Delete local files that are not present at the remote site.

-s, --allow-suid

Keep the suid/sgid bits as set on the remote site.

-n, --only-newer

Get only those files from the remote site that have more recent dates than the files on the local system. Cannot be used with the -c argument.

-r, --no-recursion

Do not get any subdirectories.

--no-umask

Do not use **umask** when getting file modes. See **umask** for more information about file modes.

-R, --reverse

Mirror files from the local system to the remote system. With this argument, make sure that you specify the local directory first and the remote directory second. If you do not specify both directories, the second is assumed to be the same as the first. If you choose neither, the operation occurs in the current working directories.

-L, --dereference

When mirroring a link, download the file the link points to rather than just the link.

-N *filename*, --newer-than *filename*

Get all files newer than the file *filename*.

-P *n*, --parallel[=*n*]

Download *n* files in parallel.

-i *regex*, --include *regex*

Get only the files whose names match the regular expression *regex*. See Chapter 7 for information about regular expressions.

-x *regex*, --exclude *regex*

Do not get the files whose names match *regex*. See Chapter 7 for information about regular expressions.

-v *n*, **--verbose=***n*
> Set the verbose level. You can set *n* from **0** (no output) to **3** (full output) using a number or by repeating the *v*. For example, **-vvv** is level 3 verbose mode.

--use-cache
> Use the cache to get directory listings.

--remove-source-files
> Move, rather than copy, files when mirroring.

set [*variable* | *value*]
> Set a preference variable for **lftp**. With no arguments, list the variables that have been changed; with no arguments and with the **-a** or **-d** flags, list all values or default values, respectively.
>
> See the **lftp** manpage for a complete list of preference variables that can be set.

wait [*n* | **all**]
> Wait for the job or jobs you specify by number, or all jobs, to terminate.

---

lftpget

lftpget [*options*] *url*

Uses the **lftp** program to fetch the specified URL, which may be HTTP, FTP, or any of the protocols supported by **lftp**.

Options

-c   Continue or restart a paused transaction.

-d   Display debugging output.

-v   Verbose mode; display more information about transactions.

---

link

link *file1* *file2*

Create a link between two files. This is the same as the **ln** command, but it has no error checking because it uses the **link( )** system call directly.

---

ln

ln [*options*] *sourcename* [*destname*]

ln [*options*] *sourcenames* *destdirectory*

Create pseudonyms (links) for files, allowing them to be accessed by different names. Links may be "hard" or "soft." A hard link creates two names for the same file, and a soft, or symbolic, link creates a second file which acts as a shortcut to the first. The default is to create hard links; use **-s** or **--symbolic** to create symbolic links.

The first form links *sourcename* to *destname*, where *destname* is usually either a new filename or (by default) a file in the current directory with the same name as *sourcename*. If *destname* is an existing file, it is overwritten; if *destname* is an existing directory, a link named *sourcename* is created in that directory. The second form creates links in *destdirectory*, each link having the same name as the file specified.

Linux
Commands

Options

-b, --backup[*=control*]

Back up any existing files. With the long version of the command, the optional *control* parameter controls the kind of backup. When no control is specified, **ln** attempts to read the control value from the **VERSION_CONTROL** environment variable. Accepted values are:

none, off

Never make backups.

numbered, t

Make numbered backups.

existing, nil

Match existing backups, numbered or simple.

simple, never

Always make simple backups.

-d, -F, --directory

Allow hard links to directories. Available to privileged users.

-f, --force

Force the link (don't prompt for overwrite permission).

--help

Print a help message and then exit.

-i, --interactive

Prompt for permission before removing files.

-n, --no-dereference

Replace symbolic links to directories instead of dereferencing them. **--force** is useful with this option.

-s, --symbolic

Create a symbolic link. This lets you link across filesystems, and also see the name of the link when you run **ls -l** (otherwise, there's no way to know the name that a file is linked to).

-S *suffix*, **--suffix**=*suffix*

Append *suffix* to files when making backups, instead of the default ~.

-t *directory*, **--target-directory**=*directory*

Create links in the specified *directory*.

-v, --verbose

Verbose mode.

--version

Print version information and then exit.

---

loadkeys

loadkeys [*options*] [*filename*]

Load a keymap from a specified file, usually one of the keymaps stored in */lib/kbd/keymaps*. If you create your own keymap file, the related commands **showkey**, **keymaps**, and **dumpkeys** will be useful as well. Note that **loadkeys** applies only to virtual consoles; to

---

change your X keyboard configuration, use **xmodmap** or **setxkbmap**, or the graphical keyboard-layout switching tools that are included with your desktop environment.

Options

-c, --clearcompose
Clear the compose, or accent, table in the kernel.

-d, --default
Load the default keymap. The same as running **loadkeys defkeymap**.

-h, --help
Display help and usage information.

-m, --mktable
Instead of loading the table, output maps as C language declarations.

-s, --clearstrings
Clear the string table in the kernel.

-v, --verbose
Operate verbosely. For extra effect, repeat.

---

locale

locale [*options*] [*names*]

Print report on current locale settings. Locales determine the country-specific settings for a system, including character encodings, the formatting of dates, honorifics, diagnostic messages, currency, printer-paper sizes, and default measurements. Locale settings are essentially a dictionary of settings specified by keyword. The keywords are grouped together into related categories whose names begin with **LC_**. Each category has a related environment variable of the same name from which it reads its locale setting. Supply keyword or category names as *names* to examine their values. You can also use the special keyword **charmap** to see the current character mapping. When executed with no arguments, **locale** prints the value of all locale-related environment variables.

Options

-a, --all-locales
Print all available locale settings installed on the system.

-c, --category-name
Print the category related to each *name* argument.

-k, --keyword-name
Print keywords along with their settings for each *name* argument.

-m, --charmaps
Print all available character maps.

Environment variables

LANG
The default value for unset internationalization variables. If not set, the system's default value is used.

LC_ADDRESS
> Postal settings, country, and language names and abbreviation.

LC_COLLATE
> String and character sorting and comparison settings.

LC_CTYPE
> Character attributes, including case conversion mappings, and categories of characters (whitespace, digit, lower, upper, punctuation, etc.).

LC_IDENTIFICATION
> Information related to the current locale definition, including its title, source, revision, and contact information for its author.

LC_MEASUREMENT
> Measurement units, metric or other.

LC_MESSAGES
> Settings for yes/no prompts and other informative and diagnostic messages.

LC_MONETARY
> Currency formats and symbols.

LC_NAME
> Formats for names and honorifics.

LC_NUMERIC
> Nonmonetary number formats.

LC_PAPER
> Default paper sizes for printing and pagination.

LC_TELEPHONE
> Telephone number formats.

LC_TIME
> Date and time formats.

LC_ALL
> When set, overrides the values of all other internationalization variables.

Examples

Print the category name and all keywords for date and time settings:

```
locale -ck LC_TIME
```

Print the strings used for days of the week and months of the year:

```
locale day mon
```

---

locate

```
locate [options] pattern
```

Search database(s) of filenames and print matches. Matches include all files that contain *pattern* unless *pattern* includes metacharacters, in which case **locate** requires an exact match. *, ?, [, and] are treated specially; / and . are not. Searches are conducted against a database of system contents that is updated periodically. To update the database, use the **updatedb** command.

Options

-b, --basename
> Look only at the basename when searching for matches.

-c, --count
> List only the match count, not the individual filenames.

-d *path*, **--database**=*path*
> Search databases in *path*. *path* must be a colon-separated list.

-h, --help
> Print a help message and then exit.

-i, --ignore-case
> Ignore case when performing matches.

-q, --quiet
> Run quietly, printing no error messages.

-r *regexp*, **--regexp** *regexp*
> Search for a basic regular expression, with no patterns allowed. May be issued more than once.

--regex
> Treat all patterns as extended regular expressions.

-S, --statistics
> Print statistics about each database and then exit.

-V, --version
> Print version information and then exit.

-w, --wholename
> Look at the entire pathname when searching for matches (the default).

---

lockfile

    lockfile [options] filenames

Create semaphore file(s), used to limit access to a file. When **lockfile** fails to create some of the specified files, it pauses for eight seconds and retries the last one on which it failed. The command processes flags as they are encountered (i.e., a flag that is specified after a file will not affect that file). This command is most often used by scripts and applications as a way to avoid multiple users changing the same file at once.

Options

-sleeptime
> Number of seconds **lockfile** waits before retrying after a failed creation attempt. Default is 8.

-!   Invert return value. Useful in shell scripts.

-l *lockout_time*
> Time (in seconds) after a lockfile was last modified at which it will be removed by force. See also **-s**.

-ml, -mu
> If the permissions on the system mail spool directory allow it or if **lockfile** is suitably setgid, **lockfile** can lock and unlock your system mailbox with the options **-ml** and **-mu**, respectively.

-**r** *retries*
> Stop trying to create *files* after this many *retries*. The default is -1 (never stop trying). When giving up, remove all created files.

-**s** *suspend_time*
> After a lockfile has been removed by force (see **-l**), a suspension of 16 seconds takes place by default. (This is intended to prevent the inadvertent immediate removal of any lockfile newly created by another program.) Use **-s** to change the default suspend time.

logger

```
logger [options] [message...]
```

TCP/IP command. Add entries to the system log (via **syslogd**). If no message is given on the command line, standard input is logged.

Options

-**d** When writing to a socket with **-s**, use a datagram instead of a stream.

-**f** *file*
> Read *message* from *file*.

-**i** Include the process ID of the **logger** process.

-**p** *pri*
> Enter message with the specified priority *pri*. Default is **user.notice**.

-**s** Log message to standard error as well as to the system log.

-**t** *tag*
> Mark every line in the log with the specified *tag*.

-**u** *socket*
> Write log to *socket* instead of to the syslog.

-- Accept no further options. Consider whatever is to the right of the hyphens as the message to be logged.

login

```
login [name | option]
```

Log into the system. **login** asks for a username (*name* can be supplied on the command line) and password (if appropriate).

If successful, **login** updates accounting files, sets various environment variables, notifies users if they have mail, and executes startup shell files.

Only the root user can log in when */etc/nologin* exists. That file is displayed before the connection is terminated. Furthermore, root may connect only on a tty that is listed in */etc/securetty*. If *~/.hushlogin* exists, execute a quiet login. If */var/adm/lastlog* exists, print the time of the last login.

Options

-**f** Suppress second login authentication.

-h *host*
> Specify name of remote host. Normally used by servers, not humans; may be used only by root.

-p Preserve previous environment.

---

logrotate

logrotate [*options*] *config_files*

System administration command. Manipulate logfiles according to commands given in *config_files*.

Options

-d, --debug
> Debug mode. No changes will be made to logfiles.

-f, --force
> Force rotation of logfiles.

-h, --help
> Describe options.

-m *command*, **--mail** *command*
> Use the specified *command* to mail logfiles. The default command is **/bin/mail -s**.

-s *file*, **--state** *file*
> Save state information in *file*. The default is */var/lib/logrotate. status*.

--usage
> Show syntax and options.

-v, --verbose
> Describe what is being done and what logfiles are affected.

Configuration commands

Logrotate directives may appear on their own or as part of logfile definitions—instructions for specific logfiles. You may use wildcards to specify those files. Enclose directives for logfile definitions in a beginning and ending curly brace. For example:

```
compress
/var/log/messages {
rotate 5
weekly
}
```

compress
> Compress old versions of logfiles with **gzip**.

compresscmd *command*
> Use *command* to compress logfiles. Default is **gzip**.

compressext *extension*
> Append filename **extension** to compressed files instead of the **compress** command's default.

compressoptions *options*
> Specify *options* to pass to the **compress** command. Default for **gzip** is **-9** for maximum compression.

copy

> Copy logfile, but do not change the original.

copytruncate

> Copy logfile, then truncate it in place. For use with programs whose logging cannot be temporarily halted.

create [*permissions*] [*owner*] [*group*]

> After rotation, re-create logfile with the specified *permissions*, *owner*, and *group*. *permissions* must be in octal. If any of these parameters is missing, the logfile's original attributes will be used.

daily

> Rotate logfiles every day.

delaycompress

> Don't compress logfile until the next rotation.

endscript

> End a **postrotate** or **prerotate** script.

extension *extension*

> Give rotated logfiles the specified *extension*. Any compression extension will be appended to this.

firstaction

> May only be used as part of a logfile definition. Begin a shell script to execute once if any files match. The script ends when the **endscript** directive is read.

ifempty

> Rotate logfile even if it is empty. Overrides the default **notifempty** option.

include *file*

> Read the *file* into current file. If *file* is a directory, read all files in that directory into the current file.

lastaction

> May only be used as part of a logfile definition. Begin a shell script to execute once after rotating all matching files and running any postrotate script. The script ends when the **endscript** directive is read.

mail *address*

> Mail any deleted logs to *address*.

mailfirst

> When using the **mail** command, mail the newly rotated log instead of the one being deleted.

maillast

> When using the **mail** command, mail the log that is about to expire. This is the default behavior.

missingok

> Skip missing logfiles. Do not generate an error.

monthly

> Rotate logfiles only the first time **logrotate** is run in a month.

nocompress
> Override **compress**.

nocopy
> Override **copy**.

nocopytruncate
> Override **copytruncate**.

nocreate
> Override **create**.

nodelaycompress
> Override **delaycompress**.

nomail
> Override **mail**.

nomissingok
> Override **missingok**.

noolddir
> Override **olddir**.

nosharedscripts
> Override **sharedscripts**. Run **prerotate** and **postrotate** scripts for each log rotated. This is the default.

notifempty
> Override **ifempty**.

olddir *directory*
> Move logs into *directory* for rotation. *directory* must be on the same physical device as the original logfiles.

postrotate
> May only be used as part of a logfile definition. Begin a shell script to apply after the logfile is rotated. The script ends when the **endscript** directive is read.

prerotate
> May only be used as part of a logfile definition. Begin a shell script to apply before a logfile is rotated. The script ends when the **endscript** directive is read.

rotate *number*
> The *number* of times to rotate a logfile before removing it.

size *n*[**k**|**M**]
> Rotate logfile when it is greater than *n* bytes. *n* can optionally be followed by **k** for kilobytes or **M** for megabytes.

sharedscripts
> Run **prescript** and **postscript** only once for the session.

start *n*
> Use *n* as the starting number for rotated logs. Default is 0.

tabooext [+] *extlist*
> Replace taboo extension list with the given *extlist*. If + is specified, add to existing list. The default list is **.rpmorig .rpmsave ,v .swp .rpmnew ~**.

weekly
> Rotate logfiles if more than a week has passed since their last rotation.

uncompresscmd *command*
> Use *command* to uncompress logfiles. Default is **gunzip**.

look

```
look [options] string [file]
```

Search for lines in *file* (*/usr/dict/words* by default) that begin with *string*.

Options

-a Use alternate dictionary, */usr/dict/web2*.

-d Compare only alphanumeric characters.

-f Search is not case-sensitive.

-t *character*
> Stop checking after the first occurrence of *character*.

losetup

```
losetup [options] loopdevice [file]
```

System administration command. Set up and control loop devices. Attach a loop device to a regular file or block device, detach a loop device, or query a loop device. A loop device can be used to mount an image file as if it were a normal device.

Options

-d Detach specified *loopdevice*.

-e *encryption*, -E*number*
> Use specified kernel *encryption* module when performing writes and reads. (Usually **NONE**, **DES**, and **XOR**.) You may also specify the encryption module by *number*. When using DES encryption, you will be prompted for an initialization passphrase.

-o *offset*
> Start reading data at *offset* bytes from the beginning of *file*.

-p *fd*
> Read the passphrase from file descriptor *fd*.

lpadmin

```
lpadmin [options]
```

System administration command. Configure CUPS printer queues. The command requires one of the following options: **-d**, **-p**, or **-x**. When a queue is configured to require a password, the **lpadmin** command will prompt for one.

Options

-d *queue*
> Set the default destination for CUPS commands like **lp** and **lpr** to the specified *queue*.

-E   Always use encryption when connecting to the server.

-h *server*
>   Apply configuration commands remotely to the specified CUPS *server*.

-p *printer print-options*
>   Apply *print-options* (documented below) to the specified *printer*.

-x *queue*
>   Delete the specified *queue*. Abort any current print job and discard any pending print jobs.

Print options

Use these additional options with the **-p** option just listed:

-c *class*
>   Add printer to the specified *class*. Create *class* if it does not already exist.

-D *description*
>   Set the text *description* of the printer.

-E   Enable printer.

-L *location*
>   Set the printer *location* text.

-i *script*
>   Use the specified System V-style interface *script*.

-m *filename*
>   Use the specified System V interface script or PPD file found in the model directory.

-o *name=value*
>   Set the *value* of PPD or server option *name*. For a list of available PPD options, use the **lpoptions** command.

-P *filename*
>   Use the PPD specified by *filename*. This option overrides the **-i** printer option.

-r *class*
>   Remove printer from the specified *class*. Remove *class* if it has no printer entries.

-u *allow:[@]name*, **-u** *deny:[@]name*
>   Set user level access control. To specify a group instead of a user *name*, preface the *name* with **@**. You may also use the special names **all** and **none**.

-v *uri*
>   Set the device universal resource indicator, *uri*. If given as a filename, the command will automatically convert it to a file URI.

lpinfo

`lpinfo` *options*

System administration command. Print information on available printer devices and drivers.

Options

-E   Force the use of encryption connecting to the server.

-l   Show a long, or verbose, listing.

-m   List available printer drivers.

-v   List available printer devices.

lpmove

`lpmove` *[option] jobdestination*

System administration command. Move the specified print *job* to a new *destination*.

Option

-E   Force the use of encryption connecting to the server.

lpq

`lpq` *[options] [+interval]*

Check the print spool queue for status of print jobs. For each job, display username, rank in the queue, filenames, job number, and total file size (in bytes). We document the CUPS printing system here; other versions will vary slightly.

Options

-a   Report on all printers listed in the server's printcap database.

-E   Use encryption when connecting to a print server.

-h *server[:port]*
Specify an alternate server and optional port.

-l   Verbose mode. Print information about each file composing a job. Use **-l** multiple times to increase the information provided.

-P *printer*
Specify which printer to query. Without this option, **lpq** uses the default printer, normally set through **lpadmin**.

-U *username*
Specify an alternate username.

+*interval*
Check the queue every *interval* seconds until it is empty. For example, **+10** reloads the queue every ten seconds.

lpr

`lpr` *[options] [files]*

Send files to be printed. If no *files* are given, accept standard input. We document the CUPS printing system here; the older LPRng and BSD systems will vary slightly. CUPS **lpr**, for example, does not accept the options **c**, **d**, **f**, **g**, **i**, **m**, **n**, **t**, **v**, or **w**, used by LPRng.

Options

-# *copies*
Set the number of copies to print, from 1 to 100.

-C, J, T *name*
Set a name for the print job.

-E Use encryption when connecting to a print server.

-H *server*[:*port*]
Specify an alternate server and optional port.

-l Expect a binary or literal file on which minimal processing should be done. The same as **-o raw**.

-m Send email when printing is complete.

-o *option*[=*value*]
Set printer-specific options. These vary by printer, but may include paper type and orientation, paper-tray selection, output order, and so forth. Check the complete CUPS user manual and your printer's PPD file for the full list.

-p Pretty-print a text document. Provides a shaded header containing page numbers, the job name, and the time and date of printing. Equivalent to **-o prettyprint**.

-P *printername*
Print to the specified printer. If no printer is given, prints to the default printer, usually set with **lpadmin**.

-q Hold job for printing.

-r Delete files after printing them.

-U *username*
Specify an alternate username.

Example

Print a simple file:

```
Lpr filename.txt
```

---

lprm

lprm [*options*] [*jobid*]

Cancel print jobs. Job IDs can be obtained from **lpq**; if no job is specified, cancels the current job on the default printer.

Options

- Remove all jobs available to the user. Same as specifying *jobid* as **ALL**.

-E Use encryption.

-h *server*[:*port*]
Specify an alternate server and optional port.

-P *printer*
Specify printer queue. If no printer is specified, the default printer is used.

-U *username*
Specify an alternate username.

lpstat

lpstat [*options*] [*queues*]

Show the status of the print queue or queues. With options that take a *list* argument, omitting the list produces all information for that option. *list* can be separated by commas or, if enclosed in double quotes, by spaces. For the LPRng print service, **lpstat** is a frontend to the **lpq** program. With no arguments, **lpstat** shows jobs queued by the current user.

Options

-a [*list*]
Show whether the *list* of printer or class names is accepting requests.

-c [*list*]
Show information about printer classes named in *list*.

-d Show the default printer destination.

-E Use encryption when connecting to the print server.

-l When showing printers, classes, or jobs, print a long listing.

-o [*list*]
Show the status of output requests. *list* contains printer names, class names, or request IDs.

-p [*list*]
Show the status of printers named in *list*.

-r Show whether the print scheduler is on or off.

-s Summarize the print status (show almost everything).

-t Show all status information (report everything).

-u [*list*]
Show request status for users on *list*. Use **all** to show information on all users.

-U *username*
Specify an alternate username.

-v [*list*]
Show printers and the devices they are attached to.

ls

ls [*options*] [*names*]

List contents of directories. If no *names* are given, list the files in the current directory. With one or more *names*, list files contained in a directory *name* or that match a file *name*. *names* can include filename metacharacters. The options let you display a variety of information in different formats. The most useful options include **-F, -R, -l**, and **-s**. Some options don't make sense together (e.g., **-u** and **-c**).

Options

-1, --format=single-column
Print one entry per line of output.

-a, --all
> List all files, including the normally hidden files whose names begin with a period.

-A, --almost-all
> List all files, including the normally hidden files whose names begin with a period. Does not include the . and .. directories.

-b, --escape
> Display nonprinting characters in octal and alphabetic format.

-B, --ignore-backups
> Do not list files ending in ~ unless given as arguments.

-c, --time=ctime, --time=status
> List files by status change time (ctime), not creation/modification time. With -l, show ctime and sort by filename; with -lt, show and sort by ctime; otherwise, sort by ctime.

-C, --format=vertical
> List files in columns (the default format).

--color[=*when*]
> Colorize the names of files depending on the type of file. Accepted values for *when* are **never**, **always**, or **auto**.

-d, --directory
> Report only on the directory, not its contents; do not dereference symbolic links.

-D, --dired
> List in a format suitable for Emacs **dired** mode.

-f
> Print directory contents in order, without attempting to sort them.

-F, --classify, --indicator-style=classify
> Flag filenames by appending / to directories, * to executable files, @ to symbolic links, | to FIFOs, and = to sockets.

--full-time
> List times in full, rather than using the standard abbreviations.

-g
> Long listing like -l, but don't show file owners.

-G, --no-group
> In long format, do not display group name.

--group-directories-first
> Display directories before files.

-h, --human-readable
> Print sizes in kilobytes and megabytes.

-H, --dereference-command-line
> When symbolic links are given on the command line, follow the link and list information from the actual file.

--help
> Print a help message and then exit.

-i, --inode
> List the inode for each file.

-I, --ignore *pattern*

Do not list files whose names match the shell pattern *pattern*, unless they are given on the command line.

--indicator-style=none

Display filenames without the flags assigned by **-p** or **-f** (default).

-k If file sizes are being listed, print them in kilobytes. This option overrides the environment variable **POSIXLY_ CORRECT**.

-l, --format=long, --format=verbose

Long format listing (includes permissions, owner, size, modification time, etc.).

-L, --dereference

List the file or directory referenced by a symbolic link rather than the link itself.

-m, --format=commas

Merge the list into a comma-separated series of names.

-n, --numeric-uid-gid

Like **-l**, but use group ID and user ID numbers instead of owner and group names.

-N, --literal

Display special graphic characters that appear in filenames.

-o Long listing like **-l**, but don't show group information.

-p, --indicator-style=slash

Mark directories by appending **/** to them.

-q, --hide-control-chars

Show nonprinting characters as **?** (default for display to a terminal).

-Q, --quote-name

Quote filenames with **"**; quote nongraphic characters.

-r, --reverse

List files in reverse order (by name or by time).

-R, --recursive

List directories and their contents recursively.

-s, --size

Print file size in blocks.

-S, --sort=size

Sort by file size, largest to smallest.

--show-control-chars

Show nonprinting characters verbatim (default for printing to a file).

--si

Similar to **-h**, but uses powers of 1000 instead of 1024.

-t, --sort=time

Sort files according to modification time (newest first).

-u, --time=atime, --time=access, --time=use
Sort files according to file-access time. With **-l**, show access time and sort by filename; with **-lt**, show and sort by access time; otherwise sort by access time.

-U, sort=none
Do not sort files.

-v, --sort=version
Interpret the digits in names such as *file.6* and *file.6.1* as versions, and order filenames by version.

--version
Print version information on standard output, then exit.

-w *n*, **--width=***n*
Format output to fit *n* columns.

-x, --format=across, --format=horizontal
List files in rows going across the screen.

-X, sort=extension
Sort by file extension, then by filename.

---

lsattr
    `lsattr [options] [files]`

Print attributes of *files* on a Linux Second Extended File System. See also **chattr**.

Options

-a   List all files in specified directories.

-d   List attributes of directories, not of contents.

-R   List directories and their contents recursively.

-v   List version of files.

-V   List version of **lsattr** and then exit.

---

lspci
    `lspci [options]`

System administration command. List all Peripheral Component Interconnect (PCI) devices. This command has many options that are useful for debugging device drivers. Here we document some of the more common options:

Options

-b   Show IRQ and addresses as seen by the cards instead of the kernel.

-t   Print a tree showing connections between devices.

-m   Print information with quoted strings suitable for use by scripts.

-n   Print vendor and device codes as numbers.

-v, -vv
List devices verbosely. Use the second form for very verbose listings.

lsmod

lsmod

System administration command. List all loaded modules: name, size (in 4 KB units), and, if appropriate, a list of referring modules. The same information is available in */proc/modules* if the */proc* directory is enabled on the system.

lsusb

lsusb [*options*]

System administration command. List all Universal Serial Bus (USB) devices. This command has many options of use for debugging device drivers. Here we document some of the more common options.

Options

-b   Show IRQ and addresses as seen by the cards instead of the kernel.

-D *device*
          Only show information about the specified *device*. This should be given as a file in the */proc/bus/usb* directory—e.g., */proc/bus/ usb/001/001*.

-t   Print a tree showing connections between devices.

-v, -vv
          List devices verbosely. Use the second form for very verbose listings.

m4

m4 [*options*] [*macros*] [*files*]

Macro processor for C and other files.

Options

-e, --interactive
          Operate interactively, unbuffered, ignoring interrupts.

-d*flags***, --debug=***flags*
          Specify *flag*-level debugging.

--help
          Print help message, then exit.

-l*n***, --arglength=***n*
          Specify the length of debugging output.

-o *file***, --error-output=***file*
          Place output in *file*. Despite the name, print error messages on standard error.

-P, --prefix-built-ins
          Prepend **m4_** to all built-in macro names.

-s, --synclines
          Insert **#line** directives for the C preprocessor.

-t*name***, --trace=***name*
          Insert *name* into symbol table as undefined. Trace macro from the point it is defined.

--version
> Print version, then exit.

-B*n*
> Set the size of the pushback and argument collection buffers to *n* (default is 4096).

-D*name*[*=value*], **--define**=*name*[*=value*]
> Define *name* as *value* or, if *value* is not specified, define *name* as null.

-E, --fatal-warnings
> Consider all warnings to be fatal, and exit after the first of them.

-F*file*, **--freeze-state**=*file*
> Record **m4**'s frozen state in *file* for later reloading.

-G, --traditional
> Behave like traditional **m4**, ignoring GNU extensions.

-H*n*, **--hashsize**=*n*
> Set symbol-table hash array to *n* (default is 509).

-I*directory*, **--include**=*directory*
> Search *directory* for include files.

-L*n*, **--nesting-limit**=*n*
> Change artificial nesting limit to *n*.

-Q, --quiet, --silent
> Suppress warning messages.

-R*file*, **--reload-state**=*file*
> Load state from *file* before starting execution.

-U*name*, **--undefine**=*name*
> Undefine *name*.

---

mail

mail [*options*] [*users*]

Read mail or send mail to other *users*. **mail** is now generally a symbolic link to **mailx**.

---

mailq

mailq [*options*]

List all messages in the **sendmail** mail queue. Equivalent to **sendmail -bp**.

Options

-Ac
> Show queue specified in */etc/mail/submit.cf* instead of queue specified in */etc/mail/sendmail.cf*.

-q[**!**]**I***substring*
> Show items in mail queue with queue ids containing *substring*. In this, and in similar options below, invert the match when **!** is specified.

-qL
> Show lost items in mail queue.

-qQ
> Show quarantined items in the mail queue.

-q[!]Q*substring*
> Show quarantined messages with quarantine reasons containing *substring*.

-q[!]R*substring*
> Show items in mail queue with recipients containing *substring*.

-q[!]S*substring*
> Show items in mail queue with senders containing *substring*.

-v   Verbose mode.

---

mailstats   `mailstats [options]`

System administration command. Display a formatted report of the current **sendmail** mail statistics.

Options

-c
> Use configuration in */etc/mail/submit.cf* instead of */etc/mail/ sendmail.cf*.

-C *file*
> Use **sendmail** configuration file *file* instead of the default *sendmail.cf* file.

-f *file*
> Use **sendmail** statistics file *file* instead of the file specified in the **sendmail** configuration file.

-o   Don't show the name of the mailer in the report.

-p   Print stats without headers or separators. Output suitable for use by other programs. Reset statistics.

-P   Print stats without headers or separators. Output suitable for use by other programs. Do not reset statistics.

---

mailx   `mailx [options] [users]`

Read mail or send mail to other *users*. **mailx** is based on the traditional **mail** command, extended to provide support for MIME, IMAP, POP3, SMTP, and S/MIME. The **mailx** command allows you to compose, send, receive, forward, and reply to mail. **mailx** has two main modes: compose mode, in which you create a message, and command mode, in which you manage your mail.

mailx is most commonly seen nowadays in scripts. Most Linux distributions include several utilities that are richer in features and easier to use: mailers built into browsers such as Mozilla and Firefox, graphical mail programs distributed with GNOME (Evolution) and KDE (Kmail), and the terminal-based, full-screen utilities **pine** and **elm**. The GNU Emacs editor can also send and receive mail.

To get you started, here are two of the most basic commands.

To enter interactive mail-reading mode, type:

> `mailx`

To begin writing a message to *user*, type:

> `mailx user`

Enter the text of the message, one line at a time, pressing Enter at the end of each line. To end the message, enter a single period (.) in the first column of a new line and press Enter.

You can also provide much of the information on the command line, as shown in the following example:

> `mailx james -s "System Log" </var/log/messages`

This command sends a message to the user *james*, with a subject line of System Log, and the text of the message read from the system logfile, */var/log/messages*.

mailx has many more options and commands than we can describe here. For complete details, as well as a full description of managing and using the command, see the manpage.

Command-line options

-~   Allow tilde escapes even when not in interactive mode.

-a *file*
> Attach the specified file to the message.

-A *account*
> Run the **account** command for the specified email account after the startup files have been read.

-b *list*
> Set blind-carbon-copy field to comma-separated *list*.

-c *list*
> Set carbon-copy field to comma-separated *list*.

-D   Start disconnected.

-e   Check for presence of mail in the system mailbox, but do not read. Returns exit status of 0 if there is mail, otherwise returns nonzero.

-E   Discard an outgoing message with no text in its first or only part.

-f [*file*]
> Process contents of *file* instead of */var/spool/mail/$user*. If *file* is omitted, process *mbox* in the user's home directory.

-H   Print message header summaries and exit.

-i   Do not respond to tty interrupt signals.

-I   Show Newsgroup: or Article-Id: fields in the header summary; used with **-f**.

-n   Do not consult */etc/mail.rc* when starting up.

-N   When printing a mail message or entering a mail folder, do not display message headers.

-q *file*

In compose mode, insert the contents of *file* at the beginning of the message.

-R   Open folders read-only.

-s *subject*

Set subject to *subject*. Use quotes around subjects that contain spaces.

-S *var*[*=value*]

Set the internal option *var*. If *var* is a string variable, assign the given value to it.

-t   Expect the message to contain To:, Cc:, and/or Bcc: fields to identify recipients and ignore any set on the command line.

-u*user*

Process contents of */var/spool/mail/$user* for the specified user.

-v   Verbose; print information about mail delivery to standard output.

Compose-mode commands

The following commands are known as tilde escapes and are only recognized at the beginning of a line in the message:

~!*command*

Execute a shell escape from compose mode and run the specified command.

~<!*command*

Execute a shell escape and run the specified command, then insert its standard output into the message.

~?   List tilde escapes.

~| *command*

Pipe message through *command*.

~: *mailx-command*

Execute *mailx-command*.

~~*string*

Insert *string* in text of message, prefaced by a single tilde (~). If string contains a ~, it must be escaped with a \.

~b *names*

Add names to or edit the Bcc: header.

~c *names*

Add names to or edit the Cc: header.

~d   Read in the *dead.letter* file.

~e   Invoke text editor.

~f *messages*

Insert *messages* into message being composed. Only the first printable part of a MIME multipart message is inserted.

~F *messages*

Similar to ~f, but include message headers and all MIME parts.

~h Add to or change To:, Cc:, Bcc:, and Subject: headers interactively.

~H Like **~h** but edit From:, Reply-To:, Sender:, and Organization: headers.

~m *messages*
Similar to **~f**, but indent with a tab.

~M *messages*
Similar to **~m**, but include message headers and all MIME parts.

~p Print message header fields, message being sent, and attachment list.

~q Abort current message composition, and save to *dead.letters* file.

~r *filename*
Include file in current message.

~s *string*
Change Subject: header to *string*.

~t *names*
Add names to or edit the To: list.

~v Invoke editor specified with the **VISUAL** environment variable.

~w *filename*
Write the message to the named file, appending it if the file already exists.

~x Like **~q**, but don't save the message to *dead.letters* file.

Command-mode commands

? List summary of commands (help screen).

! Execute a shell command.

- [*num*]
Print *num*th previous message; defaults to immediately previous.

account (ac)
Create, select, or list an email account.

alias (a)
Print or create alias lists.

alternates (alt)
Specify remote accounts on remote machines that are yours. Tell **mailx** not to reply to them.

cache
For IMAP mailboxes only, read specified messages into the IMAP cache.

chdir (c)
cd to home or specified directory.

classify

> Check contents of messages for junk mail, using Bayesian filtering, and mark as junk.

copy (co)

> Similar to **save**, but do not mark message for deletion.

delete (d)

> Delete message.

dp (dt)

> Delete current message and display next one.

edit (e)

> Edit message.

exit (ex, x)

> Exit **mailx** without updating folder or user's system mailbox.

file (fi)

> Switch folders.

folder (fold)

> Read messages saved in a file. If no file is specified, display the name of the current file. In addition to filenames, the following are allowed:
>
> #   Previous file
>
> %   System mailbox
>
> *%user*
>> *user*'s system mailbox
>
> &   *mbox*
>
> *+folder*
>> File in *folder* directory.

folders

> List folders, and subfolders with an existing folder as argument.

forward (fwd)

> Forward a message to a recipient.

from (f)

> Print headers for messages.

good (go)

> Mark messages as good (not junk mail).

headers (h)

> List message headers in groups of 18 at current prompt.

headers+ (h+)

> Move forward one window of headers.

headers- (h-)

> Move back one window of headers.

help

> Same as ?.

hold (ho)

> Hold messages in system mailbox.

ignore

Append list of fields to ignored fields. With no arguments, list currently ignored fields.

imap

Send commands to the current IMAP server.

junk (j)

Mark messages as junk mail.

list

Print list of available commands.

mail *user* **(m)**

Compose message to *user*.

mbox

Move specified messages to *mbox* on exiting (the default).

move (mv)

Like **copy**, but mark messages for deletion after the move.

next (n)

Type next message or next message that matches argument.

pipe (pi), |

Pipe messages through a shell command.

preserve (pre)

Synonym for **hold**.

print [*list*] **(p)**

Display each message in *list*. For MIME multipart messages, display parts that are labeled "text" or "message".

Print [*list*] **(P)**

Similar to **print**, but include ignored header fields and all parts of MIME multipart messages.

quit (q)

Exit **mailx** and update folder.

remove (rem)

Remove named folders.

rename (ren)

Rename an existing folder.

reply (r)

Send mail to all on distribution list.

Reply (R)

Send mail to author only.

replyall

Reply to all recipients.

respond

Same as **reply**.

retain

Always include this list of header fields when printing messages. With no arguments, list retained fields.

save (s)
> Save message to folder.

saveignore
> Remove ignored fields when saving.

saveretain
> Override **saveignore** to retain specified fields.

seen
> Mark list of messages as read.

set (se)
> Set or print **mailx** options.

shell (sh)
> Enter a new shell.

show (Sh)
> Like **print**, but show raw message text, with no decoding, for MIME or encrypted messages.

size
> Print size of each specified message.

source
> Read commands from specified file.

thread (th)
> Show current folder in threaded format.

top
> Print first few lines of each specified message.

touch
> Mark messages to be saved in *mbox*.

type (t)
> Same as **print**.

Type (T)
> Same as **Print**.

unalias
> Discard previously defined aliases.

unanswered
> Mark specified messages as unanswered.

uncollapse (unc)
> Uncollapse threaded messages so the messages and replies are visible in header summaries again.

undelete (u)
> Restore specified deleted messages.

ungood
> Undo the effect of an earlier **good** command.

unjunk
> Undo the effect of an earlier **junk** command.

unread (U)
> Mark specified messages as unread.

unset (uns)
> Unset **mailx** options.

verify (verif)
> Verify that specified messages are S/MIME signed messages.

visual (v)
> Edit message with editor specified by the **VISUAL** environment variable.

write (w)
> Write message, without headers, to file.

xit (x)
> Same as **exit**.

z

> Move **mailx**'s attention to next windowful of text. Use **z-** to move it back.

Configuration options

These options are set inside the user's *.mailrc* configuration file. The syntax is **set** *option* or **unset** *option*. The system default configuration is in */etc/mail.rc*.

append
> Append (do not prepend) messages to *mbox*.

ask, asksub
> Prompt for subject.

askattach
> Prompt at end of message for attachments.

askbcc
> Prompt for blind-carbon-copy recipients.

askcc
> Prompt for carbon-copy recipients.

asksign
> Ask if message is to be signed.

autobcc *list*
> Specify recipients who are always to receive a blind carbon copy.

autocc *list*
> Specify recipients who are always to receive a carbon copy.

autoprint
> Print next message after a delete.

autothread
> Always enter threaded mode when a folder is opened.

cmd *command*
> Specify the default command for a pipe.

crt *num*
> Use the default pager to display a message of more than *num* lines. Defaults to the height of the terminal screen.

debug
> Same as **-d** on command line.

dot
> Interpret a solitary **.** as an EOF.

encoding *value*
> The default MIME encoding to use for outgoing messages. Possible values are **8bit** (the default) or **quoted-printable**.

escape *char*
> Specify escape character to use instead of a tilde (~).

folder *dir*
> Define directory to hold mail folders.

from *addr*
> The default address to put in the From: field.

hold
> Keep message in system mailbox upon quitting.

ignore
> Ignore interrupt signals from terminal. Print them as @.

ignoreeof
> Do not treat **^D** as an EOF.

indentprefix *string*
> Use the specified string with **~m** as the prefix for indented messages.

junkdb *addr*
> Location of the junk mail database.

keep
> Do not delete user's system mailbox when empty.

metoo
> Do not remove sender from groups when mailing to them.

noheader
> Same as **-N** on command line.

nosave
> Do not save aborted letters to *dead.letter*.

pop3-use-apop
> If set, connection to POP3 server uses APOP authentication.

quiet
> Do not print version at startup.

record *file*
> Use *file* as the path to record outgoing mail. If not set, outgoing mail is not saved.

Replyall
> Switch roles of **Reply** and **reply**.

replyto *list*
> Specify addresses for the Reply-To: field.

searchheaders

When given the specifier /x:y, expand all messages that contain the string y in the x header field.

sender *addr*

Specify the address to put into the Sender: field.

showlast

Start at the last message, not the first, when folder is opened.

toplines *num*

Print *num* lines of message with the top command. Default value is 5.

verbose

Same as -v on command line.

---

make

make [*options*] [*targets*] [*macro definitions*]

Update one or more *targets* according to dependency instructions in a description file in the current directory. By default, this file is called *makefile* or *Makefile*. Options, targets, and macro definitions can be in any order. Macro definitions are typed as:

name=string

For more information on make, see Robert Mecklenburg's *Managing Projects with GNU Make* (O'Reilly).

Options

-d, --debug

Print detailed debugging information.

-e, --environment-overrides

Override *Makefile* macro definitions with environment variables.

-f *Makefile*, **--file**=*Makefile*, **--makefile**=*Makefile*

Use *Makefile* as the description file; a filename of - denotes standard input.

-h, --help

Print options to **make** command.

-i, --ignore-errors

Ignore command error codes (same as **.IGNORE**).

-j [*jobs*], **--jobs** [=*jobs*]

Attempt to execute this many *jobs* simultaneously or, if no number is specified, as many jobs as possible.

-k, --keep-going

Abandon the current target when it fails, but keep working with unrelated targets.

-l [*load*], **--load-average** [=*load*], **--max-load** [=*load*]

Attempt to keep load below *load*, which should be a floating-point number. Used with **-j**.

-n, --just-print, --dry-run, --recon

Print commands but don't execute (used for testing).

-o *file*, **--old-file**=*file*, **--assume-old**=*file*
> Never remake *file* or cause other files to be remade on account of it.

-p, **--print-data-base**
> Print rules and variables in addition to normal execution.

-q, **--question**
> Query; return 0 if file is up to date, nonzero otherwise.

-r, **--no-built-in-rules**
> Do not use default rules.

-s, **--silent**, **--quiet**
> Do not display command lines (same as **.SILENT**).

-t, **--touch**
> Touch the target files without remaking them.

-v, **--version**
> Show version of **make**.

-w, **--print-directory**
> Display the current working directory before and after execution.

--warn-undefined-variables
> Print warning if a macro is used without being defined.

-C *directory*, **--directory** *directory*
> **cd** to *directory* before beginning **make** operations. A subsequent **-C** directive will cause **make** to attempt to **cd** into a directory relative to the current working directory.

-I *directory*, **--include-dir** *directory*
> Include *directory* in list of directories containing included files.

-S, **--no-keep-going**, **--stop**
> Cancel previous **-k** options. Useful in recursive **make**s.

-W *file*, **--what-if** *file*, **--new-file** *file*, **--assume-new** *file*
> Behave as though *file* has been recently updated.

Description-file lines

Instructions in the description file are interpreted as single lines. If an instruction must span more than one input line, use a backslash (\) at the end of the line so that the next line is considered a continuation. The description file may contain any of the following types of lines:

Blank lines
> Blank lines are ignored.

Comment lines
> A pound sign (#) can be used at the beginning of a line or anywhere in the middle. **make** ignores everything after the #.

Dependency lines
> Depending on one or more targets, certain commands that follow will be executed. Possible formats include:

> ```
> targets : dependencies
> targets : dependencies ; command
> ```

Subsequent commands are executed if dependency files (the names of which may contain wildcards) do not exist or are newer than a target. If no prerequisites are supplied, then subsequent commands are always executed (whenever any of the targets are specified). No tab should precede any targets.

Conditionals

Conditionals are evaluated when the *Makefile* is first read and determine what **make** sees—i.e., which parts of the *Makefile* are obeyed and which parts are ignored. The general syntax for a conditional is:

```
Conditional
Text if true
Else
Text if false
endif
```

ifeq (*arg1*, *arg2*), **ifeq** "*arg1*" "*arg2*"

True if the two arguments are identical. The arguments should either be placed in parentheses and separated by a comma—(*arg1*, *arg2*)—or individually quoted with either single or double quotes.

ifneq (*arg1*, *arg2*), **ifneq** "*arg1*" "*arg2*"

True if the two arguments are not identical. The arguments should either be placed in parentheses and separated by a comma, or individually quoted with either single or double quotes.

ifdef *variable*

True if *variable* has a nonempty value.

ifndef *variable*

True if *variable* has an empty value.

Suffix rules

These specify that files ending with the first suffix can be prerequisites for files ending with the second suffix (assuming the root filenames are the same). Either of these formats can be used:

```
.suffix.suffix:
.suffix:
```

The second form means that the root filename depends on the filename with the corresponding suffix.

Commands

Commands are grouped below the dependency line and are typed on lines that begin with a tab. If a command is preceded by a hyphen (-), **make** ignores any error returned. If a command is preceded by an at sign (@), the command line won't echo on the display (unless **make** is called with **-n**).

Macro definitions

These have the following form:

```
name =string
```

or:

```
define name
string
endef
```

Blank space is optional around the =.

Include statements

Similar to the C include directive, these have the form:

```
include files
```

Internal macros

$? The list of prerequisites that have been changed more recently than the current target. Can be used only in normal description-file entries, not in suffix rules.

$@ The name of the current target, except in description-file entries for making libraries, where it becomes the library name. Can be used both in normal description-file entries and in suffix rules.

$< The name of the current prerequisite that has been modified more recently than the current target.

$* The name (without the suffix) of the current prerequisite that has been modified more recently than the current target. Can be used only in suffix rules.

$% The name of the corresponding *.o* file when the current target is a library module. Can be used both in normal description-file entries and in suffix rules.

$^ A space-separated list of all dependencies with no duplications.

$+ A space-separated list of all dependencies, which includes duplications.

Pattern rules

These are a more general application of the idea behind suffix rules. If a target and a dependency both contain %, GNU **make** will substitute any part of an existing filename. For instance, the standard suffix rule:

```
$(cc) -o $@ $<
```

can be written as the following pattern rule:

```
%.o : %.c
$(cc) -o $@ $<
```

Macro modifiers

D The directory portion of any internal macro name except $?. Valid uses are:

```
$(*D)   $$(@D)   $(?D)   $(<D)
$(%D)   $(@D)    $(^D)
```

F The file portion of any internal macro name except $?. Valid uses are:

```
$(*F)   $$(@F)   $(?F)   $(<F)
$(%F)   $(@F)    $(^F)
```

Functions

$(subst *from,to,string***)**
> Replace all occurrences of *from* with *to* in *string*.

$(patsubst *pattern,to,string***)**
> Similar to **subst**, but treat **%** as a wildcard within *pattern*. Substitute *to* for any word in *string* that matches *pattern*.

$(strip *string***)**
> Remove all extraneous whitespace.

$(findstring *substring,mainstring***)**
> Return *substring* if it exists within *mainstring*; otherwise, return null.

$(filter *pattern,string***)**
> Return those words in *string* that match at least one word in *pattern*. *pattern* may include the wildcard **%**.

$(filter-out *pattern,string***)**
> Remove those words in *string* that match at least one word in *pattern*. *pattern* may include the wildcard **%**.

$(sort *list***)**
> Return *list*, sorted in lexical order.

$(dir *list***)**
> Return the directory part (everything up to the last slash) of each filename in *list*.

$(notdir *list***)**
> Return the nondirectory part (everything after the last slash) of each filename in *list*.

$(suffix *list***)**
> Return the suffix part (everything after the last period) of each filename in *list*.

$(basename *list***)**
> Return everything but the suffix part (everything up to the last period) of each filename in *list*.

$(addsuffix *suffix,list***)**
> Return each filename given in *list* with *suffix* appended.

$(addprefix *prefix,list***)**
> Return each filename given in *list* with *prefix* prepended.

$(join *list1,list2***)**
> Return a list formed by concatenating the two arguments word by word (e.g., **$(join a b,.c .o)** becomes **a.c b.o**).

$(word *n,string***)**
> Return the *n*th word of *string*.

$(wordlist *start,end,string***)**
> Return words in *string* between word *start* and word *end*, inclusive.

$(words *string***)**
> Return the number of words in *string*.

$(firstword *list*)

>   Return the first word in the list *list*.

$(wildcard *pattern*)

>   Return a list of existing files in the current directory that match *pattern*.

$(foreach *variable,list,string*)

>   For each whitespace-separated word in *list*, expand its value and assign it to *variable*; then expand *string*, which usually contains a function referencing *variable*. Return the list of results.

$(if *condition,then-string[,else-string]*)

>   Expand string *condition* if it expands to a nonempty string, then expand the *then-string*. If *condition* expands to an empty string, return the empty string or, if specified, expand and return the *else-string*.

$(call *variable,parameters*)

>   Expand each item in comma-separated list *parameters* and assign it to a temporary variable, **$(**$n$**)**, where n is an incremented number beginning with 0. Then expand *variable*, a string referencing these temporary variables, and return the result.

$(origin *variable*)

>   Return one of the following strings that describes how *variable* was defined: **undefined**, **default**, **environment**, **environment override**, **file**, **command line**, **override**, or **automatic**.

$(shell *command*)

>   Return the results of *command*. Any newlines in the result are converted to spaces. This function works similarly to back-quotes in most shells.

$(error *string*)

>   When evaluated, generate a fatal error with the message *string*.

$(warning *string*)

>   When evaluated, generate a warning with the message *string*.

Macro string substitution

$(*macro:s1=s2***)**

>   Evaluates to the current definition of **$(***macro***)**, after substituting the string *s2* for every occurrence of *s1* that occurs either immediately before a blank or tab, or at the end of the macro definition.

Special target names

.DEFAULT:

>   Commands associated with this target are executed if **make** can't find any description-file entries or suffix rules with which to build a requested target.

.DELETE_ON_ERROR:

>   If this target exists in a *Makefile*, delete the target of any rule whose commands return a nonzero exit status.

.EXPORT_ALL_VARIABLES:

If this target exists, export all macros to all child processes.

.IGNORE:

Ignore error codes. Same as the **-i** option.

.INTERMEDIATE:

This target's dependencies should be treated as intermediate files.

.NOTPARALLEL:

If this target exists in a *Makefile*, run **make** serially, ignoring option **-j**.

.PHONY:

Always execute commands under a target, even if it is an existing, up-to-date file.

.PRECIOUS:

Files you specify for this target are not removed when you send a signal (such as an interrupt) that aborts **make** or when a command line in your description file returns an error.

.SECONDARY:

Like **.INTERMEDIATE**, this target's dependencies should be treated as intermediate files, but never automatically deleted.

.SILENT:

Execute commands, but do not echo them. Same as the **-s** option.

.SUFFIXES:

Suffixes associated with this target are meaningful in suffix rules. If no suffixes are listed, the existing list of suffix rules is effectively "turned off."

---

makedbm

makedbm [*options*] *infile outfile*

makedbm [*option*]

NFS/NIS command. Create or dump an NIS **dbm** file. **makedbm** will take a text *infile* and convert it to a **gdbm** database file named *outfile*. This file is suitable for use with **ypserv**. Each line of the input file is converted to a single record. All characters up to the first TAB or SPACE form the key, and the rest of the line is the data. If a line ends with **\&**, the data for that record is continued onto the next line. The **#** character is given no special treatment. *infile* can be -, in which case the standard input is read.

makedbm generates two special keys: the **YP_M*ER_NAME** key, which is the value of the current host (unless another name is specified with **-m**), and the **YP_L*_MODIFIED** key, which is the date of *infile* (or the current time if *infile* is -).

Options

-a   Add support for mail aliases.

-b   Insert **YP_INTERDOMAIN** key into map. This indicates that **ypserv** should fall back to DNS lookups when a host's address is not found in NIS.

-c   Send a **YPPROC_CLEAR** signal to **ypserv**, causing it to clear all cached entries.

-i *file_name*
    Create a **YP_INPUT_NAME** key with the value *file_name*.

-l   Convert keys of the given map to lowercase.

-m *master_name*
    Specify the value of the **YP_M*ER_NAME** key. The default value is the current hostname.

--no-limit-check
    Don't enforce NIS size limits for keys or data.

-o *file_name*
    Create a **YP_OUTPUT_NAME** key with the value *file_name*.

-r   Treat lines beginning with # as comments. Do not include them in the datafile.

-s   Add the key **YP_SECURE**, indicating that **ypserv** should accept connections to the database only from secure NIS networks.

-u *filename*
    Undo a **gdbm** file: print out a **dbm** file, one entry per line, with a single space separating keys from values.

Example

It's easy to write shell scripts to convert standard files such as */etc/passwd* to the key-value form used by **makedbm**. For example, the **awk** program:

```
BEGIN { FS =":";OFS = "\t";}{ print $1, $0}
```

takes the */etc/passwd* file and converts it to a form that can be read by **makedbm** to make the NIS file *passwd.byname*. That is, the key is a username and the value is the remaining line in the */etc/passwd* file.

---

makemap

makemap [*options*] *typename*

System administration command. Create database maps for use by **sendmail** in keyed map lookups. **makemap** will read from standard input and create a database file of type *type* with filename *name*.**db**. If the **TrustedUser** option is set in */etc/sendmail.cf* and **makemap** is invoked as root, the ouput file will be owned by **TrustedUser**.

Input should be formatted as:

    key value

Comment lines with #. Indicate parameter substitution with %*n*. Specify a literal % character by entering it twice: %%. The *type* may be **btree** or **hash**.

Options

-c *size*
    Specify hash or B-Tree cache size.

-C *file*

Look up **TrustedUser** in the specified **sendmail** configuration *file*.

-d   Allow duplicate entries. Valid only with **btree** type maps.

-D *x*

Treat *x* as the comment marker instead of *#*.

-e   Allow empty value data fields.

-f   Suppress conversion of uppercase to lowercase.

-l   List supported map types.

-N   Append the zero-byte string terminator specified in **sendmail**'s configuration file to mapped entries.

-o   Append to existing file instead of replacing it.

-r   If some keys already exist, replace them. (By default, **makemap** will exit when encountering a duplicated key.)

-s   Ignore safety checks.

-t *delimiter*

Use *delimiter* instead of whitespace.

-u   Undo a map: print out the specified database file, one entry per line.

-v   Verbose mode.

man

man [*options*] [*section*] [*title*]

Display information from the online reference manuals. **man** locates and prints the named *title* from the designated reference *section*.

Traditionally, manpages are divided into nine sections, where section 1 consists of user commands, section 2 contains system calls, and so forth (see "Section names," coming up, for the full list). By default, all sections are consulted, so the *section* option serves to bypass the most common entry and find an entry of the same name in a different section (e.g., **man 2 nice**).

Numerous other utilities—such as **info**, **xman**, and the Konqueror browser—can also display manpages.

Options

-a   Show all pages matching *title*.

-B   Specify the browser to use on HTML files. Overrides the BROWSER environment variable. The default is */usr/bin/less -is*.

-c   Reformat output even if there is a current cat file.

-C *file*

Specify a configuration file to use. Default is */etc/man.config*.

-d   Display debugging information but not the manpage.

-D   Display debugging information and also display the manpage.

-f   Same as **whatis** command.

-F, --preformat

Format the manpage but do not display it.

-h, --help

Print a help message and exit.

-H *command*

Specify a command to render HTML files as text. Overrides the HTMLPAGER environment variable. The default is */bin/cat*.

-k   Same as **apropos** command.

-K *directory*

A kind of super-**k** option. Search for a term in all manpages and display the name of each page, along with a prompt asking whether you want to view the page. This can be very slow.

-m *systems*

Search manual pages on the specified system or systems. *systems* should be a comma-separated list.

-M *path*

Search for manual pages in *path*. Ignore **-m** option.

-p *preprocessors*

Preprocess manual pages with *preprocessors* before turning them over to **nroff**, **troff**, or **groff**. Always runs **soelim** first to read in files to be included in the one currently being processed. *preprocessors* can be any combination of **e** for **eqn**, **g** for **grap**, **p** for **pic**, **r** for **refer**, **t** for **tbl**, and **v** for **vgrind**.

-P *pager*

Specify the pager to use. Overrides the MANPAGE environment variable. The default is */usr/bin/less -is*.

-S *sections*

Colon-separated list of sections to look in for an entry.

-t   Format the manual page with **/usr/bin/groff -Tgv -mandoc**.

-w, -W, --path

Print only the pathnames of entries on standard output, one per line.

Section names

Manual pages are divided into sections for various audiences:

1   Executable programs or shell commands.

2   System calls (functions provided by the kernel).

3   Library calls (functions within system libraries).

4   Special files (usually found in */dev*).

5   File formats and conventions (e.g., */etc/passwd*).

6   Games.

7   Macro packages and conventions.

8   System administration commands (usually only for a privileged user).

9   Kernel routines (nonstandard).

manpath

manpath [*options*]

Attempt to determine path to manual pages. Check **$MANPATH** first; if that is not set, consult */etc/man.conf*, user environment variables, and the current working directory. The **manpath** command is a symbolic link to **man** and is equivalent to **man --path**. Most of the options are ignored for **manpath**.

Options

-d, --debug
Print debugging information.

-h   Print help message and then exit.

---

md5sum

md5sum [*option*] [*files*]

md5sum [*option*] --check [*file*]

Compute or check 128-bit MD5 checksums. Used to verify that no change has been made to a file. With no files or - specified, read from standard input. The exit status is 0 for success and nonzero for failure.

Options

-b, --binary
Read the files in binary mode.

-c, --check
Check the MD5 sum and file information in the *file* argument (or standard input) against the corresponding files and verify that they are consistent. The input must have been generated by an earlier **md5sum** command.

--help
Print usage information and exit.

--status
Don't generate output messages; the exit code indicates success or failure. Used only with **--check**.

--string=*string*
Compute the MD5 sum for the specified string. This option does not take a *file* argument. Put quotes around the string if it contains spaces.

-t, --text
Read files in text mode. The default.

--version
Print version information and exit.

-w, --warn
Warn about improperly formatted checksum lines. Used only with **--check**.

merge

merge [*options*] *file1 file2 file3*

Perform a three-way file merge, putting the result in *file1*. The effect is easiest to understand if *file2* is considered the original version of a file, *file3* an altered version of *file2*, and *file1* a later altered version of *file2*.

After the merge, *file1* contains both the changes from *file2* to *file1* and the changes from *file2* to *file3*. In other words, *file1* keeps its changes and incorporates the changes in *file3* as well. **merge** does not change *file2* or *file3*.

If a line from *file2* was changed in different ways in both *file1* and *file3*, **merge** recognizes a conflict. By default, the command outputs a warning and puts brackets around the conflict, with lines preceded by <<<<<<< and >>>>>>>. A typical conflict looks like this:

```
<<<<<<< file1
relevant lines from file1
=======
relevant lines from file3
>>>>>>> file3
```

If there are conflicts, the user should edit the result and delete one of the alternatives.

Options

-A   Output conflicts using the -A style of **diff3**. This merges all changes leading from *file2* to *file3* into *file1* and generates the most verbose output.

-e   Don't warn about conflicts.

-E   Output conflict information in a less verbose style than -A; this is the default.

-L *label*
       Specify up to three labels to be used in place of the corresponding filenames in conflict reports. That is:

       merge -L *x* -L *y* -L *z* *file_a file_b file_c*

       generates output that looks as if it came from *x*, *y*, and *z* instead of from *file_a*, *file_b*, and *file_c*.

-p   Send results to standard output instead of overwriting *file1*.

-q   Quiet; do not warn about conflicts.

-V   Print version number.

mesg

mesg [*option*]

Change the ability of other users to send **write** messages to your terminal. With no options, display the permission status.

Options

n   Forbid **write** messages.

y   Allow **write** messages (the default).

mkdir

mkdir [*options*] *directories*

Create one or more *directories*. You must have write permission in the parent directory in order to create a directory. See also **rmdir**. The default mode of the new directory is 0777, modified by the system or user's **umask**.

Options

-m *mode*, **--mode** *mode*
> Set the access *mode* for new directories. See **chmod** for an explanation of acceptable formats for *mode*.

-p, **--parents**
> Create intervening parent directories if they don't exist.

-v, **--verbose**
> Print a message for each directory created.

--help
> Print help message and then exit.

--version
> Print version number and then exit.

-Z *context*, **--context=***context*
> Set security context in SELinux.

Examples

Create a read-only directory named **personal**:

    mkdir -m 444 personal

The following sequence:

    mkdir work; cd work
    mkdir junk; cd junk
    mkdir questions; cd ../..

can be accomplished by typing this:

    mkdir -p work/junk/questions

mkdosfs

mkdosfs [*options*] *device* [*blocks*]

mkfs.msdos [*options*] *device* [*blocks*]

System administration command. Format *device* as an MS-DOS filesystem. You may specify the number of blocks on the device or allow **mkdosfs** to guess.

Options

-A Create an Atari MS-DOS filesystem.

-b *backup-sector*
> Specify sector for backup boot sector. The default value depends on the number of reserved sectors, but is usually sector 6.

-c Scan *device* for bad blocks before execution.

-C   Create and format a file suitable for use on a floppy disk. The *device* given on the command line should be a filename, and the number of *blocks* must also be specified.

-f *n*

Specify number of File Allocation Tables (FATs) to create (either **1** or **2**).

-F *fat-size*

Create File Allocation Tables (FATs) of size *fat-size*. By default this will be between 12 and 16 bits. Set to **32** to create a FAT32 filesystem.

-i *volume-id*

Use the specified 32-bit hexadecimal *volume-id* instead of calculating a number based on the time of creation.

-I   Force installation to a device without partitions. This is useful when formating magneto-optical disks.

-l *file*

Read list of bad blocks from *file*.

-m *message-file*

Set the message to be used when the filesystem is booted without an installed operating system to the contents of the file *message-file*. The message may be up to 418 bytes in size. If filename is a hyphen, read text from standard input.

-n *label*

Set volume name for filesystem to *label*. The volume name may be up to 11 characters long.

-r *maximum-entries*

Set the *maximum-entries* allowed in the root directory. The default is 112 or 224 for floppies, and 512 for hard disks.

-R *reserved-sectors*

Create the specified number of *reserved-sectors*. The default depends on the size of the File Allocation Table (FAT). For 32-bit FAT, the default is 32; for all other sizes, the default is 1.

-s *sectors*

Set the number of disk *sectors* per cluster. The number must be a power of 2.

-S *sector-size*

Create logical sectors of *sector-size* bytes. Size must be a power of 2 and at least 512 bytes.

-v   Print verbose information about progress.

mke2fs

```
mke2fs [options] device [blocks]
mkfs.ext2 [options] device [blocks]
```

System administration command. Format *device* as a Linux Second Extended Filesystem. You may specify the number of blocks on the device or allow **mke2fs** to guess.

Options

-b *block-size*
> Specify block size in bytes.

-c Scan *device* for bad blocks before execution.

-E *featurelist*
> Specify extended features. This option's parameters may be given in a comma-separated list:

> **stride**=*size*
>> Configure filesystem for a RAID array. Set stride size to *size* blocks per stripe.

> **resize**=*blocks*
>> Reserve descriptor table space to grow filesystem to the specified number of blocks.

-f *fragment-size*
> Specify fragment size in bytes.

-F Force **mke2fs** to run even if filesystem is mounted or device is not a block special device. This option is probably best avoided.

-i *bytes-per-inode*
> Create an inode for each *bytes-per-inode* of space. *bytes-per-inode* must be 1024 or greater; it is 4096 by default.

-j Create an ext3 journal. This is the same as invoking **mkfs.ext3**.

-J *parameterlist*
> Use specified *parameterlist* to create an ext3 journal. The following two parameters may be given in a comma-separated list:

> **size**=*journal-size*
>> Create a journal of *journal-size* megabytes. The size may be between 1024 filesystem blocks and 102,400 filesystem blocks in size (e.g., 1–100 megabytes if using 1K blocks, 4–400 megabytes if using 4K blocks).

> **device**=*journal-device*
>> Use an external *journal-device* to hold the filesystem journal. The *journal-device* can be specified by name, by volume label, or by UUID.

-l *filename*
> Consult *filename* for a list of bad blocks.

-L *label*
> Set volume *label* for filesystem.

-m *percentage*
> Reserve *percentage* percent of the blocks for use by privileged users.

-M *directory*
> Set the last mounted directory for filesystem to *directory*.

-n Don't create the filesystem; just show what would happen if it were run. This option is overridden by **-F**.

-N *inodes*

> Specify number of *inodes* to reserve for filesystem. By default, this number is calculated from the number of blocks and the inode size.

-o *os*

> Set filesystem operating system type to *os*. The default value is usually **Linux**.

-O *featurelist*

> Use specified *featurelist* to create filesystem. The **sparse_super** and **filetype** features are used by default on kernels 2.2 and later. The following parameters may be given in a comma-separated list:

> **dir_index**

>> Use hashed B-trees to index directories.

> **filetype**

>> Store file type information in directory entries.

> **has_journal**

>> Create an ext3 journal. Same as using the **-j** option.

> **journal_dev**

>> Prepare an external journaling device by creating an ext3 journal on *device* instead of formatting it.

> **sparse_super**

>> Save space on a large filesystem by creating fewer super-block backup copies.

-q   Quiet mode.

-r *revision*

> Set filesystem revision number to *revision*.

-S   Write only superblock and group descriptors; suppress writing of inode table and block and inode bitmaps. Useful only when attempting to salvage damaged systems.

-T *use*

> Set bytes-per-inode based on the intended *use* of the filesystem. Supported filesystem usage types are defined in */etc/mke2fs.conf*. Common types include:

> **news**

>> Four kilobytes per inode.

> **largefile**

>> One megabyte per inode.

> **largefile4**

>> Four megabytes per inode.

-v   Verbose mode.

-V   Print version number, then exit.

mkfifo

mkfifo [option] names

Make one or more named pipes (FIFOs) with the specified names.

Options

-**m** *mode*, --**mode**=*mode*
> Set permission mode. Default is 666, with the bits in the umask subtracted.

--**help**
> Print help information and exit.

--**version**
> Print version information and exit.

---

mkfs

mkfs [options] [fs-options] filesys [blocks]

System administration command. Construct a filesystem on a device (such as a hard disk partition). *filesys* is either the name of the device or the mountpoint. **mkfs** is actually a frontend that invokes the appropriate version of **mkfs** according to a filesystem type specified by the -**t** option. For example, a Linux Second Extended Filesystem uses **mkfs.ext2** (which is the same as **mke2fs**); MS-DOS filesystems use **mkfs.msdos**. *fs-options* are options specific to the filesystem type. *blocks* is the size of the filesystem in 1024-byte blocks.

Options

-**V**   Produce verbose output, including all commands executed to create the specific filesystem.

-**t** *fs-type*
> Tells **mkfs** what type of filesystem to construct.

Filesystem-specific options

These options must follow generic options and cannot be combined with them. Most filesystem builders support these three options:

-**c**   Check for bad blocks on the device before building the filesystem.

-**l** *file*
> Read the file *file* for the list of bad blocks on the device.

-**v**   Produce verbose ouput.

---

mkfs.ext3

mkfs.ext3 [options] devicesize

Create a journaling ext3 filesystem. Options are identical to **mke2fs**. See **mkfs**.

mkisofs

mkisofs [*options*] **-o** *pathspecs*

Generate an ISO9660/Joliet/HFS filesystem for writing to a CD. (HFS is the native Macintosh Hierarchical File System.) **mkisofs** takes a snapshot of a directory tree and generates a binary image that corresponds to an ISO9660 or HFS filesystem when it is written to a block device. Each specified *pathspec* describes the path of a directory tree to be copied into the ISO9660 filesystem; if multiple paths are specified, the files in all the paths are merged to form the image.

mkisofs is now generally a symbolic link to **genisoimage**.

mklost+found

mklost+found

System administration command. Create a *lost+found* directory in the current working directory. Intended for Linux Second Extended Filesystems.

mknod

mknod [*options*] *name type* [*major minor*]

Create a special file (a file that can send or receive data). Special files can be character files (read one character at a time), block files (read several characters at a time), or FIFO pipes (see **mkfifo**).

To choose which type of device to create, use one of the following arguments:

p   Create a FIFO file (named pipe). You do not need to specify the major and minor device numbers.

b   Create a block file. You must specify the major and minor device numbers the file represents.

c *or* **u**
   Create a character file. You must specify the major and minor device numbers the file represents.

Linux's */dev/MAKEDEV* utility is useful for creating one or more devices of a given type in a single command.

Options
--help
   Print usage information and exit.

-m *mode*, **--mode=***mode*
   Set the file mode of the device, as with **chmod**. The default mode is **a=rw** unless you have chosen other settings via **umask**.

--version
   Print version information and exit.

mkswap

`mkswap [options] device`

System administration command. Prepare swapspace on *device*: a disk partition or a prepared file. This command can create old and new style swap areas. The older style provides backward compatibility with 2.2 kernels, but is less efficient and more limited in size. The **mkswap** command has some dangerous options we have omitted here. They provide backward compatibility and solutions to problems with older libraries, but can destroy a disk if specified incorrectly.

Options

-c   Check for bad blocks before creating the swapspace.

-L *label*
Create a label for use with **swapon**.

-v0   Create an old style swap area.

-v1   Create a new style swap area. (The default behavior on newer kernels.)

mktemp

`mktemp [options] [template]`

Generate a unique temporary filename for use in a script. The filename is based on the specified template, which may be any filename with at least six Xs appended (e.g., */tmp/mytemp. XXXXXX*). **mktemp** replaces the Xs with the current process number and/or a unique letter combination. The file is created with mode 0600 (unless **-u** is specified), and the filename is written to standard output. With no template specified, the default file *tmp. XXXXXXXXXX* is created.

Options

-d, --directory
Make a directory, not a file.

--help
Print usage information and exit.

-q, --quiet
Fail silently in case of error. Useful to prevent error output from being sent to standard error.

-u, --dryrun
Operate in "unsafe" mode and unlink the temporary file before **mktemp** exits. Use of this option is not recommended.

-V, --version
Print version information and exit.

Linux
Commands

modinfo

modinfo [*options*] *object-file*

System administration command. Print information about kernel module *object-file*. Information is read from tag names in the modinfo section of the module file. By default, it will print the module's filename, description, author, license, and parameters.

Options

-0, --null

Separate fields with the null character instead of newlines.

-F *fieldname*, **--field** *fieldname*

Print only the value of the specified *fieldname* (e.g., author, license, depends, etc.).

-h, --help

Print usage message, then exit.

-k *kernel*

Specify kernel to use (e.g., a kernel other than the running kernel).

-V, --version

Print version number of the module.

modprobe

modprobe [*options*] [*modules*] [*moduleoptions*]

System administration command. With no options, attempt to load the specified module, as well as all modules on which it depends. If more than one module is specified, attempt to load further modules only if the previous module failed to load. When specifying a module, use only its name without its path or trailing .o. **modprobe** will pass to the kernel any options following the module name.

Options

-a, --all

Load all modules matching the given wildcard.

-c, --showconfig

Print **modprobe**'s current configuration.

-C *file*, **--config** *file*

Read additional configuration from *file* instead of */etc/modules.conf*.

-f, --force

Ignore all versioning information during module insertion. Even if the module does not match the running kernel, **modprobe** will try to insert it anyway.

--force-modversion

Ignore module versioning mismatches.

--force-vermagic

Ignore kernel versioning mismatches.

--first-time

Return failure if told to insert a module that is already present or remove a module that is not loaded. Normally, **modprobe** will return success if asked to perform an unnecessary action.

-i, --ignore-install, --ignore-remove
Ignore any *install* and *remove* directives in the configuration file.

-l, --list
List modules matching the given wildcard (or "*" if no wildcard is given).

-n, --dry-run
Perform all of the actions except actually inserting or removing the module.

-q, --quiet
Suppress warnings during failure to load a module and continue processing other modules.

-r, --remove
Remove the specified modules, as well as the modules on which they depend.

-s, --syslog
Send error messages to **syslogd** instead of to standard error.

-t*type*, **--type** *type*
Load only a specific type of module.

-v, --verbose
Print commands as they are executed.

-V, --version
Print version, then exit.

---

more

more [*options*] [*files*]

Display the named *files* on a terminal, one screenful at a time. See **less** for an alternative to **more**.

Options

+num
Begin displaying at line number *num*.

-num *number*
Set screen size to *number* lines.

+/pattern
Search for *pattern* and begin displaying at that point.

-c   Repaint screen from top instead of scrolling.

-d   Display the prompt "[Press space to continue, 'q' to quit]" instead of ringing the bell. Also display "[Press 'h' for instructions]" in response to illegal commands.

-f   Count logical rather than screen lines. Useful when long lines wrap past the width of the screen.

-l   Ignore form-feed (Ctrl-L) characters.

-p   Page through the file by clearing each window instead of scrolling. This is sometimes faster.

-s   Squeeze; display multiple blank lines as one.

-u   Suppress underline characters.

Commands

All commands in **more** are based on **vi** commands. You can specify a number before many commands to have them executed multiple times. For instance, **3:p** causes **more** to skip back three files, the same as issuing **:p** three times. The optional number is indicated by *num* in the following list:

SPACE
> Display next screen of text.

z Display next *num* lines of text, and redefine a screenful to *num* lines. Default is one screenful.

RETURN
> Display next *num* lines of text, and redefine a screenful to *num* lines. Default is one line.

d, ^D
> Scroll *num* lines of text, and redefine scroll size to *num* lines. Default is one line.

q, Q, INTERRUPT
> Quit.

s Skip next *num* lines of text. Default is one line.

f Skip forward *num* screens of text. Default is one screen.

b, ^B
> Skip backward *num* screens of text. Default is one screen. Does not work on pipes.

' Return to point where previous search began.

= Print number of current line.

/pattern
> Search for *pattern*, skipping to *num*th occurrence if an argument is specified.

?, h
> Display a summary of commands.

n Repeat last search, skipping to *num*th occurrence if an argument is specified.

!*cmd*, :!*cmd*
> Invoke shell and execute *cmd* in it.

v Invoke an editor on the file at the current line. Use the editor in the environment variable VISUAL if defined, or EDITOR if that is defined; otherwise, default to **vi**.

^L Redraw screen.

:n Skip to next file, or *num*th file if an argument is specified.

:p Skip to previous file, or *num*th previous if an argument is specified.

:f Print current filename and line number.

. Reexecute previous command.

Examples

Page through *file* in "clear" mode, and display prompts:

```
more -cd file
```

Format *doc* to the screen, removing underlines:

```
nroff doc | more -u
```

View the manpage for the **more** command; begin at the first appearance of the word "scroll":

```
man more|more +/scroll
```

mount

mount [*options*] [[*device*] *directory*]

System administration command. Mount a file structure. The file structure on *device* is mounted on *directory*. If no *device* is specified, **mount** looks for an entry in */etc/fstab* to find out what device is associated with the given directory. The directory, which must already exist and should be empty, becomes the name of the root of the newly mounted file structure. If **mount** is invoked with no arguments, it displays the name of each mounted device, the directory on which it is mounted, its filesystem type, and any mount options associated with the device.

Options

-a   Mount all filesystems listed in */etc/fstab*. Use **-t** to limit this to all filesystems of a particular type.

--bind *olddirectory newdirectory*
       Bind a mounted subtree to a new location. The tree will be available from both the old and new directory. This binding does not include any volumes mounted below the specified directory.

-f   Fake mount. Go through the motions of checking the device and directory, but do not actually mount the filesystem.

-F   When used with **-a**, fork a new process to mount each system.

-h   Print help message, then exit.

-l   When reporting on mounted filesystems, show filesystem labels for filesystems that have them.

-L *label*
       Mount filesystem with the specified label.

--move *olddirectory newdirectory*
       Move a mounted device to a new location. Maintains options and submounts.

-n   Do not record the mount in */etc/mtab*.

-o *option*
       Qualify the mount with a mount option. Many filesystem types have their own options. The following are common to most filesystems:

       async
              Read input and output to the device asynchronously.

atime

Update inode access time for each access. This is the default behavior.

auto

Allow mounting with the **-a** option.

defaults

Use all options' default values (**async, auto, dev, exec, nouser, rw, suid**).

dev

Interpret any special devices that exist on the filesystem.

dirsync

Perform all directory updates to the filesystem synchronously.

exec

Allow binaries to be executed.

_netdev

Filesystem is a network device requiring network access.

noatime

Do not update inode access time for each access.

noauto

Do not allow mounting via the **-a** option.

nodev

Do not interpret any special devices that exist on the filesystem.

noexec

Do not allow the execution of binaries on the filesystem.

nofail

Do not report errors if device doesn't exist.

nosuid

Do not acknowledge any **suid** or **sgid** bits.

nouser

Only privileged users will have access to the filesystem.

remount

Expect the filesystem to have already been mounted, and remount it.

ro

Allow read-only access to the filesystem.

rw

Allow read/write access to the filesystem.

suid

Acknowledge **suid** and **sgid** bits.

sync

Read input and output to the device synchronously.

user

Allow unprivileged users to mount or unmount the filesystem. The defaults on such a system will be **nodev**, **noexec**, and **nosuid**, unless otherwise specified.

users

Allow any user to mount or unmount the filesystem. The defaults on such a system will be **nodev**, **noexec**, and **nosuid**, unless otherwise specified.

-O *option*

Limit systems mounted with -a by -O's filesystem options (as used with -o). Use a comma-separated list to specify more than one option, and prefix an option with **no** to exclude filesystems with that option. Options -t and -O are cumulative.

-r   Mount filesystem read-only.

--bind *olddirectory newdirectory*

Bind a mounted subtree to a new location. The tree will be available from both the old and new directory. Include any volumes mounted below the specified directory.

-s   Where possible, ignore mount options specified by -o that are not supported by the filesystem.

-t *type*

Specify the filesystem type. Possible values include **adfs**, **affs**, **autofs**, **coda**, **cramfs**, **devpts**, **efs**, **ext2**, **ext3**, **hfs**, **hpfs**, **iso9660**, **jfs**, **minix**, **msdos**, **ncpfs**, **nfs**, **nfs4**, **ntfs**, **proc**, **qnx4**, **reiserfs**, **romfs**, **smbfs**, **sysv**, **tmpfs**, **udf**, **ufs**, **umsdos**, **vfat**, **xfs**, and **xiafs**. The default type is **iso9660**. The type **auto** may also be used to set **mount** to autodetect the filesystem. When used with -a, this option can limit the types mounted. Use a comma-separated list to specify more than one type to mount. Prefix a list (or type) with **no** to exclude those types.

-U *uuid*

Mount filesystem with the specified *uuid*.

-v   Display mount information verbosely.

-V   Print version, then exit.

-w   Mount filesystem read/write. This is the default.

Files

/etc/fstab

List of filesystems to be mounted and options to use when mounting them.

/etc/mtab

List of filesystems currently mounted and the options with which they were mounted.

/proc/partitions

Used to find filesystems by label and uuid.

mountd   rpc.mountd [*options*]

NFS/NIS command. NFS mount request server. **mountd** reads the
file */etc/exports* to determine which filesystems are available for
mounting by which machines. It also provides information about
which filesystems are mounted by which clients. See also **nfsd**.

Options

-d *kind*, **--debug** *kind*
Specify debugging facility. Accepted values for *kind* are
general, **call**, **auth**, **parse**, and **all**.

-f *file*, **--exports-file** *file*
Read the export permissions from *file* instead of */etc/exports*.

-F, **--foreground**
Run **mountd** in the foreground.

-h, **--help**
Print help message, then exit.

-n, **--no-tcp**
Use UDP for mounts.

-N *n*, **--no-nfs-version** *n*
Do not offer NFS version *n*.

-o *n*, **--descriptors** *n*
Allow no more than *n* open file descriptors. The default is 256.

-p *n*, **--port** *n*
Bind to specified port instead of accepting a port from
portmapper.

-r, **--reverse-lookup**
Perform a reverse lookup on ip address when requested to
report mounting hosts (a DUMP request).

-v, **--version**
Print the version number, then exit.

-V *n*, **--nfs-version** *n*
Explicity offer NFS version *n*.

Files

/etc/exports
Information about mount permissions.

/var/lib/nfs/rmtab
List of filesystems currently mounted by clients.

mt   mt [*option*] *operation* [*count* | *arguments*]

Control a magnetic tape drive used to back up or restore system
data. The version of the **mt** command documented here is the
GNU version of **mt**. The *operation* argument determines what
action will be taken, and, unless the **-f** or **-t** option is used, the

action is applied to the default tape drive named in the TAPE environment variable. The *count* argument determines how many times the operation is to be repeated. If not specified, it defaults to 1. Some operations take one or more arguments other than a count, as noted in the descriptions below.

Options

-f *device*, **-t** *device*

> Name the tape device to use. This may be a local device, a character special file (see **mknod**), or a remote device, named in the format *host:/path/to/drive* or *user@host:path/to/drive*.

--help

> Print usage message and exit.

-V, --version

> Print version number and exit. Also tells you if you are running the GNU version of **mt** or the **mt-st** version.

Operations

mt can perform the following operations on tape drives. Unique abbreviations are allowed.

asf *n*

> Move to file number *n* on the tape. This is the same as rewinding the tape and moving forward *n* files with **fsf**.

bsf *n*

> Move backward *n* files, positioning the tape at the last block of the previous file.

bsfm *n*

> Move backward *n* file marks, to a position on the side of the file mark closer to the beginning of the tape.

bsr *n*

> Move backward *n* records.

eof, weof *n*

> Write *n* end-of-file (EOF) notations at the current location on the tape.

erase

> Erase the tape.

fsf *n*

> Move forward *n* files, positioning the tape at the first block of the next file.

fsfm *n*

> Move forward *n* file marks, to a position on the side of the file mark closer to the beginning of the tape.

fsr *n*

> Move forward *n* records.

offline, rewoffl

> Rewind and unload the tape (if drive supports unload).

retension

Used when the tape has become loosely wound, usually because it has been dropped, shaken, or transported. Rewinds the tape, moves forward to the end of the tape, then rewinds again.

rewind

Return to the beginning of the tape.

seek *n*

Seek to block *n* on the tape.

status

Display the status of the tape drive.

---

mv

mv [*option*] *sources target*

Move or rename files and directories. The source (first column) and target (second column) determine the result (third column).

Source	Target	Result
File	*name* (nonexistent)	Rename file to *name*.
File	Existing file	Overwrite existing file with source file.
Directory	*name* (nonexistent)	Rename directory to *name*.
Directory	Existing directory	Move directory to be a subdirectory of existing directory.
One or more files	Existing directory	Move files to directory.

The **mv** command is often aliased as **mv -i** in the *.bashrc* file, especially for the root account, to prevent inadvertently overwriting files.

Options

-b   Back up existing files before removing.

--backup[=*type*]

Like **-b**, but can take an argument specifying the type of version-control file to use for the backup. The value of *type* overrides the VERSION_CONTROL environment variable, which determines the type of backups made. The acceptable values for version control are:

t, numbered

Always make numbered backups.

nil, existing

Make numbered backups of files that already have them, and make simple backups of the others. This is the default.

never, simple

Always make simple backups.

none, off

Never make backups.

-f, --force
> Force the move, even if *target* file exists; suppress messages about restricted access modes. Same as **--reply=yes**.

--help
> Print a help message and then exit.

-i, --interactive
> Query user before removing files. Same as **--reply=query**.

--reply=*prompt*
> Specify how to handle prompt if the destination exists already. Possible values are **yes**, **no**, and **query**.

--strip-trailing-slashes
> Remove trailing slashes from source paths.

-S *suffix*, **--suffix=***suffix*
> Override the SIMPLE_BACKUP_SUFFIX environment variable, which determines the suffix used for making simple backup files. If the suffix is not set either way, the default is a tilde (~).

-T, --no-target-directory
> Treat the destination as a file.

--target-directory=*dir*
> Move all source files and directories into the specified directory.

-u, --update
> Do not remove a file or link if its modification date is the same as or newer than that of its replacement.

-v, --verbose
> Print the name of each file before moving it.

--version
> Print version information and then exit.

---

named

named [*options*]

TCP/IP command. Internet domain nameserver. **named** is used by resolver libraries to provide access to the Internet distributed naming database. With no arguments, **named** reads */etc/named.conf* for any initial data and listens for queries on a privileged port. See RFC 1034 and RFC 1035 for more details.

There are several **named** binaries available at different Linux archives, displaying various behaviors. Here we describe **named** as provided by Internet Software Consortium's Berkeley Internet Name Domain (BIND) version 9.2.x.

Options

-c *file*
> Read configuration information from *file* instead of */etc/named.conf*.

-d *debuglevel*

Print debugging information. *debuglevel* is a number indicating the level of messages printed.

-f   Run **named** in the foreground.

-g   Run **named** in the foreground and send all log messages to standard error.

-n *n*

Specify the number of processors in a multiprocessor system. Normally **named** can autodetect the number of CPUs.

-p *port*

Use *port* as the port number. Default is 53.

-t *dir*

Change root to specified directory after reading command arguments but before reading the configuration file. Useful only when running with option **-u**.

-u *user*

Set the user ID to *user* after completing any privileged operations.

-v   Print version, then exit.

File

/etc/named.conf

Read when **named** starts up.

---

namei

namei [*options*] *pathname* [*pathname* . . .]

Follow a pathname until a terminal point is found (e.g., a file, directory, char device, etc.). If **namei** finds a symbolic link, it shows the link and starts following it, indenting the output to show the context. **namei** prints an informative message when the maximum number of symbolic links has been exceeded, making it helpful for resolving errors resulting from too many levels of links.

Options

-m   Show mode bits of each file type in the style of **ls** (e.g., "rwxr-xr-x").

-x   Show mountpoint directories with a **D** rather than a **d**.

File-type characters

For each line of output, **namei** prints the following characters to identify the file types found:

-    A regular file.

?   An error of some kind.

b   A block device.

c   A character device.

d   A directory.

f: The pathname **namei** is currently trying to resolve.

---

l   A symbolic link (both the link and its contents are output).

p   A FIFO (named pipe).

s   A socket.

---

nameif

nameif [`options`] [`name macaddress`]

System administration command. Assign an interface *name* to a network device specified by *macaddress*, the unique serial number that identifies a network card. If no *name* and *macaddress* are given, **nameif** will attempt to read addresses from the configuration file */etc/mactab*. Each line of the configuration file should contain either a comment beginning with # or an interface name and MAC address.

Options

-c *filename*
> Read interface names and MAC addresses from *filename* instead of */etc/mactab*.

-s   Send any error messages to **syslog**.

---

nc

nc [`options`] [`host`] [`port`]

TCP/IP command. **nc** (also known as **netcat**) is a versatile networking utility that reads and writes data across network connections using TCP or UDP. It's a simple tool that has many uses. Unlike **telnet**, you can easily script **nc**. It can also be used to listen for as well as make connections.

Options

-C   Send CRLF as line ending.

-i *seconds*
> Send and read data one line at a time with a delay of the specified *interval* in seconds. By default **netcat** reads and writes in 8 KB blocks.

-k   Listen for further connections when a current connection ends. Used with **-l**.

-l   Listen for an incoming connection on the specified port or ports.

-n   Don't perform any DNS lookups.

-o *file*
> Hex-dump data sent and received to *file*.

-p [*port*]
> Read from the specified source *port*.

-r   Choose ports randomly.

-s [*address*]
> Read from the specified source IP *address*.

-u   Use UDP instead of the default TCP.

-U   Use Unix Domain Sockets instead of the default TCP.

-v   Verbose output. Use multiple times to increase verbosity. If not using **-n**, include reports on forward/reverse DNS mismatches.

-w *seconds*
> Set the inactivity timeout for a connection. Silently close a connection if idle for more than the specified *seconds*.

-x *address[:port]*
> Use the proxy found at the specified IP *address* and *port*. If no port is specified, the well-known port for the protocol is used.

-X *protocol*
> Use the specified proxy *protocol*. Valid values are **4** (SOCKS v. 4), **5** (SOCKS v. 5) and **connect** (HTTPS proxy). The default value is **5**.

-z   Scan for listening daemons. With this option *port* can be given as a port range or sets of ranges.

Examples

Connect to an SMTP port reporting connection information and timing out after 2 seconds of inactivity:

```
$ nc -w 2 -v remotehost 25
```

Copy a directory over the network, preserving permissions. On the receiving server, use this:

```
$ nc -l -p 1234 | tar xzfp -
```

On the server sending the directory files, use this:

```
$ tar czfp - /dir/ |  nc -w 3 remotehost 1234
```

Perform a simple port scan:

```
$ nc -w 1 -z remotehost 20-80 400-500
```

netstat   netstat [*options*] [*delay*]

TCP/IP command. Show network status. Print information on active sockets, routing tables, interfaces, masquerade connections, or multicast memberships. By default, **netstat** lists open sockets. When a *delay* is specified, **netstat** will print new information every *delay* seconds.

Options

The first five options (**-g**, **-i**, **-M**, **-r**, and **-s**) determine what kind of information **netstat** should display.

-g, --groups
> Show multicast group memberships.

-i, --interface[=*name*]
> Show all network interfaces, or just the interface specified by *name*.

-M, --masquerade
> Show masqueraded connections.

-r, --route
> Show kernel routing tables.

-s, --statistics
> Show statistics for each protocol.

-a, --all
> Show all entries.

-A *family*, **--protocol=**_family_
> Show connections only for the specified address *family*. Accepted values are **inet**, **unix**, **ipx**, **ax25**, **netrom**, and **ddp**. Specify multiple families in a comma-separated list.

-c, --continuous
> Display information continuously, refreshing once every second.

-C   Print routing information from the route cache.

-e, --extend
> Increase level of detail in reports. Use twice for maximum detail.

-F   Print routing information from the forward information database (FIB). This is the default.

-l, --listening
> Show only listening sockets.

-n, --numeric
> Show network addresses, ports, and users as numbers.

--numeric-hosts
> Show host addresses as numbers, but resolve others.

--numeric-ports
> Show ports as numbers, but resolve others.

--numeric-users
> Show user ID numbers for users, but resolve others.

-N, --symbolic
> Where possible, print symbolic host, port, or usernames instead of numerical representations. This is the default behavior.

-o, --timers
> Include information on network timers.

-p, --program
> Show the process ID and name of the program owning the socket.

-t, --tcp
> Limit report to information on TCP sockets.

-u, --udp
> Limit report to information on UDP sockets.

-v, --verbose
> Verbose mode.

-w, --raw
> Limit report to information on raw sockets.

newaliases   newaliases

Rebuild the mail aliases database, */etc/aliases*, after a change. Return 0 on success, or a number greater than 0 if there was an error. **newaliases** must be run whenever */etc/aliases* has been changed for the change to take effect. **newaliases** is a **sendmail** command and is identical to **sendmail -bi**.

newgrp   newgrp [-] [*group*]

Change user's current group ID to the specified group. If no group is specified, change to the user's login group. The new group is then used for checking permissions. If - is specified, also reinitialize the user's environment.

newusers   newusers *file*

System administration command. Create or update system users from entries in *file*. Each line in *file* has the same format as an entry in */etc/passwd*, except that passwords are unencrypted and group IDs can be given as a name or number. During an update, the password age field is ignored if the user already exists in the */etc/shadow* password file. If a group name or ID does not already exist, it will be created. If a home directory does not exist, it will be created.

nfsd   rpc.nfsd [*options*] *n*

System administration command. Launch *n* kernel threads for the Network File System (NFS) kernel module. The threads will handle client filesystem requests. By default, only one thread is launched. Most systems require eight or more, depending on the number of NFS clients using the system. Use **nfsstat** to check NFS performance.

Option

-H *hostname*, **--host** *hostname*
　　Specify the *hostname* or address that will accept NFS requests. The default is to accept on all addresses.

-N *version*, **--no-nfs-version** *version*
　　Do not provide support for the specified NFS version. By default support is provided for versions 2, 3, and 4.

-p *port*, **--port** *hostname*
　　Listen for NFS requests on *port* instead of the default port 2049.

-T, **--no-tcp**
　　Do not accept TCP requests.

-U, **--no-udp**
　　Do not accept UDP requests.

nfsstat   nfsstat [*options*]

System administration command. Print statistics on NFS and remote procedure call (RPC) activity for both clients and server.

Options
-2, -3, -4
Shows server statistics for version 2, 3, or 4.

-c   Display only client-side statistics.

-m, --mounts
Show statistics for mounted filesystems.

-n   Display only NFS statistics.

-o *facility*
Only display statistics for the specified *facility*. The following are valid values for *facility*:

all   All of the following facilities.

fh   Server file handle cache.

net   Network layer statistics.

nfs   Same as **-n**.

rc   Server request reply cache.

rpc   Same as **-r**.

-r   Display only RPC statistics.

-s   Display only server-side statistics.

-z   Reset statistics to zero. Use with above options to zero out specific sets of statistics (e.g., **-zr** to reset the RPC statistics).

-Z, --sleep
Take a snapshot of current stats then sleep until receiving a SIGINT signal (e.g., Ctrl-C) then take another snapshot and display a **diff** of the two.

nice   nice [*option*] [*command* [*arguments*]]

Execute a *command* (with its *arguments*) with lower priority (i.e., be "nice" to other users). With no command, **nice** prints the current scheduling priority (niceness). If **nice** is a child process, it prints the parent process's scheduling priority. Niceness has a range of -20 (highest priority) to 19 (lowest priority).

Options
--help
Print a help message and then exit.

-n *adjustment*, *-adjustment*, **--adjustment**=*adjustment*
Run *command* with niceness incremented by *adjustment* (1–19); default is 10. A privileged user can raise the priority by specifying a negative *adjustment* (e.g., –5).

--version
Print version information and then exit.

nm   nm [*options*] [*objfiles*]

Print the symbol table in alphabetical order from one or more object files. If no object files are specified, perform operations on *a.out*. Output includes each symbol's value, type, size, name, and so on. A key letter categorizing the symbol can also be displayed.

Options

-a, --debug-syms
> Print debugger symbols.

--defined-only
> Display only defined symbols.

-f *format*, **--format**=*format*
> Specify output format (**bsd**, **sysv**, or **posix**). Default is **bsd**.

-g, --extern-only
> Print external symbols only.

--help
> Print help message, then exit.

-l, --line-numbers
> Print source filenames and line numbers for each symbol from available debugging information.

-n, -v, --numeric-sort
> Sort the external symbols by address.

-p, --no-sort
> Don't sort the symbols at all.

-r, --reverse-sort
> Sort in reverse, alphabetically or numerically.

-s, --print-armap
> Include mappings stored by **ar** and **ranlib** when printing archive symbols.

--size-sort
> Sort by size.

-t *radix*, **--radix**=*radix*
> Use the specified *radix* for printing symbol values. Accepted values are **d** for decimal, **o** for octal, and **x** for hexadecimal.

--target=*format*
> Specify an object code *format* other than the system default.

-u, --undefined-only
> Report only the undefined symbols.

-A, -o, --print-file-name
> Print input filenames before each symbol.

-B   Same as **--format=bsd**.

-C, --demangle[=*style*]
> Translate low-level symbol names into readable versions. You may specify a style to use when demangling symbol names from a foreign compiler.

-D, --dynamic

> Print dynamic, not normal, symbols. Useful only when working with dynamic objects (some kinds of shared libraries, for example).

-P, --portability

> Same as **-f posix**.

-S, --print-size

> Print the size of defined symbols.

-V, --version

> Print **nm**'s version number on standard error.

---

nohup

nohup *command* [*arguments*]

nohup *option*

Run the named *command* with its optional command *arguments*, continuing to run it even after you log out (make *command* immune to hangups—i.e., **no hangup**). Terminal output is appended to the file *nohup.out* by default, or *$HOME/nohup.out* if *nohup.out* can't be written to. Modern shells preserve background commands by default; this command is necessary only in the original Bourne shell.

Options

--help

> Print usage information and exit.

--version

> Print version information and exit.

---

nslookup

nslookup

TCP/IP command. Query Internet domain nameservers. **nslookup** is deprecated; its functionality is replaced by the **dig** and **host** commands. **nslookup** may not be included in some distributions.

---

nsupdate

nsupdate [*options*] [*filename*]

System administration command. Interactively submit dynamic DNS update requests to a nameserver. Use **nsupdate** to add or remove records from a zone without manually editing the zone file. Commands may be entered interactively or read from *filename*. An update message is built from multiple commands, some establishing prerequisites, some adding or deleting resource records. Messages are executed as a single transaction. A blank line or the **send** command will send the current message. Lines beginning with a semicolon are treated as comments. For additional information on dynamic DNS updates, see RFC 2136.

Options

-d   Print additional tracing information usable for debugging.

-k *keyfile*

Read encrypted transaction signature key from *keyfile*. The key should be encrypted using the HMAC-MD5 algorithm. Keyfiles are generated by the **dnssec-keygen** command.

-r *n*

Retry UDP *n* times. Default is 3.

-t *seconds*

Set request timeout. Default is 300 seconds. 0 disables timeout.

-u *seconds*

Set UDP retry interval. Default is 3 seconds. If 0, then interval is computed from the time out and retry values.

-v   Use TCP instead of UDP to send update requests.

-y *keyname:secret*

Generate transaction signature from specified *keyname* and *secret*.

Interactive commands

answer

Print answer.

class *classname*

Set default class to *classname* instead of the normal default **IN**.

key *keyname secret*

Generate transaction signature from specified *keyname* and *secret*. This command overrides command-line options **-k** or **-y**.

local *address* [*port*]

Use local *address* and, if specified, *port* to send updates.

prereq *criteria*

Specify prerequisites for updating a domain. Provide the criteria in one of the following forms:

nxdomain *domain-name*

Perform updates only if there are no preexisting records with the name *domain-name*.

nxrrset *domain-name* [*class*] *type*

Perform updates only if there is no preexisting record of the specified *type* and *class* for *domain-name*. When no *class* is given, **IN** is assumed.

yxdomain *domain-name*

Perform updates only if there is a preexisting record with the name *domain-name*.

yxrrset *domain-name* [*class*] *type* [*data*]

Perform updates only if there is a preexisting record of the specified *type* and *class* for *domain-name*. If *data* is given, the RDATA of the specified resource must match it exactly. When no *class* is given, **IN** is assumed.

send

Send the current message. Same as entering a blank line.

server *servername* [*port*]
> Update records on DNS server *servername* instead of the master server listed in the **MNAME** field of the appropriate zone's SOA record.

show
> Print all commands in current message.

update *command*
> Update the records according to one of the following *commands*:

add *domain-name* [*ttl*] [*class*] *type data*
> Add a resource record with the specified values.

delete *domain-name* [*ttl*] [*class*] [*type* [*data*]]
> Delete resource records for *domain-name*. The *ttl* field is always ignored, but if other fields are given, only delete records that match all criteria.

zone *zonename*
> Apply updates to the specified *zonename*. If no **zone** command is given, **nsupdate** attempts to determine the correct zone based on other input.

---

objcopy

objcopy [*options*] *infile* [*outfile*]

Copy the contents of the input object file to another file, optionally changing the file format in the process (but not the endianness). If *outfile* is not specified, **objcopy** creates a temporary file and renames it to *infile* when the copy is complete, destroying the original input file. The GNU Binary File Descriptor (BFD) library is used to read and write the object files.

Options

--add-section *section=file*
> Add a new section to the output object file with the specified section name and the contents taken from the specified file. Available only for formats that allow arbitrarily named sections.

--alt-machine-code=*n*
> If the output architecture has alternate machine codes, use the *n*th code instead of the default.

-b *n*, **--byte**=*n*
> Copy only every *n*th byte. Header data is not affected. The value of *n* can be from 0 to *interleave*-1, where *interleave* is specified by **-i** (default is 4). This option is useful for creating files to program ROM and is typically used with **srec** as the output format.

-B *bfdarch*, **--binary-architecture**=*bfdarch*
> Set the output architecture to *bfdarch* (e.g., i386) for transforming a raw binary file into an object file. Otherwise, this option is ignored. After the conversion, your program can access data inside the created object file by referencing the special symbols **_binary_objfile_start**, **_binary_objfile_end**, and **_binary_objfile_size**.

--change-addresses=*incr*, **--adjust-vma**=*incr*

Change the VMA and LMA addresses of all sections, plus the start address, by adding *incr*. Changing section addresses is not supported by all object formats. Sections are not relocated.

--change-leading-char

For object formats that use a special character (such as an underscore) to begin symbols, change the leading character when converting between formats. If the character is the same in both formats, the option has no effect. Otherwise, it adds, removes, or changes the leading character as appropriate for the output format.

--change-section-address *section*{=|+|-}*val*,
--adjust-section-vma *section*{=|+|-}*val*

Set or change the VMA and LMA addresses of the specified section. With =, set the section address to the specified value; otherwise, add or subtract the value to get the new address.

--change-section-lma *section*{=|+|-}*val*

Set or change the LMA address of the specified section. With =, set the section address to the specified value; otherwise, add or subtract the value to get the new address.

--change-section-vma *section*{=|+|-}*val*

Set or change the VMA address of the specified section. With =, set the section address to the specified value; otherwise, add or subtract the value to get the new address.

--change-start *incr*, **--adjust-start** *incr*

Add *incr* to the start address to get a new start address. Not supported by all object formats.

--change-warnings, **--adjust-warnings**

Issue a warning if the section that is specified in one of the options **--change-section-address**, **--change-section-lma**, or **--change-section-vma** does not exist.

--debugging

Convert debugging information if possible.

-F *bfdname*, **--target**=*bfdname*

Set the binary format for both input and output files to the binary file descriptor name *bfdname*. No format translation is done. Use the **-h** option for a list of supported formats for your system.

-g, **--strip-debug**

Do not copy debugging information.

-G *symbol*, **--keep-global-symbol**=*symbol*

Copy only the specified global symbol, making all other symbols local to the file. May be specified multiple times.

--gap-fill=*val*

Fill gaps between sections with the specified value; applies to the load address (LMA) of the sections.

-h, --help

Print help information, including a list of supported target object formats, then exit.

-i *interleave*, **--interleave**=*interleave*

Copy one out of every *interleave* bytes. Use **-b** to set the byte to copy (default is 4). This option is ignored if **-b** is not specified.

-I *bfdname*, **--input-target**=*bfdname*

Set the binary file format of the input file using its binary file descriptor name, *bfdname*.

-j *section*, **--only-section**=*section*

Copy only the specified section. May be specified multiple times.

-K *symbol*, **--keep-symbol**=*symbol*

Copy only the specified symbol from the source file. May be specified multiple times.

--keep-global-symbols=*filename*

Apply the option **--keep-global-symbol** to each symbol listed in the specified file. The file should have one symbol per line, with comments beginning with a hash mark (#). May be specified multiple times.

--keep-symbols=*file*

Apply the option **--keep-symbol** to each symbol listed in the specified file. The file should have one symbol per line, with comments beginning with a hash mark (#). May be specified multiple times.

-L *symbol*, **--localize-symbol**=*symbol*

Make the specified symbol local. May be specified multiple times.

--localize-symbols=*filename*

Apply the option **--localize-symbol** to each symbol listed in the specified file. The file should have one symbol per line, with comments beginning with a hash mark (#). May be specified multiple times.

-N *symbol*, **--strip-symbol**=*symbol*

Do not copy the specified symbol. May be specified multiple times.

--no-change-warnings, --no-adjust-warnings

Do not issue a warning even if the section specified in one of the options **--change-section-address**, **--change-section-lma**, or **--change-section-vma** does not exist.

-O *bfdname*, **--output-target**=*bfdname*

Set the binary file format of the output file using its binary file descriptor name, *bfdname*. The format **srec** generates S-records (printable ASCII versions of object files), and **binary** generates a raw binary file. Use **-h** for other available formats.

-p, --preserve-dates

Preserve the input file's access and modification dates in the output file.

--pad-to=*addr*

Pad the output file up to the load address. Use the fill value specified by **--gap-fill** (default is 0).

-R *section*, **--remove-section=***section*

Do not copy any section with the specified name. May be specified multiple times.

--redefine-sym *old=new*

Change the name of the symbol *old* to *new*.

--remove-leading-char

If the first character of a global symbol is a special character (such as an underscore) used by the input object file format, remove it. Unlike **--change-leading-char**, this option always changes the symbol name when appropriate, regardless of the output object format.

--rename-section *oldname=newname*[*,flags*]

Rename a section from *oldname* to *newname*, optionally also changing the flags to *flags*.

-S, --strip-all

Do not copy relocation and symbol information.

--set-section-flags *section=flags*

Set flags for the specified section as a comma-separated string of flag names. Not all flags are meaningful for all object formats. The possible flags are **alloc**, **code**, **contents**, **data**, **debug**, **load**, **noload**, **readonly**, **rom**, and **share**.

--set-start=*val*

Set the start address of the new file to the specified value. Not supported by all object formats.

--srec-forceS3

Force all **srec** output records to be type S3 records.

--srec-len=*ival*

Set the maximum length of **srec** output records to the specified value. The length includes the **address**, **data**, and **crc** fields.

--strip-symbols=*filename*

Apply the option **--strip-symbol** to each symbol listed in the specified file. The file should have one symbol per line, with comments beginning with a hash mark (#). May be specified multiple times.

--strip-unneeded

Strip all symbols not needed for relocation processing.

-v, --verbose

Run in verbose mode, listing all object files modified; for archives, list all archive members.

-V, --version
> Print version information and exit.

-W *symbol*, **--weaken-symbol**=*symbol*
> Make the specified symbol weak. May be specified multiple times.

--weaken
> Make all global symbols weak.

--weaken-symbols=*filename*
> Apply the option **--weaken-symbol** to each symbol listed in the specified file. The file should have one symbol per line, with comments beginning with a hash mark (#). May be specified multiple times.

-x, --discard-all
> Do not copy nonglobal symbols.

-X, --discard-locals
> Do not copy compiler-generated local symbols (usually those starting with L or ..).

objdump

objdump [*options*] *objfiles*

Display information about one or more object files. If an archive is specified, **objdump** displays information on each object file in the archive. At least one of the options **-a, -d, -D, -f, -g, -G, -h, -H, -p, -r, -S, -t, -T, -V,** or **-x** must be given to tell **objdump** what information to show.

Options
-a, --archive-header
> If any input files are archives, display the archive header information. The output includes the object file format of each archive member.

--adjust-vma=*offset*
> Add *offset* to all section headers before dumping information. Useful if the section addresses do not correspond to the symbol table.

-b *bfdname*, **--target**=*bfdname*
> Set the binary file format using its binary file descriptor name, *bfdname*. Use the **-h** option for a list of supported formats for your system.

-C [*style*], **--demangle**[=*style*]
> Decode (demangle) low-level symbol names into user-level names, optionally specifying a mangling style. Removes any initial underscores and makes C++ function names readable.

-d, --disassemble
> Display assembler mnemonic names for the machine instructions. Disassemble only sections that are expected to contain instructions.

-D, --disassemble-all

Disassemble all sections, not just those expected to contain instructions.

-EB, --endian=big
-EL, --endian=little

Specify whether the object files are big- or little-endian, for disassembling. Useful for disassembling formats such as S-records (printable ASCII versions of object files) that do not include that information.

-f, --file-header

Display overall header summary information.

--file-start-context

When using **-S** and displaying source code from a file that hasn't been displayed yet, include context from the start of the file.

-g, --debugging

Display debugging information.

-G, --stabs

Display any stabs (debugging symbol table entries) information, in addition to the contents of any sections requested.

-h, --section-header, --header

Display section-header summary information.

-H, --help

Display help information and exit.

-i, --info

Display the architectures and object formats available on your system for use with **-b** or **-m**.

-j *name*, **--section=***name*

Display information for section *name*.

-l, --line-numbers

Label the display with filename and source code line numbers corresponding to the object code or relocation entries shown. Use with **-d**, **-D**, or **-r**.

-m *arch*, **--architecture=***arch*

Specify the architecture for disassembling object files. Useful when disassembling files such as S-records that do not include this information.

-M *options*, **--disassembler-options=***options*

Pass target-specific information to the disassembler. Supported only on some targets.

--no-show-raw-insn

Do not show instructions in hexadecimal when disassembling. This is the default with **--prefix-addresses**.

-p, --private-headers

Display information specific to the object format. For some formats, no additional information is displayed.

--prefix-addresses
When disassembling, print the complete address on each line.

-r, --reloc
Display relocation entries. With **-b** or **-D**, the entries are intermixed with the disassembly.

-R, --dynamic-reloc
Print dynamic relocation entries. Meaningful only for dynamic objects such as certain types of shared libraries.

-s, --full-contents
Display the full contents of any requested sections.

-S, --source
Display source code intermixed with disassembly, if possible. Implies **-d**.

--show-raw-insn
When disassembling, show instructions in hexadecimal as well as symbolic form. This is the default, except with **--prefix-addresses**.

--start-address=*addr*
Start displaying data at the specified address. Applies to **-d**, **-r**, and **-s**.

--stop-address=*addr*
Stop displaying data at the specified address. Applies to **-d**, **-r**, and **-s**.

-t, --syms
Print symbol table entries.

-T, --dynamic-syms
Print dynamic symbol table entries. Meaningful only for dynamic objects such as certain types of shared libraries.

-V, --version
Print version information and exit.

-w, --wide
Format lines for output devices wider than 80 characters, and do not truncate symbol table names.

-x, --all-headers
Display all available header information. Equivalent to specifying **-a -f -h -r -t**.

-z, --disassemble-zeroes
Disassemble blocks of zeroes. The default is to skip such blocks.

---

od

od [*options*] [*files*]

od --traditional [*file*] [[+]*offset* [[+]*label*]]

Dump the specified files to standard output. The default is to dump in octal format, but other formats can be specified. With multiple files, concatenate them in the specified order. If no files are specified or *file* is -, read from standard input. With the second form, using the **--traditional** option, only one file can be specified.

Options

For the following options, see the upcoming "Arguments" section for an explanation of the arguments *bytes*, *size*, and *type*. If no options are specified, the default is **-A o -t d2 -w 16**.

-a   Print as named characters. Same as **-t a**.

-A *radix*, **--address-radix=***radix*
> Specify the radix (base) for the file offsets printed at the beginning of each output line. The possible values are:
>
> **d**   Decimal.
>
> **n**   None; do not print an offset.
>
> **o**   Octal; the default.
>
> **x**   Hexadecimal.

-b   Print as octal bytes. Same as **-t o1**.

-c   Print as ASCII characters or backslash escapes. Same as **-t c**.

-d   Print as unsigned decimal shorts. Same as **-t u2**.

-f   Print as floating-point. Same as **-t fF**.

--help
> Display a usage message and exit.

-i   Print as decimal integers. Same as **-t dI**.

-j *bytes*, **--skip-bytes=***bytes*
> Skip the specified number of input bytes before starting.

-l   Print as decimal longs. Same as **-t dL**.

-N *bytes*, **--read-bytes=***bytes*
> Format and print only the specified number of input bytes.

-o   Print as octal shorts. Same as **-t o2**.

-s   Print as decimal shorts. Same as **-t d2**.

-S *bytes*, **--strings**[**=***bytes*]
> Output strings that are at least *bytes* ASCII graphic characters long (default is 3 if *bytes* is not specified for **--strings**).

-t *type*, **--format=***type*
> Format the output according to *type*, where *type* is a string of one or more of the characters listed in the "Arguments" section. If more than one type is specified, each output line is written once in each specified format. If a trailing z is appended to *type*, **od** appends any printable characters to the end of each output line.

--traditional
> Accept arguments in the traditional form, which takes a single file specification with an optional offset and label, as shown in the second form of the command. *offset* is an octal number indicating how many input bytes to skip over. *label* specifies an initial pseudo-address, which is printed in parentheses after any normal address. Both the offset and the label can begin with an optional plus sign (+), and can have a trailing decimal point

(.) to force the offset to be interpreted as a decimal number and/or a trailing **b** to multiply the number of bytes skipped by *offset* by 512.

-v, --output-duplicates

Print all lines, including duplicates. By default, only the first of a series of identical lines is printed, and an asterisk is printed at the beginning of the following line to indicate that there were duplicates.

--version

Display version information and exit.

-w *bytes*, **--width**[*=bytes*]

Dump *bytes* input bytes to each output line. Defaults to 16 if this option is omitted. If **--width** is specified but *bytes* is omitted, the default is 32.

-x   Print as hexadecimal shorts. Same as **-t x2**.

Arguments

bytes

Specify a number of bytes. Treated as hexadecimal if it begins with **0x** or **0X**, as octal if it begins with **0**, or as decimal otherwise. Append **b** to multiply by 512, **k** to multiply by 1024, or **m** to multiply by 10,248,576.

size

Specified as part of *type* to indicate how many bytes to use in interpreting each number. Types **a** and **c** do not take a size. For other types, *size* is a number. For type **f**, *size* can also be one of the following:

D   Double.

F   Float.

L   Long double.

For the remaining types (**d**, **o**, **u**, **x**), *size* can be one of the following in addition to a number:

C   Character.

I   Integer.

L   Long.

S   Short.

type

Specify the format type. The possible types are:

a   Named character.

c   ASCII character or backslash escape.

d*size*

Signed decimal, with *size* bytes per integer.

f*size*

Floating point, with *size* bytes per integer.

o*size*
> Octal, with *size* bytes per integer.

u*size*
> Unsigned decimal, with *size* bytes per integer.

x*size*
> Hexadecimal, with *size* bytes per integer.

---

openvt

openvt [*options*] [--] [*command*] [*arguments*]

Locate the first available virtual terminal (VT) and run *command* with any *arguments* given. If no command is specified, the shell $SHELL is started.

Options

-- Indicates the end of **openvt** options. Required before the command name to pass options to the command.

-c *vt*
> Use the specified VT number instead of the first available. You must have write access to *vt*.

-e Execute *command* without forking. For use in */etc/inittab*, rather than on the command line.

-l Run the command as a login shell, prepending a dash (-) to the command name.

-s Switch to the new VT when the command is started and make it the current VT.

-u Determine the owner of the current VT, and log in as that user. You must be root to use this option, which is also suitable for calling by **init**. Don't use with -l.

-v Verbose mode.

-w Wait for the command to complete. If used with -s, switch back to the controlling terminal when the command is done.

---

passwd

passwd [*options*] [*user*]

Create or change a password associated with a *user* name. Only the owner or a privileged user may change a password. Owners need not specify their *user* name. Users can change their own passwords. For all other operations, you must be root.

Options
-d, --delete
> Delete the password for the user's account.

-f, --force
> Force the operation. Overrides -u.

-?, --help
> Display a help message describing the options. See also --usage.

-i *days*, --inactive=*days*
> Set the number of days after a password has expired before the account is disabled.

-k, --keep-tokens
> Keep passwords (authentication tokens) that have not expired.

-l, --lock
> Lock the user's account.

-n *days*, **--minimum**=*days*
> Set the minimum number of days that the password is valid.

-S, --status
> Print the status of the user's password.

--stdin
> Read new passwords from standard input.

-u, --unlock
> Unlock the user's account

--usage
> Display a brief usage message. See also **--help**.

-w *days*, **--warning**=*days*
> Set the number of days of warning users will get before their password expires.

-x *days*, **--maximum**=*days*
> Set the maximum number of days that the password is valid.

---

paste

paste [*options*] *files*

Merge corresponding lines of one or more *files* into tab-separated vertical columns and write to standard output. Use - to read from standard input, instead of specifying a file. See also **cut**, **join**, and **pr**.

Options

-d*char*, **--delimiters**=*char*
> Separate columns with *char* instead of a tab. You can separate columns with different characters by supplying more than one *char*.

--help
> Print a help message and then exit.

-s, --serial
> Merge lines from one file at a time.

--version
> Print version information and then exit.

Examples

Create a three-column *file* from files *x*, *y*, and *z*:

```
paste x y z > file
```

List users in two columns:

```
who | paste - -
```

Merge each pair of lines into one line:

```
paste -s -d"\t\n" list
```

Linux Commands

patch

patch [*options*] [*original* [*patchfile*]]

Apply the patches specified in *patchfile* to *original*. Replace the original with the new, patched version; move the original to *original.orig* or *original~*. The patch file is a difference listing produced by the **diff** command.

Options

-b, --backup

Back up the original file.

-B *prefix*, **--prefix**=*prefix*

Prepend *prefix* to the backup filename.

--backup-if-mismatch, --no-backup-if-mismatch

When not backing up all original files, these options control whether a backup should be made when a patch does not match the original file. The default is to make backups unless **--posix** is specified.

-c, --context

Interpret *patchfile* as a context diff.

-d *dir*, **--directory**=*dir*

cd to directory *dir* before beginning **patch** operations.

-D *string*, **--ifdef**=*string*

Mark all changes with:

```
#ifdef
    string
#endif
```

--dry-run

Print results of applying a patch, but don't change any files.

-e, --ed

Treat the contents of *patchfile* as **ed** commands.

-E, --remove-empty-files

If **patch** creates any empty files, delete them.

-f, --force

Force all changes, even those that look incorrect. Skip patches if the original file does not exist; force patches for files with the wrong version specified; assume patches are never reversed.

-F *num*, **--fuzz**=*num*

Specify the maximum number of lines that may be ignored (fuzzed over) when deciding where to install a hunk of code. The default is 2. Meaningful only with context diffs.

-g *num*, **--get** *num*

Specify whether to check the original file out of source control if it is missing or read-only. If *num* is a positive number, get the file. If it is negative, prompt the user. If it is 0, do not check files out of source control. The default is negative or the value of the PATCH_GET environment variable when set, unless the **--posix** option is given. In that case, the default is 0.

--help
> Print help message, then exit.

-i *file*, **--input**=*file*
> Read patch from *file* instead of stdin.

-l, --ignore-whitespace
> Ignore whitespace while pattern matching.

-n, --normal
> Interpret patch file as a normal diff.

-N, --forward
> Ignore patches that appear to be reversed or to have already been applied.

-o *file*, **--output**=*file*
> Print output to *file*.

-p *num*, **--strip**=*num*
> Specify how much of preceding pathname to strip. A *num* of **0** strips everything, leaving just the filename. **1** strips the leading **/**. Each higher number after that strips another directory from the left.

--posix
> Conform more strictly to the POSIX standard.

--quoting-style=*style*
> Set the quoting style used when printing names. The default style is **shell**, unless set by the environment variable QUOTING_STYLE. *style* may be one of the following:
>
> **c** Quote as a C language string.
>
> **escape**
> > Like **c**, but without surrounding double-quote characters.
>
> **literal**
> > Print without quoting.
>
> **shell**
> > Quote for use in shell when needed.
>
> **shell-always**
> > Quote for use in shell even if not needed.

-r *file*, **--reject-file**=*file*
> Place rejects (hunks of the patch file that **patch** fails to place within the original file) in *file*. Default is *original.rej*.

-R, --reverse
> Do a reverse patch: attempt to undo the damage done by patching with the old and new files reversed.

-s, --silent, --quiet
> Suppress commentary.

-t, --batch
> Force changes as with **-f** but make different decisions. Skip patches if headers don't contain filenames; skip patches for files with the wrong version specified; assume patches are reversed if they look like they are. Also see **-Z**.

-T, --set-time

> When original file timestamps match the times given in the patch header, set timestamps for patched files according to the context diff headers. Use option **-f** to force date changes. Assume timestamps are in local time.

-u, --unified

> Interpret patch file as a unified context diff.

-v, --version

> Print version number and exit.

-V *method*, **--version-control**=*method*

> Specify method for creating backup files (overridden by **-B**):

> **t, numbered**
>> Make numbered backups.

> **nil, existing**
>> Back up files according to preexisting backup schemes, with simple backups as the default. This is **patch**'s default behavior.

> **never, simple**
>> Make simple backups.

--verbose

> Verbose mode.

-Y *prefix*, **--basename-prefix**=*prefix*

> Use the specified *prefix* with a file's basename to create backup filenames. Useful for specifying a directory.

-z *suffix*, **--suffix**=*suffix*

> Back up the original file in *original.suffix*.

-Z, --set-utc

> When original file timestamps match the times given in the patch header, set timestamps for patched files according to the context diff headers. Use option **-f** to force date changes. Assume timestamps are in Coordinated Universal Time (UTC). Also see **-T**.

---

pathchk

pathchk [*options*] *filenames*

Determine validity and portability of *filenames*. Specifically, determine if all directories within the path are searchable and if the length of the *filenames* is acceptable.

Options

--help

> Print a help message and then exit.

-p   Check for most POSIX systems.

-P   Check for empty names and names that start with -.

--portability

> Check portability for all POSIX systems. Equivalent to **-p -P**.

--version

> Print version information and then exit.

pccardctl

pccardctl *command*

System administration command. Monitor and control PCMCIA sockets. Commands operate on a named card socket number, or all sockets if no number is given.

Commands

config [*socket*]
  Display current socket configuration.

eject [*socket*]
  Prepare the system for the card(s) to be ejected.

ident [*socket*]
  Display card identification information.

info [*socket*]
  Display card identification information as Bourne shell variable definitions for use in scripts.

insert [*socket*]
  Notify system that a card has been inserted.

resume [*socket*]
  Restore power to socket and reconfigure for use.

status [*socket*]
  Display current socket status.

suspend [*socket*]
  Shut down device and cut power to socket.

---

pidof

pidof [*options*] *programs*

Display the process IDs of the listed program or programs. **pidof** is actually a symbolic link to **killall5**.

Options

-c   Return only processes running in the same root directory. Ignored for nonroot users.

-o *pid*
  Omit all processes with the specified process ID. Can be specified more than once to omit multiple IDs.

-s   Return a single process ID.

-x   Also return process IDs of shells running the named scripts.

---

ping

ping [*options*] *host*

System administration command. Confirm that a remote host is online and responding. **ping** is intended for use in network testing, measurement, and management. Because of the load it can impose on the network, it is unwise to use **ping** during normal operations or from automated scripts.

Options

-a Make **ping** audible. Beep each time response is received.

-A Adapt to return interval of packets. Like **-f ping**, sends packets at approximately the rate at which they are received. This option may be used by an unprivileged user.

-b Ping a broadcast address.

-B Bind to original source address and do not change.

-c *count*
> Stop after sending (and receiving) *count* **ECHO_RESPONSE** packets.

-f Flood **ping**-output packets as fast as they come back or 100 times per second, whichever is greater. This can be very hard on a network and should be used with caution. Only a privileged user may use this option.

-i *wait*
> Wait *wait* seconds between sending each packet. Default is to wait one second between each packet. This option is incompatible with the **-f** option.

-I *name*
> Set source address to interface *name*. *name* may also be specified as an IP address.

-l *preload*
> Send *preload* number of packets as fast as possible before falling into normal mode of behavior.

-L If destination is a multicast address, suppress loopback.

-M *hint*
> Specify Path MTU Discovery strategy. Accepted values are **do**, **want**, or **dont**.

-n Numeric output only. No attempt will be made to look up symbolic names for host addresses.

-p *digits*
> Specify up to 16 pad bytes to fill out packet sent. This is useful for diagnosing data-dependent problems in a network. *digits* are in hex. For example, **-p ff** will cause the sent packet to be filled with all 1s.

-q Quiet output—nothing is displayed except the summary lines at startup time and when finished.

-Q *tos*
> Set Quality of Service on ICMP datagrams.

-r Bypass the normal routing tables and send directly to a host on an attached network.

-R Set the IP record route option, which will store the route of the packet inside the IP header. The contents of the record route will be printed if the **-v** option is given, and will be set on return packets if the target host preserves the record route option across echoes or if the **-l** option is given.

-s *packetsize*

Specify number of data bytes to be sent. Default is 56, which translates into 64 ICMP data bytes when combined with the 8 bytes of ICMP header data.

-S *size*

Set send buffer (SNDBUF) size. The default is the size of one packet.

-t *n*

Set the IP Time to Live to *n* seconds.

-T *option*

Set IP timestamp options. Accepted *option* values are:

tsonly

Timestamps only.

tsandaddr

Timestamps and addresses.

tsprespec *hosts*

Timestamps with prespecified hops of one or more hosts.

-U Use older **ping** behavior and print full user-to-user latency instead of network round-trip time.

-v Verbose; list ICMP packets received other than **ECHO_ RESPONSE**.

-V Print version, then exit.

-w *n*

Exit **ping** after *n* seconds.

-W *n*

When waiting for a response, time out after *n* seconds.

---

pmap

pmap [*options*] *pids*

Display the memory maps of a process.

Options

-d Display the offset and device number of each mapping.

-q Be more quiet. Displays less header and footer information.

-x Provide a more detailed and verbose display.

-V Display the version number and exit.

---

portmap

rpc.portmap [*options*]

NFS/NIS command. RPC program number to IP port mapper. **portmap** is a server that converts RPC program numbers to IP port numbers. It must be running in order to make RPC calls. When an RPC server is started, it tells **portmap** which port number it is listening to and which RPC program numbers it is prepared to serve. When a client wishes to make an RPC call to a given program number, it first contacts **portmap** on the server machine to determine the port number where RPC packets should be sent. **portmap** must be the first RPC server started. On newer systems **portmap** is deprecated. Use **rpcbind** instead.

Linux Commands

Options

-d   Run **portmap** in debugging mode. Does not allow **portmap** to run as a daemon.

-l   Bind to loopback device. This only works from the localhost.

-v   Verbose mode.

---

poweroff

poweroff [*options*]

System administration command. Close out filesystems, shut down the system, and power off. Because this command immediately stops all processes, it should be run only in single-user mode. If the system is not in runlevel 0 or 6, **poweroff** calls **shutdown -h**, then performs a poweroff.

Options

-d   Suppress writing to */var/log/wtmp*.

-f   Call **reboot** or **halt** and not **shutdown**, even when **shutdown** would normally be called. This option is used to force a hard halt or reboot.

-h   Place hard drives in standby mode before **halt** or **poweroff**.

-i   Shut down network interfaces before reboot.

-n   Suppress normal call to **sync**.

-w   Suppress normal execution; simply write to */var/log/wtmp*.

---

pppd

pppd [*tty*] [*speed*] [*options*]

System administration command. PPP stands for the Point-to-Point Protocol; it allows datagram transmission over a serial connection. **pppd** attempts to configure *tty* for PPP (searching in */dev*) or, by default, the controlling terminal. You can also specify a baud rate of *speed*. **pppd** accepts many options. Only the most common options are listed here.

Options

[*local_IP_address*]:[*remote_IP_address*]
    Specify the local and/or remote interface IP addresses, as hostnames or numeric addresses.

asyncmap *map*
    Specify which control characters cannot pass over the line. *map* should be a 32-bit hex number, where each bit represents a character to escape. For example, bit 00000001 represents the character 0x00; bit 80000000 represents the character 0x1f or _. You may specify multiple characters.

auth
    Require self-authentication by peers before allowing packets to move.

call *file*

Read options from *file* in */etc/ppp/peers/*. Unlike the **file** option, **call** *file* may contain privileged options, even when **pppd** is not run by root.

connect *command*

Connect as specified by *command*, which may be a binary or shell command.

crtscts

Use hardware flow control.

debug

Log contents of control packets to **syslogd**.

defaultroute

Add a new default route in which the peer is the gateway. When the connection shuts down, remove the route.

nodetach

Operate in the foreground. By default, **pppd** forks and operates in the background.

disconnect *command*

Close the connection as specified by *command*, which may be a binary or shell command.

escape *character-list*

Escape all characters in *character-list*, which should be a comma-separated list of hex numbers. You cannot escape 0x20-0x3f or 0x5e.

file *file*

Consult *file* for options.

init *script*

Run specified command or shell script to initialize the serial line.

lock

Allow only **pppd** to access the device.

mru *bytes*

Refuse packets of more than *bytes* bytes.

mtu *bytes*

Do not send packets of more than *bytes* bytes.

passive, -p

Do not exit if peer does not respond to attempts to initiate a connection. Instead, wait for a valid packet from the peer.

silent

Send no packets until after receiving one.

Files

/var/run/pppn.pid

pppd's process ID. The *n* in *pppn.pid* is the number of the PPP interface unit corresponding to this **pppd** process.

/etc/ppp/ip-up
> Binary or script to be executed when the PPP link becomes active.

/etc/ppp/ip-down
> Binary or script to be executed when the PPP link goes down.

/etc/ppp/pap-secrets
> Contains usernames, passwords, and IP addresses for use in PAP authentication.

/etc/ppp/options
> System defaults. Options in this file are set *before* the command-line options.

~/.ppprc
> The user's default options. These are read before command-line options but after the system defaults.

/etc/ppp/options.ttyname
> Name of the default serial port.

---

pr

pr [*options*] [*files*]

Convert a text file or files to a paginated or columned version, with headers, suitable for printing. If - is provided as the filename, read from standard input.

Options

+*beg_pag*[:*end-pag*], **--pages**=*beg_pag*[:*end-pag*]
> Begin printing on page *beg_pag* and end on *end-pag* if specified.

-*num_cols*, **--columns**=*num_cols*
> Set the number of columns to print, balancing the number of lines in the columns on each page. Print vertical columns, except with **-a**.

-a, --across
> Print columns horizontally, not vertically.

-c, --show-control-chars
> Convert control characters to hat notation (such as **^C**), and other unprintable characters to octal backslash format.

-d, --double-space
> Double space.

-D *format*, **--date-format**=*format*
> Format the header date using *format*. See the **date** command for the possible formats.

-e[*tab-char*[*width*]], **--expand-tabs**[=*tab-char*[*width*]]
> Convert tabs (or *tab-chars*) to spaces. If *width* is specified, convert tabs to *width* characters (default is 8).

-f, -F, --form-feed
> Separate pages with form feeds, not newlines. With **-F**, print a three-line page header; otherwise, print a five-line header and trailer.

-h *header*, **--header=***header*
> Use *header* for the header instead of the filename. The header is centered.

--help
> Print a help message and then exit.

-i[*out-tab-char*[*out-tab-width*]],
--output-tabs[=*out-tab-char*[*out-tab-width*]]
> Replace spaces with tabs on output. You can specify an alternative tab character (default is tab) and width (default is 8).

-J, **--join-lines**
> Merge full lines; ignore **-W** if set.

-l *lines*, **--length=***lines*
> Set page length to *lines* (default is 66). If *lines* is less than 10, omit headers and footers. Thus the default number of lines of text (i.e., not header or trailer) is 56, or 63 with **-F**.

-m, **--merge**
> Print all files, one per column.

-n[*delimiter*[*digits*]], **--number-lines**[=*delimiter*[*digits*]]
> Number columns, or, with the **-m** option, number lines. Append *delimiter* to each number (default is a tab) and limit the size of numbers to *digits* (default is 5).

-N *num*, **--first-line-number=***num*
> Start counting with *num* at the first line of the first page printed. Also see **+***beg_page*.

-o *width*, **--indent=***width*
> Indent left margin to *width*. Does not affect the page width set with **-w** or **-W**.

-r, **--no-file-warnings**
> Continue silently when unable to open an input file.

-s[*delimiter*], **--separator**[=*delimiter*]
> Separate columns with the single-character *delimiter* (default is a tab) instead of spaces.

-S[*string*], **--sep-string**[=*string*]
> Separate columns with *string*. Default is a tab with **-J** and a space otherwise.

-t, **--omit-header**
> Suppress headers, footers, and fills at end of pages.

-T, **--omit-pagination**
> Like **-t** but also suppress form feeds.

-v, **--show-non-printing**
> Convert unprintable characters to octal backslash format.

-w *page_width*, **--width=***page_width*
> Set the page width to *page_width* characters for multicolumn output. Default is 72.

-**W** *page_width*, --**page-width**=*page_width*

Set the page width to always be *page_width* characters. Lines longer than the specified width are truncated unless -**J** is also specified. Default is 72.

--**version**

Print version information and then exit.

praliases

praliases [*options*] [*keys*]

System administration command. **praliases** prints the current **sendmail** mail aliases. (Usually defined in the */etc/aliases* or */etc/aliases.db* file.) Limit output to the specified *keys* when given.

Options

-**f** *file*

Read the aliases from the specified file instead of **sendmail**'s default alias files.

-**C** *file*

Read **sendmail** configuration from the specified file instead of from */etc/mail/sendmail.cf*.

printenv

printenv [*variables*]

printenv *option*

Print values of all environment variables or, optionally, only the specified *variables*.

Options

--**help**

Print usage information and exit.

--**version**

Print version information and exit.

printf

printf *formats* [*strings*]

printf *option*

Print *strings* using the specified *formats*. *formats* can be ordinary text characters, C-language escape characters, C format specifications ending with one of the letters **diouxXfeEgGcs** or, more commonly, a set of conversion arguments listed here.

Options

--**help**

Print usage information and exit.

--**version**

Print version information and exit.

Arguments

%% Print a single %.

%b Print *string* with \ escapes interpreted.

%s Print the next *string*.

%n$s
> Print the *n*th *string*.

%[-]m[.n]s
> Print the next *string*, using a field that is *m* characters wide. Optionally, limit the field to print only the first *n* characters of *string*. Strings are right-adjusted unless the left-adjustment flag, -, is specified.

Examples

```
printf '%s %s\n' "My files are in" $HOME
printf '%-25.15s %s\n' "My files are in" $HOME
```

---

ps

ps [*options*]

Report on active processes. **ps** has three types of options. GNU long options start with two hyphens, which are required. BSD options may be grouped and do not start with a hyphen, while Unix98 options may be grouped and require an initial hyphen. The meaning of the short options can vary depending on whether or not there is a hyphen. In options, list arguments should either be comma-separated or space-separated and placed inside double quotes. In comparing the amount of output produced, note that **e** prints more than **a** and **l** prints more than **f** for each entry.

Options

nums, **p** *nums*, **-p** *nums*, **--pid**=*nums*
> Include only specified processes, which are given in a space-delimited list.

-*nums*, **-s** *nums*, **--sid**=*nums*
> Include only specified session IDs, which are given in a space-delimited list.

[-]a
> As **a**, list all processes on a terminal. As **-a**, list all processes except session leaders and processes not associated with a terminal.

[-]c
> As **-c**, show different scheduler information with **-l**. As **c**, show the true command name.

-C *cmds*
> Select by command name.

--cols=*cols*, **--columns**=*cols*
> Set the output width (the number of columns to display).

-d Select all processes except session leaders.

-e, -A
> Select all processes.

e Include environment information after the command.

[-]f, --forest

As -f, display full listing. As **f** or **--forest**, display "forest" family tree format, with ASCII art showing the relationships.

-F Set extra-full format; implies **-f**.

-g *list*, **-G** *list*, **--group**=*groups*, **--Group**=*groups*

For **-g**, select by session leader if *list* contains numbers, or by group if it contains group names. For **-G**, select by the group IDs in *list*. **--group** selects by effective group and **--Group** selects by real group, where *groups* can be either group names or group IDs.

h, --no-headers

Suppress header. If you select a BSD personality by setting the environment variable PS_PERSONALITY to **bsd**, then **h** prints a header on each page.

-H Display "forest" family tree format, but without ASCII art.

H Display threads as if they were processes.

--headers

Repeat headers on every output page.

--help

Display help information and exit.

--info

Print debugging information.

[-]j

Jobs format. **j** prints more information than **-j**.

k *spec*, **--sort** *spec*

Specify sort order. Syntax for the specification is:

[+|-]*key*[,[+|-]*key*...]]

The default direction is +, for increasing numerical or alphabetic order. See "Format and sort specifiers" on page 338 for possible keys.

[-]l

Produce a long listing. **-l** prints more information than **l** and is often used with **-y**.

L Print list of field specifiers that can be used for output formatting or for sorting.

-L Show threads, possibly with LWP and NLWP columns.

--lines=*num*, **--rows**=*num*

Set the screen height to *num* lines. If **--headers** is also set, the headers repeat every *num* lines.

[-]m

Show threads after processes.

n Print user IDs and WCHAN numerically.

-n *file*, **N** *file*

Specify the *System.map* file for **ps** to use as a namelist file. The map file must correspond to the Linux kernel—e.g., */boot/ System.map-2.6.27.5-117.fc10.x86_64*.

-N, --deselect

Negate the selection, selecting all processes that do not meet the specified conditions.

[-]o *fields*, **--format**=*fields*

Specify user-defined format with a list of fields to display.

[-]O *fields*

As **-O**, this option is like **-o**, but some common fields are predefined. As **O**, this option can be either the same as **-O** in specifying fields to display, or can specify single-letter fields for sorting. For sorting, each field specified as a key can optionally have a leading + (return to default sort direction on key) or - (reverse the default direction).

--ppid=*nums*

Select by parent process IDs.

r   Show only processes that are currently running.

s   Display signal format.

S, --cumulative

Include some dead child process data in parent total.

[-]t *ttys*, **--tty**=*ttys*

Display processes running on the specified terminals. **t** with no terminal list displays processes for the terminal associated with **ps**. Specify - to select processes not associated with any terminal.

T   Display all processes on this terminal. Like **t** with no argument.

-T   Display threads, possibly with SPID column,

[-]u *[users]*, **U** *users*, **--user**=*users*

As **u** with no argument, display user-oriented output. As **-u**, **U**, or **--user**, display by effective user ID (and also support names), showing results for *users*. With no argument, **-u** displays results for the current user.

-U *users*, **--User**=*users*

Display processes for *users* by real user ID (and also support names).

v   Display virtual memory format.

[-]V, --version

Display version information and then exit.

[-]w

Wide format. Don't truncate long lines. Use twice to set an unlimited width.

--width=*cols*

Set screen width.

x   Display processes without an associated terminal.

-y   Do not show flags; show **rss** instead of **addr**. Requires **-l**.

Format and sort specifiers

The following are the keywords for formatting and for sorting with
--**sort**, followed by a desciption and the output column header in
parentheses:

%cpu, pcpu

> Percent of CPU time used recently. (%CPU)

%mem, **pmem**

> Percent of memory used. (%MEM)

args, cmd, command

> The command the process is running with all its arguments.
> (CMD for **cmd**; otherwise COMMAND)

blocked, sig_block, sigmask

> Mask, in hexadecimal, of blocked signals. (BLOCKED)

bsdstart

> Command start time. (START)

bsdtime

> Accumulated CPU time for user plus system. (TIME)

c Integer value of **%cpu**. (C)

caught, sig_catch, sigcatch

> Mask, in hexadecimal, of caught signals. (CAUGHT)

class, cls, policy

> Scheduling class. (POL for **policy**, otherwise CLS). Possible
> values are:
>
> -   Unreported
>
> ?   Unknown value
>
> **FF** SCHED_FIFO (first in, first out)
>
> **RR** SCHED_RR (round robin)
>
> **TS** SCHED_OTHER (standard time-sharing)

comm, ucmd, ucomm

> Name of the command executable. (CMD for **ucmd**; other-
> wise, COMMAND)

cp Per-mill CPU usage, where mill is 1000. Equivalent to **%cpu**
> with no decimal point. (CP)

cputime, time

> Cumulative CPU time. (TIME)

egid, gid

> Effective group ID number in decimal. (EGID or GID,
> respectively)

egroup, group

> Effective group ID; as text value if it is available and if it fits,
> otherwise shown as decimal value. (EGROUP or GROUP,
> respectively)

eip

> Effective instruction pointer. (EIP)

esp

    Effective stack pointer. (ESP)

etime

    Elapsed time since the start of the process. (ELAPSED)

euid, uid

    Effective user ID. (EUID or UID, respectively)

euser, uname, user

    Effective username; as text value if it is available and if it fits, otherwise shown as decimal value. (EUSER for **euser**; otherwise, USER)

f, flag, flags

    Process flags. Can be summed. (F) Possible values are **1** (the process forked but didn't exec) and **4** (the process used super-user privileges).

fgid, fsgid

    Filesystem access group ID. (FGID)

fgroup, fsgroup

    Filesystem access group ID; as text if available and if it fits, otherwise as a decimal number. (FGROUP)

fname

    First eight bytes of the executable's basename. (COMMAND)

fuid, fsuid

    Filesystem access user ID. (FUID)

fuser

    Filesystem access user ID; as text if available and if it fits, otherwise as a decimal number. (FUSER)

ignored, sig_ignore, sigignore

    Mask of ignored signals in hexadecimal format. (IGNORED)

lstart

    Command start time. (STARTED)

lwp, spid, tid

    Light-weight process, or thread, ID. (LWP, SPID, TID, respectively)

ni, nice

    The **nice** value of the process. A higher number indicates less CPU time. (NI)

nlwp, thcount

    Number of LWPs, or threads, in the process. (NLWP or THCNT, respectively)

nwchan

    Address of kernel function where process is sleeping. See also **wchan** to get the function by name. (WCHAN)

pending, sig, sig_pend

    Mask of pending signals. Use with the **m** or **-m** option to see both signals pending on the process and on individual threads. (PENDING)

pgid, pgrp

Process group ID or ID of process group leader, which are equivalent. (PGID or PGRP, respectively)

pid

Process ID. (PID)

ppid

Parent process ID. (PPID)

pri

Process's scheduling priority. A higher number indicates lower priority. (PRI)

psr

Current processor that the process is running on. (PSR)

rgid

Real group ID. (RGID)

rgroup

Real group name; as text if available and it fits, otherwise as a decimal number. (RGROUP)

rss, rssize, rsz

Resident set size (the amount of physical memory), in kilobytes. (RSZ for **rsz**; otherwise RSS)

rtprio

Real-time priority. (RTPRIO)

ruid

Real user ID number. (RUID)

ruser

Real user ID; as text if available and it fits, otherwise as a decimal number. (RUSER)

s, state

A single-character state display. See **stat** for the possible characters or for a multicharacter display. (S)

sched

Scheduling policy. Also see **class**. (SCH) Possible values are:

0   SCHED_OTHER

1   SCHED_FIFO

2   SCHED_RR

sess, session, sid

Session ID, or the process ID of the session leader, which is equivalent. (SID for **sid**; otherwise SESS)

sgi_p

Processor on which the process is currently running, or "*" if the process is not running. (P)

sgid, svgid

Saved group ID. (SGID or SVGID, respectively)

sgroup

Saved group name; as text if available and it fits, otherwise as a decimal number.

size

Size of virtual image. Provides a rough estimate of the swapspace required to swap the process out. Note that **sz** uses the same column header, but has a different meaning. (SZ)

stackp

Address of the stack bottom (start of the stack). (STACKP)

start

Start time of the command. (STARTED)

start_time

Starting time or date of the process. (START)

stat

Status. Multiple status characters can appear. See also **s** to display a single character. (STAT)

+	Part of foreground process group.
<	High priority (not "nice").
D	Asleep and not interruptible.
l	Multithreaded.
L	Pages locked into memory.
N	Low priority ("nice").
R	Running or runnable.
s	Session leader.
S	Asleep.
T	Stopped.
Z	Zombie.

suid, svuid

Saved user ID. (SUID or SVUID, respectively)

suser, svuser

Saved username; as text if it is available and it fits, otherwise as a decimal number. (SUSER or SVUSER, respectively)

sz

Physical page size of the core image of the process, including text, data and stack space. (SZ)

tpgid

ID of the foreground process group on the associated terminal for the process, or -1 if not connected to a terminal. (TPGID)

tt, tty, tname

Associated (controlling) terminal. (TTY for **tname**; otherwise TT)

vsz, vsize

Virtual memory size, in kilobytes of the entire process. (VSZ)

wchan

Kernel function in which process is sleeping, or "-" if running, or "*" if multithreaded process and **ps** is not displaying threads. (WCHAN)

ptx

ptx [*options*] [*infiles*]

ptx -G [*options*] [*infile* [*outfile*]]

Create a permuted index, including context, from the contents of the specified input files. If the input files are omitted, or are -, read from standard input. The results are written to standard output. In the second form, with the **-G** option, **ptx** behaves like the System V version rather than the GNU version; you specify only one input file, and you can also specify an output file. Because they show words in context, permuted indexes are often used in such places as bibliographic or medical databases, thesauruses, or websites to aid in locating entries of interest.

Options

-A, --auto-reference

Produce automatically generated references, consisting of the filename and line number, separated by a colon, and print them at the beginning of each line.

-b *file*, **--break-file=***file*

The specified file contains word-break characters—characters that are not part of words, but separate them.

-f, --ignore-case

Ignore case when sorting, by folding lowercase into uppercase.

-F *string*, **--flag-truncation=***string*

Use *string* to flag line truncations.

-g *num*, **--gap-size=***num*

Specify the number of spaces between output columns.

-G, --traditional

Behave like System V **ptx**; don't use the GNU extensions. If an output file is specified, any existing contents are lost.

--help

Display a help message and exit.

-i *file*, **--ignore-file=***file*

Read the list of words that are not to be used as keywords in the concordance output from *file*.

-M *string*, **--macro-name=***string*

Select a string for use when generating output suitable for **nroff**, **troff** or T~E~X. The default is xx.

-o *file*, **--only-file=***file*

Specify the "only" file, which contains a list of words to be used in the concordance output. Any words not in *file* are ignored. If both an only file and an ignore file are specified, a word must appear in the only file and not appear in the ignore file to be used as a keyword.

-O [roff], **--format=roff**

Format the output as **roff** directives suitable to be used as input to **nroff** or **troff**. Use **-T** for T~E~X output.

-r, --references

Use the first field of each line as a reference to identify the line in the permuted index.

-R, --right-side-refs

Put references on the right, instead of the left. Used with **-r** and **-A**. The space taken up by the references is not taken into account by **-w**, even if **-R** is specified without **-r** or **-A**.

-S *regexp*, **--sentence-regexp**=*regexp*

Specify a regular expression to identify the end of a line or a sentence. Without **-G** and without **-r**, the end of a sentence is used. With **-G**, or with **-r**, the end of a line is used. An empty *regex* disables end-of-line or end-of-sentence recognition.

-T [*tex*], **--format**=*tex*

Format the output as TEX directives suitable to be used as TEX input. Use **-O** for **roff** output.

--version

Print version information and exit.

-w *num*, **--width**=*num*

Select the maximum output-line width (excluding the width of any reference if **-R** is specified).

-W *regexp*, **--word-regexp**=*regexp*

Use the specified regular expression to match each keyword.

---

pwck

pwck [*options*] [*files*]

System administration command. Remove corrupt or duplicate entries in the */etc/passwd* and */etc/shadow* files. **pwck** will prompt for a "yes" or "no" before deleting entries. If the user replies "no," the program will exit. Alternate passwd and shadow *files* can be checked. If correctable errors are found, the user will be encouraged to run the **usermod** command.

Option

-q   Run in quiet mode. Only report serious problems.

-r   Run in noninteractive read-only mode, answering all questions **no**.

-s   Don't check integrity, just sort entries by UID.

Exit status

0   Success.

1   Syntax error.

2   One or more bad password entries found.

3   Could not open password files.

4   Could not lock password files.

5   Could not write password files.

pwconv

pwconv

pwunconv

System administration command. Convert unshadowed entries in */etc/passwd* into shadowed entries in */etc/shadow*. Replace the encrypted password in */etc/password* with an x. Shadowing passwords keeps them safer from password-cracking programs. **pwconv** creates additional expiration information for the */etc/shadow* file from entries in your */etc/login.defs* file. If you add new entries to the */etc/passwd* file, you can run **pwconv** again to transfer the new information to */etc/shadow*. Already shadowed entries are ignored. **pwunconv** restores the encrypted passwords to your */etc/passwd* file and removes the */etc/shadow* file. Some expiration information is lost in the conversion. See also **grpconv** and **grpunconv**.

pwd

pwd

Print the full pathname of the current working directory. See also the **dirs** shell command built into **bash**.

quota

quota [*options*] [*user|group*]

Display disk usage and total space allowed for a designated user or group. With no argument, the quota for the current user is displayed. Most users can display only their own quota information, but the superuser can display information for any user. This command reports quotas for all filesystems listed in */etc/mtab*. For NFS-mounted filesystems, **quota** calls **rpc.rquotad** on the server machine for the information.

Options

-A, --all-nfs
  Report quotas for all NFS filesystems.

-F *format*, **--format**=*format*
  Check quota files for the specified format.

-g, --group
  Given with a *user* argument, display the quotas for the groups of which the user is a member, instead of the user's quotas. With no argument, shows group quotas for the current user.

-i, --no-autofs
  Ignore mountpoints that are mounted by the automounter.

-l, --local-only
  Only report quotas on local filesystems.

-p, --raw-grace
  When user is in a grace period, print a timestamp (seconds since epoch) marking when the grace period expires.

-q, --quiet
  Display information only for filesystems in which the user is over quota.

-Q, --quiet-refuse

For NFS-mounted filesystems. do not print an error message if the connection to **rpc.rquotad** is refused (usually because it is not running on the server).

-s, --human-readable

Try to choose units for displaying limits, space used, and inodes used.

-u, --user

The default behavior. When used with **-g**, display both user and group quota information.

-v, --verbose

Display quotas for filesystems even if no storage is currently allocated.

-w, --no-wrap

Do not wrap line for long device names.

Formats

rpc

Quota over NFS.

vfsold

Version 1 quota.

vfsv0

Version 2 quota.

xfs

Quota on XFS filesystem.

---

quotacheck

quotacheck [*options*] [*filesystems*]

System administration command. Audit and correct quota information by building a table of current disk usage and comparing it to the recorded usage in both the kernel and the quota files. **quotacheck** will update quota information when possible and prompt the user if it requires input. Most systems that support quotas run this command at system startup. To prevent damage to *filesystems* or loss of quota data, turn off quotas with **quotaoff** and **umount** the system. **quotacheck** will attempt to remount any mounted filesystem as read-only before scanning.

Options

-a, --all

Check all non-NFS filestystems in */etc/mtab*.

-b, --backup

Back up quota files before writing new data to them.

-c, --create-files

Skip reading existing quota information; just write new files.

-f, --force

Force checking on filesystems with quotas currently enabled.

-F *format,* **--format=***format*
> Check quota files for the specified format. (See **quota** for valid formats.)

-g, --group
> Only check group quotas.

-i, --interactive
> Prompt user for input upon finding errors.

-m, --no-remount
> Don't try to remount mounted filesystems.

-M, --try-remount
> Force check to run in read-write mode if it cannot successfully remount the filesystem in read-only mode.

-n, --use-first-dquot
> If multiple entries for a user or group are found in a corrupt quota file, use the first entry found.

-R, --exclude-root
> Don't check the root filesystem when using the **-a** option.

-u, --user
> Only check user quotas. This is the default.

-v, --verbose
> Print information on the progress of the command.

---

quotaon

quotaon [*options*] [*filesystems*]

System administration command. Turn on enforcement of filesystem quotas. To work, the *filesystems* must have a **gpquota**, **quota**, or **usrquota** option listed in the */etc/fstab* file. On most filesystems, user and group quota files must also exist. XFS filesystems store quota information as metadata instead of as files. Use **edquota** or **setquota** to create the appropriate quota information.

Options

-a, --all
> Turn on quotas for all autoloading filesystems in */etc/fstab* that support them.

-f, --off
> Invoke **quotaoff** instead of **quotaon**.

-F *format,* **--format=***format*
> Check quota files for the specified format. (See **quota** for valid formats.)

-g, --group
> Turn group quotas on.

-p, --print-state
> Print current quota status, then exit.

-u, --user
> Turn user quotas on.

-v, --verbose
> Print a message for each filesystem affected by the command.

quotaoff

quotaoff [*options*] [*filesystems*]

System administration command. Turn off enforcement of file-system quotas. This command is a synonym for **quotaon -f**.

Options
-a, --all
> Turn off quotas for all filesystems in */etc/fstab*.

-F *format*, **--format=***format*
> Check quota files for the specified format. (See **quota** for valid formats.)

-g, --group
> Turn group quotas off.

-p, --print-status
> Print current quota status, then exit.

-u, --user
> Turn user quotas off.

-v, --verbose
> Print a message for each filesystem affected by the command.

-x *command*, **-xfs-command** *command*
> On an XFS system, perform one of the following *commands*:

> **delete**
>> Remove quota metadata from the XFS filesystem.

> **enforcement**
>> Turn off limit enforcement on an XFS filesystem.

quotastats

quotastats

System administration command. Print a report of quota system statistics gathered from the kernel.

ranlib

ranlib *filename*

ranlib *option*

Generate an index for archive file *filename*. This is equivalent to running **ar -s**.

Option
-v, -V, --version
> Print version information and exit.

rcp

rcp [*options*] *file1 file2*

rcp [*options*] *file ... directory*

Copy files between two machines. Each *file* or *directory* is either a remote filename of the form *rname@rhost:path*, or a local filename. Files can be copied between two remote machines, where neither *file1* nor *file2* is on the local machine. Use of **rcp** has generally been replaced by **scp**, which offers better security.

Linux
Commands

Options

-p   Preserve modification times and modes of the source files.

-r   If any of the source files are directories, descend into each directory and recursively copy all files and directories within it. The destination must be a directory.

---

rdate

rdate [*options*] [*host...*]

TCP/IP command. Retrieve the date and time from a host or hosts on the network and optionally set the local system time.

Options

-l   Send errors and output to **syslogd**.

-p   Print the retrieved dates.

-s   Set the local system time from the host; must be specified by root.

-t *n*   Timeout each retrieval attempt after *n* seconds.

-u   Use UDP instead of TCP.

---

rdist

rdist [*options*] [*names*]

System administration command. Remote file distribution client program. **rdist** maintains identical copies of files over multiple hosts. It reads commands from a file named *distfile* to direct the updating of files and/or directories. An alternative *distfile* can be specified with the **-f** option or the **-c** option.

Options

-a *num*

Do not update filesystems with fewer than *num* bytes free.

-A *num*

Specify the minimum number of inodes that **rdist** requires.

-c *name* [*login@*]*host*[*:dest*]

Interpret the arguments as a small *distfile*, where *login* is the user to log in as, *host* is the destination host, *name* is the local file to transfer, and *dest* is the remote name where the file should be installed.

-d *var=value*

Define *var* to have *value*. This option defines or overrides variable definitions in the *distfile*. Set the variable *var* to *value*.

-D   Debugging mode.

-f *file*

Read input from *file* (by default, *distfile*). If *file* is -, read from standard input.

-F   Execute all commands sequentially, without forking.

-l *options*

Specify logging options on the local machine.

-L *options*

Specify logging options on the remote machine.

-m *machine*

Update only *machine*. May be specified multiple times for multiple machines.

-M *num*

Do not allow more than *num* child **rdist** processes to run simultaneously. Default is 4.

-n Suppress normal execution. Instead, print the commands that would have been executed.

-o*options*

Specify one or more *options*, which must be comma-separated.

chknfs

Suppress operations on files that reside on NFS filesystems.

chkreadonly

Check filesystem to be sure it is not read-only before attempting to perform updates.

chksym

Do not update files that exist on the local host but are symbolic links on the remote host.

compare

Compare files; use this comparison rather than age as the criteria for determining which files should be updated.

follow

Interpret symbolic links, copying the file to which the link points instead of creating a link on the remote machine.

ignlnks

Ignore links that appear to be unresolvable.

nochkgroup

Do not update a file's group ownership unless the entire file needs updating.

nochkmode

Do not update file mode unless the entire file needs updating.

nochkowner

Do not update file ownership unless the entire file needs updating.

nodescend

Suppress recursive descent into directories.

noexec

Suppress **rdist** of executables that are in *a.out* format.

numchkgroup

Check group ownership by group ID instead of by name.

numchkowner

Check file ownership by user ID instead of by name.

quiet

Quiet mode; do not print commands as they execute.

remove

Remove files that exist on the remote host but not the local host.

savetargets

Save updated files in *name.old*.

sparse

Check for sparse files—for example, **ndbm** files.

verify

Print a list of all files on the remote machine that are out of date, but do not update them.

whole

Preserve directory structure by creating subdirectories on the remote machine. For example, if you **rdist** the file */foo/bar* into the directory */baz*, it would produce the file */baz/foo/bar* instead of the default */baz/bar*.

younger

Do not update files that are younger than the master files.

-p *path*

Specify the path to search for **rdistd** on the remote machine.

-P *path*

Specify path to the transport command to use on the local machine. This is normally **rsh**, but may also be **ssh**. The *path* argument may also be specified as a colon-separated list of acceptable transports to use in order of preference.

-t *seconds*

Specify the timeout period (default 900 seconds) after which **rdist** will sever the connection if the remote server has not yet responded.

-V Display version, then exit.

---

rdistd

rdistd *options*

System administration command. Start the **rdist** server. Note that you *must* specify the -S option unless you are simply querying for version information with -V.

Options

-D Debugging mode.

-S Start the server.

-V Display the version number and exit.

---

readcd

readcd dev=*device* [*options*]

Read or write compact discs. **readcd** is now generally a link to **readom**.

---

readelf

readelf *option*[...] *elffiles*

Display information about one or more ELF (Executable and Linking Format) object files. At least one option is required to specify the information to be displayed for each file.

Options

-a, --all
Display all. Equivalent to **-A -d -h -I -l -r -s -S -V**.

-A, --arch-specific
Display architecture-specific information, if any.

-d, --dynamic
Display the dynamic section.

-D, --use-dynamic
When displaying symbols, use the symbol table in the dynamic section, not the symbols section.

-e, --headers
Display all headers. Equivalent to **-h -l -s**.

-h, --file-header
Display the ELF header at the beginning of the file.

-H, --help
Display help information and exit.

-I, --histogram
Display a histogram of bucket bit lengths when displaying the symbol tables.

-l, --program-headers, --segments
Display the segment headers, if any.

-n, --notes
Display the NOTE segment, if any.

-r, --relocs
Display the relocation segment, if any.

-s, --symbols, --syms
Display entries in symbol table sections, if any.

-S, --section-headers, --sections
Display the section headers, if any.

-u, --unwind
Display the unwind section, if any (currently applies only to IA64 ELF files).

-v, --version
Display version information and exit.

-V, --version-info
Display the version sections, if any.

-w[*option*], **--debug-dump**[=*option*]
Display the debug sections. If specified with an option, display only that section. The options shown here in parentheses are for **-w**; the words preceding them are for **--debug-dump**. The options are **abbrev** (**a**), **frames** (**f**), **frames-interp** (**F**), **info** (**i**), **line** (**l**), **loc** (**o**), **macro** (**m**), **pub-names** (**p**), **ranges** (**r**), and **str** (**s**).

-W, --wide
> Don't break output lines at 80 columns. The default is to break them. Useful for wide terminals.

-x *num*, --hex-dump=*num*
> Display a hexadecimal dump of the section *number*.

readlink

readlink *file*

readlink *option*

Print the contents of the symbolic link *file*—that is, the name of the file to which the link points.

Options

-f, --canonicalize
> Canonicalize by recursively following symbolic links.

--help
> Print usage information and exit.

-n, --no-newline
> Do not output a trailing newline.

-q, --quiet, -s, --silent
> Suppress most error messages.

-v, --verbose
> Print all error messages.

--version
> Print version information and exit.

readom

readom dev=*device* [*options*]

Read or write compact discs. The device is usually specified as **dev=***scsibus/target/lun* or **dev=***target/lun* if the device is on the default SCSI bus. The default SCSI bus is bus 0, the *target* is the ID number, and the *lun* is the logical unit number.

Options

-c2scan
> Do a C2 error scan. If any C2 errors are found, specifying the **speed=** option to reduce the speed may help.

-clone
> Read all data and the table of contents, and put the table-of-contents data into a file with the same filename as specified with **f=** but with a *.toc* extension.

-d, debug=*num*
> Increment the debugging level by 1 with -d or set the level to *num* with **debug**. Specifying -dd is the equivalent of **debug=2**.

dev=*target*
> Set the SCSI target.

f=*filename*

Specify the file from which input should be read, or to which output should be written. If the filename is given as -, use standard input or standard output, respectively.

-factor

Print the speed factor for the **meshpoints=** option, based on the current medium's single speed. Works only if **readom** can determine the current medium type.

-fulltoc

Read the full table of contents from the current CD and display it in hexadecimal.

kd=*num*, **kdebug=***num*

Modify the kernel debugging level while SCSI commands are running, to do kernel debugging.

meshpoints=*num*

Print the read speed at *num* locations, and produce a list of values suitable for plotting. The output is written to standard output.

-nocorr

Ignore read errors, doing no error correction. Switches the drive into a mode to ignore the errors; if **readom** completes, it switches the drive back to the previous mode.

-noerror

Do not abort if an uncorrectable error is found in the data stream.

-notrunc

Do not truncate the output file on open.

-overhead

Measure SCSI command overhead. The measurement is done by running several commands 1000 times and printing the total time used for each.

retries=*num*

Set the retry count to *num*. The default is 128.

-s, -silent

Do not print a status report for SCSI command failures.

-scanbus

Scan all SCSI devices on all SCSI buses, print the results, and exit. Useful for finding the SCSI addresses of devices.

sectors=*range*

Specify the range of sectors to read.

speed=*num*

Set the reading and writing speed, as an integer value. Useful only for MMC-compliant drives. Defaults to maximum speed.

timeout=*num*

Set the default SCSI command timeout to *num* seconds. Defaults to 40 seconds.

ts=*num*
> Set the maximum transfer size for a single SCSI command to *num*. Defaults to 256 KB.

-v, -verbose
> Increment the general verbosity level by 1. Useful for displaying progress.

-V, -Verbose
> Increment the verbosity level for SCSI command transport by 1. Useful for debugging. Specifying **-VV** adds data-buffer content to the output.

-version
> Print version information and exit.

-w Switch to write mode. The default is to read from the device.

---

reboot

reboot [*options*]

System administration command. Close out filesystems, shut down the system, then reboot. Because this command immediately stops all processes, it should be run only in single-user mode. If the system is not in runlevel 0 or 6, **reboot** calls **shutdown -r**.

Options

-f Call **reboot** even when **shutdown** would normally be called.

-i Shut down network interfaces before reboot.

-n Suppress normal call to **sync**.

-w Suppress normal execution; simply write to */var/log/wtmp*.

---

reject

reject [*options*] *destination*

System administration command. Instruct printing system to reject jobs for the specified print queue *destinations*. Depending on queue settings, the system may prompt for a password. Also invoked as **cupsreject**.

Options

-E Require encryption when connecting.

-h *server*
> Apply command remotely to the specified CUPS *server*.

-r *reason*
> Reject with the specified *reason* instead of the default "Reason Unknown."

---

rename

rename *from to files*

Rename *files* by replacing the first occurrence of *from* in each filename with *to*.

Example

Rename files that start with *test* so they start with *mytest*:

```
$ rename test mytest test*
```

---

renice

renice [*priority*] [*options*] [*target*]

Control the scheduling priority of running processes. May be applied to a process, process group, or user (*target*). A privileged user may alter the priority of other users' processes. *priority* must, for ordinary users, lie between 0 and the environment variable PRIO_MAX (normally 20), with a higher number indicating increased niceness. A higher niceness value means that the process will run at a lower priority. A privileged user may set a negative priority, as low as PRIO_MIN (normally –20), to speed up processes. See the **nice** command for setting the scheduling priority for processes when they are initially run.

Options

+num

Specify number by which to increase current priority of process, rather than an absolute priority number.

-num

Specify number by which to decrease current priority of process, rather than an absolute priority number.

-g, --pgrp

Interpret *target* parameters as process group IDs.

-p, --pid

Interpret *target* parameters as process IDs (default).

-u, --user

Interpret *target* parameters as usernames.

repquota

repquota [*options*] [*filesystem*]

System administration command. Generate a report on disk usage and quotas for the specified *filesystem*.

Options

-a, --all

Generate report for all filesystems in */etc/mtab* that support quotas.

-c, --batch-translation

Translate UIDs and GIDs in batches. (Faster for */etc/passwd*.)

-C, --no-batch-translation

Translate UIDs and GIDs individually. (Faster for database lookups.)

-F *format*, **--format=**format

Report on quotas for the specified format. (See **quota** for valid formats.)

-g, --group

Report group quotas.

-i, --no-autofs

Ignore automount mount points.

-n, --no-names

Use UIDs and GIDs instead of names. (Generates faster reports.)

-p, --raw-grace

When user is in a grace period, print a timestamp (seconds since epoch) marking when the grace period expires.

-s, --human-readable

Report sizes in more human-readable units.

-t, --truncate-names

Truncate user and group names to nine characters.

-u, --user

Report user quotas. (This is the default.)

---

reset

reset [*options*] [*terminal*]

Clear screen (reset terminal). If *terminal* is specified on the command line, the value is used as the terminal type. **reset** is a symbolic link to the **tset** command. Invoking the command as **reset** is useful for clearing your terminal when a program dies and leaves the terminal in an abnormal state. You may have to run the command with a linefeed character (usually Ctrl-J) before and after it:

    Ctrl-J**reset**Ctrl-J

See the **tset** command for the available options.

---

resize2fs

resize2fs [*options*] *device* [*size*]

System administration command. Enlarge or shrink an ext2 filesystem on *device* so it has *size* blocks. The filesystem *size* cannot be larger than the underlying partition. This command changes only the filesystem size, not the underlying partition. To change the partition, use **fdisk**.

Options

-d *flags*

Print debugging information on resize activity. The value of the *flags* parameter determines what activity is reported. Compute its value by summing the numbers of the items you wish to debug:

2   Block relocations.

4   Inode relocations.

8   Inode table movement.

-f   Force resize, overriding safety checks.

-M   Shrink filesystem to minimum size.

-p   Print progress information for each resize task.

-P   Print maximum filesystem size then exit.

---

restore   restore *flag* [*options*] [*files*]

System administration command. Restore backed-up *files* from a **dump** archive. Execute this command with one of the following flags.

Flags

-C   Compare files on disk to files in the backup and print report.

-i   Restore files interactively. This will open a shell-like interface that accepts the following commands.

> **add** [*name*]
>> Add the current working directory, or the specified file or directory *name* to the list of files to extract.
>
> **cd** *directory*
>> Change the current working directory.
>
> **delete** [*name*]
>> Remove the current working directory or the specified file or directory *name* from the list of files to extract.
>
> **extract**
>> Extract selected files. This will prompt for the volume on which the files to be extracted can be found. Once the files are extracted, the system will prompt if you want to change the ownership and mode of the current directory (the one to which you extracted the files) to match the settings on the dump's original base directory.
>
> **help**
>> Print a command summary.
>
> **ls** [*name*]
>> Like the shell command, list files in the current working directory, or the specified file or directory name. A *
>> before a name indicates items marked for extraction. In verbose mode, the listing will include each item's inode.
>
> **pwd**
>> Like the shell command, print the working directory.
>
> **quit**
>> Exit the command.
>
> **setmodes**
>> Set ownership and mode of the directory to which you extract the files to match the settings on the dump's original base directory.
>
> **quit**
>> Exit the command.
>
> **verbose**
>> Verbose mode. Print inodes along with file and directory names when using **ls**.

-P *filename*

Create a Quick File Access file suitable for use with the **-Q** option.

-r   Fully restore the backup to a clean, newly created ext2 filesystem. Execute this command in the root directory of the new filesystem.

-R   Prompt for the tape volume to fully restore.

-t   Print *files* if they exist in the archive or an error if they do not. If no files are specified, list all files in the archive.

-x   Recursively extract *files* if they exist in the archive. Restore owner, modification times, and modes. If no files are specified, restore the entire backup.

Options

-a   Read all volumes to find the files to extract, beginning with volume 1. This will skip any volume prompts.

-A *file*

Read the table of contents from the specified archive *file*.

-b*blocksize*

Specify the block size in kilobytes used for a block in the archive. Restore can usually determine this when reading the dump media.

-c   Read dumps made prior to version 4.4.

-d   Print debugging information.

-D *filesystem*

When using the -C flag, compare the dump to files on the specified *filesystem*.

-f *file*

Read the backup from the specified *file*: a device file, an ordinary file, or - to read from standard input. Use *host:file* or *user@host:file* to read from a networked host using either the **rmt** program or the program specified by the RMT environment variable.

-F *script*

Run the specified *script* at the beginning of each volume. **restore** will pass the current device and volume number to the script. The script should return 0 to continue, 1 to prompt for a new tape, or any other exit value to abort the restore. The script will run with the process's real user and group ID.

-h   Do not recursively restore directory. Only restore the specified directory.

-k   Use Kerberos authentication when connecting to a remote server.

-l   Treat *file* as a regular file instead of a tape device. Use this option when restoring from remote compressed files.

-L *n*

Used with the -C flag. Abort the comparison after encountering *n* errors.

-m   Expect *filenames* to be given as inodes.

-M   Restore from a multivolume backup. Treat any filename provided with -f as a prefix.

-N   Perform all actions indicated by other flags and options, but don't write anything to the disk.

-o   Automatically set ownership and mode of the current directory to match the original base directory of the dump.

-Q *file*
     Read tape positions from the specified Quick File Access mode *file*.

-S *n*
     Read from volume *n* of a multifile backup.

-u   Unlink (remove) any existing files before writing a file with the same name.

-v   Verbose mode. Print information about files being restored.

-V   Enable multivolume mode for devices other than tapes.

-X *file*
     Read list of files and directories to extract from the specified *file*. Use - to retrieve list of files from standard input.

-y   Attempt to skip over errors without prompting for operator input.

---

rev

rev [*files*]

Reverse the order of characters on each line of the specified files and print the results on standard output. If no files are specified, **rev** reads from standard input.

---

rexec

rexec [*options*] *rhost command*

Execute commands remotely. This client program connects to a remote host running **rexecd**, and passes it *command*. It uses a login name and password for authentication. These can be passed on the command line using the options below, provided through the *$HOME/.netrc* file or the environment variables REXEC_USER and REXEC_PASS. If it cannot determine the username and password, **rexec** prompts the user for the information. Note that because **rexec** sends passwords to the remote system in cleartext, you should use it only on a secure network. See **ssh** for a more secure alternative.

Options

-a   Send both error messages and output to standard output.

-b   When received locally, only echo signals **SIGINT**, **SIGQUIT** and **SIGTERM** to the remote process.

-c   Leave remote standard input open when the local input closes.

-d   Debugging mode. Echo commands sent locally.

-l *username*
     Specify a different *username* for the remote login. Default is the same as your local username.

Linux
Commands

-n   Prompt user for name and password even if otherwise provided.

-p *password*
     Specify the *password* for the remote account.

-s   Do not echo any signals to the remote process.

rexecd

rexecd `command-line`

TCP/IP command. Server for the **rexec** routine, providing remote execution facilities with authentication based on usernames and passwords. **rexecd** is started by **inetd** and must have an entry in **inetd**'s configuration file, */etc/inetd.conf*.

Option
-D   Disable reverse DNS lookup; use IP addresses in logs.

rlogin

rlogin [`options`] `rhost`

Remote login. **rlogin** connects the terminal on the current local host to the remote host *rhost*. The remote terminal type is the same as your local terminal type. The terminal or window size is also copied to the remote system if the server supports it. Use of **rlogin** has generally been replaced with **ssh**, which offers better security.

Options
-8   Allow an 8-bit input data path at all times.

-d   Debugging mode.

-e*c* Specify escape character *c* (default is ~).

-E   Do not interpret any character as an escape character.

-l *username*
     Specify a different *username* for the remote login. Default is the same as your local username.

-L   Allow **rlogin** session to be run without any output postprocessing (i.e., run in **litout** mode).

rlogind

in.rlogind [`options`]

TCP/IP command. Server for the **rlogin** program, providing a remote login facility, with authentication based on privileged port numbers from trusted hosts. **rlogind** is invoked by **inetd** when a remote login connection is requested. The login process propagates the client terminal's baud rate and terminal type as found in the TERM environment variable.

Options
-a   Verify hostname.

-h   Permit superuser *.rhosts* files to be used. Ignored if pluggable authentication module (PAM) support is enabled. Control through */etc/pam.conf* instead.

-l Do not authenticate hosts via a nonroot *.rhosts* file. Ignored if pluggable authentication module (PAM) support is enabled. Control through */etc/pam.conf* instead.

-L Do not authenticate hosts via *.rhosts* or *hosts.equiv* files. Ignored if pluggable authentication module (PAM) support is enabled. Control through */etc/pam.conf* instead.

-n Suppress keep-alive messages.

---

rm

rm [*options*] *files*

Delete one or more *files*. To remove a file, you must have write permission in the directory that contains the file, but you need not have permission on the file itself. If you do not have write permission on the file, you will be prompted (**y** or **n**) to override. **rm** is often aliased to **rm -i**, especially for the root user, to protect against inadvertently deleting files.

Options

-d, **--directory**
> Remove directories, even if they are not empty. Available only to a privileged user.

-f, **--force**
> Remove write-protected files without prompting.

--help
> Print a help message and then exit.

-i Prompt for **y** (remove the file) or **n** (do not remove the file) for each file.

--interactive[=*when*]
> Specify when to prompt. The possible values for *when* are **never**, **no**, **none**, **once**, **always**, **yes**.

-I Prompt only once before deleting recursively or before deleting more than three files.

--no-preserve-root
> Do not treat root (/) specially. This is the default.

--one-file-system
> When removing recursively, only remove files on the same file-system as *files*.

--preserve-root
> Do not remove root (/).

-r, **-R**, **--recursive**
> If *file* is a directory, remove the entire directory and all its contents, including subdirectories. Be forewarned: use of this option can be dangerous.

-v, **--verbose**
> Verbose mode (print the name of each file before removing it).

--version
> Print version information and then exit.

-- Mark the end of options. Use this when you need to supply a filename beginning with -.

rmail

rmail [*options*] *users*

TCP/IP command. Handle remote mail received via **uucp**. **rmail** transforms trace information from mail in UUCP format to the equivalent RFC 822 format, then forwards messages to **sendmail**.

Options
-D *domain*
> Use *domain* instead of **UUCP** as the UUCP hostname in **From** fields.

-T Print debugging information.

rmdir

rmdir [*options*] *directories*

Delete the named *directories* (not the contents). *directories* are deleted from the parent directory and must be empty (if not, **rm -r** can be used instead). See also **mkdir**.

Options
--help
> Print a help message and then exit.

--ignore-fail-on-non-empty
> Ignore failure to remove directories that are not empty.

-p, --parents
> Remove *directories* and any intervening parent directories that become empty as a result. Useful for removing subdirectory trees.

-v, --verbose
> Verbose mode; print message for each directory as it is processed.

--version
> Print version information and then exit.

rmmod

rmmod [*options*] *modules*

System administration command. Unload a module or list of modules from the kernel. This command is successful only if the specified modules are not in use and no other modules are dependent on them. This simplified program provides some backward compatibility. In general, use **modprobe -r** instead.

Options
-s, --syslog
> Write messages to **syslogd** instead of to the terminal.

-v, --verbose
> Verbose mode.

-V, --version
> Print version number, then exit.

-w, --wait
> If module is in use, disable it so no new processes can use it.
> Remove the module when it is no longer in use.

rndc

rndc [*options*] [*command*]

TCP/IP command. Send commands to a BIND DNS server via a TCP connection (see the **named** command.) This command reads authentication and connection information from the file */etc/rndc. conf*, and its authentication key from */etc/rndc.key*. If entered without a *command*, display a help message listing the available commands.

Options
-c *file*
> Read configuration information from file instead of */etc/rndc.conf*.

-k *file*
> Perform command on the routing cache instead of the forwarding information base (FIB) routing table.

-p *port*
> Connect to the specified *port* instead of the default control channel port, 953.

-s *server*
> Send command to the specified *server*. There must be an entry for *server* in the configuration file.

-V Use verbose log messages.

-y *keyname*
> Specify the key to use by keyname. There must be a key entry for keyname in the */etc/rndc.conf* file.

Commands
You can send the following commands to a BIND nameserver:

dumpdb
> Dump current cache to the dump file (specified in */etc/named. conf*), or to *named_dump.db* when not specified.

flush [*view*]
> Flush all server caches, or only the cache for the specified *view*.

halt
> Stop server immediately.

querylog
> Toggle query logging.

reconfig
> Reload the configuration file and any new zones.

reload [*zone* [*class* [*view*]]]
> Reload configuration file and zones. When specified, limit the reload to the given *zone*, *class*, or *view*.

refresh *zone*
> Refresh database information for *zone*.

stats
> Write statistics to the statistics file (specified in */etc/named.conf*).

status
> Display server status.

stop
> Save any recent dynamic zone transfer updates (IXFR) to the master files, then stop the server.

trace [*debuglevel*], **notrace**
> Increase the server's debug level by 1, or set it to the specified *debuglevel*. Use the **notrace** command to set the level to 1.

---

route

route [*options*] [*command*]

TCP/IP command. Add or remove entries in the routing tables maintained by **routed**. **route** accepts two commands: **add**, to add a route, and **del**, to delete a route. The two commands have the following syntax:

> **add** [**-net** | **-host**] *address* [*modifiers*]
> **del** [**-net** | **-host**] *address* [*modifiers*]

address is treated as a plain route, unless **-net** is specified or *address* is found in */etc/networks*. **-host** can be used to specify that *address* is a plain route whether or not it is found in */etc/networks*. Using route *modifiers*, you can specify the gateway through which to route packets headed for that address, its netmask, TCP mss, or the device with which to associate the route; you can also mask certain routes. Only a privileged user may modify the routing tables.

If no command is specified, **route** prints the routing tables.

Options

-A *family*, **--family**
> Specify an address family to use with an **add** or **del** command. *family* may be **inet**, **inet6**, **ax25**, **netrom**, **ipx**, **ddp**, or **x25**.

-C, **--cache**
> Perform command on the routing cache instead of the forwarding information base (FIB) routing table.

-e, **--extend**
> Use **netstat -r** format to print routing table. Use twice to print extended information. Same as **netstat -ree**.

-F, **--fib**
> Perform command on the forwarding information base (FIB) routing table. This is the default behavior.

-h, **--help**
> Print help message, then exit.

-n, **--numeric**
> Show numerical addresses; do not look up hostnames. (Useful if DNS is not functioning properly.)

-v, --verbose
    Verbose mode.

-V, --version
    Print version and configuration options, then exit.

Route modifiers

[**dev**] *interface*
    Associate route with specified device. When the *interface* is given as the last argument on a command line, the word **dev** is optional.

netmask *mask*
    Use netmask *mask*.

gw *gateway*
    Route packets through *gateway*.

metric *n*
    Set routing metric to *n*.

mss *bytes*
    Set maximum segment size for connections over this route.

reject
    Cause route lookup for target to fail. Used to mask out networks from a default route.

Example

Add a default gateway for interface eth0:

```
route add default gw 192.168.0.1 dev eth0
```

---

rpcbind

rpcbind [*options*]

NFS/NIS command. **portmap** is renamed **rpcbind** in newer Linux systems. It maps RPC program numbers into universal addresses. This server must be running in order to make RPC calls. RPC servers run on a host register their program number with **rpcbind**. Clients wishing to make an RPC call first check with **rpcbind** to find the address for a given program number.

-a   Abort on errors if debugging (**-d**).

-d   Run in debug mode. Do not fork.

-h [*address*]
    Bind to the specified IP *address* for UDP requests. This option may be given multiple times. You need not specify the local-host. When using this option **rpcbind** automatically binds to 127.0.0.1 and ::1 (if using IPv6) as well.

-i   Insecure mode. Allow calls to SET and UNSET from any host.

-l   Enable libwrap connection logging (tcp wrappers).

-s   Change to user daemon sooner. Bind to nonprivileged ports for outgoing connections, refuse connections to privileged ports from nonprivileged clients.

-w   Warm start. Read stat from a previous **rpcbind**.

rpcgen

rpcgen [*options*] *file*

Parse *file*, which should be written in the RPC (Remote Procedural Call) language, and produce a program written in C that implements the RPC code. Place header code generated from *file.x* in *file.h*, XDR routines in *file_xdr.c*, server code in *file_svc.c*, and client code in *file_clnt.c*. Lines preceded by **%** are not parsed. By default, **rpcgen** produces Sun OS 4.1–compatible code.

-a   Produce all files (client and server).

-b   Produce SunOS 4.1–compatible code. This is the default.

-5   Produce SVR4-compatible code.

-c   Create XDR routines. Cannot be used with other options.

-C   Produce ANSI C code (the default).

-k   Produce K&R C code.

-D*name*[=*value*]
      Define the symbol *name*, and set it equal to *value* or 1.

-h   Produce a header file. With **-T**, make the file support RPC dispatch tables. Cannot be used with other options.

-I   Produce an **inetd**-compatible server.

-K *secs*
      Specify amount of time that the server should wait after replying to a request and before exiting. Default is 120. Setting *secs* to **-1** prevents the program from ever exiting.

-l   Produce client code. Cannot be used with other options.

-m   Produce server code only, suppressing creation of a "main" routine. Cannot be used with other options.

-N   New style. Allow multiple arguments for procedures. Not necessarily backward-compatible.

-o [*file*]
      Print output to *file* or standard output.

-Sc   Print sample client code to standard output.

-Ss   Create skeleton server code only.

-t   Create RPC dispatch table. Cannot be used with other options.

-T   Include support for RPC dispatch tables.

rpcinfo

rpcinfo [*options*] [*host*] [*program*] [*version*]

NFS/NIS command. Report RPC information. *program* can be either a name or a number. If a *version* is specified, **rpcinfo** attempts to call that version of the specified *program*. Otherwise, it attempts to find all the registered version numbers for the specified *program* by calling version 0, and then attempts to call each registered version.

Options

-b   Make an RPC broadcast to the specified *program* and *version* using UDP, and report all hosts that respond.

-**d**   Delete the specified *version* of *program*'s registration. Can be executed only by the user who added the registration or by a privileged user.

-**n** *portnum*
Use *portnum* as the port number for the -**t** and -**u** options, instead of the port number given by the portmapper.

-**p**   Probe the portmapper on *host* and print a list of all registered RPC programs. If *host* is not specified, it defaults to the value returned by **hostname**.

-**t**   Make an RPC call to *program* on the specified *host* using TCP, and report whether a response was received.

-**u**   Make an RPC call to *program* on the specified *host* using UDP, and report whether a response was received.

---

rpm   rpm [*options*]

The Red Hat Package Manager. A freely available packaging system for software distribution and installation. RPM packages are built, installed, and queried with the **rpm** and **rpmbuild** commands. For detailed information on RPM, see Chapter 5.

---

rsh   rsh [*options*] *host* [*command*]

Execute *command* on remote host, or, if no command is specified, begin an interactive shell on the remote host using **rlogin**. The options can be specified before or after *host*. Use of **rsh** has generally been replaced with **ssh**, which offers better security.

Options
-**d**   Enable socket debugging.

-**l** *username*
Attempt to log in as *username*. By default, the name of the user executing **rsh** is used.

-**n**   Redirect the input to **rsh** from the special device */dev/null*. (This should be done when backgrounding **rsh** from a shell prompt, to direct the input away from the terminal.)

---

rshd   rshd [*options*]

TCP/IP command. Remote shell server for programs such as **rcmd** and **rcp**, which need to execute a noninteractive shell on remote machines. **rshd** is started by **inetd** and must have an entry in **inetd**'s configuration file, */etc/inetd.conf*.

All options are exactly the same as those in **rlogind**, except for -**L**, which is unique to **rshd**.

Option
-**L**   Log all successful connections and failed attempts via **syslogd**.

rsync

rsync [*options*] *sources dest*

Transfer files; used frequently for updating files across a network. File transfer with **rsync** is fast and efficient because it checks local files against remote files in small chunks, or *blocks*, and transfers only the blocks that differ between the files.

sources and the final *dest* are in the form of:

user@host:port/filename

If the file is on the local host, a plain *filename* can be specified. If the file is on a remote host, the *host* must also be specified. *user* can optionally be specified to log in as a different user on the remote site (in which case a password prompt might appear) and *port* can optionally be specified with a remote host to make **rsync** use a TCP port other than its default, 873.

Relative filenames (names without initial slashes) are handled relative to the user's home directory. If a source directory is listed with a trailing slash, the whole directory is transferred and will appear under the destination directory; if the directory is listed without the slash, its files and subdirectories will appear directly under the destination directory. Normally, regular directories and files are transferred, but not symbolic links or other special files such as sockets and FIFOs.

Two other formats for *sources* and *dest*, which refer to files on an **rsync** server (**rsyncd**), are:

user@host::filename
rsync://*user@host:port/filename*

rsync servers are beyond the scope of this book.

Options

-0, --from0
> Specify that the file specified in options such as **--files-from** is formatted with null characters to separate the filenames; when this option is not used, the file must include each filename on a separate line.

-4, --ipv4, -6, --ipv6
> Opt for IPv4 or IPv6 when creating sockets.

-8, --8-bit-output
> Leave high-bit characters unescaped in output.

-a, --archive
> Transfer recursively, reproducing most characteristics of the files and directories being transferred, such as modification times, symbolic links, ownership, and permissions. Equivalent to **-rlptgoD**. With **--files-from**, transfer is not recursive.

--address=*addr*
> Specify the IP address of an **rsync** server to connect to; useful when multiple servers are running on the same host.

--append
> Append new data to the end of an existing file. Implies **--inplace**.

--append-verify

Like **--append**, but include existing data in full-file checksum verification.

-b, --backup

Preserve existing files at the destination by appending a suffix such as ~ while transferring new versions of those files.

-B *n*, **--block-size=**n

Change block size used for transfers.

--backup-dir

Specify where files created by the **--backup** option are stored.

--blocking-io

Use blocking I/O when starting the remote shell used for transfer.

--bwlimit=n

Set a limit to the speed of transfer, specified in kilobytes per second.

-c, --checksum

Perform a full checksum on each file transferred.

-C, --cvs-exclude

Don't transfer files that are normally considered temporary or otherwise uninteresting; obeys the same rules for ignoring files as CVS (Concurrent Versions Systems).

--compare-dest=dir

Compare source files to files of the same name in *dir* as well as the destination directory.

--compress-level=num

Set the compression level to *num*. If nonzero, -z/--**compress** is implied.

--config=configfile

When running as server, take configuration from *configfile* instead of */etc/rsyncd.conf*.

--contimeout=n

Set time in seconds to wait for a connection to an **rsync** daemon.

--copy-unsafe-links

If files to which symbolic links point are being transferred, copy even those files that exist outside the directories being transferred.

-d, --dirs

Transfer directories with no recursion unless the directory name is **.** or ends in a trailing slash (/).

-D   Equivalent to **--devices --specials**.

--daemon

Run **rsync** as server.

--devices

Transfer device (*/dev*) files; requires superuser permission on both systems.

--delete-after

After transferring files from a source directory, delete any files from the destination directory that do not exist in the source directory.

--delete

Before transferring files from a source directory, delete any files from the destination directory that do not exist in the source directory.

--delete-excluded

Invoke **--delete**, and additionally delete from the destination directory any files that match exclude options.

-e *shell*, **--rsh=***shell*

Use *shell* (which can be a complete command with arguments, enclosed in quotes) to create the connection between two systems for file transfer. **rsync** uses **rsh** by default. Nowadays, most users prefer the secure shell **ssh**. This can be made the default by setting the environment variable **RSYNC_RSH=ssh**.

--exclude=*glob-pattern*

Don't transfer files whose names match *glob-pattern*. Rules for *glob-pattern* are complex and are described in the manpage. In general, filenames can include the shell globbing characters * to match everything, ? to match a single character, and [ ] to enclose a set of matching characters. Furthermore, to specify the beginning of a filename, start the name with a / character (it does not mean the file has to be an absolute pathname).

--exclude-from=*file*

Like **--exclude**, but globbing patterns are taken from *file*; each pattern on a separate line.

--existing, --ignore-non-existing

Transfer only files that already exist on the destination host.

--files-from=*file*

Take names of files to transfer from *file*.

--force

Allow a file to replace a nonempty directory of the same name.

-g, --group

Set the group (normally identified by name, not number) of the destination file to match that of the source file, instead of using the group running the **rsync** program.

-H, --hard-links

Set hard links on destination system to match source system.

--help

Display command syntax and options, then exit.

-h, --human-readable

Output numbers in a more easily read format, using larger units with a K, M, or G suffix.

--ignore-errors

Delete files even when there are I/O errors.

--ignore-existing

Do not transfer files to replace existing files of the same name.

-I, --ignore-times

Consider files for transfer even if they have the same size and timestamp as destination files.

--include=_glob-pattern_

Specify files to be transferred even if further exclude options would cause them to be ignored. **rsync** processes the include and exclude options in the order they appear on the command line, so earlier include options override later exclude options.

--include-from=_file_

Like **--include**, but take globbing patterns from _file_, which has each pattern listed on a separate line.

--inplace

Update files in place instead of creating a new copy and then moving it.

-l, --links

Set symbolic links on destination system to match source system.

-L, --copy-links

Transfer the files to which symbolic links are made instead of just the pointer information in the links.

--log-file=_file_

Write log data to the specified file.

--log-format=_format_

Display information about each file transferred in a format specified by **%** sequences; see **rsyncd.conf** manpage for formats. Used with **--log-file**.

--max-delete=_n_

Delete at most _n_ files when deleting from destination host.

--max-size=_n_, **--min-size=**_n_

Don't transfer files that are larger than or smaller than the specified size.

-n, --dry-run

Display the names of files that would be transferred and statistics related to a transfer, without performing a transfer.

--no-blocking-io

Do not use blocking I/O when starting the remote shell used for transfer.

--no-detach

When running as a daemon, do not restart as a background process.

--no-implied-dirs

When preserving directory structures with **--relative**, do not force the creation of new directories or symbolic links if the destination host is set up differently from the source host.

--no-relative

Transfer only the plain files without preserving the entire directory structure of files whose names include directories; otherwise, **--files-from** would create the entire directory structure to contain the file.

--no-whole-file

Use **rsync**'s block checks to transfer parts of files where possible.

--numeric-ids

Set user and group IDs on destination files by number rather than name.

-o, --owner

Set the user (normally identified by name, not number) of the destination file to match that of the source file, instead of settng it to the user running the **rsync** program.

-O, --omit-dir-times

When using **--times** to preserve modification times, don't preserve directory times.

-p, --perms

Set the permissions of the destination file to match that of the source file, instead of using the existing file's permissions or the default umask of the destination user.

-P Combination of **--partial** and **--progress**.

--partial

Preserve partial files transferred if **rsync** is interrupted. The default is to delete them.

--partial-dir=_dir_

Specify a directory for keeping partial files instead of using **--partial**. Useful for speeding up the resumption of the transfer later. The file is deleted from _dir_ once the transfer is complete.

--password-file=_file_

Take password for accessing a remote **rsync** server from _file_.

--port=_n_

Use port _n_ instead of default **rsync** port.

--progress

Display ongoing statistics about the progress of the transfer of each file.

-q, --quiet

Do not display statistics or server error messages.

-r, --recursive

Copy directories with all their contents.

-R, --relative

Preserve the entire path of a specified source file or directory, instead of creating the file directly under the destination directory. That is, if *project/tmp/main.c* is specified, create *project/ tmp/main.c* instead of just *main.c*. Create intermediate directories if needed.

--read-batch=*file*

Apply all changes stored in the specified file, written by a preceding **--write-batch**.

--remove-source-files

After files have been successfully transferred, remove them from the source system. Directories are not removed.

--rsync-path=*file*

Use the **rsync** binary located in *file* on the destination system.

--safe-links

Don't copy links that point to absolute paths or to files outside the directories being transferred.

-s, --protect-args

Protect arguments sent to the remote system from intrepretation by the remote shell.

-S, --sparse

Perform special optimizations on sparse files (files that contain holes and actually contain less data than their sizes indicate).

--size-only

Skip files that have the same size on the source and destination hosts, even if their timestamps differ; usually, this check is based on both size and timestamp.

--specials

Transfer special files such as named sockets and FIFOs.

--stats

Like **-v**, but also prints a number of statistics about each file transferred, such as the number of bytes actually transferred and the number transferred to compare the files on the two hosts.

--suffix=*string*

Set the suffix placed on backup files to *string*. Default is a tilde (~).

-t, --times

Set the timestamps of the destination file to match those of the source file, instead of using the time of transfer (that is, reflecting the existence of a new file on the destination host).

-T *dir*, **--temp-dir=***dir*

Use *dir* as **rsync**'s temporary directory instead of the destination directory.

--timeout=*n*

Stop **rsync** if *n* seconds pass with no data being transferred.

-u, --update

Don't change a destination file if it is newer than the source file.

--version

Display **rsync**'s version and compiled-in features, then exit.

-v, --verbose

Display the names of files transferred and statistics related to the transfer.

-W, --whole-file

Transfer the entire files, instead of using **rsync**'s block checks to transfer just parts of files where possible.

--write-batch=_prefix_

Prepare to synchronize systems by writing files, whose names start with _prefix_, that describe the transfers to take place.

-x, --one-file-system

When traversing directories, do not transfer files on directories that are mounted on other filesystems.

-z, --compress

Use compression during transmission.

Examples

Transfer the entire directory _proj_ to the _/planning_ directory on remote host _ourhub_:

```
$ rsync -r proj/ ourhub:/planning
```

Transfer the files and subdirectories under _proj_ to the _/planning_ directory on remote host _ourhub_:

```
$ rsync -r proj ourhub:/planning
```

Return files from local directory _active_ to the _/tmp/active_ directory on remote host _ourhub_. Files to be transferred are listed in _active/current_work.txt_:

```
$ cat active/current_work.txt
workplan.doc
workplan.sxw
$ rsync -v --files-from=active/current_work.txt active \
ourhub:/tmp/active
building file list ... done
workplan.doc
workplan.sxw
...
```

Copy the source directory's OpenOffice.org (_.sxw_) files and Kim's status report, but exclude the other status reports.

```
$ ls proj
conclusion.sxw    Status_joem   Status_leigh
incentives.sxw    Status_kim    unified.sxw
$ rsync -rv --include=*kim --exclude=/proj/Status* proj \
ourhub:tmp
building file list ... done
proj/Status_kim
```

```
proj/conclusion.sxw
proj/incentives.sxw
proj/unified.sxw
...
```

rsyslogd

rsyslogd [*options*]

System administration command. **rsyslogd** provides local and remote logging functions. It is based on **sysklogd** and on some systems replaces that program. It adds support for logging over TCP, SSL, TLS, logging to databases and more. By default **rsyslogd** is command-line compatible with **sysklogd** and can be used as a drop-in replacement. In native mode, some of the old command line options have been moved to the configuration file. **rsyslogd** will log warnings for these deprecated commands. Its compatibility mode can be changed with the **-c3** option.

rsyslogd logs system messages into a set of files described by the configuration file */etc/rsyslog.conf*. Each message is one line. A message can contain a priority code, marked by a number in angle brackets at the beginning of the line.

Options

-4   Listen on IPV4 addresses only.

-6   Listen on IPV6 addresses only.

-A   If there are multiple paths to a UDP target, send to all paths.

-c*mode*
> Set compatibility *mode*. Values for *mode* are 0, for **sysklogd** and 3 to enable native **rsyslogd** options. The default value is 0 though this also generates a warning that you are not using native mode.

-d   Turn on debugging. Don't fork.

-f *configfile*
> Specify alternate configuration file.

-i *pidfile*
> Specify alternate pid file.

-l *hostlist*
> Specify hostnames that should be logged with just the hostname, not the fully qualified domain name (fqdn). Multiple hosts should be separated by a colon (:).

-n   Avoid auto-backgrounding. This is needed when starting **syslogd** from **init**.

-p *socket*
> Send log to *socket* instead of */dev/log*.

-q   If DNS is not available when determining which systems are AllowedSenders (from the configuration file), use the hostname instead of the hosts IP address.

-Q   Don't resolve hostnames to IP addresses when determining AllowedSenders.

-s *domainlist*

Strip off domain names specified in *domainlist* before logging. Multiple domain names should be separated by a colon (:).

-v   Print version number, then exit.

-w   Don't warn when receiving messages from systems not in the AllowedSender list.

-x   Don't perform DNS lookups for remote hosts sending logs.

runlevel

    runlevel [utmp]

System administration command. Display the previous and current system runlevels as reported in the *utmp* file. The default *utmp* file is */var/run/utmp*. See "Starting and Stopping the System" on page 19.

sane-find-scanner

    sane-find-scanner [options]

Locate SCSI and USB scanners and print their device files, to be sure the scanners can be detected by SANE (Scanner Access Now Easy) backends.

Options

devname

Check only the specified device for a scanner.

-f   Force the opening of any SCSI and USB devices specified with *devname*, in case the command is wrong in determining the device type.

-h, -?

Print a usage message and exit.

-p   Test for parallel-port scanners. Note that most parallel-port scanners won't be detected, even with this option.

-q   Run quietly, printing only the devices.

-v   Run verbosely. When specified as **-v**, show every device name and test result; as **-vv**, also print SCSI inquiry information and USB device descriptors.

scanimage

    scanimage [options]

Read images from devices such as scanners and cameras, writing the images to standard output in one of the PNM (Portable aNyMap) formats. **scanimage** uses the SANE interface to access the scanner and can support any device for which there is a SANE backend.

Formats

PBM

Black-and-white

PGM

Grayscale

PPM

Color

TIFF

Black-and-white, grayscale, or color

Options

--accept-md5-only

Only accept MD5 authorization requests.

-b [*format*], **--batch**[=*format*]

Work in batch mode, using a document feeder. Each page is written to a file, as specified by *format*, using a **printf**-type string. The default format is **out%d.pnm** for the PNM formats and **out%d.tif** for TIFF.

-B, --buffersize

Change the buffersize from the default 32 KB to 1 MB.

--batch-count=*num*

The number of pages to scan in batch mode. Use this option for scanners that do not signal when they are empty; the default is to continue scanning until such a signal is received.

--batch-double

Increment the page number by 2 in batch mode. Used for scanning two-sided originals on a single-sided scanner.

--batch-increment=*num*

Increment the number in the filename by *num* in batch mode.

--batch-prompt

In batch mode, prompt the user to press Return before scanning a page. Useful for manually feeding multiple pages.

--batch-start=*num*

Specify the page number in batch mode to use in the first filename. The default is 0.

-d *device*, **--device-name**=*device*

Specify the scanner device to use. See **-L** to show the available devices.

-f *format*, **--formatted-device-list**=*format*

Show the available scanner devices, as with **-L**, but also format the output. Possible format specifications are:

%d Device name

%i Index number

%m Model

%t Scanner type

%v Vendor

--format=*format*

Specify the file format of the output file. The possible values are **pnm** (default) and **tiff**.

-h, --help

> Print a help message and exit. You can get device-specific help
> by running **scanimage** as follows:
>
> > **scanimage -h -d** *device*

-i *profile*, **--icc-profile**=*profile*

> Include the specified ICC profile in the TIFF output file.

-L, --list-devices

> Display a list of available devices. The list may not be
> complete, particularly when accessing scanners across the
> network. Only scanners listed in a configuration file (typically
> in the directory */etc/sane.d*) are displayed. A scanner with no
> configuration file entry must be accessed by its full device
> name.

-n, --dont-scan

> Set the specified options, but don't actually scan anything.

-p, --progress

> Print progress information.

-T, --test

> Run some sanity tests to be sure the backend works as defined
> by the SANE API.

-v, --verbose

> Run in verbose mode, providing additional messages.

-V, --version

> Print version information and exit.

---

scp

scp [*options*] *file1* [...] *file2*

Securely copy files between hosts on a network, using **ssh**. Part of
the OpenSSH suite of network tools. **scp** requests a password or
passphrase if required. The transfer can be between two remote
hosts. If more than one file is specified for *file1*, *file2* should be a
directory; otherwise, only the last file in the list is copied. *file1* and
file2 can be specified in any of the following ways:

> file
> host:file
> user@host:file

The first format is used for a local file; a remote file can be specified in either of the other two formats.

Options

-1   Force the use of SSH protocol 1.

-2   Force the use of SSH protocol 2

-4   Use IPv4 addresses.

-6   Use IPv6 addresses.

-B   Run in batch mode. Don't ask for passwords or passphrases.

-c *cipher*

> Specify the *cipher* to be used for encrypting the data.

-C   Enable **ssh** compression.

-F *config*
> Specify an **ssh** user configuration file (default is *$HOME/.ssh/config*).

-i *file*
> Specify the file that contains the identity (private key) for RSA authentication.

-l *limit*
> Limit bandwidth used to *limit*, specified in kilobits/second.

-o *option*
> Specify an option to pass to **ssh**.

-p   Preserve modification time, access time, and mode.

-P *port*
> Connect to *port* on the remote host.

-q   Don't display the progress meter or messages.

-r   Copy directories recursively.

-S *program*
> Specify the program to use for the encrypted connection. The program must understand **ssh** options.

-v   Verbose mode.

Example

Copy the local file *user.server1.pub* to the remote system *server2*, putting it in james's home directory:

```
$ scp user.server1.pub james@server2:/home/james/
```

screen   screen [*options*] [*command* [*args*]]

Provide ANSI/VT100 terminal emulation, making it possible to run multiple full-screen pseudo-terminals from one real terminal, and letting you manipulate and save your screen input and output, copy and paste between windows, etc. **screen** allows you to detach from a running session without interrupting the processing, and reattach to it later.

Options

-a   Include all capabilities in each window's termcap.

-A   Adapt all windows to the size of the current terminal. Default is to try to use the previous window size.

-c *file*
> Use *file* as the configuration file instead of the default *$HOME/.screenrc*.

-d [*pid.tty.host*]
> Detach session running elsewhere. With **-r**, reattach to this terminal. With **-R**, reattach to this terminal or create it if it doesn't already exist. With **-RR**, use the first session when reattaching if more than one session is available.

Linux Commands

-D [*pid.tty.host*]

Detach session running elsewhere, logging out before detaching. With **-r**, reattach to this terminal. With **-R**, reattach to this terminal or create it if it doesn't already exist. With **-RR**, do whatever is necessary to create a new session.

-e *xy*

Change command characters. Specify *x* as the command character (default **Ctrl-a**) and *y* as the character that generates a literal command character (default **a**). Specify in caret notation (e.g., **-e ^Pp** to set **Ctrl-p** as the command character, which is useful for **emacs**-mode shell).

-f, -fn, -fa

Turn flow control on, off, or to automatic-switching mode.

-h *num*

Specify the size of the history scrollback buffer.

-i   Cause the interrupt key (usually **Ctrl-c**) to interrupt the display immediately when flow control is on. Use of this option is discouraged.

-l, -ln

Turn login mode on or off for */etc/utmp* updating.

-ls, -list

Print list of *pid.tty.host* strings identifying **screen** sessions.

-L   Turn on automatic output logging.

-m   Ignore the $STY environment variable and create a new session. With **-d**, start session in detached mode; useful for scripts. With **-D**, start session in detached mode but don't fork a new process; the command exits if the session terminates.

-O   Use optimal output mode for terminal rather than true VT100 emulation.

-p *window*

Preselect the specified window by number or name if it exists.

-q   Suppress error message printing on startup. Exit with nonzero return code if unsuccessful.

-r [*pid.tty.host*]

-r *sessionowner/*[*pid.tty.host*]

Resume detached session. No other options except **-d** or **-D** can be specified. With *sessionowner*, resume another user's detached session; requires setuid root.

-R   Attempt to resume the first session found, or start a new session with the specified options. Set by default if **screen** is run as a login shell.

-s *shell*

Set the default shell, overriding the $SHELL environment variable.

-S *name*

Specify a name for the session being started, for use with the **-list** and **-r** options.

-t *name*

    Set the window's title.

-T *term*

    Set $TERM to *term* instead of "screen".

-U   Run in UTF-8 mode and set the default for new windows to **utf8**.

-v   Print version information and exit.

-wipe [*match*]

    Like **-ls**, but remove destroyed sessions instead of marking them dead. If a match is specified, it should be in the same form as the argument to the **-r** option.

-x   Attach to a session that is not detached. Requires multi-display mode.

-X   Run specified command in specified session. Requires multi-display mode, and session must not be password-protected.

Key bindings

screen commands consist of a command character (**Ctrl-a** by default) followed by another character. For many of the commands, you can also specify the character as **Ctrl**-*character*—e.g., **Ctrl-a Ctrl-d** as well as **Ctrl-a d**. The default key bindings are listed here. You can change the bindings for yourself in the *$HOME/.screenrc* configuration file, or for all users in */etc/screenrc*. The term in parentheses that follows the description is the equivalent configuration-file command for changing the key binding.

Ctrl-a '

    Prompt for window name or number to switch to. (**select**)

Ctrl-a "

    List all windows for selection. (**windowlist -b**)

Ctrl-a *num*

    Switch to window *num*, where *num* is a digit in the range 0–9 or - (the blank window). (**select** *num*)

Ctrl-a Tab

    Switch input focus to next region. (**focus**)

Ctrl-a Ctrl-a

    Toggle to previously displayed window. (**other**)

Ctrl-a a

    Send the command character (**Ctrl-a**) to the window. (**meta**)

Ctrl-a A

    Prompt user to enter a name for the current window. (**title**)

Ctrl-a b

    Send a break to the window. (**break**)

Ctrl-a B

    Reopen the terminal line and send a break. (**pow-break**)

Ctrl-a c

    Create a new window with a shell and switch to it. (**screen**)

Ctrl-a C

Clear the screen. (**clear**)

Ctrl-a d

Detach screen from this terminal. (**detach**)

Ctrl-a D D

Detach and log out. (**pow-detach**)

Ctrl-a f

Toggle flow control between on, off, and auto. (**flow**)

Ctrl-a F

Resize window to current region size. (**fit**)

Ctrl-a Ctrl-g

Toggle visual bell mode. (**vbell**)

Ctrl-a h

Write contents of the current window to the file *hardcopy.n*. (**hardcopy**)

Ctrl-a H

Begin/end logging of the current window to the file *screenlog.n*. (**log**)

Ctrl-a i

Show information about this window. (**info**)

Ctrl-a k

Kill current window. (**kill**)

Ctrl-a l

Refresh current window. (**redisplay**)

Ctrl-a L

Toggle window's login slot. Requires that **screen** be configured to update the **utmp** database. (**login**)

Ctrl-a m

Redisplay last message. (**lastmsg**)

Ctrl-a M

Toggle monitoring of the current window. (**monitor**)

Ctrl-a Space
Ctrl-a n

Switch to next window. (**next**)

Ctrl-a N

Show number and title of current window. (**number**)

Ctrl-a Backspace
Ctrl-a h
Ctrl-a p

Switch to previous window. (**prev**)

Ctrl-a q

Send a start signal (associated with **Ctrl-q** by terminals) to current window. (**xon**)

Ctrl-a Q

Delete all regions except the current one. (**only**)

Ctrl-a r

Toggle current window's line-wrap setting. (**wrap**)

Ctrl-a s

Send a stop signal (associated with **Ctrl-s** by terminals) to current window. (**xoff**)

Ctrl-a S

Split current region into two new regions. (**split**)

Ctrl-a t

Show system information, including time and date. (**time**)

Ctrl-a v

Display version information. (**version**)

Ctrl-a Ctrl-v

Enter digraph for entering characters that can't normally be entered. (**digraph**)

Ctrl-a w

List all windows. (**windows**)

Ctrl-a W

Toggle 80/132 columns. (**width**)

Ctrl-a x

Lock terminal. (**lockscreen**)

Ctrl-a X

Kill the current region. (**remove**)

Ctrl-a z

Suspend **screen**. (**suspend**)

Ctrl-a Z

Reset virtual terminal to its "power-on" values. (**reset**)

Ctrl-a .

Write out a *.termcap* file. (**dumptermcap**)

Ctrl-a ?

Show all key bindings. (**help**)

Ctrl-a Ctrl-

Kill all windows and terminate **screen**. (**quit**)

Ctrl-a :

Enter command-line mode. (**colon**)

Ctrl-a [
Ctrl-a Esc

Enter copy/scrollback mode. (**copy**)

Ctrl-a]

Write contents of the paste buffer to the standard input queue of the current window. (**paste**)

Ctrl-a {
Ctrl-a }

Copy and paste a previous line. (**history**)

Ctrl-a >

Write paste buffer to a file. (**writebuf**)

Ctrl-a <
Read screen-exchange file into paste buffer. (**readbuf**)

Ctrl-a =
Remove file used by **Ctrl-a <** and **Ctrl-a >**. (**removebuf**)

Ctrl-a ,
Show where screen comes from, where it went to, and why you can use it. (**license**)

Ctrl-a _
Start/stop monitoring the current window for inactivity. (**silence**)

Ctrl-a *
List all currently attached displays. (**displays**)

---

script

script [option] [file]

Fork the current shell and make a typescript of a terminal session. The typescript is written to *file*. If no *file* is given, the typescript is saved in the file *typescript*. The script ends when the forked shell exits, usually with **Ctrl-D** or **exit**.

Options

-a   Append to *file* or *typescript* instead of overwriting the previous contents.

-c *command*
Run the specified command instead of an interactive shell.

-f   Flush output after each write. Useful if another person is monitoring the output file.

-q   Operate in quiet mode.

-t   Write timing data to standard error. Each entry has two fields: the first is the elapsed time since the last output, and the second is the number of characters in the current output.

---

sdiff

sdiff -o outfile [options] from to

Find differences between the two files *from* and *to* and merge interactively, writing the results to *outfile*.

Options

--   Treat remaining options as filenames, even if they begin with -.

-a, --text
Treat all files as text and compare line by line.

-b, --ignore-space-change
Ignore differences in whitespace.

-B, --ignore-blank-lines
Ignore added or missing blank lines.

-d, --minimal
Use a different algorithm to find fewer changes. This option causes **sdiff** to run more slowly.

-H, --speed-large-files
> Heuristically speed comparison of large files with many small scattered changes.

-i, --ignore-case
> Ignore case changes.

-I *regexp*, **--ignore-matching-lines**=*regexp*
> Ignore any changes that insert or delete lines matching the regular expression *regexp*.

--ignore-all-space
> Ignore whitespace when comparing lines.

-l, --left-column
> Print only the left column of common lines.

-o *file*, **--output**=*file*
> Write merged output to the specified file.

-s, --suppress-common-lines
> Suppress common lines.

-t, --expand-tabs
> Convert tabs to spaces in the output to preserve alignment.

-v, --version
> Print version information and exit.

-w *cols*, **--width**=*cols*
> Set the output to *cols* columns wide.

-W Ignore horizontal whitespace when comparing lines.

---

sed

sed [*options*] [*command*] [*files*]

Stream editor. Edit one or more *files* without user interaction. See Chapter 10 for more information.

---

sendmail

sendmail [*flags*] [*address...*]

System administration command. **sendmail** is a mail transfer agent (MTA) or, more simply, a mail router. It accepts mail from a user's mail program, interprets the mail address, rewrites the address into the proper form for the delivery program, and routes the mail to the correct delivery program.

Command-line flags

--   End of options marker. Only addresses should follow this option.

-Ac
> Use local submission configuration file */etc/mail/submit.cf*, even when no mail is sent from the command line.

-Am
> Use configuration file */etc/mail/sendmail.cf*, even when mail is sent from the command line.

-B_type_

Set message body type. Accepted values are **7BIT** and **8BITMIME**.

-b_x_

Set operation mode to _x_. Operation modes are:

a   Run in ARPAnet mode.

d   Run as a daemon.

D   Run as a daemon, but remain in the foreground.

h   Print persistent host status information.

H   Purge expired entries from persistent host status information.

i   Initialize the alias database.

m   Deliver mail (the default).

p   Print the mail queue.

s   Speak SMTP on input side.

t   Run in test mode.

v   Verify addresses; do not collect or deliver.

-C _file_

Use configuration file _file_.

-d _level_

Set debugging level.

-D _file_

Send debugging output to _file_ instead of stdout.

-f _name_

Sender's name is _name_.

-F _name_

Set full name of user to _name_.

-G   Relay message submission. Used by **rmail**.

-h _cnt_

Set hop count (number of times message has been processed by **sendmail**) to _cnt_.

-i   Do not interpret dots on a line by themselves as a message terminator.

-L _identifier_

Use the specified log _identifier_ for messages sent to **syslogd**.

-N _conditions_

Specify conditions for delivery status notification (DSN) as a comma-separated list. Accepted values are **never**, **delay**, **failure**, and **success**.

-n   Do not alias or forward.

-o_Xvalue_

Set an option specified by its short name _X_. Options are described in the next section.

-O *option=value*

Set an option specified by its long name. Options are described in the next section.

-p*protocol*

Receive messages via the *protocol* protocol.

-q[*time*]

Process queued messages immediately, or at intervals indicated by *time* (for example, **-q30m** for every half hour).

-qf Process saved messages in the queue using the foreground process.

-qG *group*

Process saved messages in the named queue *group*.

-q[!]**I***substring*

Process jobs for named queues containing *substring*. Use ! to process mail for all queues not containing *substring*.

-qp[*time*]

Same as **-q**, but create a persistent process to handle the queue instead of initiating a new process at each time interval.

-q[!]**Q***substring*

Process quarantined messages containing *substring*. Use ! to process mail for recipients not containing *substring*.

-q[!]**R***substring*

Process jobs with recipients containing *substring*. Use ! to process mail for recipients not containing *substring*.

-q[!]**S***substring*

Process jobs from senders containing *substring*. Use ! to process mail from senders not containing *substring*.

-Q[*reason*]

Quarantine messages for the given *reason*. Use query options above to specify the message to quarantine.

-R *portion*

When bouncing messages, return only the specified *portion* of the bounced message. *portion* may be **hdrs** for headers, or **full** for the full message.

-t Read header for **To:**, **Cc:**, and **Bcc:** lines, and send to everyone on those lists.

-v Verbose mode.

-V *envid*

Use *envid* as the original envelope ID.

-X *file*

Log all traffic to *file*. Not to be used for normal logging.

Configuration options

Command-line configuration options are the same options normally set with an **O** in the **sendmail** configuration file. On the command line, they are set using **-O** and the option's long name. Many of these options have short-name variations that are used with the **-o** option. Here, we document items most likely to be useful on the command line, providing both their short- and long-name forms. Many of the commands call for *timeout* values. These should be given as a number followed by a letter indicating the interval: **s** for seconds, **m** for minutes, **h** for hours, or **d** for days. For example, **30s** is 30 seconds, **10m** is 10 minutes, and **3d** is 3 days. The default is minutes when no letter is given.

Aliasfile=*file*, **A***file*
> Use alternate alias file.

AliasWait=*min*, **a***min*
> If the **D** option is set, wait *min* minutes for the aliases file to be rebuilt before returning an alias database out-of-date warning.

BlankSub=*char*, **B***char*
> Set unquoted space replacement character.

CheckAliases, n
> When running **newaliases**, validate the right side of aliases.

CheckpointInterval=*num*, **C***num*
> Checkpoint the queue when mailing to multiple recipients. **sendmail** will rewrite the list of recipients after each group of *num* recipients has been processed.

ClassFactor=*factor*, **z***factor*
> Multiplier for priority increments. This determines how much weight to give to a message's precedence header. **sendmail**'s default is 1800.

ConnectionCacheSize=*num*, **k***num*
> Specify the maximum number of open connections to cache.

ConnectionCacheTimeout=*timeout*, **K***timeout*
> Time out connections after *timeout*.

ConnectionRateThrottle=*num*
> Restrict SMTP connections per second to *num*.

DefaultUser=*uid*[:*gid*], **u***uid*[:*gid*]
> Use user ID and group ID for mailers instead of **1:1**. If no group ID is specified, the user's default group is used.

DefaultCharSet=*label*
> Use the specified label for 8-bit data.

DeliveryMode=*x*, **d***x*
> Set the delivery mode to *x*. Delivery modes are **d** for deferred delivery, **i** for interactive (synchronous) delivery, **b** for background (asynchronous) delivery, and **q** for queue only (i.e., deliver the next time the queue is run).

DialDelay=*seconds*
> Specify the number of seconds to wait before redialing after a connection fails.

DontPruneRoutes, R
> Don't prune route addresses.

EightBitMode=*mode*, **8***mode*

Specify how to handle 8-bit input. Accepted values for *mode* are **mimefy** (convert to 7-bit), **pass** (send as is), or **strict** (bounce the message).

ErrorHeader=*text*, **E***text*

Set error-message header. *text* is either text to add to an error message, or the name of a file. A filename must include its full path and begin with a /.

ErrorMode=*x*, **e***x*

Set error processing to mode *x*. Valid modes are **m** to mail back the error message, **w** to write back the error message, **p** to print the errors on the terminal (default), **q** to throw away error messages, and **e** to do special processing for the BerkNet.

FallbackMXhost=*host*, **V***host*

Set fallback MX host. *host* should be the fully qualified domain name of the fallback host.

ForkEachJob, Y

Deliver each job that is run from the queue in a separate process. This helps limit the size of running processes on systems with very low amounts of memory.

ForwardPath=*path*, **J***path*

Set an alternative *.forward* search path.

HelpFile=*file*, **H***file*

Specify SMTP help file to use instead of */etc/mail/helpfile*.

HoldExpensive, c

On mailers that are considered "expensive" to connect to, don't initiate immediate connection.

IgnoreDots, i

Do not take dots on a line by themselves as a message terminator.

LogLevel=*n*, **L***n*

Specify log level. Default is 9.

MatchGECOS, G

Compare local mail names to the GECOS section in the password file.

MaxDaemonChildren=*num*

Restrict incoming SMTP daemon to no more than **num** child processes.

MaxHopCount=*num*, **h***num*

Allow a maximum of *num* hops per message.

MeToo, m

Also send to **me** (the sender) if I am in an alias expansion.

MinFreeBlocks=*minblocks*, **b***minblocks*

Require at least *minblocks* on the filesystem to be free.

MinQueueAge=*timeout*

Wait the specified time before processing a new job in the queue.

NoRecipientAction=*action*

Specify what headers, if any, to add to a message without recipient headers. Accepted values are **none, add-to, add-apparently-to, add-bcc,** and **add-to-undisclosed**.

OldStyleHeaders, o

If set, this message may have old-style headers. If not set, this message is guaranteed to have new-style headers (i.e., commas instead of spaces between addresses).

PostmasterCopy=*user*, **P***user*

Send copies of all failed mail to *user* (usually postmaster).

PrivacyOptions=*optionlist*, **p***optionlist*

Adjust the privacy of the SMTP daemon. The *optionlist* argument should be a comma-separated list of the following values:

public

Make SMTP fully public (the default).

needmailhelo

Require site to send HELO or ELHO before sending mail.

needexpnhelo

Require site to send HELO or ELHO before answering an address expansion request.

needvrfyhelo

Like preceding argument, but for verification requests.

noetrn

Deny requests to reverse the connection using extended TURN.

noexpn

Deny all expansion requests.

noverb

Deny requests for verbose mode.

novrfy

Deny all verification requests.

authwarnings

Insert special headers in mail messages advising recipients that the message may not be authentic.

goaway

Set all of the previous arguments (except **public**).

nobodyreturn

Don't return message body with a delivery status notification.

noreceipts

Turn off delivery status notification on success.

restrictexpand

Deny untrusted users access to aliases, forwards, or include files. Restrict **sendmail -bv** and disallow **-v**.

restrictmailq
> Allow only users of the same group as the owner of the queue directory to examine the mail queue.

restrictqrun
> Limit queue processing to root and the owner of the queue directory.

QueueDirectory=*dir*, **Q***dir*
> Select the directory in which to queue messages.

QueueFactor=*factor*, **q***factor*
> Multiplier (factor) for high-load queuing. Default is 600000.

QueueLA=*load*, **x***load*
> Queue messages when load level is higher than *load*.

QueueTimeout=*timeout*, **T***timeout*
> Set the timeout on undelivered messages in the queue to the specified time (overridden by **Timeout.queuereturn**).

RecipientFactor=*factor*, **y***factor*
> Penalize large recipient lists by *factor*.

RefuseLA=*load*, **X***load*
> Refuse SMTP connections when load is higher than *load*.

ResolverOptions=*arg*, **I** *arg*
> Use DNS lookups and tune them. Queue messages on connection refused. The *arg* arguments are identical to resolver flags without the RES_ prefix. Each flag can be preceded by a plus or minus sign to enable or disable the corresponding nameserver option. There must be whitespace between the **I** and the first flag.

RetryFactor=*inc*, **Z***inc*
> Increment priority of items remaining in queue by *inc* after each job is processed. **sendmail** uses 90000 by default.

SaveFromLine, f
> Save Unix-style **From** lines at the front of messages.

SendMimeErrors, j
> Use MIME format for error messages.

SevenBitInput, 7
> Format all incoming messages in 7 bits.

StatusFile=*file*, **S***file*
> Save statistics in the named file.

SuperSafe, s
> Always instantiate the queue file, even when it is not strictly necessary.

TempFileMode=*mode*, **F***mode*
> Set default file permissions for temporary files. If this option is missing, default permissions are 0600.

Timeout.queuereturn=*timeout*
> Return undelivered mail that has been in the queue longer than the specified *timeout*. The default is **5d** (five days).

TimeZoneSpec=*timezone*, **t***timezone*
Set name of the time zone.

UseErrorsTo, l
Do not ignore **Errors-To** header.

UserDatabaseSpec=*database*, **U***database*
Consult the user *database* for forwarding information.

Verbose, v
Run in verbose mode.

sendmail support files

/usr/lib/sendmail
Traditional location of **sendmail** binary.

/usr/bin/newaliases
Link to */usr/lib/sendmail*; rebuilds the alias database from information in */etc/aliases*.

/usr/bin/mailq
Prints a listing of the mail queue.

/etc/mail/sendmail.cf
Configuration file, in text form.

/etc/mail/submit.cf
Configuration file used for local message submissions.

/etc/mail/helpfile
SMTP help file.

/etc/mail/statistics
Statistics file.

/etc/aliases
Alias file, in text form.

/etc/aliases.db
Alias file in **dbm** format. Created by **newaliases**.

/var/spool/mqueue
Directory in which the mail queue and temporary files reside.

---

sensors

sensors [*options*] [*chips*]

Display current readings of all sensor chips and set limits (with **-s**) as specified in the configuration file. The default configuration file is */etc/sensors.conf*.

Options

-A   Omit adapter and algorithm for each chipset.

--bus-list
Generate bus statements for use in the configuration file. If multiple chips share an address on different buses of the same type, this lets you refer to each bus by name, not number.

-c *config-file*
Specify a configuration file to use in place of the default.

-f   Print temperatures in Fahrenheit, not Celsius.

-h   Display help information and exit.

-s   Evaluate all **set** statements in the configuration file. Requires superuser privileges.

-u   Produce raw output. Used for testing and debugging.

-v   Display version information and exit.

seq

seq [*options*] [*first* [*increment*]] *last*

Print the numbers from *first* through *last* by *increment*. The default is to print one number per line to standard output. Both *first* and *increment* can be omitted and default to 1, but if *first* is omitted then *increment* must also be omitted. In other words, if only two numbers are specified, they are taken to be the first and last numbers. The numbers are treated as floating-point.

Options

-f *format*, **--format**=*format*
Write the output using the specified **printf** floating-point format, which can be one of **%e**, **%f**, or **%g** (the default).

--help
Print help message and exit.

-s *string*, **--separator**=*string*
Use *string* to separate numbers in the output. Default is newline.

-w, **--equal-width**
Equalize the width of the numbers by padding with leading zeros. (Use **-f** for other types of padding.)

--version
Print version information and exit.

setkeycodes

setkeycodes *scancode keycode*

System administration command. Assign a *keycode* event to the specified keyboard *scancode*. The kernel matches these to its own keycodes. Scancodes in the range of 1–88 are hardwired in the kernel, but the remaining scancodes can be assigned to keycodes in the range of 1–127. Use **getkeycodes** to see current assignments. Use **showkey** to discover what scancode a key is sending.

setleds

setleds [*options*]

Display or change the LED flag settings (NumLock, CapsLock, and ScrollLock) for the current virtual terminal. With no options, display the current settings for all three flags. Can be used in a startup script to set the initial state of the LEDs.

Options

+num, -num
Set or clear NumLock.

+caps, -caps
> Set or clear CapsLock

+scroll, -scroll
> Set or clear ScrollLock.

-D   Change both the current and the default flag settings. Useful for always having NumLock set, for example.

-F   Only change the flags (and their settings may be reflected by the keyboard LEDs). The default behavior.

-L   Change the LEDs but not the flags, so the leds no longer reflect the virtual terminal (VT) flags. Run **setleds -L** with no other options to restore the default behavior.

-v   Report the settings before and after the change.

---

setmetamode

setmetamode [*options*]

Display or set Meta key handling for the current virtual terminal. With no option, print the current Meta key mode. Otherwise, set the mode and display the setting before and after the change.

Options

esc, prefix, escprefix
> Set the Meta key to send an escape sequence.

meta, bit, metabit
> Set the Meta key to set the high-order bit of the character.

---

setquota

setquota [*options*] [*name*] [*limits*] *filesystems*

System administration command. Set quotas from the command line. Provide limits in the format *soft-block-limit hard-block-limit soft-inode-limit hard-inode-limit*. To disable a quota, set it to **0**. See also **edquota**, a **vi** editor interface for editing and setting quotas.

Options

-a, --all
> Apply settings to all filesystems listed in */etc/mtab* that support quotas.

-b, --batch
> Read new settings from standard input. Provide as a list, each line in the form of "name limits."

-F *format*, **--format**=*format*
> Specify filesystem quota *format* to use. See **quota** for a list of accepted values.

-g, --group
> Set group quotas instead of users.

-p *prototype*, **--prototype**=*prototype*
> Apply the same settings as used for the specified user or group: *prototype*.

-t *blockgrace inodegrace*, **--edit_period** *blockgrace inodegrace*
Specify overall grace times in seconds for block and inode quotas.

-T *name blockgrace inodegrace*, **--edit-times** *name blockgrace inodegrace*
Specify grace times in seconds for individual user or group *name*. Use the string **unset** to remove existing grace times.

-u, --user
Set user quotas. (This is the default.)

---

setsid

setsid *command* [*arguments*]

System administration command. Execute the named command and optional command *arguments* in a new session.

---

setterm

setterm [*options*]

Set terminal attributes by writing a character string to standard output to invoke the specified attributes.

Options

For Boolean options, the default value is on. Where 8-color is specified, the possible colors are black, red, green, yellow, blue, magenta, cyan, and white. Where 16-color is specified, the possible colors include the 8-color colors, plus grey, bright red, bright green, bright yellow, bright blue, bright magenta, bright cyan, and bright white.

-appcursorkeys [**on**|**off**]
Set cursor key application mode on or off. Virtual consoles only. Can cause problems with **vi**.

-append [*num*]
Write a snapshot of virtual console *num* to the file specified with the **-file** option, appending the snapshot to any existing contents. With no argument, write a snapshot of the current virtual terminal. Overridden by **-dump**.

-background *8-color*|**default**
Set background color. Virtual consoles only.

-bfreq [*freq*]
Set the bell frequency in Hz (default 0).

-blank [*min*]
Set the delay before the screen blanks to the specified number of minutes. Virtual consoles only.

-blength [*millisec*]
Set the bell duration in milliseconds (default 0). Possible values are 0–2000.

-blink [**on**|**off**]
Turn blinking mode on or off. If the terminal is not a virtual console, **-blink off** also turns off bold, half-bright, and reverse modes.

-bold [on|off]

Turn bold on or off. If the terminal is not a virtual console, **-bold off** also turns off blink, half-bright, and reverse modes.

-clear [all]

Clear the screen.

-clear rest

Clear from the current cursor position to the end of the screen.

-clrtabs [*tab1...tabn*]

With no arguments, clear all tab stops. Otherwise, clear the specified tab stops. Virtual consoles only.

-cursor [on|off]

Turn the cursor on or off.

-default

Set rendering options to defaults.

-dump [*num*]

Write a snapshot of virtual console *num* to the file specified with the **-file** option, overwriting any existing contents. With no argument, dump the current virtual console. Overrides **-append**.

-file *file*

Write output from the **-dump** or **-append** option to the specified file. If no filename is specified, write to the file *screen.dump* in the current directory.

-foreground *8-color*|default

Set foreground color. Virtual consoles only.

-half-bright [on|off]

Turn half-bright (dim) mode on or off. If the terminal is not a virtual console, **-half-bright off** also turns off bold, blink, and reverse modes.

-hbcolor *16-color*

Set color for half-bright characters. Virtual consoles only.

-initialize

Display the terminal initialization string to reset the rendering options and other attributes to their defaults.

-inversescreen [on|off]

Invert the screen colors, swapping foreground and background, and underline and half-bright. Virtual consoles only.

-linewrap [on|off]

Turn line-wrapping on or off. Virtual consoles only.

-msg [on|off]

Enable or disable the sending of kernel **printk**( ) messages to the console. Virtual consoles only.

-msglevel [*num*]

Set the console logging level for kernel **printk**( ) messages. The value of *num* can be in the range 0–8. Messages more important than the specified number are printed, with **8** printing all kernel messages, and **0** equivalent to **-msg on**. Virtual consoles only.

-powerdown [*min*]

Set the VESA powerdown interval to the specified number of minutes, from 0–60. If no value is specified for *min*, defaults to 0, disabling powerdown.

-powersave [*mode*]

Put the monitor in the specified VESA powersave mode. Specifying no mode is equivalent to **off**. The possible values of *mode* are:

on, vsync

vsynch suspend mode.

hsync

hsync suspend mode.

powerdown

Powerdown mode.

off

Turn off VESA powersaving features.

-regtabs [*num*]

Clear all existing tab stops and set a regular tab stop pattern at every *num* number (default is 8). *num* is a number in the range 1–160. Virtual consoles only.

-repeat [on|off]

Turn keyboard repeat on or off. Virtual consoles only.

-reset

Display the terminal reset string to reset the terminal to its power-on state.

-reverse [on|off]

Turns reverse-video mode on or off. If the terminal is not a virtual console, **-reverse off** also turns off bold, half-bright, and blink modes.

-store

Store the current rendering options as the defaults. Virtual consoles only.

-tabs [*tab1...tabn*]

Set tab stops at the specified cursor positions, which can range from 1 to 160. Virtual consoles only.

-term *term*

Replace the value of the TERM environment variable with *term*.

-ulcolor *16-color*

Set color for underlining. Virtual consoles only.

-underline [on|off]

Turn underlining on or off.

sftp

sftp [*options*] *host*

An interactive file transfer program, similar to **ftp** except that it uses **ssh** to perform file transfers securely. **sftp** connects to *host* and logs in, prompting for a password if required. The host can be specified in the following ways:

```
Host
[user@]host[:file [file] ...]
[user@]host[:dir[/]]
```

If *user* is specified, that username is used for the login. If any files are specified, the **sftp** client automatically retrieves them after the user has been authenticated, and then exits. If a directory *dir* is specified, the client starts in that directory on the remote host. **sftp** is part of the OpenSSH suite of network tools.

Options

-1   Use SSH1. The default is to use SSH2, which offers stronger security.

-b *file*
Run in batch mode, taking commands from the specified file. Requires the use of a noninteractive authentication mechanism.

-B *bytes*
Specify the size of the buffer **sftp** uses for file transfers. Default is 32768 bytes.

-C   Enable compression (uses **ssh -C**).

-F *file*
Use *file* as the **ssh** configuration file instead of the default system configuration file. The systemwide file is usually */etc/ssh/ssh_config*, and per-user files are *$HOME/.ssh/config*.

-o *option*
Pass an option to **ssh**. The passed option is in the format used by **ssh_config**(5) (e.g., **-o PORT=**nn, where *nn* is the port number). **-o** can appear more than once to pass multiple options to **ssh**. This option is useful for passing options that don't have an equivalent **sftp** command-line option.

-P *server_path*
Connect directly to the local **sftp** server specified in *server_path*. Useful for debugging.

-R *num*
Specify the number of requests that may be outstanding at any time (default 64).

-s *subsys|server_path*
Specify the SSH2 subsystem or path to the **sftp** server on the remote system. Specifying the path is useful for using **sftp** via SSH1 or if the remote **sshd** does not have an **sftp** subsystem configured.

-S *program*

Specify the name of a program that understands **ssh** options and that you want to use for the encrypted connection.

-v   Raise the logging level.

---

sh

sh [*options*] [*file* [*arguments*]]

The standard Unix shell, a command interpreter into which all other commands are entered. On modern versions of Linux, this is just another name for the **bash** shell. For more information, see Chapter 6. For legacy Linux versions and other Unix flavors, be careful not to rely on **sh** and **bash** being equivalent.

---

sha1sum

sha1sum [*option*] [*files*]

Compute or check 160-bit SHA1 checksums to verify file integrity. If the file is not specified, or specified as -, read from standard input.

Options

-b, --binary

Read files in binary mode.

-c, --check

Read and check the SHA1 sums in the *files* (or standard input) and verify that they are consistent. The input must have been generated by an earlier **sha1sum** command.

--help

Print usage information and exit.

--status

Don't generate output messages; the exit code indicates success or failure. Used only with **--check**.

-t, --text

Read files in text mode. The default.

--version

Print version information and exit.

-w, --warn

Warn about improperly formatted checksum lines. Used only with **--check**.

---

showkey

showkey [*options*]

Print keycodes, scancodes, or ASCII codes of keys pressed on the keyboard. The default is to show keycodes. In keycode and scancode mode, the program terminates 10 seconds after the last key is pressed. In ASCII mode, press **Ctrl-D** to exit. This command may not function properly under the X Window System, which also reads from the console device.

Options

-a, --ascii
> Print the ASCII character, decimal, octal, and hexadecimal values of keys pressed.

-h, --help
> Print version number and help message, then exit.

-k, --keycodes
> Print keycodes associated with key-press events. This is the default mode.

-s, --scancodes
> Print the keyboard scancodes associated with key-press events.

---

showmount

showmount [*options*] [*host*]

NFS/NIS command. Show information about an NFS server. This information is maintained by the **mountd** server on *host*. The default value for *host* is the value returned by **hostname**. With no options, show the clients that have mounted directories from the host. **showmount** is usually found in */usr/sbin*, which is not in the default search path.

Options

-a, --all
> Print all remote mounts in the format *hostname:directory*, where *hostname* is the name of the client and *directory* is the root of the filesystem that has been mounted.

-d, --directories
> List directories that have been remotely mounted by clients.

-e, --exports
> Print the list of exported filesystems.

-h, --help
> Provide a short help summary.

--no-headers
> Do not print headers.

-v, --version
> Report the current version of the program.

---

shred

shred [*options*] *files*

Overwrite a file to make the contents unrecoverable, and delete the file afterward if requested.

Options

-   Shred standard output.

-f, --force
> Force permissions to allow writing to *files*.

--help
> Print help message and exit.

-n*num*, **--iterations=***num*
> Overwrite files *num* times (default is 25).

--random-source=_file_
> Use _file_ as the source of random bytes for overwriting. Default is _/dev/urandom_.

-s_num_, **--size=**_num_
> Shred _num_ bytes. _num_ can be expressed with suffixes (e.g., **K**, **M**, or **G**).

-u, --remove
> Remove file after overwriting. **shred** does not remove the file unless this option is specified.

-v, --verbose
> Verbose mode.

--version
> Print version information and exit.

-x, --exact
> Shred the exact file size; do not round up to the next full block.

-z, --zero
> On the final pass, overwrite with zeros to hide the shredding.

---

shutdown

shutdown [_options_] _when_ [_message_]

System administration command. Terminate all processing. _when_ may be a specific time (in _hh:mm_ format), a number of minutes to wait (in _+m_ format), or **now**. A broadcast _message_ notifies all users to log off the system. Processes are signaled with **SIGTERM** to allow them to exit gracefully. _/etc/init_ is called to perform the actual shutdown, which consists of placing the system in runlevel 1. Only privileged users can execute the **shutdown** command, although **init** may call **shutdown** with root privileges when the Ctrl-Alt-Del key combination is pressed from the console keyboard. Broadcast messages, default or defined, are displayed at regular intervals during the grace period; the closer the shutdown time, the more frequent the message.

Options

-a   When called from **init**, shut down only if one of the users listed in the file _/etc/shutdown.allow_ is currently logged in.

-c   Cancel a shutdown that is in progress.

-f   Reboot fast, by suppressing the normal call to **fsck** when rebooting.

-F   Force a filesystem check (**fsck**) on reboot.

-h   Halt or power off the system when shutdown is complete. Which it does depends on system hardware/BIOS.

-H   Halt the system when shutdown is complete.

-k   Print the warning message, but suppress actual shutdown.

-P   Power off the system when shutdown is complete.

-r   Reboot the system when shutdown is complete.

size

size [*options*] [*objfile...*]

Print the number of bytes of each section of *objfile* and its total size. If *objfile* is not specified, *a.out* is used.

Options

-d   Display the size in decimal and hexadecimal.

--format=*format*
> Imitate the **size** command from either System V (**--format sysv**) or BSD (**--format berkeley**).

--help
> Print help message, then exit.

-o   Display the size in octal and hexadecimal.

--radix=*num*
> Specify how to display the size: in hexadecimal and decimal (if *num* is **10** or **16**) or hexadecimal and octal (if *num* is **8**).

-t, --totals
> Show object totals. Works only with Berkeley format listings.

--target=*bfdname*
> Specify object format by binary file descriptor name. Use **-h** for a list of supported object formats.

-x   Display the size in hexadecimal and decimal.

-A   Imitate System V's **size** command.

-B   Imitate BSD's **size** command.

-V, --version
> Print version, then exit.

slabtop

slabtop [*options*]

Display kernel slab cache information in real time. **slabtop** displays a listing of the top caches as sorted by a given sort criteria.

Options

-d *n*, **--delay=***n*
> Refresh the display every *n* seconds. By default, the display is refreshed every three seconds.

-s *S*, **--sort=***S*
> Sort by *S*, where *S* is one of the following sort criteria:
>
> **a**   Sort by the number of active objects in each cache.
>
> **b**   Sort by the number of objects per slab.
>
> **c**   Sort by cache size.
>
> **l**   Sort by the number of slabs in each cache.
>
> **n**   Sort by the name of each cache.
>
> **o**   Sort by the number of objects in each cache (this is the default).
>
> **p**   Sort by the number of pages per slab.

> **s**   Sort by the size of objects in each cache.
>
> **u**   Sort by cache utilization.
>
> **v**   Sort by the number of active slabs.

-o, --once
> Display once and then exit.

--help
> Display usage information and then exit.

-V, --version
> Display version information and then exit.

---

slattach

`slattach [options] [tty]`

TCP/IP command. Attach serial lines as network interfaces, thereby preparing them for use as point-to-point connections. Only a privileged user may attach or detach a network interface.

Options

-c *command*
> Run *command* when the connection is severed.

-d   Debugging mode.

-e   Exit immediately after initializing the line.

-h   Exit when the connection is severed.

-l   Create UUCP-style lockfile in */var/spool/uucp*.

-L   Enable three-wire operation.

-m   Suppress initialization of the line to 8-bit raw mode.

-n   Similar to **mesg -n**.

-p *protocol*
> Specify *protocol*, which may be **slip**, **adaptive**, **ppp**, or **kiss**.

-q   Quiet mode; suppress messages.

-s *speed*
> Specify line speed.

---

sleep

`sleep amount [units]`

`sleep option`

Wait a specified *amount* of time before executing another command. *units* may be **s** (seconds), **m** (minutes), **h** (hours), or **d** (days). The default for *units* is **s**.

Options

--help
> Print usage information and exit.

--version
> Print version information and exit.

sort   sort [*options*] [*files*]

Sort the lines of the named *files*. Compare specified fields for each pair of lines; if no fields are specified, compare them by byte, in machine-collating sequence. If no files are specified or if the file is -, the input is taken from standard input. See also **uniq**, **comm**, and **join**.

Options

-b, --ignore-leading-blanks
Ignore leading spaces and tabs.

-c, --check
Check whether *files* are already sorted and, if so, produce no output.

-C, --check=quiet, --check=silent
Like **-c**, but do not report the first bad line.

-d, --dictionary-order
Sort in dictionary order.

-f, --ignore-case
Fold; ignore uppercase/lowercase differences.

-g, --general-numeric-sort
Sort in general numeric order.

--help
Print a help message and then exit.

-i, --ignore-nonprinting
Ignore nonprinting characters (those outside ASCII range 040–176).

-k *n*[,*m*], --key=*n*[,*m*]
Skip *n*–1 fields and stop at *m*–1 fields (i.e., start sorting at the *n*th field, where the fields are numbered beginning with 1). If *m* is omitted, stop at the end of the line.

-m, --merge
Merge already sorted input files.

-M, --month-sort
Attempt to treat the first three characters as a month designation (JAN, FEB, etc.). In comparisons, treat JAN < FEB and any invalid name for a month as less than a valid month.

-n, --numeric-sort
Sort in arithmetic order.

-o*file*, --output=*file*
Put output in *file*.

-r, --reverse
Reverse the order of the sort.

-s, --stable
Stabilize sort by disabling last-resort comparison.

-S*size*, --buffer-size=*size*
Set the size of the main memory buffer to *size*, which may include a suffix—e.g., **K** (1024, the default) or **M**.

-tc, **--field-separator=**c
> Separate fields with c instead of nonblank to blank transition.

-Tdir, **--temporary-directory=**dir
> Specify the directory pathname to be used for temporary files instead of $TMPDIR or /tmp. May be given more than once for multiple directories.

-u, **--unique**
> Identical lines in input file appear only one time in output. With **-c**, check for strict ordering.

--version
> Print version information and then exit.

-z, **--zero-terminated**
> End lines with zero byte, not with newline.

Examples

List files by decreasing number of lines:

```
wc -l * | sort -r
```

Alphabetize a list of words, remove duplicates, and print the frequency of each word:

```
sort -fd wordlist | uniq -c
```

Sort the password file numerically by the third field (user ID):

```
sort -nk3,4 -t: /etc/passwd
```

---

split

```
split [options] [infile [prefix]]
```

Split *infile* into equal-sized segments. *infile* remains unchanged, and the results are written to *prefix***aa**, *prefix***ab**, and so on. The default prefix is **x**, giving the output files **xaa**, **xab**, etc. If *infile* is - or missing, standard input is read. See also **csplit**.

Options

-a n, **--suffix-length=**n
> Use suffixes of length n (default is 2).

-b n[**b**|**k**|**m**], **--bytes=**n[**b**|**k**|**m**]
> Split *infile* into n-byte segments. Alternate block sizes may be specified:

> **b**   512 bytes.

> **k**   1 kilobyte.

> **m**   1 megabyte.

-C bytes[**b**|**k**|**m**], **--line-bytes=**bytes[**b**|**k**|**m**]
> Put a maximum of *bytes* into file; insist on adding complete lines.

-d, **--numeric-suffixes**
> Use numeric suffixes instead of alphabetic suffixes for the output filenames.

-n, **-l** n, **--lines=**n
> Split *infile* into n-line segments (default is 1000).

--help
> Print a help message and then exit.

--verbose
> Print a message for each output file.

--version
> Print version information and then exit.

Examples

Break *bigfile* into 1000-line segments:

```
split bigfile
```

Concatenate four files, then split them into 10-line files named *new.aa*, *new.ab*, and so on. Note that without the -, **new.** would be treated as a nonexistent input file:

```
cat list[1-4] | split -10 - new.
```

---

ssh

ssh [*options*] *hostname* [*command*]

Securely log a user into a remote system and run commands on that system. The version of **ssh** described here is the OpenSSH client. **ssh** can use either version 1 (SSH1) or version 2 (SSH2) of the SSH protocol. SSH2 is preferable, as it provides stronger encryption methods and greater connection integrity. The hostname can be specified either as *hostname* or as *user@hostname*. If a command is specified, the user is authenticated, the command is executed, and the connection is closed. Otherwise, a terminal session is opened on the remote system. See "Escape characters," later in this command, for functions that can be supported through an escape character. The default escape character is a tilde (~). The exit status returned from **ssh** is the exit status from the remote system, or 255 if there was an error.

Commonly, authentication is handled with standard username/password credentials, but it can also be useful to authenticate with a key exchange. This is done by generating a key on the client with **ssh-keygen** and populating the *authorized_keys* file on the remote host.

Options

-1   Try only SSH1.

-2   Try only SSH2.

-4   Use only IPv4 addresses.

-6   Use only IPv6 addresses.

-a   Disable forwarding of the authentication agent connection.

-A   Allow forwarding of the authentication agent connection. Can also be specified on a per-host basis in a configuration file.

-b *bind_address*
> Specify the interface to transmit from when there are multiple available interfaces or aliased addresses.

-c blowfish|3des|des|*ciphers*

Select the cipher for encrypting the session. The default is **3des**. For SSH2, a comma-separated list of *ciphers* can also be specified, with the ciphers listed in order of preference. **des** is supported only for legacy SSH1 compatibility and otherwise should not be used.

-C   Enable compression. Useful mainly for slow connections. The default compression level can be set on a per-host basis in the configuration file with the **CompressionLevel** option.

-D [*bind_address*:]*port*

Enable dynamic application-level port forwarding using *port* on the local side. Can be specified in the configuration file. Only root can forward privileged ports. For IPv6, an alternative syntax is [*bind_address/*]*port* or the address can be enclosed in square brackets.

-e *char*|^*char*|**none**

Set the escape character (default ~). The escape character must be the first character on a line. If **none** is specified, disable the use of an escape character.

-f   Run interactively for user authentication, then go into background mode for command execution. Implies **-n**.

-F *configfile*

Specify a per-user configuration file (default is *$HOME/.ssh/config*).

-g   Allow remote hosts to connect to local forwarded ports.

-i *idfile*

Use *idfile* to read identity (private key) for RSA or DSA authentication. Default is *$HOME/.ssh/id_rsa* or *$HOME/.ssh/id_dsa* for SSH2, or *$HOME/.ssh/identity* for SSH1. You can specify more than one **-i** option on the command line or in the configuration file.

-I *device*

Specify a smartcard *device* from which to get the user's private RSA key.

-k   Disable forwarding of GSSAPI (Generic Security Service Application Programming Interface) credentials to the server. Can be set on a per-host basis in the configuration file.

-K   Enable forwarding of GSSAPI credentials to the server.

-l *user*

Log in as *user* on the remote system. Can be specified on a per-host basis in the configuration file.

-L [*bind_address*:]*port:host:hostport*

Forward *port* on the local host to the specified remote host and port. Can be specified in the configuration file. Only root can forward privileged ports. For IPv6, an alternative syntax is [*bind_address/*]*port/host/hostport* or the address can be enclosed in square brackets.

-m *macspec*

For SSH2, the contents of *macspec* specify message authentication code (MAC) algorithms to use. *macspec* is a comma-separated list of algorithms in order of preference.

-M Put the **ssh** client into master mode for connection sharing.

-n Get standard input as a redirection from */dev/null*. Used to prevent reading from standard input, which is required when running **ssh** in the background. Useful for running X programs on a remote host.

-N Do not execute a remote command. Useful with SSH2 for port forwarding.

-o *option*

Specify options in configuration-file format. Useful for specifying options that have no command-line equivalent. For details on the options, see the manpage for **ssh_config**(5).

-p *port*

Specify the port on the remote host to which **ssh** is to connect. Can be specified on a per-host basis in the configuration file.

-q Run quietly, suppressing warnings and error messages.

-R [*bind_address*:]*port:host:hostport*

Forward *port* on the remote host to the local *host:hostport*. Can be specified in the configuration file. You can forward privileged ports only if you are logged in as root on the remote host. For IPv6, an alternative syntax is [*bind_address/*]*port/host/hostport* or the address can be enclosed in square brackets.

-s For SSH2, request invocation of a subsystem on the remote host to be used for another application, such as **sftp**. The desired subsystem is specified as the remote command.

-S *ctl*

Specify the location of a control socket for connection sharing.

-t Force pseudo-tty allocation. Multiple **-t** options can be specified to force tty allocation even when **ssh** has no local tty.

-T Disable pseudo-tty allocation.

-v Verbose mode. Useful for debugging. Specify multiple **-v** options to increase verbosity.

-V Display version information and exit.

-w *local*[:*remote*]

Request tunnel device forwarding with the specified local (client) and remote (server) tunnel devices.

-x Disable X11 forwarding.

-X Enable X11 forwarding. Can be specified on a per-host basis in the configuration file.

-Y Enable trusted X11 forwarding.

Escape characters

~. Disconnect.

~~ Send a single ~.

~# List forwarded connections.

~& Run **ssh** in the background at logout, while waiting for a forwarded connection or X11 sessions to terminate.

~? Display the available escape characters.

~B Send a BREAK to the remote system. Only for SSH2 and if the remote system supports it.

~C Open a command line. Useful for adding port forwardings when using the **-L** and **-R** options.

~R Request rekeying of the connection. Useful only for SSH2 and if the peer supports it.

~^Z

    Run in the background.

---

ssh-add

ssh-add [*options*] [*files*]

ssh-add -e|-s *reader*

Add RSA or DSA identities to the authentication agent (see **ssh-agent**), which must be running and must be an ancestor of the current process. **ssh-add** reads the files created by **ssh-keygen** for private keys. It reads the information in these private keys to obtain RSA or DSA identities. With no arguments specified, **ssh-add** adds the files *$HOME/.ssh/id_rsa*, *$HOME/.ssh/id_dsa*, and *$HOME/.ssh/ identity*. If any *files* are specified, it adds those instead, prompting for a passphrase if required.

Options

-c Confirm identities being added, by running the program specified in the SSH_ASKPASS environment variable. A 0 exit status from the program indicates successful confirmation.

-d Remove an identity from the agent instead of adding one.

-D Delete all identities from the agent.

-e *reader*

    Remove key in specified smartcard *reader*.

-l List fingerprints of all identities known to the agent.

-L List public key parameters of all identities known to the agent.

-s *reader*

    Add key in smartcard *reader*.

-t *life*

    Set maximum lifetime when adding identities to an agent. The value of *life* can be in seconds or another time format specified in **sshd_config**(5).

-x Lock the agent with a password.

-X Unlock the agent.

ssh-agent

ssh-agent [options] [command [arguments]]

Hold private keys used for public key authentication. **ssh-agent** is usually executed at the beginning of an X or login session; then all other windows or programs given as *command* are run as clients of **ssh-agent**. When a command is specified, the command and any arguments are executed. The agent dies when the command completes. Use **ssh-add** to add keys (identities) to the agent. Operations that require a private key are performed by the agent, which returns the results to the requestor.

Options

-a *bind_addr*
Bind the agent to the socket *bind_addr* (default is */tmp/ssh-nnnnnnnn/agent*, where *nnnnnnnn* is a generated number).

-c   Write **csh** commands to standard output. This is the default if the environment variable SHELL looks like a **csh**-type shell.

-d   Debug mode.

-k   Kill the current agent.

-s   Write Bourne shell commands to standard output. This is the default if the environment variable SHELL does not look like a **csh**-type shell.

-t *life*
Set a default value for maximum identity lifetime for added identities. May be specified in seconds or in a format specified in **sshd**(8). This value can be overridden by a lifetime specified for an identity with **ssh-add**. The default maximum lifetime is forever.

ssh-keygen

ssh-keygen [options]

Generate, manage, and convert authentication keys for **ssh**. When using **ssh-keygen** to create a key, the **-t** option must be specified to identify the type of key to create.

Options

-b *bits*
Specify the number of bits in the key. For RSA keys, the minimum is 512, and the default is 2048. DSA keys must be exactly 1024 bits.

-B   Show the bubblebabble digest (a digest represented as a string that looks like real words) for the private or public keyfile specified with **-f**.

-c   Change the comment in the private and public keyfiles (for RSA1 keys only).

-C *comment*
Specify a new comment.

-D *reader*
Download the RSA public key from the smartcard in *reader*.

-e   Read an OpenSSH private or public keyfile and write it in SECSH Public Key File Format to standard output for exporting to a commercial SSH.

-f *file*

Specify the filename of the keyfile.

-F *hostname*

List occurrences of the specified hostname found in a *known_ hosts* file. Useful with **-H** to print keys that were found in a hashed format.

-H   Hash a *known_hosts* file.

-i   Read an SSH2-compatible unencrypted private or public keyfile and write an OpenSSH-compatible key to standard output. Used to import keys from a commercial SSH.

-l   Show fingerprint of public or private RSA1 keyfile specified with **-f**. With **-v**, also displays an ASCII art representation of the key.

-N *passphrase*

Specify the new passphrase.

-p   Change the passphrase for a private keyfile. Prompt for the file, the old passphrase, and twice for the new passphrase.

-P *passphrase*

Specify the old passphrase.

-q   Operate in quiet mode.

-t *type*

Specify the type of key to create. Possible values of *type* are **rsa1** for SSH1, and **rsa** or **dsa** for SSH2.

-U *reader*

Upload an existing RSA private key to the smartcard in *reader*.

-v   Verbose mode; print debugging messages. Use multiple **-v** options for greater verbosity.

-y   Read a private OpenSSH-format file and print a public key to standard output.

ssh-keyscan

`ssh-keyscan [options]`

Gather public and private host keys from a number of hosts. Can be used in scripts.

Options

-4   Use IPv4 addresses only.

-6   Use IPv6 addresses only.

-f *file*

Read hostnames or *addrlist namelist* pairs from *file*. If - is specified instead of a filename, read hosts or *addrlist namelist* pairs from standard input.

-H   Hash hostnames and addresses in the output.

-**p** *port*
> Specify the port to connect to on the remote host.

-**t** *type*
> Specify the type of key to get from the scanned hosts. Possible values are **rsa1** for SSH1 (default), or **rsa** or **dsa** for SSH2. Specify multiple values in a comma-separated list.

-**T** *timeout*
> Specify the timeout for attempting a connection, in seconds. Default is 5 seconds.

-**v**   Verbose mode.

---

sshd

sshd [*options*]

TCP/IP command. Server for the **ssh** program, providing a secure remote-login and remote-execution facility equivalent to **rlogin** and **rsh**. Normally started at boot, **sshd** listens for incoming connections, forking a new daemon when one is detected. The forked daemon handles authentication, command execution, and encryption. Most implementations of **sshd** support both SSH protocols 1 and 2. The following options are those used by OpenSSH, OpenBSD's Secure Shell implementation.

Options

-**4**   Use only IPv4 addresses.

-**6**   Use only IPv6 addresses.

-**b** *bits*
> Use the specified number of *bits* in the server key. Default is 768.

-**d**   Run **sshd** in the foreground and send verbose debug information to the system log. Process only one connection. Use the specified number of *bits* in the server key. This option may be specified from one to three times. Each additional -**d** increases the level of information sent to the system log.

-**D**   Do not detach from the foreground process.

-**e**   Send output to standard error instead of the system log.

-**f** *file*
> Read configuration information from *file* instead of the default configuration file */etc/ssh/sshd_config*.

-**g** *seconds*
> Set the grace time a client has to authenticate itself before the server disconnects and exits. The default is 600 seconds. A value of **0** means there is no limit.

-**h** *keyfile*
> Read the host's cryptographic key from the specified *keyfile* instead of from the default file */etc/ssh/ssh_host_key* for SSH protocol 1, and the default files */etc/ssh/ssh_host_rsa_key* and */etc/ssh/ssh_host_dsa_key* for SSH protocol 2. The -**h** option may be given more than once to specify multiple keyfiles.

-i   Use when running **sshd** from **inetd**.

-k *seconds*
> Set how often the version 1 server key should be regenerated. Default value is 3600 seconds. If set to 0 seconds, the key will never be regenerated.

-o *setting*
> Pass a configuration file setting as an option.

-p *port*
> Listen for connections on *port*. The default is 22. More than one **-p** option may be specified. This option overrides ports specified in a configuration file.

-q   Send no messages to the system log.

-t   Test configuration files and keys, then exit.

-u *namelength*
> Specify the length of the remote hostname field in the UTMP structure as specifed in *utmp.h*. A *namelength* of 0 will cause **sshd** to write dotted decimal values instead of hostnames to the *utmp* file and prevent DNS requests unless required by the authentication mechanism.

---

stat

stat [*options*] *files*

Print out the contents of an inode as they appear to the **stat** system call in a human-readable format. The error messages "Can't stat file" and "Can't lstat file" usually mean the file doesn't exist. "Can't readlink file" generally indicates that something is wrong with a symbolic link.

Options

-c *format*, **--format**=*format*
> Display the output as specified by *format*.

-f, --filesystem
> Display information about the filesystem where the file is located, not about the file itself.

--help
> Display help information and exit.

-L, --dereference
> Follow links and display information about the files found.

-t, --terse
> Print the output tersely, in a form suitable for parsing by other programs.

--version
> Print version information and exit.

Output

stat and **stat -L** display the following:

- Device number
- Inode number

- Access rights
- Number of hard links
- Owner's user ID and name, if available
- Owner's group ID and name, if available
- Device type for inode device
- Total size, in bytes
- Number of blocks allocated
- I/O block size
- Last access time
- Last modification time
- Last change time
- Security context for SELinux

If **-f** is specified, **stat** displays the following information about the filesystem:

- Filesystem type
- Filesystem block size
- Total blocks in the filesystem
- Number of free blocks
- Number of free blocks for nonroot users
- Total number of inodes
- Number of free inodes
- Maximum filename length

Format

The **printf**(3) flag characters #, 0, -, +, and space can be used in *format*. In addition, the field width and precision options can be used.

If **-c** *format* is specified, the following sequences can be used for *format*:

%a Access rights in octal.

%A Access rights in human-readable form.

%b Number of blocks allocated.

%B Size in bytes of each block reported by %b.

%d Device number in decimal.

%D Device number in hex.

%f Raw mode in hex.

%F File type.

%g Owner's group ID.

%G Owner's group name.

%h Number of hard links.

%i Inode number.

%n Filename.

%N Quoted filename. If file is a symbolic link, include path to original.

%o I/O block size.

%s Total size, in bytes.

%t Major device type in hex.

%T Minor device type in hex.

%u Owner's user ID.

%U Owner's username.

%x Last access time.

%X Last access time as seconds since the Epoch.

%y Last modification time (modification of the file contents).

%Y Last modification time as seconds since the Epoch.

%z Time of last change (modification of the inode).

%Z Time of last change as seconds since the Epoch.

If both **-c** *format* and **-f** are specified, the following sequences can be used for *format*:

%a Free blocks available to nonroot user.

%b Total data blocks in filesystem.

%c Total file nodes in filesystem.

%d Free file nodes in filesystem.

%f Free blocks in filesystem.

%i Filesystem ID, in hex.

%l Maximum filename length.

%n Filename.

%s Optimal transfer block size.

%S Fundamental block size (for block counts).

%t Type in hex.

%T Type in human-readable form.

Examples

Sample output from the command **stat /**:

```
stat /
  File: "/"
  Size: 4096          Blocks: 8          IO Block: 4096
Directory
Device: 303h/771d      Inode: 2          Links: 19
Access: (0755/drwxr-xr-x) Uid: (    0/    root)  Gid: (
0/    root)
Access: 2009-04-27 21:47:29.000000000 -0400
Modify: 2009-04-27 20:10:22.000000000 -0400
Change: 2009-04-27 20:10:22.000000000 -0400
```

Sample output with **-f**, displaying information about the filesystem:

```
stat -f /
  File: "/"
    ID: 0          0      Namelen: 255      Type: ext2/ext3
Blocks: Total: 2612475    Free: 1869472    Available:
1736735    Size: 4096
Inodes: Total: 1329696    Free: 1150253
```

statd

rpc.statd [*options*]

System administration command. The NFS status server, **statd**, reports server status to clients like the **rup** command.

Options

-d   Debugging mode; log verbose information to standard error.

-F   Run **statd** in the foreground.

-n *hostname*, **--name** *hostname*
Specify a name to use for the local hostname. By default, this is read using the **gethostname** function.

-o *port*, **--outgoing-port** *port*
Specify the *port* that **statd** should use for its outgoing requests to other servers. When not specified, a port is assigned by **portmap**.

-p *port*, **--port** *port*
Specify the incoming *port* that **statd** should listen on. When not specified, a port is assigned by **portmap**.

-P *directory*, **--state-directory-path** *directory*
Store state information in *directory* instead of the default, */var/lib/nfs*.

-V   Print version information, then exit.

-?   Print help message, then exit.

strace

strace [*options*] command [*arguments*]

Trace the system calls and signals for *command* with optional *arguments*. **strace** shows you how data is passed between the program and the kernel. With no options, **strace** prints a line for each system call. It shows the call name, given arguments, return value, and any generated error messages. A signal is printed with both its signal symbol and a descriptive string. As it shows the data transfer between user and kernel-space, **strace** is very useful as both a diagnostic utility for system administrators and a debugging tool for programmers. By default, the output is written to standard error.

Options

-a *n*
Align the return values in column *n*. The default is 40.

-c   Count system calls, errors, signals, and time and provide a summary report when the program has ended.

-d   Debug mode. Print debugging information for **strace** on stderr.

-e [*keyword=*][*!*]*values*

Pass an expression to **strace** to limit the types of calls or signals that are traced or to change how they are displayed. If no *keyword* is given, **trace** is assumed. The *values* can be given as a comma-separated list. Preceding the list with an exclamation point (!) negates the list. The special *values* **all** and **none** are valid, as are the *values* listed with the following *keywords*:

abbrev=*names*

Abbreviate output from large structures for system calls listed in *names*.

read=*descriptors*

Print all data read from the given file *descriptors*.

signal=*symbols*

Trace the listed signal *symbols* (for example, **signal**=SIGIO,SIGHUP).

trace=*sets*

sets may be a list of system call names or one of the following:

desc

File descriptor related calls.

file

Calls that take a filename as an argument.

ipc

Interprocess communication.

network

Network-related.

process

Process management.

signal

Signal-related.

raw=*names*

Print arguments for the given system calls in hexadecimal.

verbose=*names*

Unabbreviate structures for the given system calls. Default is **none**.

write=*descriptors*

Print all data written to the given file *descriptors*.

-f   Trace forked processes.

-ff   Write system calls for forked processes to separate files named *filename.pid* when using the **-o** option.

-h   Print help and exit.

-i   Print the current instruction pointer with each system call.

-o *filename*

Write output to *filename* instead of stderr. If *filename* starts with the pipe symbol |, treat the rest of the name as a command to which output should be piped.

-O *n*

Override **strace**'s built-in timing estimates, and just subtract *n* microseconds from the timing of each system call to adjust for the time it takes to measure the call.

-p *pid*

Attach to the given process ID and begin tracking. **strace** can track more than one process if more than one option -p is given. Type **Ctrl-C** to end the trace.

-q   Quiet mode. Suppress attach and detach messages from **strace**.

-r   Relative timestamp. Print time in microseconds between system calls.

-s *n*

Print only the first *n* characters of a string. Default value is 32.

-S *value*

Sort output of -c option by the given *value*. *value* may be **calls**, **name**, **time**, or **nothing**. Default is **time**.

-t   Print time of day on each line of output.

-tt   Print time of day with microseconds on each line of output.

-ttt Print timestamp on each line as the number of seconds and microseconds since the Epoch.

-T   Print time spent in each system call.

-u *username*

Run command as *username*. Needed when tracing **setuid** and **setgid** programs.

-V   Print version and exit.

-v   Verbose. Do not abbreviate structure information.

-x   Print all non-ASCII strings in hexadecimal.

-xx   Print all strings in hexadecimal.

---

strings

strings [*options*] *files*

Search each *file* specified and print any printable character strings found that are at least four characters long and followed by an unprintable character. Often used to find human-readable content within binary files.

Options

@*file*

Read command-line options as a whitespace-separated list of options from *file*.

-, -a, --all

Scan entire object files; default is to scan only the initialized and loaded sections for object files.

-e *encoding,* **--encoding=***encoding*

Specify the character encoding of the strings to be found. Possible values are:

b   16-bit big-endian

B   32-bit big-endian

l   16-bit little-endian

L   32-bit little-endian

s   Single-7-bit-byte characters, such as ASCII, ISO-8859, etc. (the default)

S   Single-8-bit-byte characters.

-f, --print-file-name

Print the name of the file before each string.

-*min-len,* **-n** *min-len,* **--bytes=***min-len*

Print only strings that are at least *min-len* characters.

-o   The same as **-t o**.

-t *base,* **--radix=***base*

Print the offset within the file before each string, in the format specified by *base*:

d   Decimal

o   Octal

x   Hexadecimal

-T *format,* **--target=***format*

Specify an alternative object code format to the system default. See **strings --help** for a list of valid target formats.

--help

Print help message and then exit. The help message includes a list of valid targets.

-v, --version

Print version information and then exit.

---

strip

```
strip [options] files
```

Remove symbols from object *files*, thereby reducing file sizes and freeing disk space.

Options

-F *bfdname,* **--target=***bfdname*

Specify object format for both input and output by binary file descriptor name *bfdname*. Use option **-h** to see a list of supported formats.

-I *bfdname,* **--input-target=***bfdname*

Expect object format *bfdname* for input.

--help
> Print help message, then exit.

-K *symbol*, **--keep-symbol**=*symbol*
> Delete all symbols except the specified *symbol*. This option may be used more than once.

-N *symbol*, **--strip-symbol**=*symbol*
> Remove *symbol* from the source file.

-O *bfdname*, **--output-target**=*bfdname*
> Use object format *bfdname* for output.

-o *file*
> Write stripped object to *file* instead of replacing the original. Only one object file at a time may be stripped when using this option.

-p, --preserve-dates
> Preserve access and modification times.

-R *section*, **--remove-section**=*section*
> Delete *section*.

-S, -g, -d, --strip-debug
> Strip debugging symbols.

-s, --strip-all
> Strip all symbols.

--strip-unneeded
> Remove symbols not needed for relocation processing.

-V, --version
> Print version and exit.

-v, --verbose
> Verbose mode.

-X, --discard-locals
> Strip local symbols that were generated by the compiler.

-x, --discard-all
> Strip nonglobal symbols.

---

stty

stty [*options*] [*modes*]

Set terminal I/O options for the current standard input device. Without options, **stty** reports the terminal settings that differ from those set by running **stty sane**, where ^ indicates the Ctrl key and ^` indicates a null value. Most modes can be negated using an optional - (shown in brackets). The corresponding description is also shown in brackets. Some arguments use non-POSIX extensions; these are marked with *.

Options

-a, --all
> Report all option settings.

-F *dev*, **--device**=*dev*
> Open the specified device and use it instead of standard input.

-g, --save
> Report settings in **stty**-readable form (i.e., hex).

--help
> Print help message and exit.

--version
> Print version information and exit.

Control modes
[-]clocal
> [Enable] disable modem control.

[-]cread
> [Disable] enable the receiver.

[-]crtscts*
> [Disable] enable RTS/CTS handshaking.

cs*bits*
> Set character size to *bits*, which must be **5**, **6**, **7**, or **8**.

[-]cstopb
> [1] 2 stop bits per character.

[-]hup, **[-]hupcl**
> [Do not] hang up connection on last close.

[-]parenb
> [Disable] enable parity generation and detection.

[-]parodd
> Use [even] odd parity.

Input modes
[-]brkint
> [Do not] signal INTR on break.

[-]icrnl
> [Do not] map CR to NL on input.

[-]ignbrk
> [Do not] ignore break on input.

[-]igncr
> [Do not] ignore CR on input.

[-]ignpar
> [Do not] ignore parity errors.

[-]imaxbel*
> When input buffer is too full to accept a new character, [flush the input buffer] beep without flushing the input buffer.

[-]inlcr
> [Do not] map NL to CR on input.

[-]inpck
> [Disable] enable input parity checking.

[-]istrip
> [Do not] strip input characters to 7 bits.

[-]**iuclc**[*]
> [Do not] map uppercase to lowercase on input.

[-]**iutf8**[*]
> [Do not] assume input characters are UTF-8 encoded.

[-]**ixany**[*]
> Allow [only XON] any character to restart output.

[-]**ixoff**, [-]**tandem**
> [Enable] disable sending of START/STOP characters.

[-]**ixon**
> [Disable] enable XON/XOFF flow control.

[-]**parmrk**
> [Do not] mark parity errors.

Output modes

bs$n$[*]
> Select style of delay for backspaces (0 or 1).

cr$n$[*]
> Select style of delay for carriage returns (0–3).

ff$n$[*]
> Select style of delay for formfeeds (0 or 1).

nl$n$[*]
> Select style of delay for linefeeds (0 or 1).

tab$n$, [-]**tabs**[*]
> Select style of delay for horizontal tabs (0–3). **tabs** is the same as **tab0** and **-tabs** is the same as **tab3**.

vt$n$[*]
> Select style of delay for vertical tabs (0 or 1).

[-]**ocrnl**[*]
> [Do not] map CR to NL on output.

[-]**ofdel**[*]
> Set fill character to [NULL] DEL.

[-]**ofill**[*]
> Delay output with [timing] fill characters.

[-]**olcuc**[*]
> [Do not] map lowercase to uppercase on output.

[-]**onlcr**[*]
> [Do not] map NL to CR-NL on output.

[-]**onlret**[*]
> On the terminal, NL performs [does not perform] the CR function.

[-]**onocr**[*]
> Do not [do] output CRs at column 0.

[-]**opost**
> [Do not] postprocess output.

Local modes

[-]echo

> [Do not] echo every character typed.

[-]echoe, [-]crterase

> [Do not] echo ERASE character as BS-space-BS string.

[-]echok

> [Do not] echo NL after KILL character.

[-]echonl

> [Do not] echo NL.

[-]icanon

> [Disable] enable canonical input (ERASE, KILL, WERASE, and RPRNT processing).

[-]iexten

> [Disable] enable extended functions for input data.

[-]isig

> [Disable] enable checking of characters against INTR, SUSPEND, and QUIT.

[-]noflsh

> [Enable] disable flush after INTR or QUIT.

[-]tostop*

> [Do not] send SIGTTOU when background processes write to the terminal.

[-]xcase*

> [Do not] change case on local output.

[-]echoprt, [-]prterase*

> When erasing characters, echo them backward, enclosed in \ and /.

[-]echoctl, [-]ctlecho*

> Do not echo control characters literally. Use hat notation (e.g., ^Z).

[-]echoke, [-]crtkill*

> Erase characters as specified by the **echoprt** and **echoe** settings (default is **echoctl** and **echok** settings).

Combination modes

[-]cooked

> Same as [**raw**]-**raw**.

[-]evenp, [-]parity

> Same as [-]**parenb** and **cs[8]7**.

ek

> Reset ERASE and KILL characters to Ctrl-h and Ctrl-u, their defaults.

[-]lcase, [-]LCASE

> [Unset] set **xcase**, **iuclc**, and **olcuc**.

[-]nl

> [Unset] set **icrnl** and **onlcr**. **-nl** also unsets **inlcr**, **igncr**, **ocrnl**, and **onlret**.

[-]oddp

> Same as [-]**parenb**, [-]**parodd**, and **cs[8]7**.

[-]raw

> [Disable] enable raw input and output (no ERASE, KILL, INTR, QUIT, EOT, SWITCH, or output postprocessing).

sane

> Reset all modes to reasonable values.

[-]cbreak

> Same as [**icanon**]**-icanon**.

[-]pass8

> Same as [**parenb**]**-parenb** [**istrip**]**-istrip cs[7]8**.

[-]litout

> Same as [**parenb**]**-parenb** [**istrip**]**-istrip** [**opost**]**-opost cs[7]8**.

[-]decctlq*

> Same as [-]**ixany**.

crt

> Same as **echoe echoctl echoke**.

dec

> Same as **echoe echoctl echoke -ixany**. Additionally, set INTERRUPT to Ctrl-C, ERASE to Del, and KILL to Ctrl-U.

Control assignments

ctrl-char c

> Set control character to *c*. *ctrl-char* is **dsusp** (flush input and then send stop), **eof**, **eol**, **eol2** (alternate end-of-line), **erase**, **intr**, **lnext** (treat next character literally), **kill**, **rprnt** (redraw line), **quit**, **start**, **stop**, **susp**, **swtch**, or **werase** (erase previous word). *c* can be a literal control character, a character in hat notation (e.g., **^Z**), in hex (must begin with 0x), in octal (must begin with 0), or in decimal. Disable the control character with values of **^-** or **undef**.

Special settings

n   Set terminal baud rate to *n* (e.g., 2400).

ispeed *speed*

> Specify input speed.

line *i**

> Set line discipline to *i* (1–126).

min *n*

> Set the minimum number of characters that will satisfy a read until the time value has expired when **-icanon** is set.

ospeed *speed*

> Specify output speed.

rows *rows**

> Specify number of rows.

---

cols *columns*, **columns** *columns**
Specify number of columns.

size*
Display current row and column settings.

speed
Display terminal speed.

time *n*
Set the number of tenths of a second before reads time out if the **min** number of characters has not been read when **-icanon** is set.

---

su

su [*option*] [*user*] [*shell_args*]

Create a shell with the effective user ID *user*. If no *user* is specified, create a shell for a privileged user (i.e., become a superuser). Enter EOF to terminate. You can run the shell with particular options by passing them as *shell_args* (e.g., if the shell runs **bash**, you can specify **-c** *command* to execute *command* via **bash**, or **-r** to create a restricted shell).

Options

-, -l, --login
Go through the entire login sequence (i.e., change to *user*'s environment).

-c *command*, **--command**=*command*
Execute *command* in the new shell and then exit immediately. If *command* is more than one word, it should be enclosed in quotes. For example:

```
su -c 'find / -name \*.c -print' nobody
```

-f, --fast
Start the shell with the **-f** option, which suppresses the reading of the *.cshrc* or *.tcshrc* file. Applies to **csh** and **tcsh**.

-m, -p, --preserve-environment
Do not reset environment variables.

-s *shell*, **--shell**=*shell*
Execute *shell*, not the shell specified in */etc/passwd*, unless *shell* is restricted.

--help
Print a help message and then exit.

--version
Print version information and then exit.

Examples

Become root and obtain all of root's user environment:

```
$ su -
```

Become root long enough to restart the Apache **httpd** web server, then revert to the current user:

```
$ su -c /etc/rc.d/init.d/httpd restart
```

sudo

sudo [*options*] [*command*]

sudoedit [*options*] *files*

If you are allowed, execute *command* as the superuser. Authorized users of **sudo** and the commands they are permitted to execute are listed in the **sudo** configuration file, */etc/sudoers*. If an unauthorized user attempts to run a command, **sudo** informs an administrator via email. By default, it sends the message to the root account. Users attempting to run commands are prompted for their password. Once authenticated, **sudo** sets a timestamp for the user. For five minutes from the timestamp, the user may execute further commands without being prompted for her password. This grace period may be overridden by settings in the */etc/sudoers* file. Also see */etc/sudoers* for configuration examples. The **sudoedit** form of **sudo** is equivalent to running **sudo -e**.

Options

-b   Execute *command* in the background.

-e   Edit one or more files instead of running a command, running the editor specified by the VISUAL or EDITOR environment variable. If a specified file does not exist, it is created.

-h   Print help message, then exit.

-H   Set the HOME environment variable to the home directory of the target user (default is root).

-i   Run the shell specified in */etc/passwd* for the user **sudo** is being run as.

-k   Revoke user's **sudo** permissions. Similar to **-K**, but changes user's timestamp to the Epoch instead of revoking it.

-K   Remove user's timestamp.

-l   List all allowed and forbidden commands for the user on the current host, then exit.

-L   List parameters that may be set as defaults for a user in the */etc/sudoers* file.

-p *promptstring*

   Use the specified *promptstring* to prompt for a password. The string may contain the following escape codes, which are replaced with the current user's login name and local hostname.

   %h Local hostname without the domain name.

   %H Local hostname with the domain name.

   %u Current user's login name

   %U Login name of the user the command will run under. The default is root.

   %% A single percent (%) character.

-P   Preserve invoking user's group membership.

-s   Run the shell specified in the SHELL environment variable, or the default shell specified in */etc/passwd*. If a command is given, it should be a shell script and not a binary file.

-S   Read password from standard input instead of from the console.

-u *user*
> Run command as the specified *user* instead of the root user. This may also be specified as a user ID number using *#uid*.

-v   Update timestamp for user to extend the timeout. Prompt for password if necessary. No command is run.

-V   Print version number, then exit. When run by the root user, print **sudo**'s defaults and the local network address as well.

--   Stop reading command-line arguments. Useful with **-s**.

---

sum

sum [*options*] *files*

Calculate and print a checksum and the number of (1 KB) blocks for *file*. If no files are specified, or *file* is -, read from standard input. Useful for verifying data transmission.

Options

-r   The default setting. Use the BSD checksum algorithm.

-s, --sysv
> Use alternate checksum algorithm as used on System V. The block size is 512 bytes.

--help
> Print a help message and then exit.

--version
> Print the version number and then exit.

---

swapoff

swapoff [*options*] [*devicelist*]

System administration command. Stop making devices and files specified in *devicelist* available for swapping and paging.

Option

-a   Consult */etc/fstab* for devices marked **sw**. Use those in place of the *device* argument.

-h   Print help message and then exit.

-V   Display version number and then exit.

---

swapon

swapon [*options*] *devices*

System administration command. Make the listed *devices* available for swapping and paging.

Options

-a   Consult */etc/fstab* for devices marked **sw**. Use those in place of the *devices* argument.

-e   Used with **-a**. Don't complain about missing devices.

-h   Print help message, then exit.

-p *priority*

> Specify a *priority* for the swap area. Higher priority areas will be used up before lower priority areas are used.

-s   Print swap usage summaries, then exit.

-V   Print version information, then exit.

sync

sync

System administration command. Write filesystem buffers to disk. **sync** executes the **sync( )** system call. If the system is to be stopped, **sync** must be called to ensure filesystem integrity. Note that **shutdown** automatically calls **sync** before shutting down the system. **sync** may take several seconds to complete, so the system should be told to **sleep** briefly if you are about to manually call **halt** or **reboot**. Note that **shutdown** is the preferred way to halt or reboot your system, as it takes care of **sync**-ing and other housekeeping for you.

sysctl

sysctl [*options*] [*key*]

System administration command. Examine or modify kernel parameters at runtime using the */proc/sys* filesystem. While many of these kernel keys can be altered by other utilities, **sysctl** provides a single interface to kernel settings.

Options

-a, -A

> Display all available values.

-e   Ignore requests for unknown keys.

-n   Print values only, no keynames.

-N   Print keynames only.

-p [*file*]

> Reset keys from information specified in */etc/sysctl.conf*, or the specified *file*.

-q   When setting values, don't print the values to **stdout**.

-w *key=value*

> Write a new value to the specified key.

sysklogd

syslogd [*options*]

System administration command. **sysklogd** provides both **syslogd** and **klogd** functionality. By default, it is meant to behave exactly like the BSD version of **syslogd**. While the difference should be completely transparent to the user, **sysklogd** supports an extended syntax. It is invoked as **syslogd**.

sysklogd logs system messages into a set of files described by the configuration file */etc/syslog.conf*. Each message is one line. A message can contain a priority code, marked by a number in angle brackets at the beginning of the line. Priorities are defined in *<sys/syslog.h>*. **syslogd** reads from an Internet domain socket specified in */etc/services*. To bring **syslogd** down, send it a terminate signal. See also **klogd**. On some newer systems **sysklogd** is replaced by **rsyslogd**.

Options

-a *socket*

Add *socket* to the list of sockets **syslogd** listens to.

-d   Turn on debugging.

-f *configfile*

Specify alternate configuration file.

-h   Forward messages from remote hosts to forwarding hosts.

-l *hostlist*

Specify hostnames that should be logged with just the hostname, not the fully qualified domain name. Multiple hosts should be separated by a colon (:).

-m *markinterval*

Select number of minutes between mark messages.

-n   Avoid auto-backgrounding. This is needed when starting **syslogd** from **init**.

-p *socket*

Send log to *socket* instead of */dev/log*.

-r   Receive messages from the network using an internet domain socket with the **syslog** service.

-s *domainlist*

Strip off domain names specified in *domainlist* before logging. Multiple domain names should be separated by a colon (:).

-u *user*

Drop root privileges and run with the privileges of *user* while logging. While it will initially open logfiles as root, upon receiving a SIGHUP it will reopen them as *user*. This will fail if the logfiles are not writable by *user*.

-v   Print version number, then exit.

---

syslogd

syslogd

System administration command. See **sysklogd**.

---

tac

tac [*options*] [*file*]

Named for the common command **cat**, **tac** prints files in reverse to standard output. Without a filename or with -, it reads from standard input. By default, **tac** reverses the order of the lines, printing the last line first.

Options

-b, --before

Print separator (by default a newline) before the string it delimits.

-r, --regex
Expect separator to be a regular expression.

-s *string*, **--separator**=*string*
Specify alternate separator (default is newline).

--help
Print a help message and then exit.

--version
Print version information and then exit.

tail

tail [*options*] [*files*]

Print the last 10 lines of each named *file* on standard output. Print from standard input with no filename or with -. If more than one file is specified, the output includes a header at the beginning of each file:

==> *filename* <==

For options that take the number of bytes or lines as an argument, you can prepend a plus sign (+) to *num* to begin printing with the *num*th item. These options can also specify a block size:

b   512 bytes

K   1 kilobyte

M   1 megabyte

G   1 gigabyte

Options

-c *num*, **--bytes** *num*
Print the last *num* bytes.

-f, --follow[=**name**|**descriptor**]
Don't quit at the end of file; "follow" file as it grows and end when the user presses Ctrl-C. Following by file descriptor is the default, so **-f**, **--follow**, and **--follow=descriptor** are equivalent. Use **--follow=name** to track the actual name of a file even if the file is renamed, as with a rotated logfile.

-F   Identical to **--follow=name --retry**.

--help
Print a help message and exit.

-n *num*, **--lines**=*num*
Print the last *num* lines.

--max-unchanged-stats=*num*
Used with **--follow**=*name* to reopen a file whose size hasn't changed after *num* iterations (default 5), to see if it has been unlinked or renamed (as with rotated logfiles).

--pid=*pid*
Used with **-f** to end when process ID *pid* dies.

-q, --quiet, --silent
Suppress filename headers.

--retry

Keep trying to open a file even if it isn't accessible when **tail** starts or if it becomes inaccessible later. Useful with **--follow**=*name*.

-s *sec*, **--sleep-interval**=*sec*

With **-f**, sleep approximately *sec* seconds between iterations. Default is 1 second.

-v, **--verbose**

With multiple files, always output the filename headers.

--version

Print version information and then exit.

Examples

Show the last 20 lines containing instances of **.Ah**:

```
grep '\.Ah' file | tail -20
```

Show the last 10 characters of variable **name**:

```
echo "$name" | tail -c
```

Print the last two blocks of **bigfile**:

```
tail -2b bigfile
```

ctrl c to quit!

---

tailf

tailf *file*

Print the last 10 lines of a file, then wait for the file to grow. **tailf** is similar to **tail -f**, but it does nothing when the file is not growing. Useful for following a logfile, particularly on a laptop when you want to conserve the battery power.

---

talk

talk *person* [*ttyname*]

Talk to another user. *person* is either the login name of someone on your own machine or *user@host* on another host. To talk to a user who is logged in more than once, use *ttyname* to indicate the appropriate terminal name. Once communication has been established, the two parties may type simultaneously, with their output appearing in separate windows. To redraw the screen, type Ctrl-L. To exit, type your interrupt character; **talk** then moves the cursor to the bottom of the screen and restores the terminal.

---

tar

tar [*options*] [*tarfile*] [*other-files*]

Copy *files* to or restore *files* from an archive medium. If any *files* are directories, **tar** acts on the entire subtree. **tar** was originally used to create tape archives and still has options related to that use. However, here we document the options commonly used today. Options need not be preceded by - (though they may be). The exception to this rule is when you are using a long-style option (such as **--touch**). In that case, the exact syntax is:

```
tar --long-option -function-options files
```

For example:

```
tar --touch -xvf tarfile.tar
```

Function options

You must use exactly one of these, and it must come before any other options:

-A, --catenate, --concatenate
> Concatenate a second tar file to the end of the first.

-c, --create
> Create a new archive.

-d, --diff, --compare
> Compare the files stored in *tarfile* with *other-files*. Report any differences: missing files, different sizes, different file attributes (such as permissions or modification time).

--delete
> Delete from the archive. This option cannot be used with magnetic tape.

-r, --append
> Append *other-files* to the end of an existing archive.

-t, --list
> Print the names of *other-files* if they are stored in the archive (if *other-files* are not specified, print names of all archived files).

-u, --update
> Add files if not in the archive or if modified.

-x, --extract, --get
> Extract *other-files* from an archive (if *other-files* are not specified, extract all files).

Options

--anchored
> Exclude patterns must match the start of the filename (the default).

--atime-preserve
> Preserve original access time on extracted files.

-b *n*, --blocking-factor=*n*
> Set block size to $n \times 512$ bytes. By default, $n=20$.

-B, --read-full-records
> Reblock while reading; used for reading from 4.2BSD pipes.

--backup[=*type*]
> Back up files rather than deleting them. If no backup type is specified, a simple backup is made with ~ as the suffix. (See also **--suffix**.) The possible values of *type* are:
>
> **t, numbered**
> > Make numbered backups.
>
> **nil, existing**
> > Make numbered backups if there are already numbered backups; otherwise, make simple backups.
>
> **never, simple**
> > Always make simple backups.

-C *directory*, **--directory**=*directory*
> **cd** to *directory* before beginning **tar** operation.

--checkpoint
> List directory names encountered.

--exclude=*pattern*
> Remove files matching *pattern* from any list of files.

-f *file*, **--file**=*file*
> Store files in or extract files from archive *file*. Note that *file* may take the form *hostname:filename*.

-F *script*, **--info-script**=*script*, **--new-volume-script**=*script*
> Implies **-M** (multiple archive files). Run *script* at the end of each file.

--force-local
> Interpret filenames in the form *hostname:filename* as local files.

-g *file*, **--listed-incremental**=*file*
> Create, list, or extract new-style incremental backup.

-G, **--incremental**
> Create, list, or extract old-style incremental backup.

--group=*group*
> Use *group* as the group for files added to the archive.

-h, **--dereference**
> Dereference symbolic links, and archive the files they point to rather than the symbolic link.

--help
> Print help message and exit.

-i, **--ignore-zeros**
> Ignore blocks of zeros (i.e., EOFs).

--ignore-case
> Ignore case when excluding files.

--ignore-failed-read
> Ignore unreadable files to be archived. Default behavior is to exit when encountering these.

--index-file=*file*
> With **-v**, send output to *file*.

-j, **--bzip2**
> Compress files with **bzip2** before archiving them, or uncompress them with **bunzip2** before extracting them.

-k, **--keep-old-files**
> When extracting files, do not overwrite files with similar names. Instead, print an error message.

-K *file*, **--starting-file**=*file*
> Begin **tar** operation at *file* in archive.

--keep-newer-files
> When extracting files, do not overwrite files that are newer than the archive files.

-m, --touch

Do not restore file modification times; update them to the time of extraction.

-M, --multivolume

Expect archive to be multivolume. With **-c**, create such an archive.

--mode=_permissions_

Use _permissions_ when adding files to an archive. The permissions are specified the same way as for the **chmod** command.

-N _date_, **--newer=**_date_, **--after-date=**_date_

Ignore files older than _date_.

--newer-mtime=_date_

Add only files whose contents have changed since _date_ to the archive.

--no-anchored

Exclude patterns may match anything following a slash.

--no-ignore-case

Do not ignore case when excluding files.

--no-same-permissions

Do not extract permissions information when extracting files from the archive. This is the default for users, and therefore affects only the superuser.

--no-recursion

Do not move recursively through directories.

--no-wildcards

Don't use wildcards when excluding files; treat patterns as strings.

--no-wildcards-match-slash

Wildcards do not match **/** when excluding files.

--null

Allow filenames to be null-terminated with **-T**. Override **-C**.

--numeric-owner

Use the numeric owner and group IDs rather than the names.

-o, --no-same-owner

When extracting, create files with yourself as owner.

-O, --to-stdout

Print extracted files to standard output.

--occurrence[=_n_]

Process only the _n_th occurrence of each file (default is 1). Use with **--delete**, **--diff**, **--extract**, or **--list**.

--one-file-system

Do not archive files from other filesystems.

--overwrite

Overwrite existing files and directory metadata when extracting from archive.

--overwrite-dir

Overwrite existing directory metadata when extracting from archive.

--owner=_owner_
> Set _owner_ as the owner of extracted files instead of the original owner. _owner_ is first assumed to be a username, then, if there is no match, a numeric user ID.

-p, --same-permissions, --preserve-permissions
> Keep permissions of extracted files the same as the originals.

-P, --absolute-names
> Do not remove initial slashes (/) from input filenames.

--posix
> Create a POSIX-compliant archive.

--preserve
> Equivalent to invoking both the **-p** and **-s** options.

-R, --block-number
> Display archive's block number in messages.

--record-size=_size_
> Treat each record as having _size_ bytes, where _size_ is a multiple of 512.

--recursion
> Move recursively through directories.

--recursive-unlink
> Remove existing directory hierarchies before extracting directories with the same name.

--remove-files
> Remove originals after inclusion in archive.

--rsh-command=_command_
> Do not connect to remote host with **rsh**; instead, use _command_.

-s, --same-order, --preserve-order
> When extracting, sort filenames to correspond to the order in the archive.

-S, --sparse
> Treat sparse files more efficiently when adding to archive.

--same-owner
> When extracting, create files with the same ownership as the originals.

--show-defaults
> Display the default **tar** options.

--show-omitted-dirs
> List directories being omitted when operating on an archive.

--strip-components=_num_, **--strip-path=**_num_
> Strip the specified number of leading components from filenames before extracting. Use **--strip-components** for **tar** versions beginning with tar-1.14.90. Earlier versions of tar-1.14 use **--strip-path**.

--suffix=_suffix_
> Use _suffix_ instead of the default ~ when creating a backup file.

-T *file*, **--files-from**=*file*
> Consult *file* for files to extract or create.

--totals
> Print byte totals.

-U, **--unlink-first**
> Remove each existing file from the filesystem before extracting from the archive.

--use-compress-program=*program*
> Compress archived files with *program*, or uncompress extracted files with *program*.

--utc
> Display file modification dates in UTC format.

-v, **--verbose**
> Verbose. Print filenames as they are added or extracted.

-V *name*, **--label**=*name*
> Name this volume *name*.

--version
> Print version information and exit.

--volno-file=*file*
> Use/update the volume number in *file*.

-w, **--interactive**, **--confirmation**
> Wait for user confirmation (**y**) before taking any actions.

-W, **--verify**
> Check archive for corruption after creation.

--wildcards
> Use wildcards when excluding files.

--wildcards-match-slash
> Wildcards match / when excluding files.

-X *file*, **--exclude-from** *file*
> Consult *file* for list of files to exclude.

-z, **--gzip**, **--gunzip**, **--ungzip**
> Compress files with **gzip** before archiving them, or uncompress them with **gunzip** before extracting them.

-Z, **--compress**, **--uncompress**
> Compress files with **compress** before archiving them, or uncompress them with **uncompress** before extracting them.

Examples

Create an archive of book chapter files (**c**), show the command working (**v**), and store the results in *Chapters.tar*:

```
tar cvf Chapters.tar chapter*
```

List the archive's contents in a format like **ls -l**:

```
tar tvf Chapters.tar
```

Extract Chapter 1:

```
tar xvf Chapters.tar chapter1
```

Create an archive of the current directory and store it in a file *backup.tar*:

```
tar cvf - `find . -print` > backup.tar
```

(The - tells **tar** to store the archive on standard output, which is then redirected.)

Create an archive and filter it through **bzip2** to compress it:

```
tar cvfj Chapters.tar.bz2 chapter*
```

Filter an existing archive through **gzip**, extracting the contents but leaving the original file compressed:

```
tar xvfz chapters.tar.gz
```

---

taskset

taskset [*options*] [*mask* | *list*] [*pid* | *command* [*args*]]

taskset is used to retrieve or set the processor affinity mask of either an existing process, given its PID, or to run a new a process, given its command name, with a specified affinity mask. The Linux scheduler will then honor the given affinity mask, ensuring that the process in question runs only on allowed processors.

Options

-c, --cpu-list
> The affinity mask is provided in list form, for example, "0,2,5-6," not as a bitmask.

-p, --pid
> Set or retrieve the mask of the given PID. Do not start a new process.

-h, --help
> Display usage information and then exit.

-V, --version
> Display version information and then exit.

---

tcpdump

tcpdump [*options*] [*expression*]

System administration command. Dump headers and packets of network traffic that match *expression*. The command continues to capture packets until it receives a SIGTERM or SIGINT signal (usually generated by typing the interrupt character **control-C**). When finished, it will generate a report on traffic captured, received, or dropped by the kernel.

Expressions

Create matching expressions using the following primitives followed by an ID or name.

direction
> A qualifier indicating whether to match source or destination information. Accepted values are **src**, **dst**, **src or dst**, and **src and dst**. When not specified, the expression will match either source or destination traffic.

Linux
Commands

protocol
> A qualifier restricting matches to a particular kind of packet. Accepted values are: **ether**, **fddi**, **tr**, **wlan**, **ip**, **ip6**, **arp**, **rarp**, **decnet**, **tcp**, and **udp**. If not specified, the match defaults to any appropriate protocol matching type.

type
> A qualifier indicating what kind of thing the ID or name references, such as a part of a hostname (**host**), IP address (**net**) or port (**port**). When not specified, the match defaults to **host**.

Options

-A Print packets in ASCII text.

-c *n*
> Exit after receiving *n* packets.

-C *n*
> When saving to a file, do not write files larger than *n* million bytes. Open a new file with the same basename appended by a number. Start with the number 1.

-d, **-dd**, **-ddd**
> Compile and dump the packet-matching code for the given expression, then exit. Use the second form to dump it as a C programming fragment. Use the third form to dump the code in decimal.

-D Print a list of the available interfaces, then exit.

-e Print the link-level header on each line.

-F *file*
> Read *expression* from the specified *file*.

-i *interface*
> Listen on the specified *interface*. If not specified, **tcpdump** will listen on the lowest-numbered interface available, other than the loopback interface. Use **any** to listen to all available interfaces.

-l Line buffer standard out.

-L Print the data link types for an interface, then exit.

-n, **-nn**
> Print IP addresses instead of converting them to hostnames. Use the second form to leave protocols and port numbers in numeric form, as well.

-N Print hostnames instead of fully qualified domain names.

-p Don't put the interface into promiscuous mode.

-q Abbreviate output, printing less protocol information.

-r *file*
> Read packets from the specified *file*. (You can create such a file with the **-w** option.)

-s *n*
> Read *n* bytes of data from each packet. (The default is 68.)

-S   Print absolute TCP sequence numbers.

-T *n*

Read *n* bytes of data from each packet. (The default is 68.)

-t, -tt, -ttt, -tttt

Change display of timestamp. Use the first form to omit the timestamp from each line. Use the second form to print an unformatted timestamp. Use the third form to print the time in seconds between the current and the previous dump line. The final form prints the date before the timestamp on each dump line.

-u   Print undecoded NFS handles.

-v, -vv, -vvv

Increase the verbosity of the printout. Each additional **v** increases the detail of the information printed.

-w *file*

Write the raw packet information to *file* without parsing or printing it. Specify - to write to standard output.

-W *n*

Wrap files creating a rotating buffer. Used with **-C**, this will set a limit on the number of files created. Upon reaching the limit, **tcpdump** will begin overwriting earlier files.

-x, -xx

Print packets in hex. Use the second form to print the packet's link level header in hex as well.

-X, -XX

Print packets in hex and ASCII text. Use the second form to print the packet's link level header in hex and ASCII as well.

-Z *user*

Drop root privileges and change to the specified user. Use the primary group of the specified user.

Examples

Place full packets into a file named *tcpdump.cap* for later analysis:

```
tcpdump -v -w tcpdump.cap -xX -s 0
```

Read all packet headers received on the eth0 interface, except for arp and SSH packets:

```
tcpdump -i eth0 not arp and not port ssh
```

tcpslice   tcpslice [*options*] [*start* [*end*]] *files*

System administration command. Reads and manipulates packet capture files created by **tcpdump -w**. Based on timestamps, extract portions of or merge together *files*. Display all packets between the given *start* and *end* times. **tcpslice** understands most time and date formats. **tcpslice** also understands a relative time format specified as a unit of time—e.g., **+1h10m** to specify the first hour and ten minutes of packets in the specified *files*. This format is named *ymdhmsu* after the letters it uses to denote units of time: years, months, days, hours, minutes, seconds, and microseconds. If no constraining dates are specified, the command will print out all packets contained in *files*.

Options

-d Print the start and end time of the specified range, then exit.

-D When merging files, don't discard duplicate packets.

-l Merge packets based on the time relative to the start of the file. The default is to merge based on the absolute timestamp.

-r Print the time and date of the first and last packet in each file, then exit.

-R Print the raw timestamp of the first and last packet in each file, then exit.

-t Print times associated with the first and last packet in each file in *ymdhmsu* format.

-w *file*
> Write output to *file* instead of standard output.

---

tee

        tee [*options*] *files*

Accept output from another command and send it both to standard output and to *files* (like a T or fork in the road).

Options

-a, --append
> Append to *files*; do not overwrite.

-i, --ignore-interrupts
> Ignore interrupt signals.

--help
> Print a help message and then exit.

--version
> Print version information and then exit.

Example

        ls -l | tee savefile   *View listing and save for later*

---

telinit

        telinit [*option*] [*runlevel*]

System administration command. Signal **init** to change the system's runlevel. **telinit** is actually just a link to **init**, the ancestor of all processes.

Option

-t *seconds*
> Send SIGKILL *seconds* after SIGTERM. Default is 20.

Runlevels

The default runlevels vary from distribution to distribution, but these are standard:

0   Halt the system.

1, s, S
   Single user.

6   Reboot the system.

a, b, c
   Process only entries in *letc/inittab* that are marked with runlevel **a, b**, or **c**.

q, Q
   Reread *letc/inittab*.

Check the *letc/inittab* file for runlevels on your system.

---

telnet

`telnet [options] [host [port]]`

Access remote systems. **telnet** is the user interface that communicates with another host using the Telnet protocol. If **telnet** is invoked without *host*, it enters command mode, indicated by its prompt, `telnet>`, and accepts and executes commands. Type ? at the command prompt to see the available commands. If invoked with arguments, **telnet** performs an **open** command (shown in the following list) with those arguments. *host* indicates the host's official name, alias, or Internet address. *port* indicates a port number (default is the Telnet port).

The Telnet protocol is often criticized because it uses no encryption and makes it easy for snoopers to pick up user passwords. Most sites now use **ssh** instead.

Options

-7   Request 7-bit operation.

-8   Request 8-bit operation.

-a   Automatic login to the remote system.

-b *hostalias*
   Use **bind** to bind the local socket to an aliased address or the address of an interface other than the one that would be chosen by **connect**.

-c   Disable reading of the user's *.telnetrc* file.

-d   Turn on socket-level debugging.

-e [*escape_char*]
   Set initial **telnet** escape character to *escape_char*. If *escape_char* is omitted, no escape character is predefined.

-E   Disable the escape character functionality.

-f   With Kerberos V5 authentication, allow forwarding of the local credentials to the remote system.

-**F** With Kerberos V5 authentication, allow local credentials to be forwarded to the remote system, including any that were already forwarded to the local environment.

-**k** *realm*
With Kerberos authentication, obtain tickets for the remote host in *realm*, instead of in the remote host's realm.

-**K** Do not allow automatic login to the remote system.

-**l** *user*
When connecting to remote system and if remote system understands ENVIRON, send *user* to the remote system as the value for variable USER. Implies the -**a** option.

-**L** Specify an 8-bit data path on output.

-**n** *tracefile*
Open *tracefile* for recording the trace information.

-**r** Emulate **rlogin**. The default escape character for this mode is a tilde (~); an escape character followed by a dot causes **telnet** to disconnect from the remote host; a ^**Z** instead of a dot suspends **telnet**; and a ^] (the default **telnet** escape character) generates a normal **telnet** prompt. These codes are accepted only at the beginning of a line.

-**x** Turn on data-stream encryption if possible.

-**X** *atype*
Disable the *atype* type of authentication.

telnetd

telnetd [*options*]

TCP/IP command. Telnet protocol server. **telnetd** is invoked by the Internet server for requests to connect to the Telnet port (port 23 by default). **telnetd** allocates a pseudo-terminal device for a client, thereby creating a login process that has the slave side of the pseudo-terminal serving as stdin, stdout, and stderr. **telnetd** manipulates the master side of the pseudo-terminal by implementing the Telnet protocol and by passing characters between the remote client and the login process.

The Telnet protocol is often criticized because it uses no encryption and makes it easy for snoopers to pick up user passwords. Most sites now use **ssh** instead.

Options

-**a** *type*
When compiled with authentication support, this option sets the authentication type. Accepted values are:

debug
Debug authentication code.

none
No authentication required, but accept it if offered. Use **login** for any further verification needed to access an account.

off
> Disable authentication.

user
> Allow only authenticated remote users with permission to access their accounts without giving a password.

valid
> Allow only authenticated remote users. Use **login** for any additional verification needed to access an account.

-debug [*port*]
> Start **telnetd** manually instead of through **inetd**. *port* may be specified as an alternate TCP port number on which to run **telnetd**.

-D *modifier(s)*
> Debugging mode. This allows **telnet** to print out debugging information to the connection, enabling the user to see what telnet is doing. Several modifiers are available for the debugging mode:

netdata
> Display data stream received by **telnetd**.

options
> Print information about the negotiation of the Telnet options.

ptydata
> Display data written to the pseudo-terminal device.

report
> Print **options** information, as well as some additional information about what processing is going on.

-edebug
> When compiled with support for encryption, enable encryption debugging code.

-h Don't print host-specific information until after login is complete.

-L *path*
> Specify path to alternative login program. By default **telnetd** uses */bin/login*.

-n Disable checking for lost connections with TCP keep-alives.

-U Refuse connections from IP addresses with no reverse DNS information.

-X *type*
> Disable authentication *type*.

---

test

test *expression*

[*expression*]

Evaluate an *expression* and, if its value is true, return a zero exit status; otherwise, return a nonzero exit status. In shell scripts, you can use the alternate form [*expression*]. This command is generally used with conditional constructs in shell programs. Also exists as a built-in in most shells.

File testers

The syntax for all of these options is **test** *option file*. If the specified file does not exist, they return false. Otherwise, they test the file as specified in the option description.

-b   Is the file block special?

-c   Is the file character special?

-d   Is the file a directory?

-e   Does the file exist?

-f   Is the file a regular file?

-g   Does the file have the set-group-ID bit set?

-G   Is the file owned by the process's effective group ID?

-k   Does the file have the sticky bit set?

-L, -h
>Is the file a symbolic link?

-O   Is the file owned by the process's effective user ID?

-p   Is the file a named pipe?

-r   Is the file readable by the current user?

-s   Is the file nonempty?

-S   Is the file a socket?

-t [*file-descriptor*]
>Is the file associated with *file-descriptor* (or 1, standard output, by default) connected to a terminal?

-u   Does the file have the set-user-ID bit set?

-w   Is the file writable by the current user?

-x   Is the file executable?

File comparisons

The syntax for file comparisons is **test** *file1 option file2*. A string by itself, without options, returns true if it's at least one character long.

-ef   Do the files have identical device and inode numbers?

-nt   Is *file1* newer than *file2*? Check modification date, not creation date.

-ot   Is *file1* older than *file2*? Check modification date, not creation date.

String tests

The syntax for string tests is **test** *option string* or **test** *string1* [!]= *string2*.

-n   Is the string at least 1 character long?

-z   Is the string 0 characters long?

string1 = *string2*
>Are the two strings equal?

string1 != *string2*
>Are the strings unequal?

Expression tests

Note that an expression can consist of any of the previous tests.

(expression)
> Is the expression true?

! expression
> Is the expression false?

expression **-a** *expression*
> Are the expressions both true?

expression **-o** *expression*
> Is either expression true?

Integer tests

The syntax for integer tests is **test** *integer1 option integer2*. You may substitute -l *string* for an integer; this evaluates to *string*'s length.

-eq Are the two integers equal?

-ge Is *integer1* greater than or equal to *integer2*?

-gt Is *integer1* greater than *integer2*?

-le Is *integer1* less than or equal to *integer2*?

-lt Is *integer1* less than *integer2*?

-ne Are the two integers unequal?

---

time

`time [options] command [arguments]`

Run the specified command, passing it any *arguments*, and time the execution. Note that there is also a shell **time** command, so you might need to specify the full path, usually */usr/bin/time*, to run this version of **time**. **time** displays its results on standard error. The output includes elapsed time, user CPU time, system CPU time, and other information such as memory used and number of I/O operations. The output can be formatted using **printf** format strings specified with the **-f** option or the TIME environment variable.

Options

--
> The end of the options. Anything after the -- is treated as the command or one of its arguments.

-a, --append
> Used with **-o** to append the output to *file* instead of overwriting it.

-f *format*, **--format=**ived*format*
> Specify the output format. Overrides any format specified in the TIME environment variable.

--help
> Print help message and exit.

-o *file*, **--output=**vived*file*
> Send the output from **time** to the specified file instead of to standard error. If *file* exists, it is overwritten.

-p, --portability
Use portable output format (POSIX).

-v, --verbose
Give verbose output, providing all available information.

-V, --version
Print version information and exit.

Resources

The following resources can be specified in format strings:

c Number of involuntary context switches because of time slice expiring.

C Name and arguments of command being timed.

D Average size of unshared data area, in kilobytes.

e Elapsed real time, in seconds.

E Elapsed real time as *hours:minutes:seconds*.

F Number of major (I/O-requiring) page faults.

I Number of filesystem inputs.

k Number of signals delivered to the process.

K Average total (data+stack+text) memory use, in kilobytes.

M Maximum resident set size, in kilobytes.

O Number of filesystem outputs.

p Average unshared stack size, in kilobytes.

P Percent of CPU used.

r Number of socket messages received.

R Number of minor (recoverable) page faults.

s Number of socket messages sent.

S Total CPU seconds used by the system on behalf of the process.

t Average resident set size, in kilobytes.

U Total CPU seconds used directly by the process.

w Number of voluntary context switches.

W Number of times the process was swapped out of main memory.

x Exit status of the command.

X Average shared text size, in kilobytes.

Z System page size, in bytes.

Example

Time the execution of the command **ls -l** and display the user time, system time, and exit status of the command:

```
/usr/bin/time -f "\t%U user,\t%S system,\t%x status" ls -Fs
```

tload

tload [*options*] [*tty*]

Display system load average in graph format. If *tty* is specified, print it to that terminal.

Options

-d *delay*
    Specify the delay, in seconds, between updates.

-s *scale*
    Specify scale (number of characters between each graph tick). A smaller number results in a larger scale.

-V   Print version information and exit.

---

tmpwatch

tmpwatch [*options*] *hours directory*

System administration command. Recursively remove regular files and directories in *directory* with access times older than *hours*. Specify the directory as an absolute path. This command is usually invoked by **cron** to remove old files in the */tmp* directory.

Options

-a, --all
    Remove all file types.

-c, --ctime
    Make decision on last inode change time for files and modification time for directories instead of access time.

-d, --nodirs
    Do not remove directories.

-f, --force
    Force removal of read-only files (similar to **rm -f**).

-l, --nosymlinks
    Don't remove symbolic links.

-m, --mtime
    Make decision on last modification time instead of access time.

-M, --dirmtime
    Make directory deletion decisions based on modification time.

-q, --quiet
    Report only fatal errors.

-s, --fuser
    Before deleting, attempt to use **fuser** to see if a file is in use.

-t, --test
    Verbosely test command, but don't actually remove files.

-u, --atime
    Make decision on access time. (This is the default.)

-U *user*, **--exclude-user** *user*
    Don't delete files owned by *user*, specified by name or user ID.

Linux
Commands

-v, --verbose
> Print more details. Use two times to further increase the detail of the output.

-x, --exclude=_path_
> Skip the specified _path_, the absolute path of a directory or file.

top

```
top [options]
```

Provide information (frequently refreshed) about the most CPU-intensive processes currently running. You do not need to include a - before options. See **ps** for explanations of the field descriptors.

Options

-b   Run in batch mode; don't accept command-line input. Useful for sending output to another command or to a file.

-c   Show command line or program name in display. **-c** is a toggle; **top** starts with the last remembered setting.

-d _delay_
> Specify delay between refreshes. Specify as _ss.tt_ (seconds and tenths).

-f   Add or remove fields or columns.

-h   Print a help message and exit.

-H   Display either all individual threads or a summary of all threads in process. **-H** is a toggle; **top** starts with the last remembered setting.

-i   Suppress display of idle and zombie processes. **-i** is a toggle; **top** starts with the last remembered setting.

-n _num_
> Update display _num_ times, then exit.

-p _pids_
> Monitor only processes with the specified process IDs.

-s   Secure mode. Disable some (dangerous) interactive commands.

-S   Cumulative mode toggle. Print total CPU time of each process, including dead child processes when on. **top** starts with the last remembered setting.

-u _user_
> Monitor only processes with the specified effective UID or username.

-U _user_
> Monitor only processes with the specified UID or username, matching real, effective, saved, and filesystem ids.

-v   Print version information and exit.

Interactive commands

=   Remove restrictions on which tasks are shown. Reverses the effect of an active **i** or **n** command.

space, Enter
> Update display immediately.

<, >
> Move the sort field. Use < to move one column left and > to move one column to the right.

A   Toggle alternate display mode between a single window or multiple windows. See the following section, "Alternate display mode commands," for the commands that work with **A**.

b   Toggle between bold and reverse display. Only works with **x** and/or **y**.

B   Globally toggle bold display.

c   Toggle display of program name or full command line.

d, s
> Change delay between refreshes. Prompt for new delay time, which should be in seconds. Suppressed in secure mode.

f   Prompt to add fields to or remove fields from the display.

F, O
> Select sort field.

G   Select another field group and make it current, or change by selecting a number from the following list:

> 1   Def
>
> 2   Job
>
> 3   Mem
>
> 4   Usr

h, ?
> Display help about commands and the status of secure and cumulative modes.

H   Toggle between displaying all individual threads and a summary of all threads in process.

I, 1
> Toggle SMP view. Use **I** to toggle IRIX/Solaris mode (divide CPU usage by number of CPUs), **1** to toggle single/separate states.

k   Prompt for process ID to kill, and signal to send (default is SIGTERM) to kill it.

i   Toggle suppression of idle and zombie processes.

l   Toggle display of load-average and uptime information.

m   Toggle display of memory information.

n, #
> Prompt for maximum number of processes to show. If **0** is entered, show as many as will fit on the screen (default).

o   Prompt to change order of displayed fields.

q   Exit.

r	Apply **renice** to a process. Prompt for PID and **renice** value. Suppressed in secure mode.
R	Toggle normal or reverse sort.
S	Toggle cumulative mode. (See the **-S** option.)
t	Toggle display of **processes** and **CPU states** lines.
u	Prompt for user to show; matches on effective UID.
U	Prompt for user to show; matches on real, effective, saved, and filesystem UID.
W	Write current setup to *~/.toprc*. This is the recommended way to write a **top** configuration file.
x	Toggle highlighting for sort field.
y	Toggle highlights for running tasks.
z	Toggle between color and mono display.
Z	Globally change color mappings.

Alternate display mode commands

=	Rebalance tasks in the current window.
+	Rebalance tasks in every window.
-	Show or hide the current window.
_	Show all invisible windows or hide all visible windows.
a	Cycle forward through all four windows.
g	Change the name of the current window or group.
w	Cycle backward through all four windows.

Field descriptions

The first five entries in the following list describe the lines that appear at the top of the **top** display. The rest are the fields that can be displayed for each task (sizes are in kilobytes). Use the interactive **f** command to add or remove fields.

top
> Display the time the system has been up, the number of users, and three load averages consisting of the average number of processes ready to run in the last 1, 5, and 15 minutes.

Tasks
> The total number of processes running when the last update was taken, shown as the number of running, sleeping, stopped, or undead tasks.

Cpu(s)
> The percentage of CPU time spent in user mode, in system mode, on tasks with a negative nice value, and idle.

Mem
> Memory statistics, including total available memory, free memory, memory used, shared memory, and memory used for buffers.

Swap

Swapspace statistics, including total, available, used, and cached.

PID

Process ID.

PPID

Parent process ID.

UID

Effective user ID of task's owner.

USER

Effective username of task's owner.

RUSER

Real username of task's owner.

GROUP

The effective group name of task's owner.

PR

Priority.

NI

Nice value.

nFLT

Page fault count.

CODE

Code size.

DATA

Data plus stack size.

RES

Resident task size.

SWAP

Size of swapped-out portion of task.

VIRT

The total amount of virtual memory used by the task.

nDRT

Number of pages marked dirty.

#C

Last-used processor, for multiprocessor systems.

SHR

Amount of shared memory used.

S State of the task. Values are **S** (sleeping), **D** (uninterruptible sleep), **R** (running), **Z** (zombies), or **T** (stopped or traced).

WCHAN

Address or name of the kernel function in which the task is currently sleeping.

TIME

Total CPU time used by task and any children.

TIME+

Like **TIME**, but shows the time down to hundredths of a second.

%CPU

Share of CPU time since last update, as percentage of total CPU time.

%MEM

Share of physical memory.

TTY

Controlling tty.

COMMAND

Command line (truncated if too long) or name of program depending on the state of the **C** toggle. Processes with no command line are shown in parentheses.

FLAGS

Task flags.

---

touch

touch [*options*] *files*

For one or more *files*, update the access time and modification time (and dates) to the current time and date. **touch** is useful in forcing other commands to handle files a certain way; for example, the operation of **make**, and sometimes **find**, relies on a file's access and modification time. If a file doesn't exist, **touch** creates it with a file size of 0.

Options

-a, --time=atime, --time=access, --time=use
Update only the access time.

-c, --no-create
Do not create any file that doesn't already exist.

-d *time*, --date=*time*
Change the time value to the specified *time* instead of the current time. *time* can use several formats and may contain month names, time zones, a.m. and p.m. strings, etc.

-m, --time=mtime, --time=modify
Update only the modification time.

-r *file*, --reference=*file*
Change times to be the same as those of the specified *file*, instead of the current time.

-t *time*
Use the time specified in *time* instead of the current time. This argument must be of the format [[*cc*]*yy*]*mmddhhmm*[.*ss*], indicating optional century and year, month, date, hours, minutes, and optional seconds.

--help
Print help message and then exit.

--version
Print the version number and then exit.

---

tr

tr [*options*] [*string1* [*string2*]]

Translate characters. Copy standard input to standard output, substituting characters from *string1* to *string2*, or deleting characters in *string1*.

Options

-c, -C, --complement
Complement characters in *string1* with respect to ASCII 001-377.

-d, --delete
Delete characters in *string1* from output.

-s, --squeeze-repeats
Squeeze out repeated output characters in *string2*.

-t, --truncate-set1
Truncate *string1* to the length of *string2* before translating.

--help
Print help message and then exit.

--version
Print the version number and then exit.

Special characters

Include brackets ([ ]) where shown.

\a   Ctrl-G (bell)

\b   Ctrl-H (backspace)

\f   Ctrl-L (form feed)

\n   Ctrl-J (newline)

\r   Ctrl-M (carriage return)

\t   Ctrl-I (tab)

\v   Ctrl-K (vertical tab)

nnn
Character with octal value *nnn*

\\   Literal backslash

char1-char2
All characters in the range *char1* through *char2*. If *char1* does not sort before *char2*, produce an error.

[*char**]
In *string2*, expand *char* to the length of *string1*.

[*char*number*]
Expand *char* to *number* occurrences. [**x*4**] expands to **xxxx**, for instance.

[:*class*:]
Expand to all characters in *class*, where *class* can be:

alnum
Letters and digits

alpha
Letters

blank
> Whitespace

cntrl
> Control characters

digit
> Digits

graph
> Printable characters except space

lower
> Lowercase letters

print
> Printable characters

punct
> Punctuation

space
> Whitespace (horizontal or vertical)

upper
> Uppercase letters

xdigit
> Hexadecimal digits

[=*char*=]
> The class of characters to which *char* belongs.

Examples

Change uppercase to lowercase in a file:

    cat file | tr 'A-Z' 'a-z'

Turn spaces into newlines (ASCII code 012):

    tr ' ' '\012' < file

Strip blank lines from **file** and save in **new.file**:

    cat file | tr -s "" "\012" > new.file

Delete colons from **file** and save result in **new.file**:

    tr -d : < file > new.file

---

tracepath tracepath [*options*] *host* [*port*]

TCP/IP command. Trace path to *host* and report the Maximum Transmission Unit (MTU). A simplified version of **traceroute** without options meant for use by unprivileged users. If specified, it will use *port* to send UDP probe packets. *host* is the destination hostname or the IP number of the host to reach.

Options

-l *n* Use alternative packet length of *n*. The default is 65536 for IPv4 and 128000 for IPv6.

-n Don't look up host names, just print IP addresses.

traceroute   traceroute [*options*] *host* [*packetsize*]

TCP/IP command. Trace route taken by packets to reach network host. **traceroute** attempts tracing by launching UDP probe packets with a small TTL (time-to-live), then listening for an ICMP "time exceeded" reply from a gateway. *host* is the destination hostname or the IP number of the host to reach. *packetsize* is the packet size in bytes of the probe datagram. Default is 40 bytes.

Options

-4, -6
  Force IPv4 or IPv6 tracerouting.

-A Perform AS path lookups.

-d Turn on socket-level debugging.

-e Show ICMP extensions.

-f *n*
  Set the initial time-to-live to *n* hops.

-F Set the "don't fragment" bit.

-g *addr*
  Enable the IP LSRR (Loose Source Record Route) option in addition to the TTL tests, to ask how someone at IP address *addr* can reach a particular target.

-i *interface*
  Specify the network interface for getting the source IP address for outgoing probe packets. Useful with a multihomed host. Also see the **-s** option.

-I Use ICMP ECHO requests instead of UDP datagrams.

-m *max_ttl*
  Set maximum time-to-live used in outgoing probe packets to *max-ttl* hops. Default is 30.

-n Show numerical addresses; do not look up hostnames. (Useful if DNS is not functioning properly.)

-N *n*
  Send *n* probe packets simultaneously. The default is 16.

-p *port*
  Set base UDP port number used for probe packets to *port*. Default is (decimal) 33434.

-q *n*
  Set number of probe packets per hop to the value *n*. Default is 3.

-r Bypass normal routing tables and send directly to a host on an attached network.

-s *src_addr*
  Use *src_addr* as the IP address that will serve as the source address in outgoing probe packets.

-t *tos*

Set the type-of-service in probe packets to *tos* (default is 0). The value must be a decimal integer in the range 0 to 255.

-T Use TCP SYN packets instead. This may help bypass some firewall rules.

-v Verbose; received ICMP packets (other than TIME_EXCEEDED and PORT_UNREACHABLE) will be listed.

-w *wait*

Set time to wait for a response to an outgoing probe packet to *wait* seconds (default is 5).

-x Toggle IP checksums, usually to turn them off. IP checksums are always calculated if **-I** is specified.

-z *msecs*

Set the delay between probes, in milliseconds. The default is 0.

---

troff

troff

See **groff**.

---

true

true

A null command that returns a successful (0) exit status. See also **false**.

---

tset

tset [*options*] [*terminal*]

reset [*options*] [*terminal*]

Initialize a terminal. The terminal to be initialized is whichever is found first from the value of *terminal*, the value of the TERM environment variable, or the default terminal type. See also the **reset** command.

Options

-c Set control characters.

-e*char*

Set the erase character to *char*.

-i*char*

Set the interrupt character to *char*.

-I Do not send terminal or tab initialization strings to the terminal.

-k*char*

Set line-kill character to *char*.

-m *arg*

Specify a mapping from a port type to a terminal, where *arg* looks like this:

[*port_type*][*operator*][*baud_rate*][:]*terminal_type*

operator can be any combination of < (less than), > (greater than), @ (equal), and ! (not). The terminal type is a string (e.g., **vt100** or **xterm**).

-q   Print the terminal type on standard output but do not initialize the terminal.

-Q   Don't display values for the erase, interrupt, and line kill characters.

-r   Print the terminal type to standard error.

-s   Print the shell commands that initialize the TERM environment variable on standard output.

-V   Print the version of **ncurses** used for this program and exit.

tsort

    tsort [*option*] [*file*]

Perform a topological sort on partially ordered strings in the specified file. If no file is specified or is -, read standard input. Multiple strings on a line are separated by spaces, where each line indicates a partial ordering. The fully ordered results are written to standard output. See the **tsort** info page for an example of the use of **tsort** for sorting lists of functions into the order they are called.

Options
--help
    Print help information and exit.

--version
    Print version information and exit.

tty

    tty [*options*]

Print the filename of the terminal connected to standard input.

Options
--help
    Print help message and exit.

-s, --silent, --quiet
    Print nothing to standard output, but return an exit status.

--version
    Display version information and exit.

tune2fs

    tune2fs [*options*] *device*

System administration command. Tune the parameters of a Linux Second Extended Filesystem by adjusting various parameters. You must specify the *device* on which the filesystem resides; it must not be mounted read/write when you change its parameters.

Options
-c *max-mount-counts*
    Specify the maximum number of mount counts between two checks on the filesystem.

-e *behavior*

Specify the kernel's behavior when encountering errors. *behavior* must be one of:

continue

Continue as usual.

remount-ro

Remount the offending filesystem in read-only mode.

panic

Cause a kernel panic.

-f Force completion even if there are errors.

-g *group*

Allow *group* (a group ID or name) to use reserved blocks.

-j Add an ext3 journal to the filesystem. If specified without **-J**, use the default journal parameters.

-J *jrnl-options*

Specify ext3 journal parameters as a comma-separated list of *option=value* pairs. The specified options override the default values. Only one size or device option can be specified for a filesystem. Possible options are:

device=*ext-jrnl*

Attach to the journal block device on *ext-jrnl*, which must exist and must have the same block size as the filesystem to be journaled. *ext-jrnl* can be specified by its device name, by the volume label (**LABEL**=*label*), or by the Universal Unique Identifier (UUID) stored in the journal's ext2 superblock (**UUID**=*uuid*; see **uuidgen**). Create the external journal with:

```
mke2fs -O jrnl-devext-jrnl
```

size=*jrnl-size*

The size of the journal in megabytes. The size must be at least equivalent to 1024 blocks and not more than 102,400 blocks.

-l Display a list of the superblock's contents.

-L *label*

Specify the volume label of filesystem. The label must be no more than 16 characters.

-m *percentage*

Specify the percentage of blocks that will be reserved for use by privileged users.

-M *dir*

Specify the filesystem's last-mounted directory.

-o *mount-options*

Set or clear the specified default *mount-options*. Mount options specified in */etc/fstab* or on the command line for **mount** will override these defaults. Specify multiple options as

a comma-separated list. Prefixing an option with a caret (^)
clears the option. No prefix or a plus sign (+) causes the
option to be set. The following options can be cleared or set:

acl

Enable Posix Acess Control Lists.

bsdgroups

Assign new files the group-id of the directory in which
they are created instead of the group-id of the process
creating them.

debug

Enable debugging code.

journal_data

When journaling, commit all data to journal before
writing to the filesystem.

journal_data_ordered

When journaling, force data to the filesystem before
committing metadata to the journal.

journal_data_writeback

When journaling, force data to the filesystem after
committing metadata to the journal.

-O *option*

Set or clear the specified filesystem options in the filesystem's
superblock. Specify multiple options as a comma-separated
list. Prefixing an option with a caret (^) clears the option. No
prefix or a plus sign (+) causes the option to be set. Run
e2fsck after changing **filetype** or **sparse_super**. The following
options can be cleared or set:

dir_index

Use B-trees to speed up lookups on large directories.

filetype

Save file type information in directory entries.

has_journal

Create an ext3 journal. Same as the **-j** option.

sparse_super

Save space on large filesystems by limiting the number of
backup superblocks. Same as **-s**.

-r *num*

Specify the number of blocks that will be reserved for use by
privileged users.

-s [0|1]

Turn the sparse superblock feature on or off. Run **e2fsck** after
changing this feature.

-u *user*

Allow *user* (a user ID or name) to use reserved blocks.

-U *uuid*

> Set the UUID of the filesystem to a UUID generated by
> **uuidgen** or to one of the following:
>
> **clear**
>
> > Clear the existing UUID.
>
> **random**
>
> > Randomly generate a new UUID.
>
> **time**
>
> > Generate a new time-based UUID.

---

tunelp

tunelp *device* [*options*]

System administration command. Control a line printer's device
parameters. Without options, print information about device(s).

Options

-a [on|off]

> Specify whether or not to abort if the printer encounters an
> error. By default, do not abort.

-c *n*

> Retry device *n* times if it refuses a character. (Default is 250.)
> After exhausting *n*, sleep before retrying.

-i *irq*

> Use *irq* for specified parallel port. Ignore **-t** and **-c**. If 0, restore
> noninterrupt-driven (polling) action.

-o [on|off]

> Specify whether to abort if device is not online or is out of
> paper.

-q [on|off]

> Specify whether to print current IRQ setting.

-r Reset port.

-s Display printer's current status.

-t *time*

> Specify a delay of *time* in jiffies to sleep before resending a
> refused character to the device. A jiffy is defined as either one
> tick of the system clock or one AC cycle time; it should be
> approximately 1/100 of a second.

-w *time*

> Specify a delay of *time* in jiffies to sleep before resending a
> strobe signal.

---

ul

ul [*options*] [*filenames*]

Translate underscores to underlining. The process will vary by
terminal type. Some terminals are unable to handle underlining.

Options

-i   When on a separate line, translate - to underline instead of translating underscores.

-t *terminal-type*
    Specify terminal type. By default, TERM is consulted.

---

umount

umount [*options*] [*directory*]

System administration command. Unmount filesystem specified by directory. You may also specify the filesystem by device name. **umount** announces to the system that the removable file structure previously mounted on the specified directory is to be removed. Any pending I/O for the filesystem is completed, and the file structure is flagged as clean. A busy filesystem cannot be unmounted.

Options

-a   Unmount all filesystems listed in */etc/mtab* other than */proc*.

-d   If the unmounted device was a loop device, free the loop device too. See also the **losetup** command.

-f   Force the unmount. This option requires kernel 2.1.116 or later.

-h   Print help message and exit.

-i   Don't execute */sbin/umount.<filesystem>* helper programs.

-l   Lazy unmount. Detach the filesystem from the hierarchy immediately, but don't clean up references until it is no longer busy. Requires kernel 2.4.11 or later.

-n   Unmount, but do not record changes in */etc/mtab*.

-O *options*
    Unmount only filesystems with the specified options in */etc/fstab*. Specify multiple options as a comma-separated list. Add **no** as a prefix to an option to indicate filesystems that should not be unmounted.

-r   If unmounting fails, try to remount read-only.

-t *type*
    Unmount only filesystems of type *type*. Multiple types can be specified as a comma-separated list, and any type can be prefixed with **no** to specify that filesystems of that type should not be unmounted.

-v   Verbose mode.

-V   Print version information and exit.

---

uname

uname [*options*]

Print information about the machine and operating system. Without options, print the name of the kernel (Linux).

Options

-a, --all
> Combine all the system information from the other options.

-i, --hardware-platform
> Print the system's hardware platform.

-m, --machine
> Print the name of the hardware that the system is running on.

-n, --nodename
> Print the machine's hostname.

-o, --operating-system
> Print the operating system name.

-p, --processor
> Print the type of processor.

-r, --kernel-release
> Print the release number of the kernel.

-s, --kernel-name
> Print the name of the kernel (Linux). This is the default action.

-v, --kernel-version
> Print build information about the kernel.

--help
> Display a help message and then exit.

--version
> Print version information and then exit.

---

unexpand   unexpand [*options*] [*files*]

Convert strings of initial whitespace, consisting of at least two spaces and/or tabs, to tabs. Read from standard input if given no file or a file named -.

Options

-a, --all
> Convert all, not just leading, strings of spaces and tabs.

--first-only
> Convert only leading spaces and tabs. Overrides **-a**.

-t *nums*, **--tabs** *nums*
> *nums* is a comma-separated list of integers that specify the placement of tab stops. If a single integer is provided, the tab stops are set to every *integer* spaces. By default, tab stops are eight spaces apart. This option implies **-a**.

--help
> Print help message and then exit.

--version
> Print the version number and then exit.

unicode_start	unicode_start [*font* [*umap*]]
	Put keyboard and console in Unicode mode, setting the font to *font* and the Unicode map to *umap* if the font doesn't have its own map. If no font is specified, use the default.
unicode_stop	unicode_stop
	Take keyboard and console out of Unicode mode.
uniq	uniq [*options*] [*file1* [*file2*]]
	Remove duplicate adjacent lines from sorted *file1* or from standard input, sending one copy of each line to *file2* (or to standard output). Often used as a filter. Specify only one of **-d** or **-u**. See also **comm** and **sort**.

Options

-c, --count
> Print each line once, prefixing number of instances.

-d, --repeated
> Print duplicate lines once but no unique lines.

-D, --all-repeated[=*method*]
> Print all duplicate lines. **-D** takes no delimiter method. The delimiter method *method* takes one of the following values: **none** (default), **prepend**, or **separate**. Blank lines are used as the delimiter.

-f *n*, **--skip-fields**=*n*
> Ignore first *n* fields of a line. Fields are separated by spaces or by tabs.

-i, --ignore-case
> Ignore case differences when checking for duplicates.

-s *n*, **--skip-chars**=*n*
> Ignore first *n* characters of a field.

-u, --unique
> Print only unique lines (no copy of duplicate entries is kept).

-w *n*, **--check-chars**=*n*
> Compare only first *n* characters per line (beginning after skipped fields and characters).

--help
> Print a help message and then exit.

--version
> Print version information and then exit.

Examples

Send one copy of each line from **list** to output file **list.new**:

```
uniq list list.new
```

Show which names appear more than once:

```
sort names | uniq -d
```

unlink

unlink *filename*

unlink *option*

Remove the specified file using the system **unlink** function.

Options

--help

> Print help information and exit.

--version

> Print version information and exit.

uptime

uptime [*option*]

Print the current time, how long the system has been running, the number of users currently logged in (which may include the same user multiple times), and system load averages. This output is also produced by the first line of **w** command output.

Option

-V   Print version information and exit.

useradd

useradd [*options*] [*user*]

System administration command. Create new user accounts or update default account information. Unless invoked with the **-D** option, *user* must be given. **useradd** will create new entries in system files. Home directories and initial files may also be created as needed.

Options

-b *dir*, **--base-dir** *dir*

> Specify base *dir* for home directories. The default is */home*.

-c *comment*, **--comment** *comment*

> Comment field.

-d *dir*, **--home** *dir*

> Home directory. The default is to use *user* as the directory name under the *home* directory specified with the **-D** option.

-D [*options*]

> Set or display defaults. If *options* are specified, set them. If no options are specified, display current defaults. The options are:

> **-b** *dir*, **--base-dir** *dir*

> > Home directory prefix to be used in creating home directories. If the **-d** option is not used when creating an account, the *user* name is appended to *dir*.

> **-e** *date*, **--expiredate** *date*

> > Expire *date*. Requires the use of shadow passwords.

> **-f** *days*, **--inactive** *days*

> > Number of *days* after a password expires to disable an account. Requires the use of shadow passwords.

-g *group*, **--gid** *group*
> Initial *group* name or ID number.

-s *shell*, **--shell** *shell*
> Default login *shell*.

-e *date*, **--expiredate** *date*
> Account expiration *date*. Use the format *MM/DD/YYYY*. Two-digit year fields are also accepted. The value is stored as the number of days since January 1, 1970. This option requires the use of shadow passwords.

-f *days*, **--inactive** *days*
> Permanently disable account this many *days* after the password has expired. A value of **-1** disables this feature. This option requires the use of shadow passwords.

-g *group*, **--gid** *group*
> Initial *group* name or ID number. If a different default group has not been specified using the **-D** option, the default group is 1.

-G *groups*, **--groups** *groups*
> Supplementary *groups* given by name or number in a comma-separated list with no whitespace.

-k [*dir*], **--skel** [*dir*]
> Copy default files to the user's home directory. Meaningful only when used with the **-m** option. Default files are copied from */etc/skel/* unless an alternate *dir* is specified.

-K *key=value*, **--key** *key=value*
> Override */etc/login.defs* defaults. This option can be given multiple times.

-l
> Keep old entries for *user* in lastlog and faillog databases. By default old user data in these are reset.

-m, **--create-home**
> Make user's home directory if it does not exist. The default is not to make the home directory.

-M
> Do not create a home directory for the user, even if the system default in */etc/login.defs* is to create one.

-o, **--non-unique**
> Override. Accept a nonunique *uid* with the **-u** option. (Probably a bad idea.)

-p *passwd*, **--password** *passwd*
> The encrypted password, as returned by **crypt**(3).

-r, **--system**
> Red Hat-specific option. Create a system account with a non-expiring password and a UID lower than the minimum defined in */etc/login.defs*. Do not create a home directory for the account unless **-m** is also specified.

-s *shell*, **--shell** *shell*
> Login *shell*.

-u *uid*, --**uid** *uid*

> Numerical user ID. The value must be unique unless the -**o** option is used. The default value is the smallest ID value greater than 99 and greater than every other *uid*.

---

userdel

userdel [*option*] *user*

System administration command. Delete all entries for *user* in system account files.

Option
-**f**, --**force**

> Remove the *user* even if they are currently logged in. Remove home directory and mail spool even if they are used by another user. Remove group too, if USERGROUPS_ENAB is set to yes in */etc/login.defs*.

-**r**, --**remove**

> Remove the home directory of *user* and any files contained in it.

---

usermod

usermod [*options*] *user*

System administration command. Modify *user* account information.

Options
-**a**, --**append**

> Used with the -**G** option. Add *user* to the specified *groups*, but don't remove *user* from groups not in the current list.

-**c** *comment*, --**comment** *comment*

> Comment field.

-**d** *dir*, --**home** *dir*

> Home directory.

-**e** *date*, --**expiredate** *date*

> Account expiration *date*. *date* is in the format *MM/DD/YYYY*; two-digit year fields are also accepted. The value is stored as the number of days since January 1, 1970. This option requires the use of shadow passwords.

-**f** *days*, --**inactive** *days*

> Permanently disable account this many *days* after the password has expired. A value of -**1** disables this feature. This option requires the use of shadow passwords.

-**g** *group*, --**gid** *group*

> Initial *group* name or number.

-**G** *groups*, --**groups** *groups*

> Supplementary *groups* given by name or number in a comma-separated list with no whitespace. *user* will be removed from any groups to which it currently belongs that are not included in *groups*.

-l *name*, --**login** *name*
> Login *name*. This cannot be changed while the user is logged in.

-L, --**lock**
> Lock user's password by putting a ! in front of it. This option cannot be used with -**p** or -**U**.

-o, --**non-unique**
> Override. Accept a nonunique *uid* with the -**u** option.

-p *pw*, -**password** *pw*
> Encrypted password, as returned from **crypt**(3).

-s *shell*, --**shell** *shell*
> Login *shell*.

-u *uid*, --**uid** *uid*
> Numerical user ID. The value must be unique unless the -**o** option is used. Any files owned by *user* in the user's home directory will have their user ID changed automatically. Files outside of the home directory will not be changed. *user* should not be executing any processes while this is changed.

-U, --**unlock**
> Unlock the user's password by removing the ! that -**L** put in front of it. This option cannot be used with -**p** or -**L**.

users

    users [file]

    users option

Print a space-separated list of each login session on the host. Note that this may include the same user multiple times. Consult *file* or, by default, */var/log/utmp* or */var/log/wtmp*.

Options
--**help**
> Print usage information and exit.

--**version**
> Print version information and exit.

usleep

    usleep [microseconds]

    usleep [option]

Sleep some number of microseconds (default is 1).

Options
-?, --**help**
> Print help information and then exit.

--**usage**
> Print brief usage message and then exit.

-v, --**version**
> Print version information.

uuidgen   uuidgen [*option*]

Create a new Universal Unique Identifier (UUID) and print it to standard output. The generated UUID consists of five hyphen-separated groups of hex digits (e.g., 3cdfc61d-87d3-41b5-ba50-32870b33dc67). The default is to generate a random-based UUID, but this requires that a high-quality random-number generator be available on the system.

Options

-**r**   Generate a random-based UUID.

-**t**   Generate a time-based UUID.

vdir   vdir [*options*] [*files*]

Verbosely list directory contents. Equivalent to **ls -lb**. By default, list the current directory. Directory entries are sorted alphabetically unless overridden by an option. **vdir** takes the same options as **ls**.

vi   vi [*options*] [*files*]

A screen-oriented text editor based on **ex**. **vi** is bi-modal, with a command mode and an insert mode. For more information on **vi**, see Chapter 9.

vidmode   vidmode [*option*] *image* [*mode* [*offset*]]

System administration command. Set the video mode for a kernel *image*. If no arguments are specified, print current *mode* value. *mode* is a 1-byte value located at offset 506 in a kernel image. You may change the *mode* by specifying the kernel *image* to change, the new *mode*, and the byte offset at which to place the new information (the default is 506). Note that **rdev -v** is a synonym for **vidmode**. If LILO is used, **vidmode** is not needed. The video mode can be set from the LILO prompt during a boot.

Modes

-**3**   Prompt

-**2**   Extended VGA

-**1**   Normal VGA

0   Same as entering **0** at the prompt

1   Same as entering **1** at the prompt

2   Same as entering **2** at the prompt

3   Same as entering **3** at the prompt

n   Same as entering **n** at the prompt

Option

-**o** *offset*
         Same as specifying an *offset* as an argument.

vim
    vim

An enhanced version of the **vi** screen editor. Both **vi** and **vim** are covered in Chapter 9.

vmstat
    vmstat [*options*] [*interval* [*count*]]

System administration command. Print report on virtual memory statistics, including information on processes, memory, paging block I/O, traps, system and CPU usage. **vmstat** initially reports average values since the last system reboot. If given a sampling period *interval* in seconds, it prints additional statistics for each interval. If specified, **vmstat** exits when it has completed *count* reports. Otherwise, it continues until it receives a Ctrl-C, printing a new header line each time it fills the screen.

Options

-a   Display active and inactive memory.

-d   Display disk statistics.

-f   Display the number of forks since the system was booted.

-m   Display the names and sizes of various kernel objects stored in a cache known as the slab layer. Also see the **slabtop** command.

-n   Don't print new header lines when the screen is full.

-p *partition*
    Display detailed statistics for the specified partition.

-s   Display various event counters and memory statistics.

-S *units*
    Switch the output units. Possible values are **k**, **K**, **m**, or **M**.

-t   Add a timestamp to output.

-V   Print version number, then exit.

VM mode fields

procs

    r   Processes waiting for runtime.

    b   Uninterruptible sleeping processes.

memory

    swpd
        Virtual memory used, in kilobytes.

    free
        Idle memory, in kilobytes.

    buff
        Memory used as buffers, in kilobytes.

    cache
        Cache memory, in kilobytes.

Linux
Commands

    inactive
        Inactive memory, in kilobytes, displayed with **-a**.

    active
        Active memory, in kilobytes; displayed with **-a**.

swap
    si   Memory swapped in from disk each second, in kilobytes.

    so Memory swapped out to disk each second, in kilobytes.

io
    bi   Blocks received from block devices each second.

    bo Blocks sent to block devices each second.

system
    in   Interrupts per second, including clock interrupts.

    cs   Context switches per second.

cpu
    us   Percentage of CPU time consumed by user processes.

    sy   Percentage of CPU time consumed by system processes.

    id   Percentage of CPU time spent idle.

    wa Percentage of CPU time spent waiting for I/O.

Disk mode fields

Reads and **Writes**
    total
        Total reads or writes completed successfully.

    merged
        Reads or writes grouped into one I/O.

    sectors
        Sectors read or written successfully.

    ms
        Milliseconds spent reading or writing.

IO
    cur I/O in progress

    s   Seconds spent doing I/O.

Disk partition mode fields

reads
    Total reads issued to this partition.

read sectors
    Total sectors read for this partition.

writes
    Total writes issued to this partition.

requested writes
    Total write requests for this partition.

Slab mode fields

cache
> Cache name.

num
> Number of currently active objects.

total
> Total number of available objects.

size
> Size of each object.

pages
> Number of pages with at least one active object.

totpages
> Total number of allocated pages.

pslab
> Number of pages per slab.

---

volname

volname [*devfile*]

Return the volume name for a device such as a CD-ROM that was formatted with an ISO-9660 filesystem. The default device file *devfile* is */dev/cdrom*.

---

w

w [*options*] [*user*]

Print summaries of system usage, currently logged-in users, and what those users are doing. **w** is essentially a combination of **uptime**, **who**, and **ps -a**. Display output for one user by specifying *user*.

Options

-**f**   Toggle printing the from (remote hostname) field.

-**h**   Suppress heading and **uptime** information.

-**s**   Use the short format.

-**u**   Ignore the username while figuring out the current process and CPU times.

-**V**   Display version information.

File

/var/run/utmp
> List of users currently logged in.

---

wall

wall [*file*]

wall [-n] [*message*]

Write to all users. Depending on your Linux distribution, **wall** uses one of the two syntaxes shown. In both versions, the default is for **wall** to read a message from standard input and send the message to all users currently logged in, preceded by "Broadcast Message from...." With the first syntax, which comes with Debian-based systems, for example, if *file* is specified, **wall** reads input from that file rather than from standard input, and only the superuser can write to a terminal if the user has disallowed messages. With the second syntax, distributed with Red Hat-based systems, for example, the text of the message can be included on the command line, and the message is limited to 20 lines. In this form, if **-n** is specified, the default banner message is replaced with "Remote broadcast message." **-n** can only be specified by the superuser, and only if **wall** was installed set-group-id.

Example

Send the message contained in the file *message.txt* to all users:

```
$ wall < message.txt
```

---

warnquota   warnquota [*options*] [*filesystem*]

System administration command. Mail warning messages to users that have exceeded their soft limit.

Options

-a *file*, **--admins-file=***file*
> Read group administrator information from *file* instead of */etc/quotagrpadmins*.

-c *file*, **--config=***file*
> Read configuration information from *file* instead of */etc/warnquota.conf*.

-d, --no-details
> Send messages without attaching quota reports.

-F *format*, **-format=***format*
> Read quota information of the specified format. (See **quota** for valid formats.)

-g, --group
> Send messages for group quotas. Send the message to the user specified in */etc/quotagrpadmins*.

-i, --no-autofs
> Ignore automount mount points.

-q *file*, **-quota-tab=***file*
> Read device description strings from *file* instead of */etc/quotagrpadmins*.

-s, --human-readable
> Report sizes in more human-readable units.

-u, --user
> Send messages for user quotas. (This is the default.)

---

watch   watch [*options*] *command* [*cmd_options*]

Run the specified command repeatedly (by default, every two seconds) and display the output so you can watch it change over time. The command and any options are passed to **sh -c**, so you may need to use quotes to get correct results.

Options

-d, --differences[=**cumulative**]

> Highlight changes between iterations. If **cumulative** is specified, the highlighting remains on the screen throughout, giving a cumulative picture of the changes.

-h, --help

> Display help message and exit.

-n *secs*, **--interval**=*secs*

> Run the command every *secs* seconds.

-t, --no-title

> Do not display the header or the blank line following the header.

-v, --version

> Print version information and exit.

WC

wc [*options*] [*files*]

Print byte, word, and line counts for each file. Print a total line for multiple *files*. If *files* is omitted or is -, read standard input. See other examples under **ls** and **sort**.

Options

-c, --bytes

> Print byte count only.

-l, --lines

> Print line count only.

-L, --max-line-length

> Print length of longest line.

-m, --chars

> Print character count only.

-w, --words

> Print word count only.

--help

> Print help message and then exit.

--version

> Print the version number and then exit.

Examples

Count the number of users logged in:

```
who | wc -l
```

Count the words in three essay files:

```
wc -w essay.[123]
```

Count lines in the file named by variable $file (don't display filename):

```
wc -l < $file
```

Linux
Commands

wget

wget [*options*] [*urls*]

Perform noninteractive file downloads from the Web. **wget** works in the background and can be used to set up and run a download without the user having to remain logged on. **wget** supports HTTP, HTTPS, and FTP, as well as downloads through HTTP proxies. **wget** uses a global startup file that you may find at */etc/wgetrc* or */usr/local/ etc/wgetrc*. In addition, users can define their own *$HOME/.wgetrc* files.

Options

-4, --inet4-only

Force connection to IPv4 hosts only.

-6, --inet6-only

Force connection to IPv6 hosts only.

-a *logfile*, **--append-output=***logfile*

Append output messages to *logfile*, instead of overwriting the contents as **-o** does. If *logfile* doesn't exist, create it.

-A *acclist*, **--accept=***acclist*

Specify a comma-separated list of filename suffixes or patterns to accept.

-b, --background

Go into the background immediately after startup, writing output to the file specified with **-o** or to **wget-log**.

-B *url*, **--base=***url*

Used with **-F** to prepend the specified URL to relative links in the input file specified with **-i**.

--bind-address=*address*

When making client TCP/IP connections, **bind( )** to the specified local address, which can be specified as a hostname or IP address. Useful if your system is bound to multiple IP addresses.

-c, --continue

Continue getting a partially downloaded file. Affects the restarting of downloads from an earlier invocation of **wget**. Works only with FTP servers and HTTP servers that support the Range header.

--connect-timeout=*seconds*

Set the timeout for a connection to be established in seconds. The default is never to time out, unless a timeout is implemented by system libraries.

--cut-dirs=*num*

Ignore the specified number of directory components when creating the local directory structure.

-d, --debug

Turn on debugging. **wget** must have been compiled with debug support.

-D *domainlist*, **--domains**=*domainlist*
> Specify a comma-separated list of domains to be followed. Does not turn on **-H**.

--delete-after
> Delete each retrieved file from the local machine after downloading it. Useful for prefetching pages through a proxy. **-k** is ignored if specified with **--delete-after**.

--dns-timeout=*seconds*
> Set the DNS lookup timeout to *seconds*. The default is to never time out.

-e *command*, **--execute**=*command*
> Execute the specified command after the commands in *.wgetrc*, overriding any *.wgetrc* commands. Can be included multiple times, once for each command to execute.

-E, **--html-extension**
> Append the suffix *.html* to the filenames of downloaded files where the URL does not include it (for example, an *.asp* file).

--exclude-domains=*domainlist*
> Specify a comma-separated list of names that are never to be followed.

-F, **--force-html**
> When reading input from a file, force the file to be treated as an HTML file.

--follow-ftp
> Follow FTP links from HTML documents. The default is to ignore FTP links.

--follow-tags=*list*
> Specify a comma-separated list of tags to be considered, overriding the internal table that **wget** normally uses during a recursive retrieval.

--ftp-user, **--ftp-password**
> Specify the user name and password on an FTP server.

-h, **--help**
> Display usage information and exit.

-H, **--span-hosts**
> Enable spanning across hosts when doing recursive retrieval.

--header=*header*
> Add an additional header to be passed to the HTTP server. The header must include a colon (:) preceded by at least one nonblank character, and with no newline characters. Can be specified multiple times. If *header* is an empty string, all user-defined headers are cleared.

--http-user=*user*, **--http-password**=*password*
> Specify the username and password on an HTTP server.

-i *file*, **--input-file**=*file*
> Read URLs from the specified file. URLs specified on the command line are accessed before URLs in the file. If *file* is given as -, read from standard input.

-I *list*, **--include-directories**=*list*

    Specify a comma-separated list of directories to follow when downloading. The list elements may contain wildcards.

--ignore-case

    Ignore case when matching files and directories. Affects the behavior of **-A**, **-I**, **-R**, **-X**, and FTP globbing.

--ignore-length

    Ignore the "Content-Length" header on the HTTP server.

--ignore-tags=*list*

    Specify a comma-separated list of tags to be ignored for recursive retrievals.

-k, **--convert-links**

    Convert document links after the download is complete so they work locally.

-K, **--backup-converted**

    When converting a file, back up the original and add an *.orig* suffix. Affects the behavior of **-N**.

--keep-session-cookies

    Causes **--save-cookies** to also save session cookies.

-l *depth*, **--level**=*depth*

    For recursive retrievals, specify the maximum recursion depth. The default depth is 5.

-L, **--relative**

    Follow relative links only.

--limit-rate=*rate*

    Set the maximum download speed, The default is to specify the rate in bytes, or add a **k** suffix for kilobytes or **m** for megabytes.

--load-cookies=*file*

    Load cookies from the specified file before the first HTTP retrieval.

-m, **--mirror**

    Turn on options suitable for mirroring a remote site. Equivalent to **-r -N -l inf --no-remove-listing**.

--max-redirect=*num*

    Set the maximum number of redirections to follow (default is 20).

-N, **--timestamping**

    Turn on timestamping.

-nc, **--no-clobber**

    Do not download a file if there is already a copy on the disk. The default is to preserve the original copy and rename successive downloads, adding *.1*, *.2*, etc. to their name. May not be specified with **-N**.

-nd, **--no-directories**

    Do not create a directory hierarchy when doing recursive retrievals.

-nH, --no-host-directories
> Disable creation of directories prefixed by the name of the host. The default is to include the hostname.

--no-cache
> Disable server-side cache for an HTTP retrieval. The default is for caching to be on.

--no-cookies
> Disable the use of cookies.

--no-dns-cache
> Disable caching of DNS lookups; look up hostname again for each new connection.

--no-glob
> Turn off FTP globbing to prevent the use of wildcards for multiple file retrievals.

--no-http-keep-alive
> Turn off the keep-alive feature for HTTP retrievals.

--np, --no-parent
> In recursive retrievals, do not ever go up to the parent directory.

--no-passive-ftp
> Do not allow use of passive FTP transfer mode.

--no-proxy
> Do not use proxies.

--no-remove-listing
> Do not remove the temporary *.listing* files generated by FTP retrievals.

-nv, --non-verbose
> Turn off verbose mode, but don't run completely quietly. Displays error messages and basic information.

-o *logfile*, **--output-file**=*logfile*
> Log output messages to *logfile*, instead of the default standard error.

-O *file*, **--output-document**=*file*
> Concatenate all documents into the specified file. If the file exists, it is overwritten. Specify the file as - to write to standard output.

-p, --page-requisites
> Download all files necessary to display an HTML page.

-P *prefix*, **--directory-prefix**=*prefix*
> Set the directory prefix to the specified value.

--post-data=*string*, **--post-file**=*file*
> Use POST as the method for HTTP requests and send the specified data in the request body. Use **--post-data** to send *string* as data and **--post-file** to send the *file* contents.

--prefer-family=*family*
> Connect to the addresses of the specified family first when there is a choice. The possible values for *family* are **IPv4** (the default), **IPv6**, and **none**.

--progress=*type*[*:style*]

> Set the progress indicator to *type*. Valid types are **dot** and **bar**; the default is **bar**. With **--progress=dot**, you can also set a style. The default style is for each dot to represent 1 KB, with 10 dots in a cluster and 50 dots per line. Alternatives are **binary**, with each dot representing 8 KB, 16-dot clusters, and 48 dots per line; **mega**, for downloading very large files, with each dot representing 64 KB, 8 dots per cluster, and 48 dots per line; and **giga**, with each dot representing 1 MB, 8 dots per cluster, and 4 clusters per line.

--protocol-directories

> Use the protocol name as part of the local filename.

--proxy-user=*user*, **--proxy-passwd**=*password*

> Specify the username and password for authentication on a proxy server.

-q, --quiet

> Run quietly; don't produce output.

-Q *quota*, **--quota**=*quota*

> Specify download quota for automatic retrievals. The default value is in bytes; add **k** suffix for kilobytes, or **m** for megabytes.

-r, --recursive

> Turn on recursive retrieving.

-R *rejlist*, **--reject**=*rejlist*

> Specify a comma-separated list of filename suffixes or patterns to reject.

--random-wait

> Set a random wait time to prevent being identified by websites that look for patterns in time between requests so they can block access.

--read-timeout=*seconds*

> Set the read (and write) timeout to the specified number of seconds. The default is 900 seconds.

--referer=*url*

> Include a "Referer: url" header in an HTTP request.

--restrict-file-names=*mode*[*,***nocontrol**]

> Restrict the characters found in remote URLs from appearing in local filenames. The value of *mode* is the operating system—e.g., **unix** or **windows** (use **unix** for Linux). Such characters are escaped with a percent sign (%). The default is to escape characters not valid on your operating system. Appending **,nocontrol** turns off escaping of control characters.

--retr-symlinks

> When retrieving FTP directories recursively, follow symbolic links and retrieve the linked-to files.

--retry-connrefused

> Retry after getting a "connection refused" error. Useful for mirroring unreliable sites whose servers are likely to go down briefly.

-S, --server-response
Print HTTP server headers and FTP server responses.

--save-cookies=*file*
Save cookies in the specified file before exiting. Does not save expired cookies, and only saves session cookies if **--keep-session-cookies** is also specified.

--save-headers
Save the headers sent by an HTTP server to the file, preceding the contents and separated by a blank line.

--spider
Behave like a web spider, checking that pages exist but not downloading them.

--strict-comments
Turn on strict parsing of HTML comments, instead of terminating comments at the first occurrence of -->.

-t *num*, **--tries=***num*
Set the number of retries to the specified value of *num*. Set *num* to **0** or **inf** to keep trying forever (infinitely) (default is 20 retries), unless there is a fatal error such as "connection refused."

-T *seconds*, **--timeout=***seconds*
Set network timeout to the specified number of seconds. Equivalent to specifying all of **--dns-timeout**, **--connect-timeout**, and **--read-timeout**.

--user=*user*, **--password=***password*
Specify the user name and password for both FTP and HTTP file retrieval.

-U *agent*, **--user-agent=***agent*
Specify an agent string to the HTTP server to replace the default identification of Wget/*version*, where *version* is the current **wget** version. This string is used in the User-Agent header field.

-v, --verbose
Turn on verbose output, printing all available data. This is the default.

-V, --version
Display version information and exit.

-w *seconds*, **--wait=***seconds*
Specify the wait in seconds between retrievals. Used to lighten server load. Use the suffix **m** to specify the wait in minutes, **h** for hours, or **d** for days.

--waitretry=*seconds*
Specify the number of seconds to wait between retries if the download fails. The default in the global configuration file is not to wait.

-x, --force-directories
Create a hierarchy of directories even if one wouldn't otherwise be created.

-X *list*, --exclude-directories=*list*
> Specify a comma-separated list of directories to exclude from download. List elements may contain wildcards.

whatis

whatis `keywords`

Search the short manual page descriptions in the **whatis** database for each *keyword* and print a one-line description to standard output for each match. Like **apropos**, except that it searches only for complete words. Equivalent to **man -f**.

whereis

whereis `[options] files`

Locate the binary, source, and manual page files for specified commands/files. The supplied filenames are first stripped of leading pathname components and any (single) trailing extension of the form *.ext* (for example, *.c*). Prefixes of *s.* resulting from use of source code control are also dealt with. **whereis** then attempts to locate the desired program in a list of standard Linux directories (*/bin*, */etc*, */usr/bin*, */usr/local/bin/*, etc.).

Options

-b   Search only for binaries.

-B *directories*
> Change or otherwise limit the directories to search for binaries.

-f   Terminate the last directory list and signal the start of filenames. Required when the **-B**, **-M**, or **-S** option is used.

-m   Search only for manual sections.

-M *directory*
> Change or otherwise limit the directories to search for manual sections.

-s   Search only for sources.

-S *directory*
> Change or otherwise limit the directories to search for sources.

-u   Search for unusual entries—that is, files that do not have one entry of each requested type. Thus, the command **whereis -m -u** * asks for those files in the current directory that have no documentation.

Example

Find all files in */usr/bin* that are not documented in */usr/share/man/man1* but that have source in */usr/src*:

```
$ cd /usr/bin
$ whereis -u -M /usr/share/man/man1 -S /usr/src -f *
```

which

which [*options*] [--] [*commands*]

List the full pathnames of the files that would be executed if the named *commands* had been run. **which** searches the user's $PATH environment variable.

Options

-a, --all
> Print all matches, not just the first.

-i, --read-alias
> Read aliases from standard input and write matches to standard output. Useful for using an alias for **which**.

--read-functions
> Read shell functions from standard input and report matches to standard output. Useful for also using a shell function for **which** itself.

--skip-alias
> Ignore **--read-alias** if present. Useful for finding normal binaries while using **--read-alias** in an alias for **which**.

--show-dot
> If a matching command is found in a directory that starts with a dot, print *./cmdname* instead of the full pathname.

--show-tilde
> Print a tilde (~) to indicate the user's home directory. Ignored if the user is root.

--skip-dot
> Skip directories that start with a dot.

--skip-functions
> Ignore **--read-functions** if present. Useful when searching for normal binaries while using **--read-functions** in an alias or function for **which**.

--skip-tilde
> Skip directories that start with a tilde (~) and executables in $HOME.

--tty-only
> Stop processing options on the right if not on a terminal.

-v, -V, --version
> Print version information and then exit.

--help
> Print help information and then exit.

Example

```
$ which cc ls
/usr/bin/cc
ls:     aliased to ls -sFC
```

who

who [*options*] [*file*]

who am i

Show who is logged into the system. With no options, list the names of users currently logged in, their terminal, the time they have been logged in, and the name of the host from which they have logged in. An optional system *file* (default is */etc/utmp*) can be supplied to give additional information.

Options

-a, --all
Equivalent to **-b -d --login -p -r -t -T -u**.

am i
Print information for the invoking user.

-b, --boot
Print time of last system boot.

-d, --dead
Print a list of dead processes.

-H, --heading
Print column headings.

--help
Print a help message and then exit.

-l, --login
Print list of system login processes.

--lookup
Attempt to include canonical hostnames via DNS.

-m   Same as **who am i**.

-p, --process
Print active processes spawned by **init**.

-q, --count
"Quick." Display all usernames and the total number of users.

-r, --runlevel
Print the current runlevel.

-s, --short
Print only name, line, and time. This is the default behavior.

-t, --time
Print the last system clock change.

-u, --users
Print a list of the users who are logged in.

--version
Print version information and then exit.

-w, -T, --mesg, --message, --writable
Include user's message status in the output:

+   **mesg y** (**write** messages allowed)

-   **mesg n** (**write** messages refused)

?   Cannot find terminal device

Example

This sample output was produced at 8 a.m. on April 17:

```
$ who -uH
NAME    LINE   TIME          IDLE   PID  COMMENTS
Earvin  ttyp3  Apr 16 08:14  16:25  2240
Larry   ttyp0  Apr 17 07:33    .    15182
```

Since Earvin has been idle since yesterday afternoon (16 hours), it appears that he isn't at work yet. He simply left himself logged in. Larry's terminal is currently in use.

---

whoami

whoami

Print current user ID. Equivalent to **id -un**.

---

whois

whois[*options*] *query*[@*server*[:*port*]]

jwhois [*options*] *query*[@*server*[:*port*]]

Search a **whois** database for a domain name, IP address, or NIC name. The information returned varies, but usually contains administrative and technical contacts so that you can find a person to handle problems at that domain. By default, the command returns information on *.com*, *.net*, and *.edu* domains, but other hosts can be queried for other domains using *host* or the **-h** option.

Options

-- Indicate the end of **whois** options. A subsequent string that begins with a hyphen on the command line is taken as a query string.

-a, --raw
Do not rewrite query according to configuration before sending to server.

-c *file*, **--config**=*file*
Specify a configuration file to use instead of the default */etc/jwhois.conf*.

-d, --disable-cache
Disable reading and writing to the cache.

-f, --force-lookup
Force the lookup query to go to the host, even if it is available from the cache.

-h *host*, **--host**=*host*
Query the **whois** server on the specified host. Same as *host* on the command line. By default, queries the server in the environment variable NICNAMESERVER or WHOISSERVER if either is set; otherwise queries *whois.internic.net*.

--help
Print help message and exit.

-i, --display-redirections
Display every step in a redirection. The default is to display only the last step.

-n, --no-redirect
> Disable redirection from one server to the next.

-p *port*, **--port**=*port*
> Connect to the specified port. Same as *port* on the command line. Default is 43.

-r, --rwhois
> Force use of the **rwhois** protocol, instead of HTTP or **whois**.

--rwhois-display=*display*
> Request receiving **rwhois** servers to display the results in the specified display instead of the default.

--rwhois-limit=*limit*
> Request receiving **rwhois** servers to limit the number of matches to the specified limit.

-s, --no-whoisservers
> Disable built-in support for *whois-servers.net*.

-v   Verbose. Print debugging information while running. Specify **-vv** to increase verbosity.

--version
> Print version information and exit.

---

wodim

wodim [*options*] *track1,track2...*

Record data or audio CD or DVD media. This program normally requires root access to the device file; run as root or install suid-root. It has a large number of options and settings; see the manpage for a complete list as well as a number of useful examples.

General options

General option flags go directly after the **wodim** command and before any track options or arguments. The general options are:

-atip
> Display the ATIP (Absolute Time In Pregroove) information for a disc. Not all drives allow you to read this information.

blank=*type*
> Erase data from a CD-RW in one of the following ways:

> **all**
>> Erase all information on the disc. May take a long time.

> **fast**
>> Perform a quick erase of the disc, erasing only the PMA, TOC, and pregap.

> **help**
>> Display a possible list of blanking methods.

> **session**
>> Blank the last session.

> **track**
>> Blank a track.

> **trtail**
>> Blank the tail of a track only.

unclose

Unclose the last session.

unreserve

Unreserve a track previously marked as reserved.

-checkdrive

Check to see if there are valid drivers for the current drive. Returns 0 if the drive is valid.

-d, **debug=***n*

Set the debug level to an integer (greater numbers are more verbose), or use multiple **-d** flags as with the **-v** and **-V** flags.

-dao, **-sao**

Disk-at-once (session-at-once) mode. Works only with MMC drives that support nonraw session-at-once modes.

dev=*target*

Set the SCSI target for the CD/DVD recorder. May be specified as a device name or as three comma-separated integers representing bus, target, and logical unit. To check the options that are available, use the **-scanbus** option. By default **wodim** looks in the CDR_DEVICE environment variable.

driver=*name*

Lets you specify a driver for your system. Suggested for experts only. The special drivers **cdr_simul** and **dvd_simul** are used for simulation and profiling tests if your drive does not support the **-dummy** option.

driveropts=*optlist*

Specify a comma-separated list of driver options. To get a list of valid options, use **driveropts=help** together with **-checkdrive**.

-dummy

Perform a dry run, doing all the steps of recording with the laser turned off. This will let you know whether the process is going to work.

-eject

Eject disc after recording. Some hardware may need to eject a disc after a dummy recording and before the actual recording.

-fix

Close ("fixate") the session, preventing future multisession recordings and allowing the disc to be played in standard audio CD players (some can also play a disc that has not been closed).

-force

Override errors if possible. May allow you to blank an otherwise broken CD-RW.

fs=*n*

Set the FIFO buffer size to *n*, in bytes. You may use **k**, **m**, **s**, or **f** to specify kilobytes, megabytes, or units of 2048 and 2352 bytes, respectively. The default is 4 MB.

gracetime=_n_

Set the number of seconds of grace time before writing. The value of _n_ should be at least 2 (default is 4 seconds).

kdebug=_n_, **kd=**_n_

Set the kernel's debug notification value to _n_ during SCSI command execution. Works through the usal-driver.

mcn=_n_

Set the Media Catalog Number to _n_.

msifile=_file_

Like **-msinfo**, but also saves the information in the specified file.

-msinfo

Get multisession information from the CD. Used only with multisession discs onto which you can still record more sessions.

-multi

Set to record in multisession mode. Must be present on all sessions but the last one for a multisession disc.

-nofix

Do not close the disc after writing.

-reset

Attempt to reset the SCSI bus. Does not work on all systems.

-s, -silent

Silent mode. Do not print any SCSI command errors.

speed=_n_

Set the speed to _n_, a multiple of the audio speed. Normally, **wodim** gets the speed from _/etc/wodim.conf_ or the CDR_SPEED environment variable. If your drive has trouble with higher numbers, try 0 as a value.

timeout=_n_

Set the SCSI command timeout to _n_ seconds. Defaults to 40.

-tao

Track-at-once (TAO) write mode. Most drives require TAO mode for multisession recording.

-toc

Display the table of contents for the CD currently in the drive. Works for CD-ROM, as well as CD-R and CD-RW drives.

ts=_n_

Set the maximum transfer size for a single SCSI command to _n_. Defaults to 63 KB.

-scanbus

Scan SCSI devices. Useful for finding the SCSI address of the drive.

-useinfo

Use _.inf_ files to override audio options set elsewhere.

-v   Verbose mode. Use one **v** for each level of verbosity. **-vv** would be very verbose, and **-vvv** would be even more so.

-V   A verbose mode counter that applies only to SCSI transport messages. This slows the application but can be useful for debugging.

-version

Print version information and exit.

-waiti

Wait for input on standard input before opening the SCSI driver. Useful for letting **wodim** read input from a pipe while writing additional sessions to a multisession disk.

Track options and arguments

Track options may be mixed with track arguments, and normally apply to the track immediately after them or to all tracks after them. The track arguments themselves should be the files that you will be writing to the CD. Options are:

-audio

Write all tracks after this track in digital audio format (playable by standard CD players). If you do not use this flag or the **-data** flag, **wodim** assumes that *.au* and *.wav* files are to be recorded as raw audio and that all other files are data.

-cdi

Write subsequent tracks in CDI format. Use with XA disks only.

-data

Record subsequent tracks as CD-ROM data. If you do not use this flag or the **-audio** flag, all files except for those that end in *.wav* or *.au* are assumed to be data.

-index=*a,b,c*

Set the index list for the next track. The values should be increasing comma-separated integers, starting with index 1 and counting in sectors (75ths of a second). For example, you could set three indices in a track with **index=0,750,7500** and they would occur at the beginning of the track, after 10 seconds, and after 100 seconds.

-isosize

The size of the next track should match the size of the ISO-9660 filesystem. This is used when duplicating CDs or copying from raw-data filesystems.

isrc=*n*

Set the International Standard Recording Number for the track argument following this option.

-mode2

Write all subsequent tracks in CD-ROM mode 2 format.

-nopad

Do not insert blank data between data tracks following this flag. This is the default behavior.

-pad

    Insert 15 sectors of blank data padding between data tracks. Applies to all subsequent tracks or until you use the **-nopad** argument, and is overridden by the **padsize=**n argument.

padsize=n

    Insert n sectors of blank data padding after the next track. Applies only to the track immediately after it.

-swab

    Declare that your data is in byte-swapped (little-endian) byte order. This is not normally necessary.

tsize=n

    Set the size of the next track. Useful only if you are recording from a raw disk for which **wodim** cannot determine the file size. If you are recording from an ISO 9660 filesystem, use the **-isosize** flag instead.

-xa, -xa1, -xa2

    Write subsequent tracks in CD-ROM XA mode 2 format. **-xa1** writes in mode 2 form 1 format, and subheaders must be supplied by the application providing the data. **-xa** and **-xa2** write in mode 2 form 1 and mode 2 form 2, respectively, and subheaders are created by the drive.

write

write *user* [*tty*]

message

Initiate or respond to an interactive conversation with *user*. A **write** session is terminated with EOF. If the user is logged into more than one terminal, specify a *tty* number. See also **talk**; use **mesg** to keep other users from writing to your terminal.

xargs

xargs [*options*] [*command*]

Execute *command* (with any initial arguments), but read remaining arguments from standard input instead of specifying them directly. **xargs** passes these arguments in several bundles to the command, allowing it to process more arguments than it could normally handle at once. The arguments are typically a long list of filenames (generated by **ls** or **find**, for example) that get passed to **xargs** via a pipe. The default command is **/bin/echo**.

Options

-0, --null

    Expect filenames to be terminated by NULL instead of whitespace. Do not treat quotes or backslashes specially.

-a *file*, --arg-file=*file*

    Read arguments from *file*, not standard input.

-E *string*

    Set EOF to *string*. Default is no EOF string.

--help

Print usage information and then exit.

-I *string*

Replace all occurrences of *string* in the initial arguments with names read from standard input. Unquoted blanks are not considered argument terminators; newline character is used. Implies **-x** and **-L 1**.

-L *lines*

Allow no more than *lines* nonblank input lines on the command line (default is 1). Implies **-x**.

-n *args*, **--max-args=***args*

Allow no more than *args* arguments on the command line. Overridden by the maximum number of characters set with **-s**.

-p, **--interactive**

Prompt for confirmation (**y** or **Y**) before running each command line. Implies **-t**.

-P *max*, **--max-procs=***max*

Allow no more than *max* processes to run at once. The default is 1. A maximum of 0 allows as many as possible to run at once.

-r, **--no-run-if-empty**

Do not run command if standard input contains only blanks.

-s *max*, **--max-chars=***max*

Allow no more than *max* characters per command line.

--show-limits

Display upper and lower limits on command-line length (based on system limits, **xarg** buffer size, and **-s** if specified) before running the command.

-t, **--verbose**

Verbose mode. Print command line on standard error before executing.

-x, **--exit**

If the maximum size (as specified by **-s**) is exceeded, exit.

--version

Print the version number of **xargs** and then exit.

Examples

grep for *pattern* in all files on the system:

```
find / | xargs grep pattern> out &
```

Run **diff** on file pairs (e.g., **f1.a** and **f1.b**, **f2.a** and **f2.b**, etc.):

```
echo $* | xargs -n2 diff
```

The previous line would be invoked as a shell script, specifying filenames as arguments. Display *file*, one word per line (same as **deroff -w**):

```
cat file | xargs -n1
```

Move files in **olddir** to **newdir**, showing each command:

```
ls olddir | xargs -i -t mv olddir/{ } newdir/{ }
```

xinetd

xinetd [*options*]

TCP/IP command. The extended Internet services daemon. **xinetd** saves system resources by listening to multiple sockets on the behalf of other server programs, invoking necessary programs as requests are made for their services. Beyond this, **xinetd** provides better logging facilities, including remote user ID, access times, and server-specific information. It also provides access-control facilities. Not limited to system administration use, it can launch services that are not listed in */etc/services*. Unprivileged users can use this tool to start their own servers.

Options

-cc *num*

> Perform an internal-state consistency check every *num* seconds.

-d Turn on debugging support.

-dontfork

> Execute in the foreground. This option automatically sets the -stayalive option.

-f *file*

> Read configuration from the specified *file* instead of */etc/xinetd.conf*.

-filelog *file*

> Write log messages to the specified *file*. Cannot be combined with -syslog or -d.

-inetd_compat

> Read the */etc/inetd.conf* file after reading */etc/xinetd.conf*.

-limit *num*

> Start no more than *num* concurrent processes.

-logprocs *num*

> Limit processes used to look up remote user IDs to *num*.

-pidfile *file*

> Write **xinetd**'s process ID to *file*.

-stayalive

> Keep running even when no services have been specified.

-syslog *facility*

> Log messages to the specified **syslogd** facility. Accepted values are **daemon**, **auth**, **user**, and **local***n*, where *n* can range from 0 to 7. Cannot be combined with -syslog or -d. The default behavior is to write messages to **syslogd** using the **daemon** facility.

-version

> Print version information, then exit.

Configuration files

By default **xinetd** reads its configuration information from file */etc/xinetd.conf*. Lines in this file beginning with # are treated as comments. The entries for each service differ completely from */etc/inetd* entries. **xinetd** configuration entries for services follow the pattern:

```
service servicename
{
    attribute1 = valueset1
    attribute2 = valueset2
}
```

Some attributes allow assignment operators other than =. Other operators are +=, to add to a value set, and -=, to remove a value from a value set. There are many attributes available to control services. The following are the most common:

cps

> Limit incoming connection rate. Accepts two numeric arguments: the number of connections per second to allow and the number of seconds to wait to accept a new connection when the rate is exceeded. The default is 50 incoming connections and a 10-second wait.

disable

> Accept a Boolean **yes** or **no**. When disabled, **xinetd** will ignore the entry.

flags

> Accept a set of the following values defining **xinetd**'s behavior:

> **IDONLY**

>> Accept only connections when the remote user's ID can be verified by an identification server. Cannot be used with USERID logging.

> **INTERCEPT**

>> Intercept packets to ensure they are coming from allowed locations. Cannot be used with internal or multithreaded services.

> **IPv4**

>> Service is an IPv4 service.

> **IPv6**

>> Service is an IPv6 service.

> **KEEPALIVE**

>> Set flag on socket, enabling periodic checks to determine if the line is still receiving data.

> **NAMEINARGS**

>> Expect the first argument for the **server_args** attribute to be the command to run. This flag is necessary to wrap services with **tcpd**.

> **NODELAY**

>> Set socket's **NODELAY** flag.

> **NOLIBWRAP**

>> Don't use **xinetd**'s internal TCP wrapping facilities.

Linux
Commands

NORETRY

If service fails to fork, don't try to fork again.

SENSOR

Instead of launching a service, add IP addresses that attempt to access this service to a list of denied addresses for a time specified by the **deny_time** attribute.

group

Specify a group ID for the server process. This may be used only when **xinetd** runs as root.

nice

Set service priority. This attribute accepts the same values as the **renice** command.

id

Specify a unique identifier for the service. Useful when creating multiple entries with the *servicename*. For example, two versions of the echo service, one supporting UDP and the other TCP, might be given the identifiers **echo-stream** and **echo-dgram**.

log_on_failure

Specify values to log when a server cannot be started. Accepted values are HOST, USERID, or just ATTEMPT.

log_on_success

Specify values to log when a server is started. Accepted values are PID, HOST, USERID, EXIT, and DURATION.

no_access

Specify hosts that should not be allowed access to a service. May be given as an IP address, a netmask, a hostname, a network name from */etc/networks*, or a group of IP addresses like so: 192.168.1.{10,11,12,15,32}.

only_from

Restrict access to the service to the specified hosts. This attribute accepts the same values as **no_access**.

per_source

Specify the maximum number of instances allowed to a single source IP address. The default is "UNLIMITED".

port

Specify the service port to listen to. This attribute is required for non-RPC services not listed in */etc/services*. If the service is listed, the value of **port** cannot differ from what is listed.

protocol

Specify protocol to use, usually **tcp** or **udp**. The protocol must be listed in */etc/protocols*. This attribute is required for RPC services, as well as services not found in */etc/services*.

rpc_version

The RPC version used by the service. This can be a single number or a range of numbers from *x-y*. This attribute is required for RPC services.

rpc_number

Specify RPC ID number. This is required only for services not listed in /etc/rpc; otherwise it's ignored.

server

The program to execute for the service. When using **tcpd** to wrap a service, also set the **NAMEINARGS** flag and use the server's program name as the first argument for **server_args**. This attribute is required for all noninternal services.

server_args

Arguments to pass to the server program.

socket_type

Specify the socket type to create. Accepted values are **stream**, **dgram**, **raw**, and **seqpacket**.

type

Describe the type of service. Accepted values are **RPC**, **INTERNAL**, and **UNLISTED**.

user

Specify a user ID for the server process. This may be used only when **xinetd** runs as root.

wait

Determine whether services should be treated as single-threaded (**yes**) and **xinetd** should wait until the server exits to resume listening for new connections, or multithreaded (**no**) and **xinetd** should not wait to resume listening. This attribute is required for all serices.

Files

/etc/xinetd.conf
Default configuration file.

/etc/xinetd.d
Common directory containing configuration files included from /etc/xinetd.conf.

---

yacc

```
yacc [options] file
```

Given a *file* containing context-free grammar, convert *file* into tables for subsequent parsing, and send output to *y.tab.c*. This command name stands for **y**et **a**nother **c**ompiler-**c**ompiler. See also **flex**, **bison**, and the book *lex & yacc* (O'Reilly).

Options

-b *prefix*
Prepend *prefix*, instead of *y*, to the output file.

-d   Generate *y.tab.h*, producing **#define** statements that relate **yacc**'s token codes to the token names declared by the user.

-g   Generate a VCG description.

-l   Exclude **#line** constructs from code produced in *y.tab.c*. (Use after debugging is complete.)

-o *outfile*
> Write generated code to *outfile* instead of the default *y.tab.c.*

-p *prefix*
> Change the symbol **yacc** uses for symbols it generates from the default **yy** to *prefix*.

-t Compile runtime debugging code.

-v Generate *y.output*, a file containing diagnostics and notes about the parsing tables.

yes

yes [*strings*]

yes [*option*]

Print the command-line arguments, separated by spaces and followed by a newline, until killed. If no arguments are given, print **y** followed by a newline until killed. Useful in scripts and in the background; its output can be piped to a program that issues prompts.

Options
--help
> Print a help message and then exit.

--version
> Print version information and then exit.

ypbind

ypbind [*options*]

NFS/NIS command. NIS binder process. **ypbind** is a daemon process typically activated at system startup time. Its function is to remember information that lets client processes on a single node communicate with some **ypserv** process. The information **ypbind** remembers is called a *binding*—the association of a domain name with the Internet address of the NIS server and the port on that host at which the **ypserv** process is listening for service requests. This information is cached in the file */var/yp/binding/domainname.version.*

Options
-broadcast
> Ignore configuration information in */etc/yp.conf* and directly request configuration information from a remote system using **ypset**.

-broken-server
> Allow connections to servers using normally illegal port numbers. Sometimes needed for compatibility with other versions of **ypserv**.

-c Check configuration file for syntax errors, then exit.

-debug
> Run in the foreground process instead of detaching and running as a daemon.

-f *file*

Read configuration information from *file* instead of */etc/yp.conf*.

-no-ping

Don't ping remote servers to make sure they are alive.

--version

Print version information, then exit.

-ypset

Allow remote machine to change the local server's bindings. This option is very dangerous and should be used only for debugging the network from a remote machine.

-ypsetme

ypset requests may be issued from this machine only. Security is based on IP address checking, which can be defeated on networks on which untrusted individuals may inject packets. This option is not recommended.

---

ypcat

ypcat [*options*] *map*

NFS/NIS command. Print values in an NIS database specified by *map* name or nickname.

Options

-d *domain*

Specify *domain* other than the default domain.

-h *host*

Specify a **ypbind** *host* other than the default.

-k   Display keys for maps in which values are null or key is not part of value.

-t   Do not translate *mname* to map name.

-x   Display map nickname table listing the nicknames (*mname*s) known and map name associated with each nickname. Do not require an *mname* argument.

---

ypinit

ypinit [*options*]

NFS/NIS command. Build and install an NIS database on an NIS server. **ypinit** can be used to set up a master server, slave server, or slave copier. Only a privileged user can run **ypinit**.

Options

-m   Indicate that the local host is to be the NIS master server.

-s *master_name*

Set up a slave server database. *master_name* should be the hostname of an NIS server, either the master server for all the maps, or a server on which the database is up to date and stable.

ypmatch   ypmatch [options] key... mname

NFS/NIS command. Print value of one or more *keys* from an NIS map specified by *mname*. *mname* may be either a map name or a map nickname.

Options

-**d** *domain*
> Specify *domain* other than default domain.

-**k**   Before printing value of a key, print the key itself, followed by a colon (:).

-**t**   Do not translate nickname to map name.

-**x**   Display map nickname table listing the nicknames (*mnames*) known, and the map name associated with each nickname. Do not require an *mname* argument.

---

yppasswd   yppasswd [options] [name]

NFS/NIS command. Change login password in Network Information Service. Create or change your password, and distribute the new password over NIS. The superuser can change the password for any *user*. This command may also be invoked as **ypchfn** and **ypchsh**.

Options

-**f**   Update the password information field (the **GECOS** field). Using this option is the same as **ypchfn**.

-**l**   Update the login shell. Using this option is the same as **ypchsh**.

-**p**   Update the password. This is the default behavior for **yppasswd**.

---

yppasswdd   rpc.yppasswdd [options]

NFS/NIS command. Server for modifying the NIS password file. **yppasswdd** handles password-change requests from **yppasswd**. It changes a password entry only if the password represented by **yppasswd** matches the encrypted password of that entry and if the user ID and group ID match those in the server's */etc/passwd* file. Then it updates */etc/passwd* and the password maps on the local server. If the server was compiled with the **CHECKROOT=1** option, the password is also checked against the root password.

Options

-**D** *dir*
> Specify a directory that contains the *passwd* and *shadow* files for **rpc.yppasswdd** to use instead of */etc/passwd* and */etc/shadow*. Useful to prevent all users in the NIS database from automatically gaining access to the NIS server.

-**e** [**chsh**|**chfn**]
> Permit users to change the shell or user information in the **GECOS** field of their *passwd* entry. By default, **rpc.yppasswdd** does not permit users to change these fields.

-E *program*

> Specify a program to edit the *passwd* and *shadow* files instead of **rpc.yppasswdd**. The program should return 0 for successful completion; 1 for successful completion, but the **pwupdate** program should not be run to update the NIS server's maps; and anything else if the change failed.

-p *pwfile*

> Specify an alternative *passwd* file to */etc/passwd*, to prevent all users in the NIS database from automatically gaining access to the NIS server.

--**port** *num*

> Specify a port that **rpc.yppasswdd** will try to register itself, allowing a router to filter packets to the NIS ports.

-s *shadowfile*

> Use *shadowfile* instead of */etc/passwd* for shadow password support.

-v

> Print version information and whether the package was compiled with **CHECKROOT**.

-x *program*

> Modify files using the specified *program* instead of using internal default functions. **rpc.yppasswdd** passes information to *program* in the following format:
>
> ```
> username o:oldpassword p:password s:shell g:gcos
> ```
>
> Any of the fields **p**, **s**, or **g** may be missing.

yppoll

yppoll [*options*] *map*

NFS/NIS command. Determine version of NIS map at NIS server. **yppoll** asks a **ypserv** process for the order number and the host-name of the master NIS server for the *map*.

Options
-h *host*

> Ask the **ypserv** process at *host* about the map parameters. If *host* is not specified, the hostname of the NIS server for the local host (the one returned by **ypwhich**) is used.

-d *domain*

> Use *domain* instead of the default domain.

yppush

yppush [*options*] *mapnames*

NFS/NIS command. Force propagation of changed NIS map. **yppush** copies a new version of an NIS map, *mapname*, from the master NIS server to the slave NIS servers. It first constructs a list of NIS server hosts by reading the NIS map **ypservers** with the **-d** option's *domain* argument. Keys within this map are the ASCII names of the machines on which the NIS servers run. A map transfer request is sent to the NIS server at each host, along with the information needed by the transfer agent to call back to

Linux
Commands

yppush. When the attempt has been completed and the transfer agent has sent **yppush** a status message, the results may be printed to standard error. Normally invoked by */var/yp/Makefile* after commenting out the **NOPUSH=true** line.

Options

-d *domain*

    Specify a *domain*.

-h *host*

    Specify one or a group of systems to which a map should be transferred instead of using the list of servers in the **ypservers** map. Multiple **-h** options can be specified to create a list of hosts.

-p *count*, **--parallel** *count*

    Send maps to *count* NIS slaves simultaneously (in parallel). By default, **yppush** sends maps to one server at a time (serially).

--port *num*

    Specify a port to listen on for callbacks. This will not work when sending maps in parallel. By default, the command chooses a random port.

-t *secs*

    Specify a timeout value in seconds. The timeout determines how long **yppush** will wait for a response from a slave server before sending a map transfer request to the next server. The default timeout is 90 seconds, but for big maps a longer timeout may be needed.

-v   Verbose; print message when each server is called and for each response. Specify twice to make **yppush** even more verbose.

---

ypserv

ypserv [*options*]

NFS/NIS command. NIS server process. **ypserv** is a daemon process typically activated at system startup time. It runs only on NIS server machines with a complete NIS database. Its primary function is to look up information in its local database of NIS maps. The operations performed by **ypserv** are defined for the implementor by the NIS protocol specification, and for the programmer by the header file *<rpcvc/yp_prot.h>*. Communication to and from **ypserv** is by means of RPC calls. On startup or when receiving the signal SIGHUP, **ypserv** parses the file */etc/ypserv.conf*. **ypserv** supports **securenets**, which can be used to restrict access to a given set of hosts.

Options

-d [*path*], **--debug** [*path*]

    Run in debugging mode without going into background mode, and print extra status messages to standard error for each request. If *path* is specified, use it instead of */var/yp*.

-i *interface*, **--iface** *interface*

    Only provide service on the specified network *interface*.

-p *port*, **--port** *port*
> Bind to the specified port. For use with a router to filter packets so that access from outside hosts can be restricted.

-v, **--version**
> Print version information and exit.

Files and directories

/etc/yp.conf
> Configuration file.

/var/yp/domainname
> Location of NIS databases for *domainname*.

/var/yp/Makefile
> *Makefile* that is responsible for creating NIS databases.

/var/yp/securenets
> **securenets** information containing netmask/network pairs separated by whitespace.

---

ypset

ypset [*options*] *server*

NFS/NIS command. Point **ypbind** at a particular server. **ypset** tells **ypbind** to get NIS services for the specified domain from the **ypserv** process running on *server*. *server* indicates the NIS server to bind to and can be specified as a name or an IP address.

Options

-d *domain*
> Use *domain* instead of the default domain.

-h *host*
> Set **ypbind**'s binding on *host* instead of the local host. *host* can be specified as a name or an IP address.

---

yptest

yptest [*options*]

NFS/NIS command. Check configuration of NIS services by calling various NIS functions. Without arguments, **yptest** queries the NIS server for the local machine.

Options

-d *domainname*
> Use *domainname* instead of the current host's default domain. This option may cause some tests to fail.

-h *host*
> Test **ypserv** on the specified *host* instead of the current host. This option may cause some tests to fail.

-m *map*
> Use the specified *map* instead of the default map.

-q Quiet mode. Print no messages.

-u *user*
> Run tests as *user* instead of as nobody.

ypwhich

ypwhich [*options*] [*host*]

NFS/NIS command. Return hostname of NIS server or map master. Without arguments, **ypwhich** cites the NIS server for the local machine. If *host* is specified, that machine is queried to find out which NIS master it is using.

Options

-**d** *domain*

Use *domain* instead of the default domain.

-**m** [*map*]

Find master NIS server for a map. No host can be specified with -**m**. *map* may be a map name or a nickname for a map. If no map is specified, display a list of available maps.

-**t** *mapname*

Inhibit nickname translation.

-**V***n*

Version of **ypbind** (default is v2).

-**x** Display map nickname table. Do not allow any other options.

ypxfr

ypxfr [*options*] *mapname*

NFS/NIS command. Transfer an NIS map from the server to the local host by making use of normal NIS services. **ypxfr** creates a temporary map in the directory */var/yp/domain* (where *domain* is the default domain for the local host), fills it by enumerating the map's entries, and fetches the map parameters and loads them. If run interactively, **ypxfr** writes its output to the terminal. However, if it is invoked without a controlling terminal, its output is sent to **syslogd**.

Options

-**c** Do not send a "Clear current map" request to the local **ypserv** process.

-**C** *tid prog ipadd port*

This option is for use only by **ypserv**. When **ypserv** invokes **ypxfr**, it specifies that **ypxfr** should call back a **yppush** process at the host with IP address *ipadd*, registered as program number *prog*, listening on port *port*, and waiting for a response to transaction *tid*.

-**d** *domain*

Specify a domain other than the default domain.

-**f** Force the transfer to occur even if the version on the master server is older than the local version.

-**h** *host*

Get the map from *host* instead of querying NIS for the map's master server. *host* may be specified by name or IP address.

-p *dir*

Use *dir* as the path to the NIS map directory instead of */var/yp*.

-s *domain*

Specify a source *domain* from which to transfer a map that should be the same across domains (such as the *services.byname* map).

---

ypxfrd   rpc.ypxfrd [*options*]

NFS/NIS command. This server is used to copy a master's NIS map using an RPC based file transfer program instead of building a local map the way **ypxfr** would. This will speed up the transfer of large maps.

Options
--debug

Debug mode. Do not fork.

-d *dir*

Use *dir* instead of */var/yp*.

-p *port*

Bind to the specified *port*.

-v, --version

Print version information and exit.

---

zcat   zcat [*options*] [*files*]

Read one or more *files* that have been compressed with **gzip** or **compress** and write them to standard output. Read standard input if no *files* are specified or if - is specified as one of the files; end input with EOF. **zcat** is identical to **gunzip -c** and takes the options described for **gzip/gunzip**.

---

zcmp   zcmp [*options*] *files*

Read compressed files and pass them uncompressed to the **cmp** command, along with any command-line options. If a second file is not specified for comparison, look for a file called *file.gz*.

---

zdiff   zdiff [*options*] *files*

Read compressed files and pass them, uncompressed, to the **diff** command, along with any command-line options. If a second file is not specified for comparison, look for a file called *file.gz*.

---

zforce   zforce [*names*]

Rename all **gzip**ped files to *filename.gz*, unless file already has a *.gz* extension.

zgrep

zgrep [*options*] [*files*]

Uncompress files and pass to **grep**, along with any command-line arguments. If no files are provided, read from (and attempt to uncompress) standard input. May be invoked as **zegrep** or **zfgrep** and will in those cases invoke **egrep** or **fgrep**.

zless

zless *files*

Uncompress files and allow paging through them. Equivalent to running **zmore** with the environment variable PAGER set to **less**. See **zmore** for the available commands.

zmore

zmore [*files*]

Similar to **more**. Uncompress files and print them one screenful at a time. Works on files compressed with **compress**, **gzip**, or **pack**, and with uncompressed files. The argument *i* in the following **zmore** commands is an optional integer argument.

Commands

space
> Print next screenful.

*i***space**
> Print next *i* lines.

Return
> Print one more line.

*i***d**, *i***^D**
> Print next *i*, or 11, lines.

*i***z** Print next *i* lines or a screenful. If *i* is specified, treat it as the new window size for the rest of the current file, then revert to the default.

*i***s** Skip *i* lines, then print the next screenful.

*i***f** Skip *i* screens, then print the next screenful.

q, Q, :q, :Q
> Go to next file or, if current file is the last, exit **zmore**.

e, q
> Exit **zmore** when the prompt "--More-- (Next file: *file*)" is displayed.

s Skip next file and continue when the prompt "--More-- (Next file: *file*)" is displayed.

= Print line number.

*i***/***expr*
> Search forward for *i*th occurrence (in all files) of *expr*, which should be a regular expression. Display occurrence, including the two previous lines of context.

*i***n** Search forward for the *i*th occurrence of the last regular expression searched for.

!*command*
> Execute *command* in shell. If *command* is not specified, execute last shell command. To invoke a shell without passing it a command, enter \!.

.   Repeat the previous command.

---

znew

znew [*options*] [*files*]

Uncompress *.Z* files and recompress them in *.gz* format.

Options

-9   Optimal (and slowest) compression method.

-f   Recompress even if *filename.gz* already exists.

-K   If the original *.Z* file is smaller than the *.gz* file, keep it.

-P   Pipe data to conversion program. This saves disk space.

-t   Test new *.gz* files before removing *.Z* files.

-v   Verbose mode.

4

Boot Methods

This chapter describes techniques for booting your Linux system. Depending on your hardware and whether you want to run any other operating systems, you can configure the system to automatically boot Linux or to provide a choice between several operating systems. Choosing between operating systems is generally referred to as *dual booting*, although you can select between more than two. We talk more about dual booting in the section "Dual-Booting Linux and Windows 2000/XP/Vista" on page 536.

An alternative to dual booting is virtualization, where you run one or more virtual operating systems inside a real operating system. The real system is known as the host, and the virtual systems are known as guests. Virtualization makes it easy to switch between systems without having to reboot. Two ways to run virtual systems are to make Linux the host system with another operating system running in a virtual machine. See Chapter 15 for an overview of virtualization concepts and for information on how to run guest systems under Linux. You can also run Linux as a guest with another operating system such as Windows as the host. Two ways to do this are with Microsoft's Virtual PC and VMware server. Both are free downloads and are available at *www.microsoft.com* and *www.vmware.com*, respectively.

Once your Linux system is installed, rebooting the system is generally straightforward. There are several possibilities for configuring your boot process. The most common choices are:

- Boot Linux from a bootable disk, most likely a CD or an installation CD/DVD, leaving another operating system to boot from the hard drive.

- Use the Linux Loader, LILO. This used to be the traditional method of booting and lets you boot both Linux and other operating systems.

- Use GRUB (GRand Unified Bootloader), the GNU graphical boot loader and command shell. Like LILO, GRUB lets you boot both Linux and other operating systems. GRUB, which has additional functionality not found in LILO, is now the *de facto* Linux boot loader.

Whatever method you choose for booting, be sure to have a working boot disk available for emergency use. In particular, don't experiment with the files and options in this chapter unless you have a boot disk, because any error could leave you unable to boot from the hard disk. Note, though, that one of the advantages of using GRUB is that if there is a problem booting from the menu, it drops you down to the command-line interface so you can enter commands directly and try to recover. In addition, your distribution CD or DVD undoubtedly has a recovery option on it. Or you can boot from a live Linux CD such as Knoppix.

The Boot Process

On an x86-based PC, the first sector of every hard disk is known as the *boot sector* and contains the partition table for that disk and possibly also code for booting an operating system. The boot sector of the first hard disk is known as the *master boot record* (MBR), because when you boot the system, the BIOS transfers control to a program that lives on that sector along with the partition table. That code is the *boot loader*, the code that initiates an operating system. When you add Linux to the system, you need to modify the boot loader, replace it, or boot from a floppy or CD to start Linux.

In Linux, each disk and each partition on the disk is treated as a device. For example, the entire first hard disk is known as */dev/hda*, and the entire second hard disk is */dev/hdb*. The first partition of the first hard drive is */dev/hda1*, and the second partition is */dev/hda2*. The first partition of the second hard drive is */dev/hdb1*, and so on. If your drives are SCSI or SATA instead of IDE, the naming works the same way, except that the devices are */dev/sda*, */dev/sda1*, and so on. Thus, if you want to specify that the Linux partition is the second partition of the first hard drive (as in the examples in this chapter), you refer to it as */dev/hda2*. Note that GRUB has its own disk naming convention, described later in this chapter in "GRUB: The Grand Unified Bootloader" on page 516.

Once you've made the decision to install LILO or GRUB, you still need to decide how it should be configured. Most Linux distributions will automatically set up the booting environment for you, whether you are installing Linux as the primary operating system or into a dual-booting environment (or in a virtual guest system where the real MBR is not modified). If for some reason your distribution doesn't do it for you, or you want to do it manually, the rest of this chapter will help you. If your distribution does set up the boot environment for you, you might still want to read the sections on LILO or GRUB to find out how the customize your boot loader.

If you want your system to dual-boot Linux and Windows, you need to know that Windows has its own loader installed on the MBR, and it expects that loader to be in charge. The standard solution described in this chapter is to add Linux as an option in the Windows loader and install LILO or GRUB in the Linux partition as a secondary boot loader. The result is that the Windows loader transfers control to the secondary loader, which then boots Linux. See "Dual-Booting Linux and Windows 2000/XP/Vista" on page 536 for more information. You can also install one of the Linux boot loaders in the MBR and use it to boot Windows. (See the "Linux+WinNT" and the "Multiboot with GRUB" mini-HOWTOs at the Linux Documentation Project [*www.tldp.org*] if you're interested in doing that.)

When you install the boot loader (either LILO or GRUB) on the MBR, it replaces the Windows boot loader. If you have problems with your installation or you simply want to restore the original boot loader, you can do one of the following:

- If you're running LILO, you can boot Linux from a boot disk (CD or floppy) and restore the boot sector, which LILO automatically backs up:

  ```
  $ /sbin/lilo -u
  ```

- For Windows 2000, XP, and Vista, boot your computer from the Windows CD. When you see "Welcome to Setup," press R (for repair) and, in Windows 2000, then press C. Select your Windows installation from the numbered list that is displayed (there may be only one entry) and enter the administrator password at the prompt. Enter the command **fixmbr** at the command-line prompt and confirm it with **y**. After the MBR has been restored, type **exit** to reboot.

The common element in both methods is that they replace the boot loader on the MBR with the original Microsoft boot loader.

Whatever boot loader is on the MBR is the one that will be used to boot the system. This means that if you want to switch from LILO to GRUB, say, or from GRUB to LILO, you don't need to uninstall the old loader; simply install the new one.

The rest of this chapter describes the various techniques for booting Linux and the options that you can specify to configure both the boot loader and the Linux kernel. Whether you use GRUB or LILO, you can pass options to the loader and specify options for the kernel.

LILO: The Linux Loader

In addition to booting Linux, LILO can boot other operating systems, such as Windows or any of the BSD systems. During installation, some Linux distributions provide the opportunity to install LILO (most now install GRUB by default). LILO can also be installed later if necessary. LILO can be installed on the MBR of your hard drive or as a secondary boot loader on the Linux partition. LILO consists of several pieces, including the boot loader itself, a configuration file (*/etc/lilo.conf*), a map file (*/boot/map*) containing the location of the kernel, and the **lilo** command (*/sbin/lilo*), which reads the configuration file and uses the information to create or update the map file and to install the files LILO needs.

One thing to remember about LILO is that it has two aspects: the boot loader and the **lilo** command. The **lilo** command configures and installs the boot loader and updates it as necessary. The boot loader is the code that executes at system boot time and boots Linux or another operating system.

You can make a rescue CD for LILO with the LILO command **mkrescue --iso** to make an image that can be burned to CD. Use **mkrescue** by itself or with other options to make a rescue floppy disk. See the **mkrescue** manpage for more information.

The LILO Configuration File

The **lilo** command reads the LILO configuration file, */etc/lilo.conf*, to get the information it needs to install LILO. Among other things, it builds a map file containing the locations of all disk sectors needed for booting.

Note that any time you change */etc/lilo.conf* or rebuild or move a kernel image, you need to rerun **lilo** to rebuild the map file and update LILO.

The configuration file starts with a section of global options, described in the next section. Global options are those that apply to every system boot, regardless of the operating system you are booting. Here is an example of a global section (a hash sign, #, begins a comment):

```
boot=/dev/hda        # The boot device is /dev/hda
map=/boot/map        # Save the map file as /boot/map
install=/boot/boot.b # The file to install as the new boot sector
prompt               # Always display the boot prompt
timeout=30           # Set a 3-second (30 tenths of a second) timeout
```

Following the global section, there is one section of options for each Linux kernel and for each non-Linux operating system that you want LILO to be able to boot. Each of these sections is referred to as an *image* section because each boots a different kernel image (shorthand for a binary file containing a kernel) or another operating system. Each Linux image section begins with an **image=** line.

```
image=/boot/vmlinuz  # Linux image file
  label=linux        # Label that appears at the boot prompt
  root=/dev/hda2     # Location of the root filesystem
  vga=ask            # Always prompt the user for VGA mode
  read-only          # Mount read-only to run fsck for a filesystem check
```

The equivalent section for a non-Linux operating system begins with **other=** instead of **image=**. For example:

```
other=/dev/hda1      # Location of the partition
  label=winxp
  table=/dev/hda     # Location of the partition table
```

Put LILO configuration options that apply to all images into the global section of */etc/lilo.conf*, and options that apply to a particular image into the section for that image. If an option is specified in both the global section and an image section, the setting in the image section overrides the global setting for that image.

Here is an example of a complete */etc/lilo.conf* file for a system that has the Linux partition on */dev/hda2*:

```
## Global section
boot=/dev/hda2
map=/boot/map
delay=30
timeout=50
prompt
vga=ask
```

```
## Image section: For regular Linux
image=/boot/vmlinuz
  label=linux
  root=/dev/hda2
  install=/boot/boot.b
  map=/boot/map
  read-only

## Image section: For testing a new Linux kernel
image=/testvmlinuz
  label=testlinux
  root=/dev/hda2
  install=/boot/boot.b
  map=/boot/map
  read-only
  optional                  # Omit image if not available when map is built

## Image section: For booting Windows XP
other=/dev/hda1
  label=winxp
  loader=/boot/chain.b
  table=/dev/hda            # The current partition table
```

Global options

In addition to the options listed here, the kernel options **append**, **read-only**, **read-write**, **root**, and **vga** (described later in "Kernel options" on page 513) can also be set as global options.

backup=*backup-file*

Copy the original boot sector to *backup-file* instead of to */boot/boot.nnnn*, where *nnnn* is a number that depends on the disk device type.

boot=*boot-device*

Set the name of the device that contains the boot sector. **boot** defaults to the device currently mounted as root, such as */dev/hda2*. Specifying a device such as */dev/hda* (without a number) indicates that LILO should be installed in the master boot record; the alternative is to set it up on a particular partition, such as */dev/hda2*.

change-rules

Begin a section that redefines partition types at boot time for hiding and unhiding partitions. See the LILO User's Guide, which comes with the LILO distribution, for detailed information on using this option and creating a new rule set.

compact

Merge read requests for adjacent disk sectors to speed up booting. Use of **compact** is particularly recommended when booting from a floppy disk. Use of **compact** may conflict with **linear**.

default=*name*

Use the image *name* as the default boot image. If **default** is omitted, the first image specified in the configuration file is used.

delay=*tsecs*

Specify, in tenths of a second, how long the boot loader should wait before booting the default image. If **serial** is set, **delay** is set to a minimum of 20. The default is not to wait. See "Boot-Time Kernel Options" on page 539 for ways to get the boot prompt if no delay is set.

disk=*device-name*

Define parameters for the disk specified by *device-name* if LILO can't figure them out. Normally, LILO can determine the disk parameters itself, and this option isn't needed. When **disk** is specified, it is followed by one or more parameter lines, such as:

```
disk=/dev/sda
  bios=0x80      # First disk is usually 0x80, second is usually 0x81
  sectors=...
  heads=...
```

Note that this option is not the same as the disk geometry parameters you can specify with the **hd** boot command-line option. With **disk**, the information is given to LILO; with **hd**, it is passed to the kernel. Note also that if either **heads** or **sectors** is specified, they must both be specified. The parameters that can be specified with **disk** are listed briefly here; they are described in detail in the LILO User's Guide.

bios=*bios-device-code*

The number the BIOS uses to refer to the device. See the previous example.

cylinders=*cylinders*

The number of cylinders on the disk.

heads=*heads*

The number of heads on the disk.

inaccessible

Tell LILO that the BIOS can't read the disk; used to prevent the system from becoming unbootable if LILO thinks the BIOS can read it. If this parameter is specified, it must be the only parameter.

partition=*partition-device*

Start a new section for a partition. The section contains one variable, **start**=*partition-offset*, which specifies the zero-based number of the first sector of the partition:

```
partition=/dev/sda1
  start=2048
```

sectors=*sectors*

The number of sectors per track.

disktab=*disktab-file*

This option has been superseded by the **disk**= option.

fix-table

If set, allow **lilo** to adjust 3-D addresses (addresses specified as sector/head/cylinder) in partition tables. This is sometimes necessary if a partition isn't track-aligned and another operating system is on the same disk. See the *lilo.conf* manpage for details.

force-backup=*backup-file*

Like **backup**, but overwrite an old backup copy if one exists.

ignore-table

Tell **lilo** to ignore corrupt partition tables.

install=*boot-sector*

Install the specified file as the new boot sector. If **install** is omitted, the boot sector defaults to */boot/boot.b*.

lba32

Generate 32-bit Logical Block Addresses instead of sector/head/cylinder addresses, allowing booting from any partition on hard disks greater than 8.4 GB (i.e., remove the 1024-cylinder limit). Requires BIOS support for the EDD packet call interface* and at least LILO version 21–4.

linear

Generate linear sector addresses, which do not depend on disk geometry, instead of 3-D (sector/head/cylinder) addresses. If LILO can't determine your disk's geometry itself, you can try using **linear**; if that doesn't work, then you need to specify the geometry with **disk=**. Note, however, that **linear** sometimes doesn't work with floppy disks, and it may conflict with **compact**.

lock

Tell LILO to record the boot command line and use it as the default for future boots until it is overridden by a new boot command line. **lock** is useful if there are kernel options that you need to enter on the boot command line every time you boot the system.

map=*map-file*

Specify the location of the map file. Defaults to */boot/map*. The map file records the location of the kernel(s) used on the system.

message=*message-file*

Specify a file containing a message to be displayed before the boot prompt. The message can include a formfeed character (**Ctrl-L**) to clear the screen. The map file must be rebuilt by rerunning the **lilo** command if the message file is changed or moved. The maximum length of the file is 65,535 bytes.

nowarn

Disable warning messages.

optional

Specify that any image that is not available when the map is created should be omitted and not offered as an option at the boot prompt. Like the per-image option **optional**, but applies to all images.

password=*password*

Specify a password that the user is prompted to enter when trying to load an image. The password is not encrypted in the configuration file, so if passwords are used, permissions should be set so that only the superuser is able to read the file. This option is like the per-image version, except that all images are password-protected and they all have the same password.

---

* As long as your BIOS is dated after 1998, it should include EDD packet call interface support.

prompt

Automatically display the boot prompt without waiting for the user to press the Shift, Alt, or Scroll Lock key. Note that setting **prompt** without also setting **timeout** prevents unattended reboots.

restricted

Can be used with **password** to indicate that a password needs to be entered only if the user specifies parameters on the command line. Like the per-image **restricted** option, but applies to all images.

serial=*parameters*

Allow the boot loader to accept input from a serial line as well as from the keyboard. Sending a break on the serial line corresponds to pressing a Shift key on the console to get the boot loader's attention. All boot images should be password-protected if serial access is insecure (e.g., if the line is connected to a modem). Setting **serial** automatically raises the value of **delay** to 20 (i.e., two seconds) if it is less than that. The parameter string *parameters* has the following syntax:

```
port[,bps[parity[bits]]]
```

For example, to initialize COM1 with the default parameters:

```
serial=0,2400n8
```

The parameters are:

port

The port number of the serial port. The default is 0, which corresponds to COM1 (*/dev/ttys0*). The value can be one of 0 through 3, for the four possible COM ports.

bps

The baud rate of the serial port. Possible values of *bps* are **110**, **300**, **1200**, **2400**, **4800**, **9600**, **19200**, **38400**, **57600**, and **115200**. The default is 2400 bps.

parity

The parity used on the serial line. Parity is specified as **n** or **N** for no parity, **e** or **E** for even parity, and **o** or **O** for odd parity. However, the boot loader ignores input parity and strips the 8th bit.

bits

Specify whether a character contains 7 or 8 bits. Default is 8 with no parity and 7 otherwise.

timeout=*tsecs*

Set a timeout (specified in tenths of a second) for keyboard input. If no key has been pressed after the specified time, the default image is booted automatically. **timeout** is also used to determine when to stop waiting for password input. The default timeout is infinite.

verbose=*level*

Turn on verbose output, where higher values of *level* produce more output. If **-v** is also specified on the **lilo** command line, the level is incremented by 1 for each occurrence of **-v**. The maximum verbosity level is 5.

Image options

The following options are specified in the image section for a particular boot image. The image can be a Linux kernel or a non-Linux operating system.

alias=*name*

Provide an alternate name for the image that can be used instead of the name specified with the **label** option.

image=*pathname*

Specify the file or device containing the boot image of a bootable Linux kernel. Each per-image section that specifies a bootable Linux kernel starts with an **image** option. See also the **range** option.

label=*name*

Specify the name that is used for the image at the boot prompt. Defaults to the filename of the image file (without the path).

loader=*chainloader*

For a non-Linux operating system, specify the chain loader to which LILO should pass control for booting that operating system. The default is */boot/ chain.b*. If the system will be booted from a drive that is neither the first hard disk nor a floppy or CD, the chainloader must be specified.

lock

Like **lock**, as described in the previous global options section; it can also be specified in an image section.

optional

Specify that the image should be omitted if it is not available when the map is created by the **lilo** command. Useful for specifying test kernels that are not always present.

other=*pathname*

Specify the path to a file that boots a non-Linux system. Each per-image section that specifies a bootable non-Linux system starts with an **other** option.

password=*password*

Specify that the image is password-protected and provide the password that the user is prompted for when booting. The password is not encrypted in the configuration file, so if passwords are used, permissions should be set so only the superuser can read the file.

range=*sectors*

Used with the **image** option, when the image is specified as a device (e.g., **image**=*/dev/fd0*), to indicate the range of sectors to be mapped into the map file. *sectors* can be given as the range *start-end* or as *start+number*, where *start* and *end* are zero-based sector numbers and *number* is the increment beyond *start* to include. If only *start* is specified, only that one sector is mapped. For example:

```
image=/dev/fd0
range=1+512   # take 512 sectors, starting with sector 1
```

restricted

Specify that a password is required for booting the image only if boot parameters are specified on the command line.

---

table=*device*

Specify, for a non-Linux operating system, the device that contains the partition table. If **table** is omitted, the boot loader does not pass partition information to the operating system being booted. Note that */sbin/lilo* must be rerun if the partition table is modified. This option cannot be used with **unsafe**.

unsafe

Can be used in the per-image section for a non-Linux operating system to indicate that the boot sector should not be accessed when the map is created. If **unsafe** is specified, then some checking isn't done, but the option can be useful for running the **lilo** command without having to insert a floppy disk when the boot sector is on a fixed-format floppy disk device. This option cannot be used with **table**.

Kernel options

The following kernel options can be specified in */etc/lilo.conf* as well as on the boot command line:

append=*string*

Append the options specified in *string* to the parameter line passed to the kernel. This typically is used to specify certain hardware parameters. For example, while BIOSes on modern systems can recognize more than 64 MB of memory, BIOSes on older systems were limited to 64 MB. If you are running Linux on such a system, you can use **append**:

```
append="mem=128M"
```

initrd=*filename*

Specify the file to load into */dev/initrd* when booting with a RAM disk. See also the options **load_ramdisk** (in "Boot-Time Kernel Options" on page 539) and **prompt_ramdisk**, **ramdisk_size**, and **ramdisk_start** in this section.

literal=*string*

Like **append**, but replace all other kernel boot options.

noinitrd

Preserve the contents of */dev/initrd* so they can be read after the kernel is booted.

prompt_ramdisk=*n*

Specify whether the kernel should prompt you to insert the floppy disk that contains the RAM disk image, for use during Linux installation. Values of *n* are:

0   Don't prompt. Usually used for an installation in which the kernel and the RAM disk image both fit on one floppy.

1   Prompt. This is the default.

ramdisk_size=*n*

Specify the amount of memory, in kilobytes, to be allocated for the RAM disk. The default is 4096, which allocates 4 MB.

ramdisk_start=*offset*

Used for a Linux installation in which both the kernel and the RAM disk image are on the same floppy. *offset* indicates the offset on the floppy where the RAM disk image begins; it is specified in kilobytes.

read-only

Specify that the root filesystem should be mounted read-only for filesystem checking (**fsck**), after which it is typically remounted read/write.

read-write

Specify that the root filesystem should be mounted read/write.

root=*root-device*

Specify the device that should be mounted as root. If the special name **current** is used as the value, the root device is set to the device on which the root filesystem currently is mounted. Defaults to the root-device setting contained in the kernel image.

vga=*mode*

Specify the VGA text mode that should be selected when booting. The mode defaults to the VGA mode setting in the kernel image. The values are case-insensitive. They are:

ask

Prompt the user for the text mode. Pressing Enter in response to the prompt displays a list of the available modes.

extended *(or* **ext***)*

Select 80×50 text mode.

normal

Select normal 80×25 text mode.

number

Use the text mode that corresponds to *number*. A list of available modes for your video card can be obtained by booting with **vga=ask** and pressing Enter.

The lilo Command

You need to run the **lilo** command to install the LILO boot loader and to update it whenever the kernel changes or to reflect changes to */etc/lilo.conf*. Note that if you replace your kernel image without rerunning **lilo**, your system may be unable to boot.

The path to the **lilo** command is usually */sbin/lilo*. The syntax of the command is:

```
lilo [options]
```

Some of the options correspond to */etc/lilo.conf* keywords:

Configuration keyword	Command option
boot=*bootdev*	**-b** *bootdev*
compact	**-c**
delay=*tsecs*	**-d** *tsecs*
default=*label*	**-D** *label*
disktab=*file*	**-f** *file*
install=*bootsector*	**-i** *bootsector*
lba32	**-L**

Configuration keyword	Command option
linear	-l
map=*mapfile*	-m *mapfile*
fix-table	-P fix
ignore-table	-P ignore
backup=*file*	-s *file*
force-backup=*file*	-S *file*
verbose=*level*	-v

These options should be put in the configuration file whenever possible; putting them on the **lilo** command line instead of in */etc/lilo.conf* is deprecated. The next section describes those options that can be given only on the **lilo** command line; the others were described earlier.

lilo Command Options

The following list describes **lilo** command options that are available only on the command line. Multiple options are given separately; for example:

```
$ lilo -q -v
```

-C *config-file*
Specify an alternative to the default configuration file (*/etc/lilo.conf*). **lilo** uses the configuration file to determine which files to map when it installs LILO.

-I *label*
Print the path to the kernel specified by *label* to standard output, or an error message if no matching label is found. For example:

```
$ lilo -I linux
/boot/vmlinuz-2.0.34-0.6
```

-q
List the currently mapped files. **lilo** maintains a file (*/boot/map* by default) containing the name and location of the kernel(s) to boot. Running **lilo** with this option prints the names of the files in the map file to standard output, as in this example (the asterisk indicates that **linux** is the default):

```
$ lilo -q
linux     *
test
```

-r *root-directory*
Specify that before doing anything else, **lilo** should **chroot** to the indicated directory. Used for repairing a setup from a boot CD or floppy; you can boot from that disk but have **lilo** use the boot files from the hard drive. For example, if you issue the following commands, **lilo** will get the files it needs from the hard drive:

```
$ mount /dev/hda2 /mnt
$ lilo -r /mnt
```

-R *command-line*
Set the default command for the boot loader the next time it executes. The command executes once and then is removed by the boot loader. This option typically is used in reboot scripts, just before calling **shutdown -r**.

Boot Methods

-t   Indicate that this is a test—do not really write a new boot sector or map file. Can be used with **-v** to find out what **lilo** would do during a normal run.

-u *device-name*

Uninstall **lilo** by restoring the saved boot sector from */boot/boot.nnnn*, after validating it against a timestamp. *device-name* is the name of the device on which LILO is installed, such as */dev/hda2*.

-U *device-name*

Like **-u**, but do not check the timestamp.

-V   Print the **lilo** version number.

LILO Boot Errors

As LILO loads itself, it displays the letters of the word LILO, one at a time as it proceeds. Once LILO is correctly loaded, you'll see the full word printed on the screen. If nothing prints, then LILO has not been loaded at all; most likely LILO isn't installed or it is installed, but on a partition that is not active. If LILO started loading, but there was a problem, you can see how far it got by how many letters printed:

L   The first stage boot loader is loaded and running, but it can't load the second stage. There should be an error code indicating the type of problem; usually the problem is a media failure or bad disk parameters. See the LILO User's Guide for the meaning of the error codes.

LI   The first stage boot loader loaded the second stage but was not able to run it. The problem is most likely bad disk parameters or the file */boot/boot.b* (the boot sector) was moved but the **lilo** command wasn't run.

LIL

The second stage boot loader was run, but it couldn't load the descriptor table from the map file. This is usually caused by a media failure or bad disk parameters.

LIL?

The second stage boot loader was loaded at an incorrect address, probably because of bad disk parameters or by moving */boot/boot.b* without running **lilo**.

LIL-

The descriptor table is corrupt. The problem is probably bad disk parameters or moving */boot/map* without running **lilo**.

LILO

LILO was successfully loaded.

GRUB: The Grand Unified Bootloader

Like LILO, the GRUB boot loader can load other operating systems in addition to Linux. GRUB has become the default bootloader for most Linux variants. It was written by Erich Boleyn to boot operating systems on PC-based hardware and is now developed and maintained by the GNU project. GRUB was intended to boot operating systems that conform to the Multiboot Specification, which was designed to create one booting method that would work on any conforming PC-based operating system. In addition to multiboot-conforming systems, GRUB can boot directly into Linux, FreeBSD, OpenBSD, and NetBSD. It can also boot other operating systems such as Microsoft Windows indirectly, through the use of a *chainloader*. The chainloader loads an intermediate file, and that file loads the operating system's boot loader.

GRUB provides a graphical menu interface. It also provides a command interface that is accessible both while the system is booting (the native command environment) and from the command line once Linux is running.

While LILO works perfectly well, especially if you usually boot the default image, GRUB has some advantages. The graphical menu interface shows you exactly what your choices are for booting, so you don't have to remember them. It also lets you easily edit an entry on the fly, or drop down into the command interface. In addition, if you are using the menu interface and something goes wrong, GRUB automatically puts you into the command interface so you can attempt to recover and boot manually. Another advantage of GRUB is that if you install a new kernel or update the configuration file, that's all you have to do; with LILO, you also have to remember to rerun the **lilo** command to reinstall the boot loader. On the other hand, if you are used to LILO, don't need to see the prompts often, and have a stable system, LILO is quick and convenient.

A GRUB installation consists of at least two and sometimes three executables, known as stages. The stages are:

Stage 1
> Stage 1 is the piece of GRUB that resides in the MBR or the boot sector of another partition or drive. Since the main portion of GRUB is too large to fit into the 512 bytes of a boot sector, Stage 1 is used to transfer control to the next stage, either Stage 1.5 or Stage 2.

Stage 1.5
> Stage 1.5 is loaded by Stage 1 only if the hardware requires it. Stage 1.5 is filesystem-specific; that is, there is a different version for each filesystem that GRUB can load. The name of the filesystem is part of the filename (*e2fs_stage1_5*, *fat_stage1_5*, etc.). Stage 1.5 loads Stage 2.

Stage 2
> Stage 2 runs the main body of the GRUB code. It displays the menu, lets you select the operating system to be run, and starts the system you've chosen.

If it was compiled with netboot support, GRUB can also be used to boot over a network. We don't describe that process here; see the file *netboot/README.netboot* in the GRUB source directory for detailed information.

One of the first things to understand about GRUB is that it uses its own naming conventions. Drives are numbered starting from 0; thus, the first hard drive is hd0, the second hard drive is hd1, the first floppy drive is fd0, and so on. Partitions are also numbered from 0, and the entire name is put in parentheses. For example, the first partition of the first drive, */dev/hda1*, is known as (hd0,0) to GRUB, and the third partition of the second drive is (hd1,2). GRUB makes no distinction between drive types; thus the first drive is hd0 regardless of whether it is IDE, SCSI, or SATA.

Files are specified either by the filename or by *blocklist*, which is used to specify files such as chainloaders that aren't part of a filesystem. A filename looks like a standard Unix path specification with the GRUB device name prepended; for example:

```
(hd0,0)/grub/grub.conf
```

If the device name is omitted, the GRUB root device is assumed. The GRUB root device is the disk or partition where the kernel image is stored, set with the **root** command. See "GRUB Commands" on page 525 for the command descriptions.

When you use blocklist notation, you tell GRUB which blocks on the disk contain the file you want. Each section of a file is specified as the offset on the partition where the block begins plus the number of blocks in the section. The offset starts at 0 for the first block on the partition. The syntax for blocklist notation is:

```
[device][offset]+length[,offset]+length...
```

In this case, too, the device name is optional for a file on the root device. With blocklist notation, you can also omit the offset if it is 0. A typical use of blocklist notation is when using a chainloader to boot Windows. If GRUB is installed in the MBR, you can chainload Windows by setting the root device to the partition that has the Windows boot loader, making it the active partition, and then using the **chainloader** command to read the Windows boot sector:

```
rootnoverify (hd0,0)
makeactive
chainloader +1
```

In this example, the blocklist notation (+1) does not include either the device name or the offset because we set the root device to the Windows partition, and the Windows loader begins at offset 0 of that partition.

GRUB also includes a *device map*. The device map is an ASCII file, usually */boot/ grub/device.map*. Since the operating system isn't loaded yet when you use GRUB to boot Linux (or any other operating system), GRUB knows only the BIOS drive names. The purpose of the device map is to map the BIOS drives to Linux devices. For example:

```
(fd0)    /dev/fd0
(hd0)    /dev/hda
```

Installing GRUB

Installing GRUB involves two stages. First, you install the GRUB files on your system, either by compiling and installing the source tarball or from a package. That puts the GRUB files in the correct locations on your system. The second step is to install the GRUB software as your boot manager. This is the step we describe in this section.

If you installed GRUB as part of your Linux installation, the distribution's installation program took care of both stages of installing GRUB, and you'll see the GRUB menu when you boot Linux. If you didn't install GRUB as part of your Linux installation, you have two choices. The easiest way to install GRUB is with the **grub-install** shell script that comes with GRUB. If **grub-install** doesn't work, or if you want to do the installation manually, you can run the **grub** command and issue the installation commands yourself.

The following sections describe how to create a GRUB boot CD, a GRUB boot floppy, and how to install GRUB. You can create a GRUB boot disk for everyday use or to have for an emergency.

Creating a GRUB boot CD

The following instructions make a CD that boots to GRUB:

1. Make a directory that will hold the GRUB iso image to be written to CD:

   ```
   $ mkdir -p grubiso/boot/grub     # make parent dirs if needed
   ```

2. Copy the file *stage2_eltorito** to the new directory from the directory where GRUB was installed (in this example */usr/lib/grub/x86_64-pc*):

   ```
   $ cp /usr/lib/grub/x86_64-pc grubiso/boot/grub
   ```

   You can move other files to the directory as well, such as *menu.lst* to display the menu when you boot.

3. Run **genisoimage** to make an ISO9660 image file, *grub.iso*:

   ```
   $ genisoimage -R -b boot/grub/stage2_eltorito -no-emul-boot \
   -boot-load-size 4 -boot-info-table -o grub.iso grubiso
   ```

   This command takes the contents of *grubiso/boot/grub* (only the top of the directory tree needs to be specified) and makes the image file *grub.iso*. See the **genisoimage** command in Chapter 3 for information on the options.

4. The image file can now be burned onto a CD (or DVD) with the burning software of your choice.

Creating a GRUB boot floppy

The following instructions make a floppy that boots to the GRUB command line:

1. From the directory where GRUB was installed (e.g., */usr/share/grub/i386-pc*), use the **dd** command to write the file *stage1* to the floppy:

   ```
   $ dd if=stage1 of=/dev/fd0 bs=512 count=1
   ```

   This command writes one block, with a block size of 512, from the input file *stage1* to the floppy device */dev/fd0*.

2. Now write the file *stage2* to the floppy, skipping over the first block (**seek=1**) so you don't overwrite *stage1*:

   ```
   $ dd if=stage2 of=/dev/fd0 bs=512 seek=1
   ```

Put together, the process looks like this:

```
$ dd if=stage1 of=/dev/fd0 bs=512 count=1
1+0 records in
1+0 records out
$ dd if=stage2 of=/dev/fd0 bs=512 seek=1
254+1 records in
254+1 records out
```

---

* El Torito is a specification that lets you create a bootable CD.

The boot floppy is now ready to boot to the GRUB command line.

You can also make a boot floppy that boots to the GRUB menu:

1. Create a GRUB configuration file (*/boot/grub/menu.lst*) if you don't already have one. The configuration file is described later in "The GRUB Configuration File" on page 521.

2. Create a filesystem on your floppy disk. For example:

   ```
   $ mke2fs /dev/fd0
   ```

3. Mount the floppy drive and create the directory */boot/grub*:

   ```
   $ mount /mnt
   $ mkdir /mnt/boot
   $ mkdir /mnt/boot/grub
   ```

4. Copy the *stage1*, *stage2*, and *grub.conf* GRUB images from */boot/grub* on your Linux partition to */mnt/boot/grub*.

5. Run the **grub** command. This example assumes the command is in */sbin/grub*, but it might be in */usr/sbin/grub* on your system:

   ```
   $ /sbin/grub --batch <<EOT
   root (fd0)
   setup (fd0)
   quit
   EOT
   ```

You should now be able to boot to the GRUB menu from the floppy disk you just created.

Using grub-install

GRUB comes with a shell script, **grub-install**, which uses the GRUB shell to automate the installation. The command syntax is:

```
grub-install options install-device
```

where *install-device* is the name of the device on which you want to install GRUB, specified as either the GRUB device name (e.g., (hd0)) or the system device (e.g., */dev/hda*). For example, you might issue the following command (as root):

```
$ grub-install /dev/hda
```

This command installs GRUB into the MBR of the first hard drive. The **grub-install** options are:

--force-lba
> Force GRUB to use LBA mode, to allow booting from partitions beyond cylinder 1024.

--grub-shell=*file*
> Specify that *file* is to be used as the GRUB shell. You might want to use this option to append options to **grub**. For example:

   ```
   $ grub-install --grub-shell="grub --read-only" /dev/fd0
   ```

-h, --help
> Print a help message on standard output and exit.

--recheck

Force probing of a device map. You should run **grub-install** with this option if you add or remove a disk from your system. The device map is found at */boot/grub/device.map*.

--root-directory=*dir*

Install GRUB images in the directory *dir* instead of the GRUB root directory.

-v, --version

Print the GRUB version number to standard output and exit.

Installing from the GRUB command line

To install GRUB from the native command environment, make a GRUB boot disk as described previously. You will use that disk to boot to the GRUB command line to do the installation. If you know which partition holds the GRUB files, you're all set. Otherwise, you can find the partition with the **find** command:

```
grub> find /boot/grub/stage1
(hd0,0)
```

Here, the files are on (hd0,0). Use that information to set the GRUB root device:

```
grub> root (hd0,0)
```

Run the **setup** command to install GRUB. To install GRUB on the MBR, run **setup** as follows:

```
grub> setup (hd0)
```

If you are going to chainload Linux and want to install GRUB on the boot sector of the Linux partition, run **setup** like this:

```
grub> setup (hd0,0)
```

The GRUB Configuration File

GRUB uses a configuration file that sets up the menu interface. The configuration file is called *menu.lst* and is found with the other GRUB files in the */boot/grub* directory. In some distributions (e.g., Fedora and Red Hat) the configuration file is called *grub.conf*, which is a symbolic link to *menu.lst*.

The configuration file begins with a section containing global commands that apply to all boot entries, followed by an entry for each Linux image or other operating system that you want to be able to boot. Here is an example of a global section (a hash sign, #, begins a comment):

```
default=0                              # default to the first entry
timeout=20                             # set the timeout to 20 seconds
splashimage=(hd0,0)/grub/splash.xpm.gz  # the splash image displayed with
                                       # the menu
```

Certain GRUB commands are available only in the global section of the configuration file, for use with the GRUB menu. These commands are described in the following list. All other commands can be used either in the configuration file or on the command line and are described later in "GRUB Commands" on page 525.

default *num*

Set the default menu entry to *num*. The default entry is started if the user does not make a selection before the timeout time. Menu entries are numbered from 0. If no default is specified, the first entry (0) is used as the default.

fallback *num*

Specify the entry to be used if for any reason the default entry has errors. If this command is specified and the default doesn't work, GRUB boots the fallback entry automatically instead of waiting for user input.

hiddenmenu

Specify that the menu is not to be displayed. The user can press Esc before the end of the timeout period to have the menu displayed; otherwise, the default entry is booted at the end of the timeout.

timeout *time*

Specify the timeout period, in seconds. The timeout is the amount of time GRUB waits for user input before booting the default entry.

title *name*

Start a new boot entry with specified *name*.

Following the global section, the configuration file includes an entry for each boot image. An entry begins with a **title** command that specifies the text that will appear on the menu for that entry when the system boots. A typical boot entry might look like this:

```
title Linux 2.6.28
root (hd0,1)
kernel /vmlinuz-2.6.28 ro root=LABEL=/
initrd /initrd-2.6.28
```

This entry provides the information GRUB needs to boot to Linux. When the menu is displayed, it will include an entry that says:

```
Linux 2.6.28
```

The GRUB root is on the second partition of the first hard drive (hd0,1). The **kernel** command specifies which Linux kernel to run and passes some parameters to the kernel, and the **initrd** command sets up an initial RAM disk.

The configuration file also provides some security features, such as the ability to set passwords and to lock certain entries so only the root user can boot them. The configuration file can be set up so that a password is required to run interactively (i.e., for editing menu entries or using the command interface) or simply to protect certain menu entries while leaving other entries available to all users. See the explanation of the **password** and **lock** commands in "GRUB Commands" on page 525.

In addition to providing a password feature, GRUB provides the command **md5crypt** to encrypt passwords in MD5 format, and a corresponding Linux command, **grub-md5-crypt**. **grub-md5-crypt** is a shell script that acts as a frontend to the **grub** shell, calling **md5crypt**. Passwords encrypted either directly with **md5crypt** or with **grub-md5-crypt** can be used with the **password** command to set up a GRUB password. **grub-md5-crypt** has three possible options:

--help
   Print help message and exit.

--grub-shell=_file_
   Specify that _file_ is to be used as the GRUB shell.

--version
   Print version information and exit.

Using the Menu Interface

The most common way to use GRUB is with the menu interface. The Stage 2 loader reads the configuration file _menu.lst_ and displays the menu. If a timeout is set in the configuration file, GRUB displays a countdown at the bottom of the window showing how much time is left before it boots to the default entry. Move the cursor to an entry and press Enter to boot; or, press **e** to edit the command line for that entry, **a** to modify the kernel arguments, or **c** to go to the command-line interface to issue commands manually.

If you go to the command line, you can return to the menu at any time by pressing Esc.

Selecting **a** and **e** are similar, except that **a** displays only the **kernel** command line and lets you append options to it, while **e** displays the entire boot entry for you to edit. In either case, the available editing commands are similar to those available on the shell command line. When you are through editing, press Esc to return to the main menu. Your changes take effect for this session only; the configuration file is not permanently changed.

One common use for editing a **kernel** command is to boot to single-user mode. To do that, select **a** from the menu and append the word "single" to the end of the **kernel** command. Then press Esc to return to the menu and select the entry.

The GRUB Shell

In addition to using the command line from within the GRUB menu interface (or booting directly to the command line), you can run a GRUB shell directly from the Linux command line with the **grub** command. For the most part, using the **grub** shell is the same as running in the native command-line environment. The major difference is that the shell uses operating system calls to emulate the BIOS calls that the native environment uses. That can lead to some differences in behavior.

The syntax of the **grub** command is:

```
grub [options]
```

For example:

```
$ grub --no-floppy
```

The **grub** command-line options are:

--batch
   Turn on batch mode for noninteractive use. Equivalent to **grub --no-config-file --no-curses --no-pager**.

--boot-drive=_drive_

Use _drive_ as the Stage 2 boot drive, specified as a decimal, hexadecimal, or octal integer. The default is hexadecimal 0x0.

--config-file=_file_

Use _file_ as the GRUB configuration file. The default is _/boot/grub/menu.lst_.

--device-map=_file_

Use _file_ for the device map. The value of _file_ is usually _/boot/grub/device.map_.

--help

Display a help message to standard output and exit.

--hold

Wait for a debugger to attach before starting **grub**.

--install-partition=_partition_

Use _partition_ as the Stage 2 installation partition, specified as a decimal, hexadecimal, or octal number. The default is hexadecimal 0x20000.

--no-config-file

Run without reading the configuration file.

--no-curses

Don't use the **curses** interface for managing the cursor on the screen.

--no-floppy

Don't probe for a floppy drive. This option is ignored if **--device-map** is also specified.

--no-pager

Don't use the internal pager.

--preset-menu

Use a preset menu, for example if your system has no console and you need to get a serial terminal set up to see messages. To use this option, compile GRUB with the **--enable-preset-menu=**_file_ option and create a menu file. See the GRUB documentation for more information.

--probe-second-floppy

Probe the second floppy drive (which is not probed by default). This option is ignored if **--device-map** is also specified.

--read-only

Do not write to any disk drives.

--verbose

Print verbose messages.

--version

Print version information and exit.

When you run **grub**, you will see something like this:

```
    GRUB  version 0.94  (640K lower / 3072K upper memory)

 [ Minimal BASH-like line editing is supported.  For the first word, TAB
 lists possible command completions.  Anywhere else TAB lists the possible
 completions of a device/filename. ]

 grub>
```

You can now enter commands at the grub> prompt. Press Tab to get a brief help message, listing all the commands:

```
grub>
Possible commands are: blocklist boot cat chainloader cmp color configfile
debug device displayapm displaymem dump embed find fstest geometry halt help
hide impsprobe initrd install ioprobe kernel lock makeactive map md5crypt
module modulenounzip pager partnew parttype password pause quit read reboot
root rootnoverify savedefault serial setkey setup terminal testload testvbe
unhide uppermem vbeprobe
```

Using Tab is a quick way to remind yourself of the commands, but it can be confusing to see them all run together and wrapping across lines. You can also run the **help** command, which lists the most frequently used commands and their syntax:

```
grub> help
    blocklist FILE                              boot
    cat FILE                                    chainloader [--force] FILE
    color NORMAL [HIGHLIGHT]                     configfile FILE
    device DRIVE DEVICE                          displayapm
    displaymem                                   find FILENAME
    geometry DRIVE [CYLINDER HEAD SECTOR [       halt [--no-apm]
    help [--all] [PATTERN ...]                   hide PARTITION
    initrd FILE [ARG ...]                        kernel [--no-mem-option] [--type=TYPE]
    makeactive                                   map TO_DRIVE FROM_DRIVE
    md5crypt                                     module FILE [ARG ...]
    modulenounzip FILE [ARG ...]                 pager [FLAG]
    partnew PART TYPE START LEN                  parttype PART TYPE
    quit                                         reboot
    root [DEVICE [HDBIAS]]                        rootnoverify [DEVICE [HDBIAS]]
    serial [--unit=UNIT] [--port=PORT] [--       setkey [TO_KEY FROM_KEY]
    setup [--prefix=DIR] [--stage2=STAGE2_       terminal [--dumb] [--timeout=SECS] [--
    testvbe MODE                                 unhide PARTITION
    uppermem KBYTES                              vbeprobe [MODE]
```

You can add the **--all** option to see all the commands.

To get help for a specific command, add the command name (e.g., **help read**). **help** treats the text you enter as a pattern; therefore, if you enter **help find**, you'll get help for the **find** command, but if you enter **help module**, you'll get help for both **module** and **modulenounzip**.

GRUB Commands

The following sections describe two sets of commands. Both can be used at the GRUB command line. In addition, the first set can be used in the global section of the menu, and the second can be used in individual menu entries. A few commands can be used only on the GRUB shell command line; this is noted in the command entry. The commands **default**, **fallback**, **hiddenmenu**, **timeout**, and **title** are available only in the configuration file, for use with the menu interface. They are described in "The GRUB Configuration File" on page 521.

When running commands, if you find that you aren't sure how to complete a pathname, you can use the Tab key to find the possible completions. For example:

```
grub> blocklist (hd0,1)/grub/[Tab]
Possible files are: grub.conf splash.xpm.gz menu.lst device.map stage1
stage2 e2fs_stage1_5 fat_stage1_5 ffs_stage1_5 jfs_stage1_5 minix_stage1_5
reiserfs_stage1_5 vstafs_stage1_5 xfs_stage1_5
grub> blocklist (hd0,1)/grub/stage2
(hd0,1)33306+24,33332+231
```

Command-Line and Global Menu Commands

The commands available at the command line and in the global section of the configuration file are as follows.

bootp	bootp [--with-configfile]
	Initialize a network device via the Bootstrap Protocol (BOOTP). This command is available only if GRUB was compiled with netboot support. If **--with-configfile** is specified, GRUB automatically loads a configuration file specified by your BOOTP server.
color	color *normal* [*highlight*]
	Specify colors for the menu. *normal* represents the color used for normal menu text, while *highlight* represents the color used to highlight the line the cursor is on. Both *normal* and *highlight* are specified as two symbolic color names, for foreground and background color, separated by a slash. For example: color light-gray/blue cyan/black You can prefix the foreground color with **blink-** (e.g., **blink-cyan/red**) to get a blinking foreground. The colors **black**, **blue**, **green**, **cyan**, **red**, **magenta**, **brown**, and **light-gray** can be specified for foreground or background. Additional colors that can be used only for the foreground are **dark-gray**, **light-blue**, **light-green**, **light-cyan**, **light-red**, **light-magenta**, **yellow**, and **white**.
device	device *drive file*

	Specify a file to be used as a BIOS drive. This command is useful for creating a disk image and/or for fixing the drives when GRUB fails to determine them correctly. The **device** command is available only from within the **grub** shell, not from the native command line. For example:
	
	    grub> **device (fd0) /floppy-image**
	    grub> **device (hd0) /dev/sd0**

dhcp

dhcp [--with-configfile]

Initialize a network device via the DHCP protocol. Currently, this command is just an alias for **bootp** and is available only if GRUB was compiled with netboot support. If specified with **--with-config-file**, GRUB will fetch and load a configuration file specified by your DHCP server.

hide

hide *partition*

Hide the specified partition. This is useful when you are booting Windows and there are multiple primary partitions on one disk. Hide all but the one you want to boot. Also see **unhide**.

ifconfig

ifconfig [--server=*server*] [--gateway=*gateway*] [--mask=*mask*] [--address=*address*]

Configure a network device manually. If no options are specified, displays the current network configuration. With the server address, gateway, netmask, and IP address specified, **ifconfig** configures the device. The addresses must be in dotted decimal format (e.g., 192.168.0.4), and the options can be specified in any order.

pager

pager [*flag*]

Enable or disable the internal pager by setting *flag* to **on** (enable) or **off** (disable).

partnew

partnew *part type from to*

Make a new primary partition, *part*, specified in GRUB syntax. *type* is the partition type, specified as a number in the range 0-0xff. *from* and *to* are the starting and ending sectors, specified as absolute numbers. Some of the common partition types are:

Type	Number
None	0
FAT 16, lt 32M	4
FAT 16, gt 32M	6
FAT 32	0xb
FAT 32, with LBA	0xc
WIN 95, extended	0xf
EXT2FS	0x83
Linux extended	0x85
Linux RAID	0xfd
FreeBSD	0xa5
OpenBSD	0xa6
NetBSD	0xfd

parttype   parttype *part type*

Change the type of partition *part* to *type*. The type must be a number in the range 0-0xff. See **partnew** for a list of partition types.

password   password [--md5] *passwd* [*file*]

Set a password for the menu interface. If used in the global section of the configuration file, outside the menu entries, GRUB prompts for a password before processing an **a**, **e**, or **c** entered by the user. Once the password *passwd* has been entered, if no *file* was specified, GRUB allows the user to proceed. Otherwise, GRUB loads the file as a new configuration file and restarts Stage 2. If **password** appears in an individual menu entry, GRUB prompts for the password before continuing. Specify **--md5** to tell GRUB that the password was encrypted with the **md5crypt** command.

rarp   rarp

Initialize a network device via the Reverse Address Resolution Protocol (RARP). This command is available only if GRUB was compiled with netboot support. The use of RARP is deprecated.

serial   serial [*options*]

Initialize a serial device. The serial port is not used for communication unless **terminal** is also specified. This command is available only if GRUB was compiled with serial support.

Options

--**device**=*device*
> Specify the tty device to be used in the host operating system. This option can be used only in the **grub** shell.

--**parity**=*parity*
> Specify the parity. The possible values are **no**, **odd**, and **even**; the default is **no**.

--**port**=*port*
> Specify the I/O port. The value of *port* overrides any value specified for --**unit**.

--**speed**=*speed*
> Specify the transmission speed (default is 9600).

--**stop**=*num*
> Specify the number of stop bits. The value of *num* is either 1 or 2 (default is 1).

--**unit**=*num*
> Specify the serial port to use. The value of *num* is a number in the range 0–3; the default is 0, corresponding to COM1.

--word=_num_

> Specify the number of data bits. The value of _num_ is a number in the range 5–8 (default is 8).

---

setkey   `setkey [to-key from-key]`

Configure the keyboard map for GRUB by mapping the key _from-key_ to the key _to-key_. With no mappings specified, reset the keyboard map. **setkey** is useful for setting up international keyboards. Possible key values are letters; digits; one of the strings **alt, backspace, capslock, control, delete, enter, escape, F**_n_ (where _n_ is one of the function key numbers), **shift, tab**; or one of the strings in the "Key value" columns of the following table.

Key value	Character	Key value	Character
ampersand	&	asterisk	*
at	@	backquote	`
backslash	\	bar	|
braceleft	{	braceright	}
bracketleft	[	bracketright	]
caret	∧	colon	:
comma	,	dollar	$
doublequote	"	equal	=
exclam	!	greater	>
less	<	minus	-
numbersign	#	parenleft	(
parenright	)	percent	%
period	.	plus	+
question	?	quote	`
semicolon	;	slash	/
space		tilde	~
underscore	_		

---

splashimage   `splashimage file`

Use the image in _file_ as the background (splash) image. The file should be a gzipped _.xpm_ (X pixmap) file, created with a 14-color palette at 640 × 480 resolution and specified with standard GRUB device syntax:

```
splashimage=(hd0,0)/grub/splash.xpm.gz
```

Programs that you can use to create _.xpm_ files include the GIMP, **xv**, and **xpaint**.

---

terminal   `terminal [options] [console] [serial]`

Specify a terminal for user interaction. This command is available only if GRUB was compiled with serial support. If both **console** and **serial** are specified, GRUB uses the first terminal where a key is pressed, or the first after the timeout has expired. If neither is specified, GRUB displays the current setting.

Options
--dumb
> The terminal is a dumb terminal; if this option is not specified, the terminal is assumed to be VT100-compatible.

--lines=*num*
> The terminal has *num* lines. The default is 24.

--silent
> Suppress the prompt to hit any key (useful if your system does not have a terminal).

--timeout=*secs*
> Specify the timeout in seconds.

---

tftpserver   tftpserver *ipaddress*

Specify a TFTP server, overriding the address returned by a BOOTP, DHCP, or RARP server. The IP address must be specified in dotted decimal format. This command is available only if GRUB was compiled with netboot support. This command is deprecated; use **ifconfig** instead.

---

unhide   unhide *partition*

Unhide the specified partition. This is useful when booting DOS or Windows when there are multiple primary partitions on one disk. You can **unhide** the partition you want to boot and **hide** the others.

Command-Line and Menu-Entry Commands

The commands available at the command line and in the individual menu entries of the configuration file are as follows.

---

blocklist   blocklist *file*

Print the specified file in blocklist notation, where *file* is an absolute pathname or a blocklist. For example:

```
grub> blocklist (hd0,1)/grub/grub.conf
(hd0,1)33746+2
```

---

boot   boot

Boot the operating system or chainloader that has been loaded. You need to run this command only if you are in the interactive command-line mode.

cat

cat *file*

Display the contents of the specified file.

chainloader

chainloader [--force] *file*

Load *file* as a chainloader. You can use blocklist notation to specify the first sector of the current partition with +1. If **--force** is specified, the file is loaded forcibly.

cmp

cmp *file1 file2*

Compare the two files *file1* and *file2*. Report differences by printing nothing if the files are identical, the sizes if they are different, or the bytes at an offset if they differ at that offset.

configfile

configfile *file*

Load *file* as the configuration file.

debug

debug

Toggle debug mode, which prints extra messages to show disk activity. The default debug mode is off.

displayapm

displayapm

Display Advanced Power Management (APM) BIOS information.

displaymem

displaymem

Display the system address space map of the machine, including all regions of physical RAM installed. For example:

```
grub> displaymem
displaymem
 EISA Memory BIOS Interface is present
 Address Map BIOS Interface is present
 Lower memory: 640K, Upper memory (to first chipset hole):
3072K
 [Address Range Descriptor entries immediately follow
 (values are 64-bit)]
   Usable RAM:  Base Address:  0x0 X 4GB + 0x0,
      Length:    0x0 X 4GB + 0xa0000 bytes
   Reserved:  Base Address:  0x0 X 4GB + 0xa0000,
      Length:    0x0 X 4GB + 0x60000 bytes
   Usable RAM:  Base Address:  0x0 X 4GB + 0x100000,
      Length:    0x0 X 4GB + 0x300000 bytes
```

dump

dump *from to*

Dump the contents of one file into another. The file you're dumping *from* is a GRUB file, and the file you're dumping *to* is an operating system file.

embed

embed *stage1.5 device*

Embed the specified Stage 1.5 file in the sectors following the MBR if *device* is a drive, or in the boot loader area if it is an FFS (Berkeley Fast File System) partition (or, in the future, a ReiserFS partition). If successful, print the number of sectors the Stage 1.5 file occupies. You don't usually need to run this command directly.

find

find *file*

Search all partitions for the specified file and print the list of devices where it was found. The filename specified should be an absolute filename, such as */boot/grub/stage1*, or a blocklist.

fstest

fstest

Toggle the filesystem test mode, which prints data for device reads and the values being sent to the low-level routines. The **install** and **testload** commands turn off filesystem test mode. The test output is in the following format:

    <partition-offset-sector, byte-offset, byte-length>

for high-level reads in a partition, and:

    [disk-offset-sector]

for low-level sector requests from the disk.

geometry

geometry *drive [cylinder head sector [total_sector]]*

Print geometry information for *drive*. From the GRUB shell, you can specify the number of cylinders, heads, sectors, and total sectors to set the drive's geometry. If *total_sector* is omitted, it is calculated from the other values.

halt

halt [--no-apm]

Shut down the computer. The computer is halted with an APM BIOS call unless the option **--no-apm** is specified.

help

help [--all] [*patterns*]

Provide help for built-in commands. With no options, show the command and any options or parameters for the most common commands. With **--all**, show the same information for all possible commands. If you specify a pattern (i.e., a partial command name) or a full command name, a more complete description of the command or commands matching the pattern is displayed.

impsprobe

impsprobe

Probe the Intel Multiprocessor Specification 1.1 or 1.4 configuration table and boot the CPUs that are found into a tight loop. This command can be used only in Stage 2.

initrd	initrd *file* [*args*]
	Load an initial ramdisk *file* and pass any arguments.
install	install [*options*] *stage1_file* [d] *dest_dev* *stage2_file* [*addr*] [p] [*config_file*] [*real_config_file*]

Perform a full GRUB install. See also the **setup** command, which acts as a frontend to **install** and is easier to use. The Stage 2 or Stage 1.5 file (both referred to as *stage2_file* here because they are loaded the same way) must be in its final install location (e.g., in the */boot/grub* directory). **install** loads and validates *stage1_file*, installs a blocklist in the Stage 1 file for loading *stage2_file* as Stage 2 or Stage 1.5, and writes the completed Stage 1 file to the first block of the device *dest_dev*.

Options

--force-lba

> If the BIOS has LBA support but might return the incorrect LBA bitmap (which sometimes happens), **--force-lba** forces **install** to ignore the incorrect bitmap.

--stage2=*os_stage2_file*

> This option is required to specify the operating system name of the Stage 2 file if the filesystem where it is located cannot be unmounted.

Parameters

addr

> Specify the address at which Stage 1 is to load Stage 2 or Stage 1.5. The possible values are 0x8000 for Stage 2 and 0x2000 for Stage 1.5. If omitted, GRUB determines the address automatically.

config_file

> Specify the location of the configuration file for Stage 2.

d   Tell Stage 1 to look for the actual disk on which *stage2_file* was installed if it's not on the boot drive.

dest_dev

> Specify the destination device. The final Stage 1 file is written to this device.

p   If present, the partition where *stage2_file* is located is written into the first block of Stage 2.

real_config_file

> If *stage2_file* is really a Stage 1.5 file, *real_config_file* specifies the real configuration filename and is written into the Stage 2 configuration file.

stage1_file

> Specify the Stage 1 file to be written.

stage2_file

> Specify the file that Stage 1 is to load for Stage 2.

ioprobe   ioprobe *drive*

Probe the I/O ports used for *drive* and write the results to standard output.

kernel   kernel [--non-mem-option] *file* [...]

Load the kernel image from *file*. Any text following *file* is passed on as the kernel command line. After running this command, you must reload any modules. The option **--type** specifies the kernel type and is required only for loading a NetBSD ELF kernel; GRUB automatically determines other types. The possible values of type are **linux, biglinux, freebsd, multiboot, netbsd**, and **openbsd**. For Linux, **--no-mem-option** tells GRUB not to pass the **mem=** option to the kernel.

lock   lock

Lock the entry until a valid password is entered. This is used in a menu entry immediately after **title** to prevent nonroot users from executing the entry. This command is most useful in conjunction with the **password** command.

makeactive   makeactive

Set the active partition on the root disk to GRUB's root device. Use only on primary PC hard disk partitions.

map   map *to from*

Map the *from* drive to the *to* drive. You need to do this when chain-loading an operating system such as Windows, if it is not on the first drive. For example, if Windows is on (hd1):

    grub> **map (hd0) (hd1)**
    grub> **map (hd1) (hd0)**

This swaps the mappings of the first and second hard drives, tricking Windows into thinking it's on the first drive so it can boot.

md5crypt   md5crypt

Prompt for a password and encrypt it in MD5 format for use with the **password** command.

module   module *file* [...]

Load the boot module *file* for a multiboot format boot image. Anything after the filename is passed as the module command line.

modulenounzip   modulenounzip *files*

Like **module**, except that automatic decompression is disabled.

pause

pause *messages*

Print the specified message and wait for a key to be pressed before continuing.

quit

quit

Used only from within the **grub** shell to exit from the shell. In the native command environment, use **reboot** instead to reboot the computer.

read

read *addr*

Read a 32-bit value from memory at the specified address and display it in hex.

reboot

reboot

Reboot the system.

root

root *device* [*hdbias*]

Set the root device to the specified *device* and attempt to mount it to get the partition size (and some additional information for booting BSD kernels). If you are booting a BSD kernel, you can specify *hdbias* to tell the kernel how many BIOS drive numbers are before the current one.

rootnoverify

rootnoverify *device* [*hdbias*]

Similar to **root**, but don't attempt to mount the partition. Used when you are booting a non-GRUB-readable partition such as Windows.

savedefault

savedefault

Save the current menu entry as the default. GRUB will default to that entry the next time you boot the system.

setup

setup [*options*] *install_device* [*image_device*]

Set up installation of GRUB and run the **install** command to actually install GRUB onto the device *install_device*. Find the GRUB images on *image_device* if it is specified; otherwise use the current root device as set by the **root** command. If *install_device* is a hard disk, embed a Stage 1.5 file in the disk if possible.

Options

--force-lba

Force **install** to use LBA mode. Specify this option if your BIOS supports LBA mode but you find that GRUB isn't working in LBA mode without it.

--prefix=*dir*

Specify the directory where the GRUB images are located. If not specified, GRUB searches for them in */boot/grub* and */grub*.

--stage2=*os_stage2_file*

Passed to **install** to tell GRUB the operating system name of the Stage 2 file.

---

testload   testload *file*

Read the contents of a *file* in different ways and compare the results to test the filesystem code. If no errors are reported and the final output reports an equal value for the reported variables **i** and **filepos**, then the filesystem is consistent and you can try loading a kernel.

---

testvbe   testvbe *mode*

For a VBE (VESA BIOS Extension) BIOS, test the specified VESA BIOS extension mode. You should see an animation loop, which you can cancel by pressing any key.

---

uppermem   uppermem *kbytes*

Tell GRUB to assume that only the specified number of kilobytes of upper memory are installed. You should need to use this command only for old systems, where not all the memory may be recognized.

---

vbeprobe   vbeprobe [*mode*]

For a VBE BIOS, probe VESA BIOS extension information. If *mode* is specified, the output shows only information for that mode; otherwise, all available VBE modes are listed.

Dual-Booting Linux and Windows 2000/XP/Vista

As mentioned earlier, when you run Windows, its boot loader expects to be the one in charge; therefore, the standard way to dual-boot Windows and Linux is to add Linux as an option on the Windows boot menu. This section describes how to do that. The information provided here applies to Windows 2000 and Windows XP, which use the Windows NT loader **ntldr** (so called because it was developed for Windows NT). Windows Vista uses a different boot loader. If you want to set up Vista to dual-boot Linux, you can use the free download EasyBCD by Neosmart Technologies (*neosmart.net*).

Note again that you do not need the information in this section if your Linux installation software set up the dual-booting for you, which it probably did.

To set up dual booting with the NT loader manually, you need to provide the loader with a copy of the Linux boot sector. We'll describe how to do that on a

---

computer running Windows with an NTFS filesystem (note that Windows should be installed on your system already). See the "Linux+NT-loader" mini-HOWTO for more information and other alternatives.

You should have a Linux boot floppy or CD available so that if necessary you can boot Linux before the Windows boot loader has been modified. You should also have a DOS-formatted floppy to transfer the boot sector to the Windows partition. If you are running LILO and it is already installed, you may need to modify */etc/lilo.conf* as described later. Otherwise, install LILO or GRUB to the boot sector of the Linux partition; once the Linux boot manager is installed and you have a configuration file, you can set up the system for dual booting.

The following instructions assume your Linux partition is on */dev/hda2*. If Linux is on another partition in your system, be sure to replace */dev/hda2* in the following examples with the correct partition. The instructions also assume that you have a floppy drive to make a diskette for transferring the boot sector to your NTFS filesystem. If you don't have a floppy drive, you will have to use some other means of doing the transfer. If you have a FAT partition, you can mount that on Linux and transfer the file there. Other possibilities include putting it on a CD, transferring it over a network to another system while you reboot to Windows, or even emailing it to yourself and reading it from the Windows side.

1. If you are running LILO, specify the Linux root partition as your boot device in */etc/lilo.conf*. If you are editing */etc/lilo.conf* manually, your entry will look like this:

   ```
   boot=/dev/hda2
   ```

   and will be the same as the **root=** entry.

   If you are running GRUB, make sure your configuration file, */boot/grub/menu.lst*, includes a menu entry for booting Linux. The exact values of the entries in the menu depend on the filename of the kernel image that you wish to boot. For example:

   ```
   title Linux 2.6.28
   root (hd0,1)
   kernel /vmlinuz-2.6.28 ro root=LABEL=/
   initrd /initrd-2.6.28
   ```

   You can then skip to Step 3.

2. Run the **lilo** command to install LILO on the Linux root partition.

3. At this point, if you need to reboot Linux, you'll have to use a boot floppy or CD because the NT loader hasn't been set up yet to boot Linux.

4. From Linux, run the **dd** command to make a copy of the Linux boot sector:

   ```
   $ dd if=/dev/hda2 of=/bootsect.lnx bs=512 count=1
   ```

   This command copies one block, with a block size of 512 bytes, from the input file */dev/hda2* to the output file */bootsect.lnx*. Note that if you are running GRUB, the boot sector is actually the *stage1* file. (The output filename can be whatever makes sense to you; it doesn't have to be *bootsect.lnx*.)

5. Copy *bootsect.lnx* to a DOS-formatted floppy disk if that is how you are going to transfer it to Windows:

```
$ mount -t msdos /dev/fd0 /mnt
$ cp /bootsect.lnx /mnt
$ umount /mnt
```

6. Reboot the system to Windows and copy the boot sector from the floppy disk to the hard disk. You can drag and drop the file to the hard drive, or use the command line to copy the file, as in the following example:

```
C:> copy a:\bootsect.lnx c:\bootsect.lnx
```

It doesn't matter where on the hard drive you put the file because you'll tell the NT loader where to find it in step 8.

7. Modify the attributes of the file *boot.ini** to remove the system and read-only attributes so you can edit it:

```
C:> attrib -s -r c:\boot.ini
```

8. Edit *boot.ini* with a text editor to add the line:

```
C:\bootsect.lnx="Linux"
```

This line adds Linux to the boot menu and tells the NT boot loader where to find the Linux boot sector. You can insert the line anywhere in the **[operating systems]** section of the file. Its position in the file determines where it will show up on the boot menu when you reboot your computer. Adding it at the end, for example, results in a *boot.ini* file that looks something like this (the second **multi(0)** entry is wrapped to fit the margins of this page):

```
[boot loader]
timeout=30
default=multi(0)disk(0)rdisk(0)partition(1)\WINNT
[operating systems]
multi(0)disk(0)rdisk(0)partition(1)\WINNT="Windows NT Server Version 4.00"
multi(0)disk(0)rdisk(0)partition(1)\WINNT="Windows NT Server Version
4.00 [VGA mode]" /basevideo /sos
C:\bootsect.lnx="Linux"
```

If you want Linux to be the default operating system, modify the **default=** line:

```
default=C:\bootsect.lnx
```

9. Rerun **attrib** to restore the system and read-only attributes:

```
C:> attrib +s +r c:\boot.ini
```

Now you can shut down Windows and reboot. Windows will prompt you with a menu that looks something like this:

```
OS Loader V4.00
Please select the operating system to start:
Windows NT Workstation Version 4.00
Windows NT Workstation Version 4.00 [VGA mode]
Linux
```

---

* *boot.ini* is the Windows counterpart to */etc/lilo.conf*. It defines which operating systems the Windows loader can boot.

Select Linux, and the NT loader will read the Linux boot sector and transfer control to LILO or GRUB on the Linux partition.

If you are using LILO and you later modify *letc/lilo.conf* or rebuild the kernel, you need to rerun the **lilo** command, create a new *bootsect.lnx* file, and replace the version of *bootsect.lnx* on the Windows partition with the new version. In other words, you need to rerun steps 2–6.

 If you have any problems or you simply want to remove LILO or GRUB later, you can reverse the installation procedure: boot to Windows, change the system and read-only attributes on *boot.ini*, re-edit *boot.ini* to remove the Linux entry, save the file, restore the system and read-only attributes, and remove the Linux boot sector from the Windows partition.

Boot-Time Kernel Options

The earlier sections of this chapter described some of the options you can specify when you boot Linux. There are many more options that can be specified. This section touches on the ways to pass options to the kernel and then describes some of the kinds of parameters you might want to use. The parameters in this section affect the kernel and therefore apply regardless of which boot loader you use.

If LILO is your boot loader, you can add to or override the parameters specified in *letc/lilo.conf* during the boot process as follows:

- If **prompt** is set in *letc/lilo.conf*, LILO always presents the boot prompt and waits for input. At the prompt, you can choose the operating system to be booted. If you choose Linux, you can also specify parameters.

- If **prompt** isn't set, press Ctrl, Shift, or Alt when the word "LILO" appears. The boot prompt will then appear. You also can press the Scroll Lock key before LILO is printed and not have to wait poised over the keyboard for the right moment.

- At the boot prompt, specify the system you want to boot, or press Tab to get a list of the available choices. You then can enter the name of the image to boot. For example:

  ```
  LILO boot: <press Tab>
  linux    test    winxp
  boot: linux
  ```

  You also can add boot command options:

  ```
  boot: linux single
  ```

- If you don't provide any input, LILO waits the amount of time specified in the **delay** parameter and then boots the default operating system with the default parameters, as set in *letc/lilo.conf*.

If you are using GRUB, you can pass parameters to the kernel on the **kernel** command line, either in the configuration file or from the command-line interface. If you are booting from the GRUB menu, you can edit or add parameters by entering **e** or **a** when the menu appears.

Some of the boot parameters have been mentioned earlier. Many of the others are hardware-specific and are too numerous to mention here. For a complete list of parameters and a discussion of the booting process, see the "BootPrompt HOWTO." Some of the parameters not shown earlier that you might find useful are listed next; many more are covered in the HOWTO. Most of the following parameters are used to provide information or instructions to the kernel, rather than to LILO or GRUB:

acpi=off
> Disable ACPI (Advanced Configuration and Power Interface) if it was to be enabled. This is useful for debugging possible hardware problems.

debug
> Print all kernel messages to the console.

hd=*cylinders,heads,sectors*
> Specify the hard drive geometry to the kernel. Useful if Linux has trouble recognizing the geometry of your drive, especially if it's an IDE drive with more than 1024 cylinders.

load_ramdisk=*n*
> Tell the kernel whether to load a RAM disk image for use during Linux installation. Values of *n* are:
>
> 0 Don't try to load the image. This is the default.
>
> 1 Load the image from a floppy disk to the RAM disk.

mem=*size*
> Specify the amount of system memory installed. Useful if your BIOS reports memory only up to 64 MB and your system has more memory installed. Specify as a number with **M** or **k** (case-insensitive) appended:
>
> ```
> mem=128M
> ```
>
> Because **mem** would have to be included on the command line for every boot, it often is specified on a command line saved with **lock** or with **append** to be added to the parameters passed to the kernel.

noinitrd
> When set, disable the two-stage boot and preserve the contents of */dev/initrd* so the data is available after the kernel has booted. */dev/initrd* can be read only once, and then its contents are returned to the system.

number
> Start Linux at the runlevel specified by *number*. A runlevel is an operating state that the system can be booted to, such as a multiuser system or a system configuration running the X Window System. A runlevel is generally one of the numbers from 1 to 6; the default is usually 3. On modern distributions using Upstart, the runlevels and their corresponding states are defined in the *ttyN* files in the directory */etc/event.d*. On older systems using SysVinit, the runlevels are defined in the file */etc/inittab*. See Chapter 2 for a discussion of the init process.

ro   Mount the root filesystem read-only. Used for doing system mainte-
      nance, such as checking the filesystem integrity, when you don't want
      anything written to the filesystem.

rw   Mount the root filesystem read/write. If neither **ro** nor **rw** is specified,
      the default value (usually **rw**) stored in the kernel image is used.

single
      Start Linux in single-user mode. This option is used for system administra-
      tion and recovery. It gives you a root prompt as soon as the system boots,
      with minimal initialization. No other logins are allowed.

initrd: Using a RAM Disk

Modern Linux distributions use a modular kernel, which allows modules to be
added without requiring that the kernel be rebuilt. If your root filesystem is on a
device whose driver is a module (as is frequently true of SCSI disks), you can use
the **initrd** facility, which provides a two-stage boot process, to first set up a
temporary root filesystem in a RAM disk containing the modules you need to add
(e.g., the SCSI driver) and then load the modules and mount the real root filesystem. The RAM disk containing the temporary filesystem is the special device
file */dev/initrd*.

Similarly, you need to use a RAM disk if your root partition uses the ext3 filesystem and ext3 was not compiled into the kernel image. In that case, the ext3
module must be loaded with **initrd**.

Before you can use **initrd**, both RAM disk support (**CONFIG_BLK_DEV_
RAM=y**) and initial RAM disk support (**CONFIG_BLK_DEV_INITRD=y**) must
be compiled into the Linux kernel. Then you need to prepare the normal root filesystem and create the RAM disk image. Your Linux distribution may have utilities
to do some of the setup for you; for example, the Red Hat distribution comes with
the **mkinitrd** command, which builds the **initrd** image. For detailed information,
see the **initrd** manpage and the file *initrd.txt* (the path may vary, but it is usually
something like */usr/src/linux/Documentation/initrd.txt*).

Once your Linux system has been set up for **initrd**, you can do one of the
following, depending on which boot loader you are using:

- If you are using LILO, add the **initrd** option to the appropriate image section:

  ```
  image=/vmlinuz
      initrd=/boot/initrd  # The file to load as the contents of /dev/initrd
      ...
  ```

- Run the **/sbin/lilo** command, and you can reboot with **initrd**.

- If you are using GRUB, add the **initrd** option to the kernel line of the
  configuration-file boot entry, or to the **kernel** command if you are booting
  from the command-line interface:

  ```
  kernel /vmlinuz-2.6.28 ro root=LABEL=/
  initrd /initrd-2.6.28
  ```

5

Package Management

This chapter describes the two major Linux packaging systems: the Red Hat Package Manager (RPM) and the Debian GNU/Linux Package Manager. It also describes the major frontend applications designed to simplify and automate package management: **yum** for RPM-based systems, and **apt**, **aptitude**, and **synaptic** for Debian-based systems (**apt** is now also available for RPM-based systems).

When you install applications on your Linux system, most often you'll find a binary or a source package containing the application you want, instead of (or in addition to) a *.tar.gz* file. A package is a file containing the files necessary to install an application. However, while the package contains the files you need for installation, the application might require the presence of other files or packages that are not included, such as particular libraries (and even specific versions of the libraries), to actually be able to run. Such requirements are known as *dependencies*.

Package-management systems offer many benefits. As a user, you may want to query the package database to find out what packages are installed on the system and their versions. As a system administrator, you need tools to install and manage the packages on your system. And if you are a developer, you need to know how to build a package for distribution.

Among other things, package managers do the following:

- Provide tools for installing, updating, removing, and managing the software on your system.
- Allow you to install new or upgraded software directly across a network.
- Tell you what software package a particular file belongs to or what files a package contains.
- Maintain a database of packages on the system and their status, so you can determine what packages or versions are installed on your system.

- Provide dependency checking, so you don't mess up your system with incompatible software.
- Provide GPG, PGP, MD5, or other signature-verification tools.
- Provide tools for building packages.

Any user can list or query packages. However, installing, upgrading, or removing packages generally requires root privileges. This is because the packages normally are installed in system-wide directories that are writable only by root. Sometimes you can specify an alternate directory to install a package into your home directory or into a project directory where you have write permission, if you aren't running as root.

Signature verification is an important feature of package-management systems that helps maintain the security of your system. An MD5 checksum is used to check the integrity of a package, making sure, for example, that it was downloaded correctly and that it was not tampered with by a malicious user. GPG (and PGP) encrypt a digital signature into the package, which is used to verify the identity of the package creator.

Most often you'll install a binary package, in which the source code has been compiled and the software is ready to run once it is installed. You may also want or need to install source packages, which provide the source code and instructions for compiling and installing it. Source code packages do not contain executable files. Packages follow certain naming conventions, and you can tell from the name whether it is a binary or source package. RPM and Debian package names contain the same information, but they are expressed slightly differently. An RPM package has the form:

```
package-version-release.architecture.rpm
```

A Debian package has the form:

```
package_version-revision_architecture.deb
```

In both cases, *package* is the name of the package, *version* is the version number of the software, *release* (RPM) and *revision* (Debian) indicate the revision number of the package for that version, and *architecture* shows what system architecture the software was packaged for (e.g., **i386** or **amd64**). The value of *architecture* may also be **noarch** for a package that is not hardware-specific or **src** for an RPM source package (Debian source packages come as **tar**red, **gzip**ped files).

All the package managers check for dependencies when you install a package. In the case of RPM, if there are missing dependencies, it prints an error and terminates without installing the package. To proceed, you need to first install the missing package (or packages). This can become an involved process if the missing package has its own dependencies. A major advantage of the high-level package managers described in this chapter (i.e., **yum**, **apt**, **aptitude**, and **synaptic**) is that they automatically resolve dependencies and install missing packages for you. Another advantage is that they locate and download the package automatically, based on information in configuration files specifying where to look for packages. With RPM, you first have to locate the package, then download it, and only then can you run RPM to do the install. On the other hand, if you already have the package file on your system or on a CD, RPM is quick and easy to run.

Both RPM and the **apt** system back up old files before installing an updated package. Not only does this let you go back if there is a problem, but it also ensures that you don't lose your changes (to configuration files, for example).

The following list shows the package-management programs described in the rest of this chapter. Which program to use is very much a matter of personal preference, and you can use more than one at different times. However, it's best to pick the program you prefer and use it consistently, so all your packages are maintained in a single database that you can query.

The Advanced Package Tool (APT)

> APT is a modern, user-friendly package-management tool that consists of a number of commands. The most frequently used of these commands is **apt-get**, which is used to download and install a Debian package. **apt-get** can be run from the command line or selected as a method from **dselect**.

> Note that there are versions of the **apt** commands that can be used on an RPM-based system. If you plan to do that, it's best to install the version of **apt** that comes with your Linux distribution.

aptitude

> High-level text-based interface to APT. Runs either from the command line or in a visual mode inside a terminal window such as an xterm.

dpkg

> The original Debian packaging tool. Used to install or uninstall packages, or as a frontend to **dpkg-deb**. Getting and installing packages is usually done with **apt-get**, but **dpkg** is still commonly used to install a package that is already on your system. In fact, **apt-get** calls **dpkg** to do the installation once it's gotten the package.

dpkg-deb

> Lower-level packaging tool. Used to create and manage the Debian package archives. Accepts and executes commands from **dpkg** or can be called directly.

dselect

> An interactive frontend to **dpkg**. With the advent of the newer tools and the increased number of packages, the use of **dselect** is deprecated.

synaptic

> A graphical frontend to APT.

RPM

> The original command-line system for installing and managing RPM packages. RPM has two commands: **rpm** for installing and managing packages, and **rpmbuild** for creating packages.

yum

> A frontend to RPM that runs from the command line.

Another RPM-based package manager, **up2date**, used to be the default for Red Hat Enterprise Linux systems. Red Hat has since switched to **yum** as the default, but **up2date** is still available if you prefer it. **up2date** has both command line and graphical interfaces, and like **yum**, it resolves dependencies as needed.

If you want to update your system regularly, to keep it current and to be sure you have the latest security fixes, you can set up a command that you can reissue at some regular interval (say, every day or once a week), or you can set it up as a **cron** job to run overnight daily or weekly. (See the descriptions of the **cron** and **crontab** commands in Chapter 3 for more information on setting up a **cron** job.)

You can set up your **cron** job to automatically download and install updated packages, but a safer approach is to have your job download the updates and email you a summary, leaving it up to you when and how to do the installation. This is particularly true in a production environment where you want to test changes thoroughly before incorporating them into your system.

Yum: Yellowdog Updater Modified

Yum is a system for managing RPM packages, including installing, updating, removing, and maintaining packages; it automatically handles dependencies between packages. Yum is derived from **yup**, an updating system written for Yellow Dog Linux, an RPM-based PowerPC distribution. Yum downloads the information in the package headers to a directory on your system, which it then uses to make decisions about what it needs to do. Yum obtains both the headers and the RPMs themselves from a collection of packages on a server, known as a *repository*.

A repository consists of a set of RPM packages and the package headers, which are on a server that can be accessed via FTP or HTTP, from an NFS server, or from a local filesystem. A single server can contain one or multiple repositories; repositories are often mirrored on many servers, and you can configure **yum** to use multiple repositories. When they are downloaded to your system, the header and package files are maintained in */var/cache/yum*.

The configuration file, */etc/yum.conf*, is where you customize **yum**. It consists of two section types. The first section, [**main**], sets configuration defaults for **yum** operation. This section is followed by [*server*] sections, where each server is named according to the repository it specifies. For example, for Fedora, you might have [**base**] for the base Fedora repository and [**development**] for the development repository.

The server sections can also be stored, one to a file, in */etc/yum.repos.d*. **yum** comes with a default *yum.conf* file, which you can use as is or as a starting point from which to add additional repositories.

The yum Command

The **yum** command is an automated system for updating **rpm**-based packages, particularly on Fedora and Red Hat Enterprise Linux. Yum can automatically install, upgrade, and remove packages. In addition to individual packages or a list of packages, **yum** can operate on an entire group of packages at a time.

When you run **yum**, it first updates the cache (unless you tell it not to with the -C option); then it proceeds to perform the requested operation.

The format of the **yum** command is:

```
yum [options] [command] [package ...]
```

Any general options are specified first, followed by a command telling **yum** what you want it to do, usually followed by a list of one or more packages. The *command* is always required, except with the **--help, -h,** and **--version** options.

Package names can be specified in various combinations of name, architecture, version, and release. For example, you could refer to the **bash** package as *bash, bash.x86_64, bash-3.2, bash-3.2-30,* or *bash-3.2-30.fc10.x86_64.*

General options

The following general options can be set on the command line. For those that can also be set in the **[main]** section of the *yum.conf* configuration file, the name of the configuration option is given.

-c *[config-file]*
> Specify the location of the **yum** configuration file. The file can be specified as a path to a local file or as an HTTP or FTP URL. The default is */etc/yum.conf.*

-C Run entirely from the local cache. Don't download or update headers unless required to complete the requested action.

-d *[num]*
> Set the debug level to *num*, which is generally a number between 0 and 10, to specify how much debugging information to print. The configuration option is **debuglevel**.

--disableexcludes=*option*
> Disable the excludes defined in *yum.conf*. The possible options are **all** to disable all excludes, **main** to disable only the excludes defined in **[main]** in *yum.conf*, or *repoid* to disable any excludes defined for the specified repository.

--disableplugin=*plugin*
> Run with the specified plugins disabled, where *plugin* is a comma-separated list of plugins.

--disablerepo=*repoid*
> Disable the repository specified by *repoid* so **yum** won't use it for this operation. The configuration option is **enabled**.

-e *[num]*
> Set the error level to *num*, where *num* is a number, generally between 0 and 10. If the value is 0, print only critical errors. If it is 1, print all errors. Values greater than 1 mean print more errors, if there are any. The configuration option is **errorlevel**.

--enablerepo=*repoid*
> Enable the specified repository that is marked as disabled (**enable=0**) in the configuration file. This allows the repository to be used for this operation. The configuration option is **enabled**.

-h *[command]*, **--help** *[command]*
> Display a help message and exit. With a command, display help for that command.

--installroot=*root*

> Specify an alternative root for package installation. All packages will be installed relative to *root*. The configuration option is **installroot**.

--nogpgcheck

> Disable GPG signature checking. The configuration option is **gpgcheck**.

--noplugins

> Disable all plugins. The configuration option is **plugins**.

--obsoletes

> Enable obsoletes processing logic, taking into consideration packages that are obsoleted by other packages in the repository. Meaningful only with the **yum update** command. The configuration option is **obsoletes**.

-q, --quiet

> Run without producing output. See also **-y**.

-R [*minutes*]

> Set the maximum amount of time in minutes that **yum** will wait before performing a command.

--showduplicates

> For the **info**, **list**, and **search** commands, show all matching packages, not just the latest versions.

--skipbroken

> If **yum** finds dependency problems in a transaction, resolve them by removing the packages causing problems. The configuration option is **skip_ broken**.

-t, --tolerant

> Currently does nothing. This option was originally intended to allow **yum** to keep going (be tolerant) in spite of any package errors on the command line. The configuration option is **tolerant**.

-v, --verbose

> Display debugging information.

--version

> Display the version of **yum** and exit.

-x [*package*], **--exclude=***package*

> Exclude the specified package from updates on all repositories. *package* can be given as a name or a glob. The configuration option is **exclude**.

-y
> Assume that the answer to any question is yes. The configuration option is **assumeyes**.

yum Command Summary

The individual **yum** commands are listed here.

---

check-update   check-update

> Determine if updates are available, without running **yum** interactively. If any package updates are available, returns an exit value of

100 and a list of packages. If there are no updates, returns 0.
Returns 1 on error.

clean

clean [*options*]

Clean up the **yum** cache directory.

Options
all

Clean everything: headers, packages, metadata, and the cache.

dbcache

Clean up the **sqlite** database cache, forcing **yum** to recreate it
the next time it runs.

headers

Remove all header files, forcing **yum** to download new headers
the next time it runs.

metadata

Remove the metadata files, which maintain information about
the packages such as package name, file size, description,
dependencies, etc. The metadata will be downloaded again the
next time **yum** is run.

packages

Remove cached packages from the system.

deplist

deplist *packages*

Generate a list of dependencies for the specified packages,
including what packages satisfy the dependencies.

groupinfo

groupinfo *groups*

Like **info**, but operates on package groups instead of individual
packages.

groupinstall

groupinstall *groups*
groupupdate *groups*

Like **install**, but operates on package groups instead of individual
packages.

grouplist

grouplist

Generate a list of installed and available groups to standard output.
You can use these groups as input parameters to the other **group**
commands, with their names in quotes (" ").

groupremove

groupremove *groups*

Like **remove**, but operates on package groups instead of individual
packages.

help

help [*command*]

Display help information for the specified command, or if no command is given, for all commands.

info

info [*options*] [*packages*]

Display version information, a summary, and a description for each package, or for all packages if none is specified. See the **list** command for a description of the options.

install

install *packages*

Install the latest version of a package or packages, ensuring that all dependencies are met. If no package matches the name as specified, the name is treated as a shell glob and any matches are installed.

list

list [*options*] [*packages*]

Display a list of packages that match the *packages* specification and that are installed or available for installation.

Options

all

List all installed or available packages.

available

List packages on the repository that are available for installation.

extras

List packages on the system that are not available on any repository specified in the configuration file.

installed

List installed packages.

obsoletes

List installed packages that are made obsolete by any packages in any repository in the configuration file.

recent

List packages that have been recently added to any repository in the configuration file.

updates

List packages that have updates available for installation.

localinstall

localinstall *packages*

Install the specified packages, which reside on the local system, rather than downloading them from a repository.

localupdate   localupdate *packages*

Update the specified packages, which reside on the local system, rather than downloading them from a repository.

makecache   makecache

Download and cache the metadata files from the repository. Once the cache has been built, you can use the -C option to run the commands that use the metadata (**check-update**, **info**, **list**, **provides**, and **search**) directly from the cache.

provides   provides *feature1* [*feature2* ...]
whatprovides *feature1* [*feature2* ...]

List packages that are available or installed that provide the specified features. The features can be specified as a name or as a wildcard in file-glob syntax format, and Perl or Python regular expressions can be used.

reinstall   reinstall *package1* [*package2* ...]

Reinstall the specified packages. The packages must already exist on the system.

remove   remove *package1* [*package2* ...]
erase *package1* [*package2* ...]

Remove the specified packages from the system. Also remove any packages that depend on the specified packages.

repolist   repolist [*option*]

Generate a list of configured repositories. With no option or if the option is **all**, list all repositories. The other options are **disabled** to list disabled repositories, and **enabled** to list enabled repositories.

resolvedep   resolvedep *dep1* [*dep2* ...]

List the packages that provide the specified dependencies.

search   search *string1* [*string2* ...]

Find packages matching the specified string or strings in the description, summary, packager, or package name fields. Perl or Python regular expressions can be used for the strings. Useful for finding a package if you don't know the name.

shell   shell [*filename*]

Run an interactive **yum** shell, allowing multiple commands to be run within one **yum** execution. A filename can be specified that contains the commands to be run.

update   update [*packages*]

With no packages specified, update all installed packages. Otherwise, update the specified packages. In either case, **yum** makes sure that all dependencies are satisfied. If no package matches, the names specified are assumed to be shell globs, and any matches are installed.

With the **--obsoletes** option, **yum** includes package obsoletes in its calculations.

upgrade   upgrade [*packages*]

Equivalent to **update --obsoletes**.

Plugins and yum-utils

You can install plugins to extend the capabilities of **yum**. Plugins are Python programs that are installed in a directory specified with the **pluginpath** option in */etc/yum.conf*. In addition, to enable plugins, set the **plugins** option in */etc/yum.conf* to 1.

One set of such plugins is **yum-utils**, a collection of tools for managing packages and repositories. The following list briefly describes each tool. For more information on a tool, run it with the **-h** or **--help** option.

debuginfo-install
Install **debuginfo** packages, which contain debugging information for programs.

package-cleanup
Clean up packages, handling duplicates, orphaned packages, and dependency problems.

repoclosure
Read the metadata of one or more repositories, check dependencies, and display a list of any unresolved dependencies.

repodiff
Compare two or more repositories and display a list of added, removed, or changed packages.

repo-graph
Display a full package dependency list in dot format.

repomanage
Manage a directory of **rpm** packages, returning a list of the newest or oldest packages in a directory.

repoquery
Query **yum** repositories for additional information.

repo-rss
Generate an RSS feed from one or more repositories.

reposync

Synchronize a remote repository to a local directory, using **yum** to retrieve packages.

repotrack

Keep track of packages and their dependencies, and download them.

yum-builddep

Install missing dependencies to build specified packages.

yum-complete-transaction

Find incomplete or aborted transactions and try to complete them.

yumdownloader

Download binary and source packages from **yum** repositories for specified packages.

The Red Hat Package Manager

The Red Hat Package Manager (RPM) is a freely available packaging system for software distribution and installation. In addition to the Red Hat Enterprise Linux and Fedora distributions, both SUSE and Mandriva are among the Linux distributions that use RPM.

Using RPM is straightforward. A single command, **rpm**, has options to perform all package-management functions except building packages.* For example, to find out if the Emacs editor is installed on your system, you could enter:

```
$ rpm -q emacs
emacs-22.2-5.fc9.x86_64
```

This command prints the full package name, confirming its presence.

The **rpmbuild** command is used to build both binary and source packages.

RPM Package Concepts

This section provides an overview of some of the parts of an RPM package. Much of the information is of primary use to developers, but because some of the terms are referenced in the RPM command descriptions, they are explained briefly here.

An RPM package has three primary components. The *header* contains all the information about the package, such as its name and version, a description, a list of included files, the copyright terms, and where the source file can be found. The *signature* contains information used to verify the integrity and authenticity of the package. The *archive* contains the actual files that make up the package.

When a package is being built, one of the requirements for its developers is to create a *spec* file. If you download the source **rpm** for a package, you can look at the spec file; it has a filename of *package.spec* (e.g., *yum.spec* for the **yum** spec file). The spec file contains all the information required to build a package,

---

* In older versions of RPM, the build options were part of the **rpm** command.

including a description of the software, instructions telling the **rpmbuild** command how to build the package, and a list of the files included and where they get installed. Some other features of spec files include the following:

Macros
> Macros are sequences of commands stored together and executed by invoking the macro name. The RPM build process provides two standard macros: **%setup** to unpack the original sources and **%patch** to apply patches. Other macros appear later in this chapter in the command descriptions and are described there.

Scripts
> Scripts are used to control the build process. Some of the scripts RPM uses include **%prep** to begin the build process, **%build** primarily to run **make** and perhaps do some configuration, **%install** to do a **make install** and **%clean** to clean up afterward. Four additional scripts may be created to run when a package is actually installed on a system. These scripts are **%pre** for scripts run before package installation, **%post** for scripts run after package installation, **%preun** for scripts run before a package is uninstalled, and **%postun** for scripts run after a package is uninstalled.

Trigger scriptlets
> Trigger scriptlets are extensions of the normal install and uninstall scripts. They provide for interaction between packages. A trigger scriptlet provided with one package will be triggered to run by the installation or removal of some other package. For example, a newly installed RPM package may cause an existing application to run or restart once installation is complete. In many cases, a newly installed package requires services to be restarted.

The rpm Command

RPM packages are built, installed, and queried with the **rpm** command. RPM package filenames usually end with a *.rpm* extension. **rpm** has a set of modes, each with its own options. The format of the **rpm** command is:

```
rpm [options] [packages]
```

With a few exceptions, as noted in the lists of options that follow, the first option specifies the **rpm** mode (install, query, update, etc.), and any remaining options affect that mode.

Options that refer to packages are sometimes specified as *package-name* and sometimes as *package-file*. The package name is the name of the program or application, such as **xpdf**. The package file is the name of the RPM file, such as *xpdf-3.00-10.1.i386.rpm*.

RPM provides a configuration file for specifying frequently used options. The default global configuration file is usually */usr/lib/rpm/rpmrc*, the local system configuration file is */etc/rpmrc*, and users can set up their own *$HOME/.rpmrc* files. You can use the **--showrc** option to show the values RPM will use by default for all the options that may be set in an *rpmrc* file:

```
rpm --showrc
```

The **rpm** command includes FTP and HTTP clients, so you can specify an *ftp://* or *http://* URL to install or query a package across the Internet. You can use an FTP or HTTP URL wherever *package-file* is specified in the commands presented here. Be careful, however, when downloading packages from the Internet. Always verify package contents by checking MD5 hashes and signatures. Whenever possible, install from trusted sites.

Any user can query the RPM database. Most of the other functions, such as installing and removing packages, require superuser privileges.

General options

The following options can be used with all modes:

--dbpath *path*
> Use *path* as the path to the RPM database instead of the default */var/lib/rpm*.

-?, --help
> Print a long usage message (run **rpm** with no options for a shorter usage message).

--pipe *command*
> Pipe the query output to the specified command.

--quiet
> Display only error messages.

--rcfile *filelist*
> Get configuration from the files in the colon-separated *filelist*. If **--rcfile** is specified, the list must contain at least one file and that file must exist. *filelist* defaults to */usr/lib/rpm/rpmrc:/usr/lib/rpm/redhat/rpmrc:/etc/rpmrc:~/.rpmrc*. Use with **--showrc** to see what options will be used if alternate configuration files are specified.

--root *dir*
> Perform all operations within the directory tree rooted at *dir*.

-v Verbose. Print progress messages.

--version
> Print the **rpm** version number.

-vv Print debugging information.

Install, upgrade, and freshen options

Use the **install** command to install or upgrade an RPM package. Upgrading with **install** leaves any existing versions on the system. The **install** syntax is:

```
rpm -i [install-options] package_file ...
rpm --install [install-options] package_file ...
```

To install a new version of a package and remove an existing version at the same time, use the **upgrade** command instead:

```
rpm -U [install-options] package_file ...
rpm --upgrade [install-options] package_file ...
```

If the package doesn't already exist on the system, **-U** acts like **-i** and installs it. To prevent that behavior, you can **freshen** a package instead; in that case, **rpm** upgrades the package only if an earlier version is already installed. The **freshen** syntax is:

```
rpm -F [install-options] package_file ...
rpm --freshen [install-options] package_file ...
```

For all forms, *package-file* can be specified as an FTP or HTTP URL to download the file before installing it. See "FTP/HTTP options" on page 563.

The installation and upgrade options are:

--aid
> If **rpm** suggests additional packages, add them to the list of package files.

--allfiles
> Install or upgrade all files.

--badreloc
> Used with **--relocate** to force relocation even if the package is not relocatable.

--excludedocs
> Don't install any documentation files.

--excludepath *path*
> Don't install any file whose filename begins with *path*.

--force
> Force the installation. Equivalent to **--replacepkgs --replacefiles --oldpackage**.

-h, --hash
> Print 50 hash marks as the package archive is unpacked. Use this option with **-v** or **--verbose** for a nicer display.

--ignorearch
> Install even if the binary package is intended for a different architecture.

--ignoreos
> Install binary package even if the operating systems don't match.

--ignoresize
> Don't check disk space availability before installing.

--includedocs
> Install documentation files. This is needed only if **excludedocs: 1** is specified in an *rpmrc* file.

--justdb
> Update the database only; don't change any files.

--nodeps
> Don't check whether this package depends on the presence of other packages.

--nodigest
> Don't verify package or header digests.

--nomanifest
> Don't process nonpackage files as manifests.

--noorder
> Don't reorder packages to satisfy dependencies before installing.

--nopost

> Don't execute any post-install script.

--nopostun

> Don't execute any post-uninstall script.

--nopre

> Don't execute any pre-install script.

--nopreun

> Don't execute any pre-uninstall script.

--noscripts

> Don't execute any pre-install or post-install scripts. Equivalent to specifying **--nopre --nopost --nopreun --nopostun**.

--nosignature

> Don't verify package or header signatures.

--nosuggest

> Don't suggest packages that provide a missing dependency.

--notriggerin

> Don't execute any install trigger scriptlet.

--notriggerun

> Don't execute any uninstall trigger scriptlet.

--notriggerpostun

> Don't execute any post-uninstall trigger scriptlet.

--notriggers

> Don't execute any scripts triggered by package installation. Equivalent to specifying **--notriggerin --notriggerun --notriggerpostun**.

--oldpackage

> Allow an upgrade to replace a newer package with an older one.

--percent

> Print percent-completion messages as files are unpacked. Useful for running **rpm** from other tools.

--prefix *path*

> Set the installation prefix to *path* for relocatable binary packages.

--relocate *oldpath=newpath*

> For relocatable binary files, change all file paths from *oldpath* to *newpath*. Can be specified more than once to relocate multiple paths.

--replacefiles

> Install the packages even if they replace files from other installed packages.

--replacepkgs

> Install the packages even if some of them are already installed.

--test

> Go through the installation to see what it would do, but don't actually install the package. This option lets you test for problems before doing the installation.

Query options

The syntax for the **query** command is:

```
rpm -q [package-selection-options] [package-query-options]
rpm --query [package-selection-options] [package-query-options]
```

There are two subsets of query options. *Package-selection options* determine which packages to query, and *package-query options* determine which information to provide.

Package-selection options

package_name
> Query the installed package *package_name*.

-a, --all
> Query all installed packages.

-f *file*, **--file** *file*
> Find out which package owns *file*.

--fileid *md5*
> Query package with the specified MD5 digest.

-g *group*, **--group** *group*
> Find out which packages have group *group*.

--hdrid *sha1*
> Query package with the specified SHA1 digest in the package header.

-p *package_file*, **--package** *package_file*
> Query the uninstalled package *package_file*, which can be a URL. If *package_file* is not a binary package, it is treated as a text file containing a package manifest, with each line of the manifest containing a path or one or more whitespace-separated glob expressions to be expanded to paths. These paths are then used instead of *package_file* as the query arguments. The manifest can contain comments that begin with a hash mark (#).

--pkgid *md5*
> Query the package with a package identifier that is the given MD5 digest of the combined header and contents.

--querybynumber *num*
> Query the *num*th database entry. Useful for debugging.

-qf, --queryformat *string*
> Specify the format for displaying the query output, using tags to represent different types of data (e.g., NAME, FILENAME, DISTRIBUTION). The format specification is a variation of the standard **printf** formatting, with the type specifier omitted and replaced by the name of the header tag inclosed in brackets ({ }). For example:

```
%{NAME}
```

The tag names are case-insensitive. Use **--querytags** (see "Miscellaneous options" on page 563) to view a list of available tags. The tag can be followed by :*type* to get a different output format type. The possible types are:

:armor

Wrap a public key in ASCII armor.

:arraysize

Display number of elements in array tags.

:base64

Encode binary data as base64.

:date

Use **%c** format as in **strftime(3)** to display the preferred date and time format for this locale.

:day

Use **%a %b %d %Y** format as in the function **strftime(3)**. This format displays the day, the month, the month as a decimal number, and the four-digit year.

:depflags

Format dependency flags.

:fflags

Format file flags.

:hex

Use hexadecimal format.

:octal

Use octal format.

:perms

Format file permissions.

:pgpsig

Display the PGP signature and time.

:shescape

Escape single quotes for use in a script.

:triggertype

Display trigger suffix (i.e., **in**, **un**, or **postun**, indicating whether it's an install, uninstall, or post-uninstall trigger).

:xml

Wrap data in simple XML markup.

--specfile *specfile*

Query *specfile* as if it were a package. Useful for extracting information from a spec file.

--tid *tid*

List packages with the specified transaction identifier (*tid*), which is a Unix timestamp. All packages installed or erased in a single transaction have the same tid.

--triggeredby *pkg*

> List packages containing triggers that are run when the installation status of package *pkg* changes. For example:

```
$ rpm -q --triggeredby glibc
redhat-lsb-3.2-2.fc10.x86_64
```

> In this example, the package **redhat-lsb-3.2-2.fc10.x86_64** contains a **triggerpostun** scriptlet that runs after **glibc** is uninstalled.

--whatrequires *capability*

> List packages that require the given capability to function. For example:

```
$ rpm -q --whatrequires popt
popt-devel-1.13-4.fc10.x86_64
logrotate-3.7.7-1.fc10.x86_64
nash-6.0.71-2.fc10.x86_64
initscripts-8.86-1.x86_64
rpm-4.6.0-0.rc1.7.x86_6
```

--whatprovides *capability*

> List packages that provide the given capability. For example:

```
$ rpm -q --whatprovides popt
popt-1.13-4.fc10.x86_64
```

Package-query options

-c, --configfiles

> List configuration files in the package. Implies **-l**.

--changelog

> Display the log of change information for the package.

-d, --docfiles

> List documentation files in the package. Implies **-l**.

--dump

> Dump information for each file in the package. The output includes the following information in this order:

```
path size mtime md5sum mode owner group isconfig isdoc rdev symlink
```

--filesbypkg

> List all files in each package.

-i, --info

> Display package information, including the name, version, and description. The results are formatted according to **--queryformat** if specified.

-l, --list

> List all files in the package.

--last

> List packages by install time, with the latest packages listed first.

--provides

> List the capabilities this package provides.

-R, --requires

> List any packages this package depends on.

-s, --state

List each file in the package and its state. The possible states are **normal, not installed**, or **replaced**. Implies **-l**.

--scripts

List any package-specific shell scripts used during installation and uninstallation of the package.

--triggers, --triggerscript

Display any trigger scripts in the package.

Uninstall options

The syntax for **erase**, the uninstall command, is:

```
rpm -e [uninstall-options] package_name ...
rpm --erase [uninstall-options] package_name ...
```

The uninstall options are:

--allmatches

Remove all versions of the package. Only one package should be specified; otherwise, an error results.

--nodeps

Don't check dependencies before uninstalling the package.

--nopostun

Don't run any post-uninstall scripts.

--nopreun

Don't run any pre-uninstall scripts.

--noscripts

Don't execute any pre-uninstall or post-uninstall scripts. This option is equivalent to **--nopreun --nopostun**.

--notriggerpostun

Don't execute any post-uninstall scripts triggered by the removal of this package.

--notriggers

Don't execute any scripts triggered by the removal of this package. Equivalent to **--notriggerun --notriggerpostun**.

--notriggerun

Don't execute any uninstall scripts triggered by the removal of this package.

--test

Don't really uninstall anything; just go through the motions. Use with **-vv** for debugging.

Verify options

The syntax for the **verify** command is:

```
rpm -V | --verify [package-selection-options] [verify-options]
```

Verify mode compares information about the installed files in a package with information about the files that came in the original package and displays any

---

discrepancies. The information compared includes the size, MD5 sum, permissions, type, owner, and group of each file. Uninstalled files are ignored.

The package selection options include those available for query mode. In addition, the following **verify** options are available:

--nodeps
> Ignore package dependencies.

--nodigest
> Ignore package or header digests.

--nofiles
> Ignore attributes of package files.

--nogroup
> Ignore group ownership errors.

--nolinkto
> Ignore symbolic-link errors.

--nomd5
> Ignore MD5 checksum errors.

--nomode
> Ignore file mode (permissions) errors.

--nordev
> Ignore major and minor device number errors.

--nomtime
> Ignore modification time errors.

--noscripts
> Ignore any verify script.

--nosignature
> Ignore package or header signatures.

--nosize
> Ignore file size errors.

--nouser
> Ignore user ownership errors.

The output is formatted as an eight-character string, possibly followed by an attribute marker, and then the filename. Each of the eight characters in the string represents the result of comparing one file attribute to the value of that attribute from the RPM database. A period (.) indicates that the file passed that test. The following characters indicate failure of the corresponding test:

5   MD5 sum

D   Device

G   Group

L   Symlink

M   Mode (includes permissions and file type)

S   File size

T   Mtime

U   User

The possible attribute markers are:

c   Configuration file

d   Documentation file

g   Ghost file (contents not included in package)

l   License file

r   Readme file

Database rebuild options

The syntax of the command to rebuild the RPM database is:

```
rpm --rebuilddb [options]
```

You also can build a new database:

```
rpm --initdb [options]
```

The options available with the database rebuild mode are the **--dbpath**, **--root**, and **-v** options described earlier under "General options" on page 546.

Signature-check options

RPM packages may have a GPG signature built into them. There are three types of digital signature options: you can check signatures, add signatures to packages, and import signatures.

The syntax of the signature check mode is:

```
rpm --checksig [options] package_file...
rpm -K [options] package_file...
```

The signature-checking options **-K** and **--checksig** check the digests and signatures contained in the specified packages to insure the integrity and origin of the packages. Note that RPM now automatically checks the signature of any package when it is read; these options are still useful, however, for checking all headers and signatures associated with a package.

The **--nosignature** and **--nodigest** options described earlier, under "Verify options" on page 560, are available for use with signature check mode.

The syntax for adding signatures to binary packages is:

```
rpm --addsign binary-pkgfile...
rpm --resign binary-pkgfile...
```

Both **--addsign** and **--resign** generate and insert new signatures, replacing any that already exist in the specified binary packages.*

The syntax for importing signatures is:

```
rpm --import public-key
```

---

* In older versions of RPM, **--addsign** was used to add new signatures without replacing existing ones, but currently both options work the same way and replace any existing signatures.

The **--import** option is used to import an ASCII public key to the RPM database so that digital signatures for packages using that key can be verified. Imported public keys are carried in headers, and keys are kept in a ring, which can be queried and managed like any package file.

Miscellaneous options

Several additional **rpm** options are available:

--querytags
> Print the tags available for use with the **--queryformat** option in query mode.

--setperms *packages*
> Set file permissions of the specified packages to those in the database.

--setugids *packages*
> Set file owner and group of the specified packages to those in the database.

--showrc
> Show the values **rpm** will use for all options that can be set in an *rpmrc* file.

FTP/HTTP options

The following options are available for use with FTP and HTTP URLs in install, update, and query modes.

--ftpport *port*
> Use *port* for making an FTP connection on the proxy FTP server instead of the default port. Same as specifying the macro **%_ftpport**.

--ftpproxy *host*
> Use *host* as the proxy server for FTP transfers through a firewall that uses a proxy. Same as specifying the macro **%_ftpproxy**.

--httpport *port*
> Use *port* for making an HTTP connection on the proxy HTTP server instead of the default port. Same as specifying the macro **%_httpport**.

--httpproxy *host*
> Use *host* as the proxy server for HTTP transfers. Same as specifying the macro **%_httpproxy**.

RPM Examples

Query the RPM database to find Emacs-related packages:

```
$ rpm -q -a | grep emacs
```

Query an uninstalled package, printing information about the package and listing the files it contains:

```
$ rpm -qpil ~/downloads/bash-3.2-29.fc10.x86_64.rpm
```

Install a package (assumes superuser privileges):

```
$ rpm -i sudo-1.6.9p17-2.fc10.x86_64.rpm
```

Do the same thing, but report on the progress of the installation:

```
$ rpm -ivh sudo-1.6. 9p17-2.fc10.x86_64.rpm
```

The rpmbuild Command

The **rpmbuild** command is used to build RPM packages. The syntax for **rpmbuild** is:

    rpmbuild -[b|t] *stage* [*build-options*] *spec-file* ...

Specify **-b** to build a package directly from a spec file, or **-t** to open a **tar**red, **gzip**ped file and use its spec file.

Both forms take the following single-character *stage* arguments, which specify the stages, or steps, required to build a package. The stages are listed in the order they would be performed:

p   Perform the prep stage, unpacking source files and applying patches.

l   Do a list check, expanding macros in the files section of the spec file and verifying that each file exists.

c   Perform the prep and build stages; generally equivalent to doing a **make**.

i   Perform the prep, build, and install stages; generally equivalent to doing a **make install**.

b   Perform the prep, build, and install stages, then build a binary package.

s   Build a source package.

a   Perform the prep, build, and install stages, then build both binary and source packages.

The difference between the build stage, which is one of the early steps, and building a binary package in **b** or **a** is the difference between building a working binary for the software and putting all the pieces together into a final **rpm** package.

rpmbuild options

The general **rpm** options described under "General options" on page 546 can be used with **rpmbuild**.

The following additional options can also be used when building an **rpm** file with **rpmbuild**:

--buildroot *dir*
> Override the **BuildRoot** tag with *dir* when building the package.

--clean
> Clean up (remove) the build files after the package has been made.

--nobuild
> Go through the motions, but don't execute any build stages. Used for testing spec files.

--rmsource
> Remove the source files when the build is done. Can be used as a standalone option to clean up files separately from creating the packages.

--rmspec
> Remove the spec file when the build is done. Can be used as a standalone option.

--short-circuit

Can be used with **-bc** and **-bi** to skip previous stages that already ran successfully. With **--short-circuit**, **-bc** starts directly at the build stage and **-bi** starts with the install stage.

--sign

Add a GPG signature to the package for verifying its integrity and origin.

--target *platform*

When building the package, set the macros **%_target**, **%_target_arch**, and **%_target_os** to the value indicated by *platform*.

Two other options can be used standalone with **rpmbuild** to recompile or rebuild a package:

--rebuild *source-pkgfile...*

Like **--recompile**, but also build a new binary package. Remove the build directory, the source files, and the spec file once the build is complete.

--recompile *source-pkgfile...*

Install the named source package, and prep, compile, and install the package.

Finally, the **--showrc** option is used to show the current **rpmbuild** configuration:

```
rpmbuild --showrc
```

This option shows the values that will be used for all options that can be set in *rpmrc* and *macros* files.

The Debian Package Manager

Debian GNU/Linux provides several package-management tools, primarily intended to facilitate the building, installation, and management of binary packages. In addition, the tools described here also work on other Debian-based systems such as Ubuntu, Xandros, Knoppix, and numerous others.

Debian package names generally end in *.deb*. The Debian package-management tools we describe include the **apt** commands, **aptitude**, **dpkg**, **dpkg-deb**, **dselect**, and **synaptic**. Each of these tools is described in detail in "Debian Package Manager Command Summary" on page 569.

Files

Some important files used by the Debian package-management tools are described briefly here:

control

Comes with each package. Documents dependencies; contains the name and version of the package, a description, maintainer, installed size, the package priority, etc.

conffiles

Comes with each package. Contains a list of the configuration files associated with the package.

preinst, postinst, prerm, postrm
> Scripts developers can include in a package to be run before installation, after installation, before removal, or after removal of the package.

/var/lib/dpkg/available
> Contains information about packages available on the system.

/var/lib/dpkg/status
> Contains information about the status of packages available on the system.

/etc/apt/sources.list
> A list for APT of package sources, used to locate packages. The sources are listed one per line, in order of preference.

/etc/apt/apt.conf
> The main APT configuration file.

/etc/apt/preferences
> A preferences file that controls various aspects of APT, such as letting a user select the version or release of a package to install.

/etc/dpkg/dpkg.cfg
> A configuration file containing default options for **dpkg**.

For a user, the important file is */etc/apt/sources.list*. This file is where you set up the paths to the package archives, telling **apt** where to go to find packages. **apt** is installed with a default file. You aren't required to modify the sources in the file, but you'll probably want to change some sources or add additional ones at some point. You might also want to change some of the options in the configuration files *apt.conf*, *preferences*, and *dpkg.config* if you aren't satisfied with the defaults. The *control*, *conffiles*, and the pre- and post-install and removal script files are created by the package developers and used internally by the package-management system.

Package Priorities

Every Debian package has a priority associated with it, indicating how important the package is to the system. The priorities are:

required
> The package is essential to the proper functioning of the system.

important
> The package provides important functionality that enables the system to run well.

standard
> The package is included in a standard system installation.

optional
> The package is one that you might want to install, but you can omit it if you are short on disk space, for example.

extra
> The package either conflicts with other packages that have a higher priority, has specialized requirements, or is one that you would want to install only if you need it.

The control file for **dpkg**, for example, shows that **dpkg** itself has a priority of **required**; **dpkg-dev** (which provides tools for building Debian packages) has a priority of **standard**; and **dpkg-doc** is **optional**.

Package and Selection States

The possible states that a package can be in are:

config-files
Only the configuration files for the package are present on the system.

half-configured
The package is unpacked, and configuration was started but not completed.

half-installed
Installation was started but not completed.

installed
The package is unpacked and configured.

not-installed
The package is not installed.

unpacked
The package is unpacked but not configured.

The possible package selection states are:

deinstall
The package has been selected for deinstallation (i.e., for removal of everything but the configuration files).

install
The package has been selected for installation.

purge
The package has been selected to be purged (i.e., for removal of everything including the configuration files).

Package Flags

Two possible package flags can be set for a package:

hold
The package should not be handled by **dpkg** unless forced with the **--force-hold** option. Holding a package keeps it at the current version, preventing it from being updated. You might hold a package, for example, if the latest version is broken and you want to stay with the version you have until a newer one is released.

reinst-required
The package is broken and needs to be reinstalled. Such a package cannot be removed unless forced with the **--force-reinstreq** option.

Scripts

In addition to the commands described in the next section, a number of shell and Perl scripts are included with the package manager for use in managing and building packages:

apt-file
> Search for packages, specifying an action and a pattern to search for. (Perl script)

apt-rdepends
> Recursively list dependencies. (Perl script)

dpkg-architecture
> Determine and set the build and host architecture for package building. (Perl script)

dpkg-checkbuilddeps
> Check installed packages against the build dependencies and build conflicts listed in the control file. (Perl script)

dpkg-buildpackage
> A control script to help automate package building. (Shell script)

dpkg-distaddfile
> Add an entry for a file to *debian/files*. (Perl script)

dpkg-divert
> Create and manage the list of diversions, used to override the default location for installing files. (Perl script)

dpkg-genchanges
> Generate an upload control file from the information in an unpacked, built source tree and the files it has generated. (Perl script)

dpkg-gencontrol
> Read information from an unpacked source tree, generate a binary package control file (by default, *debian/tmp/DEBIAN/control*), and add an entry for the binary file to *debian/files*. (Perl script)

dpkg-name
> Rename Debian packages to their full package names. (Shell script)

dpkg-parsechangelog
> Read and parse the changelog from an unpacked source tree and write the information to standard output in machine-readable form. (Perl script)

dpkg-preconfigure
> Let packages ask questions prior to installation. (Perl script)

dpkg-reconfigure
> Reconfigure a package that is already installed. (Perl script)

dpkg-scanpackages
> Create a *Packages* file from a tree of binary packages. The *Packages* file is used by **dselect** to provide a list of packages available for installation. (Perl script)

dpkg-shlibdeps
> Calculate shared library dependencies for named executables. (Perl script)

dpkg-source
> Pack and unpack Debian source archives. (Perl script)

dpkg-statoverride
> Manage the list of stat overrides, which let **dpkg** override file ownership and mode when a package is installed. (Perl script)

Debian Package Manager Command Summary

For the **apt-** commands, options can be specified on the command line or set in the configuration file. Boolean options set in the configuration file can be overridden on the command line in a number of different ways, such as **--no-***opt* and *-opt*=**no**, where *opt* is the single-character or full name of the option.

---

apt-cache

apt-cache [*options*] *command*

Perform low-level operations on the APT binary cache, including the ability to perform searches and produce output reports from package metadata.

Commands

add *files*
> Add the specified package index files to the source cache. Useful for debugging.

depends *pkgs*
> For each specified package, show a list of dependencies and packages that can fulfill them.

dotty *pkgs*
> Graph the relationships between the specified packages. The default is to trace out all dependent packages; turn this behavior off by setting the **APT::Cache::GivenOnly** configuration option.

dump
> List every package in the cache. Used for debugging.

dumpavail
> Print a list of available packages to standard output, suitable for use with **dpkg**.

gencaches
> Build source and package caches from the sources in *sources.list* and from */var/lib/dpkg/status*. Equivalent to running **apt-get check**.

madison [*pkgs*]
> Display a table showing the available versions of each specified package. Similar to **madison**, a Debian tool that checks for package versions and reports their status. This option works locally and doesn't require access to the Debian project's internal archive.

pkgnames [*prefix*]

Print a list of packages in the system. If *prefix* is specified, print only packages whose names begin with that prefix. Most useful with the **--generate** option.

policy [*pkgs*]

Print detailed information about the priority selection of each specified package. With no arguments, print the priorities of all sources. Useful for debugging issues related to the *preferences* file.

rdepends [*pkgs*]

Show a list of reverse dependencies for each specified package— i.e., list any packages that depend on the specified packages.

search *regex*

Search package names and descriptions of all available package files for the specified regular expression and print the name and short description of each matching package. With **--full**, the output is identical to that from the **show** command. With **--names-only**, only the package name is searched. Multiple regular expressions can be specified. Useful for finding packages when you don't know the actual package name.

show *pkgs*

Display the package records for each specified package. See the **-a** option for more details.

showpkg *pkgs*

Display information about the specified packages. For each package, the output includes the available versions, packages that depend on this package, and packages that this package depends on.

showsrc *pkgs*

Display source package records for each specified package.

stats

Display statistics about the cache.

unmet

Display the unmet dependencies in the package cache.

Options

-a, --all-versions

Print full records for all available versions. For use with the **show** command. The default is to show all versions; use with **--no-all-versions** to display only the version that would be installed. The configuration option is **APT::Cache::AllVersions**.

--all-names

Cause **pkgnames** to print all names, including virtual packages and missing dependencies. The configuration option is **APT::Cache::AllNames**.

-c *file*, **--config-file=**_file_
> Specify a configuration file to be read after the default configuration file.

-f, --full
> Print full package records when searching. The configuration option is **APT::Cache::ShowFull**.

-g, --generate
> Automatically regenerate the package cache rather than using the current cache. Default is to regenerate; turn it off with **--no-generate**. The configuration option is **APT::Cache::Generate**.

-h, --help
> Print usage information and exit.

-i, --important
> Print only important dependencies (Depends and Pre-Depends relations). For use with **unmet**. The configuration option is **APT::Cache::Important**.

--installed
> Only produce output for currently installed packages. For use with **depends** and **rdepends**. The configuration option is **APT::Cache::Installed**.

-n, --names-only
> Search only on package names, not long descriptions. The configuration option is **APT::Cache::NamesOnly**.

-o, --option
> Set a configuration option. Syntax is **-o** *group::tool=option*.

-p *file*, **--pkg-cache=**_file_
> Use the specified file for the package cache, the primary cache used by all operations. The configuration option is **Dir::Cache::pkgcache**.

-q, --quiet
> Operate quietly, producing output for logging but no progress indicators. Use **-qq** for even quieter operation. The configuration option is **quiet**.

--recurse
> Run **depends** or **rdepends** recursively, so all specified packages are printed once. The configuration option is **APT::Cache::RecurseDepends**.

-s *file*, **--src-cache=**_file_
> Specify the source cache file used by **gencaches**. The configuration option is **Dir::Cache::srcpkgcache**.

-v, --version
> Print version information and exit.

---

apt-cdrom

apt-cdrom [*options*] *command*

Add a new CD or DVD to **apt**'s list of available sources. The database of CD-ROM IDs that **apt** maintains is */var/lib/apt/cdroms.list*.

Commands

add

Add a disk to the source list.

ident

Print the identity of the current disk and the stored filename. Used for debugging.

Options

-a, --thorough

Do a thorough package scan. May be needed with some old Debian CDs to find all package locations.

-c *file*, **--config-file**=*file*

Specify a configuration file to be read after the default configuration file.

-d *mount-point*, **--cdrom**=*mount-point*

Specify the CD-ROM mount point, which must be listed in */etc/fstab*. The configuration option is **Acquire::cdrom::mount**.

-f, --fast

Do a fast copy, assuming the files are valid and don't all need checking. Specify this only if the disk has been run before without error. The configuration option is **APT::CDROM::Fast**.

-h, --help

Print help message and exit.

-m, --no-mount

Don't mount or unmount the mount point. The configuration option is **APT::CDROM::NoMount**.

-n, --just-print, --recon, --no-act

Check everything, but don't actually make any changes. The configuration option is **APT::CDROM::NoAct**.

-o, --option

Set a configuration option. Syntax is **-o** *group::tool=option*.

-r, --rename

Prompt for a new label and rename the disk to the new value. The configuration option is **APT::CDROM::Rename**.

-v, --version

Print the version information and exit.

---

apt-config

apt-config [*options*] shell *args*
apt-config [*options*] dump

An internal program for querying configuration information, accessing the main configuration file */etc/apt/apt.conf*.

Commands

dump

Display the contents of the configuration space.

---

shell

> Access the configuration information from a shell script. The arguments are in pairs, specifying the name of a shell variable and a configuration value to query. The value may be post-fixed with /x, where x is one of the following letters:

> **b**   Return true or false.

> **d**   Return directories.

> **f**   Return filenames.

> **i**   Return an integer.

Options

-c *file*, **--config-file**=*file*
> Specify a configuration file to be read after the default configuration file.

-h, **--help**
> Print help message and exit.

-o, **--option**
> Set a configuration option. Syntax is **-o** *group::tool=option*.

-v, **--version**
> Print the version information and exit.

---

apt-extracttemplates

apt-extracttemplates [*options*] *files*

Extract configuration scripts and templates from the specified Debian package files. For each specified file, a line of output is generated with the following information:

    package version template-file config-script

and the template files and configuration scripts are written to the directory specified with **-t** or **--temp-dir**, or by the configuration option **APT::ExtractTemplates::TempDir**. The filenames are in the form *package.template.xxxx* and *package.config.xxxx*.

Options

-c *file*, **--config-file**=*file*
> Specify a configuration file to be read after the default configuration file.

-h, **--help**
> Print help message and exit.

-o, **--option**
> Set a configuration option. Syntax is **-o** *group::tool=option*.

-t *dir*, **--tempdir**=*dir*
> Write the extracted template files and configuration scripts to the specified directory. The configuration option is **APT::ExtractTemplates::TempDir**.

-v, **--version**
> Print the version information and exit.

apt-ftparchive   `apt-ftparchive [options] command`

Generate package and other index files used to access a distribution source. The files should be generated on the source's origin site.

Commands

clean *config-file*

Clean the databases used by the specified configuration file by removing obsolete records.

contents *path*

Search the specified directory tree recursively to generate a contents file. For each *.deb* file found, read the file list, sort the files by package, and write the results to standard output. Use with **--db** to specify a binary caching database.

generate *config-file sections*

Build indexes according to the specified configuration file.

packages *path [override [pathprefix]]*

Generate a package file from the specified directory tree. The optional override file contains information describing how the package fits into the distribution, and the optional path prefix is a string prepended to the filename fields. Similar to **dpkg-scanpackages**. Use with **--db** to specify a binary caching database.

release *path*

Generate a release file from the specified directory tree.

sources *paths [override [pathprefix]]*

Generate a source index file from the specified directory tree. The optional override file contains information used to set priorities in the index file and to modify maintainer information. The optional path prefix is a string prepended to the directory field in the generated source index. Use **--source-override** to specify a different source override file. Similar to **dpkg-scansources**.

Options

-c *file*, **--config-file**=*file*

Specify a configuration file to be read after the default configuration file.

--contents

Perform contents generation. If set and if package indexes are being generated with a cache database, the file listing is extracted and stored in the database. If used with **generate**, allows the creation of any contents files. The default is on. The configuration option is **APT::FTPArchive::Contents**.

-d, **--db**

Use a binary caching database. This option has no effect on **generate**. The configuration option is **APT::FTPArchive::DB**.

--delink

Enable delinking of files when used with the **External-Links** setting. The default is on; turn off with **--no-delink**. The configuration option is **APT::FTPArchive::DeLinkAct**.

-h, --help

Print help message and exit.

--md5

Generate MD5 sums for the index files. The default is on. The configuration option is **APT::FTPArchive::MD5**.

-o, --option

Set a configuration option. Syntax is **-o** *group::tool=option*.

-q, --quiet

Run quietly, producing logging information but no progress indicators. Use **-qq** for quieter operation. The configuration option is **quiet**.

--read-only

Make the caching databases read-only. The configuration option is **APT::FTPArchive::ReadOnlyDB**.

-s *file*, **--source-override=***file*

Specify a source override file. Use with the **sources** command. See the **sources** command description for more information. The configuration option is **APT::FTPArchive::SourceOverride**.

-v, --version

Print the version information and exit.

---

apt-get

apt-get [*options*] *command* [*package*...]

A command-line tool for handling packages. Also serves as a backend to other APT tools such as **dselect**, **synaptic**, and **aptitude** (all described later in this section).

Commands

autoclean

Like **clean**, but remove only package files that can no longer be downloaded. Set the configuration option **APT::Clean-Installed** to **off** to prevent installed packages from being erased.

autoremove

Remove packages that were automatically installed to satisfy a dependency and are no longer needed.

build-dep

Install or remove packages to satisfy the build dependencies for a source package.

clean

Clear the local repository of retrieved package files. Useful for freeing up disk space.

check

Update the package cache and check for broken dependencies.

dist-upgrade

Like **upgrade**, but also handle changing dependencies for new package versions intelligently. See the **-f** option for more information.

dselect-upgrade

Used with **dselect**. Track the changes made by **dselect** to the **Status** field of available packages and take actions necessary to realize that status.

install *packages*

Install one or more packages. Specify the package name, not the full filename. Other required packages are also retrieved and installed. With a hyphen appended to the package name, the package is removed if it is already installed. Select a version to install by appending an equals sign and the version. Select a distribution to install by appending a slash and the distribution.

purge *packages*

Like **remove**, but also purge the specified packages from the system.

remove *packages*

Remove one or more packages. Specify the package name, not the full filename. With a plus sign appended to the name, the package is installed.

source *packages*

Find source packages and download them into the current directory. If specified with **--compile**, the source packages are compiled into binary packages. With **--download-only**, the source packages are not unpacked. Select a specific version by appending an equals sign and the version.

update

Resynchronize the package overview files from their sources. Must be done before an **upgrade** or **dist-upgrade**.

upgrade

Install the latest versions of all packages currently installed. Run **update** first.

Options

--arch-only

Process only architecture-dependent build dependencies. Configuration option is **APT::Get::Arch-Only**.

--auto-remove

With **install** or **remove**, remove unused dependencies; like running the **autoremove** command. Configuration option is **APT::Get::AutomaticRemove**.

-b, --compile, --build

Compile source packages after download. The configuration option is **APT::Get::Compile**.

-c *file*, **--config-file**=*file*

Specify a configuration file to read after the default.

-d, --download-only

Retrieve package files, but don't unpack or install them. The configuration option is **APT::Get::Download-only**.

--diff-only

Download only the *diff* file from a source archive. The configuration option is **APT::Get::Diff-Only**.

--dsc-only

Download only the *dsc* file from a source archive. The configuration option is **APT::GET::Dsc-Only**.

-f, --fix-broken

Try to fix a system with broken dependencies. Can be used alone or with a command. Run with the **install** command if you have problems installing packages. You can run the sequence:

```
apt-get -f install
apt-get dist-upgrade
```

several times to clean up interlocking dependency problems. The configuration option is **APT::Get::Fix-Broken**.

--force-yes

Force yes. Cause **apt** to continue without prompting even if it is doing something that could damage your system. Use with great caution and only if absolutely necessary. The configuration option is **APT::Get::force-yes**.

-h, --help

Display a help message and exit.

--ignore-hold

Ignore a hold placed on a package, which would normally prevent the package from being upgraded. Use with **dist-upgrade** to override many undesired holds. The configuration option is **APT::Get::Ignore-Hold**.

--list-cleanup

Erase obsolete files from */var/lib/apt/lists*. The default is on; use **--no-list-cleanup** to turn it off, which you would normally do only if you frequently modify your list of sources. The configuration option is **APT::Get::List-Cleanup**.

-m, --ignore-missing, --fix-missing

Ignore missing or corrupted packages or packages that cannot be retrieved. Can cause problems when used with **-f**. The configuration option is **APT::Get::Fix-Missing**.

--no-download

Disable package downloading; use with **--ignore-missing** to force APT to use only the packages that have already been downloaded. The configuration option is **APT::Get::Download**.

--no-remove

Do not remove any packages; instead, abort without prompting. The configuration option is **APT::Get::Remove**.

--no-upgrade

Do not upgrade packages. Use with **install** to prevent upgrade of packages that are already installed. The configuration option is **APT::Get::Upgrade**.

-o, --option

Set a configuration option. Syntax is **-o** *group::tool=option*.

--only-source

Do not map the names specified with the **source** or **build-dep** commands through the binary table. With this option, only source package names can be specified. The configuration option is **APT::Get::Only-Source**.

--print-uris

Print Uniform Resource Indicators (URIs) of files instead of fetching them. Prints path, destination filename, size, and expected MD5 hash. The configuration option is **APT::Get::Print-URIs**.

--purge

Tell **dpkg** to do a purge instead of a remove for items that would be removed. Purging removes packages completely, including any configuration files. The configuration option is **APT::Get::Purge**.

-q, --quiet

Quiet mode. Omit progress indicators and produce only logging output. Use **-qq** to make even quieter. The configuration option is **quiet**.

--reinstall

Reinstall packages that are already installed, upgrading them to the latest version. The configuration option is **APT::Get::ReInstall**.

-s, --simulate, --just-print, --dry-run, --recon, --no-act

Go through the motions, but don't actually make any changes to the system. The configuration option is **APT::Get::Simulate**.

-t *rel*, **--target-release=***rel*, **--default-release=***rel*

Retrieve packages only from the specified release. The value of *rel* can be a release number or a value such as "unstable." The configuration option is **APT::Default-Release**.

--tar-only

Download only the *tar* file from a source archive. The configuration option is **APT::Get::Tar-Only**.

--trivial-only

Perform only operations that are considered trivial—i.e., ones that won't harm your system, by, say, removing needed files. Unlike **--assume-yes**, which always answers "yes" to any prompts, **--trivial-only** always answers "no." The configuration option is **APT::Get::Trivial-Only**.

-u, --show-upgraded

Print a list of all packages to be upgraded. The configuration option is **APT::Get::Show-Upgraded**.

-v, --version
>   Display the version and exit.

-V, --verbose-versions
>   Show full versions for upgraded and installed packages. The configuration option is **APT::Get::Show-Versions**.

-y, --yes, --assume-yes
>   Automatically reply "yes" to prompts and run noninteractively. Abort if there is an error. The configuration option is **APT::Get::Assume-Yes**.

---

apt-sortpkgs

    apt-sortpkgs [options] indexfiles

Sort the records in a source or package index file by package name and write the results to standard output. **apt-sortpkgs** also sorts the internal fields of each record.

Options

-c *file*, **--config-file**=*file*
>   Specify a configuration file to read after the default.

-h, --help
>   Display a help message and exit.

-o, --option
>   Set a configuration option. Syntax is **-o** *group::tool=option*.

-s, --source
>   Order by source index field. The configuration option is **APT::SortPkgs::Source**.

-v, --version
>   Display the version and exit.

---

aptitude

    aptitude [options] [action [arguments]]

A text-based frontend to **apt**, which can be run either directly from the command line or from a visual mode that runs in a terminal window.

Actions

The following actions are supported. Running **aptitude** with no action invokes the visual mode. Package names can be entered individually or as search patterns. A search pattern consists of terms starting with a tilde (~), followed by a character indicating the type of term, followed by the text to be searched for. The most common usage is to use **~n** to search for a package name (e.g., **~nemacs**, to search for packages that have *emacs* in their name). You can find the full list of term types in the *Aptitude User's Manual*. The manual can be found in */usr/share/doc/aptitude/README* on a Debian-based system. On an RPM-based system with **aptitude** installed, the *README* file may be in */usr/share/aptitude* or */usr/share/doc/aptitude*.

autoclean

Clean out the cache by removing only packages that can no longer be downloaded.

changelog *package*[*=version* | */archive*] ...

Download and display the Debian changelog for each specified package.

clean

Clean out the cache by removing all previously downloaded *.deb* files.

download *package*[*=version* | */archive*] ...

Download the *.deb* file for each specified package to the current directory. With a version, install that version; with an archive, install the version from that archive.

forbid-version *package*[*=version*] ...

Don't allow **aptitude** to upgrade the package to a particular version. If no version is specified, it is assumed to be the version that would normally be used. To override later, use the **install** action.

forget-new

Remove internal information about what packages are "new."

full-upgrade

Upgrade as many installed packages as possible, installing and removing packages as needed to satisfy dependencies. Formerly called **dist-upgrade**, which is now deprecated.

help

Display help information and exit.

hold *packages*

Place a hold on each specified package.

install [*package*[*=version* | */archive*] ...]

Install the specified packages. With a version, install that version. With an archive, install the version in that archive. With no arguments, install any stored or pending actions. You can also use **install** to perform different actions on multiple packages with a single command. Append - to the package name to **remove**, + to **install**, _ to **purge**, = to **hold** a package, or : to leave the package at the current version.

keep *packages*

Cancel any scheduled action on the specified packages.

keep-all

Cancel all scheduled actions on all packages.

markauto *packages*

Mark the specified packages as automatically installed.

purge [*package*[*=version*] ...]

Remove the specified packages and their configuration files.

remove [*package*[*=version*] ...]

Remove the specified packages.

safe-upgrade

Upgrade as many packages as possible; if a package has dependency problems, avoid upgrading that package (but don't remove it).

search *patterns*

Search for packages matching each of the specified patterns and display a list of matches. The full list of search terms can be found in the *Aptitude User's Manual*.

show *patterns*

Search for packages matching each of the specified patterns and display detailed information for every match found.

unhold *packages*

Remove the hold on each specified package.

unmarkauto *packages*

Mark the specified packages as manually installed.

update

Update the list of available packages by downloading the names of new and upgradeable packages.

why, **why-not** *packages*

Display reasons why the specified packages can or cannot be installed.

Options

Most of the **aptitude** options have corresponding configuration options that can be set in the configuration file.

-d, --download-only

Download packages to the cache but do not install them. Configuration option is **Aptitude::CmdLine::Download-Only**.

-D, --show-deps

Show summaries of why packages will be automatically installed or removed. Configuration option is **Aptitude::CmdLine::Show-Deps**.

-f   Attempt to fix dependencies of broken packages. Configuration option is **Aptitude::CmdLine::Fix-Broken**.

-F *format*, **--display-format** *format*

Specify the output format for **search**. See the *Aptitude User's Manual* for details on specifying the format. Configuration option is **Aptitude::CmdLine::Package-Display-Format**.

-h, --help

Print help message and exit.

-O *order*, **--sort** *order*

Specify the sort order for **search** output. See the *Aptitude User's Manual* for details.

-P, --prompt

Always display a prompt even for actions that were explicitly requested. The corresponding configuration option is **Aptitude::CmdLine::Always-Prompt**.

--purge-unused

Purge packages that are no longer required by any installed package.

-q[=*n*], **--quiet**[=*n*]

Run in quiet mode, suppressing progress indicators. Use multiple **q**s to run even quieter, or specify a number *n* to indicate directly the degree of quietness.

-r, --with-recommends

Treat recommendations as dependencies when installing new packages. The corresponding configuration option is **Aptitude::CmdLine::Recommends-Important**.

-R, --without-recommends

Do not treat recommendations as dependencies when installing new packages. The corresponding configuration option is **Aptitude::CmdLine::Recommends-Important**.

-s, --simulate

Go through the motions, but do not actually perform the actions. Print the actions that would be performed. Configuration option is **Aptitude::Simulate**.

--schedule-only

Schedule actions to be performed later, but don't perform them now. Works with actions that modify package states; to run them later, use **aptitude install** with no arguments.

-t *release*, **--target-release** *release*

Specify the release to use for installing packages. Equivalent to adding /*release* to package names for the **changelog, download**, and **show** actions. The corresponding configuration option is **Aptitude::CmdLine::Default-Release**.

-v, --verbose

Operate verbosely, displaying additional information. Specify multiple times to get even more information displayed. The corresponding configuration option is **Aptitude::CmdLine::Verbose**.

-V, --show-versions

Display the version for packages being installed. Configuration option is **Aptitude::CmdLine::Show-Versions**.

--version

Display the version information for **aptitude** and exit.

--visual-preview

Start the visual interface and display the preview screen.

-w *width*, **--width** *width*

Specify the output display width for **search**. The default is the terminal width. The corresponding configuration option is **Aptitude::CmdLine::Package-Display-Width**.

-y, --assume-yes

Assume a yes response to a yes/no prompt and don't display the prompt. Prompts for dangerous actions are still shown. This option overrides -P. The corresponding configuration option is **Aptitude::CmdLine::Assume-Yes**.

-Z   Display the disk space that will be used or freed by the packages being acted upon. The corresponding configuration option is **Aptitude::CmdLine::Show-Size-Changes**.

Internal options

The following options are used internally for **aptitude**'s visual mode. You shouldn't need to issue them directly.

-i   Display a download preview when the program starts. Cannot be used with **-u**.

-S *filename*
Load extended state information from the specified file, not the default state file.

-u   Begin updating the package lists when the program starts. Cannot be used with **-i**.

---

dpkg

dpkg [*options*] *action*

A tool for installing, managing, and building packages. Also serves as a frontend to **dpkg-deb** and **dpkg-query**.

dpkg actions

These actions are carried out by **dpkg** itself:

-A *pkgfile*, **--record-avail** *pkgfile*
Update the record of available files kept in */var/lib/dpkg/available* with information from *pkgfile*. This information is used by **dpkg** and **dselect** to determine which packages are available. With **-R** or **--recursive**, *pkgfile* must be a directory.

-C, --audit
Search for partially installed packages and suggest how to get them working.

--clear-avail
Remove existing information about which packages are available.

--clear-selections
Set the state of every nonessential package to **deinstall** to deselect them before running **dpkg --set-selections**.

--command-fd *n*
Accept commands passed on the file descriptor given by *n*. Note that any additional options set through this file descriptor or on the command line are not reset, but remain for other commands issued during the same session.

--compare-versions *ver1 op ver2*
Perform a binary comparison of two version numbers. The operators **lt le eq ne ge gt** treat a missing version as earlier. The operators **lt-nl le-nl ge-nl gt-nl** treat a missing version as later (where **nl** is "not later"). A third set of operators (< << <= = >= >> >) is provided for compatibility with control-file syntax. **dpkg** returns zero for success (i.e., the condition is satisfied) and nonzero otherwise.

--configure [*packages* | **-a** | **--pending**]
> Reconfigure one or more unpacked *packages*. If **-a** or **--pending** is given instead of *packages*, configure all packages that are unpacked but not configured. Configuring a package involves unpacking the configuration files, backing up the old configuration files, and running the **postinst** script if one is present.

-Dh, --debug=help
> Print debugging help message and exit.

--force-help
> Print help message about the **--force-***list* options and exit. See the **--force-***list* option description for the possible values of *list*.

--forget-old-unavail
> Forget about uninstalled, unavailable packages.

--get-selections [*pattern*]
> Get list of package selections and write to standard output. With *pattern* specified, write selections that match the pattern.

--help
> Print help message and exit.

-i *pkgfile*, **--install** *pkgfile*
> Install the package specified as *pkgfile*. With **-R** or **--recursive**, *pkgfile* must be a directory.

--license, --licence
> Print **dpkg** license information and exit.

--print-architecture
> Print the target architecture.

--print-installation-architecture
> Print the host architecture for installation.

-r, --remove [*packages* | **-a** | **--pending**]
-P, --purge [*packages* | **-a** | **--pending**]
> Remove or purge one or more installed *packages*. Removal gets rid of everything except the configuration files listed in *debian/conffiles*; purging also removes the configuration files. If **-a** or **--pending** is given instead of *packages*, **dpkg** removes or purges all packages that are unpacked and marked (in */var/lib/dpkg/status*) for removing or purging.

--set-selections
> Set package selections based on input file read from standard input.

--unpack *pkgfile*
> Unpack the package, but don't configure it. When used with **-R** or **--recursive**, *pkgfile* must be a directory.

--update-avail *pkgs-file*
--merge-avail *pkgs-file*
> Update the record of available files kept in */var/lib/dpkg/available*. This information is used by **dpkg** and **dselect** to determine what packages are available. Update replaces the information with the contents of the *pkgs-file*, distributed as

Packages. Merge combines the information from *Packages* with the existing information. You can also use **dselect update** to do the same thing.

--version
Print **dpkg** version information and exit.

--yet-to-unpack
Search for uninstalled packages that have been selected for installation.

dpkg-deb actions

The following actions can be specified for **dpkg** and are passed to **dpkg-deb** for execution. Also see **dpkg-deb**.

-b *dir* [*archive*], **--build** *dir* [*archive*]
Build a package.

-c *archive*, **--contents** *archive*
List the contents of a package.

-e *archive* [*dir*], **--control** *archive* [*dir*]
Extract control information from a package.

-f *archive* [*control-fields*], **--field** *archive* [*control-fields*]
Display the control field or fields of a package.

-I *archive* [*control-files*], **--info** *archive* [*control-files*]
Show information about a package.

--fsys-tarfile *archive*
Write the filesystem tree contained in a package to standard output in *tar* format.

-x *archive dir*, **--extract** *archive dir*
Extract the files from a package.

-X *archive dir*, **--vextract** *archive dir*
Extract the files and display the filenames from a package.

dpkg-query actions

The following actions can be specified for **dpkg** and are passed to **dpkg-query** for execution. Also see **dpkg-query**.

-l, **--list** [*pkg-name-pattern*]
List all packages whose names match the specified pattern. With no pattern, list all packages in */var/lib/dpkg/available*.

-L *packages*, **--listfiles** *packages*
List installed files that came from the specified package or packages.

-p, **--print-avail** *package*
Print the details about *package* from */var/lib/dpkg/available*.

-s *packages*, **--status** *packages*
Report the status of one or more *packages*.

-S *filename-pattern*, **--search** *filename-pattern*
Search installed packages for a filename.

Options

dpkg options can be specified on the command line or set in the configuration file. Each line in the configuration file contains a single option, specified without the leading dash (-).

--abort-after=_num_
> Abort processing after _num_ errors. Default is 50.

--admindir= _dir_, **--instdir=** _dir_, **--root=**_dir_
> Change default directories. **admindir** contains administrative files with status and other information about packages; it defaults to _/var/lib/dpkg_. **instdir** is the directory into which packages are installed; it defaults to _/_. Changing the **root** directory to _dir_ automatically changes **instdir** to _dir_ and **admindir** to _/dir/var/lib/dpkg_.

-B, --auto-deconfigure
> When a package is removed, automatically deconfigure any other package that depended on it.

-D_octal_, **--debug=**_octal_
> Turn on debugging, with the _octal_ value specifying the desired level of debugging information. Use **-Dh** or **--debug=help** to display the possible values. You can OR the values to get the desired output.

-E, --skip-same-version
> Don't install the package if this version is already installed.

--force-_list_, **--no-force-**_list_, **--refuse-**_list_
> Force or refuse to force an operation. _list_ is specified as a comma-separated list of options. With **--force**, a warning is printed, but processing continues. **--refuse** and **--no-force** cause processing to stop with an error. Use **--force-help** to display a message describing the options. The force/refuse options are:

> **all**
> > Turn all force options on or off.

> **architecture**
> > Process even if intended for a different architecture.

> **bad-path**
> > Some programs are missing from the path.

> **bad-verify**
> > Install package even if it fails to verify.

> **confdef**
> > Always choose the default action for modified configuration files. If there is no default and **confnew** or **confold** is also specified, use that to decide; otherwise, ask the user.

> **configure-any**
> > Configure any unpacked but unconfigured package that the package depends on.

conflicts

Permit installation of conflicting packages. Can result in problems from files being overwritten.

confmiss

Always install a missing configuration file. Be careful using this option, since it means overriding the removal of the file.

confnew

Always install the new version of a modified configuration file, unless **confdef** is also specified. In that case, use the default action if there is one.

confold

Keep the old version of a modified configuration file, unless **confdef** is also specified. In that case, use the default action if there is one.

depends

Turn dependency problems into warnings.

depends-version

Warn of version problems when checking dependencies, but otherwise ignore.

downgrade

Install even if a newer version is already installed. Forced by default. Note that no dependency checking is done, so use of this option can cause serious system problems.

hold

Process packages even if they are marked to be held.

not-root

Try to install or remove even when not logged on as root.

overwrite

Overwrite a file from one package with the same file from another package.

overwrite-dir

Overwrite one package's directory with a file from another package.

overwrite-diverted

Overwrite a diverted file with an undiverted version.

remove-essential

Remove a package even if it is essential. Note that this can cause your system to stop working.

remove-reinstreq

Remove a package even if it is broken and is marked to require reinstallation.

-G, --refuse-downgrade

Don't install a package if a newer version is already installed.

--ignore-depends=_pkglist_

Dependency problems result only in a warning for the packages in _pkglist_.

--log=*filename*

Log status updates and actions to the specified file instead of the default */var/log/dpkg.log*.

--new

New binary package format. This is a **dpkg-deb** option.

--no-act, --dry-run, --simulate

Go through the motions, but don't actually write any changes. Used for testing. Be sure to specify before the action; otherwise, changes might be written.

--nocheck

Ignore the contents of the control file when building a package. This is a **dpkg-deb** option.

--no-debsig

Do not verify package signatures.

-O, --selected-only

Process only packages that are marked as selected for installation.

--old

Old binary package format. This is a **dpkg-deb** option.

-R, --recursive

Recursively handle *.deb* files found in the directories and their subdirectories specified with **-A, -i, --install, --unpack**, and **--avail**.

--status-fd *n*

Send the package status information to the specified file descriptor. Can be given more than once.

---

dpkg-deb

dpkg-deb *action* [*options*]

Backend command for building and managing Debian package archives. Also see **dpkg**; you'll often want to use **dpkg** to pass commands through to **dpkg-deb**, rather than call **dpkg-deb** directly.

Actions

-b *dir* [*archive*], --build *dir* [*archive*]

Create an *archive* from the filesystem tree starting with directory *dir*. The directory must have a *DEBIAN* subdirectory containing the control file and any other control information. If *archive* is specified and is a filename, the package is written to that file; if no *archive* is specified, the package is written to *dir.deb*. If the archive already exists, it is replaced. If *archive* is the name of a directory, **dpkg-deb** looks in the control file for the information it needs to generate the package name. (Note that for this reason, you cannot use **--nocheck** with a directory name.)

-c *archive*, --contents *archive*

List the filesystem-tree portion of *archive*.

-e *archive* [*dir*], **--control** *archive* [*dir*]

> Extract control information from *archive* into the directory *dir*, which is created if it doesn't exist. If *dir* is omitted, a *DEBIAN* subdirectory in the current directory is used.

-f *archive* [*control-fields*], **--field** *archive* [*control-fields*]

> Extract information about one or more fields in the control file for *archive*. If no fields are provided, print the entire control file.

-h, --help

> Print help information and exit.

-I *archive* [*control-files*], **--info** *archive* [*control-files*]

> Write information about binary package *archive* to standard output. If no control files are provided, print a summary of the package contents; otherwise, print the control files in the order they were specified. An error message is printed to standard error for any missing components.

--fsys-tarfile *archive*

> Extract the filesystem tree from *archive*, and send it to standard output in **tar** format. Can be used with **tar** to extract individual files from an archive.

--license, --licence

> Print the license information and exit.

--version

> Print the version number and exit.

-W *archive*, **--show** *archive*

> Show information about the specified archive. Display package name and version on one line or customize with the **--show-format** option.

-x *archive dir*, **--extract** *archive dir*
-X *archive dir*, **--vextract** *archive dir*

> Extract the filesystem tree from *archive* into the specified directory, creating *dir* if it doesn't already exist. **-x** (**--extract**) works silently, while **-X** (**--vextract**) lists the files as it extracts them. Do not use this action to install packages; use **dpkg** instead.

Options

-D, --debug

> Turn on debugging.

--new

> Build a new-style archive format (this is the default).

--nocheck

> Don't check the control file before building an archive. This lets you build a broken archive.

--old

> Build an old-style archive format; obsolete.

--showformat=*format*

> Specify the output format for **-W/--show**. The format can include the standard escape sequences **\n** (newline), **\r** (carriage return), or **** (backslash). Specify package fields with the syntax ${*var*[;*width*]}. Fields are right-aligned by default, or left-aligned if *width* is negative.

-z#

> Set the compression level to the value specified by **#** when building an archive.

-Z *type*

> Set the type of compression to use when building an archive. Possible values are **gzip**, **bzip2**, and **none**.

---

dpkg-query

dpkg-query [*option*] *command*

Display information about packages listed in the **dpkg** database. You can also use **dpkg-query** as a backend for **dpkg**, instead of calling **dpkg-query** directly.

Commands

--help

> Print help information and exit.

-l [*patterns*], **--list** [*patterns*]

> List packages whose names match any of the specified patterns. With no pattern specified, list all packages in */var/lib/dpkg/status*. The pattern may need to be in quotes to avoid expansion by the shell.

-L *packages*, **--listfiles** *packages*

> List files installed on your system from each of the specified packages. This command does not list files created by package-specific installation scripts.

--license, **--licence**

> Print the license information and exit.

-p *package*, **--print-avail** *package*

> Display details for the specified package, as found in */var/lib/dpkg/available*.

-s *package*, **--status** *package*

> Report on the status of the specified package.

-S *patterns*, **--search** *patterns*

> Search the installed packages for filenames matching one of the specified patterns. At least one pattern must be specified.

-W [*patterns*], **--show** [*patterns*]

> Like **-l**, but the output can be customized with the **--showformat** option.

--version

> Print version information and exit.

Options

--admindir=*dir*

Use *dir* as the location of the **dpkg** database. The default is */var/lib/dpkg*.

-f *format*, **--showformat**=*format*

Specify the output format for **-W/--show**. The format can include the standard escape sequences **\n** (newline), **\r** (carriage return), or **** (backslash). Specify package fields with the syntax ${*var*[;*width*]}. Fields are right-aligned by default, or left-aligned if *width* is negative.

---

dpkg-split

dpkg-split [*action*] [*options*]

Split a binary package into smaller pieces and reassemble the pieces, either manually or in automatic mode. The automatic mode maintains a queue of parts for reassembling.

Actions

-a -o *output part*, **--auto -o** *output part*

Add *part* to the queue for automatic reassembly, and if all the parts are available, reassemble the package as *output*. Requires the use of the **-o** (or **--output**) option, as shown.

-d [*packages*], **--discard** [*packages*]

Discard parts from the automatic-assembly queue. If any *packages* are specified, discard only parts from those packages. Otherwise, empty the queue.

-I *parts*, **--info** *parts*

Print information about the specified part file or files to standard output.

-j *parts*, **--join** *parts*

Join the parts of a package file together from the *parts* specified. The default output file is *package-version.deb*.

-l, **--listq**

List the contents of the queue of parts waiting for reassembly, giving the package name, the parts that are on the queue, and the number of bytes.

-s *full-package* [*prefix*], **--split** *full-package* [*prefix*]

Split the package *full-package* into parts *N* of *M*, named *prefix-NofM.deb*. The prefix defaults to the *full-package* name without the *.deb* extension.

-h, **--help**

Print help message and exit.

--license, **--licence**

Print license information and exit.

--version

Print version information and exit.

Options

--depotdir *dir*

Specify an alternate directory *dir* for the queue of parts waiting for reassembly. Default is */var/lib/dpkg*.

--msdos

Force **--split** output filenames to be MS-DOS-compatible.

-Q, --npquiet

Do not print an error message for a part that doesn't belong to a binary package when doing automatic queuing or reassembly.

-o *output*, **--output** *output*

Use *output* as the filename for a reassembled package.

-S *num*, **--partsize** *num*

When splitting, specify the maximum part size (*num*) in kilobytes. Default is 450 KB.

---

dselect

dselect [*options*] [*action*]

A screen-oriented user frontend to **dpkg**, used to install and manage packages. See **dpkg** and **dpkg-deb** for information on building packages.

Actions

If **dselect** is run with no action specified on the command line, it displays the following menu:

```
* 0. [A]ccess   Choose the access method to use.
  1. [U]pdate   Update list of available packages, if
                possible.
  2. [S]elect   Request which packages you want on your
                system.
  3. [I]nstall  Install and upgrade wanted packages.
  4. [C]onfig   Configure any packages that are
                unconfigured.
  5. [R]emove   Remove unwanted software.
  6. [Q]uit     Quit dselect.
```

The asterisk (on the first line) shows the currently selected option. Any of the menu items can be specified directly on the command line as an action (**access**, **update**, **select**, **install**, **config**, **remove**, **quit**) to go directly to the desired activity. For example:

$ dselect access

If you enter **quit** on the command line, **dselect** exits immediately without doing anything. An additional command-line action is **menu**, which displays the menu and is equivalent to running **dselect** with no action.

Options

Options can be specified both on the command line and in the **dselect** configuration file, */etc/dpkg/dselect.cfg*.

--admindir *dir*

> Change the directory that holds internal datafiles to *dir*. Default is */var/lib/dpkg*.

--color *colorspec*, **--colour** *colorspec*

> Set colors for different parts of the screen, as specified by *colorspec* as follows:
>
> > *screenpart*:[*fgcolor*],[*bgcolor*][:*attr*[+*attr*+...]]
>
> This option can be specified multiple times, to override the default colors for different *screenparts*. Rather than having to specify the colors on the command line each time you run **dselect**, you might prefer to set them in the configuration file. The possible screen parts (going from the top of the screen to the bottom) are:
>
> **title**
>
> > The screen title.
>
> **listhead**
>
> > The header line above the package list.
>
> **list**
>
> > The scrolling list of packages and some help text.
>
> **listsel**
>
> > The selected item in the list.
>
> **pkgstate**
>
> > The text showing the current state of each package.
>
> **pkgstatesel**
>
> > The text showing the current state of the selected package.
>
> **infohead**
>
> > The header line showing the state of the selected package.
>
> **infodesc**
>
> > The short description of the package.
>
> **info**
>
> > The text that displays information such as the package description.
>
> **infofoot**
>
> > The last line of the screen when selecting packages.
>
> **query**
>
> > Query lines.
>
> **helpscreen**
>
> > The color of help screens.
>
> Either the foreground color, the background color, or both can be specified for each screen part. The colors are given as the standard **curses** colors. After the color specification, you can specify a list of attributes separated by plus signs (+). The possible attributes are **normal**, **standout**, **underline**, **reverse**, **blink**, **bright**, **dim**, and **bold**. Not all attributes work on all terminals.

--expert
> Run in expert mode; don't print help messages.

-D [*file*], **--debug** [*file*]
> Turn on debugging. Send output to *file* if specified.

--help
> Print help message and exit.

--license, licence
> Print license information and exit.

--version
> Print version information and exit.

---

synaptic

synaptic [*options*]

Graphical frontend for APT. Use in place of **apt-get** to install, upgrade, or remove packages from your system. With **synaptic**, you can view a list of all available packages, or you can break the list down in various ways to make it more manageable. From the **synaptic** window, you can select from a list of categories. The categories are section (e.g., view only development-related packages), package status, origin, search history, or filter.

If you choose to display by filter, there is a set of predefined filters, or you can define your own. The predefined filters include ones to display all packages, packages marked for a status change, packages that can be configured with **debconf** (Debian systems only), packages with broken dependencies, and packages that can be upgraded to a later version. You can edit the existing filters or define your own, by selecting Filters from the Settings menu.

Once you've used the selection criteria to find the list of packages, you can select a single package, or you can select multiple packages by holding down the Shift or Ctrl key. Like **apt-get**, first do an **update** to update the package lists, then you can do an **install** or **upgrade**.

To start **synaptic** from Gnome, select Administration → Synaptic Package Manager from the System menu. From the KDE menu, select System → Synaptic Package Manager. You can also start the graphical interface from the command line, with the command:

> synaptic [*options*]

Options

In addition to the following options, **synaptic** accepts the standard GTK+ toolkit command-line options.

-f *filename*, **--filter-file**=*filename*
> Use the specified file as an alternative filter settings file.

-h, --help
> Print help message and exit.

-i *num*, **--initial-filter**=*num*
> Start up with the filter numbered *num* as the initial filter.

--non-interactive
> Run without prompting for user input.

*-o*option, **--option**=*option*
> Set an internal option. Don't use this option unless you are
> sure you know what you are doing.

-r Open with the file repository window displayed. This window
> lists the repositories and shows which are active.

6

The Bash Shell

The *shell* is a program that acts as a buffer between you and the operating system. In its role as a command interpreter, it should (for the most part) act invisibly. There are three main uses for the shell: interactive use; customizing your Linux session by defining *variables* and startup files; and programming, by writing and executing *shell scripts*.

The original Bourne shell became the standard shell for writing shell scripts. The Bourne shell is still found in */bin/sh* on Linux systems but is now usually a symbolic link to Bash. Because the Berkeley C shell (**csh** and later **tcsh**) offered better features for interactive use, such as command history and job control, for a long time the standard practice was to use the Bourne shell for programming and the C shell for daily use. David Korn at Bell Labs enhanced the Bourne shell by adding **csh**-like features; his shell is known as the Korn shell (**ksh**).

The Free Software Foundation developed a clone of the Bourne shell, written from scratch, named "Bash," the Bourne-Again SHell. Over time, Bash has become a POSIX-compliant version of the shell, incorporating many popular features from other shells, such as **csh**, **tcsh**, and **ksh**. Bash is the primary shell for Linux.

Another popular shell is the Z Shell, **zsh**, which is similar to **ksh** but with many extensions. **zsh** differs from Bash both in being based on **ksh** and because it does not attempt to be POSIX-compliant the way Bash does.

This chapter covers Bash. All references are to Bash version 4, which among numerous other changes includes new features such as associative arrays and coprocesses. The following topics are presented:

- Overview of features
- Invoking the shell
- Syntax
- Functions
- Variables

- Arithmetic expressions
- Command history
- Job control
- Command execution
- Restricted shells
- Built-in commands

http://www.gnu.org/software/bash/bash.html provides information about the Bash shell, as does *http://tiswww.case.edu/php/chet/bash/bashtop.html*. See also *Classic Shell Scripting* and *Learning the bash Shell* (both from O'Reilly).

Overview of Features

The Bash shell provides the following features:

- Input/output redirection
- Wildcard characters (metacharacters) for filename abbreviation
- Shell variables and options for customizing your environment
- A built-in command set for writing shell programs
- Shell functions, for modularizing tasks within a shell program
- Job control
- Command-line editing (using the command syntax of either **vi** or **emacs**)
- Access to previous commands (command history)
- Integer arithmetic
- Arrays and arithmetic expressions
- Command-name abbreviation (aliasing)
- Upward compliance with POSIX
- Internationalization facilities
- An arithmetic **for** loop
- More ways to substitute variables

Invoking the Shell

The command interpreter for the Bash shell (**bash**) can be invoked as follows:

```
bash [options] [arguments]
```

Bash can execute commands from a terminal, from a file (when the first *argument* is an executable script), or from standard input (if no arguments remain or if **-s** is specified). Bash automatically prints prompts if standard input is a terminal, or if **-i** is given on the command line.

On Linux systems, */bin/sh* is generally a link to Bash. When invoked as **sh**, Bash acts more like the traditional Bourne shell: Login shells read */etc/profile* and *~/.profile*, and regular shells read $ENV, if it's set. Full details are available on the **bash** manpage.

Options

If both single- and multi-character options appear on the command line, the multi-character options must appear first.

-, --
> End option processing.

-c *str*
> Read commands from string *str*.

-D, --dump-strings
> Print all $"..." strings in the program.

--debugger
> Read the debugging profile at startup, turn on the **extdebug** option to **shopt**, and enable function tracing. For use by the Bash debugger.

--dump-po-strings
> Same as **-D**, but output in GNU **gettext** po (portable object) format.

--help
> Print a usage message and exit successfully

-i   Create an interactive shell (prompt for input).

--init-file *file*, **--rcfile** *file*
> Use *file* as the startup file instead of ~/.bashrc for interactive shells.

--login
> Shell is a login shell.

--noediting
> Do not use the *readline* library for input, even in an interactive shell.

--noprofile
> Do not read /etc/profile or any of the personal startup files.

--norc
> Do not read ~/.bashrc. Enabled automatically when invoked as **sh**.

-O *option*
> Enable the **shopt** built-in command option *option*.

-p   Start up as a privileged user. Don't read $ENV or $BASH_ENV, don't import functions from the environment, and ignore the value of $SHELLOPTS.

--posix
> Turn on POSIX mode.

-r, --restricted
> Create a restricted shell.

-s   Read commands from standard input; output from built-in commands goes to file descriptor 1 (standard output); all other shell output goes to file descriptor 2 (standard error).

--verbose
> Same as **set -v**; the shell prints lines as it reads them.

--version
> Print a version message and exit.

The remaining options to Bash are listed under the **set** built-in command.

Arguments

Arguments are assigned in order to the positional parameters **$1**, **$2**, etc. If the first argument is an executable script, commands are read from it, and the remaining arguments are assigned to **$1**, **$2**, etc. The name of the script is available as **$0**.

Syntax

This section describes the many symbols peculiar to the Bash shell. The topics are arranged as follows:

- Special files
- Filename metacharacters
- Quoting
- Command forms
- Redirection forms
- Coprocesses

Special Files

Bash reads one or more startup files. Some of the files are read only when a shell is a login shell.

The startup files are, in the order they are read:

1. */etc/profile*. Executed automatically at login.
2. The first file found from this list: *~/.bash_profile*, *~/.bash_login*, or *~/.profile*. Executed automatically at login.
3. *~/.bashrc* is read by every shell, after the login files. However, if invoked as **sh**, Bash instead reads $ENV.

The **getpwnam**( ) and **getpwuid**( ) functions are the sources of home directories for *~name* abbreviations. (On single-user systems, the user database is stored in */etc/passwd*. However on networked systems, this information may come from NIS, NIS+, or LDAP—not your workstation password file.)

Filename Metacharacters

Characters	Meaning
*	Match any string of zero or more characters.
?	Match any single character.
[*abc...*]	Match any one of the enclosed characters; a hyphen can specify a range (e.g., **a-z, A-Z, 0-9**).
[!*abc...*], [^*abc...*]	Match any character *not* enclosed as above.
~	Home directory of the current user.
~*name*	Home directory of user *name*.
~+	Current working directory ($PWD).
~-	Previous working directory ($OLDPWD).

With the **extglob** option on:

Characters	Meaning
?(*pattern*)	Match zero or one instance of *pattern*.
*(*pattern*)	Match zero or more instances of *pattern*.
+(*pattern*)	Match one or more instances of *pattern*.
@(*pattern*)	Match exactly one instance of *pattern*.
!(*pattern*)	Match any strings that don't match *pattern*.

This *pattern* can be a sequence of patterns separated by |, meaning that the match applies to any of the patterns. This extended syntax resembles that available in **egrep** and **awk**.

Bash supports the POSIX [[=c=]] notation for matching characters that have the same weight, and [[.c.]] for specifying collating sequences. In addition, character classes, of the form [[:*class*:]], allow you to match the following classes of characters.

Class	Characters matched	Class	Characters matched
alnum	Alphanumeric characters	graph	Nonspace characters
alpha	Alphabetic characters	print	Printable characters
blank	Space or tab	punct	Punctuation characters
cntrl	Control characters	space	Whitespace characters
digit	Decimal digits	upper	Uppercase characters
lower	Lowercase characters	xdigit	Hexadecimal digits

Bash also accepts the [:**word**:] character class, which is not in POSIX. [[:**word**:]] is equivalent to [[:**alnum**:]_].

Examples

```
$ ls new*              List new and new.1
$ cat ch?              Match ch9 but not ch10
$ vi [D-R]*            Match files that begin with uppercase D through R
$ pr !(*.o|core) | lp  Print files that are not object files or core dumps
```

 On modern systems, ranges such as [**D-R**] are not portable; the system's locale may include more than just the uppercase letters from **D** to **R** in the range.

Quoting

Quoting disables a character's special meaning and allows it to be used literally, as itself. The following table displays characters that have special meaning to the Bash shell.

Character	Meaning
;	Command separator
&	Background execution
( )	Command grouping
|	Pipe
< > &	Redirection symbols
*?[]~+-@!	Filename metacharacters
"'\	Used in quoting other characters
`	Command substitution
$	Variable substitution (or command or arithmetic substitution)
space tab newline	Word separators

These characters can be used for quoting:

" " Everything between " and " is taken literally, except for the following characters that keep their special meaning:

$ Variable (or command and arithmetic) substitution will occur.

' Command substitution will occur.

" This marks the end of the double quote.

' ' Everything between ' and ' is taken literally except for another '. You cannot embed another ' within such a quoted string.

\ The character following a \ is taken literally. Use within " " to escape ", $, and '. Often used to escape itself, spaces, or newlines.

$" "

Just like " ", except that locale translation is done.

$' '

Similar to ' ', but the quoted text is processed for the following escape sequences.

Sequence	Value	Sequence	Value
\a	Alert	\t	Tab
\b	Backspace	\v	Vertical tab
\c*X*	Control character X	\n*nn*	Octal value *nnn*
\e	Escape	\x*nn*	Hexadecimal value *nn*
\E	Escape	\'	Single quote
\f	Form feed	\"	Double quote
\n	Newline	\\	Backslash
\r	Carriage return		

Examples

```
$ echo 'Single quotes "protect" double quotes'
Single quotes "protect" double quotes
$ echo "Well, isn't that \"special\"?"
Well, isn't that "special"?
```

```
$ echo "You have `ls | wc -l` files in `pwd`"
You have      43 files in /home/bob
$ echo "The value of \$x is $x"
The value of $x is 100
```

Command Forms

Syntax	Effect
cmd &	Execute *cmd* in background.
cmd1 ; *cmd2*	Command sequence; execute multiple *cmd*s on the same line.
{ *cmd1* ; *cmd2* ; }	Execute commands as a group in the current shell.
(*cmd1* ; *cmd2*)	Execute commands as a group in a subshell.
cmd1 | *cmd2*	Pipe; use output from *cmd1* as input to *cmd2*.
cmd1 `cmd2`	Command substitution; use *cmd2* output as arguments to *cmd1*.
cmd1 $(*cmd2*)	POSIX shell command substitution; nesting is allowed.
cmd $((*expression*))	POSIX shell arithmetic substitution. Use the result of *expression* as argument to *cmd*.
cmd1 && *cmd2*	AND; execute *cmd1* and then (if *cmd1* succeeds) *cmd2*. This is a "short-circuit" operation; *cmd2* is never executed if *cmd1* fails.
cmd1 || *cmd2*	OR; execute either *cmd1* or (if *cmd1* fails) *cmd2*. This is a "short-circuit" operation; *cmd2* is never executed if *cmd1* succeeds.
! *cmd*	NOT; execute *cmd*, and produce a zero exit status if *cmd* exits with a nonzero status. Otherwise, produce a nonzero status when *cmd* exits with a zero status.

Examples

```
$ nroff file > file.txt &          Format in the background
$ cd; ls                           Execute sequentially
$ (date; who; pwd) > logfile       All output is redirected
$ sort file | pr -3 | lp           Sort file, page output, then print
$ vi `grep -l ifdef *.c`           Edit files found by grep
$ egrep '(yes|no)' `cat list`      Specify a list of files to search
$ egrep '(yes|no)' $(cat list)     POSIX version of previous
$ egrep '(yes|no)' $(< list)       Faster, not in POSIX
$ grep XX file && lp file          Print file if it contains the pattern;
$ grep XX file || echo "XX not found"   Otherwise, echo an error message
```

Redirection Forms

File descriptor	Name	Common abbreviation	Typical default
0	Standard input	stdin	Keyboard
1	Standard output	stdout	Screen
2	Standard error	stderr	Screen

The usual input source or output destination can be changed, as seen in the following sections.

Simple redirection

cmd > *file*
> Send output of *cmd* to *file* (overwrite).

cmd >> *file*
> Send output of *cmd* to *file* (append).

cmd < *file*
> Take input for *cmd* from *file*.

cmd << *text*
> The contents of the shell script up to a line identical to *text* become the standard input for *cmd* (*text* can be stored in a shell variable). This command form is sometimes called a *Here document*. Input is usually typed at the keyboard or in the shell program. Commands that typically use this syntax include **cat**, **ex**, and **sed**. (If <<- is used, leading tabs are stripped from the contents of the here document, and the tabs are ignored when comparing input with the end-of-input *text* marker.) If any part of *text* is quoted, the input is passed through verbatim. Otherwise, the contents are processed for variable, command, and arithmetic substitutions.

cmd <<< *word*
> Supply text of *word*, with trailing newline, as input to *cmd*. (This is known as a *here string*, from the free version of the **rc** shell.)

cmd <> *file*
> Open *file* for reading *and* writing on the standard input. The contents are not destroyed.*

cmd >| *file*
> Send output of *cmd* to *file* (overwrite), even if the shell's **noclobber** option is set.

Redirection using file descriptors

Syntax	Effect
cmd >&*n*	Send *cmd* output to file descriptor *n*.
cmd *m*>&*n*	Same, except that output that would normally go to file descriptor *m* is sent to file descriptor *n* instead.
cmd >&-	Close standard output.
cmd <&*n*	Take input for *cmd* from file descriptor *n*.
cmd *m*<&*n*	Same, except that input that would normally come from file descriptor *m* comes from file descriptor *n* instead.
cmd <&-	Close standard input.
cmd <&*n*-	Move input file descriptor *n* instead of duplicating it.
cmd >&*n*-	Move output file descriptor *n* instead of duplicating it.

---

* With <, the file is opened read-only, and writes on the file descriptor will fail. With <>, the file is opened read-write; it is up to the application to actually take advantage of this.

Multiple redirection

Syntax	Effect
cmd 2>file	Send standard error to *file*; standard output remains the same (e.g., the screen).
cmd > file 2>&1	Send both standard error and standard output to *file*.
cmd &>>file	Append both standard error and standard output to *file*.
cmd &> file	Same. Preferred form.
cmd >& file	Same.
cmd > f1 2>f2	Send standard output to file *f1*, standard error to file *f2*.
cmd | **tee** *files*	Send output of *cmd* to standard output (usually the terminal) and to *files*. (See the example in Chapter 3 under **tee**.)
cmd 2>&1 | **tee** *files*	Send standard output and error output of *cmd* to standard output (usually the terminal) and to *files*.
cmd |&	Same as *cmd* 2>&1 | to send standard error through a pipe.

No space should appear between file descriptors and a redirection symbol; spacing is optional in the other cases.

Examples

```
$ cat part1 > book
$ cat part2 part3 >> book
$ mail tim < report
$ sed 's/^/XX /g' << END_ARCHIVE
> This is often how a shell archive is "wrapped",
> bundling text for distribution.  You would normally
> run sed from a shell program, not from the command line.
> END_ARCHIVE
XX This is often how a shell archive is "wrapped",
XX bundling text for distribution.  You would normally
XX run sed from a shell program, not from the command line.
```

To redirect standard output to standard error:

```
$ echo "Usage error:  see administrator" 1>&2
```

The following command sends output (files found) to *filelist* and error messages (inaccessible files) to file *no_access*:

```
$ find / -print > filelist 2>no_access
```

Coprocesses

A coprocess is a shell command that runs asynchronously in a subshell, connected to the originating shell by a two-way pipe. Set up a coprocess with the **coproc** reserved word:

```
coproc [NAME] command [redirections]
```

The reserved word **coproc** sets up the pipe to communicate with *command* and runs *command* in the background. *NAME* is the name of the coprocess (**COPROC** by default). If *command* is a complex command, *NAME* is optional; with a simple command, *NAME* must not be given and the default is used. If any redirections are specified, they are set up after the pipe has been set up.

The coprocess establishes an array with two values: **NAME[0]** contains the file descriptor for command output and **NAME[1]** contains the file descriptor for command input. The variable **NAME_PID** contains the process id of the coprocess. The return status is the exit status of *command*. You can use the **wait** built-in command to wait for the output of *command*.

Functions

A shell *function* is a grouping of commands within a shell script. Shell functions let you modularize your program by dividing it up into separate tasks. This way the code for each task need not be repeated every time you need to perform the task. The POSIX shell syntax for defining a function follows the Bourne shell:

```
name () {
       function body's code come here
    }
```

Functions are invoked just as are regular shell built-in commands or external commands. The command line parameters **$1**, **$2**, and so on receive the function's arguments, temporarily hiding the global values of **$1**, etc. For example:

```
# fatal --- print an error message and die:

fatal () {                          # defining function fatal
    echo "$0: fatal error:" "$@" >&2    # messages to standard error
    exit 1
}
...
if [ $# = 0 ]                       # not enough arguments
then
    fatal "not enough arguments"       # call function with message
fi
```

A function may use the **return** command to return an exit value to the calling shell program. Be careful *not* to use **exit** from within a function unless you really wish to terminate the entire program.

Bash allows you to define functions using an additional keyword, **function**, as follows:

```
function fatal {
    echo "$0: fatal error:" "$@" >&2    # messages to standard error
    exit 1
}
```

All functions share traps with the "parent" shell (except the **DEBUG** trap, if function tracing has been turned on). With the **errtrace** option enabled (either **set -E** or **set -o errtrace**), functions also inherit the **ERR** trap. If function tracing has been enabled, functions inherit the **RETURN** trap. Functions may have local variables, and they may be recursive. The syntax used to define a function is irrelevant.

Variables

This section describes the following:

- Variable substitution
- Built-in shell variables
- Other shell variables
- Arrays
- Special prompt strings

Variable Substitution

No spaces should be used in the following expressions. The colon (:) is optional; if it's included, *var* must be nonnull, as well as set.

Variable expression	Description
var=value ...	Set each variable *var* to a *value*.
${*var*}	Use value of *var*; braces are optional if *var* is separated from the following text. They are required for array variables.
${*var:-value*}	Use *var* if set; otherwise, use *value*.
${*var:=value*}	Use *var* if set; otherwise, use *value* and assign *value* to *var*.
${*var:?value*}	Use *var* if set; otherwise, print *value* and exit (if not interactive). If *value* isn't supplied, print the phrase "parameter null or not set."
${*var:+value*}	Use *value* if *var* is set; otherwise, use nothing.
${#*var*}	Use the length of *var*.
${#*}, ${#@}	Use the number of positional parameters.
${*var#pattern*}	Use value of *var* after removing *pattern* from the left. Remove the shortest matching piece.
${*var##pattern*}	Same as #*pattern*, but remove the longest matching piece.
${*var%pattern*}	Use value of *var* after removing *pattern* from the right. Remove the shortest matching piece.
${*var%%pattern*}	Same as %*pattern*, but remove the longest matching piece.
${!*prefix**}, ${!*prefix*@}	List of variables whose names begin with *prefix*.
${*var:pos*}, ${*var:pos:len*}	Starting at position *pos* (0-based) in variable *var*, extract *len* characters, or rest of string if no *len*. *pos* and *len* may be arithmetic expressions.
${*var/pat/repl*}	Use value of *var*, with first match of *pat* replaced with *repl*.
${*var/pat*}	Use value of *var*, with first match of *pat* deleted.
${*var//pat/repl*}	Use value of *var*, with every match of *pat* replaced with *repl*.
${*var/#pat/repl*}	Use value of *var*, with match of *pat* replaced with *repl*. Match must occur at beginning of the value.
${*var/%pat/repl*}	Use value of *var*, with match of *pat* replaced with *repl*. Match must occur at end of the value.

You can indirectly reference a variable by "aliasing" one variable name to affect the value of the other:

```
$ greet="hello, world"          Create initial variable
  $ friendly_message=greet       Aliasing variable
  $ echo ${!friendly_message}    Use the alias
hello, world
```

Examples

```
$ u=up d=down blank=          Assign values to three variables (last is null)
$ echo ${u}root               Braces are needed here
uproot
$ echo ${u-$d}                Display value of u or d; since u is set, it's printed
up
$ echo ${tmp-`date`}          If tmp is not set, the date command is executed
Thu May 7 02:09:09 EDT 2009
$ echo ${blank="no data"}     blank is set, so it is printed (a blank line)

$ echo ${blank:="no data"}    blank is set but null, so the string is printed
no data
$ echo $blank                 blank now has a new value
no data
$ tail=${PWD##*/}             Take the current directory name and remove the
                              longest character string ending with /, which
                              removes the leading pathname and leaves the tail
```

Built-in Shell Variables

Built-in variables are automatically set by the shell and are typically used inside shell scripts. Built-in variables can make use of the variable substitution patterns shown previously. Note that the **$** is not actually part of the variable name, although the variable is always referenced this way.

Variable	Description
$#	Number of command-line arguments.
$-	Options currently in effect (arguments supplied on command line or to **set**).
$?	Exit value of last executed command.
$$	Process number of current process.
$!	Process number of last background command.
$0	First word; that is, command name. This will have the full pathname if it was found via a PATH search.
$n	Individual arguments on command line (positional parameters). If *n* is greater than 9, it must be specified as ${*n*}.
$*, $@	All arguments on command line ($1 $2 ...).
"$*"	All arguments on command line as one string ("$1 $2 ..."). The values are separated by the first character in the IFS special variable.
"$@"	All arguments on command line, individually quoted ("$1" "$2" ...).
$_	Temporary variable; initialized to pathname of script or program being executed. Later, stores the last argument of previous command. Also stores name of matching MAIL file during mail checks.
HISTCMD	The history number of the current command.
LINENO	Current line number within the script or function.
OLDPWD	Previous working directory (set by **cd**).
OPTARG	Name of last option processed by **getopts**.
OPTIND	Numerical index of OPTARG.
PPID	Process number of this shell's parent.
PWD	Current working directory (set by **cd**).

Variable	Description
RANDOM[=n]	Generate a new random number with each reference; start with integer n, if given.
REPLY	Default reply, used by **select** and **read**.
SECONDS[=n]	Number of seconds since the shell was started, or, if n is given, number of seconds + n since the shell started.

In addition, Bash sets the following variables. Many of these variables are for use by the Bash debugger (see *http://bashdb.sourceforge.net*) or for providing programmable completion (see the section "Programmable Completion" on page 615).

Variable	Description
BASH	The full pathname used to invoke this instance of Bash.
BASH_ARGC	Array variable. Each element holds the number of arguments for the corresponding function or dot-script invocation. Set only in extended debug mode, with **shopt -s extdebug**.
BASH_ARGV	An array variable similar to BASH_ARGC. Each element is one of the arguments passed to a function or dot-script. It functions as a stack, with values being pushed on at each call. Thus, the last element is the last argument to the most recent function or script invocation. Set only in extended debug mode, with **shopt -s extdebug**.
BASH_COMMAND	The command currently executing or about to be executed. Inside a trap handler, it is the command running when the trap was invoked.
BASH_EXECUTION_STRING	The string argument passed to the -c option.
BASH_LINENO	Array variable, corresponding to BASH_SOURCE and FUNCNAME. For any given function number i (starting at 0), ${FUNCNAME[i]} was invoked in file ${BASH_SOURCE[i]} on line ${BASH_LINENO[i]}. The information is stored with the most recent function invocation first.
BASH_REMATCH	Array variable, assigned by the =~ operator of the [[ ]] construct. Index 0 is the text that matched the entire pattern. The other indices are the text matched by parenthesized subexpressions. This variable is read-only.
BASH_SOURCE	Array variable, containing source filenames. Each element corresponds with those in FUNCNAME and BASH_LINENO.
BASH_SUBSHELL	This variable is incremented by one each time a subshell or subshell environment is created.
BASH_VERSINFO[0]	The major version number, or release, of Bash.
BASH_VERSINFO[1]	The minor version number, or version, of Bash.
BASH_VERSINFO[2]	The patch level.
BASH_VERSINFO[3]	The build version.
BASH_VERSINFO[4]	The release status.
BASH_VERSINFO[5]	The machine type; same value as in MACHTYPE.
BASH_VERSION	A string describing the version of Bash.
COMP_CWORD	For programmable completion. Index into COMP_WORDS, indicating the current cursor position.
COMP_LINE	For programmable completion. The current command line.
COMP_POINT	For programmable completion. The position of the cursor as a character index in COMP_LINE.
COMP_WORDBREAKS	For programmable completion. The characters that the *readline* library treats as word separators when doing word completion.
COMP_WORDS	For programmable completion. Array variable containing the individual words on the command line.

Variable	Description
DIRSTACK	Array variable, containing the contents of the directory stack as displayed by **dirs**. Changing existing elements modifies the stack, but only **pushd** and **popd** can add or remove elements from the stack.
EUID	Read-only variable with the numeric effective UID of the current user.
FUNCNAME	Array variable, containing function names. Each element corresponds with those in BASH_SOURCE and BASH_LINENO.
GROUPS	Array variable containing the list of numeric group IDs in which the current user is a member.
HISTCMD	The history number of the current command.
HOSTNAME	The name of the current host.
HOSTTYPE	A string that describes the host system.
MACHTYPE	A string that describes the host system in the GNU *cpu-company-system* format.
OSTYPE	A string that describes the operating system.
PIPESTATUS	An array variable containing the exit statuses of the commands in the most recent foreground pipeline.
SHELLOPTS	A colon-separated list of shell options (for **set -o**). If set in the environment at startup, Bash enables each option present in the list.
SHLVL	Incremented by one every time a new Bash starts up.
UID	Read-only variable with the numeric real UID of the current user.

Other Shell Variables

The following variables are not automatically set by the shell, although many of them can influence the shell's behavior. They are typically used in your *.profile* file, where you can define them to suit your needs. Variables can be assigned values by issuing commands of the form:

```
variable=value
```

This list includes the type of value expected when defining these variables.

Variable expression	Description
CDPATH=*dirs*	Directories searched by **cd**; allows shortcuts in changing directories; unset by default.
COLUMNS=*n*	Screen's column width; used in line edit modes and **select** lists.
COMPREPLY=(*words ...*)	Array variable from which Bash reads the possible completions generated by a completion function.
EDITOR=*file*	Pathname of line-edit mode to turn on (can end in **emacs** or **vi**); used when VISUAL is not set.
EMACS	If the value starts with **t**, Bash assumes it's running in an Emacs buffer and disables line editing.
ENV=*file*	Name of script that gets executed at startup; useful for storing alias and function definitions. For example, **ENV=$HOME/.bashrc**.
FCEDIT=*file*	Editor used by **fc** command (default is */bin/ed*).
FIGNORE=*pattern*	Colon-separated list of patterns describing filenames to ignore when doing filename completion.
GLOBIGNORE=*patlist*	Colon-separated list of patterns describing the set of filenames to ignore during pattern matching.

Variable expression	Description
HISTCONTROL=*list*	Colon-separated list of values controlling how commands are saved in the history file. Recognized values are: **ignoredups**, **ignorespace**, **ignoreboth**, and **erasedups**.
HISTFILE=*file*	File in which to store command history. Default is *~/.bash_history*.
HISTFILESIZE=*n*	Number of lines to be kept in the history file. This may be different than the number of commands.
HISTIGNORE=*list*	A colon-separated list of patterns that must match the entire command line. Matching lines are *not* saved in the history file. An unescaped **&** in a pattern matches the previous history line.
HISTSIZE=*n*	Number of history commands to be kept in the history file.
HISTTIMEFORMAT=*string*	A format string for *strftime*(3) to use for printing timestamps along with commands from the **history** command. If set (even if null), Bash saves time-stamps in the history file along with the commands.
HOME=*dir*	Home directory; set by **login** (from */etc/passwd file*).
HOSTFILE=*file*	Name of a file in the same format as */etc/hosts* that Bash should use to find host-names for hostname completion.
IFS='*chars*'	Input field separators; default is space, tab, and newline.
IGNOREEOF=*n*	Numeric value indicating how many successive EOF characters must be typed before Bash exits. If null or nonnumeric value, default is 10.
INPUTRC=*file*	Initialization file for the *readline* library. This overrides the default value of *~/.inputrc*.
LANG=*dir*	Default value for locale, used if no **LC_*** variables are set.
LC_ALL=*locale*	Current locale; overrides **LANG** and the other **LC_*** variables.
LC_COLLATE=*locale*	Locale to use for character collation (sorting order).
LC_CTYPE=*locale*	Locale to use for character class functions.
LC_MESSAGES=*locale*	Locale to use for translating $"..." strings.
LC_NUMERIC=*locale*	Locale to use for the decimal-point character.
LINES=*n*	Screen's height; used for **select** lists.
MAIL=*file*	Default file to check for incoming mail; set by **login**.
MAILCHECK=*n*	Number of seconds between mail checks; default is 600 (10 minutes).
MAILPATH=*files*	One or more files, delimited by a colon, to check for incoming mail. Along with each file, you may supply an optional message that the shell prints when the file increases in size. Messages are separated from the filename by a **?** character, and the default message is **You have mail in $_. $_** is replaced with the name of the file. For example, you might have: `MAILPATH="$MAIL?Ring! Candygram!:/etc/motd?New Login Message"`
OPTERR=*n*	When set to **1** (the default value), Bash prints error messages from the built-in **getopts** command.
PATH=*dirlist*	One or more pathnames, delimited by colons, in which to search for commands to execute.
POSIXLY_CORRECT=*string*	When set at startup or while running, Bash enters POSIX mode, disabling behavior and modifying features that conflict with the POSIX standard.
PROMPT_COMMAND=*command*	If set, Bash executes this command each time before printing the primary prompt.
PS1=*string*	Primary prompt string; default is **$**.
PS2=*string*	Secondary prompt (used in multiline commands); default is **>**.
PS3=*string*	Prompt string in **select** loops; default is **#?**.

Variable expression	Description
PS4=*string*	Prompt string for execution trace (**bash -x** or **set -x**); default is +.
SHELL=*file*	Name of default shell (e.g., */bin/bash*). Bash sets this if it's not in the environment at startup.
TERM=*string*	Terminal type.
TIMEFORMAT=*string*	A format string for the output for the **time** keyword.
TMOUT=*n*	If no command is typed after *n* seconds, exit the shell. Also affects the **read** command and the **select** loop.
VISUAL=*path*	Same as EDITOR, but VISUAL is checked first.
auto_resume=*list*	Enables the use of simple strings for resuming stopped jobs. With a value of **exact**, the string must match a command name exactly. With a value of **substring**, it can match a substring of the command name.
histchars=*chars*	Two or three characters that control history expansion. The first character signals a history event. The second is the "quick substitution" character, and the third indicates the start of a comment. The default value is !^#.

Arrays

Bash supports one-dimensional arrays. Elements are referenced by an index; the first element is numbered 0 and there is no upper limit on the number of elements. Arrays are initialized with a special form of assignment:

```
message=(hi there how are you today)
```

where each value (in this example, each word) becomes an element of the array.

Elements may also be assigned individually:

```
message[0]=hi          This is the hard way
message[1]=there
message[2]=how
message[3]=are
message[4]=you
message[5]=today
```

Declaring arrays is not required. Any valid reference to a subscripted variable can create an array.

Bash also provides associative arrays, where the indices are strings instead of numbers. In this case, [and] act like double quotes. Associative arrays are created with **declare -A** *arrayname*. Unlike indexed arrays, when assigning a value to an associative array, a subscript is always required.

When referencing arrays, use the $\{ ... \} syntax. This isn't needed when referencing arrays inside (( )) (the form of **let** that does automatic quoting). Note that [and] are typed literally (i.e., they don't stand for optional syntax).

Syntax	Effect
${*name*[*i*]}	Use element *i* of array *name*. *i* can be any arithmetic expression as described under **let**.
${*name*}	Use element 0 of indexed array *name*.
${*name*[*]}, ${*name*[@]}	Use all elements of array *name*.
${#*name*[*]}, ${#*name*[@]}	Use the number of elements in array *name*.

The built-in commands **declare**, **local**, and **readonly** accept the -a option for an indexed array and the -**A** option for an associative array. Use the **unset** built-in to remove arrays or array elements. The built-ins are described in detail later in this chapter.

Special Prompt Strings

Bash processes the values of the built-in shell variables **PS1**, **PS2**, and **PS4** for the following special escape sequences:

Escape sequence	Description
\a	An ASCII BEL character (octal 07).
\A	The current time in 24-hour *HH:MM* format.
\d	The date in "weekday month day" format.
\D{*format*}	The date as specified by the *strftime*(3) format *format*. The braces are required.
\e	An ASCII Escape character (octal 033).
\h	The hostname, up to the first period.
\H	The full hostname.
\j	The current number of jobs.
\l	The basename of the shell's terminal device.
\n	A newline character.
\r	A carriage-return character.
\s	The name of the shell (basename of $0).
\t	The current time in 24-hour *HH:MM:SS* format.
\T	The current time in 12-hour *HH:MM:SS* format.
\u	The current user's username.
\v	The version of Bash.
\V	The release (version plus patch level) of Bash.
\w	The current directory, with $HOME abbreviated as ~.
\W	The basename of the current directory, with $HOME abbreviated as ~.
\!	The history number of this command.
\#	The command number of this command.
\$	If the effective UID is 0, a #; otherwise a $.
\@	The current time in 12-hour a.m./p.m. format.
\nnn	The character represented by octal value *nnn*.
\\	A literal backslash.
\[	Start a sequence of nonprinting characters, such as for highlighting or changing colors on a terminal.
\]	End a sequence of nonprinting characters.

In Bash, the escape sequences are processed first. After that, variable, command, and arithmetic substitutions are performed if the **promptvars** shell option is enabled via the **shopt** command (the default).

Arithmetic Expressions

The **let** built-in command performs integer arithmetic. You can substitute arithmetic values (for use as command arguments or in variables); base conversion is also possible.

Expression	Meaning
$((expr))	Use the value of the enclosed arithmetic expression.
B#n	Interpret integer *n* in numeric base *B*. For example, **8#100** specifies the octal equivalent of decimal 64.

Operators

The shell uses arithmetic operators from the C programming language; the following table lists the operators in decreasing order of precedence.

Operator	Description
++ --	Auto-increment and auto-decrement, both prefix and postfix.
+ - ! ~	Unary plus and minus, logical negation and binary inversion (one's complement).
**	Exponentiation.
* / %	Multiplication; division; modulus (remainder).
+ -	Addition; subtraction.
<< >>	Bitwise left shift; bitwise right shift.
< <= > >=	Less than; less than or equal to; greater than; greater than or equal to.
== !=	Equality; inequality (both evaluated left to right).
&	Bitwise AND.
^	Bitwise exclusive OR.
|	Bitwise OR.
&&	Logical AND (short-circuit).
||	Logical OR (short-circuit).
?:	Inline conditional evaluation.
= += -=	Assignment.
*= /= %=	
< <= > >=	
&= ^= |=	
,	Sequential expression evaluation.

Examples

See the **let** command for more information and examples:

```
let "count=0" "i = i + 1"              Assign i and count
let "num % 2"                          Test for an even number
(( percent >= 0 && percent <= 100 ))  Test the range of a value
```

Command History

Bash lets you display or modify previous commands. Commands in the history list can be modified using:

- Line-edit mode
- The **fc** and **hist** commands

Bash also supports a command-history mechanism very similar to that of the C shell. This mechanism uses a history expansion character (! by default) to select a line from the history. Portions of the line are then selected to be included in the current line. Because the interactive line-editing features are considerably superior we do not cover those features here. See the Bash manpage for more information.

Line-Edit Mode

Line-edit mode emulates many features of the **vi** and **emacs** editors. The history list is treated like a file. When the editor is invoked, you type editing keystrokes to move to the command line you want to execute. You can also change the line before executing it. When you're ready to issue the command, press the Enter key.

Select an editor with either **set -o vi** or **set -o emacs**; assignment to the VISUAL or EDITOR variables has no effect. Note that **vi** starts in input mode; to type a **vi** command, press the Escape key first.

Common editing keystrokes

vi	emacs	Result
k	Ctrl-P	Get previous command.
j	Ctrl-N	Get next command.
/*string*	Ctrl-R *string*	Get previous command containing *string*.
h	Ctrl-B	Move back one character.
l	Ctrl-F	Move forward one character.
b	ESC-B	Move back one word.
w	ESC-F	Move forward one word.
X	DEL	Delete previous character.
x	Ctrl-D	Delete character under cursor.
dw	ESC-D	Delete word forward.
db	ESC-H	Delete word backward.
xp	Ctrl-R	Transpose two characters.

The fc Command

fc stands for either "find command" or "fix command," since it does both jobs. Use **fc -l** to list history commands and **fc -e** to edit them. See the **fc** entry in the section "Built-in Commands" on page 619 for more information.

Examples

`$ history`	*List the last 16 commands*
`$ fc -l 20 30`	*List commands 20 through 30*
`$ fc -l -5`	*List the last five commands*
`$ fc -l cat`	*List all commands since the last command beginning with cat*
`$ fc -l 50`	*List all commands since command 50*
`$ fc -ln 5 > doit`	*Save command 5 to file doit*
`$ fc -e vi 5 20`	*Edit commands 5 through 20 using vi*
`$ fc -e emacs`	*Edit previous command using emacs*

Interactive line editing is easier to use than **fc**, since you can move up and down in the saved command history using your favorite editor commands (as long as your favorite editor is either **vi** or Emacs!). You can also use the Up and Down arrow keys to traverse the command history and the right and left arrow keys to move around in the command line.

Programmable Completion

Bash and the *readline* library provide *completion* facilities, whereby you can type part of a command name, press the Tab key, and have Bash fill in part or all of the rest of the command or filename. *Programmable completion* lets you, as a shell programmer, write code to customize the list of possible completions that Bash will present for a particular, partially entered word. This is accomplished through the combination of several facilities:

- The **complete** command allows you provide a completion specification, or *compspec*, for individual commands. You specify, via various options, how to tailor the list of possible completions for the particular command. This is simple, but adequate for many needs. (See the **complete** entry in the section "Built-in Commands" on page 619.)

- For more flexibility, you may use **complete -F** *funcname command*. This tells Bash to call *funcname* to provide the list of completions for *command*. You write the *funcname* function.

- Within the code for a **-F** function, the COMP* shell variables provide information about the current command line. COMPREPLY is an array into which the function places the final list of completion results.

- Also within the code for a **-F** function, you may use the **compgen** command to generate is a list of results, such as "usernames that begin with **a**" or "all set variables." The intent is that such results would be used with an array assignment:

```
...
COMPREPLY=( $( compgen options arguments ) )
...
```

Compspecs may be associated with either a full pathname for a command or, more commonly, with an unadorned command name (*/usr/bin/man* versus plain **man**). In the list that follows, completions are attempted based on the options provided to the **complete** command.

1. Bash first identifies the command. If a pathname is used, Bash looks to see if a compspec exists for the full pathname. Otherwise, it sets the command name to the last component of the pathname, and searches for a compspec for the command name.

2. If a compspec exists, Bash uses it. If not, Bash falls back to the default built-in completions.

3. Bash performs the action indicated by the compspec to generate a list of possible matches. Of this list, only those that have the word being completed as a prefix are used for the list of possible completions. For the **-d** and **-f** options, the variable FIGNORE is used to filter out undesirable matches.

4. Bash generates filenames as specified by the **-G** option. GLOBIGNORE is not used to filter the results, but FIGNORE is.

5. Bash processes the argument string provided to **-W**. The string is split using the characters in $IFS. The resulting list provides the candidates for completion. This is often used to provide a list of options that a command accepts.

6. Bash runs functions and commands as specified by the **-F** and **-C** options. For both, Bash sets COMP_LINE and COMP_POINT as described previously. For a shell function, COMP_WORDS and COMP_CWORD are also set.

   Also for both, **$1** is the name of the command whose arguments are being completed, **$2** is the word being completed, and **$3** is the word in front of the word being completed. Bash does *not* filter the results of the command or function.

   a. Functions named with **-F** are run first. The function should set the COMPREPLY array to the list of possible completions. Bash retrieves the list from there.

   b. Commands provided with **-C** are run next, in an environment equivalent to command substitution. The command should print the list of possible completions, one per line. An embedded newline should be escaped with a backslash.

7. Once the list is generated, Bash filters the results according to the **-X** option. The argument to **-X** is a pattern specifying files to exclude. By prefixing the pattern with a !, the sense is reversed, and the pattern instead specifies that only matching files should be retained in the list.

   An **&** in the pattern is replaced with the text of the word being completed. Use \& to produce a literal **&**.

8. Finally, Bash prepends or appends any prefixes or suffixes supplied with **-P** or **-S** options.

9. In the case that no matches were generated, if **-o dirnames** was used, Bash attempts directory name completion.

10. On the other hand, if **-o plusdirs** was provided, Bash *adds* the result of directory completion to the previously generated list.

11. Normally, when a compspec is provided, Bash's default completions are not attempted, nor are the *readline* library's default filename completions.

    a. If the compspec produces no results and **-o bashdefault** was provided, then Bash attempts its default completions.

   b. If neither the compspec, nor the Bash default completions with **-o bash-default** produced any results, and **-o default** was provided, then Bash has the *readline* library attempt its filename completions.

Ian Macdonald has collected a large set of useful compspecs, often distributed as the file */etc/bash_completion*.

Examples

Restrict files for the C compiler to C, C++ and assembler source files, and relocatable object files:

```
complete -f -X '!*.[Ccos]' gcc cc
```

For the **man** command, restrict expansions to things that have manpages:

```
# Simple example of programmable completion for manual pages.
# A more elaborate example appears in the bash_completion file.
# Assumes    man [num] command    command syntax.
```

`shopt -s extglob`	*Enable extended pattern matching*
`  _man () {`	
`     local dir mandir=/usr/share/man`	*Local variables*
`     COMPREPLY=( )`	*Clear reply list*
`     if [[ ${COMP_WORDS[1]} = +([0-9]) ]]`	*Section number provided*
`     then`	
`         # section provided: man 3 foo`	
`         dir=$mandir/man${COMP_WORDS[COMP_CWORD-1]}`	*Look in that directory*
`     else`	
`         # no section, default to commands`	
`         dir=$mandir/'man[18]'`	*Look in command directories*
`     fi`	
`     COMPREPLY=( $( find $dir -type f |`	*Generate raw file list*
`         sed 's;..*/;;' |`	*Remove leading directories*
`         sed 's/\.[0-9].*$//' |`	*Remove trailing suffixes*
`         grep "^${COMP_WORDS[$COMP_CWORD]}" |`	*Keep those that match given prefix*
`         sort`	*Sort final list*
`     ) )`	
`  }`	
`  complete -F _man man`	*Associate function with command*

Job Control

Job control lets you place foreground jobs in the background, bring background jobs to the foreground, or suspend (temporarily stop) running jobs. Many job-control commands take a *jobID* as an argument. This argument can be specified as follows:

%*n* Job number *n*.

%*s* Job whose command line starts with string *s*.

%?s

    Job whose command line contains string *s*.

%%

    Current job.

%+

    Current job (same as above).

%-

    Previous job.

The following job-control commands are described more completely in the section "Built-in Commands" on page 619.

bg   Put a job in the background.

fg   Put a job in the foreground.

jobs

    List active jobs.

kill

    Terminate a job.

stty tostop

    Stop background jobs if they try to send output to the terminal. (Note that **stty** is not a built-in command.)

suspend

    Suspend a job-control shell (such as one created by **su**).

wait

    Wait for background jobs to finish.

Ctrl-Z

    Suspend a foreground job. Then use **bg** or **fg**. (Your terminal may use something other than **Ctrl-Z** as the suspend character.)

Command Execution

When you type a command to Bash, it looks in the following places until it finds a match:

1. Keywords such as **if** and **for**.

2. Aliases. You can't define an alias whose name is a shell keyword, but you can define an alias that expands to a keyword, e.g., **alias aslongas=while**. (In non-POSIX mode, Bash does allow you to define an alias for a shell keyword.)

3. Special built-ins like **break** and **continue**. The list of POSIX special built-ins is **.** (dot), **:**, **break**, **continue**, **eval**, **exec**, **exit**, **export**, **readonly**, **return**, **set**, **shift**, **source**, **times**, **trap**, and **unset**.

4. Functions. When in non-POSIX mode, Bash finds functions before built-in commands.

5. Nonspecial built-ins like **cd** and **test**.

6. Scripts and executable programs, for which the shell searches in the directories listed in the PATH environment variable.

The distinction between "special" built-in commands and nonspecial ones comes from POSIX. This distinction, combined with the **command** command, makes it possible to write functions that override shell built-ins, such as **cd**. For example:

```
cd () {                          Shell function, found before built-in cd
        command cd "$@"          Use real cd to change directory
        echo now in $PWD         Other stuff we want to do
    }
```

Restricted Shells

A *restricted shell* is one that disallows certain actions, such as changing directory, setting PATH, or running commands whose names contain a **/** character. See the Bash manpage for the full list of restrictions.

To run a restricted shell, enter the command **bash -r**. Depending on your Linux distribution, you may also be able to enter the command as **rbash**.

You can still run shell scripts, since in that case the restricted shell calls the unrestricted version of the shell to run the script after it reads */etc/profile*, *$HOME/.profile*, and other startup files.

Restricted shells are not used much in practice, as they are difficult to set up correctly.

Built-in Commands

Examples to be entered as a command line are shown with the **$** prompt. Otherwise, examples should be treated as code fragments that might be included in a shell script. For convenience, some of the reserved words used by multiline commands are also included.

!

> ! *pipeline*
>
> Negate the sense of a pipeline. Returns an exit status of 0 if the pipeline exited nonzero, and an exit status of 1 if the pipeline exited zero. Typically used in **if** and **while** statements.
>
> **Example**
>
> This code prints a message if user **jane** is not logged on:
>
> ```
> if ! who | grep jane > /dev/null
> then
>         echo jane is not currently logged on
> fi
> ```

#

> #
>
> Ignore all text that follows on the same line. **#** is used in shell scripts as the comment character and is not really a command.

#!shell

#!*shell* [*option*]

Used as the first line of a script to invoke the named *shell*. Anything given on the rest of the line is passed *as a single argument* to the named *shell*. This feature is typically implemented by the kernel, but may not be supported on some older systems. Some systems have a limit of approximately 32 characters on the maximum length of *shell*. For example:

```
#!/bin/sh
```

:

:

Null command. Returns an exit status of 0. The line is still processed for side effects, such as variable and command substitutions, or I/O redirection. See the following Example and the Example under **case**.

Example

Check whether someone is logged in:

```
if who | grep $1 > /dev/null
then :    # Do nothing if user is found
else echo "User $1 is not logged in"
fi
```

.

. *file* [*arguments*]

Read and execute lines in *file*. *file* does not have to be executable, but must reside in a directory searched by PATH. The *arguments* are stored in the positional parameters. If Bash is not in POSIX mode and *file* is not found in PATH, Bash looks in the current directory for the *file*.

[[ ]]

[[*expression*]]

Same as **test** *expression* or [*expression*], except that [[ ]] allows additional operators. Word splitting and filename expansion are disabled. Note that the brackets ([ ]) are typed literally and that they must be surrounded by whitespace.

Additional operators

&& Logical AND of test expressions (short circuit).

|| Logical OR of test expressions (short circuit).

< First string is lexically "less than" the second.

> First string is lexically "greater than" the second.

---

alias

alias [*option*] [*name*[='*cmd*']...]

Assign a shorthand *name* as a synonym for *cmd*. If ='*cmd*' is omitted, print the alias for *name*; if *name* is also omitted, print all aliases. By itself or with **-p**, **alias** prints one alias per line on standard output as

alias *name=value*. If the value contains a trailing space, the next word on the command line also becomes a candidate for alias expansion. See also **unalias**.

Option

-p   Print the word **alias** before each alias.

Example

```
alias dir='echo ${PWD##*/}'
```

---

bg

bg [*jobIDs*]

Put current job or *jobIDs* in the background. See the section "Job Control" on page 617.

---

bind

```
bind [-m map] [options]
bind [-m map] [-q function] [-r sequence] [-u function]
bind [-m map] -f file
bind [-m map] -x sequence:command
bind [-m map] sequence:function
bind readline-command
```

Manage the *readline* library. Nonoption arguments have the same form as in an *.inputrc* file.

Options

-f *file*
    Read key bindings from *file*.

-l   List the names of all the *readline* functions.

-m *map*
    Use *map* as the keymap. Available keymaps are: **emacs, emacs-standard, emacs-meta, emacs-ctlx, vi, vi-move, vi-command,** and **vi-insert**. **vi** is the same as **vi-command**, and **emacs** is the same **emacs-standard**.

-p   Print the current *readline* bindings such that they can be reread from a *.inputrc* file.

-P   Print the current *readline* bindings.

-q *function*
    Query which keys invoke the *readline* function *function*.

-r *sequence*
    Remove the binding for key sequence *sequence*.

-s   Print the current *readline* key sequence and macro bindings such that they can be reread from a *.inputrc* file.

-S   Print the current *readline* key sequence and macro bindings.

-u *function*
    Unbind all keys that invoke the *readline* function *function*.

-v   Print the current *readline* variables such that they can be reread from a *.inputrc* file.

-V Print the current *readline* variables.

-x *sequence:command*
   Execute the shell command *command* whenever *sequence* is entered.

---

break

```
break [n]
```

Exit from a **for, while, select,** or **until** loop (or break out of *n* loops).

---

builtin

```
builtin command [ arguments ... ]
```

Run the shell built-in command *command* with the given arguments. This allows you to bypass any functions that redefine a built-in command's name. The **command** command is more portable.

Example

This function lets you do your own tasks when you change directory:

```
cd () {
        builtin cd "$@"     Actually change directory
            pwd             Report location
}
```

---

caller

```
caller [expression]
```

Print the line number and source filename of the current function call or dot file. With nonzero *expression*, prints that element from the call stack. The most recent is zero. This command is for use by the Bash debugger.

---

case

```
case value in
  pattern1) cmds1;;
  pattern2) cmds2;;
    .
    .
    .
  esac
```

Execute the first set of commands (*cmds1*) if *value* matches *pattern1*, execute the second set of commands (*cmds2*) if *value* matches *pattern2*, etc. The last command in each set ends with ;; and no further matches are attempted. If the set ends in ;& instead, execution continues with the commands for the next set of patterns; if it ends in ;;&, the next pattern in the list is tested. *value* is typically a positional parameter or other shell variable. *cmds* are typically Linux commands, shell programming commands, or variable assignments. Patterns can use file-generation metacharacters. Multiple patterns (separated by |) can be specified on the same line; in this case, the associated *cmds* are executed whenever *value*

---

matches any of these patterns. See the Examples here and under **eval**.

A pattern may be preceded by an optional open parenthesis, as in (*pattern*, necessary for balancing parentheses inside a $() construct.

Examples

Check first command-line argument and take appropriate action:

```
case $1 in      # Match the first arg
    no|yes) response=1;;
    -[tT])  table=TRUE;;
    *)      echo "unknown option"; exit 1;;
esac
```

Read user-supplied lines until user exits:

```
while :        # Null command; always true
do
    printf "Type . to finish ==> "
    read line
    case "$line" in
       .) echo "Message done"
          break ;;
       *) echo "$line" >> $message ;;
    esac
done
```

---

cd

```
cd [-LP] [dir]
cd [-LP] [-]
```

With no arguments, change to the user's home directory. Otherwise, change the working directory to *dir*. If *dir* is a relative pathname but is not in the current directory, the CDPATH variable is searched. A directory of - stands for the previous directory.

Options

-L Use the logical path (what the user typed, including any symbolic links) for **cd ..** and the value of PWD. This is the default.

-P Use the actual filesystem physical path for **cd ..** and the value of PWD.

---

command

```
command [-pvV] name [arg ...]
```

Without **-v** or **-V**, execute *name* with given arguments. This command bypasses any aliases or functions that may be defined for *name*. When used with a special built-in, it prevents the built-in from exiting the script if it fails.

Options

-p Use a predefined, default search path, not the current value of PATH.

-v Print a description of how the shell interprets *name*.

-V   Print a more verbose description of how the shell interprets *name*.

Example

Create an alias for **rm** that gets the system's version, and runs it with the **-i** option:

```
$ alias 'rm=command -p rm -i'
```

---

compgen

compgen [*options*] [*string*]

Generate possible completions for *string* according to the options and write to standard output. Options are those accepted by **complete**, except for **-p** and **-r**. For more information, see the entry for **complete**.

---

complete

complete [*options*] *command* ...

Specify the way to complete arguments for each *command*. See "Programmable Completion" on page 615 for more discussion.

Options

-A *type*

Use *type* to specify a list of possible completions. The *type* may be one of the following. Options in parentheses are alternative specifications for **-A** *type*.

alias *(-a)*
Alias names.

arrayvar
Array variable names.

binding
Bindings from the *readline* library.

builtin *(-b)*
Shell built-in command names.

command *(-c)*
Command names.

directory *(-d)*
Directory names.

disabled
Names of disabled shell built-in commands.

enabled
Names of enabled shell built-in commands.

export *(-e)*
Names of exported shell variables.

file *(-f)*
Filenames.

function
Names of shell functions.

group *(-g)*
> Group names.

helptopic
> Help topics as allowed by the **help** built-in command.

hostname
> Hostnames, as found in the file named by $HOSTFILE.

job *(-j)*
> Job names.

keyword *(-k)*
> Shell reserved keywords.

running
> Names of running jobs.

service *(-s)*
> Service names (from */etc/services*).

setopt
> Valid arguments for **set -o**.

shopt
> Valid option names for the **shopt** built-in command.

signal
> Signal names.

stopped
> Names of stopped jobs.

user *(-u)*
> Usernames.

variable *(-v)*
> Shell variable names.

-C *command*
> Run *command* in a subshell and use its output as the list of completions.

-E Remaining options and actions apply to completion attempts on a blank line.

-F *function*
> Run shell function *function* in the current shell. Upon its return, retrieve the list of completions from the COMPREPLY array.

-G *pattern*
> Expand *pattern* to generate completions.

-o *option*
> Control the behavior of the completion specification. The value for *option* is one of the following:

> **bashdefault**
>> Fall back to the normal Bash completions if no matches are produced.

> **default**
>> Use the default *readline* completions if no matches are produced.

dirnames

Do directory name completion if no matches are produced.

filenames

Inform the *readline* library that the intended output is filenames, so that the library can do any filename-specific processing, such as adding a trailing slash for directories or removing trailing spaces.

nospace

Inform the *readline* library that it should not append a space to words completed at the end of a line.

plusdirs

Attempt directory completion and add any results to the list of completions already generated.

-p With no commands, print all completion settings in a way that can be reread.

-P *prefix*

The *prefix* is added to each resulting string as a prefix after all the other options have been applied.

-r Remove the completion settings for the given commands, or all settings if no commands.

-S *suffix*

The *suffix* is added to each resulting string as a suffix after all the other options have been applied.

-W *wordlist*

Split *wordlist* (a single shell word) using $IFS. The generated list contains the members of the split list that matched the word being completed. Each member is expanded using brace expansion, tilde expansion, parameter and variable expansion, command substitution, and arithmetic expansion. Shell quoting is respected.

-X *pattern*

Exclude filenames matching *pattern* from the filename completion list. With a leading ! in the pattern, the sense is reversed, and only filenames matching *pattern* are retained.

---

continue

```
continue [n]
```

Skip remaining commands in a **for**, **while**, **select**, or **until** loop, resuming with the next iteration of the loop (or skipping *n* loops).

---

declare

```
declare [options] [name[=value]]
typeset [options] [name[=value]]
```

Declare variables and manage their attributes. In function bodies, variables are local, as if declared with the **local** command.

Options

-a Each *name* is an indexed array variable.

-A Each *name* is an associative array variable.

-f Each *name* is a function.

-F   For functions, print just the function name and attributes, not the function definition (body). Implies **-f**.

-i   Each variable is an integer; in an assignment, the value is evaluated as an arithmetic expression.

-l   Assign all values as lowercase only; convert uppercase to lowercase.

-p   With no *names*, print all variables and their values. With *names*, print the names, attributes, and values of the given variables. Used with **-f**, print all function names and attributes. This option causes all other options to be ignored.

-r   Mark *names* as read-only. Subsequent assignments will fail.

-t   Apply the *trace* attribute to each name. Traced functions inherit the **DEBUG** and **RETURN** traps from the shell. This attribute has no meaning for variables.

-u   Assign all values as uppercase only; convert lowercase to uppercase.

-x   Mark *names* for export into the environment of child processes.

With a + instead of a -, the given attribute is disabled. With no variable names, all variables having the given attribute(s) are printed in a form that can be reread as input to the shell.

Examples

```
$ declare -i val          Make val an integer
$ val=4+7                 Evaluate value
$ echo $val               Show result
11

$ declare -r z=42         Make z read-only
$ z=31                    Try to assign to it
bash: z: readonly variable   Assignment fails
$ echo $z                 
42

$ declare -p val z        Show attributes and values
declare -i val="11"
declare -r z="42"
```

---

dirs   `dirs [-clpv] [+n] [-n]`

Print the directory stack, which is managed with **pushd** and **popd**.

Options

+n Print the *n*th entry from the left; first entry is zero.

-n Print the *n*th entry from the right; first entry is zero.

-c Remove all entries from (clear) the directory stack.

-l Produce a longer listing, one that does not replace $HOME with ~.

-p Print the directory stack, one entry per line.

<table>
<tr><td></td><td>-v</td><td>Print the directory stack, one entry per line, with each entry preceded by its index in the stack.</td></tr>
</table>

| **disown** | `disown [-ahr] [job ...]` |
| | Remove *job* from the list of jobs managed by Bash. |

Options

-a   Remove all jobs. With **-h**, mark all jobs.

-h   Instead of removing jobs from the list of known jobs, mark them to *not* receive **SIGHUP** when Bash exits.

-r   With no jobs, remove (or mark) only running jobs.

| **do** | `do` |
| | Reserved word that precedes the command sequence in a **for**, **while**, **until**, or **select** statement. |

| **done** | `done` |
| | Reserved word that ends a **for**, **while**, **until**, or **select** statement. |

| **echo** | `echo [-eEn] [string]` |
| | Write *string* to standard output. (See also **echo** in Chapter 3.) |

Options

-e   Enable interpretation of the following escape sequences, which must be quoted (or escaped with a \) to prevent interpretation by the shell:

\a   Alert (ASCII BEL).

\b   Backspace.

\c   Suppress the terminating newline (same as **-n**).

\e   ASCII Escape character.

\f   Formfeed.

\n   Newline.

\r   Carriage return.

\t   Tab character.

\v   Vertical-tab character.

\\   Backslash.

\0*nnn*

   ASCII character represented by octal number *nnn*, where *nnn* is zero, one, two, or three digits and is preceded by a 0.

nnn

   ASCII character represented by octal number *nnn*, where *nnn* is one, two, or three digits.

\xHH

　　　　ASCII character represented by hexadecimal number *HH*, where *HH* is one or two hexadecimal digits.

-E　Do not interpret escape sequences, even on systems where the default behavior of the built-in **echo** is to interpret them.

-n　Do not print the terminating newline.

Examples

```
$ echo "testing printer" | lp
$ echo "Warning: ringing bell \a"
```

---

enable　　enable [-adnps] [-f *file*] [*command* ...]

Enable or disable shell built-in commands. Disabling a built-in lets you use an external version of a command that would otherwise use a built-in version, such as **echo** or **test**.

Options

-a　For use with **-p**, print information about all built-in commands, disabled and enabled.

-d　Remove (delete) a built-in previously loaded with **-f**.

-f *file*

　　　　Load a new built-in command *command* from the shared library file *file*.

-n　Disable the named built-in commands.

-p　Print a list of enabled built-in commands.

-s　Print only the POSIX special built-in commands. When combined with **-f**, the new built-in command becomes a POSIX special built-in.

---

esac　　esac

Reserved word that ends a **case** statement.

---

eval　　eval *args*

Typically, **eval** is used in shell scripts, and *args* is a line of code that contains shell variables. **eval** forces variable expansion to happen first and then runs the resulting command. This "double-scanning" is useful any time shell variables contain input/output redirection symbols, aliases, or other shell variables. (For example, redirection normally happens before variable expansion, so a variable containing redirection symbols must be expanded first using **eval**; otherwise, the redirection symbols remain uninterpreted.)

Example

This fragment of a shell script shows how **eval** constructs a command that is interpreted in the right order:

```
for option
do
```

```
                    case "$option" in           Define where output goes
                        save) out=' > $newfile' ;;
                        show) out=' | more' ;;
                    esac
                done

                eval sort $file $out
```

exec

```
exec [-a name] [-cl] [command args ... ]
```

Execute *command* in place of the current process (instead of creating a new process). **exec** is also useful for opening, closing, or copying file descriptors.

Options

-a *name*
    Use *name* for the value of **argv[0]**.

-c Clear the environment before executing the program.

-l Place a minus sign at the front of **argv[0]**, just as *login*(1) does.

Examples

```
trap 'exec 2>&-' 0          Close standard error when
                            shell script exits (signal 0)

$ exec /bin/csh             Replace shell with C shell
$ exec < infile             Reassign standard input to infile
```

exit

```
exit [n]
```

Exit a shell script with status *n* (e.g., **exit 1**). *n* can be 0 (success) or nonzero (failure). If *n* is not given, exit status is that of the most recent command. **exit** can be issued at the command line to close a window (log out). Exit statuses can range in value from 0 to 255.

Example

```
if [ $# -eq 0 ]
then
    echo "Usage: $0 [-c] [-d] file(s)" 1>&2
    exit 1                      # Error status
fi
```

export

```
export [-fn] [name=[value] ...]
export -p
```

Pass (export) the value of one or more shell variables, specified by *name*, giving them global meaning (they are local by default). For example, a variable defined in one shell script must be exported if its value is used in other programs called by the script. If a *value* is specified, the variable is set to that value. If no *names* are given, or with **-p**, **export** lists the variables exported by the current shell.

Options

-f   Names refer to functions; the functions are exported in the environment.

-n   Remove the named variables or functions from the environment.

-p   Print names and values of exported variables.

Example

In the original Bourne shell, you would type:

```
TERM=vt100
export TERM
```

In Bash, type this instead:

```
export TERM=vt100
```

---

false   false

Built-in command that exits with a false return value.

---

fc   fc [-lnr] [-e *editor*] [*first* [*last*]]
fc -s [*old=new*] [*command*]

Display or edit commands in the history list. *first* and *last* are numbers or strings specifying the range of commands to display or edit. If *last* is omitted, **fc** applies to a single command (specified by *first*). If both *first* and *last* are omitted, **fc** edits the previous command or lists the last 16. The second form of **fc** takes a history *command*, replaces *old* with *new*, and executes the modified command. If no strings are specified, *command* is just reexecuted. If no *command* is given either, the previous command is reexecuted. *command* is a number or string like *first*. See the examples in the earlier section "Command History" on page 614.

Options

Use only one of **-e**, **-l** or **-s**.

-e *editor*
      Invoke *editor* to edit the specified history commands. If no editor is specified, Bash defaults first to the value of FCEDIT, then to the value of EDITOR, then to **vi**.

-l   List the specified command or range of commands, or list the last 16.

-n   Suppress command numbering from the -l listing.

-r   Reverse the order of the -l listing.

-s [*old=new*]
      Replace the string *old* with *new* in the specified command and execute the modified command.

---

fg   fg [*jobIDs*]

Bring current job or *jobIDs* to the foreground. See the section "Job Control" on page 617.

fi

```
fi
```

Reserved word that ends an **if** statement. (Don't forget to use it!)

for

```
for x [in list]
do
   commands
done
```

For variable *x* (in optional *list* of values) do *commands*. If **in** *list* is omitted, "$@" (the positional parameters) is assumed.

Examples

Paginate files specified on the command line; save each result:

```
for file; do
      pr $file > $file.tmp
done
```

Search chapters for a list of words (like **fgrep -f**):

```
for item in `cat program_list`
do
      echo "Checking chapters for"
      echo "references to program $item..."
      grep -c "$item.[co]" chap*
done
```

Extract a one-word title from each file and use as new filename:

```
for file
do
      name=`sed -n 's/NAME: //p' $file`
      mv $file $name
done
```

for

```
for ((init; cond; incr))
do
   commands
done
```

Arithmetic **for** loop, similar to C's. Evaluate *init*. While *cond* is true, execute the body of the loop. Evaluate *incr* before retesting *cond*. Any one of the expressions may be omitted; a missing *cond* is treated as being true.

Example

Search for a phrase in each odd chapter:

```
for ((x=1; x <= 20; x += 2))
do
         grep $1 chap$x
done
```

function

[function] *name* ( ) { *commands*; }
function *name* { *commands*; }

Define *name* as a shell function. See the description of semantic issues in the section "Functions" on page 605. If the reserved word **function** is given, the parentheses following name are optional.

Example

Define a function to count files:

```
$ function fcount {
>     ls | wc -l
>}
```

getopts

getopts *string name* [*args*]

Process command-line arguments (or *args*, if specified) and check for legal options. **getopts** is used in shell-script loops and is intended to ensure standard syntax for command-line options. Standard syntax dictates that command-line options begin with -. Options can be stacked: i.e., consecutive letters can follow a single -. End processing of options by specifying -- on the command line. *string* contains the option letters to be recognized by **getopts** when running the shell script. Valid options are processed in turn and stored in the shell variable *name*. If an option is followed by a colon, the option must be followed by one or more arguments. (Multiple arguments must be given to the command as one shell *word*. This is done by quoting the arguments or separating them with commas. The application must be written to expect multiple arguments in this format.) **getopts** uses the shell variables OPTARG, OPTIND, and OPTERR.

hash

hash [-dlrt] [-p *file*] [*commands*]

As the shell finds commands along the search path ($PATH), it remembers the found location in an internal hash table. The next time you enter a command, the shell uses the value stored in its hash table.

With no arguments, **hash** lists the current hashed commands. The display shows hits (the number of times the command is called by the shell) and the command name.

With *commands*, the shell adds those commands to the hash table.

Options

-d   Remove (delete) just the specified commands from the hash table.

-l   Produce output in a format that can be reread to rebuild the hash table.

-p *file*
    Associate *file*, assumed to be the full pathname, with *command* in the hash table rather than searching $PATH.

-r   Remove all commands from the hash table.

-t   With one name, print the full pathname of the command. With more than one name, print the command name and the full path, in two columns.

Besides the **-r** option, the hash table is also cleared when PATH is assigned. Use **PATH=$PATH** to clear the hash table without affecting your search path. This is most useful if you have installed a new version of a command in a directory that is earlier in $PATH than the current version of the command.

---

help

help [-s] [*pattern*]

Print usage information on standard output for each Bash command that matches *pattern*. The information includes descriptions of each command's options. With the **-s** option, print only brief usage information.

Examples

```
$ help -s cd          Short help
cd: cd [-L|-P] [dir]
```

```
$ help true           Full help
true: true
        Return a successful result.

        Exit Status:
        Always succeeds.
```

---

history

history [*count*]
history [*options*]

Print commands in the history list or manage the history file. With no options or arguments, display the history list with command numbers. With a *count* argument, print only that number of the most recent commands.

Options

-a   Append new history lines (those executed since the beginning of the session) to the history file.

-c   Clear the history list (remove all entries).

-d *position*
        Delete the history item at position *position*.

-n   Read unread history lines from the history file into the history list.

-p *argument* ...
        Perform history substitution on each *argument*, printing the results to standard output. The results are not saved in the history list. Each argument must be quoted.

-r   Read the history file and replace the history list with its contents.

Store the *arguments* in the history list as a single entry.

-w Write the current history list to the history file, overwriting the file.

---

if

```
if condition1
then commands1
[ elif condition2
then commands2 ]
   .
   .
   .
[ else commands3 ]
fi
```

If *condition1* is met, do *commands1*; otherwise, if *condition2* is met, do *commands2* ; if neither is met, do *commands3*. Conditions are often specified with the **test** and **[[ ]]** commands. See **test** and **[[ ]]** for a full list of conditions, and see additional Examples under **:** and **exit**.

Examples

Insert a 0 before numbers less than 10:

```
if [ $counter -lt 10 ]
then number=0$counter
else number=$counter
fi
```

Make a directory if it doesn't exist:

```
if [ ! -d $dir ]; then
   mkdir $dir
   chmod 775 $dir
fi
```

---

jobs

```
jobs [options] [jobIDs]
```

List all running or stopped jobs, or list those specified by *jobIDs*. For example, you can check whether a long compilation or text format is still running. Also useful before logging out. See the section "Job Control" on page 617.

Options

-l List job IDs and process group IDs.

-n List only jobs whose status changed since last notification.

-p List process group IDs only.

-r List running jobs only.

-s List stopped jobs only.

-x *cmd*

Replace each job ID found in *cmd* with the associated process ID and then execute *cmd*.

The Bash Shell

kill

```
kill [options] IDs
```

Terminate each specified process *ID* or job *ID*. You must own the process or be a privileged user. This built-in command is similar to */usr/bin/kill*, described in Chapter 3. See the section "Job Control" on page 617.

Options

-l   List the signal names and numbers. (Used by itself.)

-n *num*
> Send the given signal number.

-s *name*
> Send the given signal name.

-signal
> The signal number or name (from **kill -l** or */usr/include/sys/ signal.h*). With a signal number of 9, the kill is absolute.

let

```
let expressions
```
or
```
((expressions))
```

Perform arithmetic as specified by one or more *expressions*. *expressions* consist of numbers, operators, and shell variables (which don't need a preceding **$**). Expressions must be quoted if they contain spaces or other special characters. The (( )) form does the quoting for you. For more information and examples, see "Arithmetic Expressions" on page 613. See also **expr** in Chapter 3.

Examples

Each of these examples adds 1 to variable **i**:

```
i=`expr $i + 1`
let i=i+1
let "i = i + 1"
(( i = i + 1 ))
(( i += 1 ))
(( i++ ))
```

local

```
local [option] [name[=value]]
```

Declares local variables for use inside functions. The *option* can be any option accepted by **declare**; see **declare** for the full list. It is an error to use **local** outside a function body.

logout

```
logout
```

Exit a login shell. The command fails if the current shell is not a login shell.

mapfile

mapfile [*options*] [*array*]
readarray [*options*] [*array*]

Populate an array by reading lines from standard input and placing them into the specified array. The default array is MAPFILE. Without the -O option, **mapfile** clears the array before assigning entries to it.

Options

-**c** *count*
> Used with -**C** to specify the number of lines read between *callback* calls.

-**C** *callback*
> Evaluate the *callback* code every time *count* lines are read, where *count* is specified by -**c** (default is 5000).

-**n** *num*
> Read in at most *num* lines, or all lines if *num* is 0.

-**O** *origin*
> Begin assigning entries to the array at index *origin* (default index is 0).

-**s** *count*
> Discard the first *count* lines read.

-**t**   Remove a trailing line from each input line.

-**u** *fd*
> Read from the given file descriptor instead of standard input.

---

name ( )

[function] *name* ( ) {*commands*; }

Define *name* as a function. POSIX syntax. The reserved word **function** is optional. The function definition can be written on one line or across many. See "Functions" on page 605 for more detailed information.

Example

```
$ count () {
> ls | wc -l
> }
```

When issued at the command line, **count** displays the number of files in the current directory.

---

popd

popd [-n] [+*count*] [-*count*]

Pop the top directory off the directory stack (as shown by the **dirs** command), and change to the new top directory, or manage the directory stack.

Options

-**n**   Don't change to the new top directory; just manipulate the stack.

+*count*

> Remove the item *count* entries from the left, as shown by **dirs**. Counting starts at zero. No directory change occurs.

-*count*

> Remove the item *count* entries from the right, as shown by **dirs**. Counting starts at zero. No directory change occurs.

---

printf

```
printf [-v var] format [val ...]
```

Format the specified values according to the format *format* and write them to standard output. The possible format character strings are those of the ANSI C **printf** function plus several additional strings.

Option

-*v var*

> Write output to the variable *var* instead of standard output.

Additional format strings

%b Expand escape sequences in strings (e.g., \t to tab, and so on).

%q Print a quoted string that can be reread later on.

Example

```
$ date                    Reformat date/time
Fri May 15 15:39:42 EDT 2009
$ printf "%(It is now %m/%d/%Y %H:%M:%S)T\n" "$(date)"
It is now 05/15/2009 15:40:10
```

---

pushd

```
pushd [-n] [directory]
pushd [-n] [+count] [-count]
```

Add *directory* to the directory stack, or rotate the directory stack. With no arguments, swap the top two entries on the stack, and change to the new top entry.

Options

-**n** Don't change to the new top directory, just manipulate the stack.

+*count*

> Rotate the stack so that the *count*'th item from the left, as shown by **dirs**, is the new top of the stack. Counting starts at zero. The new top becomes the current directory.

-*count*

> Rotate the stack so that the *count*'th item from the right, as shown by **dirs**, is the new top of the stack. Counting starts at zero. The new top becomes the current directory.

---

pwd

```
pwd [-LP]
```

Print your present working directory on standard output.

Options

Options give control over the use of logical versus physical treatment of the printed path. See also the entry for **cd**, earlier in this
section.

-L Use logical path (what the user typed, including any symbolic
       links) and the value of PWD for the current directory. This is
       the default.

-P Use the actual filesystem physical path for the current direc-
       tory with no symbolic links.

---

read

read [*options*] [*variable1*] [*variable2* ...]

Read one line of standard input and assign each word to the corresponding *variable*, with all leftover words assigned to the last
variable. If only one variable is specified, the entire line is assigned
to that variable. See the examples here and under **case**. The return
status is 0 unless EOF is reached. If no variables are given, input is
stored in the REPLY variable.

Options

-a *array*
    Read into indexed array *array*.

-d *delim*
    Read up to first occurrence of *delim*, instead of newline.

-e Use the *readline* library if reading from a terminal.

-i *text*
    If *readline* is being used, put *text* into the editing buffer.

-n *count*
    Read at most *count* bytes.

-p *prompt*
    Print *prompt* before reading input.

-r Raw mode; ignore \ as a line-continuation character.

-s Read silently; do not echo characters.

-t *timeout*
    When reading from a terminal or pipe, if no data is entered
    after *timeout* seconds, return 1. This prevents an application
    from hanging forever, waiting for user input.

-u [*n*]
    Read input from file descriptor *n* (default is 0).

Example

Read three variables:

```
$ read first last address
Sarah Caldwell 123 Main Street

$ echo "$last, $first\n$address"
Caldwell, Sarah
123 Main Street
```

readonly   readonly [-afp] [*variable*[*=value*] ...]

Prevent the specified shell variables from being assigned new values. An initial value may be supplied using the assignment syntax, but that value may not be changed subsequently. If no variables are specified, **readonly** displays a list of variables marked read-only.

Options

-a   Each *variable* must refer to an indexed array.

-A   Each *variable* must refer to an associative array.

-f   Each *variable* must refer to a function.

-p   Display the output in a format that allows the list of read-only variables to be saved for rereading later.

return   return [*n*]

Use inside a function definition. Exit the function with status *n* or with the exit status of the previously executed command.

select   select *x* [in *list*]
do
   commands
done

Display a list of menu items on standard error, numbered in the order they are specified in *list*. If no **in** *list* is given, items are taken from the command line (via "**$@**"). Following the menu is a prompt string (set by the variable PS3). At the prompt, the user selects a menu item by typing its line number, or redisplays the menu by pressing the Enter key. User input is stored in the shell variable REPLY and the value selected is stored in *x*. If a valid item number is typed, the *commands* associated with the value in *x* are executed and the prompt is redisplayed for the user to select a new value. Typing **EOF** terminates the loop.

Example

```
PS3="Select the item number: "
select event in Format Page View Exit
do
    case "$event" in
      Format) nroff $file | lp;;
      Page)   pr $file | lp;;
      View)   more $file;;
      Exit)   exit 0;;
      *   )   echo "Invalid selection";;
    esac
done
```

The output of this script looks like this:

```
1. Format
2. Page
3. View
4. Exit
Select the item number:
```

---

set

set [*options arg1 arg2 ...*]

With no arguments, **set** prints the values of all variables known to the current shell. Options can be enabled (*-option*) or disabled (*+option*). Options can also be set when the shell is invoked. (See the section "Invoking the Shell" on page 597.) Arguments are assigned in order to **$1**, **$2**, etc.

Options

-a   From now on, automatically mark variables for export after defining or changing them.

-b   Print job completion messages as soon as jobs terminate; don't wait until the next prompt.

-B   Enable brace expansion. On by default.

-C   Prevent overwriting via > redirection; use >| to overwrite files.

-e   Exit if a command yields a nonzero exit status. The **ERR** trap executes before the shell exits.

-E   Cause shell functions, command substitutions, and subshells to inherit the **ERR** trap.

-f   Ignore filename metacharacters (e.g., * ? [ ]).

-h   Locate and remember commands as they are defined. On by default.

-H   Enable **csh**-style (!-style) history substitution. On by default.

-k   Assignment of environment variables (*var=value*) takes effect regardless of where they appear on the command line. Normally, assignments must precede the command name.

-m   Enable job control; background jobs execute in a separate process group. **-m** is usually on by default.

-n   Read commands but don't execute; useful for checking syntax. Ignored if the shell is interactive.

+o [*mode*]
    With *mode*, disable the given shell option. Plain **set +o** prints the settings of all the current options in a form that can be reread by the shell later.

-o [*mode*]
    List shell modes, or turn on mode *mode*. Many modes can be set by other options. Modes are:

    allexport
        Same as **-a**.

braceexpand

Same as **-B**.

emacs

Set command-line editor to **emacs**.

errexit

Same as **-e**.

errtrace

Same as **-E**.

functrace

Same as **-T**.

hashall

Same as **-h**.

histexpand

Same as **-H**.

history

Enable command history. On by default.

ignoreeof

Don't process *EOF* signals. To exit the shell, type **exit**.

keyword

Same as **-k**.

monitor

Same as **-m**.

noclobber

Same as **-C**.

noexec

Same as **-n**.

noglob

Same as **-f**.

notify

Same as **-b**.

nounset

Same as **-u**.

onecmd

Same as **-t**.

physical

Same as **-P**.

pipefail

Change pipeline exit status to be that of the rightmost command that failed, or zero if all exited successfully.

posix

Change to POSIX mode.

privileged

Same as **-p**.

verbose

Same as **-v**.

vi Set command-line editor to **vi**.

xtrace
Same as **-x**.

+p Reset effective UID to real UID.

-p Start up as a privileged user. Don't read $ENV or $BASH_ ENV, don't import functions from the environment, and ignore the value of $SHELLOPTS.

-P Always use physical paths for **cd** and **pwd**; do not follow symbolic links.

-t Exit after one command is executed.

-T Cause shell functions, command substitutions, and subshells to inherit any **DEBUG** and **RETURN** traps.

-u In substitutions, treat unset variables as errors.

-v Show each shell command line when read.

-x Show commands and arguments when executed, preceded by the value of PS4. This provides step-by-step tracing of shell scripts.

- Turn off **-v** and **-x**, and turn off option processing. Included for compatibility with older versions of the Bourne shell.

-- Used as the last option; -- turns off option processing so that arguments beginning with - are not misinterpreted as options. (For example, you can set **$1** to -1.) If no arguments are given after --, unset the positional parameters.

Examples

```
set -- "$num" -20 -30    Set $1 to $num, $2 to -20, $3 to -30
set -vx                  Read each command line; show it;
                         execute it; show it again (with arguments)
set +x                   Stop command tracing
set -o noclobber         Prevent file overwriting
set +o noclobber         Allow file overwriting again
```

---

shift

```
shift [n]
```

Shift positional arguments (e.g., **$2** becomes **$1**). If *n* is given, shift to the left *n* places; otherwise *n* is assumed to be 1. Used in **while** loops to iterate through command-line arguments.

---

shopt

```
shopt [-opqsu] [options]
```

Set or unset shell options. With no options or just **-p**, print the option names and whether they are set or not.

Options

-o Each *option* must be one of the shell option names for **set -o**, instead of the options listed in the next section.

-p Print the option settings as **shopt** commands that can be reread later.

-q   Quiet mode. The exit status is zero if the given option is set, nonzero otherwise. With multiple options, all of them must be set for a zero exit status.

-s   Set the given *options*. With no *options*, print only those that are set.

-u   Unset the given *options*. With no *options*, print only those that are unset.

Settable shell options

The following list describes the behavior when set. Options marked with an asterisk (*) are enabled by default.

autocd

Attempt to **cd** to a directory that is given as a command name. Allowed in interactive shells only.

cdable_vars

Treat a nondirectory argument to **cd** as a variable whose value is the directory to go to.

cdspell

Attempt spelling correction on each directory component of an argument to **cd**. Allowed in interactive shells only.

checkhash

Check that commands found in the hash table still exist before attempting to use them. If not, perform a normal PATH search.

checkjobs

Display the status of any running or stopped jobs before exiting an interactive shell.

checkwinsize

Check the window size after each command and update LINES and COLUMNS if the size has changed.

cmdhist *

Save all lines of a multiline command in one history entry. This permits easy reediting of multiline commands.

compat31

Behave like version 3.1 with respect to quoted arguments to the conditional command's =~ operator.

dirspell

During filename completion, attempt to correct the spelling of directory names if the name as given is not found.

dotglob

Include filenames starting with a period in the results of filename expansion.

execfail

Do not exit a noninteractive shell if the command given to **exec** cannot be executed. Interactive shells do not exit in such a case, no matter the setting of this option.

expand_aliases *

Expand aliases created with **alias**. Disabled in noninteractive shells.

extdebug

Enable behavior needed for debuggers:

- **declare -F** displays the source filename and line number for each function name argument.

- When a command run by the **DEBUG** trap fails, the next command is skipped.

- When a command run by the **DEBUG** trap inside a shell function or script sourced with **.** (dot) or **source** returns with an exit status of 2, the shell simulates a call to **return**.

- BASH_ARGC and BASH_ARGV are set as described earlier.

- Function tracing is enabled. Command substitutions, shell functions, and subshells invoked via (...) inherit the **DEBUG** and **RETURN** traps.

- Error tracing is enabled. Command substitutions, shell functions, and subshells invoked via (...) inherit the **ERROR** trap.

extglob

Enable extended pattern-matching facilities such as +(...).

extquote *

Allow $'...' and $"..." within ${*variable*} expansions inside double quotes.

failglob

Cause patterns that do not match filenames to produce an error.

force_fignore *

When doing completion, ignore words matching the list of suffixes in FIGNORE, even if such words are the only possible completions.

globstar

During filename expansion, the pattern ** matches all directories and subdirectories, and filenames in directories, recursively. Only directories and subdirectories match if the pattern ends in **/**.

gnu_errfmt

Print error messages in the standard GNU format.

histappend

Append the history list to the file named by HISTFILE upon exit, instead of overwriting the file.

histreedit

Allow a user to reedit a failed history substitution with the *readline* library.

histverify
Place the results of history substitution into the *readline* library's editing buffer, in case the user wishes to modify it further, instead of executing it directly.

hostcomplete *
If using *readline*, attempt hostname completion when a word containing an @ is being completed.

huponexit
Send a **SIGHUP** to all running jobs upon exiting an interactive shell.

interactive_comments *
Allow words beginning with # to start a comment in an interactive shell.

lithist
If **cmdhist** is also set, save multiline commands to the history file with newlines instead of semicolons.

login_shell
Set by the shell when it is a login shell. This is a read-only option.

mailwarn
Print the message "The mail in *mailfile* has been read" when a file being checked for mail has been accessed since the last time Bash checked it.

no_empty_cmd_completion
If using *readline*, do not search $PATH when a completion is attempted on an empty line.

nocaseglob
Ignore letter case when doing filename matching.

nocasematch
Ignore case when pattern-matching in **case** or [[ ]] conditional commands.

nullglob
Expand patterns that do not match any files to the null string, instead of using the literal pattern as an argument.

progcomp *
Enable programmable completion.

promptvars *
Perform variable, command, and arithmetic substitution on the values of PS1, PS2 and PS4.

restricted_shell
Set by the shell when it is a restricted shell. This is a read-only option.

shift_verbose
Causes **shift** to print an error message when the shift count is greater than the number of positional parameters.

sourcepath *

> Causes the . (dot) and **source** commands to search $PATH in order to find the file to read and execute.

xpg_echo

> Causes **echo** to expand escape sequences, even without the **-e** or **-E** options.

---

source

```
source file [arguments]
```

Identical to the . (dot) command; see that entry.

---

suspend

```
suspend [-f]
```

Suspend the current shell. Often used to stop an **su** command.

Option

-f   Force the suspension, even if the shell is a login shell.

---

test

```
test condition
or
[ condition ]
or
[[ condition ]]
```

Evaluate a *condition* and, if its value is true, return a zero exit status; otherwise, return a nonzero exit status. An alternate form of the command uses [ ] rather than the word **test**. An additional alternate form uses [[ ]], in which case word splitting and pathname expansion are not done. (See the [[ ]] entry.) *condition* is constructed using the following expressions. Conditions are true if the description holds true.

File conditions

-a *file*, **-e** *file*
> *file* exists.

-b *file*
> *file* exists and is a block special file.

-c *file*
> *file* exists and is a character special file.

-d *file*
> *file* exists and is a directory.

-f *file*
> *file* exists and is a regular file.

-g *file*
> *file* exists, and its set-group-id bit is set.

-G *file*
> *file* exists, and its group is the effective group ID.

-h *file*, **-L** *file*
> *file* exists and is a symbolic link.

-k *file*
>   *file* exists, and its sticky bit is set.

-N *file*
>   *file* exists and was modified after it was last read.

-O *file*
>   *file* exists, and its owner is the effective user ID.

-p *file*
>   *file* exists and is a named pipe (FIFO).

-r *file*
>   *file* exists and is readable.

-s *file*
>   *file* exists and has a size greater than zero.

-S *file*
>   *file* exists and is a socket.

-t [*n*]
>   The open file descriptor *n* is associated with a terminal device; default *n* is 1.

-u *file*
>   *file* exists, and its set-user-id bit is set.

-w *file*
>   *file* exists and is writable.

-x *file*
>   *file* exists and is executable.

f1 **-ef** *f2*
>   Files *f1* and *f2* are linked (refer to same file).

f1 **-nt** *f2*
>   File *f1* is newer than *f2*.

f1 **-ot** *f2*
>   File *f1* is older than *f2*.

String conditions

string
>   *string* is not null.

-n *s1*
>   String *s1* has nonzero length.

-z *s1*
>   String *s1* has zero length.

s1 == *s2*
>   Strings *s1* and *s2* are identical. *s2* can be a wildcard pattern. Quote *s2* to treat it literally. Preferred over =.

s1 != *s2*
>   Strings *s1* and *s2* are *not* identical. *s2* can be a wildcard pattern. Quote *s2* to treat it literally.

s1 =~ *s2*

    String *s1* matches extended regular expression *s2*. Quote *s2* to keep the shell from expanding embedded shell metacharacters. Strings matched by parenthesized subexpressions are placed into elements of the BASH_REMATCH array. See the description of BASH_REMATCH earlier in this chapter.

s1 < *s2*

    ASCII value of *s1* precedes that of *s2*. (Valid only within [[ ]] construct.)

s1 > *s2*

    ASCII value of *s1* follows that of *s2*. (Valid only within [[ ]] construct.)

Internal shell conditions

-o *opt*

    Shell option *opt* for **set -o** is on.

Integer comparisons

n1 **-eq** *n2*

    n1 equals *n2*.

n1 **-ge** *n2*

    n1 is greater than or equal to *n2*.

n1 **-gt** *n2*

    n1 is greater than *n2*.

n1 **-le** *n2*

    n1 is less than or equal to *n2*.

n1 **-lt** *n2*

    n1 is less than *n2*.

n1 **-ne** *n2*

    n1 does not equal *n2*.

Combined forms

(*condition*)

    True if *condition* is true (used for grouping). For **test** and [ ], the ( )s should be quoted by a \. The form using [[ ]] doesn't require quoting the parentheses.

! *condition*

    True if *condition* is false.

condition1 **-a** *condition2*

    True if both conditions are true.

condition1 **&&** *condition2*

    True if both conditions are true. (Valid only within [[ ]] construct.)

condition1 **-o** *condition2*

    True if either condition is true.

condition1 || *condition2*

    True if either condition is true. (Valid only within [[ ]] construct.)

Examples

The following examples show the first line of various statements that might use a test condition:

```
while test $# -gt 0          While there are arguments...
while [ -n "$1" ]            While there are nonempty arguments..
if [ $count -lt 10 ]         If $count is less than 10...
if [ -d RCS ]                If the RCS directory exists...
if [ "$answer" != "y" ]      If the answer is not y...
if [ ! -r "$1" -o ! -f "$1" ]   If the first argument is not a readable
                                file or a regular file...
```

---

time

time *command*

Execute *command* and print the total elapsed time, user time, and system time (in seconds). Same as the Linux command **time** (see Chapter 3), except that the built-in version can also time other built-in commands as well as all commands in a pipeline.

---

times

times

Print accumulated process times for user and system.

---

trap

trap [*options*] [[*commands*] *signals*]

Execute *commands* if any *signals* are received. Common signals include **EXIT** (0), **HUP** (1), **INT** (2), and **TERM** (15). Multiple commands must be quoted as a group and separated by semicolons internally. If the command is the null string (i.e., **trap ""** *signals*), the signals are ignored by the shell. If the commands are omitted entirely, processing of the specified signals is reset to the default action. If the command is -, the signals are reset to their initial defaults.

If both *commands* and *signals* are omitted, list current trap assignments. See the Examples here and in **exec**.

Options

-l   List all signals and their numbers, like **kill -l**.

-p   Print the current trap settings in a form suitable for rereading later.

Signals

A list of signal names, numbers, and meanings were given earlier in the **kill** entry; see the listing there. The shell allows you to use either the signal number or the signal name (without the **SIG** prefix). In addition, the shell supports "pseudo-signals," signal names or numbers that aren't real operating system signals but which direct the shell to perform a specific action. These signals are:

DEBUG
    Execution of any command.

ERR
    Nonzero exit status.

EXIT

Exit from shell (usually when shell script finishes).

0 Same as **EXIT**, for historical compatibility with the Bourne shell.

RETURN

A **return** is executed, or a script run with . (dot) or **source** finishes.

Examples

```
trap "" INT      Ignore interrupts (signal 2)
trap INT         Obey interrupts again
```

Remove a **$tmp** file when the shell program exits, or if the user logs out, presses **Ctrl-C**, or does a **kill**:

```
trap "rm -f $tmp; exit" EXIT HUP INT TERM      POSIX style
trap "rm -f $tmp; exit" 0 1 2 15      Pre-POSIX Bourne shell style
```

Print a "clean up" message when the shell program receives signals **SIGHUP**, **SIGINT**, or **SIGTERM**:

```
trap 'echo Interrupt!  Cleaning up...' HUP INT TERM
```

---

true   true

Built-in command that exits with a true return value.

---

type   type [-afpPt] *commands*

Show whether each command name is a Linux command, a built-in command, an alias, a shell keyword, or a defined shell function.

Options

-a Print all locations in $PATH that include *command*, including aliases and functions. Use **-p** together with **-a** to suppress aliases and functions.

-f Suppress function lookup, as with **command**.

-p If **type -t** would print **file** for a given *command*, this option prints the full pathname for the executable files. Otherwise, it prints nothing.

-P Like **-p**, but force a PATH search, even if **type -t** would not print **file**.

-t Print a word describing each *command*. The word is one of **alias**, **builtin**, **file**, **function**, or **keyword**, depending upon the type of each *command*.

Example

```
$ type mv read if
mv is /bin/mv
read is a shell builtin
if is a shell keyword
```

The Bash Shell

ulimit   ulimit [*options*] [*n*]

Print the value of one or more resource limits, or, if *n* is specified, set a resource limit to *n*. Resource limits can be either hard (**-H**) or soft (**-S**). By default, **ulimit** sets both limits or prints the soft limit. The options determine which resource is acted on.

Options

-H Hard limit. Anyone can lower a hard limit; only privileged users can raise it.

-S Soft limit. Anyone can raise a soft limit up to the value of the hard limit.

-a Print all limits.

-b Maximum socket buffer size.

-c Maximum size of core files.

-d Maximum kilobytes of data segment or heap.

-e Maximum scheduling priority ("nice").

-f Maximum size of files (the default option).

-i Maximum number of pending signals.

-l Maximum size of address space that can be locked in memory.

-m Maximum kilobytes of physical memory. (Not effective on all Linux systems.)

-n Maximum number of file descriptors.

-p Maximum size of pipe buffers in 512-byte blocks. (May not be set.)

-q Maximum number of bytes in POSIX message queues.

-r Maximum real-time scheduling priority.

-s Maximum stack size.

-t Maximum CPU seconds.

-T Maximum number of threads.

-u Maximum number of processes a single user can have.

-v Maximum kilobytes of virtual memory.

-x Maximum number of file locks

---

umask   umask [-pS] [*mask*]

Display or set file creation mask. If *mask* begins with a digit, it is treated as an octal number; otherwise it is treated as a symbolic mask. The file creation mask determines which permission bits are turned off (e.g., **umask 002** produces **rw-rw-r--**). The mask is similar to that accepted by the **chmod** command.

Options

-p Output is in a form that can be reread later by the shell.

-S Print the current mask using symbolic notation.

unalias

unalias *names*
unalias -a

Remove *names* from the alias list. See also **alias**.

Option

-a   Remove all aliases.

unset

unset [*options*] *names*

Erase definitions of functions or variables listed in *names*.

Options

-f   Unset functions *names*.

-v   Unset shell variables *names* (default).

until

until *condition*
do
 commands
done

Until *condition* is met, do *commands*. *condition* is often specified with the **test** command. See the Examples under **case** and **test**.

wait

wait [*ID*]

Pause in execution until all background jobs complete (exit status 0 is returned), or pause until the specified background process *ID* or job *ID* completes (exit status of *ID* is returned). Note that the shell variable **$!** contains the process ID of the most recent background process.

Example

wait $!   *Wait for most recent background process to finish*

while

while *condition*
do
 commands
done

While *condition* is met, do *commands*. *condition* is often specified with the **test** command. See the Examples under **case** and **test**.

7

Pattern Matching

A number of Linux text-processing utilities let you search for, and in some cases change, text patterns rather than fixed strings. These utilities include the editing programs **ed**, **ex**, **vi**, and **sed**; the **gawk** programming language; and the commands **grep** and **egrep**. Text patterns (called *regular expressions* in computer science literature) contain normal characters mixed with special characters (called *metacharacters*).

Perl's regular expression support is so rich that it does not fit into this book; you can find a description in the O'Reilly books *Mastering Regular Expressions* by Jeffrey E.F. Friedl, *Regular Expression Pocket Reference* by Tony Stubblebine, *Perl in a Nutshell* by Nathan Patwardhan et al., or *Perl 5 Pocket Reference* by Johan Vromans. The Emacs editor also provides regular expressions similar to those shown in this chapter. See the O'Reilly books *Learning GNU Emacs* by Debra Cameron et al., or *GNU Emacs Pocket Reference*, also by Debra Cameron, for details.

This chapter presents the following topics:

- Filenames versus patterns
- Description of metacharacters
- List of metacharacters available to each program
- Examples

For more information on regular expressions, see the aforementioned O'Reilly book *Mastering Regular Expressions*.

Filenames Versus Patterns

Metacharacters used in pattern matching are different from metacharacters used for filename expansion (see Chapter 6). However, several metacharacters have meaning for both regular expressions and for filename expansion. This can lead to a problem: the shell sees the command line first, and can potentially interpret an unquoted regular expression metacharacter as a filename expansion. For example, the command:

```
$ grep [A-Z]* chap[12]
```

could be transformed by the shell into:

```
$ grep Array.c Bug.c Comp.c chap1 chap2
```

and **grep** would then try to find the pattern *Array.c* in files *Bug.c*, *Comp.c*, *chap1*, and *chap2*. To bypass the shell and pass the special characters to **grep**, use quotes as follows:

```
$ grep "[A-Z]*" chap[12]
```

Double quotes suffice in most cases, but single quotes are the safest bet, since the shell does absolutely no expansions on single-quoted text.

Note also that in pattern matching, ? matches zero or one instance of a regular expression; in filename expansion, ? matches a single character.

Metacharacters

Different metacharacters have different meanings, depending upon where they are used. In particular, regular expressions used for searching through text (matching) have one set of metacharacters, while the metacharacters used when processing replacement text (such as in a text editor) have a different set. These sets also vary somewhat per program. This section covers the metacharacters used for searching and replacing, with descriptions of the variants in the different utilities.

Search Patterns

The characters in the following table have special meaning only in search patterns.

Character	Pattern
.	Match any *single* character except newline. Can match newline in **gawk**.
*	Match any number (or none) of the single character that immediately precedes it. The preceding character can also be a regular expression. For example, since . (dot) means any character, .* means "match any number of any character."
^	Match the following regular expression at the beginning of the line or string.
$	Match the preceding regular expression at the end of the line or string.
[]	Match any *one* of the enclosed characters. A hyphen (-) indicates a range of consecutive characters. A circumflex (^) as the first character in the brackets reverses the sense: it matches any one character *not* in the list. A hyphen or close bracket (]) as the first character is treated as a member of the list. All other metacharacters are treated as members of the list (i.e., literally).
{n,m}	Match a range of occurrences of the single character that immediately precedes it. The preceding character can also be a regular expression. {n} matches exactly *n* occurrences, {n,} matches at least *n* occurrences, and {n,m} matches any number of occurrences between *n* and *m*. *n* and *m* must be between 0 and 255, inclusive. (The GNU programs on Linux allow a range of 0 to 32767.)
\{n,m\}	Just like {n,m}, earlier, but with backslashes in front of the braces.
\	Turn off the special meaning of the following character.

Character	Pattern
\(\)	Save the subpattern enclosed between \(and \) into a special holding space. Up to nine subpatterns can be saved on a single line. The text matched by the subpatterns can be "replayed" in substitutions by the escape sequences \1 to \9.
\n	Replay the nth subpattern enclosed in \(and \) into the pattern at this point. n is a number from 1 to 9, with 1 starting on the left. See the following Examples.
\< \>	Match characters at beginning (\<) or end (\>) of a word.
+	Match one or more instances of preceding regular expression.
?	Match zero or one instances of preceding regular expression.
|	Match one or the other of the regular expressions specified before and after the vertical bar. (This is known as alternation.)
( )	Apply a match to the enclosed group of regular expressions.

Linux allows the use of POSIX "character classes" within the square brackets that enclose a group of characters. They are typed enclosed in [: and :]. For example, [[:alnum:]] matches a single alphanumeric character.

Class	Characters matched	Class	Characters matched
alnum	Alphanumeric characters	lower	Lowercase characters
alpha	Alphabetic characters	print	Printable characters
blank	Space or Tab	punct	Punctuation characters
cntrl	Control characters	space	Whitespace characters
digit	Decimal digits	upper	Uppercase characters
graph	Non-space characters	xdigit	Hexadecimal digits

Finally, the GNU utilities on Linux accept additional escape sequences that act like metacharacters. (Because \b can also be interpreted as the sequence for the ASCII Backspace character, different utilities treat it differently. Check each utility's documentation.)

Sequence	Meaning
\b	Word boundary, either beginning or end of a word, as for the \< and \> metacharacters described earlier.
\B	Interword match; matches between two word-constituent characters.
\w	Matches any word-constituent character; equivalent to [[:alnum:]_].
\W	Matches any non-word-constituent character; equivalent to [^[:alnum:]_].
\`	Beginning of an Emacs buffer. Used by most other GNU utilities to mean unambiguously "beginning of string."
\'	End of an Emacs buffer. Used by most other GNU utilities to mean unambiguously "end of string."

Replacement Patterns

The characters in the following table have special meaning only in replacement patterns, used for example in editing, when searching for and replacing text.

Character	Pattern
\	Turn off the special meaning of the following character.
\n	Reuse the text matched by the nth subpattern previously saved by \(and \) as part of the replacement pattern. n is a number from 1 to 9, with 1 starting on the left.
&	Reuse the text matched by the search pattern as part of the replacement pattern.
~	Reuse the previous replacement pattern in the current replacement pattern. Must be the only character in the replacement pattern (**ex** and **vi**).
%	Reuse the previous replacement pattern in the current replacement pattern. Must be the only character in the replacement pattern (**ed**).
\u	Convert the first character of replacement pattern to uppercase.
\U	Convert the entire replacement pattern to uppercase.
\l	Convert the first character of replacement pattern to lowercase.
\L	Convert the entire replacement pattern to lowercase.
\e	Turn off previous \u or \l.
\E	Turn off previous \U or \L.

Metacharacters, Listed by Program

Some metacharacters are valid for one program but not for another. Those that are available are marked by a bullet (•) in the following table. Items marked with a "P" are specified by POSIX. Full descriptions were provided in the previous section.

Symbol	ed	ex	vi	sed	gawk	grep	egrep	Action
.	•	•	•	•	•	•	•	Match any character.
*	•	•	•	•	•	•	•	Match zero or more preceding characters.
^	•	•	•	•	•	•	•	Match beginning of line/string.
$	•	•	•	•	•	•	•	Match end of line/string.
\	•	•	•	•	•	•	•	Escape following character.
[ ]	•	•	•	•	•	•	•	Match one from a set.
\(\)	•	•	•	•		•		Store pattern for later replay.[a]
\n	•	•	•	•		•		Replay subpattern in match.
{ }					• P		• P	Match a range of instances.
\{ \}	•		•			•		Match a range of instances.
\< \>	•	•	•					Match word's beginning or end.
+				•			•	Match one or more preceding characters.
?				•			•	Match zero or one preceding characters.
|				•			•	Separate choices to match.
( )				•			•	Group expressions to match.

[a] Stored subpatterns can be "replayed" during matching. See the following table.

Note that in **ed**, **ex**, **vi**, and **sed**, you specify both a search pattern (on the left) and a replacement pattern (on the right). The metacharacters listed above are meaningful only in a search pattern.

In **ed**, **ex**, **vi**, and **sed**, the metacharacters in the following table are valid only in a replacement pattern.

Symbol	ex	vi	sed	ed	Action
\	•	•	•	•	Escape following character.
n	•	•	•	•	Text matching pattern stored in \(\).
&	•	•	•	•	Text matching search pattern.
~	•	•			Reuse previous replacement pattern.
%				•	Reuse previous replacement pattern.
\u \U	•	•			Change character(s) to uppercase.
\l \L	•	•			Change character(s) to lowercase.
\e	•	•			Turn off previous \u or \l.
\E	•	•			Turn off previous \U or \L.

Examples of Searching

When used with **grep** or **egrep**, regular expressions should be surrounded by quotes. (If the pattern contains a **$**, you must use single quotes; e.g., *'pattern'*.) When used with **ed**, **ex**, **sed**, and **gawk**, regular expressions are usually surrounded by **/**, although (except for **gawk**) any delimiter works. The following tables show some sample patterns.

Pattern	What does it match?
bag	The string *bag*.
^bag	*bag* at the beginning of the line.
bag$	*bag* at the end of the line.
^bag$	*bag* as the only word on the line.
[Bb]ag	*Bag* or *bag*.
b[aeiou]g	Second letter is a vowel.
b[^aeiou]g	Second letter is a consonant (or uppercase or symbol).
b.g	Second letter is any character.
^...$	Any line containing exactly three characters.
^\.	Any line that begins with a dot.
^\.[a-z][a-z]	Same, followed by two lowercase letters (e.g., **troff** requests).
^\.[a-z]\{2\}	Same as previous; **ed**, **grep**, and **sed** only.
^[^.]	Any line that doesn't begin with a dot.
bugs*	*bug*, *bugs*, *bugss*, etc.
"word"	A word in quotes.
"*word"*	A word, with or without quotes.
[A-Z][A-Z]*	One or more uppercase letters.
[A-Z]+	Same; **egrep** or **gawk** only.

Pattern	What does it match?
[[:upper:]]+	Same as previous, **egrep** or **gawk**.
[A-Z].*	An uppercase letter, followed by zero or more characters.
[A-Z]*	Zero or more uppercase letters.
[a-zA-Z]	Any letter, either lower- or uppercase.
[^0-9A-Za-z]	Any symbol or space (not a letter or a number).
[^[:alnum:]]	Same, using POSIX character class.

egrep or gawk pattern	What does it match?
[567]	One of the numbers *5*, *6*, or *7*.
five|six|seven	One of the words *five*, *six*, or *seven*.
80[2-4]?86	*8086*, *80286*, *80386*, or *80486*.
80[2-4]?86|(Pentium(-III?)?)	*8086*, *80286*, *80386*, *80486*, *Pentium*, *Pentium-II*, or *Pentium-III*.
compan(y|ies)	*company* or *companies*.

ex or vi pattern	What does it match?
\<the	Words like *theater* or *the*.
the\>	Words like *breathe* or *the*.
\<the\>	The word *the*.

ed, sed, or grep pattern	What does it match?
0\{5,\}	Five or more zeros in a row.
[0-9]\{3\}-[0-9]\{2\}-[0-9]\{4\}	U.S. Social Security number (*nnn-nn-nnnn*).
\(why\).*\1	A line with two occurrences of *why*.
\([[:alpha:]_][[:alnum:]_.]*\) =\1;	C/C++ simple assignment statements.

Examples of Searching and Replacing

The examples in the following table show the metacharacters available to **sed** or **ex**. Note that **ex** commands begin with a colon. A space is marked by a □; a tab is marked by a *tab*.

Command	Result
s/.*/(&)/	Redo the entire line, but add spaces and parentheses.
s/.*/mv & &.old/	Change a wordlist (one word per line) into **mv** commands.
/^$/d	Delete blank lines.
:g/^$/d	Same as previous, in **ex** editor.
/^[□*tab*]*$/d	Delete blank lines, plus lines containing only spaces or tabs.
:g/^[□*tab*]*$/d	Same as previous, in **ex** editor.
s/□ □*/□/g	Turn one or more spaces into one space.
:%s/□ □*/□/g	Same as previous, in **ex** editor.
:s/[0-9]/Item &:/	Turn a number into an item label (on the current line).
:s	Repeat the substitution on the first occurrence.
:&	Same as previous.
:sg	Same as previous, but for all occurrences on the line.
:&g	Same as previous.
:%&g	Repeat the substitution globally (i.e., on all lines).

Command	Result
:.,$s/Fortran/\U&/g	On current line to last line, change word to uppercase.
:.,$s/\(F\)\(ORTRAN\)/\1\L\2/g	On current line to last line, change spelling of "FORTRAN" to correct, modern usage.
:%s/.*/\L&/	Lowercase entire file.
:s/\<./\u&/g	Uppercase first letter of each word on current line. (Useful for titles.)
:%s/yes/No/g	Globally change a word to *No*.
:%s/Yes/~/g	Globally change a different word to *No* (previous replacement).

Finally, some **sed** examples for transposing words. A simple transposition of two words might look like this:

    s/die or do/do or die/   *Transpose words*

The real trick is to use hold buffers to transpose variable patterns. For example:

    s/\([Dd]ie\) or \([Dd]o\)/\2 or \1/   *Transpose, using hold buffers*

8

The Emacs Editor

The Emacs editor is found on many Unix systems, including Linux, because it is a popular alternative to **vi**. Many versions are available, but this book documents the most popular one, GNU Emacs (version 22.3), which is available from the Free Software Foundation (*http://www.gnu.org/software/emacs*).

Emacs is much more than "just an editor"—in fact, it provides a fully integrated user environment. From within Emacs, you can issue individual shell commands or open a window where you can work in the shell, read and send mail, read news, access the Internet, write and test programs, and maintain a calendar. To fully describe Emacs would require more space than we have available. In this chapter, therefore, we focus on the editing capabilities of Emacs.

This chapter presents the following topics:

- Conceptual overview
- Command-line syntax
- Summary of **emacs** commands by group
- Summary of **emacs** commands by key
- Summary of **emacs** commands by name

For more information about Emacs, see *Learning GNU Emacs*, by Debra Cameron et al. (O'Reilly).

Conceptual Overview

This section describes some Emacs terminology that may be unfamiliar if you haven't used Emacs before.

Modes

One of the features that makes Emacs popular is its editing modes. The modes set up an environment designed for the type of editing you are doing, with features such as having appropriate key bindings available and automatically indenting according to standard conventions for that type of document. There are two types of modes: major and minor. The major modes include modes for various programming languages such as C or Perl, for text processing (e.g., XML, or even straight text), and many more. One particularly useful major mode is Dired (Directory Editor), which has commands that let you manage directories. Minor modes set or unset features that are independent of the major mode, such as auto-fill (which controls word wrapping), insert versus overwrite, and auto-save. For a full discussion of modes, see *Learning GNU Emacs* (O'Reilly) or the Emacs Info documentation system (**C-h i**).

Buffer and Window

When you open a file in Emacs, the file is put into a *buffer* so you can edit it. If you open another file, that file goes into another buffer. The view of the buffer contents that you have at any point in time is called a *window*. For a small file, the window might show the entire file; for a large file, it shows only a portion of a file. Emacs allows multiple windows to be open at the same time, to display the contents of different buffers or different portions of a single buffer.

Point and Mark

When you are editing in Emacs, the position of the cursor is known as *point*. You can set a *mark* at another place in the text to operate on the region between point and mark. This is a very useful feature for such operations as deleting or moving an area of text.

Kill and Yank

Emacs uses the terms *kill* and *yank* for the concepts more commonly known today as *cut* and *paste*. You cut text in Emacs by killing it, and paste it by yanking it back. If you do multiple kills in a row, you can yank them back all at once.

Notes on the Tables

Emacs commands use the Ctrl key and the Meta key (Meta is usually the Alt key or the Escape key). In this chapter, the notation C- indicates that the Ctrl key is pressed at the same time as the character that follows. Similarly, M- indicates the use of the Meta key. When using Escape for Meta, press and release the Escape key, then type the next key. If you use Alt (or Option on the Mac) for Meta, it is just like Ctrl or Shift, and you should press it simultaneously with the other key(s).

In the command tables that follow, the first column lists the keystroke and the last column describes it. When there is a middle column, it lists the command name. If there are no keystrokes for a given command, you'll see (**none**) in the first column. Access these commands by typing **M-x** followed by the command name. If you're unsure of the name, you can type a tab or a carriage return, and Emacs lists possible completions of what you've typed so far.

Because Emacs is such a comprehensive editor, containing literally thousands of commands, some commands must be omitted for the sake of preserving a "quick" reference. You can browse the command set from within Emacs by typing **C-h** (for help) or **M-x Tab** (for command names).

Absolutely Essential Commands

If you're just getting started with Emacs, here's a short list of the most important commands.

Keystrokes	Description
C-h	Enter the online help system.
C-x C-s	Save the file.
C-x C-c	Exit Emacs.
C-x u	Undo last edit (can be repeated).
C-g	Get out of current command operation.
C-p	Move up to the previous line.
C-n	Move down to the next line.
C-f	Move forward one character.
C-b	Move backward one character.
C-v	Move forward by one screen.
M-v	Move backward by one screen
C-s	Search forward for characters.
C-r	Search backward for characters.
C-d	Delete the current character.
Del	Delete the previous character.

Command-Line Syntax

To start an Emacs editing session, type:

```
emacs [file]
```

Summary of Commands by Group

Reminder: C- indicates the Ctrl key; M- indicates the Meta key.

File-Handling Commands

Keystrokes	Command name	Description
C-x C-f	find-file	Find file and read it.
C-x C-v	find-alternate-file	Read another file; replace the one read with C-x C-f.
C-x i	insert-file	Insert file at cursor position.
C-x C-s	save-buffer	Save file (may hang terminal; use C-q to restart).
C-x C-w	write-file	Write buffer contents to file.
C-x C-c	save-buffers-kill-emacs	Exit Emacs.
C-z	suspend-emacs	Suspend Emacs (use **exit** or **fg** to restart).

Cursor-Movement Commands

Keystrokes	Command name	Description
C-f	forward-char	Move *forward* one character (right).
C-b	backward-char	Move *backward* one character (left).
C-p	previous-line	Move to *previous* line (up).
C-n	next-line	Move to *next* line (down).
M-f	forward-word	Move one word *forward*.
M-b	backward-word	Move one word *backward*.
C-a	beginning-of-line	Move to beginning of line.
C-e	end-of-line	Move to *end* of line.
M-a	backward-sentence	Move backward one sentence.
M-e	forward-sentence	Move forward one sentence.
M-{	backward-paragraph	Move backward one paragraph.
M-}	forward-paragraph	Move forward one paragraph.
C-v	scroll-up	Move forward one screen.
M-v	scroll-down	Move backward one screen.
C-x [	backward-page	Move backward one page.
C-x]	forward-page	Move forward one page.
M->	end-of-buffer	Move to end of file.
M-<	beginning-of-buffer	Move to beginning of file.
M-g g or M-g M-g	goto-line	Go to line *n* of file.
(none)	goto-char	Go to character *n* of file.
C-l	recenter	Redraw screen with current line in the center.
M-*n*	digit-argument	Repeat the next command *n* times.
C-u *n*	universal-argument	Repeat the next command *n* times.

Deletion Commands

Keystrokes	Command name	Description
Del	backward-delete-char	Delete previous character.
C-d	delete-char	Delete character under cursor.
M-Del	backward-kill-word	Delete previous word.
M-d	kill-word	Delete the word the cursor is on.
C-k	kill-line	Delete from cursor to end of line.
M-k	kill-sentence	Delete sentence the cursor is on.
C-x Del	backward-kill-sentence	Delete previous sentence.
C-y	yank	Restore what you've deleted.
C-w	kill-region	Delete a marked region (see next section).
(none)	backward-kill-paragraph	Delete previous paragraph.
(none)	kill-paragraph	Delete from the cursor to the end of the paragraph.

Paragraphs and Regions

Keystrokes	Command name	Description
C-@	set-mark-command	Mark the beginning (or end) of a region.
C-Space	(same as above)	(same as above)
C-x C-p	mark-page	Mark page.
C-x C-x	exchange-point-and-mark	Exchange location of cursor and mark.
C-x h	mark-whole-buffer	Mark buffer.
M-q	fill-paragraph	Reformat paragraph.
(none)	fill-region	Reformat individual paragraphs within a region.
M-h	mark-paragraph	Mark paragraph.

Stopping and Undoing Commands

Keystrokes	Command name	Description
C-g	keyboard-quit	Abort current command.
C-x u	advertised-undo	Undo last edit (can be done repeatedly).
(none)	revert-buffer	Restore buffer to the state it was in when the file was last saved (or auto-saved).

Transposition Commands

Keystrokes	Command name	Description
C-t	transpose-chars	Transpose two letters.
M-t	transpose-words	Transpose two words.
C-x C-t	transpose-lines	Transpose two lines.
(none)	transpose-sentences	Transpose two sentences.
(none)	transpose-paragraphs	Transpose two paragraphs.

Search Commands

Keystrokes	Command name	Description
C-s	isearch-forward	Incremental search forward.
C-r	isearch-backward	Incremental search backward
M-%	query-replace	Search and replace.
C-M-s Enter	re-search-forward	Regular expression search forward.
C-M-r Enter	re-search-backward	Regular expression search backward

Capitalization Commands

Keystrokes	Command name	Description
M-c	capitalize-word	Capitalize first letter of word.
M-u	upcase-word	Uppercase word.
M-l	downcase-word	Lowercase word.
M- - M-c	negative-argument; capitalize-word	Capitalize previous word.
M- - M-u	negative-argument; upcase-word	Uppercase previous word.
M- - M-l	negative-argument; downcase-word	Lowercase previous word.
(none)	capitalize-region	Capitalize region.
C-x C-u	upcase-region	Uppercase region
C-x C-l	downcase-region	Lowercase region.

Word-Abbreviation Commands

Keystrokes	Command name	Description
(none)	abbrev-mode	Enter (or exit) word abbreviation mode.
C-x a i g	inverse-add-global-abbrev	Type global abbreviation, then definition.
C-x a i l	inverse-add-local-abbrev	Type local abbreviation, then definition.
(none)	unexpand-abbrev	Undo the last word abbreviation.
(none)	write-abbrev-file	Write the word abbreviation file.
(none)	edit-abbrevs	Edit the word abbreviations.
(none)	list-abbrevs	View the word abbreviations.
(none)	kill-all-abbrevs	Kill abbreviations for this session.

Buffer-Manipulation Commands

Keystrokes	Command name	Description
C-x b	switch-to-buffer	Move to specified buffer.
C-x C-b	list-buffers	Display buffer list.
C-x k	kill-buffer	Delete specified buffer.
(none)	kill-some-buffers	Ask about deleting each buffer.
(none)	rename-buffer	Change buffer name to specified name.
C-x s	save-some-buffers	Ask whether to save each modified buffer.

Window Commands

Keystrokes	Command name	Description
C-x 2	split-window-vertically	Divide the current window into two, one on top of the other.
C-x 3	split-window-horizontally	Divide the current window into two, side by side.
C-x >	scroll-right	Scroll the window right.

Keystrokes	Command name	Description
C-x <	scroll-left	Scroll the window left.
C-x o	other-window	Move to the other window.
C-x 0	delete-window	Delete current window.
C-x 1	delete-other-windows	Delete all windows but this one.
(none)	delete-windows-on	Delete all windows on a given buffer.
C-x ^	enlarge-window	Make window taller.
(none)	shrink-window	Make window shorter.
C-x }	enlarge-window-horizontally	Make window wider.
C-x {	shrink-window-horizontally	Make window narrower.
C-M-v	scroll-other-window	Scroll other window.
C-x 4 f	find-file-other-window	Find a file in the other window.
C-x 4 b	switch-to-buffer-other-window	Select a buffer in the other window.
C-x 5 f	find-file-other-frame	Find a file in a new frame.
C-x 5 b	switch-to-buffer-other-frame	Select a buffer in another frame.
(none)	compare-windows	Compare two buffers; show first difference.

Special Shell Characters

Keystrokes	Command Name	Description
M-!	shell-command	Run a shell command and display the results.
(none)	shell	Start a shell buffer.
C-c C-c	comint-interrupt-subjob	Terminate the current job.
C-c C-d	comint-send-eof	End of file character.
C-c C-u	comint-kill-input	Erase current line.
C-c C-w	backward-kill-word	Erase the previous word.
C-c C-z	comint-stop-subjob	Suspend the current job.

Indentation Commands

Keystrokes	Command name	Description
C-x .	set-fill-prefix	Use characters from the beginning of the line up to the cursor column as the "fill prefix." This prefix is prepended to each line in the paragraph. Cancel the prefix by typing this command in column 1.
(none)	indented-text-mode	Major mode: each tab defines a new indent for subsequent lines.
(none)	text-mode	Exit indented text mode; return to text mode.
C-M-\	indent-region	Indent a region to match first line in region.
M-m	back-to-indentation	Move cursor to first nonblank character on line.
M-^	delete-indentation	Join this line to the previous one.
C-M-o	split-line	Split line at cursor; indent to column of cursor.
(none)	fill-individual-paragraphs	Reformat indented paragraphs, keeping indentation.

The Emacs Editor

Centering Commands

Keystrokes	Command name	Description
M-s	center-line	Center line that cursor is on.
M-S	center-paragraph	Center paragraph that cursor is on.
(none)	center-region	Center currently defined region.

Macro Commands

Keystrokes	Command name	Description
C-x (or F3 key	start-kbd-macro	Start macro definition.
C-x) or F4 key	end-kbd-macro	End macro definition.
C-x e or F4 key	call-last-kbd-macro	Execute last macro defined.
M-n C-x e	digit-argument and call-last-kbd-macro	Execute last macro defined n times.
C-u C-x (	universal-argument and start-kbd-macro	Execute last macro defined, then add keystrokes.
(none)	name-last-kbd-macro	Name last macro you created (before saving it).
(none)	insert-kbd-macro	Insert the macro you named into a file.
(none)	load-file	Load macro files you've saved and loaded.
(none)	*macroname*	Execute a keyboard macro you've saved.
C-x q	kbd-macro-query	Insert a query in a macro definition.
C-u C-x q	(none)	Insert a recursive edit in a macro definition.
C-M-c	exit-recursive-edit	Exit a recursive edit.

Detail Information Help Commands

Keystrokes	Command name	Description
C-h a	command-apropos	What commands involve this concept?
C-h d	apropos	What functions and variables involve this concept?
C-h c	describe-key-briefly	What command does this keystroke sequence run?
C-h b	describe-bindings	What are all the key bindings for this buffer?
C-h k	describe-key	What command does this keystroke sequence run, and what does it do?
C-h l	view-lossage	What are the last 100 characters I typed?
C-h e	view-echo-area-messages	Display the *Messages* buffer.
C-h w	where-is	What is the key binding for this command?
C-h f	describe-function	What does this function do?
C-h v	describe-variable	What does this variable mean, and what is its value?
C-h m	describe-mode	Tell me about the mode the current buffer is in.
C-h s	describe-syntax	What is the syntax table for this buffer?

Help Commands

Keystrokes	Command name	Description
C-h t	help-with-tutorial	Run the Emacs tutorial.
C-h i	info	Start the Info documentation reader.
C-h r	info-emacs-command	View the Emacs documentation in the Info reader.
C-h n	view-emacs-news	View news about updates to Emacs.
C-h C-c	describe-copying	View the Emacs General Public License.
C-h C-d	describe-distribution	View information on ordering Emacs from the FSF.
C-h C-w	describe-no-warranty	View the (non)warranty for Emacs.

Summary of Commands by Key

Emacs commands are presented below in two alphabetical lists. Reminder: C- indicates the Ctrl key; M- indicates the Meta key.

Control-Key Sequences

Keystrokes	Command name	Description
C-@	set-mark-command	Mark the beginning (or end) of a region.
C-Space	(same as previous)	
C-]	(none)	Exit recursive edit and exit query-replace.
C-a	beginning-of-line	Move to beginning of line.
C-b	backward-char	Move *backward* one character (left).
C-c C-c	comint-interrupt-subjob	Terminate the current job.
C-c C-d	comint-send-eof	End-of-file character.
C-c C-u	comint-kill-input	Erase current line.
C-c C-w	backward-kill-word	Erase the previous word.
C-c C-z	comint-stop-subjob	Suspend the current job.
C-d	delete-char	Delete character under cursor.
C-e	end-of-line	Move to *end* of line.
C-f	forward-char	Move *forward* one character (right).
C-g	keyboard-quit	Abort current command.
C-h	help-command	Enter the online help system.
C-h a	command-apropos	What commands involve this concept?
C-h b	describe-bindings	What are all the key bindings for this buffer?
C-h C-c	describe-copying	View the Emacs General Public License.
C-h C-d	describe-distribution	View information on ordering Emacs from FSF.
C-h C-w	describe-no-warranty	View the (non)warranty for Emacs.
C-h c	describe-key-briefly	What command does this keystroke sequence run?
C-h d	apropos	What functions and variables involve this concept?
C-h e	view-echo-area-messages	Display the *Messages* buffer.
C-h f	describe-function	What does this function do?

Keystrokes	Command name	Description
C-h i	info	Start the Info documentation reader.
C-h k	describe-key	What command does this keystroke sequence run, and what does it do?
C-h l	view-lossage	What are the last 100 characters I typed?
C-h m	describe-mode	Tell me about the mode the current buffer is in.
C-h n	view-emacs-news	View news about updates to Emacs.
C-h r	info-emacs-manual	View the Emacs documentation in the Info reader.
C-h s	describe-syntax	What is the syntax table for this buffer?
C-h t	help-with-tutorial	Run the Emacs tutorial.
C-h v	describe-variable	What does this variable mean, and what is its value?
C-h w	where-is	What is the key binding for this command?
C-k	kill-line	Delete from cursor to end of line.
C-l	recenter	Redraw screen with current line in the center.
C-M-\	indent-region	Indent a region to match first line in region.
C-M-c	exit-recursive-edit	Exit a recursive edit.
C-M-o	split-line	Split line at cursor; indent to column of cursor.
C-M-v	scroll-other-window	Scroll other window.
C-n	next-line	Move to *next* line (down).
C-p	previous-line	Move to *previous* line (up).
C-r	isearch-backward	Start incremental search backward.
C-s	isearch-forward	Start incremental search forward.
C-t	transpose-chars	Transpose two letters.
C-u *n*	universal-argument	Repeat the next command *n* times.
C-u C-x (	universal-argument and start-kbd-macro	Execute last macro defined, then add keystrokes.
C-u C-x q	(none)	Insert recursive edit in a macro definition.
C-v	scroll-up	Move forward one screen.
C-w	kill-region	Delete a marked region.
C-x (	start-kbd-macro	Start macro definition.
C-x)	end-kbd-macro	End macro definition.
C-x [	backward-page	Move backward one page.
C-x]	forward-page	Move forward one page.
C-x ^	enlarge-window	Make window taller.
C-x {	shrink-window-horizontally	Make window narrower.
C-x }	enlarge-window-horizontally	Make window wider.
C-x <	scroll-left	Scroll the window left.
C-x >	scroll-right	Scroll the window right.
C-x .	set-fill-prefix	Use characters from the beginning of the line up to the cursor column as the "fill prefix." This prefix is prepended to each line in the paragraph. Cancel the prefix by typing this command in column 1.
C-x 0	delete-window	Delete current window.
C-x 1	delete-other-windows	Delete all windows but this one.

Keystrokes	Command name	Description
C-x 2	split-window-vertically	Divide the current window into two, one on top of the other.
C-x 3	split-window-horizontally	Divide the current window into two, side by side.
C-x 4 b	switch-to-buffer-other-window	Select a buffer in the other window.
C-x 4 f	find-file-other-window	Find a file in the other window.
C-x 5 b	switch-to-buffer-other-frame	Select a buffer in another frame.
C-x 5 f	find-file-other-frame	Find a file in a new frame.
C-x C-b	list-buffers	Display the buffer list.
C-x C-c	save-buffers-kill-emacs	Exit Emacs.
C-x C-f	find-file	Find file and read it.
C-x C-l	downcase-region	Lowercase region.
C-x C-p	mark-page	Mark page.
C-x C-q	(none)	Toggle read-only status of buffer.
C-x C-s	save-buffer	Save file (may hang terminal; use C-q to restart).
C-x C-t	transpose-lines	Transpose two lines.
C-x C-u	upcase-region	Uppercase region
C-x C-v	find-alternate-file	Read an alternate file, replacing the one read with C-x C-f.
C-x C-w	write-file	Write buffer contents to file.
C-x C-x	exchange-point-and-mark	Exchange location of cursor and mark.
C-x DEL	backward-kill-sentence	Delete previous sentence.
C-x a i g	inverse-add-global-abbrev	Type global abbreviation, then definition.
C-x a i l	inverse-add-local-abbrev	Type local abbreviation, then definition.
C-x b	switch-to-buffer	Move to the buffer specified.
C-x e	call-last-kbd-macro	Execute last macro defined.
C-x h	mark-whole-buffer	Mark buffer.
C-x i	insert-file	Insert file at cursor position.
C-x k	kill-buffer	Delete the buffer specified.
C-x o	other-window	Move to the other window.
C-x q	kbd-macro-query	Insert a query in a macro definition.
C-x s	save-some-buffers	Ask whether to save each modified buffer.
C-x u	advertised-undo	Undo last edit (can be done repeatedly).
C-y	yank	Restore what you've deleted.
C-z	suspend-emacs	Suspend Emacs (use **exit** or **fg** to restart).

Meta-Key Sequences

Keystrokes	Command name	Description
Meta	(none)	Exit a query-replace or successful search.
M- - M-c	negative-argument; capitalize-word	Capitalize previous word.
M- - M-l	negative-argument; downcase-word	Lowercase previous word.
M- - M-u	negative-argument; upcase-word	Uppercase previous word.

Keystrokes	Command name	Description
M-$	spell-word	Check spelling of word after cursor.
M-<	beginning-of-buffer	Move to beginning of file.
M->	end-of-buffer	Move to end of file.
M-{	backward-paragraph	Move backward one paragraph.
M-}	forward-paragraph	Move forward one paragraph.
M-^	delete-indentation	Join this line to the previous one.
M-*n*	digit-argument	Repeat the next command *n* times.
M-*n* C-x e	digit-argument and call-last-kbd-macro	Execute the last defined macro *n* times.
M-a	backward-sentence	Move backward one sentence.
M-b	backward-word	Move one word *backward*.
M-c	capitalize-word	Capitalize first letter of word.
M-d	kill-word	Delete word that cursor is on.
M-DEL	backward-kill-word	Delete previous word.
M-e	forward-sentence	Move forward one sentence.
M-f	forward-word	Move one word *forward*.
M-g g or M-g M-g	goto-line	Go to line *n* of file.
M-h	mark-paragraph	Mark paragraph.
M-k	kill-sentence	Delete sentence the cursor is on.
M-l	downcase-word	Lowercase word.
M-m	back-to-indentation	Move cursor to first nonblank character on line.
M-q	fill-paragraph	Reformat paragraph.
M-s	center-line	Center line that cursor is on.
M-S	cemter-paragraph	Center paragraph that cursor is on.
M-t	transpose-words	Transpose two words.
M-u	upcase-word	Uppercase word.
M-v	scroll-down	Move backward one screen.
M-x	(none)	Access command by command name.

Summary of Commands by Name

The Emacs commands below are presented alphabetically by command name. Use **M-x** to access the command name. Reminder: C- indicates the Ctrl key; M-indicates the Meta key.

Command name	Keystrokes	Description
macroname	(none)	Execute a keyboard macro you've saved.
abbrev-mode	(none)	Enter (or exit) word abbreviation mode.
advertised-undo	C-x u	Undo last edit (can be done repeatedly).
apropos	(none)	What functions and variables involve this concept?
back-to-indentation	M-m	Move cursor to first nonblank character on line.
backward-char	C-b	Move *backward* one character (left).
backward-delete-char	Del	Delete previous character.

Command name	Keystrokes	Description
backward-kill-paragraph	(none)	Delete previous paragraph.
backward-kill-sentence	C-x Del	Delete previous sentence.
backward-kill-word	C-c C-w	Erase previous word.
backward-kill-word	M-Del	Delete previous word.
backward-page	C-x [	Move backward one page.
backward-paragraph	M-{	Move backward one paragraph.
backward-sentence	M-a	Move backward one sentence.
backward-word	M-b	Move backward one word.
beginning-of-buffer	M-<	Move to beginning of file.
beginning-of-line	C-a	Move to beginning of line.
call-last-kbd-macro	C-x e	Execute last macro defined.
capitalize-region	(none)	Capitalize region.
capitalize-word	M-c	Capitalize first letter of word.
center-line	M-s	Center line that cursor is on.
center-paragraph	M-S	Center paragraph that cursor is on.
center-region	(none)	Center currently defined region.
comint-interrupt-subjob	C-c C-c	Terminate the current job.
comint-kill-input	C-c C-u	Erase current line.
comint-send-eof	C-c C-d	End of file character.
comint-stop-subjob	C-c C-z	Suspend current job.
command-apropos	C-h a	What commands involve this concept?
compare-windows	(none)	Compare two buffers; show first difference.
delete-char	C-d	Delete character under cursor.
delete-indentation	M-^	Join this line to previous one.
delete-other-windows	C-x 1	Delete all windows but this one.
delete-window	C-x 0	Delete current window.
delete-windows-on	(none)	Delete all windows on a given buffer.
describe-bindings	C-h b	What are all the key bindings for in this buffer?
describe-copying	C-h C-c	View the Emacs General Public License.
describe-distribution	C-h C-d	View information on ordering Emacs from the FSF.
describe-function	C-h f	What does this function do?
describe-key	C-h k	What command does this keystroke sequence run, and what does it do?
describe-key-briefly	C-h c	What command does this keystroke sequence run?
describe-mode	C-h m	Tell me about the mode the current buffer is in.
describe-no-warranty	C-h C-w	View the (non)warranty for Emacs.
describe-syntax	C-h s	What is the syntax table for this buffer?
describe-variable	C-h v	What does this variable mean, and what is its value?
digit-argument and call-last-kbd-macro	M-n C-x e	Execute the last defined macro n times.
digit-argument	M-n	Repeat next command n times.
downcase-region	C-x C-l	Lowercase region.

Command name	Keystrokes	Description
downcase-word	M-l	Lowercase word.
edit-abbrevs	(none)	Edit word abbreviations.
end-kbd-macro	C-x) or F4 key	End macro definition.
end-of-buffer	M->	Move to end of file.
end-of-line	C-e	Move to end of line.
enlarge-window	C-x ^	Make window taller.
enlarge-window-horizontally	C-x }	Make window wider.
exchange-point-and-mark	C-x C-x	Exchange location of cursor and mark.
exit-recursive-edit	C-M-c	Exit a recursive edit.
fill-individual-paragraphs	(none)	Reformat indented paragraphs, keeping indentation.
fill-paragraph	M-q	Reformat paragraph.
fill-region	(none)	Reformat individual paragraphs within a region.
find-alternate-file	C-x C-v	Read an alternate file, replacing the one read with C-x C-f.
find-file	C-x C-f	Find file and read it.
find-file-other-frame	C-x 5 f	Find a file in a new frame.
find-file-other-window	C-x 4 f	Find a file in the other window.
forward-char	C-f	Move *forward* one character (right).
forward-page	C-x]	Move forward one page.
forward-paragraph	M-}	Move forward one paragraph.
forward-sentence	M-e	Move forward one sentence.
forward-word	M-f	Move forward one word.
goto-char	(none)	Go to character *n* of file.
goto-line	M-g g or M-g M-g	Go to line *n* of file.
help-command	C-h	Enter the online help system.
help-with-tutorial	C-h t	Run the Emacs tutorial.
indent-region	C-M-\	Indent a region to match first line in region.
indented-text-mode	(none)	Major mode: each tab defines a new indent for subsequent lines.
info	C-h i	Start the Info documentation reader.
info-emacs-manual	C-h r	View the Emacs documentation in the Info reader.
insert-file	C-x i	Insert file at cursor position.
insert-kbd-macro	(none)	Insert the macro you named into a file.
inverse-add-global-abbrev	C-x a i g	Type global abbreviation, then definition.
inverse-add-local-abbrev	C-x a i l	Type local abbreviation, then definition.
isearch-backward	C-r	Start incremental search backward.
isearch-backward-regexp	C-r	Same, but search for regular expression.
isearch-forward	C-s	Start incremental search forward.
isearch-forward-regexp	C-r	Same, but search for regular expression.
kbd-macro-query	C-x q	Insert a query in a macro definition.
keyboard-quit	C-g	Abort current command.
kill-all-abbrevs	(none)	Kill abbreviations for this session.
kill-buffer	C-x k	Delete the buffer specified.

Command name	Keystrokes	Description
kill-line	C-k	Delete from cursor to end of line.
kill-paragraph	(none)	Delete from cursor to end of paragraph.
kill-region	C-w	Delete a marked region.
kill-sentence	M-k	Delete sentence the cursor is on.
kill-some-buffers	(none)	Ask about deleting each buffer.
kill-word	M-d	Delete word the cursor is on.
list-abbrevs	(none)	View word abbreviations.
list-buffers	C-x C-b	Display buffer list.
load-file	(none)	Load macro files you've saved.
mark-page	C-x C-p	Mark page.
mark-paragraph	M-h	Mark paragraph.
mark-whole-buffer	C-x h	Mark buffer.
name-last-kbd-macro	(none)	Name last macro you created (before saving it).
negative-argument; capitalize-word	M- - M-c	Capitalize previous word.
negative-argument; downcase-word	M- - M-l	Lowercase previous word.
negative-argument; upcase-word	M- - M-u	Uppercase previous word.
next-line	C-n	Move to *next* line (down).
other-window	C-x o	Move to the other window.
previous-line	C-p	Move to *previous* line (up).
query-replace	M-%	Search and replace.
query-replace-regexp	C-% Meta	Query-replace a regular expression.
recenter	C-l	Redraw screen, with current line in center.
rename-buffer	(none)	Change buffer name to specified name.
replace-regexp	(none)	Replace a regular expression unconditionally.
re-search-backward	(none)	Simple regular expression search backward.
re-search-forward	(none)	Simple regular expression search forward.
revert-buffer	(none)	Restore buffer to the state it was in when the file was last saved (or auto-saved).
save-buffer	C-x C-s	Save file (may hang terminal; use C-q to restart).
save-buffers-kill-emacs	C-x C-c	Exit Emacs.
save-some-buffers	C-x s	Ask whether to save each modified buffer.
scroll-down	M-v	Move backward one screen.
scroll-left	C-x <	Scroll the window left.
scroll-other-window	C-M-v	Scroll other window.
scroll-right	C-x >	Scroll the window right.
scroll-up	C-v	Move forward one screen.
set-fill-prefix	C-x .	Use characters from the beginning of the line up to the cursor column as the "fill prefix." This prefix is prepended to each line in the paragraph. Cancel the prefix by typing this command in column 1.
set-mark-command	C-@ or C-Space	Mark the beginning (or end) of a region.

Command name	Keystrokes	Description
shell	(none)	Start a shell buffer.
shell-command	M-!	Run a shell command and display the results.
shrink-window	(none)	Make window shorter.
shrink-window-horizontally	C-x {	Make window narrower.
spell-buffer	(none)	Check spelling of current buffer.
spell-region	(none)	Check spelling of current region.
spell-string	(none)	Check spelling of string typed in minibuffer.
spell-word	M-$	Check spelling of word after cursor.
split-line	C-M-o	Split line at cursor; indent to column of cursor.
split-window-vertically	C-x 2	Divide the current window into two, one on top of the other.
split-window-horizontally	C-x 3	Divide the current window into two, side by side.
start-kbd-macro	C-x (or F3 key	Start macro definition.
suspend-emacs	C-z	Suspend Emacs (use **exit** or **fg** to restart).
switch-to-buffer	C-x b	Move to the buffer specified.
switch-to-buffer-other-frame	C-x 5 b	Select a buffer in another frame.
switch-to-buffer-other-window	C-x 4 b	Select a buffer in the other window.
text-mode	(none)	Exit indented text mode; return to text mode.
transpose-chars	C-t	Transpose two letters.
transpose-lines	C-x C-t	Transpose two lines.
transpose-paragraphs	(none)	Transpose two paragraphs.
transpose-sentences	(none)	Transpose two sentences.
transpose-words	M-t	Transpose two words.
unexpand-abbrev	(none)	Undo the last word abbreviation.
universal-argument	C-u *n*	Repeat the next command *n* times.
universal-argument and start-kbd-macro	C-u C-x (	Execute last macro defined, then add keystrokes to it.
upcase-region	C-x C-u	Uppercase region.
upcase-word	M-u	Uppercase word.
view-emacs-news	C-h n	View news about updates to Emacs.
view-lossage	C-h l	What are the last 100 characters I typed?
where-is	C-h w	What is the key binding for this command?
write-abbrev-file	(none)	Write the word abbreviation file.
write-file	C-x C-w	Write buffer contents to file.
yank	C-y	Restore what you've deleted.

9

The vi, ex, and vim Editors

The **vi** and **ex** editors are the "standard" editors on Unix systems. You can count on there being some version of them, no matter what Unix flavor you are using. The two editors are in fact the same program; based on how it was invoked, the editor enters full-screen mode or line mode.

vim is a popular extended version of **vi**. On some Linux distributions, the **vi** command invokes **vim** in a **vi**-compatible mode.

This chapter presents the following topics:

- Conceptual overview
- Command-line syntax
- Review of **vi** operations
- Alphabetical list of keys in command mode
- **vi** commands
- **vi** configuration
- **ex** basics
- Alphabetical summary of ex commands

vi is pronounced "vee eye."

Besides the original Unix **vi**, there are a number of freely available **vi** clones (including **vim**). Both the original **vi** and the clones are covered in *Learning the vi and Vim Editors* by Arnold Robbins et al. (O'Reilly).

Conceptual Overview

vi is the classic screen-editing program for Unix. A number of enhanced versions exist, including **nvi**, **vim**, **vile**, and **elvis**. On GNU/Linux systems, the **vi** command is usually one of these programs (either a copy or a link). The Emacs editor, covered in Chapter 8, has several **vi** modes that allow you to use many of the same commands covered in this chapter.

The **vi** editor operates in two modes: command mode and insert mode. The dual modes make **vi** an attractive editor for users who separate text entry from editing. For users who edit as they type, the modeless editing of Emacs can be more comfortable. However, **vim** supports both ways of editing, through the **insert-mode** option.

vi is based on an older line editor called **ex**. (**ex**, in turn, was developed by Bill Joy at the University of California, Berkeley, from the primordial Unix line editor, **ed**.) A user can invoke powerful editing capabilities within **vi** by typing a colon (:), entering an **ex** command, and pressing the Enter key. Furthermore, you can place **ex** commands in a startup file called *~/.exrc*, which **vi** reads at the beginning of your editing session. Because **ex** commands are such an important part of **vi**, they are also described in this chapter.

One of the most common versions of **vi** found on Linux systems is Bram Moolenaar's Vi IMproved, or **vim**. On some Linux distributions, **vim** is the default version of **vi** and runs when you invoke **vi**. **vim** offers many extra features, and optionally changes some of the basic features of **vi**, most notoriously changing the undo key to support multiple levels of undo.

Fully documenting **vim** is beyond the scope of this chapter, but we do cover some of its most commonly used options and features. Beyond what we cover here, **vim** offers enhanced support to programmers through an integrated build and debugging process, syntax highlighting, extended **ctags** support, and support for Perl and Python, as well as GUI fonts and menus, function-key mapping, independent mapping for each mode, and more. Fortunately, **vim** comes with a powerful internal help system that you can use to learn more about the things we just couldn't fit into this chapter. See *http://www.vim.org* for more information.

Command-Line Syntax

The three most common ways of starting a **vi** session are:

```
vi [options] file
vi [options] +num file
vi [options] +/pattern file
```

You can open *file* for editing, optionally at line *num* or at the first line matching *pattern*. If no *file* is specified, **vi** opens with an empty buffer.

Command-Line Options

Because **vi** and **ex** are the same program, they share the same options. However, some options only make sense for one version of the program. Options specific to **vim** are so marked.

+[*num*]

Start editing at line number *num*, or the last line of the file if *num* is omitted.

+/*pattern*

Start editing at the first line matching *pattern*. (For **ex**, fails if **nowrapscan** is set in your *.exrc* startup file, since **ex** starts editing at the last line of a file.)

-b Edit the file in binary mode. {vim}

-c *command*

Run the given **ex** command upon startup. Only one **-c** option is permitted for **vi**; **vim** accepts up to 10. An older form of this option, +*command*, is still supported.

--cmd *command*

Like **-c**, but execute the command before any resource files are read. {vim}

-C **vim**: Start the editor in **vi**-compatible mode.

-d Run in diff mode. Can also be invoked by running the command **vimdiff**. {vim}

-D Debugging mode for use with scripts. {vim}

-e Run as **ex** (line editing rather than full-screen mode).

-h Print help message, then exit. {vim}

-i *file*

Use the specified *file* instead of the default (~/.viminfo) to save or restore **vim**'s state. {vim}

-l Enter Lisp mode for running Lisp programs (not supported in all versions).

-L List files that were saved due to an aborted editor session or system crash (not supported in all versions). For **vim**, this option is the same as **-r**.

-m Start the editor with the **write** option turned off so the user cannot write to files. {vim}

-M Do not allow text in files to be modified. {vim}

-n Do not use a swapfile; record changes in memory only. {vim}

--noplugin

Do not load any plug-ins. {vim}

-N Run **vim** in a non-**vi**-compatible mode. {vim}

-o[*num*]

Start **vim** with *num* open windows. The default is to open one window for each file. {vim}

-O[*num*]

Start **vim** with *num* open windows arranged horizontally (split vertically) on the screen. {vim}

-r [*file*]

Recovery mode; recover and resume editing on *file* after an aborted editor session or system crash. Without *file*, list files available for recovery.

-R Edit files read-only.

-s Silent; do not display prompts. Useful when running a script. This behavior also can be set through the older - option. For **vim**, only applies when used together with **-e**.

-s *scriptfile*

Read and execute commands given in the specified *scriptfile* as if they were typed in from the keyboard. {vim}

-S *commandfile*

Read and execute commands given in *commandfile* after loading any files for editing specified on the command line. Shorthand for the option **vim -c** 'source *commandfile*'. {vim}

-t *tag*

Edit the file containing *tag* and position the cursor at its definition. (See **ctags** in Chapter 3 for more information.)

-T *type*

Set the terminal type. This value overrides the $TERM environment variable. {vim}

-u *file*

Read configuration information from the specified resource file instead of default *.vimrc* resource file. If the *file* argument is **NONE**, **vim** will read no resource files, load no plug-ins, and run in compatible mode. If the argument is **NORC**, it will read no resource files, but it will load plug-ins. {vim}

-v   Run in full-screen mode (default for **vi**).

--version

Print version information, then exit. {vim}

-V[*num*]

Verbose mode; print messages about what options are being set and what files are being read or written. You can set a level of verbosity to increase or decrease the number of messages received. The default value is 10 for high verbosity. {vim}

-w *rows*

Set the window size so *rows* lines at a time are displayed; useful when editing over a slow dial-up line (or long distance Internet connection). Older versions of **vi** do not permit a space between the option and its argument. **vim** does not support this option.

-W *scriptfile*

Write all typed commands from the current session to the specified *scriptfile*. The file created can be used with the **-s** command. {vim}

-x   Prompt for a key that will be used to try to encrypt or decrypt a file using **crypt** (not supported in all versions).*

-y   Modeless **vi**; run **vim** in insert mode only, without a command mode. {vim}

-Z   Start **vim** in restricted mode. Do not allow shell commands or suspension of the editor. {vim}

While most people know **ex** commands only by their use within **vi**, the editor also exists as a separate program and can be invoked from the shell (for instance, to edit files as part of a script). Within **ex**, you can enter the **vi** or **visual** command to start **vi**. Similarly, within **vi**, you can enter **Q** to quit the **vi** editor and enter **ex**.

---

* The **crypt** command's encryption is weak. Don't use it for serious secrets.

You can exit **ex** in several ways:

:x Exit (save changes and quit).

:q! Quit without saving changes.

:vi Enter the **vi** editor.

Review of vi Operations

This section provides a review of the following:

- **vi** modes
- Syntax of **vi** commands
- Status-line commands

Command Mode

Once the file is opened, you are in command mode. From command mode, you can:

- Invoke insert mode
- Issue editing commands
- Move the cursor to a different position in the file
- Invoke **ex** commands
- Invoke a Unix shell
- Save the current version of the file
- Exit **vi**

Insert Mode

In insert mode, you can enter new text in the file. You normally enter insert mode with the **i** command. Press the Escape key to exit insert mode and return to command mode. The full list of commands that enter insert mode is provided later, in the section "Insert Commands" on page 686.

Syntax of vi Commands

In **vi**, editing commands have the following general form:

> [*n*] *operator* [*m*] *motion*

The basic editing *operators* are:

c Begin a change.

d Begin a deletion.

y Begin a yank (or copy).

If the current line is the object of the operation, the *motion* is the same as the operator: **cc**, **dd**, **yy**. Otherwise, the editing operators act on objects specified by cursor-movement commands or pattern-matching commands. (For example, **cf**.

changes up to the next period.) *n* and *m* are the number of times the operation is performed, or the number of objects the operation is performed on. If both *n* and *m* are specified, the effect is *n* × *m*.

An object of operation can be any of the following text blocks:

word
> Includes characters up to a whitespace character (space or tab) or punctuation mark. A capitalized object is a variant form that recognizes only whitespace.

sentence
> Is up to ., !, or ?, followed by two spaces.

paragraph
> Is up to the next blank line or paragraph macro defined by the **para=** option.

section
> Is up to the next **nroff/troff** section heading defined by the **sect=** option.

motion
> Is up to the character or other text object as specified by a motion specifier, including pattern searches.

Examples

2cw
> Change the next two words.

d} Delete up to next paragraph.

d^ Delete back to beginning of line.

5yy
> Copy the next five lines.

y]]
> Copy up to the next section.

cG Change to the end of the edit buffer.

More commands and examples may be found in the section "Changing and deleting text" on page 687.

Visual mode (vim only)

vim provides an additional facility, "visual mode." This allows you to highlight blocks of text which then become the object of edit commands such as deletion or saving (yanking). Graphical versions of **vim** allow you to use the mouse to highlight text in a similar fashion. See the **vim** help file *visual.txt* for the full story.

v Select text in visual mode one character at a time.

V Select text in visual mode one line at a time.

Ctrl-V
> Select text in visual mode in blocks.

Status-Line Commands

Most commands are not echoed on the screen as you input them. However, the status line at the bottom of the screen is used to edit these commands:

/   Search forward for a pattern.

?   Search backward for a pattern.

:   Invoke an **ex** command.

!   Invoke a Unix command that takes as its input an object in the buffer and replaces it with output from the command. You type a motion command after the ! to describe what should be passed to the Unix command. The command itself is entered on the status line.

Commands that are entered on the status line must be entered by pressing the Enter key. In addition, error messages and output from the **Ctrl-G** command are displayed on the status line.

vi Commands

vi supplies a large set of single-key commands when in command mode. **vim** supplies additional multi-key commands.

Movement Commands

Some versions of **vi** do not recognize extended keyboard keys (e.g., arrow keys, Page Up, Page Down, Home, Insert, and Delete); some do. All, however, recognize the keys in this section. Many users of **vi** prefer to use these keys, as it helps them keep their fingers on the home row of the keyboard. A number preceding a command repeats the movement. Movement commands are also used after an operator. The operator works on the text that is moved.

Character

Command	Action
h, j, k, l	Left, down, up, right ($\leftarrow$, $\downarrow$, $\uparrow$, $\rightarrow$)
Space	Right
Backspace	Left
Ctrl-H	Left

Text

Command	Action
w, b	Forward, backward by "word" (letters, numbers, and underscore make up words).
W, B	Forward, backward by "WORD" (only whitespace separates items).
e	End of word.
E	End of WORD.
ge	End of previous word. {vim}

Command	Action
gE	End of previous WORD. {vim}
), (	Beginning of next, current sentence.
}, {	Beginning of next, current paragraph.
]], [[	Beginning of next, current section.
][, []	End of next, current section. {vim}

Lines

Long lines in a file may show up on the screen as multiple lines. (They *wrap* around from one screen line to the next.) While most commands work on the lines as defined in the file, a few commands work on lines as they appear on the screen. The **vim** option **wrap** allows you to control how long lines are displayed.

Command	Action
0, $	First, last position of current line.
^, _	First nonblank character of current line.
+, -	First nonblank character of next, previous line.
Enter	First nonblank character of next line.
num|	Column *num* of current line.
g0, g$	First, last position of screen line. {vim}
g^	First nonblank character of screen line. {vim}
gm	Middle of screen line. {vim}
gk, gj	Move up, down one screen line. {vim}
H	Top line of screen (Home position).
M	Middle line of screen.
L	Last line of screen.
*num*H	*num* lines after top line.
*num*L	*num* lines before last line.

Screens

Command	Action
Ctrl-F, Ctrl-B	Scroll forward, backward one screen.
Ctrl-D, Ctrl-U	Scroll down, up one-half screen.
Ctrl-E, Ctrl-Y	Show one more line at bottom, top of screen.
z Enter	Reposition line with cursor to top of screen.
z.	Reposition line with cursor to middle of screen.
z-	Reposition line with cursor to bottom of screen.
Ctrl-L	Redraw screen (without scrolling).
Ctrl-R	**vi:** Redraw screen (without scrolling).
	vim: Redo last undone change.

Searches

Command	Action
/pattern	Search forward for *pattern*. End with Enter.
/pattern/+num	Go to line *num* after *pattern*.
?pattern	Search backward for *pattern*. End with Enter.
?pattern?-num	Go to line *num* before *pattern*.
:noh	Suspend search highlighting until next search. {vim}.
n	Repeat previous search.
N	Repeat search in opposite direction.
/	Repeat previous search forward.
?	Repeat previous search backward.
*	Search forward for word under cursor. Matches only exact words. {vim}
#	Search backward for word under cursor. Matches only exact words. {vim}
g*	Search backward for word under cursor. Matches the characters of this word when embedded in a longer word. {vim}
g#	Search backward for word under cursor. Matches the characters of this word when embedded in a longer word. {vim}
%	Find match of current parenthesis, brace, or bracket.
f*x*	Move cursor forward to *x* on current line.
F*x*	Move cursor backward to *x* on current line.
t*x*	Move cursor forward to character before *x* in current line.
T*x*	Move cursor backward to character after *x* in current line.
,	Reverse search direction of last **f**, **F**, **t**, or **T**.
;	Repeat last **f**, **F**, **t**, or **T**.

Line numbering

Command	Action
Ctrl-G	Display current line number.
gg	Move to first line in file. {vim}
*num***G**	Move to line number *num*.
G	Move to last line in file.
:num	Move to line number *num*.

Marks

Command	Action
m*x*	Place mark *x* at current position.
`*x*	(backquote) Move cursor to mark *x*.
'*x*	(apostrophe) Move to start of line containing *x*.
``	(backquotes) Return to position before most recent jump.
''	(apostrophes) Like preceding, but return to start of line.
'"	(apostrophe quote) Move to position when last editing the file. {vim}

Command	Action
`` `[,`] ``	(backquote bracket) Move to beginning/end of previous text operation. {vim}
`` '[,'] ``	(apostrophe bracket) Like preceding, but return to start of line where operation occurred. {vim}
`` `. ``	(backquote period) Move to last change in file. {vim}
`` '. ``	(apostrophe period) Like preceding, but return to start of line. {vim}
`` `0 ``	Position where you last exited **vim**. {vim}
:marks	List active marks. {vim}

Insert Commands

Command	Action
a	Append after cursor.
A	Append to end of line.
c	Begin change operation.
C	Change to end of line.
gI	Insert at beginning of line. {vim}
i	Insert before cursor.
I	Insert at beginning of line.
o	Open a line below cursor.
O	Open a line above cursor.
R	Begin overwriting text.
s	Substitute a character.
S	Substitute entire line.
ESC	Terminate insert mode.

The following commands work in insert mode.

Command	Action
Backspace	Delete previous character.
Delete	Delete current character.
Tab	Insert a tab.
Ctrl-A	Repeat last insertion. {vim}
Ctrl-D	Shift line left to previous shift width. {vim}
Ctrl-E	Insert character found just below cursor. {vim}
Ctrl-H	Delete previous character (same as Backspace).
Ctrl-I	Insert a tab.
Ctrl-K	Begin insertion of multi-keystroke character.
Ctrl-N	Insert next completion of the pattern to the left of the cursor. {vim}
Ctrl-P	Insert previous completion of the pattern to the left of the cursor. {vim}
Ctrl-T	Shift line right to next shift width. {vim}
Ctrl-U	Delete current line.
Ctrl-V	Insert next character verbatim.

Command	Action
Ctrl-W	Delete previous word.
Ctrl-Y	Insert character found just above cursor. {vim}
Ctrl-[	(Escape) Terminate insert mode.

Some of the control characters listed in the previous table are set by **stty**. Your terminal settings may differ.

Edit Commands

Recall that **c**, **d**, and **y** are the basic editing operators.

Changing and deleting text

The following table is not exhaustive, but it illustrates the most common operations.

Command	Action
cw	Change word.
cc	Change line.
c$	Change text from current position to end of line.
C	Same as **c$**.
dd	Delete current line.
*num*dd	Delete *num* lines.
d$	Delete text from current position to end of line.
D	Same as **d$**.
dw	Delete a word.
d}	Delete up to next paragraph.
d^	Delete back to beginning of line.
d/*pat*	Delete up to first occurrence of pattern.
dn	Delete up to next occurrence of pattern.
df*a*	Delete up to and including *a* on current line.
dt*a*	Delete up to (but not including) *a* on current line.
dL	Delete up to last line on screen.
dG	Delete to end of file.
gqap	Reformat current paragraph to **textwidth**. {vim}
g~w	Switch case of word. {vim}
guw	Change word to lowercase. {vim}
gUw	Change word to uppercase. {vim}
p	Insert last deleted or yanked text after cursor.
gp	Same as **p**, but leave cursor at end of inserted text. {vim}
]p	Same as **p**, but match current indention. {vim}
[p	Same as **P**, but match current indention. {vim}
P	Insert last deleted or yanked text before cursor.
gP	Same as **P**, but leave cursor at end of inserted text. {vim}

Command	Action
r*x*	Replace character with *x*.
R*text*	Replace with new *text* (overwrite), beginning at cursor. Escape ends replace mode.
s	Substitute character.
4s	Substitute four characters.
S	Substitute entire line.
u	Undo last change.
Ctrl-R	Redo last change. {vim}
U	Restore current line.
x	Delete current cursor position.
X	Delete back one character.
5X	Delete previous five characters.
.	Repeat last change.
~	Reverse case and move cursor right.
Ctrl-A	Increment number under cursor. {vim}
Ctrl-X	Decrement number under cursor. {vim}

Copying and moving

Register names are the letters **a–z**. Uppercase names append text to the corresponding register.

Command	Action
Y	Copy current line.
yy	Copy current line.
"*x*yy	Copy current line to register *x*.
ye	Copy text to end of word.
yw	Like **ye**, but include the whitespace after the word.
y$	Copy rest of line.
"*x*dd	Delete current line into register *x*.
"*x*d	Delete into register *x*.
"*x*p	Put contents of register *x*.
y]]	Copy up to next section heading.
ye	Copy to end of word.
"*x*p	Put contents of register *x*.
J	Join current line to next line.
gJ	Same as **J**, but without inserting a space. {vim}
:j	Same as **J**.
:j!	Same as **gJ**.

Saving and Exiting

Writing a file means overwriting the file with the current text.

Command	Action
ZZ	Quit **vi**, writing the file only if changes were made.
:x	Same as **ZZ**.
:wq	Write file and quit.
:w	Write file.
:w *file*	Save copy to *file*.
:*n,m*w *file*	Write lines *n* to *m* to new *file*.
:*n,m*w >> *file*	Append lines *n* to *m* to existing *file*.
:w!	Write file (overriding protection).
:w! *file*	Overwrite *file* with current text.
:w %.*new*	Write current buffer named *file* as *file.new*.
:q	Quit **vi** (fails if changes were made).
:q!	Quit **vi** (discarding edits).
Q	Quit **vi** and invoke **ex**.
:vi	Return to **vi** after **Q** command.
%	Replaced with current filename in editing commands.
#	Replaced with alternate filename in editing commands.

Accessing Multiple Files

Command	Action
:e *file*	Edit another *file*; current file becomes alternate.
:e!	Return to version of current file at time of last write.
:e + *file*	Begin editing at end of *file*.
:e +*num file*	Open *file* at line *num*.
:e #	Open to previous position in alternate file.
:ta *tag*	Edit file at location *tag*.
:n	Edit next file in the list of files.
:n!	Force next file.
:n *files*	Specify new list of *files*.
:rewind	Edit first file in the list.
Ctrl-G	Show current file and line number.
:args	Display list of files to be edited.
:prev	Edit previous file in the list of files.

Window Commands

The following table lists common commands for controlling windows in **vim**. See also the **split**, **vsplit**, and **resize** commands in the "Alphabetical Summary of ex Commands" on page 697. For brevity, control characters are marked in the following list by ^.

Command	Action
:new	Open a new window.
:new *file*	Open *file* in a new window.
:sp [*file*]	Split the current window. With *file*, edit that file in the new window.
:sv [*file*]	Same as :sp, but make new window read-only.
:sn [*file*]	Edit next file in file list in new window.
:vsp [*file*]	Like :sp, but split vertically instead of horizontally.
:clo	Close current window.
:hid	Hide current window, unless it is the only visible window.
:on	Make current window the only visible one.
:res *num*	Resize window to *num* lines.
:wa	Write all changed buffers to file.
:qa	Close all buffers and exit.
^W s	Same as :sp.
^W n	Same as :new.
^W ^	Open new window with alternate (previously edited) file.
^W c	Same as :clo.
^W o	Same as :only.
^W j, ^W k	Move cursor to next/previous window.
^W p	Move cursor to previous window.
^W h, ^W l	Move cursor to window on left/right.
^W t, ^W b	Move cursor to window on top/bottom of screen.
^W K, ^W B	Move current window to top/bottom of screen.
^W H, ^W L	Move current window to far left/right of screen.
^W r, ^W R	Rotate windows down/up.
^W +, ^W -	Increase/decrease current window size.
^W =	Make all windows same height.

Interacting with the System

Command	Action
:r *file*	Read in contents of *file* after cursor.
:r !*command*	Read in output from *command* after current line.
:*num*r !*command*	Like above, but place after line *num* (0 for top of file).
:!*command*	Run *command*, then return.
!*motion command*	Send the text covered by *motion* to Unix *command*; replace with output.
:n,m! *command*	Send lines *n-m* to *command*; replace with output.
num!!*command*	Send *num* lines to Unix *command*; replace with output.
:!!	Repeat last system command.
:sh	Create subshell; return to file with *EOF*.
Ctrl-Z	Suspend editor, resume with **fg**.
:so *file*	Read and execute **ex** commands from *file*.

Macros

Command	Action
:ab *in out*	Use *in* as abbreviation for *out* in insert mode.
:unab *in*	Remove abbreviation for *in*.
:ab	List abbreviations.
:map *string sequence*	Map characters *string* as *sequence* of commands. Use #1, #2, etc., for the function keys.
:unmap *string*	Remove map for characters *string*.
:map	List character strings that are mapped.
:map! *string sequence*	Map characters *string* to input mode *sequence*.
:unmap! *string*	Remove input mode map (you may need to quote the character with **Ctrl-V**).
:map!	List character strings that are mapped for input mode.
q*x*	Record typed characters into register specified by letter *x*. If letter is uppercase, append to register. {vim}
q	Stop recording. {vim}
@*x*	Execute the register specified by letter *x*. Use @@ to repeat the last @ command.

In **vi**, the following characters are unused in command mode and can be mapped as user-defined commands:

Letters
   g K q V v

Control keys
   ^A ^K ^O ^W ^X ^_ ^\

Symbols
   _ * \ = #

> The = is used by **vi** if Lisp mode is set. Different versions of **vi** may use some of these characters, so test them before using.
>
> **vim** does not use ^K, ^_, _, or \.

Miscellaneous Commands

Command	Action
<	Shift text described by following motion command left by one shiftwidth. {vim}
>	Shift text described by following motion command right by one shiftwidth. {vim}
<<	Shift line left one shift width (default is eight spaces).
>>	Shift line right one shift width (default is eight spaces).
>}	Shift right to end of paragraph.
<%	Shift left until matching parenthesis, brace, or bracket. (Cursor must be on the matching symbol.)
==	Indent line in C-style, or using program specified in **equalprg** option. {vim}

Command	Action
g	Start many multiple character commands in **vim**.
K	Look up word under cursor in manpages (or program defined in **keywordprg**). {vim}
^O	Return to previous jump. {vim}
q	Record keystrokes. {vim}
^Q	Same as **^V**. {vim} (On some terminals, resume data flow.)
^T	Return to the previous location in the tag stack. (**vim**)
^]	Perform a tag lookup on the text under the cursor.
^\	Enter **ex** line-editing mode.
^^	(Caret key with Ctrl key pressed) Return to previously edited file.

vi Configuration

This section describes the following:

- The **:set** command
- Options available with **:set**
- Sample *.exrc* file

The :set Command

The **:set** command allows you to specify options that change characteristics of your editing environment. Options may be put in the *~/.exrc* file or set during a **vi** session.

The colon does not need to be typed if the command is put in *.exrc*:

Command	Action
:set *x*	Enable Boolean option *x*, show value of other options.
:set no*x*	Disable option *x*.
:set *x=value*	Give *value* to option *x*.
:set	Show changed options.
:set all	Show all options.
:set *x*?	Show value of option *x*.

Options Used by :set

Table 9-1 contains brief descriptions of the important **set** command options. In the first column, options are listed in alphabetical order; if the option can be abbreviated, that abbreviation is shown in parentheses. The second column shows the default setting. The last column describes what the option does, when enabled.

This table lists **set** options for **vi**, with the addition of important **vim** options. Other versions of **vi** may have more or fewer or different options. See your local documentation, or use **:set all** to see the full list. Options that receive a value are marked with an =.

Table 9-1. :set options

Option	Default	Description
autoindent (ai)	noai	In insert mode, indent each line to the same level as the line above or below. Use with the **shiftwidth** option.
autoprint (ap)	ap	Display changes after each editor command. (For global replacement, display last replacement.)
autowrite (aw)	noaw	Automatically write (save) the file if changed before opening another file with a command such as **:n**, or before giving Unix command with **:!**.
background (bg)		Describe the background so the editor can choose appropriate highlighting colors. Default value of **dark** or **light** depends on the environment in which the editor is invoked. {vim}
backup (bk)	nobackup	Create a backup file when overwriting an existing file. {vim}
backupdir= (bdir)	.,~/tmp/,~/	Name directories in which to store backup files if possible. The list of directories is comma-separated and in order of preference. {vim}
beautify (bf)	nobf	Ignore all control characters during input (except tab, newline, or formfeed).
backupext= (bex)	~	String to append to filenames for backup files. {vim}
cindent (cin)	nocindent	In insert mode, indent each line relative to the one above it, as is appropriate for C or C++ code. {vim}
compatible (cp)	cp	Make **vim** behave more like **vi**. Default is **nocp** when a ~/ *.vimrc* file is found. {vim}
directory (dir)	*/tmp*	Name of directory in which **ex/vi** stores buffer files. (Directory must be writable.) This can be a comma-separated list for **vim**.
edcompatible	noedcompatible	Remember the flags used with the most recent substitute command (global, confirming) and use them for the next substitute command. Despite the name, no version of **ed** actually does this.
equalprg= (ep)		Use the specified program for the = command. When the option is blank (the default), the key invokes the internal C indention function or the value of the **indentexpr** option. {vim}
errorbells (eb)	errorbells	Sound bell when an error occurs.
exrc (ex)	noexrc	Allow the execution of *.exrc* files that reside outside the user's home directory.
formatprg= (fp)		The **gq** command will invoke the named external program to format text. It will call internal formatting functions when this option is empty (the default). {vim}
gdefault (gd)	nogdefault	Set the **g** flag on for substitutions by default. {vim}
hardtabs= (ht)	8	Define boundaries for terminal hardware tabs.
hidden (hid)	nohidden	Hide buffers rather than unload them when they are abandoned. {vim}
hlsearch (hls)	hlsearch	Highlight all matches of most recent search pattern. Use **:nohlsearch** to remove highlighting. {vim}
history= (hi)	20	Number of **ex** commands to store in the history table. {vim}
ignorecase (ic)	noic	Disregard case during a search.

Table 9-1. :set options (continued)

Option	Default	Description
incsearch (is)	noincsearch	Highlight matches to a search pattern as it is typed. {vim}
lisp	nolisp	Insert indents in appropriate Lisp format. ( ), { }, [[, and]] are modified to have meaning for Lisp.
list	nolist	Print tabs as ^I; mark ends of lines with $. (Use **list** to tell if end character is a tab or a space.)
magic	magic	Wildcard characters; . (dot), * (asterisk), and [ ] (brackets) have special meaning in patterns.
mesg	mesg	Permit system messages to display on terminal while editing in **vi**.
mousehide (mh)	mousehide	When characters are typed, hide the mouse pointer. {vim}
novice	nonovice	Require the use of long **ex** command names, such as **copy** or **read**.
number (nu)	nonu	Display line numbers on left of screen during editing session.
open	open	Allow entry to *open* or *visual* mode from **ex**. Although not in **vim**, this option has traditionally been in **vi**, and may be in your version of **vi**.
optimize (opt)	noopt	Abolish carriage returns at the end of lines when printing multiple lines; speed output on dumb terminals when printing lines with leading whitespace (spaces or tabs).
paragraphs (para)	IPLPPPQPP LIpplpipnpbp	Define paragraph delimiters for movement by { or }. The pairs of characters in the value are the names of **troff** macros that begin paragraphs.
paste	nopaste	Change the defaults of various options to make pasting text into a terminal window work better. All options are returned to their original value when the **paste** option is reset. {vim}
prompt	prompt	Display the **ex** prompt (:) when **vi** 's **Q** command is given.
readonly (ro)	noro	Any writes (saves) of a file fail unless you use **!** after the write (works with **w**, **ZZ**, or **autowrite**).
redraw (re)		**vi** redraws the screen whenever edits are made. **nore-draw** is useful at slow speeds on a dumb terminal: the screen isn't fully updated until you press Escape. Default depends on line speed and terminal type.
remap	remap	Allow nested map sequences.
report=	5	Display a message on the status line whenever you make an edit that affects at least a certain number of lines. For example, **6dd** reports the message "6 lines deleted."
ruler (ru)	ruler	Show line and column numbers for the current cursor position. {vim}
scroll=	[1/2 *window*]	Number of lines to scroll with ^**D** and ^**U** commands.
sections= (sect)	SHNHH HUnhsh+c	Define section delimiters for [[and]] movement. The pairs of characters in the value are the names of **troff** macros that begin sections.
shell= (sh)	/bin/sh	Pathname of shell used for shell escape (**:!**) and shell command (**:sh**). Default value is derived from shell environment, which varies on different systems.
shiftwidth= (sw)	8	Define number of spaces used when the indent in increased or decreased.

Table 9-1. :set options (continued)

Option	Default	Description
showmatch (sm)	nosm	In **vi**, when) or } is entered, cursor moves briefly to matching (or {. (If no match, rings the error message bell.) Very useful for programming.
showmode	noshowmode	In insert mode, display a message on the prompt line indicating the type of insert you are making. For example, "OPEN MODE" or "APPEND MODE."
slowopen (slow)		Hold off display during insert. Default depends on line speed and terminal type.
smartcase (scs)	nosmartcase	Override the **ignorecase** option when a search pattern contains uppercase characters. {vim}
tabstop= (ts)	8	Define number of spaces a tab indents during editing session. (Printer still uses system tab of 8.)
taglength= (tl)	0	Define number of characters that are significant for tags. Default (zero) means that all characters are significant.
tags=	*tags /usr/lib/tags*	Define pathname of files containing tags. (See the Unix **ctags** command.) (By default, **vi** searches the file *tags* in the current directory and */usr/lib/tags*.)
tagstack	tagstack	Enable stacking of tag locations on a stack. (Solaris **vi** and **vim**.)
term=		Set terminal type.
terse	noterse	Display shorter error messages.
textwidth= (tw)	0	The maximum width of text to be inserted; longer lines are broken after whitespace. Default (zero) disables this feature, in which case **wrapmargin** is used. {vim}
timeout (to)	timeout	Keyboard maps timeout after 1 second.[a]
timeoutlen= (tm)	1000	Number of milliseconds after which keyboard maps timeout. Default value of 1000 provides traditional **vi** behavior. {vim}
ttytype=		Set terminal type. This is just another name for **term**.
undolevels= (ul)	1000	Number of changes that can be undone. {vim}
warn	warn	Display the warning message, "No write since last change."
window (w)		Show a certain number of lines of the file on the screen. Default depends on line speed and terminal type.
wrap		When on, long lines wrap on the screen. When off, only the first part of the line is displayed. {vim}
wrapmargin (wm)	0	Define right margin. If greater than zero, **vi** automatically inserts carriage returns to break lines.
wrapscan (ws)	ws	Searches wrap around either end of file.
writeany (wa)	nowa	Allow saving to any file.
writebackup (wb)	wb	Back up files before attempting to overwrite them. Remove the backup when the file has been successfully written, unless the **backup** option is set. {vim}

[a] When you have mappings of several keys (for example, **:map zzz 3dw**), you probably want to use **notimeout**. Otherwise, you need to type **zzz** within 1 second. When you have an insert mode mapping for a cursor key (for example, **:map! ^[OB ^[ja**), you should use **timeout**. Otherwise, **vi** won't react to Escape until you type another key.

Sample .exrc File

The following lines of code are an example of a customized *.exrc* file:

```
set nowrapscan              " Searches don't wrap at end of file
set wrapmargin=7            " Wrap text at 7 columns from right margin
set sections=SeAhBhChDh nomesg " Set troff macros, disallow message
map q :w^M:n^M              " Alias to move to next file
map v dwElp                 " Move a word
ab ORA O'Reilly Media, Inc. " Input shortcut
```

 The **q** alias isn't needed for **vim**, which has the **:wn** command. The **v** alias would hide the **vim** command **v**, which enters character-at-a-time visual-mode operation.

ex Basics

The **ex** line editor serves as the foundation for the screen editor **vi**. Commands in **ex** work on the current line or on a range of lines in a file. Most often, you use **ex** from within **vi**. In **vi**, **ex** commands are preceded by a colon and entered by pressing Enter.

You can also invoke **ex** on its own—from the command line—just as you would invoke **vi**. (You could execute an **ex** script this way.) You can also use the **vi** command **Q** to quit the **vi** editor and enter **ex**.

Syntax of ex Commands

To enter an **ex** command from **vi**, type:

```
:[address] command [options]
```

An initial : indicates an **ex** command. As you type the command, it is echoed on the status line. Execute the command by pressing the Enter key. *address* is the line number or range of lines that are the object of *command*. *options* and *addresses* are described below. **ex** commands are described in the next section "Alphabetical Summary of ex Commands" on page 697.

You can exit **ex** in several ways:

:x   Exit (save changes and quit).

:q!   Quit without saving changes.

:vi   Switch to the **vi** editor on the current file.

Addresses

If no address is given, the current line is the object of the command. If the address specifies a range of lines, the format is:

x,y

where *x* and *y* are the first and last addressed lines (*x* must precede *y* in the buffer). *x* and *y* may each be a line number or a symbol. Using ; instead of , sets the current line to *x* before interpreting *y*. The notation **1,$** addresses all lines in the file, as does **%**.

Address Symbols

Symbol	Meaning
1,$	All lines in the file.
x,y	Lines *x* through *y*.
x;y	Lines *x* through *y*, with current line reset to *x*.
0	Top of file.
.	Current line.
num	Absolute line number *num*.
$	Last line.
%	All lines; same as 1,$.
x-n	*n* lines before *x*.
x+n	*n* lines after *x*.
-[*num*]	One or *num* lines previous.
+[*num*]	One or *num* lines ahead.
'*x*	Line marked with *x*.
"	Previous mark.
/*pattern*/	Forward to line matching *pattern*.
?*pattern*?	Backward to line matching *pattern*.

See Chapter 7 for more information on using patterns.

Options

! Indicates a variant form of the command, overriding the normal behavior. The ! must come immediately after the command.

count
> The number of times the command is to be repeated. Unlike in **vi** commands, *count* cannot precede the command, because a number preceding an **ex** command is treated as a line address. For example, **d3** deletes three lines beginning with the current line; **3d** deletes line 3.

file
> The name of a file that is affected by the command. **%** stands for the current file; **#** stands for the previous file.

Alphabetical Summary of ex Commands

ex commands can be entered by specifying any unique abbreviation. In this listing, the full name appears in the margin, and the shortest possible abbreviation is used in the syntax line. Examples are assumed to be typed from **vi**, so they include the **:** prompt.

---

abbreviate   ab [*string text*]
> Define *string* when typed to be translated into *text*. If *string* and *text* are not specified, list all current abbreviations.

Examples

Note: **^M** appears when you type **^V** followed by Enter.

```
:ab ora O'Reilly Media, Inc.
:ab id Name:^MRank:^MPhone:
```

---

append

[address] a[!]
text
.

Append new *text* at specified *address*, or at present address if none is specified. Add a **!** to toggle the **autoindent** setting that is used during input. That is, if **autoindent** was enabled, **!** disables it. Enter new text after entering the command. Terminate input of new text by entering a line consisting of just a period.

Example

```
:a                        Begin appending to current line.
Append this line
and this line too.
.                         Terminate input of text to append.
```

---

args

ar
args *file* ...

Print the members of the argument list (files named on the command line), with the current argument printed in brackets ([ ]).

The second syntax is for **vim**, which allows you to reset the list of files to be edited.

---

bdelete

[num] bd[!] *[num]*

Unload buffer *num* and remove it from the buffer list. Add a **!** to force removal of an unsaved buffer. The buffer may also be specified by filename. If no buffer is specified, remove the current buffer. {vim}

---

buffer

[num] b[!] *[num]*

Begin editing buffer *num* in the buffer list. Add a **!** to force a switch from an unsaved buffer. The buffer may also be specified by filename. If no buffer is specified, continue editing the current buffer. {vim}

---

buffers

buffers[!]

Print the members of the buffer list. Some buffers (e.g., deleted buffers) will not be listed. Add **!** to show unlisted buffers. **ls** is another abbreviation for this command. {vim}

---

cd

cd *dir*
chdir *dir*

Change current directory within the editor to *dir*.

---

center

[*address*] ce [*width*]

Center line within the specified *width*. If *width* is not specified, use **textwidth**. {vim}

---

change

[*address*] c[!]
text
.

Replace the specified lines with *text*. Add a ! to switch the **autoindent** setting during input of *text*. Terminate input by entering a line consisting of just a period.

---

close

clo[!]

Close current window unless it is the last window. If buffer in window is not open in another window, unload it from memory. This command will not close a buffer with unsaved changes, but you may add ! to hide it instead. {vim}

---

copy

[*address*] co *destination*

Copy the lines included in *address* to the specified *destination* address. The command **t** (short for "to") is a synonym for **copy**.

Example

:1,10 co 50   *Copy first 10 lines to just after line 50*

---

delete

[*address*] d [*register*]

Delete the lines included in *address*. If *register* is specified, save or append the text to the named register. Register names are the lowercase letters **a–z**. Uppercase names append text to the corresponding register.

Examples

:/Part I/,/Part II/-1d   *Delete to line above "Part II"*
:/main/+d   *Delete line below "main"*
:.,$d x   *Delete from this line to last line into register x*

---

edit

e[!] [*+num*] [*filename*]

Begin editing on *filename*. If no *filename* is given, start over with a copy of the current file. Add a ! to edit the new file even if the current file has not been saved since the last change. With the *+num* argument, begin editing on line *num*. Or *num* may be a pattern, of the form */pattern*.

Examples

:e file   *Edit file in current editing buffer*
:e +/^Index #   *Edit alternate file at pattern match*
:e!   *Start over again on current file*

vi, ex, and vim

file

f [*filename*]

Change the filename for the current buffer to *filename*. The next time the buffer is written, it will be written to file *filename*. When the name is changed, the buffer's "not edited" flag is set, to indicate you are not editing an existing file. If the new filename is the same as a file that already exists on the disk, you will need to use **:w!** to overwrite the existing file. When specifying a filename, the **%** character can be used to indicate the current filename. A **#** can be used to indicate the alternate filename. If no *filename* is specified, print the current name and status of the buffer.

Example

```
:f%.new
```

fold

address fo

Fold the lines specified by *address*. A fold collapses several lines on the screen into one line, which later can be unfolded. It doesn't affect the text of the file. {vim}

foldclose

[*address*] foldc[!]

Close folds in specified *address*, or at present address if none is specified. Add a **!** to close more than one level of folds. {vim}

foldopen

[*address*] foldo[!]

Open folds in specified *address*, or at present address if none is specified. Add a **!** to open more than one level of folds. {vim}

global

[*address*] g[!]/*pattern*/[*commands*]

Execute *commands* on all lines which contain *pattern* or, if *address* is specified, on all lines within that range. If *commands* are not specified, print all such lines. Add a **!** to execute *commands* on all lines *not* containing *pattern*. See also **v**.

Examples

```
:g/Unix/p            Print all lines containing "Unix"
:g/Name:/s/tom/Tom/  Change "tom" to "Tom" on all lines
                     containing "Name:"
```

hide

hid

Close current window unless it is the last window, but do not remove the buffer from memory. This is a safe command to use on an unsaved buffer. {vim}

insert	[*address*] i[!] *text* .
	Insert *text* at line before the specified *address*, or at present address if none is specified. Add a ! to switch the **autoindent** setting during input of *text*. Terminate input of new text by entering a line consisting of just a period.
join	[*address*] j[!] [*count*]
	Place the text in the specified range on one line, with whitespace adjusted to provide two space characters after a period (.), no space characters before a), and one space character otherwise. Add a ! to prevent whitespace adjustment.

Example

:1,5j!   *Join first five lines, preserving whitespace*

jumps	ju
	Print jump list used with Ctrl-I and Ctrl-O commands. The jump list is a record of most movement commands that skip over multiple lines. It records the position of the cursor before each jump. {vim}
k	[*address*] k *char*
	Same as **mark**; see **mark**, later in this list.
left	[*address*] le [*count*]
	Left-align lines specified by *address*, or current line if no address is specified. Indent lines by *count* spaces. {vim}
list	[*address*] l [*count*]
	Print the specified lines so that tabs display as **^I**, and the ends of lines display as **$**. l is like a temporary version of **:set list**.
map	map[!] [*string commands*]
	Define a keyboard macro named *string* as the specified sequence of *commands*. *string* is usually a single character, or the sequence #*num*, representing a function key on the keyboard. Use a ! to create a macro for input mode. With no arguments, list the currently defined macros.

Examples

:map K dwwP	*Transpose two words*
:map q :w^M:n^M	*Write current file; go to next*
:map! + ^[bi(^[ea)	*Enclose previous word in parentheses*

map | 701

vim has **K** and **q** commands, which the above aliases would hide.

---

mark

[*address*] ma *char*

Mark the specified line with *char*, a single lowercase letter. Return later to the line with **'x** (where *x* is the same as *char*). **vim** also uses uppercase and numeric characters for marks. Lowercase letters work the same as in **vi**. Uppercase letters are associated with filenames and can be used between multiple files. Numbered marks, however, are maintained in a special *viminfo* file and cannot be set using this command. Same as **k**.

---

marks

marks [*chars*]

Print list of marks specified by *chars*, or all current marks if no chars specified. {vim}

Example

:marks abc   *Print marks a, b and c.*

---

mkexrc

mk[!] *file*

Create an *.exrc* file containing **set** commands for changed **ex** options and key mappings. This saves the current option settings, allowing you to restore them later.

---

move

[*address*] m *destination*

Move the lines specified by *address* to the *destination* address.

Example

:.,/Note/m /END/   *Move text block to after line containing "END"*

---

new

[*count*] new

Create a new window *count* lines high with an empty buffer. {vim}

---

next

num[!] [[+num] *filelist*]

Edit the next file from the command-line argument list. Use **args** to list these files. If *filelist* is provided, replace the current argument list with *filelist* and begin editing on the first file. With the *+num* argument, begin editing on line *num*. Or *num* may be a pattern, of the form */pattern*.

Example

:n chap*   *Start editing all "chapter" files*

---

nohlsearch	noh
	Temporarily stop highlighting all matches to a search when using the **hlsearch** option. Highlighting is resumed with the next search. {vim}
number	[*address*] nu [*count*]
	Print each line specified by *address*, preceded by its buffer line number. Use # as an alternate abbreviation for **number**. *count* specifies the number of lines to show, starting with *address*.
only	on [!]
	Make the current window be the only one on the screen. Windows open on modified buffers are not removed from the screen (hidden), unless you also use the ! character. {vim}
open	[*address*] o [/*pattern*/]
	Enter open mode (**vi**) at the lines specified by *address*, or at the lines matching *pattern*. Exit open mode with **Q**. Open mode lets you use the regular **vi** commands, but only one line at a time. It can be useful on slow dial-up lines (or on very distant Internet **ssh** connections).
preserve	pre
	Save the current editor buffer as though the system were about to crash.
previous	prev[!]
	Edit the previous file from the command-line argument list. {vim}
print	[*address*] p [*count*]
	Print the lines specified by *address*. *count* specifies the number of lines to print, starting with *address*. **P** is another abbreviation.

Example

    :100;+5p   *Show line 100 and the next five lines*

put	[*address*] pu [*char*]
	Restore previously deleted or yanked lines from named register specified by *char*, to the line specified by *address*. If *char* is not specified, the last deleted or yanked text is restored.
qall	qa[!]
	Close all windows and terminate current editing session. Use ! to discard changes made since the last save. {vim}

quit	q[!]
	Terminate current editing session. Use ! to discard changes made since the last save. If the editing session includes additional files in the argument list that were never accessed, quit by typing **q!** or by typing **q** twice. **vim** only closes the editing window if there are still other windows open on the screen.
read	[*address*] r *filename*
	Copy the text of *filename* after the line specified by *address*. If *filename* is not specified, the current filename is used.
	Example
	:0r $HOME/data *Read file in at top of current file*
read	[*address*] r !*command*
	Read the output of shell *command* into the text after the line specified by *address*.
	Example
	:$r !spell % *Place results of spell checking at end of file*
recover	rec [*file*]
	Recover *file* from the system save area.
redo	red
	Restore last undone change. Same as **Ctrl-R**. {vim}
resize	res [[±]*num*]
	Resize current window to be *num* lines high. If + or - is specified, increase or decrease the current window height by *num* lines. {vim}
rewind	rew[!]
	Rewind argument list and begin editing the first file in the list. Add a ! to rewind even if the current file has not been saved since the last change.
right	[*address*] ri [*width*]
	Right-align lines specified by *address*, or current line if no address is specified, to column *width*. Use **textwidth** option if no *width* is specified. {vim}

sbnext

[*count*] `sbn` [*count*]

Split the current window and begin editing the *count*'th next buffer from the buffer list. If no count is specified, edit the next buffer in the buffer list. {vim}

sbuffer

[*num*] `sb` [*num*]

Split the current window and begin editing buffer *num* from the buffer list in the new window. The buffer to be edited may also be specified by filename. If no buffer is specified, open the current buffer in the new window. {vim}

set

`se` *parameter1* *parameter2* ...

Set a value to an option with each *parameter*, or, if no *parameter* is supplied, print all options that have been changed from their defaults. For Boolean options, each *parameter* can be phrased as *option* or **no***option*; other options can be assigned with the syntax *option=value*. Specify **all** to list current settings. The form **set** *option*? displays the value of *option*. See the list of **set** options in the section "The :set Command" on page 692.

Examples

```
:set nows wm=10
:set all
```

shell

`sh`

Create a new shell. Resume editing when the shell terminates.

snext

[*count*] `sn` [[+*num*] *filelist*]

Split the current window and begin editing the next file from the command-line argument list. If *count* is provided, edit the *count*'th next file. If *filelist* is provided, replace the current argument list with *filelist* and begin editing the first file. With the +*n* argument, begin editing on line *num*. Alternately, *num* may be a pattern of the form */pattern*. {vim}

source

`so` *file*

Read (source) and execute **ex** commands from *file*.

Example

```
:so $HOME/.exrc
```

split

[*count*] `sp` [+*num*] [*filename*]

Split the current window and load *filename* in the new window, or the same buffer in both windows if no file is specified. Make the new window *count* lines high, or, if *count* is not specified, split the window into equal parts. With the +*n* argument, begin editing on line *num*. *num* may also be a pattern of the form */pattern*. {vim}

sprevious	`[count] spr [+num]`

Split the current window and begin editing the previous file from the command-line argument list in the new window. If *count* is specified, edit the *count*'th previous file. With the *+num* argument, begin editing on line *num*. *num* may also be a pattern of the form */pattern*. {vim}

stop	`st`

Suspend the editing session. Same as **Ctrl-Z**. Use the shell **fg** command to resume the session.

substitute	`[address] s [/pattern/replacement/] [options] [count]`

Replace the first instance of *pattern* on each of the specified lines with *replacement*. If *pattern* and *replacement* are omitted, repeat last substitution. *count* specifies the number of lines on which to substitute, starting with *address*. See additional examples in Chapter 7.

Options

c   Prompt for confirmation before each change.

g   Substitute all instances of *pattern* on each line (global).

p   Print the last line on which a substitution was made.

Examples

`:1,10s/yes/no/g`	*Substitute on first 10 lines*
`:%s/[Hh]ello/Hi/gc`	*Confirm global substitutions*
`:s/Fortran/\U&/ 3`	*Uppercase "Fortran" on next three lines*
`:g/^[0-9][0-9]*/s//Line &:/`	*For every line beginning with*
	one or more digits, add "Line" and a colon

suspend	`su`

Suspend the editing session. Same as **Ctrl-Z**. Use the shell **fg** command to resume the session.

sview	`[count] sv [+num] [filename]`

Same as the **split** command, but set the **readonly** option for the new buffer. {vim}

t	`[address] t destination`

Copy the lines included in *address* to the specified *destination* address. **t** is equivalent to **copy**.

Example

`:%t$`	*Copy the file and add it to the end*

tag	[*address*] ta *tag*
	In the *tags* file, locate the file and line matching *tag*, and start editing there.

Example

Run **ctags**, then switch to the file containing *myfunction*:

```
:!ctags *.c
:tag myfunction
```

tags	tags
	Print list of tags in the tag stack. {vim}

unabbreviate	una *word*
	Remove *word* from the list of abbreviations.

undo	u
	Reverse the changes made by the last editing command. In **vi**, the undo command will undo itself, redoing what you undid. **vim** supports multiple levels of undo. Use **redo** to redo an undone change in **vim**.

unhide	[*count*] unh
	Split screen to show one window for each active buffer in the buffer list. If specified, limit the number of windows to *count*. {vim}

unmap	unm[!] *string*
	Remove *string* from the list of keyboard macros. Use **!** to remove a macro for input mode.

v	[*address*] v/*pattern*/[*command*]
	Execute *command* on all lines *not* containing *pattern*. If *command* is not specified, print all such lines. **v** is equivalent to **g!**. See **global**.

Example

:v/#include/d	*Delete all lines except "#include" lines*

version	ve
	Print the editor's current version number and date of last change.

view	vie[[+*num*] *filename*]
	Same as **edit**, but set file to **readonly**. When executed in **ex** mode, return to normal or visual mode. {vim}

visual

[*address*] vi [*type*] [*count*]

Enter visual mode (**vi**) at the line specified by *address*. Return to **ex** mode with **Q**. *type* can be one of -, ^, or . (see the **z** command). *count* specifies an initial window size.

visual

vi [+*num*]*file*

Begin editing *file* in visual mode (**vi**), optionally at line *num*.

vsplit

[*count*] vs [+*num*] [*filename*]

Same as the **split** command, but split the screen vertically. The *count* argument can be used to specify a width for the new window. {vim}

wall

wa[!]

Write all changed buffers with filenames. Add **!** to force writing of any buffers marked **readonly**. {vim}

wnext

[*count*] wn[!] [[+*num*] *filename*]

Write current buffer and open next file in argument list, or the *count*'th next file if specified. If *filename* is specified, edit it next. With the +*num* argument, begin editing on line *num*. *num* may also be a pattern of the form */pattern*. {vim}

write

[*address*] w[!] [[>>] *file*]

Write lines specified by *address* to *file*, or write full contents of buffer if *address* is not specified. If *file* is also omitted, save the contents of the buffer to the current filename. If >> *file* is used, append lines to the end of the specified *file*. Add a **!** to force the editor to write over any current contents of *file*.

Examples

`:1,10w name_list`	*Copy first 10 lines to file name_list*
`:50w >> name_list`	*Now append line 50*

write

[*address*] w !*command*

Write lines specified by *address* to *command*.

Example

`:1,66w !pr -h myfile	lp`	*Print first page of file*

wq

wq[!]

Write and quit the file in one movement. The file is always written. The **!** flag forces the editor to write over any current contents of *file*.

wqall	wqa[!] Write all changed buffers and quit the editor. Add ! to force writing of any buffers marked **readonly**. **xall** is another alias for this command. {vim}
X	X Prompt for an encryption key. This command can be preferable to **:set key**, as typing the key is not echoed to the console. To remove an encryption key, just reset the **key** option to an empty value. {vim}
xit	x Write the file if it was changed since the last write, then quit.
yank	[*address*] y [*char*] [*count*] Place lines specified by *address* in named register *char*. Register names are the lowercase letters **a-z**. Uppercase names append text to the corresponding register. If no *char* is given, place lines in general register. *count* specifies the number of lines to yank, starting with *address*. **Example** **:101,200 ya a** *Copy lines 100–200 to register "a"*

z	[*address*] z [*type*] [*count*]
	
	Print a window of text with the line specified by *address* at the top. *count* specifies the number of lines to be displayed.
	
	Type
	
	  + Place specified line at the top of the window (default).
	  - Place specified line at the bottom of the window.
	  . Place specified line in the center of the window.
	  ^ Print the previous window.
	  = Place specified line in the center of the window and leave the current line at this line.

!	[*address*] !*command*
	
	Execute Unix *command* in a shell. If *address* is specified, use the lines contained in *address* as standard input to *command*, and replace the lines with the output and error output. (This is called *filtering* the text through the *command*.)
	
	Examples
	
	  :!ls *List files in the current directory*
	  :11,20!sort -f *Sort lines 11–20 of current file*

=	`[address] =` Print the line number of the line indicated by *address*. Default is line number of the last line.

< >	`[address] < [count]`
	`[address] > [count]`
	
	Shift lines specified by *address* either left (<) or right (>). Only leading spaces and tabs are added or removed when shifting lines. *count* specifies the number of lines to shift, starting with *address*. The **shiftwidth** option controls the number of columns that are shifted. Repeating the < or > increases the shift amount. For example, :>>> shifts three times as much as :>.

address	*address* Print the lines specified in *address*.
Enter	Print the next line in the file. (For **ex** only; not from the : prompt in **vi**.)
@	`[address] @ [char]` Execute contents of register specified by *char*. If *address* is given, move cursor to the specified address first. If *char* is @, repeat the last @ command.
&	`[address] & [options] [count]` Repeat the previous substitute (**s**) command. *count* specifies the number of lines on which to substitute, starting with *address*. *options* are the same as for the substitute command. **Examples** `:s/Overdue/Paid/` *Substitute once on current line* `:g/Status/&` *Redo substitution on all "Status" lines*
~	`[address] ~ [count]` Replace the last-used regular expression (even if from a search, and not from an **s** command) with the replacement pattern from the most recent **s** (substitute) command. This is rather obscure; see Chapter 6 of *Learning the vi and Vim Editors* by Arnold Robbins et al. (O'Reilly) for details.

10

The sed Editor

The **sed** "stream editor" is one of the most prominent text-processing tools on Unix and Linux. It is most often used for performing simple substitutions on data streams going through pipelines, but **sed** scripts can be written to do much more.

This chapter presents the following topics:

- Conceptual overview of **sed**
- Command-line syntax
- Syntax of **sed** commands
- Group summary of **sed** commands
- Alphabetical summary of **sed** commands

The version of **sed** provided with Linux systems is the GNU version written by the Free Software Foundation; its home page is *http://www.gnu.org/software/sed/sed. html.* For more information on **sed**, see Dale Dougherty and Arnold Robbins's *sed & awk* (O'Reilly).

Conceptual Overview

The stream editor, **sed**, is a noninteractive editor. It interprets a script and performs the actions in the script. **sed** is stream-oriented because, like many Unix programs, input flows through the program and is directed to standard output. For example, **sort** is stream-oriented; **vi** is not. **sed**'s input typically comes from a file or pipe, but it can also be taken from the keyboard. Output goes to the screen by default, but it can be captured in a file or sent through a pipe instead. GNU **sed** can edit files that use multibyte character sets.

Typical Uses of sed

- Editing one or more files automatically.
- Simplifying repetitive edits to multiple files.
- Writing conversion programs.

sed Operation

sed operates as follows:

- Each line of input is copied into a *pattern space*, an internal buffer where editing operations are performed.
- All editing commands in a **sed** script are applied, in order, to each line of input.
- Editing commands are applied to all lines (globally) unless line addressing restricts the lines affected.
- If a command changes the input, subsequent commands and address tests are applied to the current line in the pattern space, not the original input line.
- The original input file is unchanged because the editing commands modify an in-memory copy of each original input line. The copy is sent to standard output (but can be redirected to a file).
- **sed** also maintains the *hold space*, a separate buffer that can be used to save data for later retrieval.

Command-Line Syntax

The syntax for invoking **sed** has two forms:

```
sed [-n] [-e] 'command' file(s)
sed [-n]  -f  scriptfile file(s)
```

The first form allows you to specify an editing command on the command line, surrounded by single quotes. The second form allows you to specify a *scriptfile*, a file containing **sed** commands. Both forms may be used together, and they may be used multiple times. If no *file (s)* is specified, **sed** reads from standard input.

Standard Options

The following options are recognized:

-n   Suppress the default output; **sed** displays only those lines specified with the **p** command or with the **p** flag of the **s** command.

-e *cmd*

Next argument is an editing command. Necessary if multiple scripts or commands are specified.

-f *file*

Next argument is a file containing editing commands.

If the first line of the script is **#n**, **sed** behaves as if **-n** had been specified.

Multiple **-e** and **-f** options may be provided, and they may be mixed. The final script consists of the concatenation of all the *script* and *file* arguments.

GNU sed Options

GNU **sed** accepts a number of additional command-line options, as well as long-option equivalents for the standard options. The GNU **sed** options are:

-e *cmd*, **--expression** *cmd*
> Use *cmd* as editing commands.

-f *file*, **--file** *file*
> Obtain editing commands from *file*.

--help
> Print a usage message and exit.

-i[*suffix*], **--in-place**[*=suffix*]
> Edit files in place, overwriting the original file. If optional *suffix* is supplied, use it for renaming the original file as a backup file. See the GNU **sed** online Info documentation for the details.

-l *len*, **--line-length** *len*
> Set the line length for the **l** command to *len* characters.

-n, **--quiet**, **--silent**
> Suppress the default output; **sed** displays only those lines specified with the **p** command or with the **p** flag of the **s** command.

--posix
> Disable *all* GNU extensions. Setting POSIXLY_CORRECT in the environment merely disables those extensions that are incompatible with the POSIX standard.

-r, **--regexp-extended**
> Use Extended Regular Expressions instead of Basic Regular Expressions. See Chapter 7 for more information.

-s, **--separate**
> Instead of considering the input to be one long stream consisting of the concatenation of all the input files, treat each file separately. Line numbers start over with each file, the address **$** refers to the last line of each file, files read by the **R** command are rewound, and range addresses (/**x**/,/**y**/) may not cross file boundaries.

-u, **--unbuffered**
> Buffer input and output as little as possible. Useful for editing the output of **tail -f** when you don't want to wait for the output.

--version
> Print the version of GNU **sed** and a copyright notice, and then exit.

Syntax of sed Commands

sed commands have the general form:

> [*address*[*,address*]][!]*command* [*arguments*]

commands consist of a single letter or symbol; they are described later, by group and alphabetically. *arguments* include the label supplied to **b** or **t**, the filename supplied to **r** or **w**, and the substitution flags for **s**. *addresses* are described next.

Pattern Addressing

A **sed** command can specify zero, one, or two addresses. In POSIX **sed**, an address has one of the forms in the following table. Regular expressions are described in Chapter 7. Additionally, **\n** can be used to match any newline in the pattern space (resulting from the **N** command), but not the newline at the end of the pattern space.

Address	Meaning
/pattern/	Lines that match *pattern*.
\;pattern;	Like previous, but use semicolon as the delimiter instead of slash. Any character may be used. This is useful if *pattern* contains multiple slash characters.
n	Line number *n*.
$	The last input line.

If the command specifies:	Then the command is applied to:
No address	Each input line.
One address	Any line matching the address. Some commands accept only one address: **a**, **i**, **r**, **q**, and **=**.
Two comma-separated addresses	First matching line and all succeeding lines up to and including a line matching the second address.
An address followed by **!**	All lines that do *not* match the address.

GNU **sed** allows additional address forms:

Address	Meaning
/pattern/i	Match pattern, ignoring case. **I** may be used instead of **i**.
/pattern/m	Match pattern, allowing **^** and **$** to match around an embedded newline. **M** may be used instead of **m**.
0,/pattern/	Similar to **1**,/pattern/, but if line 1 matches *pattern*, it will end the range.
address,+n	Matches line matching *address*, and the *n* following lines.
address~incr	Matches line matching *address* and every *incr* lines after it. For example, **42~3** matches 42, 45, 48, and so on.

Pattern Addressing Examples

Command	Action performed
s/xx/yy/g	Substitute on all lines (all occurrences).
/BSD/d	Delete lines containing **BSD**.
/^BEGIN/,/^END/p	Print between **BEGIN** and **END**, inclusive.
/SAVE/!d	Delete any line that doesn't contain **SAVE**.
/BEGIN/,/END/!s/xx/yy/g	Substitute on all lines, except between **BEGIN** and **END**.

Braces ({ }) are used in **sed** to nest one address inside another or to apply multiple commands at a single matched address:

```
[/pattern/[,/pattern/]]{
command1
command2
}
```

The opening curly brace must end its line, and the closing curly brace must be on a line by itself. Be sure there are no spaces after the braces.

GNU sed Regular Expression Extensions

With the **-r** option, GNU **sed** uses Extended Regular Expressions instead of Basic Regular expressions. (See Chapter 7 for more information.) However, even without **-r**, you can use additional escape sequences for more powerful text matching. The following escape sequences are valid only in regular expressions:

\b   Matches on a word boundary, where of the two surrounding characters (*x*\b*y*), one is a word-constituent character and the other is not.

\B   Matches on a nonword boundary, where both of the two surrounding characters (*x*\b*y*) are either word-constituent or not word-constituent.

\w   Matches any word-constituent character (i.e., a letter, digit, or underscore).

\W   Matches any nonword-constituent character (i.e., anything that is *not* a letter, digit, or underscore).

\'   Matches the beginning of the pattern space. This is different from ^ when the **m** modifier is used for a pattern or the **s** command.

\'   Matches the end of the pattern space. This is different from $ when the **m** modifier is used for a pattern or the **s** command.

The following escape sequences may be used anywhere.

\a   The ASCII BEL character.

\f   The ASCII formfeed character.

\n   The ASCII newline character.

\r   The ASCII carriage-return character.

\v   The ASCII vertical tab character.

\d*nn*
    The character whose ASCII decimal value is *nn*.

\o*nn*
    The character whose ASCII octal value is *nn*.

\x*nn*
    The character whose ASCII hexadecimal value is *nn*.

Group Summary of sed Commands

In the lists that follow, the **sed** commands are grouped by function and are described tersely. Full descriptions, including syntax and examples, can be found afterward in the "Alphabetical Summary of sed Commands" on page 717. Commands marked with a † are specific to GNU **sed**.

Basic Editing

Command	Action
a\	Append text after a line.
c\	Replace text (usually a text block).
i\	Insert text before a line.
d	Delete lines.
s	Make substitutions.
y	Translate characters (like Unix **tr**).

Line Information

Command	Action
=	Display line number of a line.
l	Display control characters in ASCII.
p	Display the line.

Input/Output Processing

Command	Action
e†	Execute commands.
n	Skip current line and go to the next line.
r	Read another file's contents into the output stream.
R †	Read one line from a file into the output.
w	Write input lines to another file.
W †	Write first line in pattern space to another file.
q	Quit the **sed** script (no further output).
Q †	Quit without printing the pattern space.
v †	Require a specific version of GNU **sed** to run the script.

Yanking and Putting

Command	Action
h	Copy into hold space; wipe out what's there.
H	Copy into hold space; append to what's there.
g	Get the hold space back; wipe out the destination line.
G	Get the hold space back; append to the pattern space.
x	Exchange contents of the hold and pattern spaces.

Branching Commands

Command	Action
b	Branch to *label* or to end of script.
t	Same as **b**, but branch only after substitution.
T†	Same as **t**, but branch only if no successful substitutions.
:label	Label branched to by **t** or **b**.

Multiline Input Processing

Command	Action
N	Read another line of input (creates embedded newline).
D	Delete up to the embedded newline.
P	Print up to the embedded newline.

Alphabetical Summary of sed Commands

GNU **sed** lets you use the filenames */dev/stdin*, */dev/stdout* and */dev/stderr* to refer to standard input, output, and error, respectively, for the **r**, **R**, **w**, and **W** commands and the **w** flag to the **s** command.

GNU-specific commands or extensions are noted with {G} in the command synopsis. When the GNU version allows a command to have two addresses, the command is performed for each input line within the range.

#

> #
>
> Begin a comment in a **sed** script. Valid only as the first character of the first line. (Some versions, including GNU **sed**, allow comments anywhere, but it is better not to rely on this.) If the first line of the script is **#n**, **sed** behaves as if **-n** had been specified.

:

> :*label*
>
> Label a line in the script for the transfer of control by **b** or **t**. According to POSIX, **sed** must support labels that are unique in the first eight characters. GNU **sed** has no limit, but some older versions support up to only seven characters.

=

> [/*pattern*/]=
> [*address1*[,*address2*]]={G}
>
> Write to standard output the line number of each line addressed by *pattern*.

a

> [*address*]a\
> *text*
> [*address1*[,*address2*]]a \ {G}
> *text*

Append *text* following each line matched by *address*. If *text* goes over more than one line, newlines must be "hidden" by preceding them with a backslash. The *text* is terminated by the first newline that is not hidden in this way. The *text* is not available in the pattern space, and subsequent commands cannot be applied to it. The results of this command are sent to standard output when the list of editing commands is finished, regardless of what happens to the current line in the pattern space.

The GNU version accepts two addresses and allows you to put the first line of *text* on the same line as the **a** command.

Example

```
$ a\
This goes after the last line in the file\
(marked by $).  This text is escaped at the\
end of each line, except for the last one.
```

b

> [*address1*[,*address2*]]b[*label*]

Unconditionally transfer control to :*label* elsewhere in script. That is, the command following the *label* is the next command applied to the current line. If no *label* is specified, control falls through to the end of the script, so no more commands are applied to the current line.

Example

```
# Ignore HTML tables; resume script after </table>:
/<table/,/<\/table>/b
```

c

> [*address1*[,*address2*]]c\
> *text*

Replace (change) the lines selected by the address(es) with *text*. (See a for details on *text*.) When a range of lines is specified, all lines are replaced as a group by a single copy of *text*. The contents of the pattern space are, in effect, deleted, and no subsequent editing commands can be applied to the pattern space (or to *text*).

Example

```
# Replace first 100 lines in a file:
1,100c\
\
<First 100 names to be supplied>
```

d

[*address1*[,*address2*]]d

Delete the addressed line (or lines) from the pattern space. Thus, the line is not passed to standard output. A new line of input is read, and editing resumes with the first command in the script.

Example

```
# Delete all empty lines, including lines with just
whitespace:
/^[#tab]*$/d
```

D

[*address1*[,*address2*]]D

Delete the first part (up to embedded newline) of a multiline pattern space created by the **N** command, and resume editing with the first command in the script. If this command empties the pattern space, then a new line of input is read, as if the **d** command had been executed.

Example

```
# Strip multiple blank lines, leaving only one:
/^$/{
N
/^\n$/D
}
```

e

[*address1*[,*address2*]]e [*command*]{G}

With *command*, execute the command and send the result to standard output. Without *command*, execute the contents of the pattern space as a command, and replace the pattern space with the results.

g

[*address1*[,*address2*]]g

Paste the contents of the hold space (see **h** and **H**) back into the pattern space, wiping out the previous contents of the pattern space. The Example shows a simple way to copy lines.

Example

This script collects all lines containing the word Item: and copies them to a place marker later in the file. The place marker is overwritten:

```
/Item:/H
/<Replace this line with the item list>/g
```

G

[*address1*[,*address2*]]G

Same as **g**, except that a newline and the hold space are pasted to the end of the pattern space instead of overwriting it. The Example shows a simple way to "cut and paste" lines.

Example

This script collects all lines containing the word Item: and moves them after a place marker later in the file. The original Item: lines are deleted.

```
/Item:/{
H
d
}
/Summary of items:/G
```

h

[*address1*[,*address2*]]h

Copy the pattern space into the hold space, a special temporary buffer. The previous contents of the hold space are obliterated. You can use **h** to save a line before editing it.

Example

```
# Edit a line; print the change; replay the original
/Linux/{
h
s/.* Linux \(.*\) .*/\1:/
p
x
}
```

Sample input:

```
This describes the Linux ls command.
This describes the Linux cp command.
```

Sample output:

```
ls:
This describes the Linux ls command.
cp:
This describes the Linux cp command.
```

H

[*address1*[,*address2*]]H

Append a newline and then the contents of the pattern space to the contents of the hold space. Even if the hold space is empty, **H** still appends a newline. **H** is like an incremental copy. See Examples under **g** and **G**.

i

[*address*]i\
text
[*address1*[,*address2*]]i \ {G}
text

Insert *text* before each line matched by *address*. (See **a** for details on *text*.)

The GNU version accepts two addresses and allows you to put the first line of *text* on the same line as the **i** command.

Example

```
/Item 1/i\
The five items are listed below:
```

l

```
[address1[,address2]]l
[address1[,address2]]l [len]{G}
```

List the contents of the pattern space, showing nonprinting characters as ASCII codes. Long lines are wrapped. With GNU **sed**, *len* is
the character position at which to wrap long lines. A value of **0**
means to never break lines.

n

```
[address1[,address2]]n
```

Read the next line of input into pattern space. The current line is
sent to standard output, and the next line becomes the current line.
Control passes to the command following **n** instead of resuming at
the top of the script.

Example

In DocBook/XML, titles follow section tags. Suppose you are using
a convention where each opening section tag is on a line by itself,
with the title on the following line. To print all the section titles,
invoke this script with **sed -n**:

```
/<sect[1-4]/{
n
p
}
```

N

```
[address1[,address2]]N
```

Append the next input line to contents of pattern space; the new
line is separated from the previous contents of the pattern space by
a newline. (This command is designed to allow pattern matches
across two lines.) By using **\n** to match the embedded newline, you
can match patterns across multiple lines. See the Example under **D**.

Examples

Like the Example in **n**, but print the section tag line as well as
header title:

```
/<sect[1-4]/{
N
p
}
```

Join two lines (replace newline with space):

```
/<sect[1-4]/{
N
s/\n/ /
p
}
```

p

[*address1*[,*address2*]]p

Print the addressed line(s). Note that this can result in duplicate output unless default output is suppressed by using **#n** or the **-n** command-line option. Typically used before commands that change control flow (**d**, **n**, **b**), which might prevent the current line from being output. See the Examples under **h**, **n**, and **N**.

P

[*address1*[,*address2*]]P

Print first part (up to embedded newline) of multiline pattern space created by **N** command. Same as **p** if **N** has not been applied to a line.

Example

Suppose you have function references in two formats:

```
function(arg1, arg2)
function(arg1,
        arg2)
```

The following script changes argument **arg2**, regardless of whether it appears on the same line as the function name:

```
s/function(arg1, arg2)/function(arg1, XX)/
/function(/{
N
s/arg2/XX/
P
D
}
```

q

[*address*]q
[*address*]q [*value*]**{G}**

Quit when *address* is encountered. The addressed line is first written to the output (if default output is not suppressed), along with any text appended to it by previous **a** or **r** commands. GNU **sed** allows you to provide *value*, which is used as the exit status.

Examples

Delete everything after the addressed line:

```
/Garbled text follows:/q
```

Print only the first 50 lines of a file:

```
50q
```

Q

[*address*]Q [*value*]**{G}**

Quits processing, but without printing the pattern space. If *value* is provided, it is used as **sed**'s exit status.

r

[*address*]r *file*
[*address1*[,*address2*]]r *file*{**G**}

Read contents of *file* and append to the output after the contents of the pattern space. There must be exactly one space between the **r** and the filename. The GNU version accepts two addresses.

Example

```
/The list of items follows:/r item_file
```

R

[*address1*[,*address2*]]R *file*{**G**}

Read one line of *file* and append to the output after the contents of the pattern space. Successive **R** commands read successive lines from *file*.

s

[*address1*[,*address2*]]s/*pattern*/*replacement*/[*flags*]

Substitute *replacement* for *pattern* on each addressed line. If pattern addresses are used, the pattern // represents the last pattern address specified. Any delimiter may be used. Use \ within *pattern* or *replacement* to escape the delimiter. The following flags can be specified (those marked with a † are specific to GNU **sed**):

n   Replace *n*th instance of *pattern* on each addressed line. *n* is any number in the range 1 to 512, and the default is 1.

e†   If the substitution was made, execute the contents of the pattern space as a shell command and replaces the pattern space with the results.

g   Replace all instances of *pattern* on each addressed line, not just the first instance.

i *or* **I**†
Do a case-insensitive regular expression match.

m *or* **M**†
Allow ^ and $ to match around a newline embedded in the pattern space.

p   Print the line if the substitution is successful. If several successful substitutions are successful, **sed** prints multiple copies of the line.

w *file*
Write the line to *file* if a replacement was done. In the traditional Unix **sed**, a maximum of 10 different *files* can be opened.

GNU **sed** allows you to use the special filenames **/dev/stdout** and **/dev/stderr** to write to standard output or standard error, respectively.

Within the *replacement*, GNU **sed** accepts special escape sequences, with the following meanings:

\L   Lowercase the replacement text until a terminating \E or \U.

\l   Lowercase the following character only.

\U   Uppercase the replacement text until a terminating \E or \L.

\u   Uppercase the following character only.

\E   Terminate case conversion from \L or \U.

Examples

Here are some short, commented scripts:

```
# Change third and fourth quote to ( and ):
/function/{
s/"/)/4
s/"/(/3
}


# Remove all quotes on a given line:
/Title/s/"//g


# Remove first colon and all quotes; print resulting lines:
s/://p
s/"//gp


# Change first "if" but leave "ifdef" alone:
/ifdef/!s/if/    if/
```

---

t   [*address1*[,*address2*]]t [*label*]

Test if successful substitutions have been made on addressed lines, and if so, branch to the line marked by :*label*. (See **b** and **:**.) If *label* is not specified, control branches to the bottom of the script. The **t** command is like a case statement in the C programming language or the various shell programming languages. You test each case; when it's true, you exit the construct.

Example

Suppose you want to fill empty fields of a database. You have this:

```
ID: 1    Name: greg    Rate: 45
ID: 2    Name: dale
ID: 3
```

You want this:

```
ID: 1    Name: greg    Rate: 45    Phone: ??
ID: 2    Name: dale    Rate: ??    Phone: ??
ID: 3    Name: ????    Rate: ??    Phone: ??
```

You need to test the number of fields already there. Here's the script (fields are tab-separated):

```
#n
/ID/{
s/ID: .* Name: .* Rate: .*/&    Phone: ??/p
t
s/ID: .* Name: .*/&    Rate: ??    Phone: ??/p
t
s/ID: .*/&    Name: ????    Rate: ??    Phone: ??/p
}
```

T

[*address1*[,*address2*]]T [*label*]**{G}**

Like **t**, but only branches to *label* if there *not* any successful substitutions. (see **b**, **t**, and **:**). If *label* is not specified, control branches to the bottom of the script.

v

[*address1*[,*address2*]]v [*version*]**{G}**

This command doesn't do anything. You use it to require GNU **sed** for your script. This works, because non-GNU versions of **sed** don't implement the command at all, and will therefore fail. If you supply a specific *version*, GNU **sed** fails if the required version is newer than the one executing the script.

w

[*address1*[,*address2*]]w *file*

Append contents of pattern space to *file*. This action occurs when the command is encountered rather than when the pattern space is output. Exactly one space must separate the **w** and the filename. This command will create the file if it does not exist; if the file exists, its contents will be overwritten each time the script is executed. Multiple write commands that direct output to the same file append to the end of the file.

GNU **sed** allows you to use the special filenames **/dev/stdout** and **/dev/stderr** to write to standard output or standard error, respectively.

Example

```
# Store HTML tables in  a file
/<table/,/<\/table>/w tables.html
```

W

[*address1*[,*address2*]]W *file*

Like **w**, but only writes the contents of the first line in the pattern space to the file.

x

[*address1*[,*address2*]]x

Exchange the contents of the pattern space with the contents of the hold space. See **h** for an example.

y

[*address1*[,*address2*]]y/*abc*/*xyz*/

Translate characters. Change every instance of *a* to *x*, *b* to *y*, *c* to *z*, etc.

Example

```
# Change item 1, 2, 3 to Item A, B, C ...
/^item [1-9]/y/i123456789/IABCDEFGHI/
```

11

The gawk Programming Language

gawk is the GNU version of **awk**, a powerful utility often used for text and string manipulation within shell scripts, particularly when input data may be viewed as records and fields. **awk** is also an elegant and capable programming language that allows you to accomplish a lot with very little work.

This chapter presents the following topics:

- Conceptual overview
- Command-line syntax
- Patterns and procedures
- Built-in variables
- Operators
- Variables and array assignment
- User-defined functions
- **gawk**-specific facilities
- Implementation limits
- Group listing of **awk** functions and commands
- Alphabetical summary of **awk** functions and commands
- Source code

Conceptual Overview

awk is a pattern-matching program for processing files, especially when each line has a simple field-oriented layout. Linux provides the GNU version of **awk**, called **gawk**, which provides a number of additional features. This utility can be invoked either through the standard name **awk** or through **gawk**.

This chapter describes functionality that is found in **gawk**. Most of this discussion applies to all versions of **awk**, but items marked "gawk-specific" or as an "extension" may not apply to versions of **awk** other than GNU's. If portability to older, non-Linux systems is important, do not use gawk-specific features.

With **gawk**, you can:

- Think of a text file as made up of records and fields in a textual database.
- Perform arithmetic and string operations.
- Use programming constructs, such as loops and conditionals.
- Produce formatted reports.
- Define your own functions.
- Execute Unix commands from a script.
- Process the results of Unix commands.
- Process command-line arguments gracefully.
- Work easily with multiple input streams.
- Flush open output files and pipes.
- Sort arrays.
- Retrieve and format system time values.
- Do bit manipulation.
- Internationalize your **gawk** programs, allowing strings to be translated into a local language at runtime.
- Perform two-way I/O to a coprocess.
- Open a two-way TCP/IP connection to a socket.
- Dynamically add built-in functions.
- Profile your **gawk** programs.

Command-Line Syntax

The syntax for invoking **awk** has two forms:

```
awk  [options]  'script'  var=value  file(s)
awk  [options]  -f scriptfile  var=value  file(s)
```

You can specify a *script* directly on the command line, or you can store a script in a *scriptfile* and specify it with **-f**. **gawk** allows multiple **-f** scripts. Variables can be assigned a value on the command line. The value can be a string or numeric constant, a shell variable (**$name**), or a command substitution (`` `cmd` ``), but the value is available only after the **BEGIN** statement is executed.

awk operates on one or more *files*. If none are specified (or if - is specified), **awk** reads from standard input.

Standard Options

The standard options are:

-F*fs*

> Set the field separator to *fs*. This is the same as setting the built-in variable **FS**. **gawk** allows *fs* to be a regular expression. Each input line, or *record*, is divided into fields by whitespace (spaces or tabs) or by some other user-definable field separator. Fields are referred to by the variables **$1**, **$2**,..., **$n**. **$0** refers to the entire record.

-v *var=value*

> Assign a *value* to variable *var*. This allows assignment before the script begins execution.

For example, to print the first three (colon-separated) fields of each record on separate lines:

```
awk -F: '{ print $1; print $2; print $3 }' /etc/passwd
```

Numerous examples are shown in "Simple Pattern-Procedure Examples" on page 730.

Important gawk Options

Besides the standard command line options, **gawk** has a large number of additional options. This section lists those of most value in day-to-day use. Any unique abbreviation of these options is acceptable.

--dump-variables[=*file*]

> When the program has finished running, print a sorted list of global variables, their types, and their final values to *file*. The default file is *awkvars.out*.

--gen-po

> Read the **awk** program and print all strings marked as translatable to standard output in the form of a GNU **gettext** Portable Object file. See the section "Internationalization" on page 736 for more information.

--help

> Print a usage message to standard error and exit.

--lint[=**fatal**]

> Enable checking of nonportable or dubious constructs, both when the program is read and as it runs. With an argument of **fatal**, lint warnings become fatal errors.

--non-decimal-data

> Allow octal and hexadecimal data in the input to be recognized as such. This option is not recommended; use **strtonum**( ) in your program, instead.

--profile[=*file*]

> With **gawk**, put a "prettyprinted" version of the program in *file*. Default is *awkprof.out*. With **pgawk** (see "Profiling" on page 735), put the profiled listing of the program in *file*.

--posix
> Turn on strict POSIX compatibility, in which all common and **gawk**-specific extensions are disabled.

--source='*program text***'**
> Use *program text* as the **awk** source code. Use this option with **-f** to mix command-line programs with **awk** library files.

--traditional
> Disable all **gawk**-specific extensions, but allow common extensions (e.g., the ** operator for exponentiation).

--version
> Print the version of **gawk** on standard error and exit.

Patterns and Procedures

awk scripts consist of patterns and procedures:

```
pattern  {procedure }
```

Both *pattern* and { *procedure* } are optional. If *pattern* is missing, { *procedure* } is applied to all lines. If { *procedure* } is missing, the matched line is printed.

Patterns

A pattern can be any of the following:

```
general expression
/regular expression/
relational expression
pattern-matching expression
BEGIN
END
```

- General expressions can be composed of quoted strings, numbers, operators, function calls, user-defined variables, or any of the predefined variables described in "Built-in Variables" on page 731.

- Regular expressions use the extended set of metacharacters, as described in Chapter 7.

- The **^** and **$** metacharacters refer to the beginning and end of a string (such as the fields), respectively, rather than the beginning and end of a line. In particular, these metacharacters will *not* match at a newline embedded in the middle of a string.

- Relational expressions use the relational operators listed in "Operators" on page 732. For example, **$2 > $1** selects lines for which the second field is greater than the first. Comparisons can be either string or numeric. Thus, depending upon the types of data in **$1** and **$2**, **awk** will do either a numeric or a string comparison. This can change from one record to the next.

- Pattern-matching expressions use the operators **~** (match) and **!~** (don't match). See "Operators" on page 732.

- The **BEGIN** pattern lets you specify procedures that will take place *before* the first input line is processed. (Generally, you process the command line and set global variables here.)
- The **END** pattern lets you specify procedures that will take place *after* the last input record is read.
- **BEGIN** and **END** patterns may appear multiple times. The procedures are merged as if there had been one large procedure.

Except for **BEGIN** and **END**, patterns can be combined with the Boolean operators || (or), && (and), and ! (not). A range of lines can also be specified using comma-separated patterns:

```
pattern,pattern
```

Procedures

Procedures consist of one or more commands, function calls, or variable assignments, separated by newlines or semicolons, and are contained within curly braces. Commands fall into five groups:

- Variable or array assignments
- Input/Output commands
- Built-in functions
- Control-flow commands
- User-defined functions

Simple Pattern-Procedure Examples

Print first field of each line:

```
{ print $1 }
```

Print all lines that contain *pattern*:

```
/pattern/
```

Print first field of lines that contain *pattern*:

```
/pattern/ { print $1 }
```

Select records containing more than two fields:

```
NF > 2
```

Interpret input records as a group of lines up to a blank line. Each line is a single field:

```
BEGIN { FS = "\n"; RS = "" }
```

Print fields 2 and 3 in switched order, but only on lines whose first field matches the string **URGENT**:

```
$1 ~ /URGENT/ { print $3, $2 }
```

Count and print the number of *pattern* found:

```
/pattern/ { ++x }
END { print x }
```

Add numbers in second column and print the total:

```
{ total += $2 }
END { print "column total is", total}
```

Print lines that contain less than 20 characters:

```
length($0) < 20
```

Print each line that begins with **Name:** and that contains exactly seven fields:

```
NF =  = 7 && /^Name:/
```

Print the fields of each record in reverse order, one per line:

```
{
        for (i = NF; i >= 1; i--)
              print $i
}
```

Built-in Variables

All **awk** variables are included in **gawk**.

Version	Variable	Description
awk	ARGC	Number of arguments on the command line.
	ARGV	An array containing the command-line arguments, indexed from 0 to **ARGC - 1**.
	ENVIRON	An associative array of environment variables.
	FILENAME	Current filename.
	FNR	Like **NR**, but relative to the current file.
	FS	Field separator (a space).
	NF	Number of fields in current record.
	NR	Number of the current record.
	OFMT	Output format for numbers ("**%.6g**").
	OFS	Output field separator (a space).
	ORS	Output record separator (a newline).
	RLENGTH	Length of the string matched by **match( )** function.
	RS	Record separator (a newline).
	RSTART	First position in the string matched by **match( )** function.
	SUBSEP	Separator character for array subscripts ("**\034**").
	$0	Entire input record.
	$n	nth field in current record; fields are separated by **FS**.
gawk	ARGIND	Index in **ARGV** of current input file.
	BINMODE	Controls binary I/O for input and output files. Use values of **1**, **2**, or **3** for input, output, or both kinds of files, respectively. Set it on the command line to affect standard input, standard output, and standard error.
	ERRNO	A string indicating the error when a redirection fails for **getline** or if **close( )** fails.

Version	Variable	Description
	FIELDWIDTHS	A space-separated list of field widths to use for splitting up the record, instead of **FS**.
	IGNORECASE	When true, all regular expression matches, string comparisons, and **index( )** ignore case.
	LINT	Dynamically controls production of "lint" warnings. With a value of **"fatal"**, lint warnings become fatal errors.
	PROCINFO	An array containing information about the process, such as real and effective UID numbers, process ID number, and so on.
	RT	The text matched by **RS**, which can be a regular expression in **gawk**.
	TEXTDOMAIN	The text domain (application name) for internationalized messages (**"messages"**).

Operators

The following table lists the operators, in order of increasing precedence, that are available in **awk**.

Symbol	Meaning
= += -= *= /= %= ^= **=	Assignment.
?:	C conditional expression.
||	Logical OR (short-circuit).
&&	Logical AND (short-circuit).
in	Array membership.
~ !~	Match regular expression and negation.
< <= > >= != ==	Relational operators.
(blank)	Concatenation.
+ -	Addition, subtraction.
* / %	Multiplication, division, and modulus (remainder).
+ - !	Unary plus and minus, and logical negation.
^ **	Exponentiation.
++ --	Increment and decrement, either prefix or postfix.
$	Field reference.

While ** and **= are common extensions, they are not part of POSIX **awk**.

Variable and Array Assignment

Variables can be assigned a value with an equals sign. For example:

```
FS = ","
```

Expressions using the operators +, -, /, and % (modulo) can be assigned to variables.

Arrays can be created with the **split( )** function (described later), or they can simply be named in an assignment statement. Array elements can be subscripted with numbers (*array*[**1**], ..., *array*[*n*]) or with strings. Arrays subscripted by strings are called *associative arrays.*[*] For example, to count the number of widgets you have, you could use the following script:

```
/widget/ { count["widget"]++ }      Count widgets
    ND   { print count["widget"] }  Print the count
```

You can use the special **for** loop to read all the elements of an associative array:

```
for (item in array)
    process array[item]
```

The index of the array is available as **item**, while the value of an element of the array can be referenced as **array[item]**.

You can use the operator **in** to test that an element exists by testing to see if its index exists. For example:

```
if (index in array)
    ...
```

tests that **array[index]** exists, but you cannot use it to test the value of the element referenced by **array[index]**.

You can also delete individual elements of the array using the **delete** statement. (See also the **delete** entry in "Alphabetical Summary of awk Functions and Commands" on page 738.)

Escape sequences

Within string and regular-expression constants, the following escape sequences may be used.

Sequence	Meaning	Sequence	Meaning
\a	Alert (bell)	\v	Vertical tab
\b	Backspace	\\	Literal backslash
\f	Form feed	\nnn	Octal value nnn
\n	Newline	\xnn	Hexadecimal value nn
\r	Carriage return	\"	Literal double quote (in strings)
\t	Tab	\/	Literal slash (in regular expressions)

 The \x escape sequence is a common extension; it is not part of POSIX **awk**.

---

[*] In fact, all arrays in **awk** are associative; numeric subscripts are converted to strings before being used as array subscripts. Associative arrays are one of **awk**'s most powerful features.

Octal and Hexadecimal Constants in gawk

gawk allows you to use octal and hexadecimal constants in your program source code. The form is as in C: octal constants start with a leading **0**, and hexadecimal constants with a leading **0x** or **0X**. The hexadecimal digits **a–f** may be in either uppercase or lowercase.

```
$ gawk 'BEGIN { print 042, 42, 0x42 }'
    34 42 66
```

Use the **strtonum( )** function to convert octal or hexadecimal input data into numerical values.

User-Defined Functions

gawk allows you to define your own functions. This makes it easy to encapsulate sequences of steps that need to be repeated into a single place and reuse the code from anywhere in your program.

The following function capitalizes each word in a string. It has one parameter, named **input**, and five local variables, which are written as extra parameters:

```
# capitalize each word in a string
function capitalize(input, result, words, n, i, w)
{
    result = ""
    n = split(input, words, " ")
    for (i = 1; i <= n; i++) {
        w = words[i]
        w = toupper(substr(w, 1, 1)) substr(w, 2)
        if (i > 1)
                result = result " "
        result = result w
    }
    return result
}

# main program, for testing
{ print capitalize($0) }
```

With this input data:

```
A test line with words and numbers like 12 on it.
```

This program produces:

```
A Test Line With Words And Numbers Like 12 On It.
```

 For user-defined functions, no space is allowed between the function name and the left parenthesis when the function is called.

gawk-Specific Features

This section describes features unique to **gawk**.

Coprocesses and Sockets

gawk allows you to open a two-way pipe to another process, called a *coprocess*. This is done with the |& operator used with **getline** and **print** or **printf**.

```
print database command |& "db_server"
"db_server" |& getline response
```

If the *command* used with |& is a filename beginning with **/inet/**, **gawk** opens a TCP/IP connection. The filename should be of the following form:

```
/inet/protocol/lport/hostname/rport
```

The parts of the filename are:

protocol
> One of **tcp**, **udp** or **raw**, for TCP, UDP, or raw IP sockets, respectively. Note: **raw** is currently reserved but unsupported.

lport
> The local TCP or UPD port number to use. Use **0** to let the operating system pick a port.

hostname
> The name or IP address of the remote host to connect to.

rport
> The port (application) on the remote host to connect to. A service name (e.g., **tftp**) is looked up using the C **getservbyname( )** function.

Profiling

When **gawk** is built and installed, a separate program named **pgawk** (*profiling gawk*) is built and installed with it. The two programs behave identically; however, **pgawk** runs more slowly because it keeps execution counts for each statement as it runs. When it is done, it automatically places an execution profile of your program in a file named *awkprof.out*. (You can change the filename with the **--profile** option.)

The execution profile is a "prettyprinted" version of your program, with execution counts listed in the left margin. For example, after running this program:

```
$ pgawk '/bash$/ { nusers++ }
> END { print nusers, "users use Bash." }' /etc/passwd
16 users use Bash.
```

the execution profile looks like this:

```
# gawk profile, created Mon Nov  1 14:34:38 2004

# Rule(s)
```

```
35  /bash$/ { # 16
16          nusers++
    }

    # END block(s)
    END {
1           print nusers, "users use Bash."
    }
```

If sent **SIGUSR1**, **pgawk** prints the profile and an **awk** function call stack trace, and then keeps going. Multiple **SIGUSR1** signals may be sent; the profile and trace will be printed each time. This facility is useful if your **awk** program appears to be looping and you want to see if something unexpected is being executed.

If sent **SIGHUP**, **pgawk** prints the profile and stack trace, and then exits.

File Inclusion

The **igawk** program provides a file-inclusion facility for **gawk**. You invoke it the same way you do **gawk**: it passes all command line arguments on to **gawk**. However, **igawk** processes source files and command-line programs for special statements of the form:

```
@include file.awk
```

Such files are searched for along the list of directories specified by the AWKPATH environment variable. When found, the @**include** line is replaced with the text of the corresponding file. Included files may themselves include other files with @**include**.

The combination of the AWKPATH environment variable and **igawk** makes it easy to have and use libraries of **awk** functions.

Internationalization

You can *internationalize* your programs if you use **gawk**. This consists of choosing a text domain for your program, marking strings that are to be translated, and, if necessary, using the **bindtextdomain( )**, **dcgettext( )**, and **dcngettext( )** functions.

Localizing your program consists of extracting the marked strings, creating translations, and compiling and installing the translations in the proper place. Full details are given in *sed & awk* by Dale Dougherty and Arnold Robbins (O'Reilly).

The internationalization features in **gawk** use GNU **gettext**. You may need to install the GNU **gettext** tools to create translations if your system doesn't already have them. Here is a very brief outline of the steps involved:

1. Set **TEXTDOMAIN** to your text domain in a **BEGIN** block:
   ```
   BEGIN { TEXTDOMAIN = "whizprog" }
   ```
2. Mark all strings to be translated by prepending a leading underscore:
   ```
   printf(_"whizprog: can't open /dev/telepath (%s)\n",
                   dcgettext(ERRNO)) > "/dev/stderr"
   ```
3. Extract the strings with the **--gen-po** option:
   ```
   $ gawk --gen-po -f whizprog.awk > whizprog.pot
   ```

4. Copy the file for translating, and make the translations:

```
$ cp whizprog.pot esperanto.po
$ ed esperanto.po
```

5. Use the **msgfmt** program from GNU **gettext** to compile the translations. The binary format allows fast lookup of the translations at runtime. The default output is a file named *messages*:

```
$ msgfmt esperanto.po
$ mv messages esperanto.mo
```

6. Install the file in the standard location. This is usually done at program installation. The location can vary from system to system.

That's it! **gawk** will automatically find and use the translated messages, if they exist.

Implementation Limits

Many versions of **awk** have various implementation limits, on things such as:

- Number of fields per record
- Number of characters per input record
- Number of characters per output record
- Number of characters per field
- Number of characters per **printf** string
- Number of characters in literal string
- Number of characters in character class
- Number of files open
- Number of pipes open
- The ability to handle 8-bit characters and characters that are all zero (ASCII NUL)

gawk does not have limits on any of the above items, other than those imposed by the machine architecture and/or the operating system.

Group Listing of awk Functions and Commands

The following table classifies **awk** functions and commands.

Function type	Functions or commands				
Arithmetic	atan2	cos	exp	int	log
	rand	sin	sqrt	srand	
String	asort[a]	asorti[a]	gensub[a]	gsub	index
	length	match	split	sprintf	strtonum[a]
	sub	substr	tolower	toupper	
Control flow	break	continue	do/while	exit	for
	if/else	return	while		

Function type	Functions or commands				
I/O	close	fflush[b]	getline	next	nextfile[b]
	print	printf			
Programming	extension[a]	delete	function	system	

[a] Available in **gawk**.
[b] Available in Bell Labs **awk** and **gawk**.

The following functions are specific to **gawk**.

Function type	Functions or commands				
Bit manipulation	and	compl	lshift	or	rshift
	xor				
Time	mktime	strftime	systime		
Translation	bindtext- domain	dcgettext	dcngettext		

Alphabetical Summary of awk Functions and Commands

The following alphabetical list of keywords and functions includes all that are available in POSIX **awk** and **gawk**. Extensions that aren't part of POSIX **awk** but that are in both **gawk** and the Bell Laboratories **awk** are marked as {E}. Cases where **gawk** has extensions are marked as {G}. Items that aren't marked with a symbol are available in all versions.

#

#

Ignore all text that follows on the same line. # is used in **awk** scripts as the comment character and is not really a command.

---

and

and(*expr1, expr2*) {G}

Return the bitwise AND of *expr1* and *expr2*, which should be values that fit in a C **unsigned long**.

---

asort

asort(*src* [,*dest*]) {G}

Sort the array *src* based on the element values, destructively replacing the indices with values from one to the number of elements in the array. If *dest* is supplied, copy *src* to *dest* and sort *dest*, leaving *src* unchanged. Returns the number of elements in *src*.

---

asorti

asorti(*src* [,*dest*]) {G}

Like **asort( )**, but the sorting is done based on the indices in the array, not based on the element values. For **gawk** 3.1.2 and later.

atan2	`atan2(y, x)`
	Return the arctangent of *y*/*x* in radians.

bindtextdomain	`bindtextdomain(dir [,domain]) {G}`
	Look in directory *dir* for message translation files for text domain *domain* (default: value of TEXTDOMAIN). Returns the directory where *domain* is bound.

break	`break`
	Exit from a **while**, **for**, or **do** loop.

close	`close(expr)`
	`close(expr, how) {G}`
	In most implementations of **awk**, you can only have up to ten files and one pipe open simultaneously. Therefore, POSIX **awk** provides a **close( )** function that allows you to close a file or a pipe. It takes the same expression that opened the pipe or file as an argument. This expression must be identical, character by character, to the one that opened the file or pipe—even whitespace is significant.
	In the second form, close one end of either a TCP/IP socket or a two-way pipe to a coprocess. *how* is a string, either **"from"** or **"to"**. Case does not matter.

compl	`compl(expr) {G}`
	Return the bitwise complement of *expr*, which should be a value that fits in a C **unsigned long**.

continue	`continue`
	Begin next iteration of **while**, **for**, or **do** loop.

cos	`cos(x)`
	Return the cosine of *x*, an angle in radians.

dcgettext	`dcgettext(str [, dom [,cat]]) {G}`
	Return the translation of *str* for the text domain *dom* in message category *cat*. Default text domain is value of TEXTDOMAIN. Default category is "LC_MESSAGES".

dcngettext	`dcngettext(str1, str2, num [, dom [,cat]]) {G}`
	If *num* is one, return the translation of *str1* for the text domain *dom* in message category *cat*. Otherwise, return the translation of *str2*. Default text domain is value of TEXTDOMAIN. Default category is "LC_MESSAGES". For **gawk** 3.1.1 and later.

delete

delete *array*[*element*]
delete *array* {E}

Delete *element* from *array*. The brackets are typed literally. The second form is a common extension, which deletes *all* elements of the array in one shot.

do

do
  statement
while (*expr*)

Looping statement. Execute *statement*, then evaluate *expr* and if true, execute *statement* again. A series of statements must be put within braces.

exit

exit [*expr*]

Exit from script, reading no new input. The **END** procedure, if it exists, will be executed. An optional *expr* becomes **awk**'s return value.

exp

exp(*x*)

Return exponential of *x* (*ex*).

extension

extension(*lib*, *init*) {G}

Dynamically load the shared object file *lib*, calling the function *init* to initialize it. Return the value returned by the *init* function. This function allows you to add new built-in functions to **gawk**. See Arnold Robbins's *Effective awk Programming* (O'Reilly) for the details.

fflush

fflush([*output-expr*]) {E}

Flush any buffers associated with open output file or pipe *output-expr*.

gawk extends this function. If no *output-expr* is supplied, it flushes standard output. If *output-expr* is the null string (""), it flushes all open files and pipes.

for

for (*init-expr*; *test-expr*; *incr-expr*)
  statement

C-style looping construct. *init-expr* assigns the initial value of a counter variable. *test-expr* is a relational expression that is evaluated each time before executing the *statement*. When *test-expr* is false, the loop is exited. *incr-expr* is used to increment the counter variable after each pass. All of the expressions are optional. A missing *test-expr* is considered to be true. A series of statements must be put within braces.

for

for (*item* in *array*)
  statement

Special loop designed for reading associative arrays. For each element of the array, the *statement* is executed; the element can be referenced by *array* [*item*]. A series of statements must be put within braces.

function

function *name*(*parameter-list*) {
  statements
}

Create *name* as a user-defined function consisting of **awk** *statements* that apply to the specified list of parameters. No space is allowed between *name* and the left parenthesis when the function is called.

gensub

gensub(*regex*, *str*, *how* [, *target*]) {G}

General substitution function. Substitute *str* for matches of the regular expression *regex* in the string *target*. If *how* is a number, replace the *how*th match. If it is "**g**" or "**G**", substitute globally. If *target* is not supplied, **$0** is used. Return the new string value. The original *target* is *not* modified. (Compare with **gsub** and **sub**.) Use **&** in the replacement string to stand for the text matched by the pattern.

getline

getline
getline [*var*] [< *file*]
command | getline [*var*]
command |& getline [*var*] {G}

Read next line of input.

The second form reads input from *file*, and the third form reads the output of *command*. All forms read one record at a time, and each time the statement is executed, it gets the next record of input. The record is assigned to **$0** and is parsed into fields, setting NF, NR and FNR. If *var* is specified, the result is assigned to *var* and **$0** and NF are not changed. Thus, if the result is assigned to a variable, the current record does not change. **getline** is actually a function, and it returns 1 if it reads a record successfully, 0 if end-of-file is encountered, and -1 if for some reason it is otherwise unsuccessful.

The fourth form reads the output from coprocess *command*. See the section "Coprocesses and Sockets" on page 735 for more information.

gsub

gsub(*regex*, *str* [, *target*])

Globally substitute *str* for each match of the regular expression *regex* in the string *target*. If *target* is not supplied, defaults to **$0**. Return the number of substitutions. Use **&** in the replacement string to stand for the text matched by the pattern.

if
    if (*condition*)
     statement1
    [else
     statement2]

If *condition* is true, do *statement1*; otherwise do *statement2* in optional **else** clause. The *condition* can be an expression using any of the relational operators <, <=, = =, !=, >=, or >, as well as the array membership operator **in**, and the pattern-matching operators ~ and !~ (e.g., **if ($1 ~ /[Aa].*/)**). A series of statements must be put within braces. Another **if** can directly follow an **else** in order to produce a chain of tests or decisions.

index
    index(*str, substr*)

Return the position (starting at 1) of *substr* in *str*, or zero if *substr* is not present in *str*.

int
    int(*x*)

Return integer value of *x* by truncating any fractional part.

length
    length([*arg*])

Return length of *arg*, or the length of **$0** if no argument.

log
    log(*x*)

Return the natural logarithm (base *e*) of *x*.

lshift
    lshift(*expr, count*) {G}

Return the result of shifting *expr* left by *count* bits. Both *expr* and *count* should be values that fit in a C **unsigned long**.

match
    match(*str, regex*)
    match(*str, regex* [, *array*]) {G}

Function that matches the pattern, specified by the regular expression *regex*, in the string *str* and returns either the position in *str* where the match begins, or 0 if no occurrences are found. Sets the values of RSTART and RLENGTH to the start and length of the match, respectively.

If *array* is provided, **gawk** puts the text that matched the entire regular expression in *array*[0], the text that matched the first parenthesized subexpression in *array*[1], the second in *array*[2], and so on.

mktime
    mktime(*timespec*) {G}

Turns *timespec* (a string of the form *YYYY MM DD HH MM SS*[*DST*] representing a local time) into a time-of-day value in seconds since midnight, January 1, 1970, UTC.

next

next

Read next input line and start new cycle through pattern/procedures statements.

nextfile

nextfile {E}

Stop processing the current input file and start new cycle through pattern/procedures statements, beginning with the first record of the next file.

or

or(*expr1*, *expr2*) {G}

Return the bitwise OR of *expr1* and *expr2*, which should be values that fit in a C **unsigned long**.

print

print [*output-expr*[, ...]] [*dest-expr*]

Evaluate the *output-expr* and direct it to standard output followed by the value of ORS. Each comma-separated *output-expr* is separated in the output by the value of OFS. With no *output-expr*, print **$0**. The output may be redirected to a file or pipe via the *dest-expr*, which is described in "Output Redirections" on page 746.

printf

printf(*format* [, *expr-list*]) [*dest-expr*]

An alternative output statement borrowed from the C language. It has the ability to produce formatted output. It can also be used to output data without automatically producing a newline. *format* is a string of format specifications and constants. *expr-list* is a list of arguments corresponding to format specifiers. As for **print**, output may be redirected to a file or pipe. See "printf Formats" on page 746 for a description of allowed format specifiers.

Like any string, *format* can also contain embedded escape sequences: **\n** (newline) or **\t** (tab) being the most common. Spaces and literal text can be placed in the *format* argument by quoting the entire argument. If there are multiple expressions to be printed, there should be multiple formats specified.

Examples

Using the script:

```
{ printf("The sum on line %d is %.0f.\n", NR, $1+$2) }
```

The following input line:

```
5   5
```

produces this output, followed by a newline:

```
The sum on line 1 is 10.
```

rand

rand( )

Generate a random number between 0 and 1. This function returns the same series of numbers each time the script is executed, unless the random number generator is seeded using **srand( )**.

return	`return [expr]`
	Used within a user-defined function to exit the function, returning the value of *expr*. The return value of a function is undefined if *expr* is not provided.
rshift	`rshift(expr, count) {G}`
	Return the result of shifting *expr* right by *count* bits. Both *expr* and *count* should be values that fit in a C **unsigned long**.
sin	`sin(x)`
	Return the sine of *x*, an angle in radians.
split	`split(string, array [, sep])`
	Split *string* into elements of array *array*[1],...,*array*[n]. Return the number of array elements created. The string is split at each occurrence of separator *sep*. If *sep* is not specified, FS is used.
sprintf	`sprintf(format [, expressions])`
	Return the formatted value of one or more *expressions*, using the specified *format*. Data is formatted but not printed. See "printf Formats" on page 746 for a description of allowed format specifiers.
sqrt	`sqrt(arg)`
	Return the square root of *arg*.
srand	`srand([expr])`
	Use optional *expr* to set a new seed for the random number generator. Default is the time of day. Return value is the old seed.
strftime	`strftime([format [,timestamp]]) {G}`
	Format *timestamp* according to *format*. Return the formatted string. The *timestamp* is a time-of-day value in seconds since midnight, January 1, 1970, UTC. The *format* string is similar to that of **sprintf**. If *timestamp* is omitted, it defaults to the current time. If *format* is omitted, it defaults to a value that produces output similar to that of the Unix **date** command. See the **date** entry in Chapter 3 for a list.
strtonum	`strtonum(expr) {G}`
	Return the numeric value of *expr*, which is a string representing an octal, decimal, or hexadecimal number in the usual C notations. Use this function for processing nondecimal input data.

sub

sub(*regex*, *str* [, *target*])

Substitute *str* for first match of the regular expression *regex* in the string *target*. If *target* is not supplied, defaults to **$0**. Returns 1 if successful, 0 otherwise. Use **&** in the replacement string to stand for the text matched by the pattern.

substr

substr(*string*, *beg* [, *len*])

Return substring of *string* at beginning position *beg* (counting from 1), and the characters that follow to maximum specified length *len*. If no length is given, use the rest of the string.

system

system(*command*)

Function that executes the specified *command* and returns its exit status. The status of the executed command typically indicates success or failure. A value of 0 means that the command executed successfully. A nonzero value indicates a failure of some sort. The documentation for the command will give you the details.

awk does *not* make the output of the command available for processing within the **awk** script. Use *command* | **getline** to read the output of a command into the script.

systime

systime( ) {G}

Return a time-of-day value in seconds since midnight, January 1, 1970, UTC.

Examples

Log the start and end times of a data-processing program:

```
BEGIN {
        now = systime( )
        mesg = strftime("Started at %m/%d/%Y %H:%M:%S",
now)
        print mesg
}
process data ...
    END {
            now = systime( )
            mesg = strftime("Ended at %m/%d/%Y %H:%M:%S",
now)
            print mesg
        }
```

tolower

tolower(*str*)

Translate all uppercase characters in *str* to lowercase and return the new string.[*]

---

[*] Very early versions of **nawk** don't support **tolower( )** and **toupper( )**. However, they are now part of the POSIX specification for **awk**.

toupper	toupper(*str*)
	Translate all lowercase characters in *str* to uppercase and return the new string.

while	while (*condition*) *statement*
	Do *statement* while *condition* is true (see **if** for a description of allowable conditions). A series of statements must be put within braces.

xor	xor(*expr1, expr2*) {G}
	Return the bitwise XOR of *expr1* and *expr2*, which should be values that fit in a C **unsigned long**.

Output Redirections

For **print** and **printf**, *dest-expr* is an optional expression that directs the output to a file or pipe.

> *file*
> Direct the output to a file, overwriting its previous contents.

>> *file*
> Append the output to a file, preserving its previous contents. In both this case and the > *file* case, the file will be created if it does not already exist.

| *command*
> Direct the output as the input to a system command.

|& *command*
> Direct the output as the input to a coprocess. **gawk** only.

Be careful not to mix > and >> for the same file. Once a file has been opened with >, subsequent output statements continue to append to the file until it is closed.

Remember to call **close( )** when you have finished with a file, pipe, or coprocess. If you don't, eventually you will hit the system limit on the number of simultaneously open files.

printf Formats

Format specifiers for **printf** and **sprintf** have the following form:

```
%[posn$][flag][width][.precision]letter
```

The control letter is required. The format-conversion control letters are given in the following table.

Character	Description
c	ASCII character.
d	Decimal integer.
i	Decimal integer (added in POSIX).
e	Floating-point format ([-]d.precisione[+-]dd).
E	Floating-point format ([-]d.precisionE[+-]dd).
f	Floating-point format ([-]ddd.precision).
g	e or f conversion, whichever is shortest, with trailing zeros removed.
G	E or f conversion, whichever is shortest, with trailing zeros removed.
o	Unsigned octal value.
s	String.
u	Unsigned decimal value.
x	Unsigned hexadecimal number. Uses a-f for 10 to 15.
X	Unsigned hexadecimal number. Uses A-F for 10 to 15.
%	Literal %.

gawk allows you to provide a *positional specifier* after the % (*posn$*). A positional specifier is an integer count followed by a **$**. The count indicates which argument to use at that point. Counts start at one and don't include the format string. This feature is primarily for use in producing translations of format strings. For example:

```
$ gawk 'BEGIN { printf "%2$s, %1$s\n", "world", "hello" }'
hello, world
```

The optional *flag* is one of the following.

Character	Description
-	Left-justify the formatted value within the field.
space	Prefix positive values with a space and negative values with a minus.
+	Always prefix numeric values with a sign, even if the value is positive.
#	Use an alternate form: %o has a preceding 0; %x and %X are prefixed with 0x and 0X, respectively; %e, %E and %f always have a decimal point in the result; and %g and %G do not have trailing zeros removed.
0	Pad output with zeros, not spaces. This only happens when the field width is wider than the converted result. This flag applies to all output formats, even nonnumeric ones.
'	**gawk** 3.1.4 and later only. For numeric formats, in locales that support it, supply a thousands-separator charater.

The optional *width* is the minimum number of characters to output. The result will be padded to this size if it is smaller. The 0 flag causes padding with zeros; otherwise, padding is with spaces.

The *precision* is optional. Its meaning varies by control letter, as shown in the following table.

Conversion	Precision means
%d, %i, %o, %u, %x, %X	The minimum number of digits to print.
%e, %E, %f	The number of digits to the right of the decimal point.
%g, %G	The maximum number of significant digits.
%s	The maximum number of characters to print.

12

Source Code Management: An Overview

Chapters 13 and 14 describe two popular source code management systems for Linux: Subversion (SVN) and Git. This chapter introduces the major concepts involved with using these systems for users who may never have used one. If you're already familiar with source code management, feel free to skip ahead to the particular software suite that interests you.

This chapter covers the following topics:

- Introduction and terminology
- Usage models
- Source code management systems
- Other source code management systems

Introduction and Terminology

Source code management systems let you store and retrieve multiple versions of a file. While originally designed for program source code, they can be used for any kind of file: source code, documentation, configuration files, and so on. Modern systems allow you to store binary files as well, such as image or audio data.

Source code management systems let you compare different versions of a file, as well as do "parallel development." In other words, you can work on two different versions of a file at the same time, with the source code management system storing both versions. You can then merge changes from two versions into a third version. This will become more clear shortly. We'll start by defining some terms:

Repository
    A *repository* is where the source code management system stores its copy of your file. Usually one file in the source code management system is used to hold all the different versions of a source file. Each source code management system uses its own format to allow it to retrieve different versions easily and to track who made what changes, and when.

Sandbox

A *sandbox* is your personal, so-called "working copy" of the program or set of documents under development. You edit your private copy of the file in your own sandbox, returning changes to the source code management system when you're satisfied with the new version.

Check in, check out

You "check out" files from the repository, edit them, and then "check them in" when you're satisfied with your changes. Other developers working against the same repository will not see your changes until after you check them back in. Another term used for check-in is *commit*.

Log message

Every time you check in a file, you are prompted for a message describing the changes you made. You should do so in a concise fashion. If your software development practices include the use of a bug tracking system, you might also wish to include the bug number or problem report (PR) number that your change resolves.

Keyword substitutions

When you check out a file, the source code management system can replace special *keywords* with values representing such things as the file's version number, the name of the user who made the most recent change, the date and time the file was last changed, the file's name, and so on. Each of the systems described in this book uses an overlapping set of keywords. Some systems always do keyword substitution, while others require that you explicitly enable the feature for each file.

Branch

A *branch* is a separate development path. For example, once you've released version 1.0 of **whizprog**, you will wish to proceed with the development for version 2.0. The main line of development is often called the *trunk*.

Now consider what happens when you wish to make a bug-fix release to **whizprog** 1.0, to be named version 1.1. You create a separate branch, based on the original 1.0 code, in a new sandbox. You perform all your development *there*, without disturbing the development being done for the 2.0 release.

Tag

A *tag* is a name you give to a whole group of files at once, at whatever version each individual file may be, in order to identify those files as being part of a particular group. For example, you might create tags **WHIZPROG-1_0-ALPHA**, **WHIZPROG-1_0-BETA**, **WHIZPROG-1_0-RELEASE** and so on. This is a powerful facility that should be used well, since it allows you to retrieve a "snapshot" of your entire development tree as it existed at different points in time.

Merging

Most typically, when development along a branch is completed, it becomes necessary to *merge* the changes from that branch back into the main line of development. In our hypothetical example, all the bugs fixed in **whizprog** 1.0 to create version 1.1 should also be fixed in the ongoing 2.0 development. Source code management systems can help you automate the process of merging.

Conflict

A *conflict* occurs when two developers make inconsistent changes to the same part of a source file. Modern source code management systems detect the conflict, usually marking the conflicting parts of the file in your working copy using special markers. You first discuss the conflict with the other developer, in order to arrive at a correct resolution of the conflict. Once that's done, you then resolve the conflict manually (by making the appropriate changes) and check in the new version of the file.

Client/Server

As with other "client/server" networking models, the idea here is that the repository is stored on one machine, the *server*, and that different developers may access the repository from multiple *client* systems. This powerful feature facilitates distributed development, allowing developers to work easily on their local systems, with the repository kept in a central place where it can be easily accessed and administered.

Usage Models

Different systems have different conceptual "models" as to how they're used.

Older systems such as SCCS and RCS use a "check out with locking" model. These systems were developed before client/server computing, when software development was done on centralized minicomputers and mainframes. In this model, the repository is a central directory on the same machine where the developers work, and each developer checks out a private copy into their own sandbox. In order to avoid two developers making conflicting changes to a file, the file must be *locked* when it's checked out. Only one user may lock a particular version of a file at a time. When that user has checked in their changes, they *unlock* the file so that the next user can check in changes. If necessary, the second user may "break" the first user's lock, in which case the first user is notified via electronic mail.

This model works well for small projects where developers are co-located and can communicate easily. As long as one developer locks a file when she checks it out, another developer wishing to work with the file will know that he can't until the first one is done. The drawback is that such locking can slow down development significantly.

Newer systems, such as CVS and Subversion, use a "copy, modify, merge" model. In practice, when two developers wish to work on the same file, they usually end up changing different, unrelated parts of the file. Most of the time, each developer can make changes without adversely affecting the other. Thus, files are not locked upon checkout into a sandbox. Instead, the source code management system detects conflicts and disallows a check-in when conflicts exist.

For example, consider two developers, *dangermouse* and *penfold*, who are both working on *whizprog.c*. They each start with version 1.4 of the file. *dangermouse* commits his changes, creating version 1.5. Before *penfold* can commit his changes, the source code management system notices that the file has changed in the repository. *penfold* must first merge *dangermouse*'s changes into his working copy.

If there are no conflicts, he can then commit his changes, creating version 1.6. On the other hand, if there are conflicts, he must first resolve them (they'll be marked in the working copy), and only then may he commit his version.

The combination of the "copy, modify, merge" model with a networked client/server facility creates a powerful environment for doing distributed development. Developers no longer have to worry about file locks. Because the source code management system enforces serialization (making sure that new changes are based on the latest version in the repository), development can move more smoothly, with little danger of miscommunication or that successive changes will be lost.

Source Code Management Systems

There are several source code management systems used in the Unix community:

SCCS
> The Source Code Control System. SCCS is the original Unix source code management system. It was developed in the late 1970s for the Programmer's Workbench (PWB) Unix systems within Bell Labs. It is still in use at a few large longtime Unix sites. However, for a long time it was not available as a standard part of most commercial or BSD Unix systems, and it did not achieve the widespread popularity of other, later systems. (It is still available with Solaris.) SCCS uses a file storage format that allows it to retrieve any version of a source file in constant time.

RCS
> The Revision Control System. RCS was developed in the early 1980s at Purdue University by Walter F. Tichy. It became popular in the Unix world when it was shipped with 4.2 BSD in 1983. At the time, Berkeley Unix was the most widely used Unix variant, even though to get it, a site had to have a Unix license from AT&T.
>
> RCS is easier to use than SCCS. Although it has a number of related commands, only three or four are needed for day-to-day use, and they are quickly mastered. A central repository is easy to use: you first create a directory for the sandbox. In the sandbox, you make a symbolic link to the repository named *RCS*, and then all the developers can share the repository. RCS uses a file format that is optimized for retrieving the most recent version of a file.

CVS
> The Concurrent Versions System. CVS was initially built as a series of shell scripts sitting atop RCS. Later it was rewritten in C for robustness, although still using RCS commands to manage the storage of files. However, for quite some time, CVS has had the RCS functionality built into it, and it no longer requires that RCS be available. The file format continues to be the same. CVS was the first distributed source code management system and was until recently the standard one for Unix systems—in particular for collaborative, distributed, free and open source development projects.

The repository is named when you create a sandbox and is then stored in the files in the sandbox, so that it need not be provided every time you run a CVS command. Unlike SCCS and RCS, which provide multiple commands, CVS has one main command (named **cvs**), which you use for just about every operation.

Subversion

With increasing use, it became clear that CVS lacked some fundamental capabilities. The Subversion project was started by several longtime CVS users and developers with the explicit goal to "build a better CVS," not necessarily to explore uncharted territory in source code management systems. Subversion is thus intentionally easy to learn for CVS users. Subversion uses its own format for data storage, based on the Berkeley DB in-process data library. Distributed use was designed in from day one, providing useful facilities that leverage the capabilities of the well-known Apache HTTP server.

Git

Git is a source control system originally developed by Linus Torvalds as the source control system to manage the Linux kernel. Today, it is maintained by a community of developers and used for many diverse projects. Unlike the previous source control systems, Git is distributed. A distributed system differs from a centralized one such as CVS in several ways. The most notable is that in distributed systems, individual check outs of the source tree, called clones in distributed systems, are themselves complete and fully functioning repositories. Instead of submitting changes to a centralized server, changes are pushed and pulled among repositories.

RCS, CVS, and Subversion represent a progression, each one building on the features of its predecessors. For example, all three share a large subset of the same keyword substitutions, and command names are similar or identical in all three. They also demonstrate the progression from locking-based development to conflict-resolution-based development. Git is a radical departure from the centralized model.

Other Source Code Management Systems

Besides the source code management systems covered in this book, several other systems are worth knowing about. The following list, though, is by no means exhaustive:

Arch

GNU Arch is a distributed source code management system similar to CVS and Subversion. One of its significant strengths is that you can do offline development with it, working on multiple versions even on systems that are not connected to the Internet and that cannot communicate with the central repository. For more information, see *http://www.gnu.org/software/gnu-arch/*.

Codeville

Codeville is a distributed version-control system in the early stages of development. It is written in Python, is easy to set up and use, and shows a lot of promise. For more information, see *http://codeville.org/*.

CSSC

CSSC is a free clone of SCCS. It intends to provide full compatibility with SCCS, including file format, command names and options, and "bug for bug" compatible behavior. If you have an existing SCCS repository, you should be able to drop CSSC into your environment, in place of SCCS. CSSC can be used to migrate from a commercial Unix system to a freely available clone, such as GNU/Linux or a BSD system. For more information, see *http:// directory.fsf.org/project/cssc.*

Monotone

The web page for **monotone** describes it well:

> **monotone** is a free distributed version control system. It provides a simple, single-file transactional version store, with fully disconnected operation and an efficient peer-to-peer synchronization protocol. It understands history-sensitive merging, lightweight branches, integrated code review, and third party testing. It uses cryptographic version naming and client-side RSA certificates. It has good internationalization support, has no external dependencies, runs on [Linux, Solaris, Mac OS X, NetBSD, and Windows], and is licensed under the GNU GPL.

For more information, see *http://monotone.ca.*

The Subversion Version Control System

The Subversion version control system is a powerful, open source system for management of file and directory versions. Designed from the ground up to support distributed development, it offers many leading-edge features.

This chapter covers the following topics:

- Conceptual overview
- Using Subversion: a quick tour
- The Subversion command line client: **svn**
- Repository administration: **svnadmin**
- Examining the repository: **svnlook**
- Providing remote access: **svnserve**

Version control was introduced in Chapter 12, which contains a comparison of Subversion, GIT, and other popular systems. The material in the current chapter is adapted from *Version Control with Subversion*, Second Edition, by C. Michael Pilato et al. (O'Reilly). See that book for much more information on Subversion.

Conceptual Overview

Subversion is a version-control system. It lets you track changes to an entire project directory tree. Every change made to the tree is recorded and can be retrieved.

Basic Version-Control Operations

Project data is kept in a *repository*, a set of directories and files managed by Subversion. Users use the **svn** client program to access the repository and make changes to it.

Subversion uses the *copy-modify-merge* development model. You make a private copy of a given project in a *sandbox*. (This is often called *checking out* a copy.) This private copy is not locked in the repository. You then make all the changes you like to the copy within the sandbox, without having to worry about what other developers are doing. As you work, you can compare your changes to the version you started with, as well as the version currently in the repository. Once you're satisfied with the changes, you *commit* them, sometimes referred to as a *check-in*.

In the event that another developer has modified part of a file that you were working on and checked it in, when you commit your changes, Subversion notices and indicates that a *conflict* exists. Conflicts are marked as such in the file, and Subversion creates pristine copies of the file as it exists in the repository and of the file as you modified it, so that you can do full comparisons. Once you have resolved the conflict, you tell Subversion about it, and then commit the final version.

Subversion lets you create a development *branch*, a separate stream of development versions. You can periodically merge changes from the main development stream (the *trunk*) into your branch, and also merge changes from your branch back into the trunk.

Finally, you can *tag* a particular copy of the project. For instance, when a project is ready for a release, you can create a snapshot of the project and give it a descriptive tag that allows you to re-create the project tree exactly as it was for the release. This is particularly valuable when you need to produce a bug fix for an older version of the project, or when you have to attempt to retrofit a fix or feature from current development into an older version.

Key Features

Directory versioning
> Subversion implements a virtual versioned filesystem that tracks changes to whole directory trees over time. Files *and* directories are versioned. Because it tracks the history of the directory tree rather than just the files, you can add, delete, copy, and rename both files and directories. Every newly added file begins with a fresh, clean history all its own, even if the filename was previously used.

Atomic commits
> A collection of modifications either goes into the repository completely, or not at all. This allows developers to construct and commit changes as logical chunks, and prevents problems that can occur when only a portion of a set of changes is successfully sent to the repository.

Versioned metadata
> Each file and directory has a set of properties—keys and their values—associated with it. You can create and store any arbitrary key/value pairs. Properties are versioned over time, just like file contents.

Choice of network layers
> Subversion has an abstracted notion of repository access, making it easy for people to implement new network mechanisms. Subversion can plug into the

Apache HTTP Server as an extension module. A more lightweight, stand-alone Subversion server process is also available. This server speaks a custom protocol that can be easily tunneled over SSH.

Consistent data handling

Subversion expresses file differences using a binary differencing algorithm, which works identically on both text (human-readable) and binary (human-unreadable) files. Both types of files are stored equally compressed in the repository, and only the differences are transmitted in both directions across the network.

Efficient branching and tagging

The cost of branching and tagging need not be proportional to the project size. Subversion creates branches and tags by simply copying the project, using a mechanism similar to a hard link. Thus these operations take only a very small, constant amount of time.

Hackability

Subversion is implemented as a collection of shared C libraries with well-defined APIs. This makes Subversion extremely maintainable and usable by other applications and languages. Subversion is an open source project as well. You can contribute to its development.

Special File Properties

Subversion allows you to associate *properties* with files or directories. A property is just a keyword/value pair associated with the file. Subversion reserves property names starting with **svn:** for its own use. The special properties in Subversion 1.5.4 are:

svn:author

The username of the person who committed a particular revision.

svn:date

The server time when the transaction for a revision was created.

svn:eol-style

Different operating systems use different conventions to mark the end of lines in text files. It should be set to one of the following values:

CR Clients should always use carriage return (CR) line terminators, no matter what the native format is.

CRLF

Clients should always use carriage return and line feed (CR-LF) line terminators, no matter what the native format is.

LF Clients should always use linefeed (LF) line terminators, no matter what the native format is.

native

Clients should use the native format when checking out files.

Subversion always stores files in normalized, LF-only format in the repository.

svn:executable

Valid only for files. It indicates that the file should be made executable when it's checked out or updated from the repository. It has no effect on filesystems, such as FAT-32 or NTFS, that don't have the concept of an execute bit.

svn:externals

This property, when set on a directory under version control, allows you to specify other, external repositories to use for particular local subdirectories. You set this property with **svn propset** or **svn propedit** (see "svn Subcommands" on page 766). The value is a multiline table of directories and fully qualified Subversion URLs. For example:

```
$ svn propget svn:externals calc
third-party/sounds              http://sounds.red-bean.com/repos
third-party/skins               http://skins.red-bean.com/repositories/
skinproj
third-party/skins/toolkit -r21 http://svn.red-bean.com/repos/skin-maker
```

Once set, anyone else who checks out a working copy will also get the third party files checked out automatically.

svn:ignore

Used to tell Subversion to not place certain file types under version control. This property is set on a directory and should contain a list of file patterns that certain Subversion operations (like **svn status**, **svn add**, and **svn import**.) will ignore.

svn:keywords

A list of keywords for which Subversion should perform *keyword expansion* when checking out the file. The valid keywords are listed below.

svn:log

The log message associated with the commit of a particular revision.

svn:mime-type

An indication of the type of data stored in the file. This prevents an attempt to perform a "merge" on data that can't be merged. This property also influences how the Subversion Apache module sets the HTTP **Content-type:** header. In general, if it does not begin with **text/**, Subversion assumes that the file contains binary data. For updates, this causes Subversion to rename a modified working copy of the file with a **.orig** extension and replace the file with the current version from the repository.

svn:realmstring

A specialized property that describes the "authentication realm" for a file in Subversion's cached copy of the authentication credentials. See Chapter 6 of *Version Control with Subversion* for more information.

Valid subversion keywords

Subversion defines the list of keywords available for substitution. That list contains the following five keywords, some of which have shorter aliases that you can also use:

Date

This keyword describes the last time the file was changed in the repository and looks like **$Date: 2009-02-23 21:42:37 -0700 (Mon, 23 Feb 2009) $**. It may also be given as **LastChangedDate**.

Revision

> This keyword describes the last revision in which this file changed in the repository and looks like **$Revision$**. It may also be given as **LastChanged-Revision** or abbreviated as **Rev**.

Author

> This keyword describes the last user to change this file in the repository, and looks like **$Author$**. It may be given as **LastChangedBy**.

HeadURL

> This keyword describes the full URL to the latest version of the file in the repository. It looks like **$HeadURL: http://svn.collab.net/repos/trunk/ README $**. It may be abbreviated as **URL**.

Id This keyword is a compressed combination of the other keywords. Its substitution looks like **Id: ch14.xml,v 1.5 2005/08/12 21:21:32 sally Exp sally $**, and is interpreted to mean that the file *calc.c* was last changed in revision 148 on the evening of July 28, 2005 by the user *sally*.

Obtaining Subversion

The Subversion project website is *http://subversion.tigris.org*. It contains links to project documentation, Frequently Asked Questions (FAQs), and project source code.

Most GNU/Linux systems come with Subversion available on the installation CDs. Thus, you may be able to install a prebuilt binary for your system or use a package manager to download and install it.

Using Subversion: A Quick Tour

This section provides a very quick tour of using Subversion for version control. We start with the initial version of a project for importing into Subversion:

```
$ find /tmp/hello -print        Show directory layout
/tmp/hello
/tmp/hello/branches             Directory for branch development
/tmp/hello/tags                 Directory for tagged releases
/tmp/hello/trunk
/tmp/hello/trunk/hello.c        Mainline development is done on the trunk
/tmp/hello/trunk/Makefile
/tmp/hello/trunk/README
```

The next steps are to create the repository and then to import the project into it:

```
$ svnadmin create /path/to/svnrepos
$ svn import /tmp/hello file:///path/to/svnrepos -m "initial import"
Adding         /tmp/hello/trunk
Adding         /tmp/hello/trunk/hello.c
Adding         /tmp/hello/trunk/Makefile
Adding         /tmp/hello/trunk/README
Adding         /tmp/hello/branches
Adding         /tmp/hello/tags

Committed revision 1.
```

Now that the project exists in Subversion, we check out a working copy into a sandbox underneath our home directory and start making changes:

```
$ cd                                          Move to home directory
$ svn checkout file:///path/to/svnrepos hello   Check out working copy
A  hello/trunk
A  hello/trunk/hello.c
A  hello/trunk/README
A  hello/trunk/Makefile
A  hello/branches
A  hello/tags
Checked out revision 1.

$ cd hello/trunk                              Change to sandbox
$ vi message.c hello.c Makefile               Make changes
3 files to edit

$ cat message.c                               Show newly created file
const char message[  ] = "hello, world!";
$ make                                        Compile program and test it
cc     -c -o hello.o hello.c
cc     -c -o message.o message.c
cc -O hello.o message.o -o hello
$ hello
hello, world!
```

One of the most common operations is to compare the changed copy with the original. The result is in *unified diff* format, the equivalent of the regular **diff -u** command:

```
$ svn diff hello.c
Index: hello.c
================================================================
====
--- hello.c     (revision 1)
+++ hello.c     (working copy)
@@ -1,7 +1,9 @@
#include <stdio.h>

+extern const char message[  ];
+
int main(void)
{
-       printf("hello, world!\n");
+       printf("%s\n", message);
        return 0;
}
```

Now that we're comfortable with the changes, we schedule the new file, *message.c*, for addition to the repository, and then we actually commit our changes:

```
$ svn add message.c                Schedule message.c for addition
A         message.c
$ svn commit                       Commit all the changes
Sending        trunk/Makefile
Sending        trunk/hello.c
```

```
Adding          trunk/message.c
Transmitting file data ...
Committed revision 2.
```

Finally, we can view *all* our changes relative to the initial revision:

```
$ svn diff -r 1
Index: hello.c
===================================================================
--- hello.c     (revision 1)
+++ hello.c     (working copy)
@@ -1,7 +1,9 @@
 #include <stdio.h>

+extern const char message[   ];
+
 int main(void)
 {
-        printf("hello, world!\n");
+        printf("%s\n", message);
         return 0;
     }
Index: Makefile
===================================================================
==
--- Makefile    (revision 1)
+++ Makefile    (working copy)
@@ -1,2 +1,2 @@
-hello: hello.c
-        $(CC) -O $< -o $@
+hello: hello.o message.o
+        $(CC) -O hello.o message.o -o $@
Index: message.c
===================================================================
==
--- message.c   (revision 0)
+++ message.c   (revision 2)
@@ -0,0 +1 @@
+const char message[   ] = "hello, world!";
```

The Subversion Command Line Client: svn

The syntax for the Subversion command line client, **svn**, consists of options and a subcommand. **svn**'s *options* and *subcommand* may be provided in any order.

Common svn Options

While Subversion subcommands have different valid options, all options mean the same thing regardless of the subcommand you use it with. For example, **--verbose** (**-v**) always means verbose output, regardless of the subcommand you use it with.

--accept *arg*

Specify action for automatic conflict resolution. Possible actions are post-pone, base, mine-full, theirs-full, edit, and launch.

--auto-props

Automatically set properties an newly added or imported files, overriding the **enable-auto-props** directive in the *config* file. By default this is disabled.

--change *arg*, **-c** *arg*

Apply subcommand to specified change (a.k.a. revision.) This can be used as shorthand for "-r *arg*-1:*arg*".

--changelist *name*, **-cl** *name*

Limit subcommand to files belonging to changelist *name*. You use the **changelist** subcommand to name the set of files to which you are making changes. A file can only belong to one changelist at a time. Changelists are local and are not saved in the repository. The name is usually discarded after committing. This option can be repeated to include more than one set of files.

--config-dir *dir*

Read configuration information from the specified directory instead of the default location (*.subversion* in the user's home directory).

--depth *arg*

Control the tree-depth to which the subcommand should be recursively applied. When used with the checkout command this will set the depth property of the checked out files as well, affecting what you receive and what future commands will affect in the repository. To change this "ambient depth" use the **--set-depth** option. This option replaces the --**recursive** and --**non-recursive** options. *arg* may be one of the following:

empty

Apply to specified target only.

files

Apply to the immediate file children of the target.

immediates

Apply to the immediate file and directory children of target.

infinity

Apply recursively to all file and directory children of target.

--diff-cmd *cmd*

Use *cmd* as the external program to show differences between files instead of Subversion's internal **diff** engine. (Use **--extensions** to pass options to the external **diff** program.)

--diff3-cmd *cmd*

Use *cmd* as the external program to merge files.

--dry-run

Run a command, but make no actual changes—either on disk or in the repository.

--editor-cmd *cmd*

Use *cmd* as the program for editing a log message or a property value. If not set, Subversion checks the environment variable SVN_EDITOR, the runtime configuration (usually *~/.subversion/config*), then environment variables VISUAL and EDITOR for the name of the editor to use.

--encoding *enc*

Use *enc* as the encoding for the commit message. The default encoding is your operating system's native locale, and you should specify the encoding if your commit message is in any other encoding.

--extensions *args*, **-x** *args*

Pass *args* to an external **diff** command when providing differences between files. To pass multiple arguments, enclose all of them in quotes (for example, **svn diff --diff-cmd /usr/bin/diff -x "-b -E"**). This option can be used *only* if you also pass the **--diff-cmd** option.

--file *filename*, **-F** *filename*

Use the contents of *filename* for the specified subcommand. How it's used depends on the subcommand.

--force

Force a particular command or operation to run. There are some operations that Subversion prevents you from doing in normal usage, but you can pass this option to tell Subversion that you know what you're doing, as well as the possible repercussions of doing it, so do it anyway. Use with caution.

--force-log

Force a suspicious parameter passed to the **--message** (**-m**) or **--file** (**-F**) options to be accepted as valid. This can be used to pass a versioned file as the source for the commit log message, something Subversion would usually consider a mistake and reject.

--help, **-h**, **-?**

If used with one or more subcommands, show the built-in help text for each subcommand. If used alone, display the general client help text.

--ignore-ancestry

Ignore ancestry when calculating differences (i.e., rely on path contents alone).

--ignore-externals

Ignore external definitions and external working copies managed by them.

--incremental

Print output in a format suitable for concatenation.

--keep-changelists

Don't delete the changelist association after committing.

--keep-local

Keep the local copy of a file when using the **delete** subcommand to remove a file from the repository.

--limit *num*, **-l** *num*

Only show the first *num* log messages.

--message *message*, **-m** *message*

Use *message* as the commit message. For example:

```
$ svn commit -m "They don't make Sunday."
```

--native-eol *format*

Used with the **export** subcommand sets the end of line marker to use for all files with the **svn:eol-style** property set to **native**. You can specify LR, CR or CRLF for *format*.

--new *arg*

Use *arg* as the newer target when producing a diff.

--no-auth-cache

Do not cache authentication information (e.g., username and password) in the Subversion administrative directories.

--no-auto-props

Disable auto-props, overriding the **enable-auto-props** directive in the *config* file.

--no-diff-deleted

Do not print differences for deleted files. The default behavior when you remove a file is for **svn diff** to print the same differences that you would see if you had left the file but removed all the content.

--no-ignore

Show files in the status listing that would normally be omitted because they match a pattern in the **svn:ignore** property.

--no-unlock

Do not unlock files on commit.

--non-interactive

In the case of an authentication failure, or insufficient credentials, do not prompt for credentials (e.g., username or password). This is useful if you're running Subversion inside of an automated script where it's better to have Subversion fail instead of trying to prompt for more information.

--non-recursive, -N

Stop a subcommand from recursing into subdirectories. Most subcommands recurse by default, but some subcommands—usually those that have the potential to remove or undo your local modifications—do not. This command is deprecated. You should use **--depth** instead.

--notice-ancestry

Pay attention to ancestry when calculating differences.

--old *arg*

Use *arg* as the older target when producing a diff.

--parents

Create and add nonversioned parent directories to the working copy or the repository. Useful for creating directories on commit.

--password *pass*

Use *pass* as the password for authentication on the command line; otherwise, if it is needed, Subversion prompts you for it.

--quiet, -q

Print only essential information while performing an operation.

--record-only

Mark a revision as merged.

--reintegrate

Used with the **svn merge** subcommand, merges changes in a specified source URL into the working copy. This can be used to merge changes from a branch back into its original line.

--recursive, -R

Make a subcommand recurse into subdirectories. Most subcommands recurse by default. This option is deprecated. Use **--depth** instead.

--relocate *from to [path ...]*

Used with the **svn switch** subcommand to change the location of the repository that your working copy references. This is useful if the location of your repository changes and you have an existing working copy that you'd like to continue to use. See **svn switch** in "svn Subcommands" on page 766 for an example.

--revision *rev*, **-r** *rev*

Use *rev* as the revision (or range of revisions) for a particular operation. You can provide revision numbers, revision keywords, or dates (in curly braces) as arguments to the revision option. To provide a range of revisions, provide two revisions separated by a colon. For example:

```
$ svn log -r 1729
$ svn log -r 1729:HEAD
$ svn log -r 1729:1744
$ svn log -r {2001-12-04}:{2002-02-17}
$ svn log -r 1729:{2002-02-17}
```

The acceptable revision keywords for **--revision** are:

BASE

The original, unmodified version of the working copy. This keyword cannot refer to a URL.

COMMITTED

The last revision, before or at **BASE**, at which an item actually changed. This keyword cannot refer to a URL.

HEAD

The most recent revision in the repository.

PREV

The revision just before that at which an item changed. Equivalent to **COMMITTED** - 1. This keyword cannot refer to a URL.

Revision Date

A date specification enclosed in curly braces, { and }, such as {2002-02-17}, {15:30}, {"2002-02-17 15:30"}, {2002-02-17T15:30}, or {20020217T1530-0500}. See *Version Control with Subversion* for full details.

--revprop

Operate on a revision property instead of a Subversion property specific to a file or directory. This option requires that you also pass a revision with the **--revision** (**-r**) option.

--set-depth *arg*

Use *arg* as the new recursive depth for the target. This accepts the same values as the **--depth** command.

--show-revs *arg*

Used with **svn mergeinfo**, specifies which collection of merge information to display. *arg* may be either merged or eligible.

--show-updates, -u

Display information about which files in your working copy are out of date. This doesn't actually update any of your files; it just shows you which files will be updated if you run **svn update**.

--stop-on-copy

Cause a Subversion subcommand that is traversing the history of a versioned resource to stop harvesting that historical information when it encounters a copy—that is, a location in history where that resource was copied from another location in the repository.

--strict

Use strict semantics. See *Version Control with Subversion* for more information.

--summarize

Use with **diff** to get a summary of changes without a list of the changes themselves.

--targets *filename*

Retrieve the list of files to operate on from *filename* instead of listing all the files on the command line.

--username *name*

Use *name* as the username for authentication; otherwise, if it is needed, Subversion prompts you for it.

--verbose, -v

Print out as much information as possible while running any subcommand. This may result in Subversion printing out additional fields, detailed information about every file, or additional information regarding its actions.

--version

Print the client version info. This information not only includes the version number of the client, but also a listing of all repository access modules that the client can use to access a Subversion repository.

--with-revprop *property*

Set a revision property when writing to the repository (specify in NAME=VALUE format). When used with **svn log –xml**, display the value of the specified property name in the log output.

--xml

Prints output in XML format.

svn Subcommands

The **svn** command is the main user interface to Subversion. It works by accepting subcommands with arguments. Five of the previous options are global in version 1.5.

All subcommands will accept **--config-dir**, **--no-auth-cache**, **--non-interactive**, **--password**, and **--username**. Even commands for which these are meaningless will accept these options without fail. This is intended to make scripting easier. Because all subcommands accept these, we don't list them in options the below.

The general form of a subcommand is:

svn *subcommand* [*options*] *arguments*

---

add

svn add *path* ...

Add files and directories to your working copy and schedule them for addition to the repository. They will be uploaded and added to the repository on your next commit. If you add something and change your mind before committing, you can unschedule the addition using **svn revert**.

Alternate names: none

Changes: working copy

Accesses repository: no

Options
   --auto-props
   --depth *arg*
   --no-auto-props
   --no-ignore
   --no-parents
   --non-recursive (-N)
   --quiet (-q)
   --targets *filename*

Examples
To add a file to your working copy:

```
$ svn add foo.c .
A         foo.c
```

You can add a directory without adding its contents:

```
$ svn add -depth empty otherdir
A         otherdir
```

---

blame

svn blame *target* ...

Show author and revision information inline for the specified files or URLs. Each line of text is annotated at the beginning with the author (username) and the revision number for the last change to that line.

Alternate names: **praise, annotate, ann**

Changes: nothing

Accesses repository: yes

Options

--extensions *args*, -x *args*
--force
--incremental
--revision *rev*, -r *rev*
--use-merge-history, -g
--verbose, -v
--xml

---

cat

svn cat *target* ...

Output the contents of the specified files or URLs. For listing the contents of directories, see **svn list**.

Alternate names: none

Changes: nothing

Accesses repository: yes

Options

--revision *rev*, -r *rev*

Examples

To view *readme.txt* in your repository without checking it out:

```
$ svn cat http://svn.red-bean.com/repos/test/readme.txt
This is a README file.
You should read this.
```

 If your working copy is out of date (or if you have local modifications) and you want to see the **HEAD** revision of a file in your working copy, **svn cat** automatically fetches the **HEAD** revision when you give it a path.

```
$ cat foo.c
This file is in my local working copy
and has changes that I've made.
```

```
$ svn cat foo.c
Latest revision fresh from the repository!
```

---

changelist

svn changelist *name target*...
svn changelist --remove *name target*...

Group files for operations into named collections. This makes it easier to work or multiple groups of files.

Alternate names: **cl**

Changes: working copy

Accesses repository: no

Options

    --changelist *name*, -cl *name*
    --depth *arg*
    --quiet (-q)
    --remove
    --targets *filename*

Examples

Edit three files, add them to a changelist, then commit only files in that changelist.:

```
$ svn changelist issue1729 foo.c bar.c baz.c
Path "foo.c" is now a member of changelist 'issue1729'.
Path "bar.c" is now a member of changelist 'issue1729'.
Path "baz.c" is now a member of changelist 'issue1729'.

$ svn status
A  someotherfile.c
A  test/sometest.c

--Changelist 'issue1729':
A  foo.c
A  bar.c
A  baz.c

$ svn commit --changelist issue1729 -m "Fixing Issue 1729"
Adding      foo.c
Adding      bar.c
Adding      baz.c
Transmitting file data...
Committed revision 2

$ svn status
A  someotherfile.c
A  test/sometest.c
```

---

checkout

`svn checkout URL ... [path]`

Check out a working copy from a repository. If *path* is omitted, the basename of the URL is used as the destination. If multiple URLs are given, each one is checked out into a subdirectory of *path*, with the name of the subdirectory being the basename of the URL.

Alternate names: **co**

Changes: creates a working copy

Accesses repository: yes

Options

    --depth *arg*
    --force
    --ignore-externals
    --quiet (-q)
    --revision *rev*, -r *rev*

Examples

Check out a working copy into a directory called *mine*:

```
$ svn checkout file:///tmp/repos/test mine
A  mine/a
A  mine/b
Checked out revision 2.
$ ls
mine
```

If you interrupt a checkout (or something else interrupts your checkout, such as loss of connectivity, etc.), you can restart it either by issuing the identical checkout command again or by updating the incomplete working copy:

```
$ svn checkout file:///tmp/repos/test test
A  test/a
A  test/b
^C
svn: The operation was interrupted
svn: caught SIGINT

$ svn checkout file:///tmp/repos/test test
A  test/c
A  test/d
^C
svn: The operation was interrupted
svn: caught SIGINT

$ cd test
$ svn update
A  test/e
A  test/f
Updated to revision 3.
```

---

cleanup

```
svn cleanup [path ...]
```

Recursively clean up the working copy, removing locks and resuming unfinished operations. If you ever get a working-copy-locked error, run this command to remove stale locks and get your working copy into a usable state again.

If, for some reason, an **svn update** fails due to a problem running an external **diff** program (e.g., user input or network failure), pass the **--diff3-cmd** option to allow cleanup to complete any merging with your external **diff** program. You can also specify any configuration directory with the **--config-dir** option, but you should need these options extremely infrequently.

Alternate names: none

Changes: working copy

Accesses repository: no

Options:

--**diff3-cmd** *cmd*

---

commit

svn commit [*path* ...]

Send changes from your working copy to the repository. If you do not supply a log message with your commit by using either the **--file** or **--message** option, **svn** starts your editor for you to compose a commit message.

 If you begin a commit and Subversion starts your editor to compose the commit message, you can still abort without committing your changes. To cancel your commit, just quit your editor without saving your commit message and Subversion prompts you to abort the commit, continue with no message, or edit the message again.

Alternate names: **ci** (short for check in—not **co**, which is short for checkout)

Changes: working copy, repository

Accesses repository: yes

Options

--changelist *name*, -cl *name*
--depth *arg*
--editor-cmd *cmd*
--encoding *enc*
--file *file*, -F *file*
--force-log
--keep-changelists
--message *text*, -m *text*
--no-unlock
--quiet (-q)
--targets *filename*
--with-revprop *property*

Examples

Commit a simple modification to a file with the commit message on the command line and an implicit target of your current directory (.):

```
$ svn commit -m "added howto section."
Sending        a
Transmitting file data.
Committed revision 3.
```

To commit a file scheduled for deletion:

```
$ svn commit -m "removed file 'c'."
Deleting       c
Committed revision 7.
```

copy

svn copy *src dst*

Copy a file in a working copy or in the repository. *src* and *dst* can each be either a working-copy (WC) path or a URL:

WC→WC
> Copy and schedule an item for addition (with history).

WC→URL
> Immediately commit a copy of WC to URL.

URL→WC
> Check out URL into WC, and schedule it for addition.

URL→URL
> Complete server-side copy. This is usually used to branch and tag.

 You can only copy files within a single repository. Subversion does not support cross-repository copying.

Alternate names: **cp**

Changes: repository if destination is a URL; working copy if destination is a WC path

Accesses repository: if source or destination is in the repository, or if needed to look **up** the source revision number

Options

> --**editor-cmd** *editor*
> --**encoding** *enc*
> --**file** *file*, **-F** *file*
> --**force-log**
> --**message** *text*, **-m** *text*
> --**parents**
> --**quiet** (**-q**)
> --**revision** *rev*, **-r** *rev*
> --**with-revprop** *property*

Examples

Copy an item within your working copy (just schedules the copy; nothing goes into the repository until you commit):

```
$ svn copy foo.txt bar.txt
A         bar.txt
$ svn status
A  +  bar.txt
```

Copy an item from the repository to your working copy (just schedules the copy; nothing goes into the repository until you commit):

```
$ svn copy file:///tmp/repos/test/far-away near-here
A         near-here
```

 This is the recommended way to resurrect a dead file in your repository!

And finally, copying between two URLs:

```
$ svn copy file:///tmp/repos/test/far-away \
> file:///tmp/repos/test/over-there -m "remote copy."
Committed revision 9.
```

 This is the easiest way to tag a revision in your repository; just **svn copy** that revision (usually **HEAD**) into your tags directory.

```
$ svn copy file:///tmp/repos/test/trunk \
>           file:///tmp/repos/test/tags/0.6.32-prerelease \
>           -m "tag tree"
Committed revision 12.
```

delete

```
svn delete path ...
svn delete URL ...
```

Items specified by *path* are scheduled for deletion upon the next commit. Files (and directories that have not been committed) are *immediately* removed from the working copy. The command will not remove any unversioned or modified items; use the **--force** option to override this behavior.

Items specified by URL are deleted from the repository via an immediate commit. Multiple URLs are committed atomically.

Alternate names: **del, remove, rm**

Changes: working copy if operating on files; repository if operating on URLs

Accesses repository: only if operating on URLs

Options

--editor-cmd *editor*
--encoding *enc*
--file *file*, -F *file*
--force
--force-log
--keep-local
--message *text*, -m *text*
--quiet (-q)
--targets *filename*
--with-revprop *property*

diff

```
svn diff [-r N[:M]] [--old old-tgt] [--new new-tgt] [path ...]
svn diff -r N:M URL
svn diff [-r N[:M]] URL1[@N] URL2[@M]
```

Display the differences between two paths. The three different ways you can use **svn diff** are:

svn diff [-r N[:M]] [**--old** old-tgt] [**--new** new-tgt] [path ...]
> Display the differences between old-tgt and new-tgt. If paths are given, they are treated as relative to old-tgt and new-tgt, and the output is restricted to differences in only those paths. old-tgt and new-tgt may be working copy paths or URL[@rev]. old-tgt defaults to the current working directory, and new-tgt defaults to old-tgt. N defaults to **BASE** or, if old-tgt is a URL, to **HEAD**. M defaults to the current working version or, if new-tgt is a URL, to **HEAD**. **svn diff -r** N sets the revision of old-tgt to N, whereas **svn diff -r** N:M also sets the revision of new-tgt to M.

svn diff -r N:M URL
> A shorthand for **svn diff -r** N:M --old=URL --new=URL.

svn diff [-r N[:M]] URL1[@N] URL2[@M]
> A shorthand for **svn diff [-r** N[:M]] --old=URL1 --new=URL2.

If target is a URL, then revisions N and M can be given either via the **--revision** option or by using @ notation as described earlier.

If target is a working copy path, then the **--revision** option means:

--revision N:M
> The server compares target@N and target@M.

--revision N
> The client compares target@N against the working copy.

No **--revision** option
> The client compares the base and working copies of target.

If the alternate syntax is used, the server compares URL1 and URL2 at revisions N and M respectively. If either N or M are omitted, a value of **HEAD** is assumed.

By default, **svn diff** ignores the ancestry of files and merely compares the contents of the two files being compared. If you use **--notice-ancestry**, the ancestry of the paths in question is taken into consideration when comparing revisions. (That is, if you run **svn diff** on two files with identical contents but different ancestry you will see the entire contents of the file as having been removed and added again.)

Alternate names: **di**

Changes: nothing

Accesses repository: for obtaining differences against anything but the **BASE** revision in your working copy.

Options

--**change** *args*, **-c** *args*
--**changelist** *name*, **-cl** *name*
--**depth** *arg*
--**diff-cmd** *cmd*
--**extensions** *args*, **-x** *args*
--**force**
--**new** *new-target*
--**no-diff-deleted**
--**notice-ancestry**
--**old** *old-target*
--**revision** *rev*, **-r** *rev*
--**summarize**
--**xml**

Examples

Compare **BASE** and your working copy:

```
$ svn diff COMMITTERS
Index: COMMITTERS
===================================================
==================
--- COMMITTERS   (revision 4404)
+++ COMMITTERS   (working copy)
...
```

See how your working copy's modifications compare against an older revision:

```
$ svn diff -r 3900 COMMITTERS
Index: COMMITTERS
===================================================
==================
--- COMMITTERS   (revision 3900)
+++ COMMITTERS   (working copy)
...
```

Use --**diff-cmd** *cmd* and **-x** to pass arguments directly to the external **diff** program:

```
$ svn diff --diff-cmd /usr/bin/diff -x "-i -b" COMMITTERS
Index: COMMITTERS
===================================================
==================
0a1,2
> This is a test
>
```

---

export

```
svn export [-r rev] URL [path]
svn export path1 path2
```

The first form exports a clean directory tree into *path* from the repository specified by URL, at revision *rev* if it is given—otherwise at **HEAD**. If *path* is omitted, the last component of the URL is used for the local directory name.

The second form exports a clean directory tree from the working copy specified by *path1* into *path2*. All local changes are preserved, but files not under version control are not copied.

This command will also take the unique --**native-eol** option.

Alternate names: none

Changes: local disk

Accesses repository: only if exporting from a URL

Options

    --**depth** *arg*
    --**force**
    --**ignore-externals**
    --**native-eol** *format*
    --**quiet (-q)**
    --**revision** *rev*, -**r** *rev*

---

help

`svn help [`*subcommand* `...]`

Provide a quick usage summary. With *subcommand*, provide information about the given subcommand.

Alternate names: **?**, **h**

Changes: nothing

Accesses repository: no

---

import

`svn import [`*path*`] URL`

Recursively commit a copy of *path* to *URL*. If *path* is omitted, . is assumed. Parent directories are created in the repository as necessary.

Alternate names: none

Changes: repository

Accesses repository: yes

Options

    --**auto-props**
    --**depth** *arg*
    --**editor-cmd** *editor*
    --**encoding** *enc*
    --**file** *file*, -**F** *file*
    --**force**
    --**force-log**
    --**message** *text*, -**m** *text*
    --**no-auto-props**
    --**no-ignore**

Examples

Import the local directory *myproj* into the root of your repository:

```
$ svn import -m "New import" myproj \
> http://svn.red-bean.com/repos/test
```

```
Adding          myproj/sample.txt
...
Transmitting file data ........
Committed revision 16.
```

Import the local directory *myproj* into *trunk/vendors* in your repository. The directory *trunk/vendors* need not exist before you import into it; **svn import** will recursively create directories for you:

```
$ svn import -m "New import" myproj \
> http://svn.red-bean.com/repos/test/trunk/vendors/myproj
Adding          myproj/sample.txt
...
Transmitting file data ........
Committed revision 16.
```

After importing data, note that the original tree is *not* under version control. To start working, you still need to **svn checkout** a fresh working copy of the tree.

---

info

```
svn info [path ...]
svn info URL
```

Print information about paths in your working copy or specified URLs, including:

- Path
- Name
- URL
- Repository root
- Repostiory UUID
- Revision
- Node kind
- Last changed author
- Last changed revision
- Last changed date
- Last token
- Lock owner
- Lock created (date)
- Lock expires (date)
- Schedule
- Copied from URL
- Copied from rev
- Text last updated
- Properties last updated
- Checksum

Alternate names: none

Changes: nothing

Accesses repository: no

Options

--**changelist** *name*, -**cl** *name*
--**depth** *arg*
--**incremental**
--**revision** *rev*, -**r** *rev*
--**targets** *filename*
--**xml**

---

list

svn list [*target* ...]

List each *target* file and the contents of each *target* directory as they exist in the repository. If *target* is a working copy path, the corresponding repository URL is used. The default *target* is ., meaning the repository URL of the current working-copy directory.

With --**verbose**, the following fields show the status of the item:

- Revision number of the last commit
- Author of the last commit
- Size (in bytes)
- Date and time of the last commit

Alternate names: **ls**

Changes: nothing

Accesses repository: yes

Options

--**depth** *arg*
--**incremental**
--**revision** *rev*, -**r** *rev*
--**verbose** (-**v**)
--**xml**

Examples

To see what files a repository has without downloading a working copy:

```
$ svn list http://svn.red-bean.com/repos/test/support
README.txt
INSTALL
examples/
...
```

Pass the --**verbose** option for additional information:

```
$ svn list --verbose file:///tmp/repos
      16 sally          28361 Jan 16 23:18 README.txt
      27 sally              0 Jan 18 15:27 INSTALL
      24 harry                Jan 18 11:27 examples/
```

lock

```
svn lock path ...
svn lock URL
```

Set a lock token on a specified file to prevent other users or even the same user on another system from updating the file. Only the system with the lock token may commit changes. Locks are useful when working on binary files that cannot be merged. By default, Subversion's locks are not strict, however. Locks can be broken or taken over by other users by using the **--force** option.

Alternate names: none

Changes: working copy; repository

Accesses repository: yes

Options

--**encoding** *enc*
--**file** *file*, **-F** *file*
--**force**
--**force-log**
--**message** *text*, **-m** *text*
--**targets** *filename*

log

```
svn log [path]
svn log URL [path ...]
```

The default target is the path of your current directory. If no arguments are supplied, **svn log** shows the log messages for all files and directories inside of (and including) the current working directory of your working copy. You can refine the results by specifying a path, one or more revisions, or any combination of the two. The default revision range for a local path is **BASE:1**.

If you specify a URL alone, the command prints log messages for everything that the URL contains. If you add paths past the URL, only messages for those paths under that URL are printed. The default revision range for a URL is **HEAD:1**.

With **--verbose**, **svn log** also prints all affected paths with each log message. With **--quiet**, **svn log** does not print the log message body itself (this is compatible with **--verbose**).

Each log message is printed just once, even if more than one of the affected paths for that revision were explicitly requested. Logs follow copy history by default. Use **--stop-on-copy** to disable this behavior, which can be useful for determining branch points.

Alternate names: none

Changes: nothing

Accesses repository: yes

Options

--change *arg*, -c *arg*
--incremental
--limit *num*, -l *num*
--quiet (-q)
--revision *rev*, -r *rev*
--stop-on-copy
--targets *filename*
--use-merge-history, -g
--verbose (-v)
--with-all-revprops
--with-revprop *property*
--xml

Examples

To see the log messages for all the paths that changed in your working copy, run **svn log** from the top:

```
$ svn log
------------------------------------------------------------
--------------
r20 | harry | 2003-01-17 22:56:19 -0600 (Fri, 17 Jan 2003)
| 1 line

Tweak.
------------------------------------------------------------
--------------
r17 | sally | 2003-01-16 23:21:19 -0600 (Thu, 16 Jan 2003)
| 2 lines
...
```

If you don't have a working copy handy, you can log a URL:

```
$ svn log http://svn.red-bean.com/repos/test/foo.c
------------------------------------------------------------
--------------
r32 | sally | 2003-01-13 00:43:13 -0600 (Mon, 13 Jan 2003)
| 1 line

Added defines.
------------------------------------------------------------
--------------
r28 | sally | 2003-01-07 21:48:33 -0600 (Tue, 07 Jan 2003)
| 3 lines
...
```

If you run **svn log** on a specific path and provide a specific revision and get no output at all:

```
$ svn log -r 20 http://svn.red-bean.com/untouched.txt
------------------------------------------------------------
--------------
```

That just means that the path was not modified in that revision. If you log from the top of the repository, or know the file that changed in that revision, you can specify it explicitly:

```
$ svn log -r 20 touched.txt
------------------------------------------------------------
--------------
r20 | sally | 2003-01-17 22:56:19 -0600 (Fri, 17 Jan 2003)
| 1 line

Made a change.
------------------------------------------------------------
--------------
```

merge

```
svn merge sourceURL1[@N] sourceURL2[@M] [wcpath]
svn merge sourceWCPATH1@N sourceWCPATH2@M [wcpath]
svn merge -r N:M source [path]
```

In the first form, the source URLs are specified at revisions *N* and *M*. These are the two sources to be compared. The revisions default to **HEAD** if omitted.

In the second form, the URLs corresponding to the source working copy paths define the sources to be compared. The revisions must be specified.

In the third form, *source* can be a URL or working-copy item, in which case the corresponding URL is used. This URL, at revisions *N* and *M*, defines the two sources to be compared.

wcpath is the working-copy path that will receive the changes. If *wcpath* is omitted, a default value of "." is assumed, unless the sources have identical basenames that match a file within ".", in which case, the differences are applied to that file.

Unlike **svn diff**, this command takes the ancestry of a file into consideration when performing a merge operation. This is very important when you're merging changes from one branch into another and you've renamed a file on one branch but not the other.

Alternate names: none

Changes: working copy

Accesses repository: only if working with URLs

Options

    --accept *arg*
    --change *arg*, -c *arg*
    --depth *arg*
    --diff3-cmd *cmd*
    --dry-run
    --extensions *args*, -x *args*
    --force
    --ignore-ancestry
    --quiet (-q)
    --record-only
    --reintegrate
    --revision *rev*, -r *rev*

Examples

Merge a branch back into the trunk (assuming that you have a working copy of the trunk and that the branch was created in revision 250):

```
$ svn merge -r 250:HEAD \
> http://svn.red-bean.com/repos/branches/my-branch
U  myproj/tiny.txt
U  myproj/thhgttg.txt
U  myproj/win.txt
U  myproj/flo.txt
```

If you branched at revision 23, and you want to merge changes from the trunk into your branch, you could do this from inside the working copy of your branch:

```
$ svn merge -r 23:30 file:///tmp/repos/trunk/vendors
U  myproj/thhgttg.txt
...
```

To merge changes to a single file:

```
$ cd myproj
$ svn merge -r 30:31 thhgttg.txt
U  thhgttg.txt
```

---

mergeinfo   svn mergeinfo *sourceURL*[@*rev*] [*target* ...]

Query information about merges or potential merges between *sourceURL* and *target*. By default it shows merged information. The option *--show-revs* can be used to get information about eligible merges.

Alternate names: none

Changes: nothing

Accesses repository: yes

Options

> **--revision** *rev*, **-r** *rev*
> **--show-revs** *arg*

Examples

Find out which changesets your trunk directory has already received as well as what changesets it's still eligible to receive:

```
$ svn mergeinfo branches/test
Path: branches/test
  Source path: /trunk
    Merged ranges: r2:13
    Eligible ranges: r13:15
```

---

mkdir   svn mkdir *path* ...
             svn mkdir *URL* ...

Create a directory with a name given by the final component of the *path* or URL. A directory specified by a working copy *path* is scheduled for addition in the working copy. A directory specified by a

---

URL is created in the repository via an immediate commit. Multiple directory URLs are committed atomically. In both cases, all the intermediate directories must already exist.

Alternate names: none

Changes: working copy; repository if operating on a URL

Accesses repository: only if operating on a URL

Options

--editor-cmd *editor*
--encoding *enc*
--file *file*, -F *file*
--force-log
--message *text*, -m *text*
--parents
--quiet (-q)
--with-revprop *property*

move

svn move *src dst*

This command moves (renames) a file or directory in your working copy or in the repository.

This command is equivalent to an **svn copy** followed by **svn delete**.

WC→WC
   Move and schedule a file or directory for addition (with history).

URL→URL
   Complete server-side rename.

Subversion does not support moving between working copies and URLs. In addition, you can move files only within a single repository; Subversion does not support cross-repository moving.

Alternate names: **mv**, **rename**, **ren**

Changes: working copy; repository if operating on a URL

Accesses repository: only if operating on a URL

Options

--editor-cmd *editor*
--encoding *enc*
--file *file*, -F *file*
--force
--force-log
--message *text*, -m *text*
--revision *rev*, -r *rev*
--revprop
--with-revprop *property*

propdel

```
svn propdel propname [path ...]
svn propdel propname --revprop -r rev [URL]
```

This removes properties from files, directories, or revisions. The first form removes versioned properties in your working copy, while the second removes unversioned remote properties on a repository revision.

Alternate names: **pdel, pd**

Changes: working copy; repository only if operating on a URL

Accesses repository: only if operating on a URL

Options

--**changelist** *name*, -**cl** *name*
--**depth** *arg*
--**quiet** (-**q**)
--**revision** *rev*, -**r** *rev*
--**revprop**

Examples

Delete a property from a file in your working copy:

```
$ svn propdel svn:mime-type some-script
property 'svn:mime-type' deleted from 'some-script'.
```

Delete a revision property:

```
$ svn propdel --revprop -r 26 release-date
property 'release-date' deleted from repository revision
'26'
```

---

propedit

```
svn propedit propname path ...
svn propedit propname --revprop -r rev [URL]
```

Edit one or more properties using your favorite editor. The first form edits versioned properties in your working copy, while the second edits unversioned remote properties on a repository revision.

Alternate names: **pedit, pe**

Changes: working copy; repository only if operating on a URL

Accesses repository: only if operating on a URL

Options

--**editor-cmd** *editor*
--**encoding** *enc*
--**force**
--**force-log**
--**password** *pass*
--**revision** *rev*, -**r** *rev*
--**revprop**
--**with-revprop** *property*

propget

```
svn propget propname [path ...]
svn propget propname --revprop -r rev [URL]
```

Print the value of a property on files, directories, or revisions. The first form prints the versioned property of an item or items in your working copy, while the second prints the unversioned remote property on a repository revision.

Alternate names: **pget, pg**

Changes: working copy; repository only if operating on a URL

Accesses repository: only if operating on a URL

Options

--**changelist** *name*, **-cl** *name*
--**depth** *arg*
--**revision** *rev*, **-r** *rev*
--**revprop**
--**strict**
--**xml**

---

proplist

```
svn proplist [path ...]
svn proplist --revprop -r rev [URL]
```

List all properties on files, directories, or revisions. The first form lists versioned properties in your working copy, while the second lists unversioned remote properties on a repository revision.

Alternate names: **plist, pl**

Changes: working copy; repository only if operating on a URL

Accesses repository: only if operating on a URL

Options

--**changelist** *name*, **-cl** *name*
--**depth** *arg*
--**quiet** (-q)
--**revision** *rev*, **-r** *rev*
--**revprop**
--**verbose** (-v)
--**xml**

Examples

You can use **svn proplist** to see the properties on an item in your working copy:

```
$ svn proplist foo.c
Properties on 'foo.c':
  svn:mime-type
  svn:keywords
  owner
```

But with the **--verbose** flag, **svn proplist** is extremely handy, as it also shows you the values for the properties:

```
$ svn proplist --verbose foo.c
Properties on 'foo.c':
  svn:mime-type : text/plain
  svn:keywords : Author Date Rev
  owner : sally
```

propset

```
svn propset propname [propval] path ...
svn propset propname --revprop -r rev [propval] [URL]
```

Set *propname* to *propval* on files, directories, or revisions. The first example creates a versioned, local property change in the working copy, and the second creates an unversioned, remote property change on a repository revision. The new property value, *propval*, may be provided literally, or using the **-F** *valfile* option.

Alternate names: **pset, ps**

Changes: working copy; repository only if operating on a URL

Accesses repository: only if operating on a URL

Options

    --changelist *name*, **-cl** *name*
    --depth *arg*
    --encoding *enc*
    --file *file*, **-F** *file*
    --force
    --quiet (**-q**)
    --revision *rev*, **-r** *rev*
    --revprop
    --targets *filename*

Examples

Set the mimetype on a file:

```
$ svn propset svn:mime-type image/jpeg foo.jpg
property 'svn:mime-type' set on 'foo.jpg'
```

On a Unix system, if you want a file to have the executable permission set:

```
$ svn propset svn:executable ON somescript
property 'svn:executable' set on 'somescript'
```

By default, you cannot modify revision properties in a Subversion repository. Your repository administrator must explicitly enable revision property modifications by creating a hook named **pre-revprop-change**.

resolve

`svn resolve` *path* ...

Remove the conflicted state on working-copy files or directories. This command does not semantically resolve conflict markers; instead it replaces *path* and then removes conflict-related artifact files. Use the **--accept** argument to specify what version to use when replacing *path*. This command allows *path* to be committed again by telling Subversion that the conflicts have been resolved. Use it after you have resolved the conflict in the file. You can pass the following arguments to the **--accept** option:

Alternate names: none

Changes: working copy

Accesses repository: no

Options

> **--accept** *arg*
> **--depth** *arg*
> **--quiet** (**-q**)
> **--recursive, -R**
> **--targets** *filename*

Example

If you get a conflict on an update, your working copy will contain three additional files:

```
$ svn update
Conflict discovered in 'foo.c'.
Select: (p) postpone, (df) diff-full, (e) edit,
        (h) help for more options: p
C    foo.c
Updated to revision 31
$ svn resolve --accept mine-full foo.c
Resolved conflicted state of 'foo.c'
```

You *can* just remove the conflict files and commit, but **svn resolve** fixes up some bookkeeping data in the working-copy administrative area in addition to removing the conflict files, so you should use this command.

---

resolved

`svn resolved` *path* ...

Deprecated. Remove the conflicted state on working-copy files or directories. Symantically it is the same as '**svn resolve --accept working** *path*', which you should now use instead.

Alternate names: none

Changes: working copy

Accesses repository: no

Options

--**depth** *arg*
--**quiet** (-**q**)
--**recursive** (-**R**)
--**targets** *filename*

---

revert

svn revert *path* ...

Revert any local changes to a file or directory, and resolve any conflicted states. **svn revert** reverts not only the contents of an item in your working copy, but also any property changes. Finally, you can use it to undo any scheduling operations that you may have done (e.g., files scheduled for addition or deletion can be unscheduled).

Alternate names: none

Changes: working copy

Accesses repository: no

Options

--**changelist** *name*, -**cl** *name*
--**depth** *arg*
--**quiet** (-**q**)
--**recursive** (-**R**)
--**targets** *filename*

Examples

Discard changes to a file:

```
$ svn revert foo.c
Reverted foo.c
```

If you want to revert a whole directory of files, use the --**depth**=**infinity** flag:

```
$ svn revert --depth=infinity .
Reverted newdir/afile
Reverted foo.c
Reverted bar.txt
```

 If you provide no targets to **svn revert**, it does nothing; to protect you from accidentally losing changes in your working copy, **svn revert** requires you to provide at least one target.

---

status

svn status [*path* ...]

Print the status of working-copy files and directories. With no arguments, it prints only locally modified items (no repository access). With --**show-updates**, add working revision and server out-of-date information. With --**verbose**, print full revision information on every item.

The first five columns in the output are each one character wide, and each column gives you information about different aspects of each working-copy item.

The first column indicates that an item was added, deleted, or otherwise changed:

space
> No modifications.

A   Item is scheduled for addition.

D   Item is scheduled for deletion.

M   Item has been modified.

R   Item has been replaced in your working copy. This means the file was scheduled for deletion, and then a new file with the same name was scheduled for addition in its place.

C   The contents of the item conflicts with updates received from the repository.

X   Item is related to an externals definition.

I   Item is being ignored (e.g., with the **svn:ignore** property).

?   Item is not under version control.

!   Item is missing (e.g., you moved or deleted it without using **svn**). This also indicates that a directory is incomplete (a checkout or update was interrupted).

~   Item is versioned as a directory but has been replaced by a file, or vice versa.

The second column tells the status of a file's or directory's properties:

space
> No modifications.

M   Properties for this item have been modified.

C   Properties for this item are in conflict with property updates received from the repository.

The third column is populated only if the working copy directory is locked:

space
> Item is not locked.

L   Item is locked.

The fourth column is populated only if the item is scheduled for addition-with-history:

space
> No history scheduled with commit.

+   History scheduled with commit.

The fifth column is populated only if the item is switched relative to its parent:

space
> Item is a child of its parent directory.

S   Item is switched.

The sixth column is populated with lock information:

space
> When **--show-updates** is used, the file is not locked. Otherwise, it merely means that the file is not locked in this working copy.

K
> File is locked in this working copy.

O
> File is locked by another user or in another working copy. This will only appear when **--show-updates** is used.

T
> File is locked in this working copy, but the lock has been stolen and is invalid. The file is locked in the repository. This will only appear when **--show-updates** is used.

B
> File is locked in this working copy, but the lock has been broken and is invalid. The file is no longer locked. This will only appear when **--show-updates** is used.

If you pass the **--show-updates** option, then out-of-date information appears in the seventh column:

space
> The item in your working copy is up to date.

*
> A newer revision of the item exists on the server.

The remaining fields are variable width and delimited by spaces. The working revision is the next field if the **--show-updates** or **--verbose** options are passed.

If the **--verbose** option is passed, the last committed revision and last committed author are displayed next.

The working-copy path is always the final field, so it can include spaces.

Alternate names: **stat, st**

Changes: nothing

Accesses repository: only if using **--show-updates**

Options

> --changelist *name*, -cl *name*
> --depth *arg*
> --ignore-externals
> --incremental
> --no-ignore
> --non-recursive (-N)
> --quiet (-q)
> --show-updates (-u)
> --no-ignore
> --xml

Examples

To find out what changes you have made to your working copy:

```
$ svn status wc
 M      wc/bar.c
A  +    wc/qax.c
```

To find out what files in your working copy are out of date, pass the **--show-updates** option (this does *not* make any changes to your working copy). Here you can see that *wc/foo.c* has changed in the repository since we last updated our working copy:

```
$ svn status --show-updates wc
M            965    wc/bar.c
      *      965    wc/foo.c
A  +         965    wc/qax.c
Status against revision:   981
```

 --show-updates places an asterisk *only* next to items that are out of date (that is, items that will be updated from the repository if you run **svn update**). **--show-updates** does *not* cause the status listing to reflect the repository's version of the item.

And finally, the most information you can get out of the status subcommand:

```
$ svn status --show-updates --verbose wc
M            965        938 sally      wc/bar.c
      *      965        922 harry      wc/foo.c
A  +         965        687 harry      wc/qax.c
             965        687 harry      wc/zig.c
Head revision:    981
```

switch

svn switch URL [*path*]

This subcommand updates your working copy to mirror a new URL—usually a URL that shares a common ancestor with your working copy, although not necessarily. This is the Subversion way to move a working copy to a new branch.

As with most subcommands, you can limit the scope of the switch operation to a particular tree depth using the **--depth** option. Alternatively, you can use the **--set-depth** option to set a new "sticky" working copy depth on the switch target. Currently, the depth of a working copy directory can only be increased (telescoped more deeply); you cannot make a directory more shallow.

Alternate names: **sw**

Changes: working copy

Accesses repository: yes

Options

--accept *arg*
--depth *arg*
--diff3-cmd *cmd*
--force
--ignore-externals
--quiet (-q)
--relocate
--revision *rev*, -r *rev*
--set-depth *arg*

Examples

If you're currently inside the directory *vendors*, which was branched to *vendors-with-fix*, and you'd like to switch your working copy to that branch:

```
$ svn switch http://svn.red-bean.com/repos/branches/ \
> vendors-with-fix .
U  myproj/foo.txt
U  myproj/bar.txt
U  myproj/baz.c
U  myproj/qux.c
Updated to revision 31.
```

And to switch back, just provide the URL to the location in the repository from which you originally checked out your working copy:

```
$ svn switch http://svn.red-bean.com/repos/trunk/vendors .
U  myproj/foo.txt
U  myproj/bar.txt
U  myproj/baz.c
U  myproj/qux.c
Updated to revision 31.
```

 You can just switch part of your working copy to a branch if you don't want to switch your entire working copy.

Sometimes an administrator might change the "base location" of your repository; in other words, the contents of the repository don't change, but the main URL used to reach the root of the repository does. For example, the hostname may change, or the URL schema, or perhaps just the path that leads to the repository. Rather than checking out a new working copy, you can have the **svn switch** command "rewrite" the beginnings of all the URLs in your working copy. Use the **--relocate** command to do the substitution. No file contents are changed, nor is the repository contacted. It's similar to running a **sed** script over your working copy *.svn/* directories, which runs **s/*OldRoot*/*NewRoot*/**:

```
$ cd /tmp
$ svn checkout file:///tmp/repos test
A  test/a
A  test/b
...

$ mv repos newlocation
$ cd test/

$ svn update
svn: Unable to open an ra_local session to URL
svn: Unable to open repository 'file:///tmp/repos'
```

```
$ svn switch --relocate file:///tmp/repos file:///tmp/
newlocation .
$ svn update
At revision 3.
```

unlock

svn unlock *path* ...
svn unlock *URL*

Remove the lock token from the specified files. This command will print a warning if the target is locked by another user or no lock token exists, but will continue to unlock files it can unlock. Use the **--force** option to break a lock belonging to another user or working copy.

Alternate names: none

Changes: working copy; repository

Accesses repository: yes

Options

--**force**
--**targets** *filename*

update

svn update [*PATH* ...]

svn update brings changes from the repository into your working copy. If no revision is given, it brings your working copy up to date with the **HEAD** revision. Otherwise, it synchronizes the working copy to the revision given by the **--revision** option.

For each updated item Subversion prints a line starting with a specific character reporting the action taken. These characters have the following meaning:

A   Added

B   Broken lock (third column only)

D   Deleted

U   Updated

C   Conflicted

G   Merged

E   Existed

A character in the first column signifies an update to the actual file, while updates to the file's properties are shown in the second column. Lock information is printed in the third column.

If you want to examine an older revision of a single file, you may want to use **svn cat**.

Alternate names: **up**

Changes: working copy

Accesses repository: yes

Options

--accept *arg*
--changelist *name*, -cl *name*
--depth *arg*
--diff3-cmd *cmd*
--editor-cmd *editor*
--force
--ignore-externals
--quiet (-q)
--revision *rev*, -r *rev*
--set-depth *arg*

Repository Administration: svnadmin

svnadmin is the administrative tool for monitoring and repairing your Subversion repository.

Common svnadmin Options

--bdb-log-keep
: (Berkeley DB specific) Disable automatic log removal of database logfiles.

--bdb-txn-nosync
: (Berkeley DB specific) Disable use of **fsync( )** when committing database transactions.

--bypass-hooks
: Bypass the repository hook system.

--clean-logs
: Remove unused Berkeley DB logs.

--force-uuid
: By default, when loading data into a repository that already contains revisions, **svnadmin** ignores the UUID from the dump stream. This option causes the repository's UUID to be set to the UUID from the stream.

--ignore-uuid
: By default, when loading an empty repository, **svnadmin** uses the UUID from the dump stream. This option causes that UUID to be ignored.

--incremental
: Dump a revision only as a diff against the previous revision, instead of the usual full text.

--parent-dir *dir*
: When loading a dumpfile, root paths at *dir* instead of /.

--quiet
: Do not show normal progress; show only errors.

--revision *rev*, -r *rev*
: Specify a particular revision to operate on.

Common svnadmin Subcommands

The **svnadmin** command creates and administers the repository. As such, it always operates on local paths, not on URLs.

---

create

svnadmin create *repos_path*

Create a new, empty repository at the path provided. If the provided directory does not exist, it is created for you.

Options
> --bdb-log-keep
> --bdb-txn-nosync

Example
Creating a new repository is just this easy:

> $ **svnadmin create /usr/local/svn/repos**

---

deltify

svnadmin deltify [-r*lower*[:*upper*]]*repos_path*

svnadmin deltify only exists in 1.0.x due to historical reasons. This command is deprecated and no longer needed.

It dates from a time when Subversion offered administrators greater control over compression strategies in the repository. This turned out to be a lot of complexity for *very* little gain, and the feature was deprecated.

Options
> --quiet
> --revision *rev*, -r *rev*

---

dump

svnadmin dump *repos_path* [-r *lower*[:*upper*]] [--incremental]

Dump the contents of filesystem to standard output in a dumpfile portable format, sending feedback to standard error. Dump revisions *lower* rev through *upper* rev. If no revisions are given, dump all revision trees. If only *lower* is given, dump that one revision tree.

Options
> --incremental
> --quiet
> --revision *rev*, -r *rev*

Examples
Dump your whole repository:

> $ **svnadmin dump /usr/local/svn/repos**
> SVN-fs-dump-format-version: 1
> Revision-number: 0
> * Dumped revision 0.
> Prop-content-length: 56
> Content-length: 56
> ...

Incrementally dump a single transaction from your repository:

```
$ svnadmin dump /usr/local/svn/repos -r 21 --incremental
* Dumped revision 21.
SVN-fs-dump-format-version: 1
Revision-number: 21
Prop-content-length: 101
Content-length: 101
...
```

help

svnadmin help [*subcommand* ...]

Provide a quick usage summary. With *subcommand*, provide information about the given subcommand.

Alternate names: ?, **h**

hotcopy

svnadmin hotcopy *old_repos_path new_repos_path*

This subcommand makes a full hot backup of your repository, including all hooks, configuration files, and, of course, database files. If you pass the **--clean-logs** option, **svnadmin** performs a hotcopy of your repository, and then removes unused Berkeley DB logs from the original repository. You can run this command at any time and make a safe copy of the repository, regardless of whether other processes are using the repository.

Option

    --clean-logs

list-dblogs

svnadmin list-dblogs *repos_path*

List Berkeley DB logfiles. Berkeley DB creates logs of all changes to the repository, which allow it to recover in the face of catastrophe. Unless you enable DB_LOGS_AUTOREMOVE, the logfiles accumulate, although most are no longer used and can be deleted to reclaim disk space.

list-unused-dblogs

svnadmin list-unused-dblogs *repos_path*

List unused Berkeley DB logfiles (see **svnlook list-dblogs**).

Example

Remove all unused logfiles from a repository:

```
$ svnadmin list-unused-dblogs /path/to/repos | xargs rm
## disk space reclaimed!
```

load

svnadmin load *repos_path*

Read a dumpfile-formatted stream from standard input, committing new revisions into the repository's filesystem. Send progress feedback to standard output.

Options
>   --force-uuid
>   --ignore-uuid
>   --parent-dir
>   --quiet (-q)

Examples

This shows the beginning of loading a repository from a backup file (made, of course, with **svn dump**):

```
$ svnadmin load /usr/local/svn/restored < repos-backup
<<< Started new txn, based on original revision 1
     * adding path : test ... done.
     * adding path : test/a ... done.
...
```

Or, to load into a subdirectory:

```
$ svnadmin load --parent-dir new/subdir/for/project \
>    /usr/local/svn/restored < repos-backup
<<< Started new txn, based on original revision 1
     * adding path : test ... done.
     * adding path : test/a ... done.
...
```

---

lslocks

svnadmin lslocks *repos_path* [*path*]

Print descriptions of all locks in repository *repos_path* underneath *path*. If *path* isn't given it defaults to the root directory of the repository.

---

lstxns

svnadmin lstxns *repos_path*

Print the names of all uncommitted transactions.

---

recover

svnadmin recover *repos_path*

Run this command if you get an error indicating that your repository needs to be recovered. This command requires a database lock. Normally failure to obtain a lock will cause an error. Use the **--wait** option to cause the command to wait indefinitely for a database lock.

Options
>   --wait

---

rmlocks

svnadmin rmlocks *repos_path* *locked_path*...

Unconditionally remove locks from each locked path.

---

rmtxns

svnadmin rmtxns *repos_path* *txn_name* ...

Delete outstanding transactions from a repository.

Options

--quiet (-q)

Examples

Remove all uncommitted transactions from your repository, using **svn lstxns** to provide the list of transactions to remove:

```
$ svnadmin rmtxns /usr/local/svn/repos/ \
>`svnadmin lstxns /usr/local/svn/repos/`
```

---

setlog

svnadmin setlog *repos_path* -r *revision file*

Set the log message on revision *revision* to the contents of *file*.

This is similar to using **svn propset --revprop** to set the **svn:log** property on a revision, except that you can also use the option **--bypass-hooks** to avoid running any pre- or post-commit hooks, which is useful if the modification of revision properties has not been enabled in the pre-revprop-change hook.

 Revision properties are not under version control, so this command permanently overwrites the previous log message.

Options

--bypass-hooks
--revision *rev*, -r *rev*

Example

Set the log message for revision 19 to the contents of the file *msg*:

```
$ svnadmin setlog /usr/local/svn/repos/ -r 19 msg
```

---

setrevprop

svnadmin setrevprop *repos_path* -r *revision name file*

Set the property *name* on revision *revision* to the contents of *file*.

Options

--revision *rev*, -r *rev*

Example

Set the revision property *repository-photo* to the contents of the file *repo.png*:

```
$ svnadmin setrevprop /var/svn/repos/ -r 0 repository-
photo repo.png
```

---

setuuid

svnadmin setuuid *repos_path* [*new_uuid*]

Reset the repository UUID to *new_uuid*. If no new uuid is given generate a new one.

---

verify	`svnadmin verify repos_path`
	Run this command to verify the integrity of your repository. This iterates through all revisions in the repository by internally dumping all revisions and discarding the output.

Examining the Repository: svnlook

svnlook is a command-line utility for examining different aspects of a Subversion repository. It does not make any changes to the repository. **svnlook** is typically used by the repository hooks, but a repository administrator might find it useful for diagnostic purposes.

Since **svnlook** works via direct repository access (and thus can only be used on the machine that holds the repository), it refers to the repository with a path, not a URL.

If no revision or transaction is specified, **svnlook** defaults to the youngest (most recent) revision of the repository.

svnlook Options

Options in **svnlook** are global, just as in **svn** and **svnadmin**; however, most options apply to only one subcommand because the functionality of **svnlook** is (intentionally) limited in scope.

--**copy-info**
: Used with the **changed** command to show detailed copy source information.

--**no-diff-deleted**
: Do not print differences for deleted files. The default behavior when a file is deleted in a transaction/revision is to print the same differences that you would see if you had left the file but removed all the content.

--**no-diff-added**
: Do not print differences for added files. The default behavior is to print the same differences that you would see if you added the entire contents of an existing but empty file.

--**revision** *rev*, -**r** *rev*
: Examine revision number *rev*.

--**revprop**
: Operate on a revision property rather than the property of a file or directory. You must also specify a revision using --**revision** when using this option.

--**show-ids**
: Show the filesystem node revision IDs for each path in the filesystem tree.

--**transaction** *tid*, -**t** *tid*
: Examine transaction ID *tid*.

svnlook Subcommands

author	`svnlook author` *repos_path*

Print the author of a revision or transaction in the repository.

Options

    --revision *rev*, **-r** *rev*
    --transaction *tid*, **-t** *tid*

---

cat	`svnlook cat` *repos_path path_in_repos*

Print the contents of a file.

Options

    --revision *rev*, **-r** *rev*
    --transaction *tid*, **-t** *tid*

---

changed	`svnlook changed` *repos_path*

Print the paths that were changed in a particular revision or transaction, as well as an **svn update**-style status letter in the first column: **A** for added, **D** for deleted, and **U** for updated (modified).

Options

    --copy-info
    --revision *rev*, **-r** *rev*
    --transaction *tid*, **-t** *tid*

Example

Show a list of all the changed files in revision 39 of a test repository:

```
$ svnlook changed -r 39 /usr/local/svn/repos
A   trunk/vendors/deli/
A   trunk/vendors/deli/chips.txt
A   trunk/vendors/deli/sandwich.txt
A   trunk/vendors/deli/pickle.txt
```

---

date	`svnlook date` *repos_path*

Print the datestamp of a revision or transaction in a repository.

Options

    --revision *rev*, **-r** *rev*
    --transaction *tid*, **-t** *tid*

---

diff	`svnlook diff` *repos_path*

Print GNU-style differences of changed files and properties in a repository. If a file has a nontextual **svn:mime-type** property, the differences are explicitly not shown.

Options

> **--no-diff-added**
> **--no-diff-deleted**
> **--revision** *rev*, **-r** *rev*
> **--transaction** *tid*, **-t** *tid*

---

dirs-changed

svnlook dirs-changed *repos_path*

Print the directories that were themselves changed (property edits) or whose file children were changed.

Options

> **--revision** *rev*, **-r** *rev*
> **--transaction** *tid*, **-t** *tid*

---

help

svnlook help [*subcommand*]
svnlook -h [*subcommand*]
svnlook -? [*subcommand*]

Provide a quick usage summary. With *subcommand*, provide information about the given subcommand.

Alternate names: **?**, **h**

---

history

svnlook history *repos_path* [*path_in_repos*]

Print information about the history of a path in the repository (or the root directory if no path is supplied).

Options

> **--limit** *num*, **-l** *num*
> **--revision** *rev*, **-r** *rev*
> **--show-ids**

Example

This shows the history output for the path */tags/1.0*, as of revision 20 in our sample repository.

```
$ svnlook history -r 20 /usr/local/svn/repos /tags/1.0 \
> --show-ids
REVISION   PATH <ID>
--------   ---------
      19   /tags/1.0 <1.2.12>
      17   /branches/1.0-rc2 <1.1.10>
      16   /branches/1.0-rc2 <1.1.x>
      14   /trunk <1.0.q>
     ...
```

---

info

svnlook info *repos_path*

Print the author, datestamp, log message size, and log message.

Options

> **--revision** *rev*, **-r** *rev*
> **--transaction** *tid*, **-t** *tid*

lock

svnlook lock *repos_path path_in_repos*

Print available information about existing lock for **path_in_repos**. If no lock exists, print nothing.

---

log

svnlook log *repos_path*

Print the log message.

Options

--**revision** *rev*, -**r** *rev*
--**transaction** *tid*, -**t** *tid*

---

propget

svnlook propget *repos_path propname path_in_repos*

List the value of a property on a path in the repository.

Alternate names: **pg, pget**

Options

--**revision** *rev*, -**r** *rev*
--**transaction** *tid*, -**t** *tid*

Example

Show the value of the seasonings property on the file */trunk/ sandwich* in the **HEAD** revision:

```
$ svnlook pg /usr/local/svn/repos seasonings /trunk/
sandwich
mustard
```

---

proplist

svnlook proplist *repos_path path_in_repos*

List the properties of a path in the repository. With --**verbose**, show the property values too.

Alternate names: **pl, plist**

Options

--**revision** *rev*, -**r** *rev*
--**revprop**
--**transaction** *tid*, -**t** *tid*
--**verbose** (-**v**)

Examples

Show the names of properties set on the file */trunk/README* in the **HEAD** revision:

```
$ svnlook proplist /usr/local/svn/repos /trunk/README
original-author
svn:mime-type
```

This is the same command as in the previous example, but this time it shows the property values as well:

```
$ svnlook proplist --verbose /usr/local/svn/repos \
> /trunk/README
original-author : fitz
svn:mime-type : text/plain
```

tree   svnlook tree *repos_path* [*path_in_repos*]

Print the tree, starting at *path_in_repos* (if supplied; at the root of
the tree otherwise), optionally showing node revision IDs.

Options

> --full-paths
> --non-recursive, -N
> --revision *rev*, -r *rev*
> --show-ids
> --transaction *tid*, -t *tid*

Example

This shows the tree output (with node IDs) for revision 40 in our
sample repository:

```
$ svnlook tree -r 40 /usr/local/svn/repos --show-ids
/ <0.0.2j>
 trunk/ <p.0.2j>
  vendors/ <q.0.2j>
   deli/ <1g.0.2j>
    egg.txt <1i.e.2j>
    soda.txt <1k.0.2j>
    sandwich.txt <1j.0.2j>
```

uuid   svnlook uuid *repos_path*

Print the UUID for the repository. The UUID is the repository's
Universal Unique IDentifier. The Subversion client uses this identifier to differentiate between one repository and another.

youngest   svnlook youngest *repos_path*

Print the youngest revision number of a repository.

Providing Remote Access: svnserve

svnserve allows access to Subversion repositories using the **svn** network protocol.
You can run **svnserve** either as a standalone server process, or by having another
process—such as **inetd**, **xinetd**, or **sshd**—start it for you.

Once the client has selected a repository by transmitting its URL, **svnserve** reads a
file named *conf/svnserve.conf* in the repository directory to determine repository-
specific settings, such as what authentication database to use and what authorization policies to apply. The details are provided in *Version Control with Subversion*.

svnserve Options

Unlike the previous commands we've described, **svnserve** has no subcommands; **svnserve** is controlled exclusively by options.

--daemon, -d

Run in daemon mode. **svnserve** backgrounds itself, and accepts and serves TCP/IP connections on the **svn** port (3690, by default).

--foreground

When used together with **-d**, this option causes **svnserve** to stay in the foreground. This option is mainly useful for debugging.

--help, -h

Display a usage summary and exit.

--inetd, -i

Use the standard input/standard output file descriptors, as appropriate for a server running out of **inetd**.

--listen-host=*host*

Listen on the interface specified by *host*, which may be either a hostname or an IP address.

--listen-once, -X

Accept one connection on the **svn** port, serve it, and exit. This option is mainly useful for debugging.

--listen-port=*port*

Listen on *port* when run in daemon mode.

--pid-file *filename*

Write process ID to *filename*.

--root=*root*, **-r=***root*

Set the virtual root for repositories served by **svnserve** to *root*. The pathname in URLs provided by the client are interpreted relative to this root and are not allowed to escape this root.

--threads, -T

When running in daemon mode, spawn a thread instead of a process for each connection. The **svnserve** process still backgrounds itself at startup time.

--tunnel, -t

Run in tunnel mode, which is just like the **inetd** mode of operation (serve one connection over standard input/standard output), except that the connection is considered to be pre-authenticated with the username of the current UID. This flag is selected by the client when running over a tunnelling agent such as **ssh**.

--tunnel-user *username*

Used with **–tunnel** to specify an alternate username for pre-authentication.

14

The Git Version Control System

Git is a powerful, open source, distributed version control system (DVCS). It is not considered as user-friendly as Subversion but has many advanced features, including elegant merges of contributions from multiple independent sources and the ability to access the entire project history, even when not connected to a central server.

This chapter covers the following topics:

- Conceptual overview
- Using Git: a quick tour
- The Git command line client: **git**

Version control was introduced in Chapter 12, which contains a comparison of Subversion, Git, and other popular systems. A more thorough discussion on Git can be found in Jon Loeliger's *Version Control with Git* (O'Reilly).

Conceptual Overview

Git was originally created in 2005 by Linus Torvalds as a system for managing changes to the Linux kernel. Although it is used for many of the same tasks as other version control systems like Subversion, Git's internal workings are very different. It's important to understand some of these concepts in order to use Git successfully.

Git maintains a *repository*; a directory structure that tracks the historical contents of a set of files. Generally, the repository is stored in a *.git* directory (or another directory named by **$GIT_DIR**) along with the files themselves.

Unlike other version control systems, Git does not enforce the concept of a "central repository." Instead, every set of files tracked by Git has its own *.git* repository, and revisions can be easily *pushed* and *pulled* from one repository to another.

The set of files currently being tracked by Git is called the *working tree*. The working tree is where most of your daily work takes place. By default, the working tree starts in the parent directory of the *.git* directory. (You can override this by setting **$GIT_WORK_TREE**.) The operation of creating a working tree from a repository is called *checking out* the files, which is done by **git checkout**. After modifying the files in the working tree, you save the changes back to the repository by *committing* them with **git commit** (this is also called *checking in*).

Unlike other systems, Git introduces an extra, intermediate state between the repository and the working tree called the *index*. (You might see the index called the *cache* in a few places, but this terminology is obsolete and should be avoided.) Initially, the index tracks the set of files as they were at checkout time. As you become confident that changes you made to the working tree are correct, you add them to the index using **git add**. Then, when the set of changes forms a coherent batch, you commit the index into the repository (along with a log message) using **git commit**. The main advantage of this two-step process is it's easy to limit a commit to only some of the changes you've been working on, which leads to more coherent individual commits. Git's working style—including the index—encourages many small commits instead of large batches.

Git Repository Format

The set of commits in a Git repository is stored in the form of a *directed acyclic graph*, or *DAG*. This simply means that each commit can reference one or more earlier "parent" commits, and more than one commit can refer to the same parents. The word "acyclic" refers to the fact that the structure is not allowed to contain loops; no parent commit can refer back to a commit that lists it as a parent.

The structure of the DAG defines the repository's *history*. Normally, each commit has exactly one *parent*, which describes the repository exactly as it was before the new commit was made. By comparing a commit to its parent, you can produce a *diff*, which is a precise set of changes that were applied to the parent in order to produce the new version.

Some commits have more than one parent. These commits are called *merge commits* because they express a merging of two separate branches of history. If two people have a copy of a particular repository and start making commits, those two histories will start to diverge, which is called *forking*. Eventually, someone will need to rejoin the two histories into one, which is called *merging*. (As with other version control systems, you can also create additional named *branches* in each repository if you want. For example, you might create a maintenance branch for each major release of your software.)

Referring to Commits

Each commit in Git can be uniquely identified by its *commitid*, a SHA-1 hash code made up of 40 hexadecimal digits. Unlike revisions in centralized systems like Subversion, Git revision numbers cannot be sequential, since there's no central server to assign the sequential IDs. Because it's impossible for a human to remember strings of 40 digits, Git provides several more convenient ways to refer to commits.

Any Git command that can accept a revision can accept any of the following forms:

Full 40-digit hash

You can always simply supply the full 40-digit hash code, such as *da87b5990c03a799ae7a581c2edb1287dba08a43*.

Abbreviated hash

Since the 40 digits of a hash code are effectively random, it's very unlikely (though not impossible) that there will be more than one commit with the same hash. Thus, you can refer to any commit by the first few digits of its name, as long as only one commit starts with those digits. People often choose seven digits as a reasonably safe length. For example, *da87b59*.

Tags

Using the **git tag** command, you can create user-friendly names for individual commits. For example, if you released version v1.1 of your software after making commit *da87b59*, you could run **git tag v1.1 da87b59** so that in the future, you can always refer to a commit named *v1.1*. Tag names can be shared between repositories, but you have to do it explicitly using **git push** and **git pull**.

Local branches

Branches are similar to tags, in that they name a particular commit. However, branches are special because if you check out a branch and make a new commit, the branch advances automatically to point at the new commit.

Unlike with other version control systems, branch names in Git are maintained locally for every copy of a repository. That means if you clone someone else's repository, you take a copy of the branch called *master* (the default Git branch name). They may continue committing to their *master* branch, and you might commit to yours, and then there will exist two branches called *master*, each with different contents. You can resync them using **git push** and **git pull**.

Remote tracking branches

When you clone a central repository, you will frequently want to keep track of the branches as they exist in that respository, even as you make changes to them in your own repository. Git helps do this by naming repositories using the **git remote** command. After that, a particular branch on a particular remote would be named *remotename/branchname*. (Git automatically creates a remote named *origin* to identify the repository you originally cloned from, and the default branch in a repository is usually *master*. So you might have a local branch called *master* corresponding to a remote tracking branch called *origin/master*.)

HEAD

HEAD is a special name that always refers to the currently checked-out commit.

FETCH_HEAD

FETCH_HEAD is a special name that refers to the most recent commit retrieved by **git** fetch.

commit^n notation

For any commit, you can refer to its *n*-th direct parent by giving its name (using any acceptable form of a commit name, such as a branch name, tag, or hash), followed by ^, followed by the parent number you want. Most commits (other than merge commits) have only one parent, so if *n* is omitted, the immediate parent is returned. For example, **da87b59^** is the first parent of *da87b59*; **HEAD^2^1** is the first parent of the second parent of *HEAD*; **origin/master^^^^** is four parents up from *origin/master*, taking the first parent at each step.

commit~n notation

You can refer to a parent *n* steps up the tree using **commit~n** notation. For example, **HEAD~4** is four parents up from *HEAD*, and is equivalent to **HEAD^^^^**. Note that you can combine ~ and ^ notation, so **HEAD^2~4** is four steps up the tree from the second direct parent of *HEAD*.

branch@{n} notation

Because branch names can be retargeted at any time to refer to a different commit, you run the risk of accidentally losing a lot of work if you change or delete a branch name incorrectly. *branch@{n}* notation is designed to fix this; it refers to the commit *branch* referred to *n* commits ago. For example, if you use **git reset** or **git merge** and then change your mind, you can refer to the commit before the most recent change using **HEAD@{1}**.

Unlike ^ and ~ notation, the name here must really be a branch name, not an arbitrary commit, since it makes no sense to refer to the old meaning of a particular commit. However, you can use ^ and ~ on the output of *commit@{n}*, however. For example, **HEAD@{1}^2~4**.

You can see the history of a branch name in a format suitable for use with *commit@{n}*, using **git reflog**.

Using Git: A Quick Tour

Git permits a staggering number of different workflow styles, from "almost centralized" (everyone frequently pushes and pulls to the same central server) to entirely email-based (people exchange patches using a mailing list). It would be impossible to explain all the different Git workflows here, so we'll focus on just one: a simple push/pull workflow with a single shared repository.

Before You Start

Before you start using Git for the first time, you need to set two global configuration values, *user.email* and *user.name*, or else you won't be able to make new commits. Here's how:

```
$ git config --global user.name 'John Smith'
$ git config --global user.email 'jsmith@example.com'
```

These settings will remain in place across all your repositories, so you don't have to reset them every time. You can also override them on a per-repository basis if you want, by running the commands in a particular repository and omitting the **--global** option.

Example: The Linux Kernel Repository

As our first example, let's clone a copy of the Linux kernel into */tmp/linux-2.6*:

```
$ cd /tmp
$ git clone git://git.kernel.org/pub/scm/linux/kernel/git/torvalds/
linux-2.6.git linux-2.6
Initialized empty Git repository in /tmp/linux-2.6/.git/
remote: Counting objects: 1177432, done.
remote: Compressing objects: 100% (189064/189064), done.
remote: Total 1177432 (delta 982454), reused 1176803 (delta 981879)
Receiving objects: 100% (1177432/1177432), 288.00 MiB | 406 KiB/s, done.
Resolving deltas: 100% (982454/982454), done.
Checking out files: 100% (27842/27842), done.
```

Now you have a copy of the entire Linux kernel and its development history, including many different tags and branches. You've started out on branch *master*, which is the latest version. Check out the *v2.6.20* tag to get an older version:

```
$ cd linux-2.6
$ git checkout v2.6.20
Checking out files: 100% (33554/33554), done.
Note: moving to 'v2.6.20' which isn't a local branch
If you want to create a new branch from this checkout, you may do so
(now or later) by using -b with the checkout command again. Example:
  git checkout -b <new_branch_name>
HEAD is now at 62d0cfc... Linux 2.6.20
```

You can't make changes to tags, and you haven't created a local branch for your work, so Git has given you what it calls a *disconnected HEAD*. You can make commits, but they won't be attached to any branch at all. That's a bit dangerous, since it's easy to lose track of your work that way. Let's name our work so it doesn't get lost:

```
$ git checkout -b my-test-branch
Switched to a new branch "my-test-branch"
```

And look at the list of local branches:

```
$ git branch
  master
* my-test-branch
```

You can make a test commit:

```
$ echo 'hello world' >hello.txt
$ git add hello.txt
$ git commit -m 'my first hello commit'
Created commit 22b0a19: my first hello commit
 1 files changed, 1 insertions(+), 0 deletions(-)
 create mode 100644 hello.txt
```

Remember, this new commit hasn't been shared with anyone; you've only committed it to your local repository.

Try pulling in the changes from *v2.6.20* to *v2.6.21*:

```
$ git pull origin v2.6.21
Merge made by recursive.
...
$ ls hello.txt
hello.txt
```

All the changes from *v2.6.21* have been merged into your branch, but your new *hello.txt* is still there too. Success! If you had permission to push your new branch back to the central kernel repository, which you probably don't, you could do it now:

```
$ git push origin my-test-branch
Counting objects: 228, done.
Delta compression using 2 threads.
Compressing objects: 100% (165/165), done.
Writing objects: 100% (228/228), 38.66 KiB, done.
Total 228 (delta 142), reused 77 (delta 60)
To git://git.kernel.org/pub/scm/linux/kernel/git/torvalds/linux-2.6.git
linux-2.6
 * [new branch]      my-test-branch -> my-test-branch
```

Someone could then pull your branch into theirs and receive your *hello.txt* changes.

Creating and Sharing a New Repository

If you have a project that isn't already in Git, you will need to first create a local repository for it. Let's say you have a directory called *my-project* in which you already have a set of files. You want to keep it under version control. Here's what you do:

```
$ cd my-project
$ git init
Initialized empty Git repository in .git/
$ git add .
$ git commit -m 'Initial commit'
```

(The **git add** command above won't work unless there is at least one file to add, and **git commit** won't work until you've **git add**ed at least one file.)

For personal projects, that might be all you need; you can now create commits, branches, and tags, compare differences, and so on.

If you want to share your project with someone else, however, you will need to create a bare repository (i.e., one with no work tree of its own) and give other people access to it. In this example, we'll create a new bare repository in */home/ git/my-project.git*, copied from */tmp/my-project*, and give access to everyone in the mygroup Unix group:

```
$ git clone --bare /tmp/my-project /home/git/my-project.git
Initialized empty Git repository in .git/
$ cd /home/git/my-project.git
$ git config core.sharedRepository group
$ chgrp -R mygroup .
$ chmod -R g+rwX .
```

By convention, bare repositories have pathnames that end in a *.git* suffix. This is because they don't contain a *.git* subdirectory—the *.git* subdirectory contents are in the root of the bare repository, since there's no work tree.

People in *mygroup* can now **git clone /home/git/my-project.git** and push and pull from it.

If you want to host an open source project that everyone on the Internet can share, you have several options:

git daemon
> You can run the Git daemon on your server. The **git daemon** command is beyond the scope of this book, but you can find instructions in **git help daemon**.

Gitosis
> *Gitosis* is a separate tool that lets you create a single SSH account and give multiple people access to a Git repository through that.

git shell
> The **git shell** command (see **git help shell**) is included with Git and does a similar job to Gitosis. Most people prefer Gitosis.

http://github.com
> A commercial service, *github.com*, offers free hosting services for open source projects and reasonably priced hosting of proprietary projects.

Gitorious
> *Gitorious* is an open source tool similar to *github.com*. You can use it to create your own *github.com*-like hosting service.

http://repo.or.cz
> *repo.or.cz* was the original public Git hosting service. It provides basic push/ pull access, although it isn't as user friendly as the other alternatives.

Because Git repositories are fully distributed, you can choose to host your project in more than one place at a time for added reliability, in case a server is unavailable or loses its data.

The Git Command Line Client: git

The git Command

Everything you do with Git is accomplished using the **git** command. The **git** main program doesn't actually do anything itself; instead, it runs subcommands based on the first word on the command line, often executing a subprogram based on that name. For example, if you run **git add**, Git might end up executing a program called *git-add*. In fact, if you create additional *git-** commands in your **$PATH**, Git will add them to its repertoire automatically.

Git contains a daunting number of subcommands—well over 100 of them. Most of these commands are meant to be used internally to create other subcommands. We'll cover only the most important commands in this book.

Accessing Git's Online Help

You can ask the **git** command for help using the **git help** command. By default, it just gives a list of the most common commands:

```
$ git help
The most commonly used git commands are:
   add          Add file contents to the index
   apply        Apply a patch on a git index file and a working tree
   archive      Create an archive of files from a named tree
...
```

You can also get a complete list of all the commands:

```
$ git help -a
git commands available in '/usr/bin'
------------------------------------------
   add                gui            reflog
   add--interactive   hash-object    relink
   am                 http-fetch     remote
...
```

Finally, you can get the Unix manpage for a particular command (every Git command, even the obscure ones, has a manpage). For example, to get help for the **git add** command:

```
$ git help add
```

git Subcommands

add

git add *filename* ...

Add or update a file in the index so its changes will be committed upon the next call to **git** commit. This is called *staging* the change. Unlike other systems, Git commits only the exact file contents that you have added, so if you make further changes to a file, you will need to add it again before running **git** commit.

With the **-p** option, Git lets you stage individual changes ("hunks") interactively, even inside a particular file. You can use this to help break your commits into smaller, more understandable pieces.

Options

-**n** (no-op)
-**v** (verbose)
-**f** (force)
-**p** (partial)

Examples

To stage a new or updated file in the index:

```
$ git add myfile.c
```

To stage all the files in the current directory, except the ones ignored by *.gitignore*:

```
$ git add.
```

To add a file even though it is ignored by *.gitignore*:

```
$ git add myfile.o
The following paths are ignored by one of your .gitignore
files:
myfile.o
Use -f if you really want to add them.
fatal: no files added
$ git add -f myfile.o
```

To add only part of a file:

```
$ git add -p README
diff --git a/README b/README
index 42644cd..e2ad5c3 100644
--- a/README
+++ b/README
@@ -1 +1,2 @@
...
Stage this hunk [y,n,q,a,d,/,e,?]? y
```

---

archive

```
git archive [--remote=repository-path] [--format=zip] revision
-- [path ...] >outputfile
```

Create a tar or zip format archive from the current repository or from the repository at repository-path if **--remote** is specified. The default output file format is (uncompressed) tar, but **git archive** can also produce a zip file instead if you specify **--format=zip**.

git archive always writes the new archive to standard output, so you should redirect or pipe its output somewhere.

You must specify the revision from which to take the files. If you want to use the current revision, use **HEAD**.

If you specify one or more paths, only those paths are included in the produced archive.

Options

--list
--remote
--format=tar|zip

Examples

To list the available options for **--format**:

```
$ git archive --list
tar
zip
```

To create a *tar.gz* file of the currently checked-out revision:

```
$ git archive HEAD | gzip >my-release.tar.gz
```

To create a zip file of tag *v1.2* in a repository from another computer named *myserver* (where you have Unix shell access via ssh):

```
$ git archive --format=zip --remote=myserver:src/myapp.git
v1.2 >myapp-1.2.zip
```

bisect

```
git bisect start [bad-commit [good-commit ...]] -- [path ...]
git bisect bad [commit ...]
git bisect good [commit ...]
git bisect skip [commit ...]
git bisect reset
git bisect view
git bisect run cmd [args ...]
```

Go back in history to find the first commit that introduced a problem. **git bisect** uses a binary search algorithm to narrow down which commit caused a problem using as few steps as possible. If there are *n* commits to consider, **git bisect** can find the exact culprit with approximately *log2 n* attempts. For example, with 100 commits, it will take about 7 tries; with 1,000 commits, it will take about 10 tries.

git bisect start [*bad-commit* [*good-commit* ...] -- [*path* ...]
> Use this command to start the bisection. You can optionally specify one known *bad-commit* (which exhibits the problem) and one or more known *good-commits* (which do not exhibit the problem). If you know the bug is in a particular set of files or directory, specify them as *paths* to further narrow the set of commits to consider.

git bisect bad [*commit* ...]
> Mark the given *commit(s)* as bad and check out the next candidate. If no *commits* are provided, the default is the currently checked-out **HEAD**.

git bisect good [*commit* ...]
> Mark the given *commit(s)* as good and check out the next candidate. If no *commits* are provided, the default is the currently checked-out **HEAD**.

git bisect skip [*commit* ...]
> Mark the given *commit(s)* as untestable and check out the next candidate. You need this if some other bug exists in the current commit that prevents you from testing the bug you're looking for. If no *commits* are provided, the default is the currently checked-out **HEAD**.

git bisect reset
> Abort the bisection and check out the commit you were using when you ran **git bisect** start.

git bisect view
> Show the current bisection status using **gitk**.

git bisect run *cmd* [*args* ...]
> Continue the bisection automatically by running the given **cmd** on each candidate. If the command returns an error, the commit is considered bad; otherwise, it is considered good.

Examples

To look for a problem when you know revisions *v2.0* and *v1.1* are good, but the current version is bad, and the bug is probably in the *mymodule* subdirectory:

```
$ git bisect start HEAD v2.0 v1.1 -- mymodule
Bisecting: 100 revisions left to test after this (roughly
7 steps)
[fa16ab36ad014bcc03acc4313bb0918fb241b54d] Fix the widget
$ make test
...
$ git bisect bad
Bisecting: 50 revisions left to test after this (roughly
6 steps)
[49cf82288aac5f0dcb152e2d75cd340e48d9e760] Change some
bits
$ make test
...
$ git bisect good
fa16ab36ad014bcc03acc4313bb0918fb241b54d is first bad
commit
```

To find a bug that was introduced somewhere between *v1.1* and *v2.0*, and that could be in any file:

```
$ git bisect start
$ git bisect good v1.1
$ git bisect bad v2.0
Bisecting: 97 revisions left to test after this (roughly
7 steps)
[fa16ab36ad014bcc03acc4313bb0918fb241b54d] Fix the widget
$ git bisect run make test
...
1f73862f3b63bbc9f0a8a8a12dd58e1a39a3355f is first bad commit
bisect run success
```

---

branch

```
git branch [-r] [-a] [--contains commit]
git branch [-f] [--track] branchname [commit]
git branch -m oldname newname
git branch -d|-D [-r] branchname
```

List, create, rename, and delete branches.

git branch [-r] [-a] [--contains *commit*]
> List the existing branches. By default, lists only local branches (*.git/refs/heads/**). With **-r**, list remote tracking branches instead (*.git/refs/remotes/*/**). With **-a**, list all local and remote tracking branches. With **--contains**, list only the branches that contain the given *commit*.

git branch [-f] [--track|--no-track] *branchname* [*commit*]

Create a new branch, *branchname*, that points at the given *commit*. The default for *commit* is **HEAD**. If *branchname* already exists, the operation will fail unless **-f** is specified. If you specify **--track** (the default in newer versions of Git) and *commit* is a remote tracking branch, you will be able to type simply **git merge** or **git pull** in the future to merge remote changes into your branch.

 This command does not check out your new branch. If you want to create a new branch and check it out in one step, use **git checkout -b**.

git branch -m|-M *oldname newname*

Rename a branch from *oldname* to *newname*. If *newname* already exists, **-m** will fail while **-M** will overwrite it.

git branch -d|-D [-r] *branchname*

Delete *branchname*. If **-r** is specified, *branchname* is a remote tracking branch (*.git/refs/remotes/*/*/**); otherwise it is a local branch (*.git/refs/heads/**). If you use **-d**, the branch will only be deleted if your current **HEAD** already includes everything in *branchname*; otherwise, it will fail. If you use **-D**, this safety check doesn't occur.

Examples

To get the list of all branches:

```
$ git branch -a
```

To create a new branch that starts off pointing at your current **HEAD**:

```
$ git branch savepoint1
```

To later delete the *savepoint1* branch:

```
$ git branch -d savepoint1
```

To create and check out a new branch *test* based on remote tracking branch *origin/master*:

```
$ git branch --track test origin/master
$ git checkout test
Switched to branch 'test'
```

---

checkout

git checkout [*revision*] *path* ...

Copy files from the repository into your working tree and possibly switch branches. **git checkout** does one of four different things, depending on which options are provided:

revision but no *path*

Switch branches to the one named by *revision*. If files are modified in the working tree and also changed in the new branch, the operation will fail. The next commit will be in the new branch.

If *revision* is a valid commit but not the name of a local branch, Git still switches **HEAD** to the given commit but does not give the new branch a name. This is called a *detached HEAD*. You can later name the new branch with **git checkout -b**.

In either case, if the **-b** option is given, a new branch is created from the given *revision*, and Git switches to that branch.

path(s) but no *revision*
> Destroys all working tree changes in the named files or directories, replacing them with their contents from the index.

revision and *path(s)*
> Destroys all working tree changes in the named files or directories, replacing them with their contents from the given *revision*. This does *not* switch branches; instead, it replaces contents of the given files in the index. The next **git commit**, will affect the same branch as before, but the named paths will be considered modified.

no revision and no *path(s)*
> No changes. Prints a list of files that have been modified in the working tree.

Options

-**q** (quiet)
-**f** (force)
-**b** *new_branch_name*
--**track** (-**t**)
--**no-track**
-**m** (merge)

Examples

To revert all the files in directory *docs* to their version from the index:

```
$ git checkout docs
```

To switch to the branch called *new-feature*, which must already exist:

```
$ git checkout new-feature
Switched to branch "new-feature"
```

To switch to the remote branch *origin/master*, creating a new branch called *new-feature*:

```
$ git checkout -b new-feature origin/master
Branch new-feature set up to track remote branch refs/
remotes/origin/master.
Switched to a new branch "new-feature"
```

---

cherry-pick

git cherry-pick *commit*

Take the changes from an individual *commit* (usually one from another branch) and apply it to the current branch. Note that unlike **git merge**, **git cherry-pick** applies only a single change, not all the history leading up to that change.

The newly created commit is completely independent of the original, although it has the same commit message by default. **git cherry-pick** *commit* is the rough equivalent of **git show** *commit* | patch -p1

Options

> -e, --edit
> -x (extend commit message)
> -m *parent-number*
> -n, --no-commit
> -s, --signoff

Examples

To cherry-pick commit *1a48191* onto the current branch and edit the commit message:

```
$ git cherry-pick -e 1a48191
Finished one cherry-pick.
```

---

clean

```
git clean -n|-f [-d] [-x]
```

Removes files from the work tree that are not in the Git index. By default, it only removes files that are not listed in *.gitignore* and does not remove directories. (To undo work tree changes to files that are in the index, use **git checkout**.)

You must provide one of **-n** or **-f**.

Options

> -n (print only, do not remove)
> -f (force removal of files)
> -d (also remove extra directories)
> -x (also remove files skipped by *.gitignore*)
> -X (only remove files skipped by *.gitignore*)
> -q (quiet)

Examples

To remove all extra files in the work tree so the only files remaining are ones that would be there after a fresh **git clone**:

```
$ git clean -f -d -x
Removing foo
```

To see what would happen if you ran the above command:

```
$ git clean -n -d -x
Would remove foo
```

---

clone

```
git clone repository [local-directory]
```

Make a copy of repository (which can be a local or remote Git repository) in local-directory. By default, if repository is on the local filesystem, Git will use hardlinks to copy the *.git/objects* folder to minimize disk space waste.

Available forms for *repository* are:

/path/repo.git
rsync://hostname/path/repo.git
http://hostname/path/repo.git
https://hostname/path/repo.git
git://host/path/repo.git
ssh://host/path/repo.git
ssh://user@host:port/path/repo.git
host:path/repo.git
user@host:path/repo.git

Options

-s, --shared
--no-hardlinks
--reference *other-parent-repository*
-q, --quiet
-n, --no-checkout
--bare
-o *origin-name*, --origin *origin-name*
--depth *shallow-clone-depth*

Examples

To clone the Linux kernel repository:

```
$ git clone git://git.kernel.org/pub/scm/linux/kernel/git/
torvalds/linux-2.6.git linux-2.6
```

commit

git commit [-- *file* ...]

Commit the changes that have already been staged in the index, updating **HEAD**.

If **-a** is given, all changed files in the work tree—not only staged changes—will be committed. (**-a** is the common behavior in systems like Subversion.)

If files are specified, exactly those files are committed, regardless of the state of the index.

You cannot commit a file for the first time, even with **-a**, unless it has first been added with **git add**.

Options

-a (all files, not just added ones)
--amend
-m *commit-message*, --message=*commit-message*
-F *commit-message-file*
-q, --quiet
-s, --signoff

Examples

To commit changes only to files in the *mylib* directory:

```
$ git commit -- mylib
Created commit 90716b6: my new commit
 1 files changed, 13 insertions(+), 0 deletions(-)
 create mode 100644 test-file
```

---

config

```
git config [--global] --list
git config [--global] name
git config [--global] name value
```

List, get, or set configuration values. If **--global** is given, uses your account-wide default settings (in *~/.gitconfig*); otherwise uses the settings for the current repository (in *.git/config*). Instead of using **git config**, you can also just view or edit these files directly.

The most important settings are:

core.autocrlf
> If true, converts LF line endings to CRLF on files when checking out and converts the line endings back to LF when committing.

core.bare
> Makes this repository a bare repository, which means it has no work tree. (Public shared repositories are usually bare.)

core.sharedRepository
> Set to either **all**, **group**, or **false**. If **group**, the files in *.git* will be group readable and writable. If all, the files will also be readable (but not writable) by everyone.

core.editor
> The path of your favourite text editor, for editing commit messages. The **$EDITOR** environment variable overrides this.

gc.autopacklimit
> Controls how frequently Git will automatically run **git gc** after common operations. To disable it completely, use **0**.

rerere.enabled
> When committing a conflicted merge, Git will remember how you resolved the conflict and attempt to reuse the recorded resolution if it encounters it again in the future.

user.email
> Your email address. This will be attached to commit messages automatically. The **$EMAIL** environment variable overrides this.

user.name
> You full name. This will be attached to commit messages automatically. The **$GIT_COMMITTER_NAME** and **$GIT_AUTHOR_NAME** environment variables override this.

Options

--unset

To set your email address and name for future commits:

```
$ git config --global user.name 'John Smith'
$ git config --global user.email 'jsmith@example.com'
```

To list all your global settings:

```
$ git config --global --list
user.name=John Smith
user.email=jsmith@example.com
gc.autopacklimit=0
```

diff

```
git diff first-commit [second-commit] [-- path ...]
git diff --cached [first-commit] [-- path ...]
```

Show the differences between two revisions. If paths are specified, restricts the comparison to only the given files or directories.

The default *first-commit* is **HEAD**.

The default *second-commit* is normally the work tree. With **--cached**, the default *second-commit* is the index.

Options

    --name-only
    --name-status
    --stat (show diffstat instead of patch)
    -a, --text
    -M (detect renames)
    -C (detect copies and renames)
    --find-copies-harder
    -R (reverse patch)
    -w, --ignore-all-space
    --exit-code
    -Un, --unified=n

Examples

To see which changes are already staged in the index:

```
$ git diff --cached
```

To see which changes are in the work tree but not yet staged:

```
$ git diff
```

To see a summary of changes between two tags (*v1.1* and *v2.0*):

```
$ git diff --stat v1.1 v2.0
```

To see the changes between *v1.1* and the current work tree:

```
$ git diff v1.1
```

To see the changes between *v1.1* and **HEAD**:

```
$ git diff v1.1 HEAD
```

Git

fetch

```
git fetch [remote-name]
git fetch repository [remoteref[:localref]]
```

Fetch commits from a remote Git repository and adds it to the local one.

In the first form, fetch all branches and tags from the given *remote-name* (a remote repository set up using **git remote**). The default remote name is **origin**.

In the second form, fetch a particular *remoteref* from repository and store it as local branch *localref*. The default *localref* is **FETCH_HEAD**. The default *remoteref* is **HEAD**.

Options

    -f, --force
    -n, --no-tags
    -t, --tags

Examples

To fetch the latest Linux kernel release and compare it against your current work tree:

```
$ git fetch git://git.kernel.org/pub/scm/linux/kernel/git/
torvalds/linux-2.6.git linux-2.6 master
From git://git.kernel.org/...
 * branch          master -> FETCH_HEAD
$ git diff FETCH_HEAD
```

To update all the remote tracking branches attached to the remote named *origin*:

```
$ git fetch origin
remote: Counting objects: 15, done.
remote: Compressing objects: 100% (10/10), done.
remote: Total 10 (delta 8), reused 0 (delta 0)
Unpacking objects: 100% (10/10), done.
From git://git.kernel.org/...
   6544ab2..e3498f3  master     -> origin/master
```

To retrieve the branch *test1* from someone's repository and save it as the local branch *mytest1*:

```
$ git fetch git://git.kernel.org/... test1:mytest1
```

---

gc

```
git gc [--prune] [--aggressive]
```

Pack the *.git/objects* directory to save disk space and increase speed.

git gc is run automatically from time to time, so it is rarely needed unless you want to use the **--prune** or **--aggressive** options or want to force packing to happen at a particular time (such as before making a backup).

Options

    --aggressive (take extra time to save even more space)
    --prune (delete unused objects)

Examples

To aggressively repack the current repository and save as much space as possible:

```
$ git gc --aggressive --prune
Generating pack...
Done counting 3299 objects.
Deltifying 3299 objects...
 100% (3299/3299) done
Writing 3299 objects...
 100% (3299/3299) done
Total 3299 (delta 2225), reused 0 (delta 0)
Pack pack-4eb8f89a145f826ef93923fe97c4ab23bd8abb62
created.
Removing unused objects 100%...
Done.
```

---

gitk

gitk [*git-log options*...]

Display a graphical browser showing the Git history. **gitk** takes all the same options as **git log**.

Examples

To show the history of all changes to the *mylib* directory on branches *test1* and *test2*, but leave out all changes that are included in *v1.1*:

```
$ gitk test1 test2 ^v1.1 -- mylib
```

---

grep

git grep [-e] *pattern* [--cached|*commit* ...] [-- *path* ...]

Search the given commits for the given regular expression pattern(s).

If no *commits* are specified, normally searches the current work tree. With **--cached**, searches the index instead. If *paths* are specified, restricts the search to the given files or directories.

The main advantage of **git grep** over plain **grep** is that it ignores files (such as compiler output and editor backups) that have not been added with **git add**.

When multiple patterns are specified (using **-e**), the default combination is **--or**, unless **--and** or **--not** is specified.

Options

-e *pattern*
--and
--or
--not
(
)
-E (act like egrep)
-F (act like fgrep)
-i, --ignore-case

-v, --invert-match
-w, --word-regexp
-l, --files-with-matches
-L, --files-without-matches

Examples

To search the work tree for lines containing *chicken* without considering case:

```
$ git grep -i chicken
```

To search the top of branches *test1* and *test2* for lines containing *alpha* and either *beta* or *gamma*:

```
$ git grep -e alpha --and \( -e beta -e gamma \) test1
test2
```

To search only the *mylib* directory for files starting with the word *chicken*:

```
$ git grep '^chicken' -- mylib
```

---

init

```
git init [-q] [--bare] [--shared=false|group|all]
```

Create a new Git repository in the current directory.

Options

-q, --quiet
--bare
--shared=false|group|all

Examples

To create a new repository with default settings:

```
$ git init
```

To create a new bare repository that will be shared with everyone in your Unix group:

```
$ git init –bare --shared=group
```

---

log

```
git [revision ...] [-- path ...]
```

Show the commit history. If *paths* are specified, show only the history related to the given files or directories. If *revisions* are specified, show the history starting from the given *revisions*. The default *revision* is **HEAD**. With **--all**, the default is to show all revisions in all local branches.

Each *revision* can be specified in one of the following formats:

commit
    Include the history for the given commit.

^*commit*
    Exclude the history starting at the given commit.

a..b
    Includes all commits in *b* that are not in *a*. Equivalent to *b* ^*a*.

a...b
    Includes all commits in *a* and *b* that are not in both.

Options

--all
-p (show patch)
-U*n*, --unified=*n*
-a, --text
--raw
--stat
-M (detect renames)
-C (detect copies)
--find-copies-harder
-R (reverse patch)
-w, --ignore-all-space
-*n*, --max-count=*n* (show up to only *n* commits)
--pretty=(oneline|short|medium|full|fuller|email|raw|
format:...)
--abbrev-commit
--full-history
--no-merges
--first-parent
--parents
--left-right
--graph
--author=*regex*
--committer=*regex*
--grep=*regex*
--reverse

Examples

To show the commits on this branch, starting with the most recent:

```
$ git log
commit 3ad3a1c1866bef36461d549d87fe39babe412d61
Author: John Smith <jsmith@example.com>
Date:   Sun Jan 18 18:41:32 2009 -0500

    Make some changes.

commit 529fc80df85a5ec7c88552bcb27bc0770a84e336
Author: John Smith <jsmith@example.com>
Date:   Sun Jan 17 12:13:06 2009 -0500

    Do the first thing.
...
```

To show what was changed by the most recent commit:

```
$ git log -1 -p
diff --git a/server/hello.html b/server/hello.html
index 63ede62..e26d280 100644
--- a/server/hello.html
+++ b/server/hello.html
@@ -1,17 +1 @@
...
```

To show all commits in all local branches where the commit
message contains the word *hello*:

```
$ git log --grep=hello --all
commit 3ad3a1c1866bef36461d549d87fe39babe412d61
Author: John Smith <jsmith@example.com>
Date:   Sun Jan 18 18:41:32 2009 -0500

    Undo changes to hello.html.
...
```

---

merge

git merge *commit* ...

Merge one or more other branches into the current **HEAD**. For
each specified *commit*, Git calculates the set of changes on that
branch that are not currently in **HEAD** and attempts to apply those
changes to the current **HEAD**. If the changes cannot be applied
successfully, Git will leave conflicts in the index, which you will
need to resolve by hand (using an editor, **git add**, and **git commit**).

Almost always, you will supply exactly one *commit*. In some situations, you may wish to merge more than one branch at the same
time; this is called an *octopus* merge and is allowed only if none of
the merges cause any conflicts. It is equivalent to merging the given
commits one by one, except that the merged result produces only
one new commit.

You can override the merge strategy to be used, but this is almost
never necessary. When more than one commit is specified, the only
allowed strategy is *octopus*.

Normally, Git combines the branch histories so **git log** will show
all the commits from all branches that have been merged. With
--squash, it eliminates the history of the branches other than
HEAD. This simplifies the **git log** output, but prevents successful
merges from that branch in the future, so it is usually a bad idea.

Options

--no-commit
--squash
--log
--no-ff
-s (resolve|recursive|octopus|ours|subtree)
-m *msg*

Examples

To merge feature branches *feature1* and *feature2* into your current
branch using an *octopus* merge:

```
$ git merge feature1 feature2
Already up-to-date with
aa871d4ef9657e03b2ef7053dc13a16777955499
Trying simple merge with
bdd84225b4f7c282731aed540171e7cbe392c00d
Merge made by octopus.
 58 files changed, 1371 insertions(+), 195 deletions(-)
```

To merge the branch production into the current **HEAD**, resulting in a conflict:

```
$ git merge production
Auto-merging testfile.c
Auto-merging server/hello.html
CONFLICT (content): Merge conflict in server/hello.html
Auto-merging test2.c
Recorded preimage for 'server/hello.html'
Automatic merge failed; fix conflicts and then commit the
result.
```

To resolve the conflict above and commit the completed merge:

```
(edit server/hello.html)
$ git add server/hello.html
$ git commit
```

---

mv

```
git mv oldfile newfile
git mv oldfiles ... newdir
```

Rename *oldfile* to *newfile* or move a series of *oldfiles* into the directory *newdir*, which must already exist. **git mv** updates both the work tree and the index.

 There is no need for a **git cp** (copy) command. Just copy the file using Unix **cp** and **git add**. Git is still able to track the history of files moved and copied in this way.

Options

-**f** (overwrite even if newfile exists)
-**n**, --**dry-run**

Examples

To rename *file1.c* to *file1b.c*:

```
$ git mv file1.c file1b.c
```

To move *file1.c* and *file2.c* into the *mylib* directory:

```
$ git mv file1.c file2.c mylib/
```

---

pull

```
git pull
git pull repository branch
```

Fetch the given branch then merge it into **HEAD**. **git pull** is just a short form for **git fetch** followed by **git merge**.

If no *repository* or *branch* is specified, **git pull** attempts to pull from the remote tracking branch associated with your current branch, if any. (Associations are set up using the --**track** option when creating a branch with **git branch**. You can also add them later with **git config**.)

The *repository* can be a local repository path, a repository URL (see **git clone**), or a remote name (see **git remote**). The *branch* must be a valid branch or tag name in the remote repository.

For more information about how pull works, see **git fetch** and **git merge**.

Options

    --no-commit
    --squash
    --log
    --no-ff
    -s (resolve|recursive|octopus|ours|subtree)
    --tags
    --no-tags

Examples

To pull the latest Linux kernel changes into your current branch:

```
$ git pull git://git.kernel.org/pub/scm/linux/kernel/git/
torvalds/linux-2.6.git master
From git://git.kernel.org/...
 * branch            master      -> FETCH_HEAD
Merge made by recursive.
 21 files changed, 932 insertions(+), 66 deletions(-)
```

---

push

```
git push [--all] [--tags] [repository [localref][:remoteref]]
```

Push changes from one or more branches or tags into the specified remote repository.

Repository can be a local repository path, a repository URL (see **git clone**), or a remote name (see **git remote**). If repository is omitted, it defaults to **origin**.

If *localref* is omitted, it defaults to pushing all the refs that currently exist on the remote. For example, if you have local branches named A, B, C, and D, and the remote has branches named A, C, and E, then Git will push branches A and C unless you specify a specific *localref*.

As an alternative to providing *localref*, you can provide **--all** or **--tags**. With **--all**, Git pushes all the local branches. With **--tags**, Git pushes all the local tags.

If *remoteref* is omitted, it defaults to the same name as *localref*. If you supply *remoteref*, it needs to be the full refname, such as *refs/heads/master*, not just the base branch name.

If you supply a *remoteref* without a *localref*, Git deletes *remoteref* in the remote repository. This is useful if the remote end refuses to update a ref because it is not a fast forward; you can delete the remote ref, and then re-create it.

Options

    --all
    --tags
    --dry-run
    --thin

Examples

To push the current branch (master) to the remote named **origin**:

```
$ git push origin master
```

To push all local branches to the default remote (**origin**), as long as they already exist there:

```
$ git push
```

To push all the local branches to a particular remote repository:

```
$ git push --all server:/git/myrepo.git
```

To delete the branch *test1* on a remote named *myremote*:

```
$ git push myremote :test1
```

To push the current **HEAD** to a branch named *test1* on **myremote**:

```
$ git push myremote HEAD:refs/heads/test1
```

---

rebase

```
git rebase [-i] [--onto onto-commit] base-commit [switch-branch]
git rebase --continue | --skip | --abort
```

Automatically cherry-pick a series of commits between *base-commit* and *switch-branch* onto *onto-commit*, leaving the result in *switch-branch*.

If *switch-branch* is omitted, the default is **HEAD**. If *onto-commit* is omitted, the default is *base-commit*.

 Using **git rebase** can completely disrupt future merges to and from the rebased branch. Use **git rebase** only for changing commits that have never been shared with others, such as before a new branch has been pushed to a shared repository.

git rebase is a powerful alternative to **git merge**. You can use it to simplify and rewrite the history of your changes in order to make them easier to review, audit, and share. However, because **git rebase** rewrites the history of your repository, misuse can cause hard-to-resolve errors, including duplicate commits and merge conflicts.

You can imagine **git rebase** as a series of commands that looks something like this:

```
git checkout switch-branch
git reset --hard onto-commit
for commit in base-commit..switch-branch
    git cherry-pick commit
done
```

The end result is a new branch that contains *onto-branch* plus a linear series of commits (i.e., with no merges). The new commits consist of all the commits that were previously part of *switch-branch* but not *base-commit*.

With **-i**, **git rebase** opens an interactive editor before the rebase operation starts. The editor contains a list of all the commits in *base-commit..switch-branch*. You can rearrange the list, add/delete individual entries, or merge (squash) multiple commits into a single one, thus allowing you to produce a set of commits that is easier for others to review.

During a rebase operation, cherry-picking a particular commit may result in a conflict. In that case, you need to do one of the following:

- Resolve the conflict, commit it with **git commit**, and then run **git rebase --continue**.
- Run **git rebase --skip** to skip this commit entirely.
- Run **git rebase --abort** to cancel the rebase operation and change the Git history back to the way it started.

Options

-i, --interactive
--onto *onto-commit*
-p, --preserve-merges

Examples

To take all the patches in **HEAD** that are not in *origin/master*, and apply them on top of the current *origin/master*:

```
$ git rebase origin/master
```

To do the same as the above, but interactively reorder, edit, and squash the patches:

```
$ git rebase -i origin/master
```

To take all the patches in the *feature1* branch that are not in *origin/master*, and add them on top of *feature2*, resulting in a new *feature1*:

```
$ git rebase --onto feature2 origin/master feature1
```

To do the same as the above in two steps for clarity:

```
$ git checkout feature1
$ git rebase --onto feature2 origin/master
```

To resolve a conflict that arose during the rebase operation:

```
(edit test1.c)
$ git add test1.c
$ git commit
$ git rebase --continue
```

---

reflog

git reflog show [*branch*]

Show entries from the *reflog*, which tracks changes to local refs (branches). If *branch* is omitted, shows the reflog for **HEAD**.

The reflog tracks the "history of history." Although commands like **git reset** can be used to undo a commit, the old commit still stays around in the reflog until it eventually expires. This allows you to undo many Git operations you might have performed by accident.

You can refer to entries in the reflog using *branch@{n}* notation. For example, **HEAD@{5}** means to use **HEAD** as it existed five changes ago.

Examples

To list all the recent changes to **HEAD**:

```
$ git reflog
```

To undo the most recent merge operation:

```
$ git reset HEAD@{1}
```

---

remote

```
git remote add [-f] name repository-url
git remote rm name
git remote show name
git remote prune [--dry-run] name
git remote update [name ...]
```

Manipulate remotes, which act as short forms for tracking repository URLs and branches. This command takes one of several forms:

git remote add *name repository-url*
> Register a new remote *name* at *repository-url*. With **-f**, also **git fetch** the set of remote branches from the new remote.

git remote rm *name*
> Unregister the remote *name*.

git remote show *name*
> Show information about the given remote *name*.

git remote prune *name*
> Delete remote tracking branches that no longer exist on the remote *name*. To prevent accidental data loss, remote tracking branches in the local repository are never deleted unless you run this command.

git remote update [*name ...*]
> Equivalent to running **git fetch** *name* for each of the names individually. If no *names* are provided, fetches all the registered remotes.

Examples

To show information about the remote named *origin* (which is created automatically by **git clone**):

```
$ git remote show origin
* remote origin
  URL: git://git.kernel.org/pub/scm/linux/kernel/git/
torvalds/linux-2.6.git
  HEAD branch: master
  Remote branches:
    master     tracked
    production tracked
  Local branches configured for 'git pull':
    master     merges with remote master
    production merges with remote production
```

```
Local refs configured for 'git push':
  master      pushes to master      (up to date)
  production pushes to production (local out of date)
```

To replace *origin* with a pointer to a new server and fetch the branches on the new server:

```
$ git remote rm origin
$ git remote add -f origin myserver:/git/myproj.git
Updating origin
From myserver:/git/myproj.git
 * [new branch]      master      -> origin/master
 * [new branch]      production -> origin/production
```

To update all registered remotes:

```
$ git remote update
Updating origin
```

---

reset

git reset [--soft|--hard] [*commit*] [-- *path* ...]

If no *paths* are given, update **HEAD** to point at the given *commit*. This can be used to undo one or more *commits* as if they had never happened. If *paths* are given, **HEAD** is not changed; only the listed files and directories are modified.

 git reset is extremely dangerous and can cause you to lose track of portions of your repository's history. Use it only on branches that have never been shared with anyone else. If you make a mistake with **git reset**, you can usually undo it using **git reflog**.

With **--soft**, neither the index nor the work tree are modified, and only the **HEAD** pointer is changed. Thus, the difference between **HEAD** and the index is the set of changes needed to convert the new **HEAD** into the original **HEAD**. If you then run **git commit**, a new commit will be created that changes the files back to the way they were before you ran **git reset**.

With **--hard**, both the index and the work tree are modified to match the given *commit*; any changes from the given *commit* to **HEAD** are lost.

If neither **--soft** nor **--hard** is specified, then the index is updated, but not the work tree.

Examples

To undo the most recent commit without losing the changes to the files themselves (so they can be committed again):

```
$ git reset HEAD^
```

To change the current branch to point at the same place as *origin/ master*, destroying anything else that might have happened in the current branch previously:

```
$ git reset --hard origin/master
```

To undo the above **git reset** operation by recovering the previous
HEAD from the reflog:

```
$ git reset --hard HEAD@{1}
```

To undo the most recent five commits and recommit their changes
as a single commit:

```
$ git reset --soft HEAD~5
$ git commit
```

revert

git revert [-n] commit

Create a new commit that reverses the effect of *commit*.

Options

> **-n, --no-commit**
> **-s, --signoff**

Examples

To undo the most recent commit:

```
$ git revert HEAD
[master ae3f932] Revert "Say hello."
 1 files changed, 0 insertions(+), 50 deletions(-)
```

To undo commit *ae3f932*, even if it is not the most recent commit:

```
$ git revert ae3f932
[master ae3f932] Revert "Say hello."
 1 files changed, 0 insertions(+), 50 deletions(-)
```

rm

git rm [-f] [-r] -- *path* ...

Remove files from the work tree and index. They will be permanently removed when you run **git commit**.

With **-f**, forces removal of a file even if it doesn't match **HEAD**.
With **-r**, removes entire directories and all their contained files.

Options

> **-f** (force)
> **-r** (recursive)
> **--cached** (ignore work tree)
> **-n, --dry-run**

Examples

To remove the *mylib* directory:

```
$ git rm -r mylib
rm 'mylib/test1.c'
rm 'mylib/test2.c'
```

stash

```
git stash
git stash list
git stash show [stashid]
git stash apply [stashid]
```

Save, list, or reapply the set of uncommitted changes from a work tree and index.

This command takes one of four forms:

git stash
> Save the current set of uncommitted changes and undo them. The index and work tree are reset to match **HEAD**.

git stash list
> Show the list of all stashes that have previously been saved.

git stash show [*stashid*]
> Show the exact set of changes that are saved as *stashid*. If *stashid* is omitted, uses the most recently saved changes.

git stash apply [*stashid*]
> Brings back the changes from the given *stashid* and applies them to the current index and work tree. If *stashid* is omitted, uses the most recently saved changes.

Examples

To save the current set of uncommitted changes, switch branches, and apply those changes to the new branch:

```
$ git stash
Saved working directory and index state "WIP on master:
44951b7... Say hello"
(To restore them type "git stash apply")
HEAD is now at 44951b7 Say hello

$ git checkout feature1
Switched to a new branch "feature1"

$ git stash apply
Removed test1.c
```

status

```
git status [path ...]
```

Check what would happen if you ran **git commit**. If *paths* are specified, check what would happen if you ran **git commit** *paths*.

Examples

To check the status of the current branch:

```
$ git status
# On branch master
# Changed but not updated:
#   (use "git add <file>..." to update what will be
committed)
#
#       modified:   test1.c
```

```
#        modified:   test2.c
#
no changes added to commit (use "git add" and/or "git
commit -a")
```

To see what would happen if you ran **git commit test1.c**:

```
$ git status test1.c
# On branch master
# Changes to be committed:
#   (use "git reset HEAD <file>..." to unstage)
#
#        modified:   test1.c
#
# Changed but not updated:
#   (use "git add <file>..." to update what will be
committed)
#
#        modified:   test2.c
#
```

tag

git tag [-a|-s|-u *gpg-key-id*] [-f] [-m *msg* | -F *msg-file*]
tagname commit
git tag -d *tagname*
git tag -l [*glob-pattern*]
git tag -v *tagname* ...

Manipulate tags. A tag is simply a user-friendly name for a particular commit. The command takes one of four forms:

git tag [-a|-s|-u *gpg-key-id*] **[-m** *msg* **| -F** *msg-file*] *tagname commit*
Create a new tag named *tagname* based on the given *commit*.
With **-a**, the tag is annotated (i.e., it has a commit message
attached) but not signed. With **-s** or **-u**, the tag is annotated
and signed with the default or specified gpg private key,
respectively. With **-m** or **-F**, use the given commit message or
filename containing the commit message, respectively. If none
of **-a**, **-s**, or **-u** is specified, the tag has no annotation. (Tags
you shared with other people should always have an annotation and should usually be gpg signed.)

git tag -d *tagname*
Delete the given *tagname* from the local repository. Note that
if the tag has already been pushed to a remote repository,
there is no way to make sure everyone erases it.

git tag -l [*glob-pattern*]
List all the tags matching the *glob-pattern*. If *glob-pattern* is
omitted, lists all the tags.

git tag -v *tagname* ...
Verifies the gpg signature of each requested tag.

Examples

To mark the current version with a *v1.1* tag and sign it with your gpg key:

```
$ git tag -s v1.1 HEAD
```

To delete the *v1.1* tag (only useful if it has never been pushed):

```
$ git tag -d v1.1
```

To list all tags for version *1.x*:

```
$ git tag -l 'v1.*'
```

15

Virtualization Command-Line Tools

This chapter covers common tools used with Linux to run many virtual servers on a single physical server. We cover the two dominant hypervisors used with Linux: Xen and KVM. We also cover libvirt-based tools used to manage both Xen and KVM. Although it isn't strictly a Linux solution, VMware uses a Linux operating system for the Service Console of their ESX server and recent vSphere products, so we have included basic console commands they provide.

This chapter covers the following topics:

- Conceptual overview
- Basic virtualization operations
- The Xen Hypervisor
- The KVM Hypervisor
- The libvirt virtualization API
- VMware command line interface

We do not provide a tutorial or in-depth information on virtualization here. This is meant as a quick reference to virtualization concepts, commands, and utilities. Refer to the following locations for more in-depth coverage on each of these technologies.

The Xen hypervisor	*http://www.xen.org/*
The KVM hypervisor	*http://www.linux-kvm.org/*
libvirt virtualization API	*http://libvirt.org/*
VMware Documentation	*http://www.vmware.com/support/pubs/*

Conceptual Overview

All of the virtualization programs we cover in this chapter provide full system virtualization. They use a software layer to present a virtualized hardware system. This layer, called the virtual machine monitor (VMM) or hypervisor, makes it possible to run multiple operating systems simultaneously. The operating system at the base—running directly on the hardware and interacting with it directly—is called the *host*, and the software instances that run on top of it—interacting only indirectly with hardware—are called the *guests*.

Virtualization isn't a new topic. As a means to divide a computer's resources into multiple running environments, virtualization has been around since the 60s. Back then, IBM used it to partition mainframe computers into separate virtual machines, allowing it to run multiple applications and processes simultaneously. Although low-cost PC hardware generally replaced mainframe hardware virtualization in the 80s and 90s, virtual machines were still commonly used to provide a virtualized environment for a process: e.g., creating a security sandbox or providing greater portability. The Java Virtual Machine (JVM) is a good example of process virtualization. This kind of virtualization also includes tools like **chroot** and **virtfs**.

Another popular type of virtualization creates a new instance of the same operating system on top of the host. This technology is often called *containers*. It typically includes such projects as Solaris Zones and User Mode Linux (UML). We don't cover containers in this chapter.

Here, we cover the tools of industrial-strength server virtualization. The solutions in this chapter offer environments that look like complete, independent hardware computers even though they are just software instances running on a common hardware base. While hardware costs for PCs remain fairly low, systems with multiple CPUs or CPU cores can easily handle the task of running dozens of highly available virtualized servers simultaneously. Businesses use virtualization to reduce deployment and administration costs. Many businesses also use virtualized-desktop systems to replace physical desktops, simplifying management tasks throughout the company.

Configuring virtualization requires administrative access to systems, CPUs with built-in virtualization technology, or even modified operating systems. The tools covered here are intended for large-scale server deployments. Although these tools might allow you to run an alternative operating system on your desktop or notebook, if you are just looking to run a single guest you will find that easier to do with another kind of tool. VMware Player or VirtualBox, for example, both run in user space, require no kernel modifications or special CPU, and are available for free.

System Requirements

To run the tools covered in this chapter you should have at minimum:

- A processor that supports virtualization technology (Intel VT or AMD-V). Support should be enabled in the system BIOS.
- At least 2 GB of memory.
- At least 6 GB of disk space.

Xen can run paravirtualized guests without virtualization technology in the CPU, but it requires it for full virtualization. You can check whether your existing CPU supports virtualization by grepping */proc/cpuinfo* as follows:

```
$ egrep '(vmx|svm)' /proc/cpuinfo
```

If nothing shows up, your CPU does not support virtualization. If something does appear, you may still need to enable it in BIOS to use it.

Each solution has additional requirements or limitations. Before making a hardware purchase you should check the requirements and supported hardware for the solution you plan to use.

If you want to support migration (moving a running guest from one host to another) you will also want some kind of shared-storage solution. That might be an iSCSI or SAN volume to which all servers have access. You don't need that to get started though.

Virtualization Technology

In full virtualization, the guest operating system doesn't need to be aware that it is running in a virtual environment. It interacts with the virtual hardware in the same way it would physical hardware. Some tasks in a fully virtualized environment, however, are computationally expensive. One way to handle the expensive tasks is to use a modified processor that performs these tasks for the hypervisor.

Paravirtualization provides another way to handle these expensive tasks. In paravirtualization the guest operating system is modified to hand these expensive tasks to the hypervisor, which can handle the task without having to emulate hardware.

Network Concepts

For your virtual server to connect to the Internet it must have a way to use the physical connection of the host. Xen, KVM, and VMware will all create a default bridge interface to handle mapping the virtual systems to the physical interface. A virtual machine could also be assigned directly to a physical device, but for most situations a bridge is what you want. More complex network configurations can be made by defining a kind of virtual switch or router. We will cover some commands that can do this here.

libvirt Tools and Terminology

Xen, KVM, and other Linux-based hypervisors support a single generic API called **libvirt**. For most tasks, it doesn't matter which Linux hypervisor you are using. You can use the same basic tools. libvirt has its own terminology which will be helpful to know when reading the libvirt section.

- A **node** is a single physical machine.
- A **hypervisor** is a layer of software that virtualizes a node, providing a set of virtual machines that may differ from the node itself.
- A **domain** is an instance of an operating system running on a virtualized machine provided by the hypervisor.

Throughout this chapter, though, we'll stick to more common industry terminology, referring to a **domain** as a **guest** and the **node** running the guest as a **host**.

Basic Virtualization Operations

The complexity of virtualization prevents us from covering everything in a small chapter within this book. Fortunately, developers have written tools that handle much of the complexity for you. They have worked hard to make the defaults do the right thing for your system and have written scripts to simplify the tasks. Here we cover the higher-order tools that will help you create and manage virtual systems and networks.

Creating Virtual Systems

For VMware you will use the VI Client GUI interface to create your virtual systems. We won't cover that task here. With Xen and KVM you can use virt-manager's **virt-install** to install a new guest. At minimum you must tell **virt-install**:

- the name of the new guest domain
- whether the guest will be paravirtualized or fully virtualized (**-p** or **-v**)
- the amount of RAM to give to the new system (**-r**)
- what to use as a system disk and if creating a disk, how large it should be (**-f** and **-s**)
- whether to support graphics or not (**--vnc** or **--nographics**)
- where to find the installation files (**-c**, **-l**, or **--pxe**)

virt-install will prompt for any values you do not provide to it on the command line. The name should be a short unique identifier; whatever helps you distinguish it from other virtual machines controlled by the same hypervisor. Paravirtualization or full virtualization depends on what your OS supports. If you do not have an installation already prepared for virtualization, you need full virtualization.

The system disk can be stored anywhere in your filesystem. Use a full path to specify where, or just a filename to have it stored in the default location for your hypervisor.

You will need a way to connect to the new system. See the section "Graphic and Console Interfaces" on page 842. If you are installing a fully virtualized system, use the **--vnc** option. If you aren't installing on a system running X Window System, you may need to connect to your guest remotely from a system that does. If you are installing a paravirtualized system and the guest system supports it, you can use either **--vnc** or **--nographics**. If using **--nographics** fails, you may need to use **virsh** to **destroy** the domain and start over as you will have no way to connect to it.

What you use for installation files will depend on what kind of virtualization you are using. For a fully virtualized system you may want to install from a CDROM drive or an installation disk ISO. You can use the **-c** option to point to a physical device on the host (*/dev/cdrom*) or to an ISO file.

To install a paravirtualized Linux or UNIX system, you will instead use the -l option with **virt-install** to point to the location of the initial boot image. For some distributions, you can point this to an ISO image, but the -l option does not configure a virtual CDROM, so after the boot you will need to tell the install program where to find a mirror of the installation media. You can use HTTP, NFS, or FTP to connect to that media. This means you will have already had to have set up a server to provide these files. You can quickly prepare an installation ISO for this by mounting it via the loop back device and either exporting the directory via NFS or serving the files through HTTP. We'll provide examples.

virt-install has many other options that can help you customize your virtual server. If you are using KVM, you might want to use the **--accelerate** option to better take advantage of the hypervisor. You might want to use **--os-type** option to optimize guest configuration. You can provide more detailed information on how to configure the network interface (without any options, it just connects the guest to the default bridge interface). See **virt-install**'s entry in this chapter for further information.

Some distributions come with wrapper-scripts that call **virt-install** with default options to install a basic Linux operating system. Ubuntu, for example, provides a **vm-builder** script that will install a stripped-down version of Ubuntu, ready to run.

Examples

Mounting a Red Hat ISO for export via NFS:

```
# mkdir /mount/rhel5.3
# mount -o ro,loop RHEL-5.3.iso /mount/jeos-8
# exportfs *:/mount/rhel5.3/
```

Mounting a Red Hat ISO for HTTP access:

```
# mkdir /var/www/html/rhel5.3
# mount -o ro,loop RHEL-5.3.iso /var/www/html/rhel5.3
```

Full virtualization install from an installation iso:

```
# virt-install -name rhel-fv -v -r 256 -f /images/rhel-fv.img -s 8 -vnc \
    -c RHEL-5.3.iso
```

Paravirtual installation via HTTP using a serial console:

```
# virt-install -name rhel-pv -p -r 256 -f /images/rhel-pv.img -s 6 \
    --nographics -l http://example.com/rhel-5.3/
```

Managing Virtual Systems

While hypervisors can control the starting and stopping of virtual machines, they can't always shut them down gracefully. You may want to power off your systems by connecting to each system and initiating a shutdown in the normal way. Sometimes you can't do that, though, and you need to do the virtual equivalent of pulling the plug on a system that isn't responding. The commands listed here cover these basic operations.

Xen and KVM virtual guests can be managed with **virsh** commands. Use **virsh list --all** to get a list of all managed domains. The **start**, **shutdown**, **reboot**, and **destroy** commands are your virtual power and reset buttons. From the service console in Vmware's ESX server you can do similar things with **vmware-cmd**.

Graphic and Console Interfaces

You need some way to interact with the virtual systems. Generally, you will use a VNC or SDL graphic interface set up by your guest installation tool. VMware provides its own client software to handle this. For Xen and KVM you will likely use the VNC client **virt-viewer** or the GUI management tool **virt-manager** to connect to a virtual system. As an alternative, you could interact with a virtual system through a text-based console connected to a virtual system's serial device. The **virt-install** command has a **--nographics** option that will attempt to set this console up for you, but it works only with paravirtualized guests. If your guest system has a properly functioning network connection, you may also be able to use **ssh** to connect to it.

Configuring Networks

Your basic network options are to use bridging or Network Address Translation (NAT). In bridging, a special bridge interface transparently connects your virtual interfaces to your host's physical interface(s). Your virtual servers will share the physical interface.

Using NAT, your virtual servers are assigned private network IP addresses, and another interface then provides the NAT for your system. This NAT interface is essentially a bridge as well. A bridge is really any interface used to hook your virtual interfaces up to your physical interfaces. Still, these two approaches are commonly referred to as bridging and NAT.

VMware uses a third option. It creates a virtual switch to which you connect your guests' interfaces. The default switch, however, simply bridges the switch to the server's network interface card. Neither Xen or KVM come with a ready-made virtual switch solution, although some vendors may offer virtual switch solutions you could add to your system.

Upon installation of the hypervisor and libvirt, most distributions will automatically configure basic networking support. They will likely configure both a NAT and bridge interface. Xen's tools will use the bridge interface by default, but virt-manager's tools will likely use NAT.

The approach you want to use will depend on the kind of system on which you have installed the host operating system. If you are installing on a system that might frequently change networks (for example, a notebook you move between home and work) or want to keep your virtual systems separate from your physical network, you will probably want NAT. If you are using a wireless card, you must use NAT. Bridging will not work with wireless interfaces because wireless chipsets reject foreign MAC addresses. If you are installing on a server and want your virtual systems to interact with your network the way any physical system would, you want to use bridging.

While we don't cover it in this chapter, the Net:Bridge or (bridge-utils) package contains the **brctl** command. This command can help you build and manage more complex bridges. You can find more information on this package at:

> http://www.linuxfoundation.org/en/Net:Bridge

We highly recommend you read that page and explore the tool if you want to dig any deeper into configuring your bridges.

The basic concept to keep in mind for virtual networking is that your host systems will have interfaces for physical devices, virtual devices, and bridge devices. What they are named by default depends on your distribution and hypervisor. The following are the interfaces you might find running if you used **ifconfig** on a CentOS system running Xen.

vifX.Y
> A vif interface on the host connects to the virtual interface on a guest domain. Consider it the server's representation of that virtual Network Interface Card (NIC). vif0.0 is Domain-0's first interface. vif0.1 would be its second. vif1.0 is the first interface on the first running guest (Domain 1).

eth0
> The virtual interface for Domain-0, which is connected to vif0.0.

peth0
> This device performs packet distribution for guest systems, including Domain-0. It is bound to the bridge device, the physical network card. It has no IP address of its own, but instead acts as a simple switch. This is how packets get to the appropriate vif device.

xenbr0
> Xen's default bridge device that connects vif interfaces to the physical interface (peth0).

virbr0
> An interface providing NAT. This is the default bridge device for virt-manager tools. You may need to enable packet forwarding in Domain-0 to make this device work.

You will likely find these devices on an Ubuntu system running KVM:

eth0
> The physical interface for the host. Note that it doesn't have an IP address. The host's interface is bridged to this device.

vnet0
> An interface providing NAT. The default bridge device for virt-manager.

vnetX
> Interfaces connected to a guest's virtual interface, where X is numbered 1 or higher. These are bridged through vnet0 by default.

br0
> The host system's bridge device. This one has the host's IP address and connects to the physical interface, eth0.

You can set the interface to be used by a virtual domain when using **virt-install** with the **--network** option.

MAC Addresses

You may want to set a MAC address on a virtual interface manually. This is a special hexadecimal number that uniquely identifies your interface card. If not set, your configuration tool will generate a random number for it, but knowing what it will be ahead of time can help you configure DHCP or a PXE boot. With **virt-install** you can set it with the **--mac** option. VMware's VI Client provides an option as well.

There are some restrictions. The first three sets of numbers in a MAC address identify the vendor. When setting them, use the following vendor addresses:

Xen	00:16:3e
KVM/Qemu	54:52:00
VMware	12:50:56 AM

Making Changes to Virtual Machines

VMware's VI Client can be used to edit virtual machine configurations. Making changes to a virtual machine under Xen or KVM can be a little trickier. You can make some changes (such as memory settings) using **xm** or **virsh**. For more complex changes with Xen, you could change the configuration files located under */etc/xen/*. These are in a text format, and most of the settings you will want to change will be easy to figure out.

virsh provides one common way to make complex changes:

1. Run **virsh dumpxml** to get an XML configuration file for the domain you wish to change.
2. Use a text editor to edit the XML file.
3. Shut down the virtual system if it is still running.
4. Run **virsh define** to remove the old configuration from the hypervisor and replace it with the configuration in your edited XML file.

You can now start the domain with your new configuration.

Creating and Manipulating Disk Image Files

Tools such as **virt-install** will create disks as needed when installing a new virtual server, but you might want to add a disk to an existing server. One common form of disk image for virtual machines is a sparse file. The simplest tool for creating this is the **dd** command documented in Chapter 3. For instance, to create a 10,000 MB sparse file suitable for use as a disk image you can use the following command:

```
# dd if=/dev/zero of=newdisk.img bs=1M seek=10000 count=1
```

Change the system's configuration file to add the new drive. You can use the guest's system tools (such as **fdisk**) to configure the new disk.

You can easily increase the size of a sparse file by using **dd** to create a new sparse file then append the existing file with the new file. Don't try this with an image file currently in use by a running guest, though: shut down the guest system first. Here we use **dd** and **cat** to add a 5000 MB extension to the original image.

```
# dd if=/dev/zero of=diskextension.img bs=1M seek=5000 count=1
# cat diskextension.img >> newdisk.img
```

You will need to use a tool appropriate to the guest operating system to take advantage of the new space. For example, **resize2fs** makes the space available to an ext3 filesystem.

For more advanced features on a disk image, you can use **qemu-img**, a tool we don't document here. It can create and convert disk images to a several different formats, including to VMware's *.vmdk* format. If you are using KVM you should already have it installed on your system. If you do not, you can install it via the qemu package.

Xen

Xen is the most common hypervisor used on Red Hat Advanced Server 5, Fedora, and distributions based on these, such as CentOS 5. Assuming you are using one of these, to use Xen you must install the **xen** and **kernel-xen** packages from your package repository:

```
# yum install xen kernel-xen
```

Other operating systems will probably have similar packages. Some offer a **groupinstall** that will include all the necessary packages:

```
# yum groupinstall Virtualization
```

Once installed, reboot your system using the Xen kernel. You may want to modify your */boot/grub/grub.conf* file to boot the Xen kernel by default. Usually this means changing the **default=** entry to **default=0**, where 0 refers to the first boot configuration described by the file. See Chapter 4 for details on configuring **grub** and modifying the *grub.conf* file.

The installation of the previously mentioned packages should also configure two services to run: the Xen daemon (**xend**) and the **xendomains** script that the system uses to automatically start and stop your guest domains.

Once the new kernel and **xend** service is running, you should be able to run the command

```
# xm list
```

to list your current nodes. At first you will have one domain running, Domain-0.

To understand Domain-0, it helps to know that your system is not really running Linux directly. It's running Xen's own kernel, a virtual machine monitor based on the Nemesis microkernel. Xen's kernel doesn't provide an administrative interface; it depends on a modified operating system running as a guest to do this. This privileged guest also provides guest domains access to hardware devices. In our case, Domain-0 is running a modified version of Linux. Your OS is actually the controlling domain in a cluster of guest domains.

In Xen, these other guest domains are referred to as unprivileged domains, or DomU (the U stands for unprivileged). Domain-0 can also delegate control of hardware devices to other privileged domains, but that's a more advanced topic we won't cover here.

Paravirtualization and Architecture

Xen supports paravirtualized guests that run on the same architecture as Domain-0. Thus, if Domain-0 is running X86_64, paravirtualized guests must be X86_64 as well. To run a 32-bit guest on a 64-bit system, you must run it fully virtualized.

Like Domain-0, paravirtualized Linux guests run the Xen kernel instead of the regular kernel.

Xen Networking

Mixing libvirt and Xm tools can lead to some confusion when it comes to networking. Guest domains installed using Xen's tools bridge to device **xenbr0** by default. Those installed by libvirt's **virt-install** bridge to device **virbr0**. To cut down on confusion and take full advantage of libvirt, you may want to disable Xen's bridge networking altogether. Details on how to configure networking for Xen using libvirt can be found on the libvirt wiki: *http://wiki.libvirt.org/page/ Networking*. Altertnatively you can tell **virt-install** to bridge to device **xenbr0** using the -w option (-w **bridge:xenbr0**).

Xen Commands

Xen has its own special commands for installing and managing domains, but for most things you can use the **libvirt** tools documented in this chapter. Here, we will cover the most commonly used **xm** subcommands and the **xentop** command.

---

xm   xm [*options*] *command*

Xen hypervisor management interface. Generally you will use **virsh** to control VMs, but there are a few useful functions you can get from **xm** but not **virsh**. We cover the most common commands here.

xm can be used to configure virtual machine access rights and security policies. Policies are given labels and the labels applied to domains. This is an advanced topic we do not cover in this book.

Commands
console *domain*
    Connect to serial console on domain, if available. Use **ctrl-]** to exit a console.

create [-c] *configfile* [*settings*]
    Start the guest domain described in configfile. This command is generally used to start a previously installed domain that is not currently running. By default, a domain will have a configuration file of the same name in */etc/xen/*. You can specify the configfile with a full path, or a path relative to */etc/xen/*. The configuration file, a Python executable file, largely consists

of *name=value* pairs. These can also be given in a space-separated list on the command line. The manpage for **xmdomain.cfg** contains details on configuration file format and valid entries. The **-c** option causes **xm** to connect to the console as soon as the machine starts.

destroy *domain*

Immediately kill any running instance of the domain and free its resources to the hypervisor. (You usually want to use **shutdown** instead.)

dmesg [-c]

Print the Xen message buffer. This buffer contains informational, warning, and error messages. The **-c** option clears the message buffer.

help [--long]

Print a list of **xm** commands. If **--long** is given, print all commands grouped by function.

info

Print information about host system.

list [*options*] [*domains*]

List information about one or more *domains* (a space-separated list of domain names, ids or UUIDs). This is a more verbose listing than that provided by **libvirt**. It includes resource allocation and running time information.

Options

-*l*, --**long**

Print detailed information about domains in a format that can easily be consumed by external programs.

--**label**

Include security label information.

log

Print the contents of the **xend** log. This log is also found at */var/log/xen/xend.log*.

top

Run the **xentop** command (described next).

list [*options*] [*domains*]

List information about one or more *domains* (a space-separated list of domain names, ids or UUIDs). This is a more verbose listing than that provided by **libvirt**. It includes resource allocation and running time information as well as state. There are six possible states: running, blocked, paused, shutdown, crashed, and dying.

Options

-l, --**long**

Print detailed information about domains in a format that can easily be consumed by external programs.

--**label**

Include security label information.

pause *domain*

> Cease hypervisor scheduling for domain.

shutdown [*options*] *domain*

> Begin a graceful shutdown on *domain*. For guests that support this, it is the same as running **shutdown** on the guest. It may not succeed. By default, the command does not wait for the shutdown to complete. **xm list** will reveal the guest's current state.

Options

-a Print detailed information about domains in a format that can easily be consumed by external programs.

-w Wait for domain to complete shutdown before exiting.

unpause *domain*

> Resume hypervisor scheduling for *domain*.

---

xentop

xentop [*options*]

Provide frequently updated information about current domains. This program performs a function similar to the Linux **top** command, only with information about the hypervisor and domains instead of processes. Its various options change what information is displayed. Like **top**, **xentop** also has some interactive commands to change what information **xentop** displays as it runs.

Options

-b, --batch

> Run in batch mode; don't accept command-line input. Useful for sending output to another command or to a file.

-d *seconds*, **--delay=***seconds*

> Set the delay between refreshes. Default is 3.

-i *num*, **--iterations=***num*

> Update display num times, then exit.

-n, --networks

> Show network information.

-r, --repeat-header

> Repeat the table header before each domain.

-v, --vcpus

> Show virtual CPU information.

-x, --vbds

> Show virtual block device information.

Interactive commands

All interactive commands are case-insensitive.

B Toggle display of virtual block device information.

D Prompt for a new delay setting.

N Toggle display of network information.

Q, Esc
> Quit.

R   Toggle display of table header before each domain.

S   Change sort order by cycling through the available columns.

V   Toggle display of virtual CPU information.

Up, Down
> Scroll through displayed domains.

KVM

The Kernel-based Virtual Machine (KVM) is a full virtualization hypervisor for Linux. The work of the KVM hypervisor is handled by the Linux kernel. Each guest in KVM runs as a process and can be managed by Linux tools such as **top** and **kill**.

KVM isn't a complete virtualization solution. It depends on both the libvirt tools for management and the open source processor emulator QEMU for hardware emulation. Therefore, you will need those installed as well.

KVM is the most popular hypervisor on Ubuntu distributions. Assuming you are using Ubuntu, you can use **apt-get** to install the necessary packages:

```
$ sudo apt-get install kvm libvirt-bin ubuntu-vm-builder qemu bridge-utils
```

You may also want the **virt-viewer** and **virt-manager** packages, though these will require the X Window System as well. As of Ubuntu version 8.10 (Intrepid) you can install the meta package **ubuntu-virt-server** for the basic tools mentioned previously and **ubuntu-virt-mgmt** for the GUI management tools.

You will likely want to provide your controlling user account with access to network devices created by libvirt. Use **usermod** to add your account to the **libvirtd** user group.

Restart your system. If all goes well, you should be able to run the following command without error:

```
$ virsh -c qemu:///system list
```

Also check to make sure KVM is working:

```
    sudo kvm
```

This will confirm that you have enabled virtualization support in BIOS properly.

QEMU

QEMU is really its own virtualization solution that works in user space. Combining it with KVM speeds it up considerably, providing a robust hypervisor running at the kernel level. QEMU comes with some of its own commands for the installation and launching of virtual systems. Some older tutorials show how to use them. We won't cover those here; instead use libvirt tools to handle these tasks.

Ubuntu Builder Scripts

Ubuntu comes with tools to help you quickly build guest systems. In older systems these tools are in the **ubuntu-vm-builder** package; in newer systems, they are in the **python-vm-builder** package. These tools handle the defaults for installing a simple Ubuntu guest. In most cases all you need to provide is a name for your new domain.

libvirt and Red Hat Virtual Machine Manager

The libvirt virtualization API provides an open source programming interface to hypervisors like Xen and KVM. It comes with **virsh**, a management interface for controlling hypervisors. A closely related project, the Red Hat Virtual Machine Manager application, is a collection of tools built using libvirt. This includes a few command-line tools as well as the GUI **virt-manager** application.

Whether you are using Xen or KVM, these **libvirt** based tools will handle most of the tasks of creating and managing your guests. Except for some minor differences in what each hypervisor supports and the connection string used to get to the hypervisor, these commands work the same regardless of what hypervisor you choose. You'll want to know these tools well.

XML Configuration Files

libvirt uses XML files to define or describe the capabilities and configuration of domains, networks, and hardware devices. Many of the command tools expect to receive information from an XML file. You don't have to know the XML tags to get started, as the tools will build the required files for you, but you may want to edit an XML file directly to change the configuration of a guest.

The XML formats, as well as more in-depth information on **virsh** and the API, can be found on the **libvirt** website: *http://libvirt.org*.

Connection URIs

To control a hypervisor, **libvirt** tools must first connect to it. You will use a URI to specify the location of the hypervisor. For KVM use a **qemu://** URI and for Xen use **xen://**. For backwards compatibility **virsh** will also accept just plain **xen**, which it will treat as **xen:///**. If no connection option is given, **virsh** will try to connect to the URI given in the environment variable **LIBVIRT_DEFAULT_URI**. If none exists, it will probe the defaults in whatever hypervisor drivers it has available.

You can also make a connection to a remote server. For security reasons you will usually use SSH to do this by using an **xen+ssh://** or **qemu+ssh://** URI.

Connection URI Examples

Connect to the local Xen hypervisor:

```
xen:///
```

Use SSH to connect to the Xen hypervisor running on *xenhost.yoyodyne.com*:

```
xen+ssh://xenhost.yoyodyne.com/
```

Connect as root to the local KVM hypervisor:

```
qemu:///system
```

Connect as an unprivileged user to the local KVM hypervisor:

```
qemu:///session
```

Use SSH to connect as user john to the KVM hypervisor on *kvmhost.yoyodyne.com*.

```
ssh+qemu://john@kvmhost.yoyodyne.com/system
```

Remote GUI control

Installing the X Window System on your server nodes will consume resources you might rather give to a virtual machine, as well as increase the security risk to your servers. Instead, consider creating a server to control your nodes. That system can be a desktop system with a full X Window installation. Install the libvirt tools and **virt-manager** to that system and use a URI connection string to connect to your client. Using SSH will keep the connection secure. Use the **VIRSH_DEFAULT_CONNECT_URI** environment variable to hold the connection string. **virsh** will look there before trying the default connection URIs.

You may have problems connecting with **virt-manager** over SSH. If you launch **virt-manager** as an unprivileged user, it will usually try to switch you to the root user. This will clear environment settings like your **ssh-agent** settings. If prompted for the root password, select the "run unprivileged" option. This will preserve your current SSH settings. You don't need to run as root because you aren't controlling a hypervisor on the local system. For privileged access you will connect to a privileged user on the remote node.

At this time, **virt-manager** does not support creating new guests on remote systems. But you can manage your system just fine.

IP Forwarding and libvirt Networking

libvirt's default network configures an isolated bridge device to be used by guest domains. This default bridge creates a private network for the virtual machines, but does not connect that private network to your physical network. The simplest way to complete that connection is to enable IP Forwarding in the kernel. You can quickly enable IP Forwarding using **sysctl** like so:

```
# sysctl -w net.ipv4.ip_forward=1
```

To set your system to enable IP forwarding upon bootup, edit the **net.ipv4.ip_forward** setting in */etc/sysctl.conf*.

While IP forwarding can get you running quickly, for production environments you probably want to configure a more robust bridge network. Information on creating bridge networks for libvirt can be found on the libvirt wiki at:

http://wiki.libvirt.org/page/Networking

libvirt and Virtual Machine Manager Commands

virsh

virsh [*options*] [*command* [*command-options*]]

libvirt management interface. **virsh** uses the **libvirt** API to connect to a hypervisor and manipulate the configuration and state of virtual machines controlled by that hypervisor. If invoked with a command, it will execute the command and then exit. If invoked without a command, **virsh** enters a shell mode from which you can execute commands.

This manager will work with any hypervisor that has libvirt support. However, not all **virsh** commands are supported by all hypervisors. Nor will they work on all guests. Still, if a hypervisor can do something, you can generally use **virsh** to do it. Some hypervisors, including Xen, come with their own tools for managing virtual machines, but we still recommend you use **virsh** instead.

Most **virsh** commands expect a *domain* option. A domain refers to a virtual machine. You can use the virtual machine's name or UUID. If the machine is running, it should also have an ID number within the hypervisor, and you can use this for the *domain* option as well. Use the **list** command to see names and IDs of domains managed by the hypervisor.

Options

--c *uri*, --**connect**=*uri*
Connect to a hypervisor specified by *uri*.

-d *level*, --**debug**=*level*
Set the level of debugging information to be printed to standard output. Accepted values are 0–5. 0 disables debugging messages and is the default. 5 prints all debugging messages.

-h, --**help**
Print a brief description of options and commands.

-l *file*, --**log**=*file*
Log debugging information and errors to the specified *file*.

-q, --**quiet**
Quiet mode. Do not print informational messages to standard out.

-r, --**readonly**
Connect to hypervisor in read-only mode.

-t, --**timing**
Print timing information.

-v, --**version**
Print version information, and exit.

Commands

attach-device *domain xmlfile*
Attach device defined in *xmlfile* to *domain*.

attach-disk *domain source target* [*options*]

Attach disk device to *domain*. *source* and *target* are paths for the files and devices.

Options

--driver *name*

Set the driver *name* attribute. Valid values include **file**, **tap** (network tap), or **phy** (physical).

--subdriver *type*

Set the driver *type* attribute. The valid values depend on the driver. It's common to use **aio** with the **tap** driver.

--mode *mode*

Set the *mode* of device. Valid values include **readonly** and **shareable**.

--type *type*

Set the *type* of device. Valid values include **cdrom** and **floppy**.

attach-interface *domain type source* [*options*]

Attach interface device to *domain*. Usually *type* will be either **network** or **bridge**. The source is the host's network or bridge device to which the virtual network should connect, or default, to use the default gateway.

Options

--mac *macaddress*

Assign an address to the virtual interface.

--target *name*

Assign the target interface *name* to use in the guest.

--script *path*

Provide the *path* to a script to handle the bridge.

autostart [**--disable**] *domain*

Automatically start *domain* at system boot.

capabilities

Print hypervisor capabilities in XML format.

connect [*uri*] [**--readonly**]

Connect or reconnect to a hypervisor.

console *domain*

If a serial console is available on *domain*, connect to it. Use **ctrl-]** to exit a console.

create *xmlfile*

Start a domain described in the specified *xmlfile*.

start *domain*

Start an inactive domain.

destroy *domain*

Immediately kill any running instance of the domain and free its resources to the hypervisor. (You usually want to use **shutdown** instead.)

define *xmlfile*

> Add persistent domain information described in the specified XML file. The domain is added but not started.

detach-device *domain file*

> Detach device defined in *file*.

detach-disk *domain target*

> Detach disk device *target* from *domain*.

detach-interface *domain type* [*--mac macaddress*]

> Detach network interface from *domain*. Use *macaddress* to distinguish between multiple interfaces of the specified *type*.

domblkstat *domain device*

> Print basic stats for block *device* on *domain*.

domid *domain*

> Given the domain name, print the *domain*'s ID.

domifstat *domain interface*

> Print basic stats for network *interface* device on *domain*.

dominfo *domain*

> Print basic information on *domain*.

domuuid *domain*

> Print the *domain*'s UUID.

domname *domain*

> Given the domain ID, print the *domain*'s name.

domstate *domain*

> Print the *domain*'s state.

dump *domain file*

> Dump *domain*'s core to *file*.

dumpxml *domain*

> Print the *domain*'s information in XML. Output is suitable for use with the **create** and **define** commands.

freecell [*number*]

> Print available memory on the machine, or if specified, available memory in Non-Uniform Memory Access (NUMA) cell *number*.

help [*command*]

> Print a list of available commands or information on a specified *command*.

hostname

> Print the hypervisor's hostname.

list [*option*]

> Print a list of active domains and their current state. Use option **--inactive** to list inactive domains, or **--all** to list both active and inactive domains. There are six possible states: running, blocked, paused, shutdown, crashed, and dying.

migrate [*--live*] *domain destination* [*transport*]

> Migrate a *domain* to a new *destination* host. The *destination* should be given as a connection URI. If the transport method differs it can be given as a separate URI, though this isn't usually necessary. Use **--live** to migrate an active domain without interruption.

net-autostart [--disable] *network*
> Automatically start *network* at system boot.

net-create *xmlfile*
> Create and activate a network described in the specified *xmlfile*.

net-define *xmlfile*
> Define a network described in the specified *xmlfile* but don't start it.

net-destroy *network*
> Immediately stop an active *network*.

net-dumpxml *network*
> Print the *network*'s information in XML.

net-list [*option*]
> Print a list of active networks. Use option **--inactive** to list inactive networks, or **--all** to list both active and inactive networks.

net-name *uuid*
> Print the name of the network specified by *uuid*.

net-start *network*
> Start a previously defined but inactive network.

net-undefine *network*
> Remove *network*'s definition.

net-uuid *name*
> Print the UUID of the network specified by *name*.

nodeinfo
> Print basic information about the physical system.

quit
> Exit **virsh**'s interactive terminal.

reboot *domain*
> Reboot the *domain* as if a reboot command was run from the console.

restore *file*
> Restore a domain from a domain state saved in *file* by the **save** command.

resume *domain*
> Resume execution of a suspended *domain*.

save *domain file*
> Save a *domain*'s state to *file*. This will suspend the domain, similar to hibernating a system.

schedinfo [*options*] *domain*
> Set or show CPU scheduler settings.

Options

> **--weight** *n*
> > Set scheduler weight. Valid values of *n* are between 1 and 65535.

> **--cap** *percent*
> > Set the maximum *percent* that any one physical CPU *domain* can consume.

setmem *domain size*

> Change *domain*'s current memory allocation to the *size* given in kilobytes.

setmaxmem *domain size*

> Change *domain*'s maximum memory allocation to the *size* given in kilobytes. The new size can't be larger than was specified when the virtual machine was created.

setvcpus *domain n*

> Change the number of active virtual CPUs. *n* cannot exceed the number of CPUs specified in *domain*'s configuration file at boot time.

shutdown *domain*

> Shut down the *domain* as if the shutdown command was run from the console.

suspend *domain*

> Pause execution of *domain*.

ttyconsole *domain*

> Print *domain*'s tty console device if it has one.

undefine *domain*

> Remove *domain*'s definition.

uri

> Print hypervisor's URI.

vcpuinfo *domain*

> Print information about *domain*'s virtual CPU.

vcpupin *domain vcpu cpulist*

> Control domain virtual CPU affinity. Assign the given *vcpu* number to the physical *cpulist* given as a comma-separated list of numbers or number ranges: e.g., 0,2 or 0–2,5,6.

version

> Print library API version number and the hypervisor URI.

vncdisplay *domain*

> Print the IP address and port number of *domain*'s display, if available.

---

virt-clone   virt-clone [*options*]

Clone a virtual machine. **virt-clone** copies hard drives and duplicates the virtual hardware configuration of an existing virtual machine. Elements that must be unique, such as the MAC address of a virtualized network interfaces, are updated so as to avoid conflicts with the old system. This system to be cloned must be shut off, as an active system cannot be safely cloned.

If no options are given, **virt-clone** will query for the needed information.

virt-clone writes debugging information to **$HOME/**.*virtinst/virt-clone.log*.

Options

--connect=*uri*
> The hypervisor connection *uri*.

-d, --debug
> Print debugging information to standard output.

-f *path*, --file=*path*
> The path to the file, disk partition, or logical volume to use to store the new guests virtual disk. If the original system has multiple disks, this option should be run once per disk.

--force
> Run without prompting. Assume a yes response to any yes/no prompt. For all other prompts, exit.

-n *name*, --name=*name*
> The new domain *name* for the copied system.

-o *domain*, --original=*domain*
> The name or UUID of the original *domain* to copy.

--preserve-data
> Preserves any data that exists on the target of an **-f** option.

-m *address*, --mac=*address*
> The new hardware MAC *address* for the network interface on the copied system.

-u *uuid*, --uuid=*uuid*
> The new *uuid* for the copied system. This is a 32-digit hexadecimal number. If not specified, a random UUID is used.

---

virt-image

`virt-image [options] xmlfile`

Create a guest machine from the image descriptor in *xmlfile*. Attributes for the new guest are taken from the descriptor file, although some missing information can be provided on the command line. Command-line options supersede information in the image descriptor file.

Options

--boot=*n*
> If image has multiple boot descriptors, use descriptor *n*. The first descriptor is descriptor **0**. When omitted, the one that best fits the current hypervisor is chosen.

--check-cpu
> Warn if the number of virtual CPUs for the guest exceeds the number of physical CPUs in the host system.

--connect=*uri*
> The hypervisor connection *uri*.

-d, --debug
> Print debugging information to standard output.

-h, --help
> Print information on the command and options, then exit.

-k *map*, **--keymap**=*map*

> Set the *map* to use for the graphical console. By default, an English keymap is used.

-m *address*, **--mac**=*address*

> The hardware MAC *address* for the network interface on the copied system. If none is specified or the address is given as **RANDOM**, assign a random address.

-n *name*, **--name**=*name*

> The domain *name* for the new guest.

--noacpi

> Disable Advanced Configuration and Power Interface (ACPI).

--noapic

> Disable Advanced Programmable Interrupt Controller (APIC).

--nographics

> Do not set up graphic support.

-r *size*, **--ram**=*size*

> Allocate *size* in megabytes of memory for guest.

--sdl

> Use Simple DirectMedia Layer for graphic access.

-u *uuid*, **--uuid**=*uuid*

> The *uuid* for the new guest system. This is a 32-digit hexadecimal number. If not specified, a random UUID is used.

--vnc

> Use permanent port *n* for VNC instead of a random port. Note that specifying a port may cause clashes with other guests.

--vncport=*n*

> Use port *n* for VNC. Note that specifying a port may cause clashes with other guests.

--vcpus *n*

> Configure the new system with *n* virtual CPUs.

-w *type*[:*name*], **--network**=*type*[:*name*]

> Configure the guest's network connection. The type of network may be **bridge**, **network**, or **user**. For **bridge** and **network** you should also provide the network name as configured in the hypervisor. (Use **virsh net-list** to see configured network names.) **user** is supported by **qemu**'s unprivileged mode. It provides limited NAT by way of SliRP, a SLIP/PPP emulator.

---

virt-install

```
virt-install [options]
```

Create a guest machine completely from the command line. Virt-install does not require an XML image descriptor file. **virt-install** will prompt for any required information not provided on the command line. Following is the required information.

Options

--accelerate

Use KVM or KQEMU kernel acceleration if available. Recommended when the guest OS is compatible.

--boot=*n*

If an image has multiple boot descriptors, use descriptor *n*. The first descriptor is descriptor **0**. When omitted, the one that best fits the current hypervisor is chosen.

-c *path*, **--cdrom=***path*

File to use for virtual CDROM device. The file may be an ISO file, CDROM device, or a URL that refers to an ISO image to fetch.

--check-cpu

Warn if the number of virtual CPUs for the guest exceeds the number of physical CPUs in the host system.

--connect=*uri*

The hypervisor connection *uri*.

--cpuset=*set*

Allow guest to use only the given *set* of CPUs. A set is a comma-separated list of numbers or number ranges: e.g., 0,2 or 0–2,5,6.

-d, **--debug**

Print debugging information to standard output.

-f *path*, **--file=***path*

Required. The path to the file, disk partition, or logical volume to use to store the new guest's virtual disk. If the original system has multiple disks, this option should be given once per disk.

-h, **--help**

Print information on the command and options, then exit.

-k *map*, **--keymap=***map*

Set the keymap to use for the virtual console. By default, an English keymap is used.

-l *path*, **--location=***path*

Specify the location of the installation source. *path* may be given as a URI. Use this instead of **-c** when installing from a kernel/initrd pair instead of a CDROM. Required for installing paravirtualized guests.

--livecd

The guest will always use a live CDROM image. Configure guest to boot from CDROM drive by default. Commonly used with **--nodisks** option.

-m *address*, **--mac=***address*

The hardware MAC *address* for the network interface on the copied system. If none is specified or address is given as **RANDOM**, assign a random address.

-n *name*, **--name=***name*

Required. The domain *name* for the new guest.

--noacpi

> Disable Advanced Configuration and Power Interface (ACPI).

--noapic

> Disable Advanced Programmable Interrupt Controller (APIC).

--noautoconsole

> Don't automatically launch a console for the installation. By default, **virt-install** launches a VNC client or **virsh console** to connect to the guest.

--nodisks

> Guest is being created without disks. Do not prompt for disk setup.

--nographics

> Don't prompt for virtual console setup if neither **--sdl** nor **--vnc** is specified. Set up a text based console on the first serial port (or equivalent console device) instead.

--nonsparse

> Fully allocate space for the virtual disk. This takes longer to initialize, but results in a faster disk and ensures you don't run out of space. Recommended.

--os-type=*type*

> Optimize guest for the specified guest OS *type*. Valid values for *type* include **linux**, **windows**, **unix**, and **other**.

-p, --paravirt

> Guest will be a paravirtualized system.

--pxe

> Use PXE boot protocol to load initial kernel.

-r *size*, **--ram=***size*

> Required. Allocate *size* in megabytes of memory for guest.

-s *size*, **--file-size=***size*

> Required when creating a new file. Create a file of *size* in gigabytes. Size may be given as a decimal, for example: **2.5**. By default, virt-install creates a sparse file. The full size will be allocated, though, if used with the **--nonsparse** option.

--sdl

> Set up a virtual console and export it using Simple Direct-Media Layer (SDL).

-u *uuid*, **--uuid=***uuid*

> The *uuid* for the new guest system. This is a 32-digit hexadecimal number. If not specified, a random UUID is used.

-v, --hvm

> Configure guest with full virtualization. Don't use paravirtualization if available.

--vnc

> Set up a virtual console and export it using VNC.

--vncport=*n*

> Use permanent port *n* for VNC instead of a random port. Note that specifying a port may cause clashes with other guests.

--vcpus *n*
> Configure new system with *n* virtual CPUs.

-w *type*[*:name*], **--network**=*type*[*:name*]
> Configure guest's network connection. The type of network may be **bridge, network,** or **user.** For **bridge** and **network** you should also provide the network name as configured in the hypervisor. (Use **virsh net-list** to see configured network names.) **user** is supported by **qemu**'s unprivileged mode. It provides limited NAT by way of SliRP, a SLIP/PPP emulator. If this option is omitted, a single NIC is created to a bridge device or to the default network. Specify the option multiple times to set up multiple network interfaces.

-x *kernelargs*, **--extra-args**=*kernelargs*
> Pass additional kernel arguments to a Linux kernel. Used with the **-l** option. Commonly used to pass a Kickstart file to the kernel.

---

virt-viewer

`virt-viewer [options] domain`

Use VNC to open the console of a virtual machine. The domain may be given by name, ID, or UUID.

Options

--c *uri*, **--connect**=*uri*
> Connect to a hypervisor specified by *uri*.

--d, --direct
> Don't tunnel the VNC connection over SSH, even if the connection URI uses SSH.

--v, --verbose
> Print information about the connection to standard output.

--w, --wait
> Wait for the domain to start up before connecting to the console.

---

virt-manager

`virt-manager [options]`

Launch GUI virtual machine manager. This manager visually displays domain and hypervisor stats. Like **virsh,** it can manage domains, and when run on the same system as the hypervisor, it can even be used to configure new systems. It has a couple of useful options for controlling how it starts.

Options

--c *uri*, **--connect**=*uri*
> Connect to a hypervisor specified by *uri*.

--no-fork
> Run without forking a new process. This can be useful for debugging connection problems.

VMware ESX 3.5

While VMware isn't exactly a Linux product and isn't free, it does provide access to a Service Console, which is something like Xen's Domain-0. The Service Console runs a modified version of Red Hat Enterprise Server 3.0. So even though it is a commercial product, we want to include some information on it in this chapter.

Here, we will cover useful Service Console commands for administrators using the commercial ESX 3.5 product. VMware has also provided a free version of ESX, named ESXi. ESXi does not technically have a Service Console, though you can launch an unsupported Linux interface similar to the Service Console that has many of the same commands. Many of the commands listed in this section will work in the unsupported console, although in keeping with the unsupported nature of this console, nothing is guaranteed. VMware also provides a remote command line interface (rCLI), which is a collection of Perl utilities that mostly mimic the Service Console commands.

As we are writing this, VMware is preparing to release vSphere, the new version of ESX. It too, has a Service Console and remote CLI, the vCLI. VMware has deprecated some commands in vSphere moving functionality to the vCLI. still, they continue to provide the Service Console for troubleshooting and technical support sessions. Most of what we document here still works in vSphere.

You will need to install ESX or ESXi on a bare system. Its installation is nearly identical to an older Red Hat installation. Given your network information, it should be able to configure a default network switch that will provide your guest systems with network access.

ESX Management Client

While we cover some of the common commands below, you won't use these for most of your management tasks. Once installed and booted, the initial screen will give you a URL you can connect to in order to perform some basic configuration. That URL will also direct you to where you can find a Virtual Infrastructure Client (VI Client) to manage your ESX server. It's that client you will use to manage your servers. VI Client runs on Microsoft Windows.

Virtual Center

If you are using VMware servers, you are probably going to use multiple servers to take advantage of the High Availability features VMware offers, such as Vmotion. To coordinate those servers you will need to run a Microsoft Windows Server system with VMware's virtual center installed. It's rumored that vSphere will have a Linux-based Virtual Center, but this has not been announced for the initial release. It still requires Microsoft Windows.

VMware is GUI driven and VMware expects you will primarily use VI Client to interact with your systems. You will need to run at least one windows system to manage VMware ESX servers. The Service Console won't let you get around this requirement. However, when your network stops working right or you need to take a closer look at a system's performance, you will be glad to have the service console available.

VMware Networking

When configuring a virtual network switch, you will configure three different network connection types: Virtual Machine, VMkernel, and Service Console. VMware refers to these as different kinds of *port groups*. A port group specifies port configuration options, such as VLAN tagging or bandwidth limitations for devices assigned to that group. The switch handles the mapping of virtual devices to physical devices. In a default installation of ESX you should have a Service Console and Virtual Machine port group.

The **Service Console** port group provides network access to the service console and is used by the virtual center or VI Client to control the server. The **Virtual Machine** port group is a default port group that will bridge your virtual machines to your physical network devices. Each network card on a virtual machine must be assigned to a virtual machine port group. For a high availability cluster of ESX servers, you will need to add a **VMkernel** port group as well. This is the port group the hypervisors will use to speak with each other and for moving virtual machines between servers.

Physical interfaces on a server are given a name beginning with **vmnic**. The service console's interfaces are given names beginning with **vswif**. Both of these will show up if you run **ifconfig** from the service console.

We won't cover virtual switch configuration further, but these terms will help you better understand the network and switch-related commands.

Shared Disks

To run multiple ESX servers, you need a shared data store. It can be SAN-based block storage (e.g., Fibre Channel or iSCSI) or a NAS connection (NFS), but you need some place the servers can all access the same data. For block storage, VMware uses a shared filesystem, **vmfs**, which is designed to handle multiple systems reading and writing to the same drive.

Snapshots

ESX can take snapshots of a running system. This process essentially freezes machine state and begins tracking changes to the system in a separate file. Later you can apply those changes or discard them to revert your system to the state it had when you took the snapshot. This is commonly used to test a configuration change or system update.

Because it preserves a system's state at a specific time, you want your virtual machine doing as little as possible when taking the snapshot. Activity such as network file transfers and database transactions will fail if you decide to revert to the snapshot. Depending on virtual machine configuration, some disk activity may not be included in the snapshot.

The file tracking changes can grow quickly, so you will need sufficient space to hold the file, and you will probably not want to keep snapshots for very long. Having a snapshot may also limit your ability to migrate a system between servers.

Restoring the snapshot on a new system may not work. VMware will generate warnings when you try to migrate a system with a snapshot. Generally you want to remove all snapshots before migration.

VMware Tools

Paravirtualization on ESX depends on VMware tools. This is a collection of drivers and daemons that allow the hypervisor to communicate with the guest system. VMware tools can synchronize the guests clock with the ESX server's clock, initiate graceful shutdowns when needed, provide better access to an X Window System running on a guest, and more. You almost always want to install these.

ESX Server Commands

Most commands for ESX server begin with either **vm** or **esx**. Commands that begin with **vm** all have something to do with manipulating virtual machines. Commands that begin with **esx** manipulate the server and its configuration. The commands may have more options than those we document here. Here, we focus on the most useful commands and command options.

---

esxcfg-firewall   `esxcfg-firewall [options]`

Configure a firewall for the service console. ESX uses **iptables** to provide the firewall. Don't use the **iptables** command to configure it, though; use this command instead. In its default configuration, it denies all incoming or outgoing connections except for the ports required for the server to function:

--**allowIncoming**
> Allow incoming connections by default.

--**allowOutgoing**
> Allow outgoing connections by default.

--**blockIncoming**
> Block incoming connections by default.

--**blockOutgoing**
> Block outgoing connections by default.

-**c** *port type direction*, --**close** *port,type,direction*
> Close a *port*. The *type* may be **tcp** or **udp**, The *direction* may be **in** or **out**.

-**d** [*service*], --**disableService** [*service*]
> Close the ports required by the specified *service*.

-**e** [*service*], --**enableService** [*service*]
> Open the ports required by the specified *service*.

-**h**, --**help**
> Print a usage message. This is the default if no options are given.

-**l**, --**load**
> Load current firewall settings into **iptables**.

-q [*service*], **--query** [*service*]
> Print all current settings or the state of a *service* specified by name. Instead of a service you can query the default settings for **incoming** or **outgoing** packets.

-o *port type direction name*, **--open** *port,type,direction,name*
> Open a *port*. The type may be **tcp** or **udp**, The *direction* may be **in** or **out**. You must give the service you have opened a *name*.

-r, **--resetDefaults**
> Reset all parameters to the installed defaults.

-s, **--services**
> List known service names.

Example

Allow vmware-cmd to connect to remote hosts by opening outgoing connections to port 443:

```
# esxcfg-firewall -o 443,tcp,out,vmware-cmd
```

---

esxcfg-vswif

esxcfg-vswif *options* [*interface*]

Configure the service console network interface. Don't use **ifconfig** or manipulate */etc/sysconfig/network-script* files directly; use this command instead. Service console interface names start with **vswif** followed by a number. For example: **vswif0** or **vswif1**.

Options
-a, **--add**
> Add a service console interface. Requires the **--ip** and **--port-group** options.

-b *address*, **--broadcast** *address*
> Set the broadcast address.

-d, **--del**
> Remove a service console interface.

-D, **--disable-all**
> Disable all service console interfaces.

-e, **--enable**
> Enable a disabled interface.

-E, **--enable-all**
> Enable all service console interfaces.

-i *address*, **--ip** *address*
> Set the IP address for the interface. You can also specify **DHCP** for *address*.

-l, **--list**
> List service console interfaces along with current configuration and state.

-n *mask*, **--netmask** *mask*
> Set the netmask.

-p *name*, **--portgroup** *name*
> Set the interface's portgroup name.

-s, --disable
> Disable an interface.

esxcfg-vswitch   esxcfg-vswitch *options* [*switch*]

> Configure a virtual switch. The virtual switch handles port groups and VLAN tagging, and sets the uplink for virtual port groups. By default, there is a single virtual switch: vSwitch0. You can add additional switches and assign them to different physical network interfaces.

Options
-a, --add
> Add a new virtual switch. You must provide a switch name.

-A *name*, **--add-pg** *name*
> Add port group *name* to the switch.

-b, --get-cdp
> Print the current Cisco Discovery Protocol (CDP) for the switch.

-B *status*, **--set-cdp** *status*
> Set the CDP *status* for the switch. This may be **down**, **listen**, **advertise**, or **both**.

-d, --delete
> Delete a virtual switch. If the switch has any ports in use, this will fail.

-D *name*, **--del-pg** *name*
> Remove port group *name* from the switch.

-l, --list
> List switches and their port groups.

-L *interface*, **--link** *interface*
> Attach an uplink interface to a virtual switch. This should be an unused physical interface or **vmnic**.

-m *size*, **--mtu** *size*
> Set the size of the Maximum Transfer Unit (MTU) for the switch. This will affect all interfaces attached to the virtual switch.

-M *interface*, **--add-pg-uplink** *interface*
> Add an uplink *interface* to a port group.

-N *interface*, **--del-pg-uplink** *interface*
> Remove an uplink *interface* from a port group.

-p *name*, **--pg** *name*
> Specify name of the port group to use with the **--vlan** option. Specify ALL to apply to all port groups on the switch.

-U *interface*, **--unlink** *interface*
> Remove an uplink *interface* from a virtual switch.

-v *id*, **--vlan** *id*
> Set the VLAN *id* for a port group. Use with the **--pg** option. Setting *id* to **0** disables VLAN tagging for the port group.

esxcfg-nics

esxcfg-nics *options* [*interface*]

Display information about physical network interfaces and manage some interface settings.

Options

-a, --auto
> Set the interface to auto-negotiate speed and duplex settings.

-d *mode*, **--duplex** *mode*
> Set duplex *mode* for the interface. Value may be **full** or **half**.

-l, --list
> Print current configuration of all network interfaces on the system.

-s *n*, **--speed** *n*
> Set the speed of the interface to *n*. Valid values are **10**, **100**, **1000**, or **10000** and are measured in megabits per second.

---

esxtop

esxtop [*options*]

Provide frequently updated information about resource usage on the ESX server. This program performs a function similar to the Linux **top** command. Where **top** shows information on processes and process IDs, **esxtop** shows information on hypervisor resource pools, and resource pool groups. A resource pool is any item the hypervisor must schedule. For example, each virtual CPU, has a resource pool ID, and each virtual processor on a single virtual machine belongs to the same resource pool group.

esxtop's various options change what information is displayed. Like **top**, **esxtop** also offers interactive commands to change what information it displays as it runs. **esxtop** has more interactive commands than we'll show here. We are just covering the basic screens and common commands. The **h** command, however, will always show you the currently valid interactive commands.

Options

-a Override configuration file settings and show all statistics.

-b Run in batch mode; don't accept command-line input. Useful for sending output to another command or to a file.

-c *file*
> Use alternative configuration *file*. This also becomes the default file for the interactive command **W**.

-d *seconds*
> Set the delay between refreshes. Default is 3.

-n *num*
> Update display *num* times, then exit.

-s Secure mode. Disable the interactive command **s**.

Interactive commands

Prompt for number of rows to show.

c   Switch to CPU resource screen.

d   Switch to storage device screen.

f, F
Add or remove fields.

h   Show information on currently available commands.

m   Switch to memory resource screen.

o, O
Change field order.

Q, Esc
Quit.

s   Prompt for a new delay setting.

n   Switch to network resource usage screen.

v   Switch to virtual machine disk usage screen.

W   Write a configuration file matching current setup to ~/.esxtop3rc.

---

vmware-cmd

vmware-cmd [*options*][*vmxpath command*]

Console-based virtual machine manager. This command can work on the local system, or connect to a remote system using the Simple Object Access Protocol (SOAP). To connect to a remote system you may need to alter your firewall settings on the system issuing the commands so that it will allow outgoing connections to port 443. See the example in **esxcfg-firewall**.

The guest you want to work on is identified by the full path to its *.vmx* configuration file (*vmxpath*). The path must include the UUID of the vmfs volume and so can be quite long. Use the -l option to get the correct path for all registered virtual machines. While **vmware-cmd** has options for getting and setting virtual machine configuration values, we don't cover those here.

Options

-h   Print basic usage and commands.

-H *host*
Connect to remote *host*. This can be given as a domain name or IP address.

-s [**un**]**register** *configfile*
Add or remove the guest described in *.vmx* file found at *path* from server control.

-l   List virtual machines registered with server.

-O *port*
Connect to alternative *port*, specified by port number. The default is port **443**.

-P *password*
Provide *password* for the user specified in the -U option.

-q   Quiet mode. Minimize output.

-U *username*
> Connect with the given *username*.

-v   Verbose mode.

Command

Return values for the command generally show the command function and whether they succeed (value 1) or fail (value 0.) Power-related commands generally take an option power operation *mode* of **soft**, **hard**, or **trysoft**. **soft** power operations use **vmware-tools** to generally do the right thing to the guest, such as gracefully shutting it down before pulling the virtual plug, or running special scripts to prepare the system for suspension. **hard** operations just perform the requested action immediately. **trysoft** operations will attempt to use **vmware-tools** for its operations, but if that fails, will force the operation without using tools.

connectdevice *name*
> Connect device *name* to system. Valid device names can be found in the system's *.vmx* configuration file.

createsnapshot *name description quiesce memory*
> Take a snapshot of the system, setting the new snapshot's *name* and *description*. If these values contain spaces, enclose them in quotes. You can quiesce drive activity and save memory state while taking the snapshot. *quiesce* and *memory* should be **0** for false or **1** for true. You usually will want both to be 1.

getstate
> Report whether the virtual machine is off, on, suspended, or stuck.

getuptime
> Report how long, in minutes, a machine has been running.

hassnapshot
> Report whether virtual machine has a snapshot.

reset [*mode*]
> Restart virtual machine.

removesnapshots
> Apply saved changes and delete all snapshots.

revertsnapshot
> Discard changes and restore virtual machine to most recent snapshot. Begin tracking changes again from the snapshot state.

start [*mode*]
> Power up virtual machine.

stop [*mode*]
> Power off virtual machine.

suspend
> Save virtual machine's state and suspend its operation.

Examples

List registered virtual machines:

```
vmware-cmd -l
```

Register the yoyodyne system with the hypervisor:

```
vmware-cmd -s register /vmfs/volumes/uuid/yoyodyne/
yoyodyne.vmx
```

Start a registered virtual machine:

```
vmware-cmd /vmfs/volumes/uuid/yoyodyne/yoyodyne.vmx start
```

Create a snapshot of the yoyodyne system:

```
vmware-cmd /vmfs/volumes/uuid/yoyodyne/yoyodyne.vmx \
createsnapshot beforeupdate "state before system update" 1 1
```

Connect a virtual IDE CDROM to yoyodyne system:

```
vmware-cmd /vmfs/volumes/uuid/yoyodyne/yoyodyne.vmx \
connectdevice ide0:0
```

---

vmkfstools

```
vmkfstools options [target]
```

Manipulate disk images and vmfs filesystems. As with other commands, you generally use VI Client to perform these tasks. But you must use the command line when importing a disk from another VMware product, such as VMware Workstation. Use this command to create or extend a VMFS system or to extend, rename, or remove a disk image. It can also set or query disk image properties. Use **vmkfstools** instead of **mv** and **cp** to move and copy virtual disks.

You generally do not want to perform virtual disk operations on disks currently in use by a virtual machine. Shut down virtual machines first. Changes in a virtual disk will often require changes in a virtual machine's configuration or changes in the virtual machine's operating system. One example is changing virtual machine partition information to take advantage of an extended disk.

Targets

The *target* will be a device, partition, or file, depending on what you intend to do.

device

A device *target* will begin with */vmfs/devices/*, the mount point of the device filesystem. This will include SAN-based disks, logical volumes, and SCSI devices attached to the ESX server.

partition

A partition *target* begins with **vmhba** followed by numbers that signify *adapter:target: LUN:partition[:filepath]*. For example, **vmhba0:1:14:2** would be the 2nd partition of LUN 14 on target 1 HBA 0. You can also target a file on a partition by appending the *filepath*.

path

A path *target* is simply a path to a *.vmdk* virtual disk file. This path can be given relative to the */vmfs* directory. The path to the file target isn't required if it is in the current working directory.

Options

We have grouped options that are commonly used together, generally following the order used in the manpages.

VMFS options:

-b *size*, **--blocksize** *size*

> Set new VMFS volume block size. Default is 1m for 1 megabyte. Other valid options are 2m, 4m and 8m. Used with the **-C** option.

-C *type*, **--createfs** *type*

> Create a VMFS filesystem on a partition *target*. In ESX 3.5, the only valid type is **vmfs3**.

-S *label*, **-setfsname** *label*

> Set the label for a new VMFS filesystem. This is used only with the **-C** option.

-Z *partition*, **--extendfs** *partition*

> Extend existing vmfs3 filesystem by adding the specified *partition* to it. vmfs3 filesystems can have at most 32 partitions.

-P, **--queryfs**

> List attributes of a VMFS filesystem. The target of this command may be the path to any directory or file on a VMFS filesystem.

-h, **--human-readable**

> Used in conjunction with the **-P** option. Print sizes in a more easily read form.

Virtual disk options:

-c *size*, **--createvirtualdisk** *size*

> Create a new virtual disk of the specified *size* in bytes (by default). You can also append g, m, or k to give numbers in gigabytes, megabytes, or kilobytes, respectively. For example: 8g for 8 gigabytes.

-a *[type]*, **--adaptertype** *[type]*

> Specify adapter *type* to use with the virtual disk. The only valid types are **buslogic** or **lsilogic**. Default is **buslogic**, but for Linux you probably want **lsilogic**.

-d *format*, **--diskformat** *format*

> Set virtual disk **format**. This option is used when creating and cloning virtual disks (**-c** and **-i** options). See later options for valid virtual disk formats. When cloning, this option can be used to specify the format of the target disk; for example, when cloning a VMFS virtual disk file to a 2 GB sparse file useable by other VMware products.

-U, **--deletevirtualdisk**

> Delete a virtual disk and any associated files.

-E *source*, **--renamevirtualdisk** *source*

> Rename *source* virtual disk and associated files to *target*.

-i *source*, **--clonevirtualdisk** *source*

Clone *source* virtual disk and associated files to *target*. This is commonly used to import disks from other VMware products. You can use **-d** to specify the format of the source.

-X *size*, **--extendvirtualdisk** *size*

Extend an existing disk to the specified *size* in bytes (by default). You can also append g, m, or k to give numbers in gigabytes, megabytes, or kilobytes respectively. This action will break snapshots and the guest will need some way to recognize and take advantage of the new disk size (such as by resizing a partition with **resize2fs**).

-r *device*, **--createrdm** *device*

Create a virtual raw device mapping. (See the following section, "Virtual disk formats.") Give *device* as the full path to a device under */vmfs/devices*.

-q, **--queryrdm**

Print attributes of an existing raw disk mapping.

-z *device*, **--createrdmpassthrough** *device*

Create a physical raw device mapping. (See the following section, "Virtual disk formats.") Give *device* as the full path to a device under */vmfs/devices*.

-g, **--geometry**

Print geometry information for a virtual disk.

-w, **--writezeroes**

Initialize a virtual disk with zeroes. This will wipe any existing data from the disk.

-j, **--inflatedisk**

Convert a thin virtual disk to a preallocated virtual disk, preserving existing data and zeroing out unallocated blocks.

Virtual disk formats

This section lists the valid target disk formats to use with the **-d** option when creating or cloning a virtual disk. Created disks may be in any of the ESX vmdk formats. When cloning a disk, use **-d** if you need to export to an alternate format or target a raw device.

ESX vmdk formats:

zeroedthick

Allocate all space and wipe any previous contents of that space during virtual machine read and write operations. This is the default format.

eagerzeroedthick

Like **zeroedthick**, only the allocated space is wiped at creation time.

thick

Allocate all space, but don't bother cleaning any existing content on the disk.

thin

Supply and zero out space for the filesystem as it is used by the virtual machine.

VMware compatible formats:

2gbsparse
> Sparse disk with 2 GB maximum extent size (the Virtual disk will be split into 2 GB sections). This is a useful format when writing to disks that don't support files larger than 2 GB.

monosparse
> One monolithic disk file.

monoflat
> One monolithic flat file.

Raw device mappings:

rdm:*device*
> Virtual raw device mapping. These are treated by a guest as any other virtual disk.

rdmp:*device*
> Physical raw device mapping. A virtual machine is given direct access to a physical raw device and interacts with it as it would any SCSI device. LUN listing requests are virtualized, however, so only the system that owns the virtual device can access it.

raw:*device*
> A raw SCSI device, like a tape archive or an unmapped LUN.

Examples

Export a VMFS virtual disk to 2 GB sparse file:

```
# vmkfstools -i original.vmdk -d 2gbsparse new.vmdk
```

Index

We'd like to hear your suggestions for improving our indexes. Send email to *index@oreilly.com*.

C

c command, gdb, 164
c command, sed, 716, 718
c++ compiler (see g++ compiler)
\c control character escape
    sequence, 601
C language
    generating from RPC code, 366
    preprocessor for, 92–98
cache command, lftp, 245
cache command, mailx, 269
cal command, 68
calendar, printing, 68
caller command, Bash, 622
cameras, reading images from, 376
Cameron, Debra
    GNU Emacs Pocket Reference, 654
    Learning GNU Emacs, 654, 662
capitalization commands, Emacs, 666
caret (^)
    exponentiation operator, 732
    match at beginning of line or
        string, 655
caret, equals sign (^=) assignment
    operator, 732
case command, Bash, 622
case command, ftp, 149
cat command, 68
cat command, GRUB, 531
cat command, svn, 768
cat command, svnlook, 800
cc compiler (see gcc compiler)
cd command, Bash, 623
cd command, ex, 698
cd command, ftp, 149
cd command, gdb, 164
CDDA (Compact Disc Digital Audio)
    converting to WAV, 69
    converting to WAV format, 200–203
cdda2wav command, 69
cdparanoia command, 69–71
CDPATH built-in variable, 609
cdrdao command, 71–75
cdrecord command, 75
CD-Rs, writing in DAO mode, 71–75
CDs
    commands for, list of, 9
    converting from CDDA to WAV
        format, 200–203
    ejecting, 128
    reading and writing, 350, 352

recording audio files to, 69–71, 75
recording data files to, 75
recording data or audio to, 484–488
cdup command, ftp, 149
center command, ex, 699
centering commands, Emacs, 668
cfdisk command, 75
c++filt command, 67
C-h command (help), Emacs, 663
chage command, 76
chainloader, 517
chainloader command, GRUB, 531
chains, 29
change command, ex, 699
changed command, svnlook, 800
changelist command, svn, 768
Chapman, D. Brent (Building Internet
    Firewalls), 29
character classes
    Bash, 600
    pattern matching, 656
character files, creating, 292
chattr command, 77
chdir (c) command, mailx, 269
checkout command, git, 816
checkout command, svn, 769
checksums, calculating and
    printing, 427
check-update command, yum, 547
cherry-pick command, git, 817
chfn command, 78
chgrp command, 78
chkconfig command, 79
chmod command, 80
chmod command, ftp, 149
chown command, 82
chpasswd command, 83
chroot command, 83
chrt command, 83
chsh command, 84
chvt command, 84
CIDR (Classless Inter-Domain
    Routing), 24
cksum command, 84
Classic Shell Scripting (Robbins;
    Beebe), 597
classify command, mailx, 270
Classless Inter-Domain Routing
    (CIDR), 24
clean command, git, 818
clean command, yum, 548

F

W